Stablecoins and the Future of Financial Regulation

Jane Thomason
https://orcid.org/0009-0007-3123-7851
University College London, UK

IGI Global
Scientific Publishing
Publishing Tomorrow's Research Today

Vice President of Editorial Melissa Wagner
Director of Acquisitions Mikaela Felty
Director of Book Development Jocelynn Hessler
Production Manager Mike Brehm
Cover Design Jose Rosado

Published in the United States of America by
IGI Global Scientific Publishing
701 East Chocolate Avenue
Hershey, PA, 17033, USA
Tel: 717-533-8845 | Fax: 717-533-7115
Website: https://www.igi-global.com E-mail: cust@igi-global.com

Library of Congress Cataloging-in-Publication Data

Names: Thomason, Jane, 1958- editor
Title: Stablecoins and the future of financial regulation / [edited by] Jane Thomason.
Description: Hershey, PA : IGI Global Scientific Publishing, [2026] | Includes bibliographical references and index. | Summary: "This book demystifies stablecoins and explains why smart regulation is crucial for financial stability, inclusion, and mitigating systemic risk, offering clear insights and real-life case studies for policymakers, business leaders, technologists, and curious readers alike"-- Provided by publisher.
Identifiers: LCCN 2025052888 (print) | LCCN 2025052889 (ebook) | ISBN 9798337366555 hardcover | ISBN 9798337366562 paperback | ISBN 9798337366579 ebook
Subjects: LCSH: Cryptocurrencies | Finance--Government policy
Classification: LCC HG1710.3 .S73 2026 (print) | LCC HG1710.3 (ebook) | DDC 332.4--dc23/eng/20260130
LC record available at https://lccn.loc.gov/2025052888
LC ebook record available at https://lccn.loc.gov/2025052889
British Cataloguing in Publication Data
A Cataloguing in Publication record for this book is available from the British Library.

Table of Contents

Detailed Table of Contents

This chapter translates the Commonwealth Model Law on Stablecoins into an actionable, technically focused supervisory playbook by linking its legal mandates to the technical realities that drive financial stability outcomes. It deconstructs the stablecoin technology stack—blockchain infrastructure, smart contracts, oracle dependencies, and custody/wallet controls—to identify discrete risk surfaces and the cross-layer failure paths that can trigger rapid, system-wide losses. Anchored in recent case studies of algorithmic collapse and governance-enabled exploits, the chapter advances the principle that technological risk is financial risk and shows how vulnerabilities in bridges, oracle design, key management, and protocol governance can undermine reserves, redemption, and peg maintenance.

Stablecoins represent a defining innovation in twenty-first-century finance. Their market capitalisation, which peaked above USD 180 billion in 2022, continues to hover around USD 150–160 billion. These instruments now sit at the intersection of technology, money, and systemic risk. While their adoption accelerates financial innovation and cross-border efficiency, their rapid growth introduces challenges analogous to those historically associated with unregulated money-market instruments and private banknotes. This chapter provides a comprehensive examination of the financial-stability implications of stablecoins, integrating the policy and legal logic embedded within the Commonwealth Model Law on Stablecoins (July 2025). It expands prior analyses by introducing explicit macroprudential stress-testing regimes, systemic-risk surveillance, and potential central-bank liquidity arrangements to ensure complete conceptual convergence between economic assessment and legislative design (Financial Stability Board, 2023).

This chapter analyses cross-border coordination in the regulation and supervision of stablecoins. Stablecoins challenge jurisdiction-based regulatory frameworks by operating across multiple legal and monetary regimes. Drawing upon the perspectives of the FSB, FATF, and the CPMI, the chapter explores how these international standard-setting bodies converge on the need for globally consistent oversight to mitigate systemic, prudential, and financial integrity risks. It examines the macroeconomic and microeconomic vulnerabilities associated with fragmented regulation, including risks to monetary sovereignty, financial stability, and consumer protection. The chapter further identifies implementation challenges in supervision and enforcement, proposes key policy principles for achieving coordinated oversight, and highlights emerging models of international cooperation such as supervisory colleges, memoranda of understanding, and mutual-recognition frameworks. Ultimately, it argues that structured, institutionalised cooperation is the cornerstone of credible global stablecoin governance.

Stablecoins are rapidly transforming digital finance by enabling fast, low-cost transactions, cross-border payments, and greater financial inclusion in remittance-dependent Commonwealth economies. However, their pseudonymous nature, integration with decentralised finance, and global accessibility introduce significant vulnerabilities to money laundering, terrorist financing, and proliferation financing. Illicit actors increasingly exploit stablecoins to bypass traditional financial controls, sanctions, and oversight. This chapter evaluates these emerging risks and advances a coherent regulatory response anchored in the Commonwealth Model Law. It recommends risk-based supervision, stronger licensing and enforcement for issuers and intermediaries, Travel Rule compliance, enhanced due diligence, and mandatory transparency in reserves and governance. It also calls for improved data sharing, cyber-resilience standards, and capacity building for smaller jurisdictions. Case studies from across the Commonwealth illustrate both challenges and successful approaches.

This chapter provides a comprehensive roadmap for designing robust licensing and supervisory frameworks for stablecoins. The authors examine at a high level who should be licensed, licensing requirements, proportionate supervision, exemptions, innovation support, enforcement, cross-border cooperation, and future directions. Drawing on international principles from the Financial Stability Board, International Organization of Securities Commissions, Financial Action Task Force, and comparative experiences from the EU's Markets in Crypto-Assets Regulation, Singapore's Payment Services Act, and Commonwealth jurisdictions, this chapter argues for functional, risk-based, and technologically neutral frameworks. The authors emphasize that licensing establishes accountability rather than control, enabling innovation within appropriate guardrails. Key themes include proportionality through tiered requirements, technology-enabled supervision via RegTech and SupTech tools, graduated enforcement, and essential cross-border coordination for inherently global instruments

This chapter outlines the legal and institutional process required to implement virtual asset legislation—including stablecoins—with a focus on jurisdictions adopting the Commonwealth Secretariat's Model Laws. It presents a modular, principle-based approach to legislative design, emphasising legal clarity, proportionality, and adaptability. Drawing on comparative practices and implementation case studies, the chapter explores how governments can translate conceptual ambition into enforceable law—through legal scoping, stakeholder engagement, modular drafting, and capacity-building. The goal is to equip policymakers, legal drafters, and institutional leaders with a roadmap for embedding digital asset frameworks into domestic law while preserving sovereignty, enabling innovation, and ensuring cross-border coherence.

Stablecoins have firmly established themselves in the core of global digital finance. They now function as payment infrastructure, liquidity tools, and potential public-purpose digital money. Viewed through regulatory, technical, economic, and humanitarian lenses, the chapters in this volume present a consistent conclusion: stablecoins offer significant opportunities for efficiency, inclusion, and financial innovation, but these benefits can only be realised when supported by strong governance frameworks, transparent and high-quality reserves, enforceable redemption rights, and coherent cross-border oversight. At the same time, substantial differences remain in national implementation, supervisory capability, and the treatment of high-risk models such as algorithmic stablecoins. The Commonwealth

Model Law on Stablecoins (Commonwealth Secretariat, 2025), outlined in this volume, is a forward-looking regulatory blueprint. Its principles of proportionality, transparency, and interoperability offer jurisdictions a foundation for building safe, inclusive, and resilient systems

Foreword

The financial world stands on the threshold of a transformation as profound as the rise of the internet itself. The convergence of blockchain technology, digital currencies, and regulatory innovation is rewriting the rules of money, value, and trust. At the heart of this transformation lies the stablecoin, an innovation that combines the efficiency of decentralised finance with the stability and confidence of traditional money. Yet, as this book compellingly demonstrates, stablecoins are not simply a technical curiosity or a speculative tool; they are a cornerstone of the next era of financial inclusion, sovereignty, and cross-border cooperation.

Stablecoins and the Future of Financial Regulation arrives at a decisive moment. The global market for stablecoins now exceeds hundreds of billions of dollars, their circulation and trading volumes rivalling those of major national currencies. From Africa to Asia, stablecoins are already reducing remittance costs, enhancing payment efficiency, and expanding digital finance to previously unbanked populations. But these same characteristics, speed, borderlessness, and programmability, introduce new vulnerabilities: cyber risk, regulatory arbitrage, and systemic contagion. The challenge before policymakers is therefore not whether to regulate stablecoins, but *how* to do so in a way that safeguards consumers and stability without stifling innovation.

This volume provides that roadmap. Anchored in the *Commonwealth Model Law on Stablecoins*, it provides a unified, principle-based framework that governments of all sizes and stages of development can adapt to local needs. Across its three parts, the book moves from foundational clarity to applied governance, and finally to global cooperation and implementation.

The opening chapters define what stablecoins are, dissecting their technological design, economic purpose, and distinctions from other digital assets. Readers gain a lucid understanding of the taxonomies of fiat-backed, algorithmic, and crypto-collateralised models, as well as the unique risks each presents. The subsequent comparative analysis of regulatory frameworks, spanning the European Union's

MiCA, the United States' GENIUS Act, and Asia's licensing regimes, illuminates both the convergences and tensions that define today's policy landscape.

Part Two turns to the *Commonwealth Model Law on Stablecoins.* Its tiered licensing framework, proportionate supervision, and technology-neutral design illustrate how innovation and regulation can coexist. The chapters on technology and cyber resilience, financial stability, and cross-border coordination move beyond theory to practice, demonstrating how policymakers can translate legal principles into operational safeguards. Particularly compelling is the treatment of *cybersecurity and operational risk*, where the authors show that trust in digital money depends as much on secure code and resilient infrastructure as it does on legal compliance.

In Part Three, the book broadens its lens to explore global case studies and policy innovations. Here we see how stablecoins intersect with issues of humanitarian aid, remittances, and digital identity, transforming what was once a niche fintech phenomenon into a tool for inclusive growth. Chapters on the GENIUS Act, MiCA, and cross-jurisdictional stress-testing expose the urgent need for regulatory alignment. At the same time, contributions from emerging markets illustrate how smaller nations can leapfrog legacy systems by adopting model-law principles.

Perhaps most powerfully, this collection reveals that stablecoins are not merely about digital transactions; they are about redesigning trust in a digital age. The themes of transparency, consumer protection, and good governance resonate across every chapter. In doing so, the book speaks to the very ethos of the Commonwealth, collaboration, fairness, and shared prosperity, offering a model that promotes both innovation and responsibility.

As a global community, we face a choice: to allow digital finance to evolve in a fragmented, high-risk environment, or to shape it into a resilient, interoperable system that serves humanity. *Stablecoins and the Future of Financial Regulation* provides the intellectual and practical foundation for the latter. It is a timely and essential guide for regulators, central banks, financial institutions, and innovators who recognise that the future of money must be built on stability, transparency, and trust.

The next generation of finance will not be defined by technology alone, but by the wisdom with which we govern it.

As stablecoins evolve from fintech innovation to financial infrastructure, Stablecoins and the Future of Financial Regulation offers the first globally coordinated response to their opportunities and risks. Anchored in the Commonwealth Model Law, it equips policymakers, regulators, and financial institutions with a clear roadmap for designing trustworthy digital money systems. This book bridges the gap between aspiration and implementation. It demonstrates how stablecoins can become the foundation of an inclusive, transparent, and resilient financial ecosystem, one that empowers both advanced and developing economies.

- For regulators, it serves as a governance toolkit.
- For lawmakers, a legislative blueprint.
- For academics and innovators, a cross-disciplinary research anchor.
- For investors and industry, a vision of how compliant innovation can scale safely.

In an era where digital assets are redefining sovereignty, finance, and trust, this book stands as the essential reference for anyone shaping the next generation of money. I commend it to you.

Anthony St John
House of Lords, UK

Preface

OVERVIEW

Stablecoins and the Future of Financial Regulation is a global compendium built on the foundation of the Commonwealth Model Law on Stablecoins (Model Law). The book provides a practical approach to how to regulate and harness stablecoins as safe, inclusive, and interoperable forms of digital money.

This volume emerged from a series of expert dialogues convened under the Commonwealth Secretariat in preparation for the Model Law. The contributions to this volume reflect the interdisciplinary and collaborative nature of that endeavour. This book contributes to the growing scholarly literature examining the reconfiguration of monetary sovereignty and the evolution of financial regulation in the digital era. The Model Law offers a framework that bridges theoretical discourse and regulatory implementation.

Relevance in the World Today

As digital finance transforms economies, Stablecoins and the Future of Financial Regulation provides the first comprehensive global roadmap for building trustworthy, transparent, and inclusive frameworks for digital money. Anchored in the Model Law, this landmark volume unites law, technology, and economics to answer the most pressing question in modern finance: How can we regulate digital assets without stifling innovation?

Drawing on contributions from central bankers, technologists, policymakers, and academics across more than 20 countries, the book explains what stablecoins are, why they matter, and how nations can harness them for financial inclusion, efficiency, and resilience. It extends ongoing scholarly debates on digital sovereignty, algorithmic governance, and the transformation of monetary institutions in the era of programmable finance.

Who Should Read It

1. Regulators & Policymakers: A guide to implementing compliant, innovation-friendly frameworks.
2. Central Banks & Finance Ministries: Strategic insights for balancing sovereignty with interoperability.
3. Financial Institutions & Fintech Leaders: Regulatory intelligence on the evolving digital-asset landscape.
4. Academics & Researchers: Foundational reference for interdisciplinary study of digital currencies and financial governance.

From cross-border remittances and humanitarian aid to cybersecurity frameworks and consumer protection, this book demonstrates how stablecoins can become the foundation of an inclusive, transparent, and resilient financial ecosystem, one that empowers both advanced and developing economies. For regulators, it serves as a governance toolkit. For lawmakers, a legislative blueprint. For academics and innovators, a cross-disciplinary research reference. For investors and industry, a vision of how compliant innovation can scale safely.

Key Elements

Spanning three integrated parts, the volume offers: (i) Conceptual and regulatory foundations, precise definitions, global comparisons, and analysis of systemic risks. (ii) A detailed exposition of the Model Law, a ready-to-adopt legislative architecture aligning with FATF, FSB, and BIS standards. (iii) Global case studies and frontier research, exploring cross-border interoperability, consumer protection, public-good applications, and next-generation frameworks like the U.S. GENIUS Act (2024).

It includes:

1. Model-Law Foundation: The only publication structured around the Model Law, offering an adaptable, ready-to-implement legislative framework.
2. Comparative Global Coverage: Analyses and contrasts the US GENIUS Act, EU MiCA (2023), and Asian regulatory regimes, revealing convergence and fragmentation risks.
3. Cross-Disciplinary Insight: Integrates perspectives from regulation, cybersecurity, monetary policy, and blockchain engineering.

4. Public-Good Focus: Reframes stablecoins as enablers of financial inclusion, humanitarian aid, and digital identity, not just instruments of private finance.
5. Practical Toolkit: Provides templates for licensing, supervision, and AML/CFT compliance, bridging the gap between policy and implementation.
6. Future-Ready Vision: Explores how AI, RegTech, and SupTech can strengthen digital-asset oversight and build global trust in programmable money.

WHY THIS BOOK MATTERS

This volume provides one of the first comprehensive, globally coordinated analyses of stablecoin regulation, synthesising comparative frameworks and the Commonwealth Model Law. Stablecoins now settle trillions in digital transactions annually and are reshaping global liquidity, remittances, and monetary policy. Yet regulation remains fragmented. This book delivers the clarity, coherence, and coordination that financial leaders have been waiting for.

Model-Law Core: It is the only global publication structured around the Model Law, offering a practical regulatory framework adaptable across jurisdictions.

Holistic Scope: The book encompasses law, economics, and technology, from reserve management and AML/CFT risks to blockchain security, consumer protection, and systemic stability.

Cross-Jurisdictional Analysis: It compares the world's major stablecoin regimes, the U.S. GENIUS Act (2024), EU MiCA (2023), and Hong Kong's licensing frameworks, mapping convergence, conflicts, and gaps.

Public-Good Perspective: The book goes beyond regulation to explore how stablecoins can enable financial inclusion, humanitarian aid, remittances, and digital identity systems.

Interdisciplinary Voice: It features contributors from over 20 countries, regulators, central bankers, technologists, and legal scholars, making it a truly international and policy-relevant dialogue.

Forward-Looking Themes: The book is forward-looking and examines how AI, supervisory and regulatory technologies (RegTech and SupTech), and tools will define the next generation of supervisory systems for digital assets.

This book provides a structured analytical foundation for policymakers and scholars seeking to navigate the evolution of digital monetary systems. The evolution of money as a programmable digital infrastructure presents a defining challenge for regulatory scholarship.

As stablecoins transition from technological novelty to systemic financial infrastructure, their regulation poses a defining challenge for twenty-first-century governance. This volume offers both a conceptual framework and a model legislative architecture for managing that transition. By integrating comparative legal analysis, economic theory, and technological insight, it aims to inform scholarly inquiry and guide policy evolution toward a safe, inclusive, and interoperable digital financial system. In doing so, it lays the groundwork for future empirical and comparative studies of digital currency regulation and the evolving relationship between law and code.

CHAPTER OVERVIEW

Chapter 1: Why Stablecoins Matter outlines the core value proposition of stablecoins, their accelerating adoption across public and private sectors, and the critical need for a coherent regulatory framework that balances innovation with safety. It introduces the Commonwealth Model Law on Stablecoins as a flexible, principles-based regulatory blueprint that supports trusted digital money at scale and ensures that stablecoin development advances economic resilience, interoperability, and equitable access to financial services.

Chapter 2: What are Stablecoins? explores the conceptual foundations, typologies, and functional dynamics of stablecoins. It traces their evolution from experimental constructs to integral components of the global financial system, examining how international standard-setting bodies and national regulators define and categorise them. Through a comparative analysis of frameworks adopted by jurisdictions including the European Union, United States, United Kingdom, Singapore, Hong Kong, and the United Arab Emirates, the chapter highlights convergences in definitions and divergences shaped by monetary sovereignty and policy priorities. It further analyses the operational lifecycle of stablecoins, from issuance and reserve management to redemption, and delineates their distinctions from other digital assets such as cryptocurrencies, CBDCs, and security tokens. Ultimately, the chapter establishes the conceptual groundwork necessary for understanding the legal, regulatory, and economic implications of stablecoins in an evolving financial landscape.

Chapter 3: Global Regulatory Approaches examines how jurisdictions globally are regulating stablecoins and integrating them into existing financial frameworks. It traces the evolution from voluntary market practices to comprehensive legal regimes guided by principles of prudential oversight, consumer protection, and financial stability. Beginning with international standard-setting bodies such as the FSB, FATF, IOSCO, and BIS, the chapter outlines global benchmarks for proportionate, function- based, and technology-neutral regulation. It then analyses key national frameworks, including those of the EU, UK, US, Singapore, Hong Kong, Bahrain, and the UAE, highlighting convergences in reserve, redemption, and licensing requirements, as well as divergences driven by monetary sovereignty and market priorities. Finally, the chapter explores the role of regulatory sandboxes as instruments for controlled innovation. Collectively, these developments demonstrate a maturing global consensus on stablecoin governance that balances innovation with systemic integrity.

Chapter 4: A Stablecoin Framework for the Future presents a modular legislative framework designed to accommodate diverse capacities while promoting legal interoperability and cross-border enforceability. It also examines the consequences of regulatory inertia—including financial instability, loss of sovereignty, and exclusion from innovation ecosystems. Drawing on comparative case studies and international standards, the chapter provides actionable recommendations for policymakers, emphasizing the strategic imperative of proactive reform in the digital asset space.

Chapter 5: Technology, Security, and Cyber Risks Implementing the Commonwealth Model Law on Stablecoins translates the Commonwealth Model Law on Stablecoins into an actionable, technically focused supervisory playbook by linking its legal mandates to the technical realities that drive financial stability outcomes. It deconstructs the stablecoin technology stack—blockchain infrastructure, smart contracts, oracle dependencies, and custody/wallet controls—to identify discrete risk surfaces and the cross-layer failure paths that can trigger rapid, system-wide losses. Anchored in recent case studies of algorithmic collapse and governance-enabled exploits, the chapter advances the principle that technological risk is financial risk and shows how vulnerabilities in bridges, oracle design, key management, and protocol governance can undermine reserves, redemption, and peg maintenance.

Chapter 6: Financial Stability and Systemic Risks of Stablecoins provides a comprehensive examination of the financial-stability implications of stablecoins, integrating the policy and legal logic embedded within the Commonwealth Model Law on Stablecoins (July 2025). It expands prior analyses by introducing explicit macroprudential stress-testing regimes, systemic-risk surveillance, and potential central-bank liquidity arrangements to ensure complete conceptual convergence between economic assessment and legislative design (Financial Stability Board, 2023).

Chapter 7: Cross Border Coordination analyses cross-border coordination in the regulation and supervision of stablecoins. Stablecoins challenge jurisdiction-based regulatory frameworks by operating across multiple legal and monetary regimes. Drawing upon the perspectives of the FSB, FATF, and the CPMI, the chapter explores how these international standard-setting bodies converge on the need for globally consistent oversight to mitigate systemic, prudential, and financial integrity risks. It examines the macroeconomic and microeconomic vulnerabilities associated with fragmented regulation, including risks to monetary sovereignty, financial stability, and consumer protection. The chapter further identifies implementation challenges in supervision and enforcement, proposes key policy principles for achieving coordinated oversight, and highlights emerging models of international cooperation such as supervisory colleges, memoranda of understanding, and mutual-recognition frameworks. Ultimately, it argues that structured, institutionalised cooperation is the cornerstone of credible global stablecoin governance.

Chapter 8: Strengthening AML/CFT and Proliferation Financing Frameworks for Stablecoins: Global Policy Recommendations Anchored in the Commonwealth Model Law evaluates these emerging risks and advances a coherent regulatory response anchored in the Commonwealth Model Law. It recommends risk-based supervision, stronger licensing and enforcement for issuers and intermediaries, Travel Rule compliance, enhanced due diligence, and mandatory transparency in reserves and governance. It also calls for improved data sharing, cyber-resilience standards, and capacity building for smaller jurisdictions. Case studies from across the Commonwealth illustrate both challenges and successful approaches.

Chapter 9: Licensing and Supervision Made Simple: The Why and How We Need Licensing provides a comprehensive roadmap for designing robust licensing and supervisory frameworks for stablecoins. The authors examine at a high level who should be licensed, licensing requirements, proportionate supervision, exemptions, innovation support, enforcement, cross-border cooperation, and future directions. Drawing on international principles from the Financial Stability Board, International Organization of Securities Commissions, Financial Action Task Force, and comparative experiences from the EU's Markets in Crypto-Assets Regulation, Singapore's Payment Services Act, and Commonwealth jurisdictions, this chapter argues for functional, risk-based, and technologically neutral frameworks. The authors emphasize that licensing establishes accountability rather than control, enabling innovation within appropriate guardrails. Key themes include proportionality through tiered requirements, technology-enabled supervision via RegTech and SupTech tools, graduated enforcement, and essential cross-border coordination for inherently global instruments

Chapter 10: How to Implement a Stablecoin Framework outlines the legal and institutional process required to implement virtual asset legislation—including stablecoins—with a focus on jurisdictions adopting the Commonwealth Secretariat's Model Laws. It presents a modular, principle-based approach to legislative design, emphasising legal clarity, proportionality, and adaptability. Drawing on comparative practices and implementation case studies, the chapter explores how governments can translate conceptual ambition into enforceable law—through legal scoping, stakeholder engagement, modular drafting, and capacity-building. The goal is to equip policymakers, legal drafters, and institutional leaders with a roadmap for embedding digital asset frameworks into domestic law while preserving sovereignty, enabling innovation, and ensuring cross-border coherence.

Chapter 11: Global Stablecoin Regulation: Where to From Here? Details how stablecoins have firmly established themselves in the core of global digital finance. They now function as payment infrastructure, liquidity tools, and potential public-purpose digital money. Viewed through regulatory, technical, economic, and humanitarian lenses, the chapters in this volume present a consistent conclusion: stablecoins offer significant opportunities for efficiency, inclusion, and financial innovation, but these benefits can only be realised when supported by strong governance frameworks, transparent and high-quality reserves, enforceable redemption rights, and coherent cross-border oversight. At the same time, substantial differences remain in national implementation, supervisory capability, and the treatment of high-risk models such as algorithmic stablecoins. The Commonwealth Model Law on Stablecoins (Commonwealth Secretariat, 2025), outlined in this volume, is a forward-looking regulatory blueprint. Its principles of proportionality, transparency, and interoperability offer jurisdictions a foundation for building safe, inclusive, and resilient systems.

REFERENCES

Commonwealth Secretariat, . (2025). *Commonwealth Model Law on Stablecoins (draft)*. Commonwealth Secretariat.

Financial Stability Board. (2023). *High-level recommendations for the regulation, supervision and oversight of global stablecoin arrangements*. Financial Stability Board.

Acknowledgement

No book is ever written alone, and this work is the result of a collective journey across time zones, events, disciplines, and digital frontiers.

With deep appreciation, we extend our sincere thanks to all contributors to *Stablecoins and the Future of Financial Regulation*. Your dedication, insight, and expertise have transformed the foundational work of the Commonwealth Model Law on Stablecoins into a scholarly reference that will inform, educate, and inspire.

Each of you has played an invaluable role in translating complex regulatory frameworks and practical experience into an accessible, academic resource that will serve policymakers, scholars, and practitioners around the world. By bridging the gap between policy innovation and educational dissemination, you have helped ensure that the principles of transparency, stability, and inclusion at the heart of the Model Law reach far beyond its original context.

This book stands as a testament to your commitment to responsible innovation and to your collective vision of a more resilient and equitable global financial system.

To collaborators from across the world, thank you for lending your perspectives to make this a truly global work.

I extend deep appreciation to the reviewers, especially external colleagues who have given freely of their time: Michael Bacina, Helen Disney, Johnny Fry, Emily Landis Walker, Carlos Lozano, Louise Maladay, Netan Mangal, Ian Matthews, Jai Patel, Cheng-Yun Tsang, and Ronald Tucker.

Loretta Joseph has been an unwavering source of inspiration and a true powerhouse in the world of emerging technology and policy. Her fearless advocacy, trailblazing regulatory work, and global influence have opened doors for countless people seeking to build a more inclusive and ethical digital future. Loretta's ability to cut through complexity with clarity and conviction is matched only by her warmth, loyalty, and generosity of spirit. Beyond her professional brilliance, she has been a close friend and steadfast ally throughout my journey, offering encouragement, laughter, and wisdom at every turn. I am deeply grateful for her companionship and her tireless dedication to making the world better through technology and humanity.

Much of the knowledge in this book does not come from traditional academic texts or published papers; it has been gathered through lived experience, direct engagement, and immersion in the rapidly evolving world of innovation. The learning has come from countless hours spent at conferences and summits, listening to panels and engaging in deep conversations with the ecosystem. Insights have come from firsthand experience in developing digital assets. This book brings together that collective knowledge that lives in the minds of the contributors, where tomorrow is being imagined today.

Dr. Jane Thomason

The editor used ChatGPT, a language model developed by OpenAI, for language editing, citation checking, and quality assurance during the preparation of this volume. The final content was reviewed and edited by the editor.

Chapter 1
Why Stablecoins Matter

Loretta Joseph
Mcdonell-Nadeau Consultants, Australia

Anson Zeall
Nexusdesk, Singapore

Jane Thomason
https://orcid.org/0009-0007-3123-7851
University College London, UK

ABSTRACT

Stablecoins are one of the most transformative innovations in modern finance, combining the price stability of money with the programmability and efficiency of blockchain networks. They now underpin large segments of the digital asset economy, powering fast, low-cost payments, remittances, and decentralised finance, while offering new pathways to financial inclusion in underserved regions. However, their rapid growth introduces material risks to consumers, market integrity, and global financial stability, especially where governance is weak or regulation is fragmented. This chapter outlines the core value proposition of stablecoins, their accelerating adoption across public and private sectors, and the critical need for a coherent regulatory framework that balances innovation with safety. It introduces the Commonwealth Model Law on Stablecoins as a flexible, principles-based regulatory blueprint that supports trusted digital money at scale and ensures that stablecoin development advances economic resilience, interoperability, and equitable access to financial services.

DOI: 10.4018/979-8-3373-6655-5.ch001

INTRODUCTION

Money has continually evolved with technology. From shells and silver to paper notes and plastic cards, each leap has made transactions faster, more secure, and more inclusive. Stablecoins are digital assets designed to maintain a stable value, often pegged to a fiat currency such as the US dollar or the euro. Stablecoins offer predictability, making them increasingly popular for payments, remittances, savings, and decentralised finance (DeFi). A blockchain-based financial ecosystem that operates without centralised intermediaries such as banks or brokers. By providing the best of both worlds, the stability of traditional currency and the speed of blockchain technology, stablecoins are quietly redefining what money can be.

Stablecoins are already reshaping global finance in the following ways:

Payments: For global businesses, stablecoins allow real-time, low-cost international payments. Traditional cross-border transactions can take days and incur substantial fees. Stablecoins settle in minutes or even seconds, with transparent, auditable records.

Remittances: Migrant workers sending money home often face high fees and delays. Stablecoin-powered remittance platforms, especially when integrated with mobile money, can reduce costs by up to 80%, increasing income for families across the developing world (BIS, 2023)

DeFi (Decentralised Finance): Stablecoins are the backbone of the DeFi ecosystem. They power lending platforms, savings protocols, and insurance models, without the need for a financial intermediary.

Financial Inclusion: In regions with unstable currencies or limited banking infrastructure, stablecoins offer an accessible alternative. All that's needed is a smartphone and internet access. For millions of unbanked people, they represent an opportunity to participate in the global economy.

Opportunities and Risks

The promise of stablecoins is significant: faster, cheaper, more inclusive financial services; programmable money that unlocks new business models; and a pathway toward financial innovation in emerging markets. Programmable money is a form of digital currency in which *the transfer, storage, and use of value are governed by code-based conditions*, enabling the automation of payments and integration with smart contracts (Arner et al., 2020). However, the risks are substantial.

Consumer Protection: What happens when a stablecoin issuer fails, or when reserves backing a token are misrepresented? Users risk losing savings or being unable to redeem tokens.

Financial Stability: As stablecoins grow in scale and popularity, their failure could ripple through global markets. The collapse of TerraUSD in 2022 wiped out billions in value, shaking investor confidence and prompting urgent calls for regulation (See Chapter 6).

Regulatory Arbitrage: Without clear rules, stablecoin issuers can base themselves in loosely regulated jurisdictions, evading oversight and creating cross-border systemic vulnerabilities.

Illicit Finance: Like other digital assets, stablecoins can be exploited for money laundering, terrorist financing, or tax evasion, particularly when offered without identity checks or adequate surveillance.

Governments and regulators across the globe are grappling with urgent questions of: Who should be allowed to issue stablecoins? What safeguards are needed to protect users and the broader financial system? Can privately issued digital money coexist with Central Bank Digital Currencies (CBDCs)? How to prevent abuse, fraud, terrorism financing, or systemic collapse?

Why Now?

The past decade of digital innovation has redefined what money can be: programmable, borderless, and instantaneous. Stablecoins make global money transfers far cheaper and faster, bypassing many of the intermediaries that add cost and delay in the traditional payments stack. According to the 2025 "State of Crypto" report (Gemini, 2025), stablecoins handled approximately $46 trillion in transaction volume last year, up significantly year-on-year. Stablecoins offer global reach, 24/7 settlement, and programmability (so payments can be embedded in apps, smart contracts, and workflows), and are increasingly used for remittances, corporate treasury flows, and fintech rails. If stablecoins scale and integrate with mainstream finance, they could dramatically reduce costs and friction across cross-border commerce, remittances, and digital financial services.

Stablecoins now process billions of dollars in daily transactions, underpin DeFi, enable low-cost remittances, and increasingly interface with traditional payment systems. However, the same features that make stablecoins powerful - speed, borderless, and algorithmic governance - also expose vulnerabilities. Unregulated issuers pose risks to consumers, prudential stability, and the macroeconomy. Without coherent global governance, innovation risks collapse into fragility.

Stablecoins' rapid adoption demands thoughtful policy responses. Regulate too heavily and risk stifling innovation. Regulate too little and risk financial chaos, exclusion, or exploitation.

That is why this book, and its discussion of the Commonwealth's Model Law on Stablecoins, matters. They provide a path forward: a balanced, flexible, and future-proof approach to regulating a new form of money that is already here. By understanding what stablecoins are, how they work, and why they matter, we can shape a digital financial future that is safer, more inclusive, and better for all.

THE COMMONWEALTH MODEL LAW ON STABLECOINS

The Commonwealth Model Law on Stablecoins is a pragmatic response to these challenges. Developed through collaboration among policymakers, technologists, and financial regulators, it proposes a harmonised yet flexible framework for the safe development of digital money.

The Model Law introduces proportionate licensing, reserve segregation, audit requirements, consumer redress, and transparency standards aligned with the principles of the Financial Action Task Force (FATF), the Financial Stability Board (FSB), the Bank for International Settlements (BIS), and the International Organisation of Securities Commissions (IOSCO). Marrying legal clarity with technological neutrality, it enables both small and large jurisdictions to build resilient ecosystems without ceding monetary sovereignty.

This model represents a decisive step toward a global regulatory approach that transforms fragmented national rules into an interoperable framework for trust and confidence.

The conversation about stablecoins is not merely regulatory; it is ethical and developmental. Properly designed, they can become public financial infrastructure, accelerating cross-border payments, reducing remittance costs, and enabling humanitarian disbursements during crises. In a world where over a billion people remain unbanked, stablecoins could serve as the rails for a new era of inclusive finance. In this sense, stablecoins are not just a product of fintech innovation; they are a potential instrument of financial justice. They democratise access to stable value and empower users, not just institutions.

However, global coherence remains elusive. The world is fragmenting into competing regulatory zones, the EU's MiCAR, the U.S. GENIUS Act, Singapore's Payment Services framework, and Hong Kong's new licensing regime. Each aims to ensure stability, but their divergence threatens to fracture liquidity and hinder cross-border interoperability. The Commonwealth's initiative offers a middle path: principles-based coordination that respects sovereignty while promoting interoperability. The goal is not uniformity but alignment, to ensure that no jurisdiction becomes an island of risk or a haven for opacity.

History shows that financial regulation often follows a crisis. Stablecoins invite us to invert that sequence, to design safety before failure, to legislate foresight rather than hindsight. As digital assets move from the margins to the core of the financial system, regulators, innovators, and policymakers share a collective responsibility to define the rules of engagement.

PURPOSE OF THE BOOK

In response to these challenges, the Commonwealth Secretariat, with legal and technical experts from around the world, has developed a Model Law on Stablecoins. This landmark document provides a flexible, risk-based framework that any country, large or small, developed or developing, can adapt to regulate stablecoins responsibly.

This book is a guided tour through that model law. However, it is not written only for lawyers. It is for policy makers, innovators, regulators, economists, entrepreneurs, educators, and everyday citizens trying to make sense of a fast-changing financial future. The book aims to:

1. Demystify stablecoins for policymakers, business leaders, technologists, and the interested public.
2. Explain why regulation matters, linking it to financial stability, inclusion, and systemic risk.
3. Present the Model Law as a flexible, interoperable framework.
4. Provide case studies and real-world applications.
5. Offer a global perspective with local relevance, especially for emerging markets.

This book convenes voices from across the Commonwealth and beyond to articulate a vision for stablecoins that is both innovative and safe, global yet inclusive. Together, the contributors dissect legal taxonomies, examine comparative regulatory regimes, propose supervisory frameworks, and explore cross-border coordination, consumer protection, and the prevention of financial crime. They show how well-governed stablecoins can coexist with Central Bank Digital Currencies, serve as infrastructure for digital identity and remittances, and ultimately rebuild trust in the architecture of money.

Stablecoins are more than a monetary instrument; they embody a design philosophy for the digital age. Their evolution will determine whether the next generation of money serves the few or the many. This book, Stablecoins and the Future of Financial Regulation, marks a watershed in that journey. It lays the intellectual, legal, and ethical foundations for a world where digital money can be both stable and free, a world where innovation and integrity advance together.

OVERVIEW OF THE BOOK

Part I – Understanding Stablecoins

1. Overview of the Book – Why Stablecoins Matter

Chapter 1 provides an overview of stablecoins and why a book like this matters. The rise of stablecoins represents a significant turning point in global finance, offering the stability needed for digital assets to function as reliable instruments of exchange. Unlike volatile cryptocurrencies, stablecoins are pegged to fiat currencies, commodities, or asset baskets, allowing their use in payments, remittances, and market transactions. In developing economies, they hold particular promise for advancing financial inclusion and reducing transaction costs. However, their rapid cross-border scalability introduces complex risks. Failures in governance, reserve management, or algorithmic design can trigger systemic instability, while weak oversight exposes consumers to fraud and financial crime, including money laundering and terrorism financing.

To address these challenges, the Commonwealth Secretariat developed the Model Law on Stablecoins, a harmonised legal framework that balances innovation with prudential safeguards. Building on the Commonwealth Model Law on Virtual Assets, it establishes tiered licensing, reserve requirements, and transparency obligations aligned with global standards set by the FATF, FSB, IOSCO, and BIS. The law promotes proportional regulation, lighter regimes for smaller innovators and stringent oversight for systemically important issuers, supported by audits, disclosures, and consumer protection mechanisms.

By recognising the coexistence of public and private digital money and maintaining a technology-neutral approach, the Model Law complements emerging CBDC initiatives. This book builds upon that framework, examining the implications of stablecoins for monetary policy, financial stability, inclusion, and sovereignty. Through comparative analysis and case studies, it explores how the Model Law can guide coherent global regulation—fostering innovation while safeguarding financial integrity and trust.

2. What Are Stablecoins?

Chapter 2 establishes a rigorous conceptual foundation for understanding and defining stablecoins, providing the analytical basis for their consistent treatment across jurisdictions. It first clarifies essential terminology—such as reference assets, stabilisation mechanisms, redemption rights, and reserve assets—before examining definitions adopted by leading international bodies, including the FATF, FSB, IOS-

CO, OECD, and BIS. The chapter then compares approaches under major regulatory frameworks, including the EU's Markets in Crypto-Assets (MiCA) Regulation, as well as those of the U.S., the U.K., Singapore, Hong Kong, and the UAE, identifying areas of convergence, divergence, and explicit exclusions.

It categorises stablecoins by design: fiat-, asset-, commodity-, crypto-backed, and algorithmic, linking each to its corresponding risk profile and economic use case. The chapter also analyses operational models across the stablecoin lifecycle, including issuance, distribution, and redemption, and identifies distinct policy implications for relevant market participants.

Further, it distinguishes stablecoins from other digital assets, including CBDCs, securities, and utility tokens, highlighting conceptual boundaries that are critical for regulatory clarity. Concluding with forward-looking insights, the chapter emphasises that evolving hybrid and programmable stablecoin models require adaptable, technology-neutral frameworks. By grounding analysis in legal, functional, and economic principles, this chapter provides policymakers and scholars with a shared foundation for coherent, future-ready regulation.

3. Global Regulatory Framework

Chapter 3 compares leading jurisdictions, EU (MiCA), UK, US, Singapore, Hong Kong, UAE, and outlines international principles from FATF, FSB, IOSCO, and BIS. Highlights trends toward proportionate, risk-based, and technology-neutral regulation while exposing gaps in global consistency.

Part II – The Commonwealth Model Law on Stablecoins

4. A Framework for the Future

Chapter 4 presents a modular legislative framework designed to accommodate diverse capacities while promoting legal interoperability and cross-border enforceability. It also examines the consequences of regulatory inertia -including financial instability, loss of sovereignty, and exclusion from innovation ecosystems.

5. Technology, Security, and Cyber Risks

Chapter 5 examines the technology, security, and cyber risks inherent in stablecoin ecosystems, providing policymakers and regulators with a practical framework to operationalise the Commonwealth Model Law on Stablecoins. While the Model Law outlines high-level principles for stability and consumer protection, its effectiveness depends on understanding the technological layers that underpin stablecoin arrangements and the cybersecurity controls necessary to safeguard them.

The chapter deconstructs the stablecoin technology stack, including blockchain infrastructure, smart contracts, oracles, and custody systems, and identifies vulnerabilities within each layer. It highlights critical risks, including software flaws, protocol-level economic exploits, and weaknesses in external data dependencies. Emerging issues such as key management, third-party risk, and contagion effects from interconnected Web3 systems are explored, underscoring the importance of secure operational resilience.

In addition, the chapter emphasises the need for effective governance structures encompassing risk management, service provider oversight, and continuous security assurance. It advocates for advanced regulatory practices such as formal code verification and multi-layered key protection standards.

Ultimately, the chapter bridges the gap between legal principles and technical realities, proposing a supervisory assurance framework that equips regulators to evaluate the cyber resilience of stablecoin issuers and service providers through a consistent, risk-based, and technology-informed approach.

6. Financial Stability and Systemic Risk

Chapter 6 provides a comprehensive analysis of the financial stability and systemic risks associated with stablecoins, a rapidly expanding asset class that is beginning to challenge established monetary systems. While stablecoins offer the potential to enhance efficiency, inclusion, and innovation in global finance, their growing scale introduces new channels of contagion and systemic vulnerability. With market capitalisation exceeding USD 130 billion in 2024, stablecoins have become systemically relevant, necessitating rigorous examination of their potential impact on global financial stability.

The chapter examines recent market disruptions, including the Terra/Luna collapse, to illustrate how failures in design, governance, or reserve management can lead to market-wide instability. It analyses risk transmission mechanisms—such as liquidity mismatches, reserve asset exposures, and interconnections with traditional finance—and highlights the dangers of regulatory fragmentation and cross-border spillovers. A comparative analysis between stablecoins and Central Bank Digital Currencies (CBDCs) highlights differences in their systemic risk profiles and implications for both retail and wholesale monetary frameworks.

Concluding with forward-looking policy recommendations, the chapter emphasises the need for globally coordinated regulation, robust prudential standards, and sustained dialogue between regulators, industry leaders, and policymakers to balance innovation with financial stability—ensuring that stablecoins evolve safely alongside, rather than in conflict with, traditional monetary systems.

7. Cross-Border Coordination

Chapter 7 examines the cross-border coordination and supervisory challenges posed by stablecoins, which operate seamlessly across jurisdictions and often fall outside the regulatory perimeter of any single authority. As digital, borderless instruments, stablecoins can be issued in one country and used globally, creating complex risks for financial stability, monetary sovereignty, and market integrity. Without practical international cooperation, regulatory gaps and inconsistencies may enable arbitrage, illicit finance, and systemic contagion.

The chapter analyses the macro- and microeconomic risks arising from cross-border stablecoin activity, including currency substitution, reserve opacity, redemption uncertainty, and the amplification of operational and cyber risks. It highlights persistent challenges, including limited data access, divergent regulatory definitions, weak enforcement capacity, and inadequate information sharing between supervisory authorities.

Building on guidance from the IMF, FSB, and BIS, the chapter proposes a set of policy principles to strengthen cross-border regulatory coordination. These include harmonised disclosure standards, joint supervisory mechanisms, mutual recognition frameworks, and structured information-sharing agreements. Case studies from leading jurisdictions, including the Dubai International Financial Centre (DIFC), the Dubai Virtual Assets Regulatory Authority (VARA), the Abu Dhabi Global Market (ADGM), the Hong Kong Monetary Authority (HKMA), the Monetary Authority of Singapore (MAS) and the Financial Conduct Authority (FCA) in the United Kingdom - illustrate emerging best practices.

Concluding with a forward-looking outlook, the chapter underscores that international cooperation and technical capacity-building are essential to ensure that stablecoins develop within a coherent, secure, and globally consistent regulatory framework.

8. Anti-Money Laundering (AML), Counter-Financing of Terrorism (CFT), and Preventing Abuse

Chapter 8 outlines the AML and CFT risks associated with stablecoins and explains how the Commonwealth Model Law is designed to mitigate them. Recent findings from the Financial Action Task Force (FATF) indicate that criminal actors are increasingly turning to stablecoins for illicit purposes, so much so that "most on-chain illicit activity now involves stablecoins" (FATF, 2025). Historically, financial regulation has often been reactive, responding to crises or discovered criminal typologies after they have already caused harm. The Commonwealth Model Law on Stablecoins changes the paradigm by explicitly framing the regulatory goal as anticipating and mitigating risks before widespread misuse becomes entrenched. This philosophy recognises that waiting for a problem to become systemic is too late; therefore, it requires frameworks to be designed that prevent the conditions that would allow for widespread illicit use from the outset.

9. Licensing and Supervision Made Simple

Chapter 9 provides a clear and practical overview of licensing and supervisory frameworks for stablecoin issuers and intermediaries across key jurisdictions. It begins by examining licensing as a core regulatory mechanism—defining who may operate within the stablecoin ecosystem and under what conditions. The chapter outlines how leading frameworks, including the EU's Markets in Crypto-Assets (MiCA) Regulation, the Monetary Authority of Singapore (MAS) regime, New York's BitLicense, and the Commonwealth Model Law on Virtual Assets, establish foundational rules for authorisation, supervision, and compliance.

A central focus is the need for technology-neutral, function-based licensing that regulates activities by their economic role rather than their technical form. The chapter also highlights how proportionate, risk-based supervision - supported by RegTech (Regulatory Technology) and SupTech (Supervisory Technology) tools - can enhance compliance efficiency and adapt to market innovation.

Special consideration is given to the implementation challenges faced by Commonwealth jurisdictions, where regulatory capacity and digital infrastructure vary widely. Through a comparative analysis and synthesis of global best practices, the chapter proposes a conceptual licensing framework and a compliance checklist designed to assist policymakers and compliance officers. It concludes by emphasising balanced regulation that supports innovation while safeguarding market integrity, consumer protection, and cross-border regulatory consistency.

10. How to Implement a Stablecoin Framework

Chapter 10 presents a practical roadmap for implementing a stablecoin framework designed to promote financial inclusion, resilience, and adaptability by breaking it down into configurable components: issuance, compliance, interoperability, governance, and access. It also identifies solutions and recommendations for overcoming implementation challenges.

Part III – Global Lessons for Stablecoins Regulation and Governance

Global Lessons for Stablecoin Regulation and Governance (IGI Global Forthcoming) consolidates the book's applied and policy-oriented focus, illustrating how theory, law, and technology intersect in the real-world regulation and governance of stablecoins. This section presents a comprehensive synthesis of global frameworks, case studies, and regulatory innovations shaping the emerging landscape of digital money. Across its chapters, it examines stablecoins' economic foundations, systemic risks, legal architecture, public-good potential, and governance paradoxes—offering an integrated understanding of how stability, innovation, and sovereignty can coexist in a digitised financial ecosystem.

The first set of chapters provides a technical and economic taxonomy of stablecoins, classifying them into fiat-backed, crypto-collateralised, algorithmic, and hybrid models. Using case studies such as USDC, USDT, DAI, and TerraUSD, it analyses stabilisation mechanisms, reserve management, and governance models, contrasting their efficiency and fragility. Empirical evidence confirms the resilience of fiat-backed models compared with the volatility of algorithmic approaches, while emerging hybrid frameworks offer promising, though largely experimental, alternatives. A comparative analysis with CBDCs underscores how private and public forms of digital money can complement one another within a programmable, transparent, and inclusive financial architecture.

Subsequent chapters focus on financial stability and systemic risk, highlighting that stablecoins—now exceeding USD 130 billion in market capitalisation- are increasingly systemically important. Episodes such as the Terra/Luna collapse demonstrate the contagion potential of poor design, mismanaged reserves, and uncoordinated regulation. Through comparative case studies, the text analyses transmission channels of instability, including liquidity mismatches, market concentration, and reserve opacity. The section argues that comprehensive prudential standards, interoperable oversight, and cross-border cooperation are essential to prevent a new class of "too-big-to-fail" digital assets.

Another central theme is cross-border regulatory coordination. Because stablecoins operate across jurisdictions, domestic supervision alone is insufficient. The chapters examine guidance from the IMF, BIS, and FSB, advocating harmonised definitions, data-sharing agreements, and joint supervisory mechanisms. Jurisdictional studies—covering Dubai's VARA, ADGM, DIFC, Singapore's MAS, Hong Kong's HKMA, and the UK FCA—illustrate diverse yet converging approaches to licensing, interoperability, and enforcement. The section concludes that effective coordination requires both formal instruments (MoUs, mutual recognition, passporting regimes) and informal mechanisms (regulatory sandboxes, capacity building, and peer dialogue).

Licensing and supervisory frameworks are explored in depth through comparative analysis of MiCA (EU), BitLicense (US), MAS (Singapore), and the Commonwealth Model Law on Virtual Assets. A central insight is the shift toward function-based, technology-neutral licensing supported by RegTech and SupTech tools to ensure adaptive, real-time supervision. Special attention is paid to Commonwealth and emerging-market jurisdictions, where capacity gaps demand modular, proportionate frameworks that balance innovation with consumer protection.

The later chapters broaden the lens, positioning stablecoins as instruments of public good capable of improving remittances, humanitarian aid distribution, and digital identity-linked inclusion—provided that governance, AML/CFT, and privacy safeguards are upheld. Finally, a unifying governance analysis reframes stablecoins as both a solution and a risk, emphasising that trust in digital money depends on transparent reserves, sound legal frameworks, technological resilience, and international coordination.

Together, the chapters in Global Lessons for Stablecoin Regulation and Governance, (IGI Global Forthcoming) form a coherent narrative: stablecoins are not merely financial innovations but structural catalysts reshaping the global monetary order. Achieving their promise demands a delicate equilibrium between regulatory rigour, technological adaptability, and international cooperation—ensuring that the digital future of money is stable, inclusive, and globally coherent.

CONCLUSION

The concluding chapter synthesises the book's central insights and outlines the key challenges that will determine whether stablecoins can achieve safe and sustainable scale. It emphasises that trust, transparency, and regulatory confidence are the cornerstones of widespread adoption. To be seen as credible, every major stablecoin must demonstrate that high-quality, liquid assets fully back its tokens and that redemptions into fiat currency are reliable under all conditions.

As stablecoins become more deeply embedded in global finance, their potential to generate systemic risk increases. This calls for robust supervisory, resolution, and contingency frameworks to ensure market stability and enable orderly wind-downs during crises. The chapter also underscores the importance of interoperability—both across blockchain networks and between digital and traditional financial infrastructures—to unlock the full economic potential of stablecoins.

Finally, the chapter highlights the need for regulatory agility. The Commonwealth Model Law and similar frameworks advocate a shift from rigid, prescriptive regulation to principles-based approaches that can evolve with technology. As innovations such as new algorithmic models and AI-driven finance emerge, regulators must remain adaptive and forward-looking. The chapter concludes that only through transparency, coordination, and flexible governance can stablecoins become a safe, trusted foundation for the future of digital finance.

REFERENCES

Arner, D. W., Buckley, R. P., & Zetzsche, D. A. (2020). *Programmable Money, Smart Contracts, and the Future of Financial Regulation. Law Working Paper Series*, University of Hong Kong Faculty of Law. https://doi.org/DOI: 10.2139/ssrn.3539057

Financial Action Task Force. (2025). *Virtual Assets: Targeted Update on the Implementation of the FATF Standards on VAs and VASPs* [Press release]. FATF. https://www.fatf-gafi.org/en/publications/fatfrecommendations/targeted-update-virtual-assets-vasps-2025.html

Gemini. (2025). *2025 Global State of Crypto Report.* Gemini. https://www.gemini.com/state-of-crypto

KEY TERMS AND DEFINITIONS

AML / CFT (Anti-Money Laundering / Countering the Financing of Terrorism): Legal and regulatory measures designed to prevent the misuse of financial systems for illicit or terrorist activities, as applied by the FATF to both virtual assets and so-called stablecoins.

Asset-Backed Stablecoin: A stablecoin whose value is supported by a diversified basket of assets—such as multiple fiat currencies, commodities, or tokenised instruments—managed to preserve stability.

Asset-Referenced Token (ART): Under the EU MiCA framework, a crypto-asset maintains a stable value by referencing several currencies, commodities, or other assets rather than a single fiat currency.

Bank for International Settlements (BIS): The global institution promoting monetary and financial stability, through its CPMI reports it sets standards for the safe use of stablecoin arrangements in payments and settlements.

Central Bank Digital Currency (CBDC): A digital form of central bank money that is a direct liability of the central bank. CBDCs may coexist with, complement or compete with private stablecoins within a digital monetary ecosystem.

Collateralisation: The process of backing a stablecoin with reserves—fiat, crypto, or commodities—to maintain its peg and redemption at par value.

Correspondent Banking Relationship (CBR): A relationship between banks in different countries in which one bank holds deposits for and provides payment and other services to another bank. The withdrawal of CBRs – de-risking – has in some cases pushed households and businesses towards stablecoins and other virtual assets for cross-border payments.

Cross-Chain Bridge: A technical mechanism that allows assets to be transferred or represented between two or more blockchains. Bridges may lock or burn tokens on a source chain and mint or release tokens on a destination chain, and are frequent targets of hacks and exploits.

Crypto-Collateralised Stablecoin: A stablecoin backed by other crypto-assets held as collateral, usually in excess of the value of the stablecoins issued. The peg is maintained through collateral management, liquidation mechanisms and market incentives.

DeFi (Decentralised Finance): An ecosystem of financial services – including trading, lending, derivatives and asset management – built on public blockchains using smart contracts, often without a traditional central intermediary. DeFi systems frequently rely on stablecoins as a unit of account and settlement asset.

Electronic Money Token (EMT): Under MiCA, a crypto-asset pegged to a single official currency and functioning as tokenised e-money must be issued by a licensed e-money or credit institution.

Fiat-Backed Stablecoin: A stablecoin fully collateralised by fiat currency or high-quality liquid assets held in regulated financial institutions and redeemable at par value.

Fiat-Referenced Token (FRT): Defined by ADGM's Financial Services and Markets Regulations 2015 as a digital asset referencing a fixed amount of fiat currency and granting holders direct redemption rights.

Financial Action Task Force (FATF): The intergovernmental body setting AML/CFT standards. It treats stablecoins within existing virtual-asset definitions and stresses the "travel rule" for cross-border transfers.

Financial Stability Board (FSB): An international body developing global standards for financial stability; author of the 2023 High-Level Recommendations for Global Stablecoin Arrangements.

Global Stablecoin (GSC): A stablecoin with potential cross-border reach and systemic importance, distinguished by its stabilisation mechanism, payment usability, and global adoption footprint.

Governance Framework: Rules and decision-making processes that ensure accountability, transparency, and risk management in stablecoin issuance and reserve operations.

Hong Kong Monetary Authority (HKMA): Hong Kong's de facto central bank defines stablecoins as distributed ledger tokens that serve as a medium of exchange and maintain a stable value relative to single or basket assets.

Issuance: The act of creating and delivering new stablecoin units to users in exchange for fiat or assets, thereby generating a redemption obligation.

Markets in Crypto-Assets Regulation (MiCA): The EU's 2023 regulation governing crypto-assets defines and regulates EMTs and ARTs with detailed reserve, capital, and transparency requirements.

Minting: The blockchain operation by which new tokens are created and recorded, usually following receipt of fiat funds by the issuer.

Monetary Authority of Singapore (MAS): Singapore's central bank and regulator. Its 2023 framework recognises "Single-Currency Stablecoins" (SCS) pegged to the SGD or G10 currencies.

Multi-Chain Stablecoin: A stablecoin that exists on more than one blockchain, either through native issuance on several networks or through wrapped and bridged representations. Multi-chain designs raise specific AML/CFT, PF and operational risks due to cross-chain bridges and fragmented liquidity.

Operational Resilience: The ability of a stablecoin arrangement to maintain core functions through operational, cyber, or market disruptions.

Payment Stablecoin: As defined in the U.S. GENIUS Act (2025), a fiat-pegged digital asset used for payments or settlements, legally redeemable on demand at a fixed value and barred from paying interest.

Payment Token: Defined by the Central Bank of the UAE as a virtual asset pegged to fiat value, used for payments, and divided into Domestic Payment Tokens (AED-linked) and Foreign Payment Tokens.

PF Dashboard: A structured data and analytics platform that aggregates information on stablecoin and other virtual-asset flows from multiple sources – including VASPs, banks, customs, FIUs and analytics providers – to support strategic and operational analysis of PF and related risks.

Proliferation Financing (PF): The act of providing funds or financial services used for the manufacture, acquisition, development, transport or use of nuclear, chemical or biological weapons and their means of delivery, and related materials. In this chapter, PF includes the use of stablecoins and other virtual assets to facilitate such activities or to evade sanctions related to proliferation.

Prudential Regulation: Oversight ensuring issuers maintain adequate capital, liquidity, and sound reserve management to protect holders and systemic stability.

Redemption / Redemption Rights: The legal right of a token holder to exchange a stablecoin for its underlying reference asset at par value; cornerstone of user protection and peg credibility.

Regulatory Arbitrage: Exploiting inconsistencies between jurisdictions to reduce compliance or oversight burdens; a key concern in cross-border stablecoin activity.

Regulatory Sandbox: A controlled environment in which firms can test innovative products, services or business models with real customers under regulatory oversight and with specific safeguards. Sandboxes can be useful for piloting stablecoin-based remittances, payments or tokenisation use-cases before full-scale licensing.

Reserve Assets / Reserve Management: The portfolio of eligible, liquid assets backing a stablecoin; management covers safekeeping, liquidity, segregation, and disclosure to support redemption.

Self-Hosted Wallet: A wallet in which the user controls the private keys, in contrast to a custodial wallet where a VASP or other intermediary holds the keys on behalf of the customer. Self-hosted wallets raise specific AML/CFT and PF challenges because they sit outside traditional account-based frameworks.

Single-Currency Stablecoin (SCS): A stablecoin pegged one-to-one to a single fiat currency (e.g., USD, SGD) and authorised under MAS rules.

Stabilisation Mechanism: The method (collateral-based, algorithmic, or hybrid) by which a stablecoin sustains parity with its reference asset.

Stablecoin: A digital token engineered to maintain a stable value relative to a reference asset—usually fiat currency—serving as a medium of exchange, store of value, and settlement instrument in digital ecosystems.

Supervisory Oversight: Ongoing regulatory monitoring of issuers, custodians, and distributors to ensure compliance, financial soundness, and consumer protection.

Systemic Risk: The risk is that the failure of a major stablecoin or issuer could trigger wider financial instability due to interconnected markets and reliance on digital liquidity.

Tokenisation: The process of creating a digital representation of rights or interests in an asset (such as a security, loan, commodity or real estate) in the form of a cryptographic token on a distributed-ledger or blockchain system.

Transparency and Disclosure: Requirements mandating the timely publication of reserve composition, audits, governance, and redemption procedures.

Travel Rule: The requirement, derived from FATF Recommendation 16, for financial institutions and VASPs to ensure that originator and beneficiary information accompanies cross-border transfers of funds or virtual assets and is available to competent authorities.

Utility Token: A token granting access to a digital service or network function rather than serving as a stable store of value or payment instrument.

Virtual Asset Service Provider (VASP): A natural or legal person who, as a business, conducts one or more of the following for or on behalf of another person: exchange between virtual assets and fiat; exchange between one or more forms of virtual assets; transfer of virtual assets; safekeeping or administration of virtual assets; or participation in and provision of financial services related to an issuer's offer or sale of a virtual asset.

Virtual Asset: A digital representation of value that can be digitally traded, transferred and used for payment or investment purposes, as defined broadly in the CMLVA and FATF standards.

Wrapped Token Algorithmic Stablecoin: A type of stablecoin that seeks to maintain price stability without holding collateral. It uses A stablecoin that relies primarily on algorithmic supply adjustments, market incentives or other formula-based mechanisms to maintain its peg, rather than fully backed reserves. Algorithmic stablecoins are generally considered higher risk from both prudential and financial-integrity perspectives.

Wrapped Token: A token on one blockchain that represents an asset native to another blockchain, typically backed one-to-one by the locked original. Wrapped tokens depend on the security and governance of the bridge or custodian that manages the wrap.

Chapter 2
What Are Stablecoins?

Kokila Alagh
KARM Legal Consultants, UAE

ABSTRACT

This chapter explores the conceptual foundations, typologies, and functional dynamics of stablecoins. It traces their evolution from experimental constructs to integral components of the global financial system, examining how international standard-setting bodies and national regulators define and categorise them. Through a comparative analysis of frameworks adopted by jurisdictions including the European Union, United States, United Kingdom, Singapore, Hong Kong, and the United Arab Emirates, the chapter highlights convergences in definitions and divergences shaped by monetary sovereignty and policy priorities. It further analyses the operational lifecycle of stablecoins, from issuance and reserve management to redemption, and delineates their distinctions from other digital assets such as cryptocurrencies, CBDCs, and security tokens. Ultimately, the chapter establishes the conceptual groundwork necessary for understanding the legal, regulatory, and economic implications of stablecoins in an evolving financial landscape.

INTRODUCTION

Stablecoins have journeyed from the fringes of cryptocurrency culture to the centre of global financial debate. Unlike Bitcoin or Ether, which derive their value purely from market dynamics, stablecoins are built around the pursuit of stability rather than speculation. Their core premise is simple yet powerful: to maintain a steady value by pegging each token to a reference asset, most commonly a fiat currency. That simple promise has scaled fast: by the middle of 2025, the aggregate market capitalisation of stablecoins will have reached into the hundreds of billions, while on-chain data revealed a transformation in their use. No longer confined to trading

DOI: 10.4018/979-8-3373-6655-5.ch002

and liquidity provision within crypto markets, stablecoins were facilitating real economic activity (Singh, 2025). Over the previous year alone, they had supported more than twenty trillion dollars in on-chain transaction volume, signalling their evolution from a niche experiment into an integral component of the digital asset ecosystem (Das, 2025).

The attraction is obvious. Stablecoins promise instantaneous cross-border transfers, continuous settlement beyond the limitations of traditional banking hours, and greater financial inclusion by offering a digitally native unit of value accessible to anyone with a smartphone and an internet connection. Their programmability and borderless reach have positioned them not merely as an innovation within payments but as a foundational layer for the next generation of financial infrastructure. Yet their very success has also exposed profound regulatory and legal challenges. The proliferation of stablecoins across multiple jurisdictions, often operating in regulatory grey zones, has raised questions about their proper classification, the adequacy of their reserves, and the potential risks they pose to financial stability and consumer protection. Policymakers are still grappling with a central question: should stablecoins be treated as payment instruments, securities, deposits, or a new category of digital asset altogether?

A major obstacle to regulatory clarity lies in the absence of a universally accepted definition of "stablecoin" (Financial Stability Board, 2023). Different countries and international bodies have adopted varying terminologies and definitional approaches shaped by their own legal traditions, policy objectives, and supervisory perimeters. What one jurisdiction calls a "stablecoin" might be termed an "e-money token" or simply treated as a type of crypto-asset elsewhere. This definitional inconsistency complicates cross-border activity and hinders the development of coherent international oversight. It also risks leaving certain stablecoin arrangements outside the scope of regulation in one jurisdiction, even as they fall squarely in another, which could result in regulatory arbitrage.

The objective of this chapter is therefore to demystify the concept of the stablecoin and to establish a common analytical foundation from which subsequent regulatory and policy discussions can proceed. By unpacking the definitional variations found across international and domestic frameworks, the chapter seeks to identify the essential characteristics that distinguish stablecoins from other digital assets. In doing so, it clarifies which types of stablecoin arrangements fall squarely within prevailing regulatory definitions and which remain at their margins. This groundwork is essential for understanding the regulatory implications of stablecoin activity across diverse legal environments.

To that end, the chapter unfolds in several stages. First, it sets out a working definition of stablecoins and explains key terms (such as reference asset, reserve, redemption, etc.) that are essential to understanding how stablecoins operate. It then analyses how major international standard-setting bodies (like the Financial Stability Board (FSB), International Organization for Securities Commission (IOSCO), Financial Action Task Force (FATF), Organisation for Economic Co-operation and Development (OECD) and Bank for International Settlements (BIS)) have defined or described stablecoins, as these global perspectives inform national approaches and highlight areas of consensus (or lack thereof). Next, it compares jurisdiction-specific definitions under several prominent regulatory regimes, including the European Union, the United States of America, the United Kingdom, Hong Kong, Singapore, and the United Arab Emirates, to illustrate points of convergence and divergence. Building on this definitional groundwork, the chapter then analyses the main types of stablecoins and their associated risk. It examines how differences in reference assets or stabilisation mechanisms (for instance, fiat-backed vs. algorithmic stablecoins) influence the regulatory classification and oversight of these stablecoins.

The chapter further outlines the operational lifecycle of a stablecoin, from issuance and reserve management to distribution and redemption. Mapping this lifecycle and the key participants involved (issuers, custodians, exchanges, etc.) is crucial for understanding where regulatory responsibilities and risks arise in practice. In addition, emerging variations such as interest-bearing stablecoins or other hybrid models are discussed, as they present novel questions (e.g., if a stablecoin pays interest like a bank deposit or money market fund, should it be regulated as such?). The chapter also delineates the boundaries between stablecoins and other categories of digital assets, including cryptocurrencies, central bank digital currencies (hereinafter referred to as CBDCs), security tokens, and utility or governance tokens. By contrasting their functional and legal characteristics, we clarify at what point a token ceases to be treated as a "stablecoin" under existing frameworks (for example, if it confers shareholder-like rights or fluctuates in value, it might be deemed a security or other instrument rather than a stablecoin). Finally, the chapter offers a forward-looking discussion on how stablecoin definitions and regulatory approaches may need to evolve. Given the pace of innovation, regulators may have to periodically revisit definitions to ensure they remain technologically neutral and adequately capture new manifestations of stablecoin arrangements.

In essence, this chapter serves as both foundation and framework. It provides a comprehensive overview of what stablecoins are, how they are categorised, and why they matter, not only to the crypto ecosystem but also to the future architecture of money and payments. Establishing a shared conceptual understanding is a prerequisite for the deeper legal, policy, and economic analysis that follows in subsequent chapters. Only by defining stablecoins with precision can we meaningfully address the questions they raise about financial stability, consumer protection, and the future of monetary sovereignty in the digital age.

DEFINING STABLECOINS: CONCEPTS AND REGULATORY PERSPECTIVES

Stablecoins can be broadly defined as digital assets that aim to maintain a stable value relative to a specified asset (or basket of assets). The essence of a stablecoin lies in its attempt to merge the advantages of cryptocurrencies (instant settlement, global reach, and programmable transactions) with the purchasing power stability of conventional money. In practical terms, the goal is straightforward: each stablecoin unit should hold steady value against whatever it references, whether that's one US dollar, one euro, or an ounce of gold. Most of the stablecoins circulating today achieve this stability through reserve backing and redemption rights. Each token corresponds to an underlying unit of fiat currency (or other assets) held in custody by the issuer or its trustee. Holders can redeem tokens for the reference asset, usually at a one-to-one ratio. Others rely on more complex mechanisms, such as crypto collateralisation where digital assets are locked in smart contracts as backing, or algorithmic control, where supply automatically expands or contracts in response to price movements.

Why do the terms differ? The term carries technological and market meaning but, as yet, no single universal legal definition. This ambiguity has been highlighted by several International standard setting bodies (SSBs). The FSB, in its *High-level Recommendations for the Regulation, Supervision, and Oversight of Global Stablecoin Arrangements*, described stablecoins functionally as *"a crypto-asset that aims to maintain a stable value relative to a specified asset, or a pool or basket of assets"* (FSB, 2023). This broad definition captures the essential purpose (value stability relative to something) without tying the definition to any specific mechanism or technological implementation. In the FSB's view, a stablecoin may be pegged to a single currency, multiple currencies, or even commodities. What matters is its intent to stabilise value, not the method by which it does so. The IOSCO has used similar language in its discussions of crypto-assets, effectively focusing on the intended *economic function* of stablecoins as stability mechanisms within the crypto market (The International Organization of Securities Commissions, 2023).

In contrast, the FATF has adopted a more cautious stance. In its *Report to G20 on So-called Stablecoins*, FATF referred to stablecoins as *"so-called stablecoins"*, deliberately avoiding endorsement of the term as a standalone category (The Financial Action Task Force (FATF), 2020). FATF also noted that *"the term 'stablecoin' is not a clear legal or technical category but primarily a marketing term used by promoters"* (FATF, 2020). In other words, FATF treats stablecoins within its existing definitions of virtual assets or traditional financial assets depending on their exact characteristics, rather than carving out a new category. This stance ensures that activities involving stablecoins are subject to the same anti-money laundering/

countering the financing of terrorism (AML/CFT) controls as other virtual assets, sidestepping debates over nomenclature. Some stablecoin structures may also exploit the ambiguity in definitions to operate beyond the regulatory perimeter, especially when no single regulatory authority may have complete jurisdiction, and further, "global stablecoins", those with potential for mass adoption across borders, may pose elevated money laundering and terrorist financing risks if not properly regulated (FATF, 2020).

The notion of the "Global Stablecoin" (GSC) has become central in international policy discussions. The FSB defines a GSC as a stablecoin with a potential for wide cross-border reach and systemic importance in one or more jurisdictions (FSB, 2023). This designation is less about scale in numbers and more about influence: how such a token could affect monetary systems, payment flows, and financial stability globally. The FSB identifies three distinguishing characteristics of GSCs: (1) a stabilisation mechanism (e.g., reserve assets or an algorithm that stabilises value); (2) usability as a widely accepted means of payment and/or store of value; and (3) cross-jurisdictional reach and adoption (FSB, 2023).

In effect, a GSC is not just another crypto token; it is a digital instrument that could, in theory, rival sovereign money in reach or function. That prospect makes regulators uneasy. It explains why the conversation around stablecoins quickly evolved from niche technical debates to high-level discussions among central banks and finance ministries. The FSB's position is clear: stability in name does not guarantee safety in practice. Only when robust governance, risk management, and legal certainty exist can a stablecoin credibly operate at a systemic scale.

In the years since FSB first coined the term "GSC", this framework has influenced nearly every national regulator that has developed a stablecoin regime. Even jurisdictions that don't use the term explicitly have borrowed the logic: the greater the scale and cross-border use, the stricter the oversight should be.

These international perspectives reveal an important truth: definitions shape regulation, compliance, and market behaviour. How a jurisdiction defines "stablecoin" determines who can issue it, what reserves must be held, who oversees redemption, and what disclosures are mandatory.

DOMESTIC REGULATORY DEFINITIONS AND APPROACHES

When we shift from the global stage to national regulators, the picture becomes more intricate. Each jurisdiction has attempted to define stablecoins in a way that fits comfortably within its legal and policy architecture. Although many of these definitions are inspired by the same international principles, the details vary, sometimes subtly, sometimes significantly. There is, at best, a partial convergence around core ideas such as stability, backing, and redemption; yet significant differences remain in how broadly or narrowly each authority interprets the concept.

The European Union's *Markets in Crypto-Assets* (MiCA) introduces two categories that together capture what the market would generally regard as stablecoin instruments (The European Parliament and the Council of the European Union, 2023). *First, "electronic money tokens" (*EMTs*)* are defined as cryptoassets that purport to maintain a stable value by referencing a single official currency. In essence, an EMT is a tokenised form of fiat currency (e.g., a Euro-stablecoin). Issuers must be authorised as credit institutions or e-money institutions, reflecting the EU's view of such tokens as akin to electronic money. *Second, "asset-referenced tokens"* (ART(s)) are crypto-assets that maintain a stable value by referencing any other value or right or combination thereof; this can include a basket of currencies or asset commodities. For example, a token pegged to a mix of USD and gold, or to an index, would be an ART rather than an EMT. ART issuers face requirements that are no less demanding: they must have robust reserve asset policies and meet capital, governance, and white paper obligations. The distinction between EMTs and ARTs lies mainly in the nature of their reference assets. MiCA also draws clear boundaries: tokens that already qualify as securities, deposits, or securitisations under existing EU law are explicitly excluded. The goal is to avoid overlapping regimes. In short, MiCA places both fiat-pegged and asset-pegged tokens under a unified regime comparable to that governing e-money, ensuring that issuers hold sufficient reserves, honour redemption at par, and operate with full transparency.

The United States' Guiding and Establishing National Innovation for U.S. Stablecoins Act (GENIUS Act) has taken a more pragmatic and incremental route (United States Congress, 2025). The GENIUS ACT introduces the term "payment stablecoin" to describe fiat-pegged assets intended for settlement purposes. The GENIUS Act defines a "payment stablecoin" as a digital asset that is (a) designed to be used as a means of payment or settlement; (b) the issuer has a legal obligation of redeeming it on demand for a fixed amount of monetary value (typically a fiat currency); and (c) such stablecoin will maintain a stable value relative to a fixed amount of monetary value. Notably, payment stablecoins do not include a digital asset that is a national currency - meaning stablecoins are recognised as private instruments. The U.S. approach therefore centres on redemption obligation and payment functionality, treating stability as a precondition rather than a defining trait in isolation.

The United Kingdom, meanwhile, has chosen a deliberately phased approach. Under the *Draft Financial Services and Markets Act 2000 (Regulated Activities and Miscellaneous Provision) (Cryptoassets) Order 2025* (Draft Order), "qualifying stablecoin" is defined as a subset of crypto-assets that references fiat currency value and purports to maintain stability by holding or backing with assets of equal value (HM Treasury, 2025b). In practice, this means the regime focuses squarely on fiat-referenced stablecoins. Thus, like the EU and US, the UK is concentrating on fiat-backed stablecoins for mainstream use, leaving other types outside the regulated category for now. The HM Treasury's policy note on "*Future financial services regulatory regime for crypto assets*" acknowledges that payments using stablecoins will remain unregulated for the time being, pending further development of use cases and consumer adoption (HM Treasury, 2025a). The idea is to observe how stablecoins behave under partial supervision before expanding the regime into adjacent areas such as payments infrastructure and cross-border settlement.

The Monetary Authority of Singapore (MAS) in 2023 finalised a stablecoin regulatory framework focusing on Single-Currency Stablecoins (SCS) pegged to the Singapore dollar or a G10 currency (Monetary Authority of Singapore, 2023). Under this framework, only issuers of SCS that fulfil certain criteria can label their product as "MAS-regulated stablecoins". The MAS model limits the regulatory perimeter to the forms of stablecoins most relevant to Singapore's economy, such as those pegged to globally liquid currencies or its own sovereign currency. This ensures that stablecoins circulating within Singapore's financial system remain tightly linked to trusted monetary anchors.

The Hong Kong Monetary Authority (HKMA) has adopted a definition that is both expansive and functionally grounded. Under its *Stablecoin Ordinance* (Ordinance), a cryptographically secured digital representation of value must satisfy 5 conditions to constitute a stablecoin: (a) it is a unit of account or store of economic value; (b) it can be used as a medium of exchange for the purposes of payment for goods or services, discharge of debt or investment; (c) it can be transferred, stored or traded; (d) it is operated on a distributed ledger technology (DLT); and (e) it purports to maintain a stable value against a single or basket of assets. Notably, the Ordinance excludes CBDCs and tokens that constitute securities, futures contracts, or deposits, among others (Hong Kong Monetary Authority, 2023).

The United Arab Emirates (UAE) offers a case of multiple regulatory jurisdictions with distinct stablecoin approaches. The Central Bank of the UAE (CBUAE) regulates Payment Tokens under the *Payment Token Services Regulation* (PTSR). The CBUAE defines a *"Payment Token"* essentially as a type of virtual asset that purports to maintain a stable value by referencing the value of the same fiat currency the Payment Token is denominated in or another Payment Token also denominated in the same fiat currency(Central Bank of the UAE [CBUAE], 2024). In particular, it distinguishes Domestic Payment Tokens (DPT) and Foreign Payment Tokens (FPT), with the DPT referencing AED and the FPT referencing any other fiat currency. This framework brings stablecoins that peg to fiat (whether AED or USD) under its supervision; the CBUAE asserts its role as the gatekeeper of monetary sovereignty. Any issuer or service provider dealing in these tokens must be licensed and comply with prudential safeguards consistent with protecting the value stability of the payment token.

Meanwhile, in the Abu Dhabi Global Market (ADGM), a financial free zone in the UAE with its own financial regulator – the Financial Services Regulatory Authority (ADGM FSRA) has taken a parallel but distinct approach. The FSRA regulates Fiat-Referenced Tokens (FRTs) under the *Financial Services and Markets Regulations 2015* (FSMR) (Abu Dhabi Global Market, 2015). An FRT, as defined by the FSMR, is a digital asset, whose transfer and storage are achieved through DLT, and its purpose is to be used as a medium of exchange with a stable store of value. Further, under the FSMR, an FRT has two characteristics: (a) it references a fixed amount of single fiat currency, and (b) it ensures that FRT holders have the right of redemption against the issuer on demand. Two core characteristics follow from this: the token is fully backed, and the holder has a direct redemption claim on the issuer. This structure closely resembles what most observers would regard as a classic fiat-backed stablecoin. Crucially, an FRT issued from within the ADGM cannot reference the value of the AED, as this falls under the exclusive regulatory purview of the CBUAE. The ADGM's regulatory framework requires issuers to maintain reserves in safe, liquid assets and to segregate those reserves with an authorised custodian.

Across these jurisdictions, we see a shared understanding that stablecoins are digital assets designed to maintain stable value. Yet, their definitional boundaries differ markedly in terms of the underlying reference assets, scope of coverage, and regulatory intent. The European Union's *MiCA* adopts the most expansive approach, distinguishing between EMTs, which are tied to a single fiat currency, and ARTs, which may be pegged to a basket of currencies, commodities, or other assets. This dual classification enables the EU to accommodate a wide range of stablecoin models, from fiat-backed instruments functioning as e-money equivalents to complex, multi-asset structures designed for cross-border or diversified value stability. In contrast, other authorities adopt narrower definitions that focus primarily on fiat-referenced tokens intended for use as a means of payment or settlement, excluding commodity or multi-asset-backed variants. These jurisdictions emphasise financial stability, consumer protection, and the prevention of monetary substitution; hence, the exclusion of speculative or investment-orientated stablecoins.

The MAS' framework further refines this approach by recognising only SCS pegged to the Singapore dollar or any G10 currency, underscoring a strong link between regulatory oversight and macroeconomic stability. This mirrors a broader trend toward limiting systemic risk by tethering stablecoin value to highly liquid and internationally trusted fiat currencies. Meanwhile, HKMA's Ordinance offers a comparatively inclusive definition, capturing both single and basket-pegged models, provided they serve as a unit of account, store of value, and medium of exchange on distributed ledger infrastructure. The UAE's multi-regulator approach also illustrates the jurisdictional fragmentation that can emerge in complex financial centres. The CBUAE regulates payment tokens, distinguishing between DPTs (AED-referenced) and FPTs (foreign fiat-referenced), to preserve monetary sovereignty. The ADGM FSRA regulates FRTs pegged to a single fiat currency (excluding the AED), requiring full reserve backing and redemption rights, thereby aligning closely with prudential payment regulation principles.

What emerges from this comparative landscape is not uniformity, but a kind of structured diversity. There may be no single, global definition of a stablecoin, yet an unmistakable consensus is taking shape around its economic essence:

- A stablecoin is a digital token that aims to maintain a stable value relative to a clearly identified reference asset, serving as a reliable medium of exchange and store of value in a digital environment.

The technological details—whether blockchain type, reserve composition, or algorithmic mechanism—may vary. The legal categories—EMT, ART, Payment Token, FRT, or SCS—may differ. But the conceptual anchor remains the same: stability, redeemability, and trust.

Stablecoins, then, are best understood as function-driven instruments. Their identity lies not in their technological form but in their *purpose*: to enable predictable, reliable, stable-value exchange in a digital world. That shared function is what allows regulators—despite their differences—to see the same object through different legal lenses.

TYPOLOGIES OF STABLECOINS AND THEIR RISK PROFILES

As the term 'stablecoin' spread through financial and policy circles, it quickly became clear that it was not describing a single, uniform product but rather an entire spectrum of designs, each built upon a different logic of stability, degree of decentralisation, and level of risk. The word "stable" might suggest simplicity, yet the architectures behind it are remarkably diverse. Some stablecoins are anchored in fiat reserves held in bank accounts; others derive their value from baskets of assets, volatile cryptocurrencies, or even self-adjusting algorithms. Beneath their shared promise of price stability lies a range of mechanisms that vary not only in sophistication but also in reliability.

To understand this diversity, one must classify stablecoins according to what supports their value and how they maintain their peg. The distinctions are more than theoretical. They determine how each type behaves under stress, how regulators might treat it, and where vulnerabilities may lie. A fiat-backed stablecoin fails in very different ways than an algorithmic one. Recognising these nuances is therefore essential to understanding both the promise and the fragility of this new form of digital money.

Fiat-Collateralised Stablecoins (Fiat-Backed)

These tokens are the most straightforward and widely adopted form. Each token is backed by an equivalent amount of fiat currency or short-term liquid instruments held in reserve. For every digital dollar issued, there should exist one actual dollar, or its near-equivalent, held safely in a regulated institution. This design underpins some of the largest stablecoins in circulation, such as Tether (USDT) and USD Coin (USDC), both of which are pegged to the United States dollar and redeemable at par. The reserves supporting these tokens often consist of cash, bank deposits, treasury bills, and other short-duration, high-quality assets.

The apparent simplicity of this model conceals intricate dependencies. Its success rests entirely on the integrity of the reserves, the credibility of the issuer, and the reliability of the banking partners that safeguard those reserves. If the issuer's disclosures are inaccurate or if the underlying assets include riskier instruments such as long-dated commercial paper, redemption pressures could quickly overwhelm liquidity. Similarly, if an issuer becomes insolvent or loses access to its custodial banks, redemptions could halt and the peg could break. Though these coins exist on distributed ledgers, their stability is rooted in the conventional financial system, and they inherit its vulnerabilities.

The risks embedded in fiat-backed models fall into three broad categories: the sufficiency and quality of reserves, the operational and solvency risk of the issuer, and the dependency on traditional banks for custody. Despite these challenges, fiat-collateralised stablecoins remain the most trusted and widely integrated type. Their mechanics resemble those of familiar instruments like stored value or electronic money, making them easier to regulate. Yet they can also concentrate on risk. When a few issuers hold tens of billions of dollars across a small cluster of banks, their stability begins to matter for the broader financial ecosystem.

Asset-Backed Stablecoins

These tokens derive their value not from a single currency but from a basket of assets, which may include multiple fiat currencies, commodities such as gold, or tokenised financial instruments. The rationale is diversification. By anchoring value to a range of assets, issuers aim to avoid dependence on the stability of any one currency. However, this diversification comes at the cost of complexity. Managing a reserve composed of several asset classes introduces valuation and liquidity challenges. The token's price may appear stable relative to its basket but fluctuates in relation to any particular currency.

An investor holding such a coin might find it stable in theory but not in practice. When the U.S. dollar appreciates against the basket, for example, the token's value in dollars will fall, even if it remains perfectly balanced within its reference index. Moreover, including commodities or bonds in the reserve portfolio exposes the issuer to market risk. A decline in the market value of these assets could render the token under-collateralised, forcing the issuer to liquidate positions at inopportune times. These dynamics resemble those faced by investment funds, and regulators have taken notice.

The European Union's treatment of ARTs under MiCA reflects precisely this concern. By imposing reserve, governance, and capital requirements—and by limiting issuance size for significant tokens—the EU aims to prevent large basket-based coins from undermining monetary policy or financial stability. Asset-backed stablecoins, in other words, may diversify away from single-currency dependence, but they invite new exposures in return. Their stability depends as much on asset management as on technical design.

Crypto-Collateralised Stablecoins

Instead of relying on fiat or physical assets, these tokens are backed by cryptocurrencies and held in decentralised smart contracts. In theory, they remove the need for trusted intermediaries, since all reserve operations occur transparently on the blockchain. A well-known example is DAI, which is issued by the MakerDAO protocol. Users deposit volatile assets such as Ether as collateral and mint a smaller amount of DAI against it, creating an over-collateralised position—perhaps 150 dollars' worth of Ether for every 100 DAI issued.

This mechanism is ingenious but precarious. The system's solvency depends entirely on the value of its crypto collateral. When markets are calm, overcollateralisation provides sufficient protection. When volatility spikes, however, the peg can come under severe pressure. Falling collateral prices trigger automated liquidations, which can flood markets and depress prices further, amplifying instability. In extreme conditions, the feedback loop can become self-destructive, leading to what analysts call a "death spiral".

Because these structures operate through code, they introduce a different class of risk—technical and governance vulnerabilities. Smart contracts can contain coding flaws or depend on unreliable data feeds known as oracles. Attacks or errors in these systems can instantly drain reserves or disable redemptions. Moreover, the question of accountability remains unresolved. If no identifiable issuer exists, regulators face difficulty in assigning responsibility for compliance, consumer protection, or redress. This dilemma has made crypto-collateralised stablecoins the most conceptually challenging for regulators to categorise. They are neither fully decentralised nor fully accountable, existing in the twilight between algorithm and institution.

Algorithmic Stablecoins

These occupy the fourth and most controversial position in this taxonomy. These tokens attempt to achieve price stability without holding any collateral at all. Instead, they rely on algorithmic mechanisms and market incentives to expand or contract supply in response to price fluctuations. In essence, they try to replace monetary backing with mathematical control.

The idea evokes the image of an autonomous digital central bank, adjusting token supply to maintain equilibrium. When demand increases, the system mints new tokens to bring the price down; when demand falls, it burns tokens or issues a secondary volatility token to absorb excess supply. The architecture is often elegant in theory but brittle in practice. Without real reserves to anchor confidence, the system's stability depends entirely on collective belief in the mechanism itself. Once that belief falters, collapse is swift.

The case of TerraUSD (UST) in 2022 remains the most vivid illustration. When redemptions surged and market participants lost faith in the stabilising algorithm, the peg dissolved almost overnight, wiping out tens of billions in value. The episode confirmed that confidence alone is not a sufficient stabilisation mechanism. Regulatory bodies such as the Financial Stability Board have since declared that algorithmic models fail to meet the criteria for effective stabilisation under global standards. Many jurisdictions now prohibit or severely restrict such tokens, viewing them not as stablecoins but as speculative instruments masquerading as money.

Despite repeated failures, experimentation continues. Developers have tried hybrid models that combine partial reserves with algorithmic features, seeking a balance between efficiency and credibility. None, however, has yet demonstrated the resilience required for mainstream adoption. Algorithmic stability remains an aspiration rather than an achievement.

"Privacy" or Anonymity-Enhanced Stablecoins

Combine value stability with varying degrees of transactional anonymity. Unlike traditional stablecoins, whose transactions are recorded on public ledgers for anyone to trace, these instruments use privacy-preserving technologies such as zero-knowledge proofs or specialised privacy blockchains to conceal details of transactions. Some projects wrap existing fiat-backed tokens in privacy layers, while others issue entirely new tokens with native privacy features.

From a technological perspective, these designs aim to recreate one of cash's defining attributes—privacy. From a regulatory perspective, they create a serious dilemma. Anonymous digital money invites misuse for illicit purposes, undermining global standards for anti-money laundering and counter-terrorism financing. The FATF's "travel rule", which requires that identifying information accompany digital asset transfers, is fundamentally incompatible with privacy-enhanced architectures. Regulators therefore view such models as inherently non-compliant. Exchanges have delisted them, payment providers have blocked them, and in most regulated markets they now exist only at the margins.

Yet their existence underscores an unresolved tension in the digital age: how to reconcile the individual's right to privacy with the state's obligation to maintain financial integrity. Stablecoins have made money transparent, traceable, and programmable. Privacy-focused variants attempt to restore what digitisation has eroded, even if doing so places them in permanent conflict with regulation.

When viewed together, these five typologies reveal the extraordinary breadth of experimentation taking place under the stablecoin banner. The first type relies on traditional financial institutions to guarantee value; the second blends financial innovation with portfolio management; the third turns to decentralised infrastructure; the fourth places faith in self-correcting code; and the fifth challenges the very premise of regulatory transparency. Each is a response to the same question: how can digital systems recreate the stability and trust once provided by sovereign money?

The implications for regulators are profound. Fiat-backed coins fit comfortably within existing regimes for electronic money, where well-established rules on reserves, segregation, and redemption already exist. Asset-backed models, depending on their structure, may resemble collective investment schemes or money-market funds, demanding disclosure, valuation, and capital rules akin to securities regulation. Crypto-collateralised designs push oversight into uncharted territory, raising questions about who is legally responsible for a decentralised protocol. Algorithmic and privacy-enhanced designs often fall outside permissible boundaries entirely, facing de facto exclusion from regulated financial systems.

Each typology represents a different balance between innovation and assurance. The more centralised and regulated the model, the safer it tends to be for consumers, but the less revolutionary it becomes. The more decentralised and autonomous the design, the more it embodies the ideals of open finance, yet the thinner its layer of legal protection is. Understanding this continuum is essential for policymakers and participants alike.

It is not enough to call a token "stable". One must examine the foundation of that stability, the identity of the guarantor, and the consequences of failure. Those questions reveal whether a stablecoin is a trustworthy medium of exchange or merely another speculative construct in disguise. Stablecoins are not a single invention but an ongoing experiment in the re-creation of trust through technology. Some designs have succeeded in replicating the discipline of traditional money; others have collapsed under the weight of their own abstraction. Together, they form an evolving laboratory, perhaps the most significant in the history of monetary innovation since the birth of the modern central bank.

FUNCTIONAL AND ECONOMIC CHARACTERISTICS OF STABLECOINS

To understand the regulatory and market significance of stablecoins, one must look beyond their technical construction and examine how they function within the wider financial system. A stablecoin is not merely a token on a blockchain. It is a bridge between traditional money and the digital economy, a conduit for payments, settlement, and liquidity across borders and platforms. Its economic characteristics determine not only its value proposition but also its policy implications. The way a stablecoin behaves in practice—how it moves, who uses it, and for what purpose—reveals as much about its regulatory treatment as its underlying design.

Stablecoins play several distinct yet interconnected roles in the modern financial ecosystem. The OECD, in its report on *Central Bank Digital Currencies and Payments: A Review of Domestic and International Implications*, identifies two fundamental elements that stablecoins share with fiat currencies: (a) stable medium of exchange and (b) unit of account (Organisation for European Economic Co-operation [OECD], 2021).

Their appeal lies in their ability to combine the stability of fiat currency with the efficiency and programmability of blockchain technology. This dual nature makes them uniquely positioned to serve both traditional finance and the emerging digital-asset economy.

In Cross-Border Payments, stablecoins have demonstrated extraordinary utility. Traditional international transfers remain expensive, slow, and fragmented, constrained by correspondent banking networks and time-zone boundaries. A stablecoin transaction, by contrast, can move value globally within seconds, twenty-four hours a day, at a fraction of the cost. This efficiency has made them attractive to businesses that operate internationally, to financial institutions seeking instant settlement, and to individuals remitting funds to their families abroad. In many emerging markets, where banking access is limited and payment infrastructure is weak, stablecoins have quietly become a de facto alternative to the traditional banking system. Both Visa and Mastercard have started integrating stablecoin settlement into their payment networks for certain transactions (Schaaf, 2025). These changes show that stablecoin payment technology is becoming more like regular finance. This newfound convenience, however, brings new policy tensions. Cross-border use of stablecoins challenges the ability of governments to monitor capital flows, enforce foreign-exchange regulations, and protect consumers. It also raises questions of monetary sovereignty when foreign-currency stablecoins begin circulating within domestic economies. The efficiency that makes stablecoins attractive to users can also make them disruptive to existing financial controls. The European Central Bank (ECB) has warned that wide use of foreign stablecoins in Europe could undermine the ECB's control over euro area monetary conditions (Schaaf, 2025). While stablecoins offer a revolutionary improvement in payment efficiency, their rise forces regulators to rethink international cooperation, data sharing for transactions (to ensure AML compliance), and the interplay with monetary sovereignty.

Beyond payments, stablecoins today form the liquidity backbone of the crypto-asset markets (Adachi et al., 2022). They provide the liquidity that enables continuous trading on cryptocurrency exchanges, serving as the cash leg in millions of daily transactions. Without them, the digital-asset ecosystem would be far less liquid and far more volatile. Stablecoins function as the settlement asset of choice between exchanges, brokers, and traders, providing a neutral medium of value when national currencies cannot move quickly enough through banking channels. Their presence has effectively created a parallel layer of dollar liquidity that operates entirely on-chain.

This central role in liquidity creation also exposes new systemic risks. If a major stablecoin were to lose its peg or experience a redemption freeze, the resulting loss of confidence could ripple through the entire digital-asset market. The collapse of a large issuer would not merely affect its users; it could trigger a cascade of price dislocations and liquidity shortfalls across platforms.

Stablecoins have also begun to play a growing role in the settlement of tokenised real-world assets. As financial instruments such as bonds, equities, and real estate are increasingly issued on distributed ledgers, they require a form of digital cash to complete transactions. The stablecoin serves as that digital settlement asset, enabling delivery-versus-payment transactions in a fully digital environment. Its reliability, redeemability, and legal recognition determine whether such settlements can achieve finality comparable to traditional clearing systems. If the stablecoin fails or becomes illiquid, the integrity of tokenised markets themselves could be compromised. Hence, stablecoins are not merely financial instruments; they are part of the infrastructure of tomorrow's financial market.

The ECB emphasises that stablecoins are increasingly used for settling trades in tokenised asset markets and even interbank transactions in pilot cases, due to their speed and global accessibility (Schaaf, 2025). There are also legal questions: does delivery vs payment in stablecoin confer the same finality and legal certainty as settlement? Regulators may be concerned that if stablecoins are not robust (credit risk-free), using them for settling high-value tokenised trades could introduce counterparty risk into securities settlement. In response, bodies like the BIS Committee on Payments and Markets Infrastructure (hereinafter referred to as CPMI) have emphasised that systematically important stablecoin arrangements should have minimal credit and liquidity risks and that such stablecoin arrangements should provide for clear and certain final settlement, irrespective of the mechanism used for operational settlement (The Committee on Payments and Market Infrastructures [CPMI], 2023).

As the tokenisation of financial assets expands, stablecoins could become deeply integrated into financial infrastructure. This makes it imperative to ensure those stablecoins have appropriate safeguards and are integrated with appropriate oversight.

In the context of financial inclusion, stablecoins have offered an unexpected form of resilience. In regions where local currencies are unstable or access to the formal banking system is limited, dollar-denominated stablecoins provide an accessible store of value and a medium of exchange resistant to domestic inflation. For many users in emerging markets, they represent not a speculative tool but a lifeline to monetary stability. Yet this phenomenon introduces a paradox: while stablecoins can empower individuals, they can also erode the effectiveness of domestic monetary policy. When residents of a country begin using foreign-currency stablecoins as their preferred means of payment and savings, the local currency loses relevance, and with it, the central bank's control over money supply and interest rates. Thus, financial inclusion achieved through foreign-currency stablecoins can come at the cost of national monetary autonomy.

Corporate treasury operations are another area where stablecoins are gaining ground. What began as a tool for crypto firms to settle trades has evolved, with mainstream companies now exploring their use to improve efficiency in cross-border transactions and liquidity management. Large firms like Walmart and Amazon reportedly tested stablecoin applications in payments and settlements (Schaaf, 2025), while financial institutions such as BlackRock have invested in stablecoin issuer Circle, recognising their potential in short-term liquidity and tokenised money markets (Circle Internet Financial, 2022).

For corporates, the appeal lies in 24/7 liquidity and faster intra-group fund transfers, along with possible yield opportunities on idle balances. However, challenges persist with accounting standards, regulatory treatment and operational risks (such as token freezes or blockchain outages) remain unresolved. Corporate treasurers continue to approach adoption cautiously, awaiting regulatory clarity and safeguards. Nonetheless, moves such as PayPal's launch of its USD stablecoin (hereinafter referred to as PYUSD) indicate that stablecoins are entering mainstream payment ecosystems, a development likely to prompt regulators to subject large-scale stablecoin arrangements to payment system-level oversight and resilience standards (PayPal Inc., n.d.).

Stablecoins are equally central to the architecture of decentralised finance, commonly known as DeFi. In the realm of DeFi, stablecoins act as a foundational layer for numerous applications, from lending and borrowing to yield farming and derivatives. In lending protocols like Aave, users frequently post stablecoins as collateral or borrow stablecoins to avoid exposure to volatility (Aave Protocol., n.d.). Additionally, many DeFi yield farming strategies involve stablecoins: users provide liquidity in stablecoin pools or stake stablecoins in protocols to earn interest and rewards. Because demand to borrow stablecoins can be high, interest rates in DeFi for lending stablecoins are often attractive.

The ECB has pointed out that if stablecoins were to pay interest and be widely adopted by businesses, this could result in a diversion from bank deposits and pose financial stability issues, especially in bank-centric systems like Europe (Schaaf, 2025). In DeFi specifically, a key risk is smart contract risk and lack of investor protection. Participants intending to generate high yields with stablecoins can lose money if a protocol is hacked or a Ponzi-like yield scheme collapses.

Stablecoins have evolved from a simple concept into a multifaceted tool embedded in various financial activities. They serve as money in the crypto economy, a unit of account and store of value for blockchain transactions, and are bridging into real-world use cases. This functional versatility is part of their appeal but also why they are now under the microscope of financial regulation. Each case surfaces different policy considerations. Use of stablecoin in payments raises issues of consumer protection, AML / CFT, and monetary sovereignty; market liquidity usage raises issues of systemic risk and market integrity; DeFi usage raises issues around investor protection and AML / CFT risks. A critical point is that stablecoins can no longer be viewed in isolation. Their risks and impacts must be considered in the context of the larger systems they are integrated into.

In the end, stablecoins embody a paradox at the heart of modern finance. They promise freedom from intermediaries yet depend on trust in new forms. They aspire to be borderless yet constantly encounter the boundaries of national law. They claim stability yet exist within markets defined by change. Understanding their functional and economic roles is not simply a matter of classification. It is a recognition that stablecoins represent a new layer in the architecture of money itself—one that blends code, law, and confidence into a single, evolving instrument.

OPERATIONAL MODELS AND LIFECYCLE OF STABLECOINS

To truly understand the practical nature of stablecoins, one must look beyond their conceptual design and explore the way they actually function from creation to redemption. A stablecoin is not merely a line of code representing value; it is part of an operational ecosystem that links technology, finance, and regulation. Its lifecycle mirrors, in many respects, that of traditional electronic money, but it is executed in a new technological paradigm that transforms how value is issued, circulated, and redeemed.

Each stage of this lifecycle—minting, issuance, distribution, reserve management, and redemption—is intertwined with the others. Together they define not only the efficiency of a stablecoin system but also the points at which risk and regulatory responsibility arise. To fully grasp the significance of stablecoins, it is therefore necessary to trace this lifecycle step by step, while recognising that the process is supported by a wide network of intermediaries, custodians, exchanges, and technology providers whose actions collectively sustain the illusion of simplicity that stablecoins present to the end user.

The process begins with minting, which in blockchain terminology refers to the creation of new tokens and their inscription on a distributed ledger in a transferable form. The UK's Financial Conduct Authority (FCA) defines minting in its *Consultation Paper on Stablecoin Issuance and Cryptoasset Custody* (FCA Consultation Paper) as *"the process of putting a cryptoasset on a blockchain or network using DLT or similar technology in a transferable form"* (Financial Conduct Authority, 2025). In practical terms, for fiat-backed stablecoins, minting occurs when an issuer receives fiat currency from a user and creates the equivalent amount of tokens representing a claim on that fiat.

Generally, the activity of minting is not directly regulated as a standalone activity, as it may simply be considered as a technological service. For instance, under the Draft Order, the FCA proposes to exclude the minting of a qualifying stablecoin from the regulated activity of issuance of qualified stablecoins (HMT, 2025b). However, the controls around minting are crucial to prevent unauthorised or excessive issuance.

From a regulatory stance, while the blockchain mint operation itself isn't regulated, the circumstances prompting it are, i.e., taking customer funds (as part of issuance). Regulators will likely expect issuers to have internal controls and audits around their mint/burn smart contracts to prevent mismanagement or fraud. Moreover, network validators (like miners or stakers) who record these transactions aren't usually directly regulated in their capacity as validators, but they form part of the broader stablecoin ecosystem.

Following minting, the next stage is issuance. Issuance in a stablecoin context means the process by which the issuer sends or allocates an agreed amount of stablecoins to a customer's account or wallet (Baughman et al., 2022). Issuance transforms the newly minted token from a technical construct into a financial instrument. The issuer becomes liable to the holder for redemption, and the stablecoin enters circulation. In virtually all major jurisdictions, issuance of stablecoins is now recognised as a regulated activity, requiring authorisation or licensing by a competent financial authority. The rationale is simple: issuance involves accepting customer funds and creating a claim on an issuer, a process that mirrors deposit-taking or the creation of electronic money.

The conditions under which issuance can take place are subject to increasing scrutiny. Regulators demand that issuers always maintain full backing, disclose the composition of their reserves, and provide clear redemption terms to users. The obligation to redeem at par value—meaning that one token must always be exchangeable for one unit of the reference currency—is central to preserving confidence in the system. A failure at the issuance stage, whether through under-collateralisation or operational error, can cascade into systemic instability.

Once issued, stablecoins begin to circulate through a complex network of intermediaries. This phase is known as distribution. In traditional monetary terms, distribution is akin to the movement of currency from the central bank to commercial banks and then to the public. In the digital context, however, distribution often occurs through various platforms. Many retail customers do not mint coins directly from the issuer but rather obtain them through crypto exchanges or brokers. For instance, a user might deposit cash on a crypto exchange and trade it for USDT or simply buy USDC from a broker or OTC desk. These intermediaries play a role in distributing stablecoins broadly. Distribution channels are significant because they are points where regulatory oversight like AML/CFT and consumer protection can be applied indirectly. Distributors are typically required to conduct due diligence on the stablecoin to ensure such stablecoin's suitability. One risk in distribution is concentration and liquidity: if one exchange holds a huge portion of a stablecoin's circulating supply in its wallets (on behalf of users), issues at that exchange (hacks, freezes) could affect many holders. Another aspect is cross-border distribution, as stablecoins can flow into jurisdictions where they aren't formally approved. A stablecoin might be freely circulating among users in a country even if the local regulator hasn't decided how to treat it.

The distribution and operation of secondary trading platforms is generally a regulated activity in most jurisdictions, requiring an authorisation from the appropriate regulator. For instance, under the Dubai Virtual Asset Regulatory Authority (hereinafter referred to as VARA), distribution of virtual assets may only be undertaken by licensed distributors holding a 'Broker-Dealer Services' license (Virtual Assets Regulatory Authority 2025). In other jurisdictions, distribution may be undertaken by firms holding authorisations "Dealing in Investments as Agent" or "Dealing in Investments as Principal", depending on the fund flows.

Furthermore, in most jurisdictions (such as ADGM, VARA, MiCA, and FCA's proposed framework), operating a crypto-asset exchange is also a regulated financial activity.

The distribution phase also highlights a critical tension between accessibility and control. The ease with which stablecoins can cross borders and change hands enhances their global utility but simultaneously complicates compliance with anti-money-laundering and sanctions regimes. The same attributes that make stablecoins frictionless for legitimate commerce can render them ideal instruments for regulatory evasion if not properly supervised.

Beneath the visible layer of circulation lies the often-overlooked function of reserve management, which is the cornerstone of every stablecoin system. The credibility of a stablecoin, particularly fiat-backed and asset-backed ones, relies on the management of its reserve assets. Reserve management entails deciding what assets to hold and back the stablecoin, where to hold them, how to keep them liquid, and how to secure them against loss. Most regulatory frameworks now specify what qualifies as eligible reserve assets. For fiat-backed coins, it is generally expected (or mandated) that reserves be held in cash or high-quality liquid assets with minimal credit, liquidity and market risk. Reserve management also involves having an external custodian or trustee to hold the assets, ensuring they are legally ring-fenced for the benefit of the stablecoin holders. The risk if reserves are mismanaged is a classic run-on-the-bank scenario. If holders doubt the reserves are fully there or liquid, they may rush to redeem, forcing fire sales of assets that could render the stablecoin insolvent. This is exactly the scenario regulators want to prevent by strict reserve rules. Furthermore, most regulatory frameworks require robust reserve management, including transparency and reporting obligations.

Redemption marks the final and most critical phase in the stablecoin lifecycle. Redemption is the process whereby a stablecoin holder returns the token to the issuer in exchange for the underlying fiat or asset at par value. This is the mirror image of issuance and is crucial for maintaining the price peg (Baughman et al., 2022). Redemption rights to token holders provide for a consumer protection mechanism. Regulators see guaranteed redemption as fundamental. Most regulatory frameworks, such as the European Union under MiCA, CBUAE under the PTSR, the c States under the GENIUS Act and HKMA under the Ordinance, explicitly require that redemption at par be available at any time (or within a prescribed short timeframe) and with minimal fees or hurdles. Some current issuers impose certain minimum redemption sizes, but regulatory trends are toward making this process as smooth as a bank withdrawal. From an operational standpoint, redemption entails the burning of the returned tokens (removing them from circulation on-chain) and releasing the corresponding reserve assets (sending fiat to the user's bank account, for example). The FCA Consultation Paper defines burning as "*the process by which a cryptoasset is permanently removed from circulation on the blockchain*".

This contraction of supply is recorded and often visible on-chain (burn events). The ability to meet redemptions depends on good reserve management. If redemption requests exceed the liquid assets on hand, an issuer could face default. That's why having a portion of reserves in cash is critical – to meet daily liquidity needs. For instance, the MiCA requires that at least 30% of the funds received by EMT issuers must be deposited in separate accounts in credit institutions.

Another crucial element is legal enforceability. Holders must have a clear legal right to redeem. Most regulatory frameworks impose a legal obligation on stablecoin issuers to redeem stablecoins at par value. While most regulatory frameworks share the core element of obligating issuers to redeem stablecoins at par value, they differ in nuances in relation to the timelines to process redemption requests and the fees that an issuer can impose in relation to such redemption requests.

In practice, an orderly redemption process is also key to market discipline. Thus, from a financial stability perspective, authorities want to avoid any scenario where an issuer suspends redemptions. Many stablecoin holders never directly redeem with the issuer. Retail customers may just trade on an exchange for another asset, and only market makers actually do the redeeming with the issuer. But the presence of open redemption to those market makers is enough to enforce the peg for all, indirectly.

Surrounding this core lifecycle is a constellation of intermediaries and market infrastructure that sustain stablecoin operations. Beyond issuers and users, stablecoin arrangements involve various market intermediaries and infrastructure providers that ensure the system runs smoothly. These include custodians who are key for safeguarding reserves. Regulators may require that custodians be independent and highly rated institutions to mitigate issuer fraud or bankruptcy risk. If a custodian fails, there could be a loss of reserves. Payment processors/gateways play an important role in integrating stablecoins into payment flows, e.g., merchant acquirers that let businesses accept stablecoin payments and convert to fiat. These entities might need licences from the relevant monetary authorities depending on jurisdiction. Exchanges and brokers, as mentioned under distribution, facilitate liquidity and price discovery for stablecoins. They often coordinate with issuers (some exchanges are authorised redemption agents). Custodial service providers safeguard stablecoin holdings for users and carry the responsibility of secure storage of stablecoins.

Each of these participants might be subject to different regulations. Policymakers seek to ensure there are no blind spots, i.e., that every significant function in a stablecoin's operation is covered by regulatory remit to prevent responsibility gaps. The FSB's calls for jurisdictions to regulate and supervise all associated functions and activities of a GSC arrangement (FSB, 2023). Coordination among regulators (banking, securities, payments, competition authorities, etc.) is highly required given this network of intermediaries.

EMERGING OPERATIONAL MODELS

A recent innovation in stablecoin design involves models where holding a stablecoin can generate a return or share of revenue, blurring the line between a payment instrument and an investment product. For example, some issuers have contemplated sharing a portion of the interest income earned on reserve assets with stablecoin holders. Generally, issuers generate profit from the interest earned from reserve assets comprising highly liquid financial instruments. But competitive pressures or new entrants could lead to stablecoins that pass some of that yield to users, perhaps via the coin's value slowly increasing or through periodic dividends. Such a yield-bearing stablecoin might attract more users, but it may also constitute a different instrument legally, potentially a security, because holders are now investing for profit, not just using a payment tool. Regulators have indeed drawn this line: the US GENIUS Act flatly prohibits stablecoin issuers from paying interest to holders, precisely to avoid this scenario and keep stablecoins transactional in nature rather than investment vehicles. Similarly, the MiCA also prohibits the distribution of interest from reserve assets to EMT and ART holders. On the other hand, the ADGM FSRA and Central Bank of Bahrain (hereinafter referred to as CBB), under its Stablecoin Issuance and Offering Module (hereinafter referred to as SIO Module), allow for issuers to incentivise holders through monetary and non-monetary benefits, subject to certain safeguards.

Additionally, some programmable stablecoins might embed smart contract features that alter how they function in certain conditions. Programmability could be beneficial (enforcing rules automatically) but also complicates classification – is a highly programmed coin still a simple payment instrument or something more complex?

Crucially, as stablecoin operational models evolve, policy must adapt. For example, if stablecoins start offering embedded insurance or other novel features, those might trigger insurance regulation or consumer law issues. If stablecoins integrate with social media or other platforms deeply, operational oversight might extend to tech infrastructure and data privacy concerns.

The bottom line is that the design of the stablecoin lifecycle – from minting to redemption – is integral to understanding its risk profile and regulatory needs. A stablecoin that is centrally issued and redeemed through KYC channels might be easier than a decentralised stablecoin, which spreads functions across users and code, reducing single-point failure but making regulation of any entity tricky. By mapping out these operations in detail, regulators and stakeholders can identify where to impose requirements and where new rules may be needed.

STABLECOINS VS. OTHER DIGITAL ASSETS: KEY DISTINCTIONS

To avoid conflating concepts, it is important to delineate what stablecoins contrast with other forms of digital assets circulating in today's markets. Stablecoins occupy a unique niche: they are chiefly characterised by their stable value function and their use as a medium of exchange or value storage unit within digital systems. Other digital assets – from cryptocurrencies like Bitcoin to CBDCs to tokenised securities – have different purposes, value dynamics, and regulatory classifications. Drawing clear lines between these categories helps prevent regulatory arbitrage and ensures that discussions about stablecoins remain properly scoped. Here, we compare stablecoins to several other prominent categories of digital assets, highlighting both overlaps and differences:

Stablecoins vs. Unbacked Cryptocurrencies (Virtual Assets)

The FATF defines virtual assets as "*a digital representation of value that can be digitally traded or transferred and can be used for payment or investment purposes*" (The Financial Action Task Force [FATF], 2021). Traditional cryptocurrencies such as Bitcoin, Ether, or Litecoin are not stable in value because their prices float based on market supply and demand, often with high volatility. They typically have no underlying asset or issuer guaranteeing any value, and their value derives from scarcity. Stablecoins, by contrast, explicitly aim to eliminate that volatility by tying value to an external reference (like a fiat currency). A stablecoin holder expects that 1 stablecoin will purchase what 1 unit of the reference asset would, whereas a Bitcoin holder accepts that the purchasing power can swing wildly. From a functional perspective, this makes stablecoins much more suitable as a medium of exchange and unit of account. It also makes them preferred for savings in the crypto context (to avoid volatility). In contrast, virtual assets behave more like speculative commodities or investment assets. FATF classifies both as virtual assets for AML, but regulators often carve out stablecoins for additional scrutiny due to their payment-like nature and also attribute additional AML/CFT risks to stablecoins due to their potential for mass adoption (FATF, 2020).

Stablecoins vs. CBDCs

The BIS defines CBDCs as *"a central bank liability, denominated in an existing unit of account, which serves both as a medium of exchange and a store of value."* CBDCs can further be categorised into retail CBDCs (digital cash for the public) and wholesale CBDCs (for interbank settlements). The differences between stablecoins and CBDCs are significant: issuance and guarantee. A CBDC is a liability of the central bank, effectively carrying a sovereign guarantee. A stablecoin is a claim on a private entity or pool of assets; its stability is only as good as that private backing. Thus, CBDCs are often considered the safest digital money. A key aspect is that CBDCs are being designed with public policy objectives (financial inclusion, privacy balanced with traceability, etc.), whereas stablecoin technology evolved in the open market (sometimes prioritising speed innovation over, say, accessibility by minorities).

Stablecoins vs. Security Tokens

Security tokens are digital assets that represent "securities" or share characteristics similar to securities and confer rights like dividends, interest, ownership of a share of a company, voting rights, or claims on assets. They typically confer rights such as ownership interests or entitlements in assets or enterprises, such as equity shares, bonds, or investment funds, recorded on a blockchain. Essentially, they mirror traditional securities but in digital token form. Stablecoins, on the other hand, typically do not give you any such rights or interest, and holding a stablecoin doesn't give you a share in the issuer's profits or any governance over the issuer. It simply gives you the ability to redeem for a reference asset (for asset-backed stablecoins) or to use the token at stable face value. This is a crucial legal distinction: stablecoins are generally not meant to be investment products, whereas security tokens explicitly are investments. For example, if a token gives you a cut of a project's revenue, that's likely a security. A number of jurisdictions, such as the CBUAE, MiCA and the GENIUS Act, prohibit the distribution of interest to token holders.

Stablecoins vs. Utility Tokens

Utility tokens are digital tokens that provide access to a product or service or otherwise have a use case within a certain ecosystem – for example, a token that must be spent to use a decentralised storage platform, or tokens used to pay fees on a blockchain, or a token that grants access to a social network feature. They are not primarily meant as stores of value or investment (though they often become speculative). Utility tokens typically derive value from the expectation of future utility or demand. Stablecoins differ in that their value proposition is explicit stability and general use as money, not specialised functionality. From a regulatory viewpoint, utility tokens are sometimes unregulated or given lighter treatment if they function only within a limited context. However, many so-called utility tokens have strayed into investment territory in practice, leading regulators to be sceptical of the label. The key difference is issuer obligations: a stablecoin issuer promises redemption (a specific duty), whereas a utility token issuer doesn't promise the token's value or redemption and only has to maintain the service the token is used for.

Stablecoins vs. Governance Tokens

Governance tokens are tokens that confer voting rights or decision-making power in a decentralised protocol or blockchain project, such as DeFi platforms and decentralised autonomous organisations (hereinafter referred to as DAOs). They typically allow holders to vote on proposals, such as changes to protocol parameters or treasury use. Some governance tokens also entitle holders to a share of fees generated by the protocol (like some decentralised exchange (hereinafter referred to as DEX) governance tokens do). These tokens derive value from the perceived influence and possibly dividends from a decentralised platform's success. Stablecoins serve a transactional role, and governance tokens serve a coordination role for a community. If a stablecoin started giving governance rights (say an algorithmic stablecoin where holders can vote on policies), it might then be treated more like a share in a collective scheme.

Given these distinctions, regulators often frame definitions to ensure a token that has features of another category does not slip by simply by claiming to be a stablecoin. Many jurisdictions also explicitly exclude stablecoins that constitute securities, futures contracts, bank deposits, vouchers, or other forms of stored value from their stablecoin definitions if those are already covered elsewhere – to avoid overlap (e.g., a prepaid card balance in a wallet technically is a stable electronic value, but it's not a crypto token and is regulated as e-money, so they don't want to call that a stablecoin).

In conclusion, stablecoins are best thought of as part of a broader digital asset taxonomy to serve as digital cash or monetary tokens in the ecosystem. They stand apart from investment tokens (securities) by having no inherent profit participation for holders, apart from any interest that could be distributed (which, as we noted, is being curtailed by regulation). They stand apart from pure utility tokens by not being consumptive in nature. And they stand apart from sovereign digital currencies by virtue of private issuance and associated risks. These distinctions clarify why regulatory frameworks are being tailored for stablecoins as a class. As the digital asset landscape evolves, these boundaries will be continually tested; a token could emerge that blurs stablecoin and security (e.g., a stablecoin that pays a variable return based on some index). When that happens, regulators will need to decide which rules prevail or if new hybrid rules are needed. But for now, the conceptual clarity achieved in this chapter will guide our subsequent analyses: we know what we mean by stablecoin and what falls outside that definition into other regulatory buckets.

FORWARD-LOOKING CONSIDERATIONS

The stablecoin ecosystem is dynamic and fast-moving. Innovations in design and usage are constantly emerging, which means that any definition or regulatory framework devised today may need revisiting in the near future. As we look ahead, several trends stand out that could challenge the current understanding of stablecoins and blur the lines between stablecoins and other digital assets.

Hybrid Stablecoin Models

Projects are experimenting with stablecoins that combine features of multiple types discussed earlier. For instance, some are exploring partially collateralised, partially algorithmic stablecoins, aiming to get capital efficiency higher than fully reserved coins but more robust than purely algorithmic. If successful, these blur the clear-cut categories of "fiat-backed" vs "algorithmic". Regulators so far tend to treat anything less than fully backed with caution, but as models evolve, a more nuanced approach might be needed.

Programmable and Smart Stablecoins

While current stablecoins are just value holders, future iterations could embed smart contract logic. For example, a stablecoin that can carry attached conditions (only spendable for certain goods, or that self-executes tax reporting on each transaction, etc.). Token standards such as the ERC-3643 are now integrating AML/CFT and other compliance checks into the token's architecture (ERC3643 Association, 2025). Regulators would need to decide if such an instrument fall under stablecoin rules or not.

Interest-Bearing Stablecoins

Despite some prohibitions, the market may try new angles, such as distributing new tokens as rewards rather than interest on the base token to circumvent rules. If such interest-bearing stablecoins emerge, it could effectively create a class of instruments that share characteristics with money market funds. An interest-bearing stablecoin could attract huge inflows as an alternative to bank deposits, especially if offering higher yields due to lower regulatory costs than banks. If they become large, they could divert funds from banks, as noted by the ECB, potentially reducing bank lending capacity and shifting systemic risk to this new product (Schaaf, 2025). Some market participants argue that sharing some interest (under strict limits) could make stablecoins safer by giving holders an incentive to stick around and not run at the first sign of trouble, but authorities likely prefer the simple route of prohibition of payment of interest.

Real World Asset Tokenisation and the Stablecoins

As more real-world assets get tokenised (bonds, loans, real estate), there could be sector-specific stablecoins or integrated stablecoin-like functions. For example, a real estate token marketplace where transactions happen in a stablecoin tied to that ecosystem. These niche stablecoins might not fit generic regulatory categories and could pose new risks by tying a stablecoin's value to illiquid underlying assets. If those become prevalent, regulators might have to decide: do we bring those under stablecoin rules or treat them as funds/securities?

Global Regulatory Convergence

In the forward horizon, we may see global convergence toward best practices. Most jurisdictions move towards adopting the core FATF recommendations, leading to an international consensus on core themes. On the other hand, divergence could hamper the interoperability of stablecoin networks. Thus, it is imperative for policymakers and regulators to promote consistent taxonomy and risk assessments so that regulatory arbitrage is minimised.

In conclusion, stablecoins represent an evolving subject of financial innovation. As such, definitions and regulations cannot be static. A degree of flexibility must be built into regulatory regimes to adapt to unforeseen innovations. One can imagine regulators instituting "innovation sandbox" provisions. Industry standards bodies might also help by creating best practices for new stablecoin types before laws catch up.

The coming years will likely see refinement and expansion of stablecoin frameworks, rather than radical overhauls, as regulators absorb lessons from initial implementations and market developments. The foundational concepts laid out in this chapter are likely to endure as cornerstones. However, the edges of what qualifies as a stablecoin and how rules apply will be tested by innovation. Regulators must remain vigilant and proactive, periodically recalibrating legal definitions and requirements to ensure they remain effective, relevant, and technology-neutral in achieving the core policy goals: monetary and financial stability, consumer protection, integrity of payments, and fostering beneficial innovation. By establishing fundamental conceptual ground now and acknowledging the need for ongoing review, regulators and market participants must equip themselves to handle the evolution of stablecoins and their role in the future of finance.

REFERENCES

Aave Protocol. (n.d.). *Aave — open-source non-custodial liquidity protocol* [Computer software]. https://aave.com/

Abu Dhabi Global Market. (2015, October 4). *Financial Services and Markets Regulations 2015* (ADGM Law No. 4 of 2013) [Regulations]. https://en.adgm.thomsonreuters.com/rulebook/financial-services-and-markets-regulations-2015-0

Adachi, M., Bento Pereira Da Silva, P., Born, A., Cappuccio, M., Czák-Ludwig, S., Gschossmann, I., Pellicani, A., Philipps, S.-M., Plooij, M., Rossteuscher, I., & Zeoli, P. (2022). *Stablecoins' Role in Crypto and Beyond: Functions, Risks and Policy* (Policy Report No. Vol. 18; Macroprudential Bulletin). European Central Bank. https://www.ecb.europa.eu/press/financial-stability-publications/ macroprudential-bulletin/html/ecb.mpbu202207_2~836f682ed7.en.html

Baughman, G., Carapella, F., Gerszten, J., & Mills, D. C. (2022). *The stable in stablecoins*. Board of Governors of the Federal Reserve System., DOI: 10.17016/2380-7172.3224

Central Bank of the UAE. (2024). *Payment Token Services Regulation* (No. 2/2024; p. 101) [Regulations]. https://rulebook.centralbank.ae/en/rulebook/payment-token-services-regulation

Circle Internet Financial. (2022). *Circle Announces $400M Funding Round* [Press Release]. Circle Internet Group, Inc. https://www.circle.com/pressroom/circle-announces-400m-funding-round

Das, A. (2025, November 12). Social Capital Markets. *Stablecoin Statistics 2025*. https://socialcapitalmarkets.net/crypto-trading/stablecoin-statistics

ERC3643 Association. (2025). *ERC-3643 (T-REX Protocol): The standard for permissioned tokens* (Version 4.1.3) [Computer Software]. https://github.com/ERC-3643/ERC-3643

Financial Conduct Authority. (2025). *Stablecoin Issuance and Cryptoasset Custody* (Consultation Paper No. CP25/14; p. 239). https://www.fca.org.uk/publications/consultation-papers/cp25-14-stablecoin-issuance-cryptoasset-custody

Financial Stability Board. (2023). *High-level Recommendations for the Regulation, Supervision and Oversight of Global Stablecoin Arrangements* (Reports to the G20, p. 24). https://www.fsb.org/uploads/P170723-3.pdf

Hong Kong Monetary Authority. (2023). *Legislative proposal to implement regulatory regime for stablecoin issuers and announcement on introduction of sandbox arrangement* [Consultation]. https://www.hkma.gov.hk/eng/news-and-media/press-releases/2023/12/20231227-4/

Monetary Authority of Singapore. (2023). *Proposed Regulatory Approach for Stablecoin-Related Activities* (Consultation Nos P009-2022; p. 128). https://www.mas.gov.sg/publications/consultations/ 2022/consultation-paper-on-proposed-regulatory-approach-for-stablecoin-related-activities

Organisation for European Economic Co-operation. (2021). *Central Bank Digital Currencies and payments: A review of domestic and international implications* (OECD Economics Department Working Papers, Vol. 1655). DOI: 10.1787/18151973

PayPal Inc. (n.d.). *PayPal USD Stablecoin*. PayPal. https://www.paypal.com/us/digital-wallet/manage-money/crypto/pyusd

Schaaf, J. (2025, July 28). European Central Bank. *From Hype to Hazard: What Stablecoins Mean for Europe*.https://www.ecb.europa.eu/press/blog/date/2025/html/ecb.blog20250728~e6cb3cf8b5.en.html

Singh, R. (2025, April 7). J.P. Morgan Wary of Stablecoins' Trillion-Dollar Growth Bets, Cuts Them by Half. *Reuters*. https://www.reuters.com/business/finance/jpmorgan-wary-stablecoins-trillion-dollar-growth-bets-cuts-them-by-half-2025-07-03/

The Committee on Payments and Market Infrastructures. (2023). *Considerations for the Use of Stablecoin Arrangements in Cross-Border Payments* (CPMI Report No. 220; CPMI Papers, p. 37). Bank for International Settlements. https://www.bis.org/cpmi/publ/d220.pdf

The European Parliament and the Council of the European Union. (2023, May 31). *Regulation (EU) 2023/1114 Of the European Parliament and of the Council of 31 May 2023 on markets in crypto-assets and amending Regulations (EU) No 1093/2010 and (EU) No 1095/2010 and Directives 2013/36/EU and (EU) 2019/1937*. Official Journal of the European Union (OJ). https://eur-lex.europa.eu/eli/reg/2023/1114/oj/eng

The Financial Action Task Force. (2020). *FATF Report to G20 on So-called Stablecoins* (p. 32). https://www.fatf-gafi.org/content/dam/fatf-gafi/reports/Virtual-Assets-FATF-Report-G20-SoCalled-Stablecoins.pdf.coredownload.pdf

The Financial Action Task Force. (2021). *Updated Guidance for a Risk-Based Approach to Virtual Assets and Virtual Asset Service Providers* (p. 111). https://www.fatf-gafi.org/content/dam/fatf-gafi/guidance/Updated-Guidance-VA-VASP.pdf.coredownload.inline.pdf

The International Organization of Securities Commissions. (2023). *Policy Recommendations for Crypto and Digital Asset Markets* (No. 747; p. 77). https://www.iosco.org/library/pubdocs/pdf /IOSCOPD747.pdf

Treasury, H. M. U. K. (2025a). *Future Financial Services Regulatory Regime for Cryptoassets (Regulated Activities)* (p. 19) [Policy Note]. https://assets.publishing.service.gov.uk/media/ 680f6397b0d43971b07f5bfd/20250428_RAO_SI_draft_policy_note.pdf

Treasury, H. M. U. K. (2025b). *The Financial Services and Markets Act 2000 (Regulated Activities and Miscellaneous Provisions) (Cryptoassets) Order 2025* (No. 2025 No. 000; p. 27). [Draft Statutory Instrument].https://assets.publishing.service.gov.uk/media/680f6387faff81833fcae94b/0302425_draft_RAO_SI.pdf

United States Congress. (2025). *Guiding and Establishing National Innovation for U.S. Stablecoins Act (GENIUS Act)* (Pub. L. No. 119-27, S. 1582). https://www.congress.gov/bill/119th-congress/senate-bill/1582/textVirtual Assets Regulatory Authority. (2025). *Virtual Assets and Related Activities Regulations 2023* (p. 50) [Rulebook]. Government of Dubai. https://rulebooks.vara.ae/rulebook/virtual-assets-and-related-activities-regulations-2023

Chapter 3
Global Regulatory Approaches

Kokila Alagh
KARM Legal Consultants, UAE

ABSTRACT

This chapter examines how jurisdictions globally are regulating stablecoins and integrating them into existing financial frameworks. It traces the evolution from voluntary market practices to comprehensive legal regimes guided by principles of prudential oversight, consumer protection, and financial stability. Beginning with international standard-setting bodies such as the FSB, FATF, IOSCO, and BIS, the chapter outlines global benchmarks for proportionate, function- based, and technology-neutral regulation. It then analyses key national frameworks, including those of the EU, UK, US, Singapore, Hong Kong, Bahrain, and the UAE, highlighting convergences in reserve, redemption, and licensing requirements, as well as divergences driven by monetary sovereignty and market priorities. Finally, the chapter explores the role of regulatory sandboxes as instruments for controlled innovation. Collectively, these developments demonstrate a maturing global consensus on stablecoin governance that balances innovation with systemic integrity.

INTRODUCTION

Having explored in the preceding chapter what stablecoins are, how they function, and how they differ from other classes of digital assets, this chapter turns to the question of how the world's regulators have responded. The definitional complexity surrounding stablecoins has translated into an equally intricate regulatory landscape shaped by competing priorities of innovation, consumer protection, financial stability, and monetary sovereignty. Stablecoins have evolved from a technological

DOI: 10.4018/979-8-3373-6655-5.ch003

experiment to an influential component of global finance, prompting policymakers to determine where, within existing financial frameworks, these instruments should sit and, increasingly, to create new regimes when existing laws fall short.

Today, stablecoins occupy a prominent place in modern financial discourse. No longer confined to the realm of crypto-asset enthusiasts, they are now integrated into mainstream financial operations, serving as a medium of payment, a liquidity bridge, and even a settlement layer for tokenized financial instruments. Their presence is felt in cross-border transactions, institutional treasury management, decentralized finance, and emerging tokenized asset markets. Yet with this expansion comes profound regulatory significance. The use of privately issued, digitally transferable units of value inevitably intersects with questions of monetary control, prudential oversight, and systemic risk. The frameworks governing the issuance, circulation, and redemption of stablecoins, therefore, form one of the defining challenges of contemporary financial regulation.

Around the world, jurisdictions grapple with the best approach for integrating stablecoins into their legal and supervisory systems. Some have developed bespoke regimes designed specifically to address their unique features, while others have opted to adapt existing payment, securities, or e-money laws to cover stablecoin activities. In doing so, regulators are converging, at least in principle, on several shared objectives. This includes ensuring that stablecoins are issued responsibly, that reserves are of high quality and fully segregated, that redemption is reliable and enforceable, and that activities involving stablecoins meet robust anti-money-laundering and counter-terrorist-financing standards. Yet beneath this convergence lie striking divergences. Domestic policy prioritises whether to preserve monetary sovereignty, promote fintech innovation, or maintain global competitiveness, having shaped national choices leading to a regulatory mosaic rather than a uniform global model.

This chapter examines that mosaic in depth by comparing and contrasting the regulatory approaches taken by key jurisdictions, while identifying the principles that unite them and the policy considerations that divide them. In addition, it analyses how stablecoins and stablecoin-related activities are treated under different legal systems, and what kinds of authorizations or licenses are required for entities performing them. Also, the chapter considers how jurisdictions approach foreign-issued stablecoins, assessing whether non-domestic issuers are required to obtain local authorization or satisfy additional conditions before offering their tokens within a national market.

Before turning to country-specific frameworks, the discussion First outlines the high-level principles set forth by SSBs that inform and guide national stablecoin regulation. These include recommendations from the FSB, FATF, IOSCO, and BIS. Their recommendations emphasize proportionality, technology-neutrality, and the fundamental doctrine of "same activity, same risk, same regulation". These international standards do not impose binding law but provide an important benchmark against which national frameworks are measured and harmonized.

Second, the chapter conducts a comparative survey of leading national regimes. It explores the European Union's MiCA, the United Kingdom, the United States, Singapore, Hong Kong, the Kingdom of Bahrain, and the UAE. Collectively, these case studies demonstrate how similar principles (licensing of issuers, full reserve backing, redemption at par, robust governance, and AML/CFT compliance) are expressed through different regulatory architectures.

Third, the chapter considers regulatory sandboxes as a policy instrument that enables innovation under supervision. Jurisdictions such as Hong Kong have leveraged sandbox environments to test stablecoin-related applications in controlled settings, allowing both regulators and innovators to observe risk dynamics before broader market deployment. Such initiatives reveal how supervisory agility can coexist with prudential discipline, providing valuable lessons for regulators seeking to encourage experimentation without sacrificing consumer protection or systemic stability.

Ultimately, this chapter aims to identify the threads of convergence that run through global stablecoin regulation while recognizing the deliberate divergences that persist. Across nearly all jurisdictions, certain safeguards have become universal: mandatory licensing or registration of issuers, the maintenance of high-quality and segregated reserves, legally enforceable redemption rights, and strict compliance with AML/CFT obligations. These common pillars embody a shared international vision of stability, transparency, and accountability. Yet meaningful differences endure, and these differences are not mere technicalities but reflections of sovereign priorities. Some states impose limits on foreign-currency-referenced stablecoins to defend monetary sovereignty; others encourage their development to stimulate fintech ecosystems or attract cross-border capital.

By mapping both alignment and divergence, this chapter provides a panoramic view of the global policy landscape for stablecoins. It shows that while jurisdictions may vary in form, they increasingly converge in intent: to harness the benefits of innovation while containing its risks. The future of stablecoin regulation will depend not merely on domestic lawmaking but on the degree to which nations can coordinate these parallel efforts.

BACKGROUND

International Standards and Principles for Stablecoin Regulation

SSBs play a pivotal role in shaping the regulatory direction of national authorities. Over the period from 2019 to 2023, SSBs like the FSB, FATF, IOSCO, and BIS have addressed the risks posed by virtual assets and stablecoins. Such SSBs' collective guidance has become the intellectual foundation of modern regulatory approaches, promoting consistency while encouraging jurisdictions to adapt principles that suit their own policy objectives and institutional contexts. The work of these SSBs is grounded in three recurring themes: (1) applying a risk-proportionate regulatory approach; (2) adopting functional, activity-based oversight; and (3) ensuring technological neutrality.

Rather than prescribing a single model for regulation, the international community has instead articulated high-level expectations that jurisdictions are encouraged to implement domestically. The FSB's *High-Level Recommendations for the Regulation, Supervision and Oversight of Global Stablecoin Arrangements* (FSB, 2020) is perhaps the most influential of these. In that report, the FSB set out ten overarching recommendations for what it terms GSC. It emphasizes that authorities must have the necessary powers and resources to regulate GSCs effectively. This includes authority over governance, issuers, custody providers, exchanges, and other intermediaries that play a significant role in the stablecoin ecosystem. Authorities, the FSB notes, must have access to all relevant information and, where necessary, the power to restrict or prohibit operations that fail to meet applicable requirements.

A core element of the FSB's guidance is its insistence on a comprehensive, function-based approach to oversight. The FSB urges regulators to rely on existing frameworks wherever possible, extending or adapting them only when the unique features of stablecoin activity create gaps in supervision. It also stresses the need for close cross-border cooperation, reflecting the inherently global character of most stablecoins. Information-sharing and mutual recognition among regulators are essential, the FSB argues, for preventing regulatory arbitrage and ensuring that stablecoin arrangements operating across multiple jurisdictions are subject to coherent oversight. To this end, it encourages authorities to formalize their collaboration through memoranda of understanding or ad hoc cooperative mechanisms suited to the scale and structure of each arrangement.

The FSB further highlights the importance of sound governance and accountability. Where a stablecoin arrangement relies on third-party service providers, its governing body should assess and disclose how such dependencies affect its capacity to meet regulatory obligations and performance standards. Individuals occupying control functions are expected to satisfy fit-and-proper criteria. The FSB also calls for comprehensive risk-management frameworks covering operational, cybersecurity, and financial crime risks. Stablecoins that promise stability must, in their view, maintain effective stabilization mechanisms and robust reserve backing to prevent loss of value and to mitigate the risk of redemption runs. For single-currency stablecoins, redemption must occur at par with the referenced fiat currency, and the redemption process must not impose undue costs or delays on holders.

In recognition of the systemic interconnections that stablecoins can create, the FSB recommends that issuers and governing bodies establish recovery and resolution plans. These plans should ensure the orderly wind-down of an issuer or a key service provider without disrupting critical functions or transmitting shocks to the wider financial system. In essence, the FSB positions stablecoin arrangements within the same prudential paradigm as other systemically important financial institutions, demanding transparency, resilience, and clear lines of accountability.

The BIS has reinforced these themes through its report *Application of the Principles for Financial Market Infrastructure for Stablecoin Arrangements* (BIS, 2022). The BIS emphasizes that systemically important stablecoin arrangements should have appropriate governance, facilitating timely human intervention and clear accountability for all functions. The BIS has also highlighted the need for continuous monitoring of the interdependencies between a stablecoin's components, warning that weaknesses in one function can propagate risk to others. It calls for an integrated approach to risk mitigation, one that recognizes that stablecoin arrangements do not operate in isolation but within a broader network of financial infrastructures.

The IOSCO, in its *Policy Recommendations for Crypto and Digital Assets,* reiterates the principle of "*same activities, same risks, same regulation/regulatory outcomes*," and stresses that while many of the risks associated with traditional crypto-assets (such as conflicts of interest, market manipulation, or operational fragility) apply equally to stablecoins, the latter introduce additional vulnerabilities. These include a lack of transparency in reserve management, insufficient verification of collateral, and the potential for rapid destabilization if confidence erodes. IOSCO's guidance implies that regulators should address these risks through mandatory disclosure, independent audits of reserve assets, and enforceable redemption guarantees. In this way, IOSCO situates stablecoin oversight within the broader context of market conduct and transparency regulation.

AML/CFT considerations form another pillar of the international framework. The FATF, in its *Report to G20 on So-called Stablecoins* and *Updated Guidance for a Risk-Based Approach to Virtual Assets and Virtual Asset Services Providers* (FATF, 2020), warns that stablecoins present the same ML/TF risks as other virtual assets, but that these risks may be magnified by their global reach and potential for mass adoption. and could heighten such risks due to their global reach and potential for mass adoption. A widely used stablecoin, if insufficiently regulated, could facilitate illicit flows by providing a stable and liquid medium of exchange outside traditional financial controls. FATF, therefore, insists that its standards apply fully to stablecoin arrangements. Any governance body, issuer, or intermediary typically falls within the definition of a financial institution or a virtual asset service provider (VASP) and is consequently subject to the same obligations of customer due diligence, record-keeping, suspicious transaction reporting, and the implementation of the "travel rule" for fund transfers.

FATF's approach is functionally oriented: even if a stablecoin system is technologically decentralized, authorities are expected to identify the entities that perform regulated functions, such as development, issuance, or distribution, and ensure that these entities comply with AML and CFT requirements. FATF further expects jurisdictions to empower authorities to freeze and confiscate illicit assets and to cooperate internationally in enforcement. These expectations have led many jurisdictions to amend their AML laws to expressly include stablecoin issuers and intermediaries, aligning their compliance obligations with those of other financial institutions.

Taken together, these initiatives represent a broad consensus among standard-setting bodies. Each recognizes that stablecoins, because of their hybrid nature, require robust oversight to safeguard financial stability, monetary integrity, and consumer protection. Regulation should be proportionate to the risks presented, agnostic to technology or corporate form, and centred on the functions performed rather than the entities' labels. Authorities must ensure clear allocation of responsibility within and across jurisdictions, closing regulatory gaps so that stablecoin activities are subject to the same standards as equivalent traditional financial activities.

The cumulative effect of these principles has been to shape the contours of national regulatory frameworks. Many jurisdictions now require the authorisation of stablecoin issuers and intermediaries, mandate full reserve backing with high-quality liquid assets, and enshrine redemption rights at par. Governance standards, disclosure obligations, and AML compliance have become nearly universal. Yet while the influence of international standards is unmistakable, the way in which each jurisdiction translates these high-level principles into law varies according to domestic priorities and institutional design. The next section of this chapter explores these national adaptations, tracing how the recommendations of the FSB, FATF, IOSCO, and BIS have been interpreted across the European Union, the United States, the United Kingdom, Asia, and the Middle East, and how global principles are being shaped into distinct regulatory realities.

Regulatory Approaches in Key Jurisdictions

The evolution of stablecoin regulation has been marked by a remarkable diversity of national responses. While most major economies recognise the importance of establishing clear rules for stablecoin issuance and use, the manner in which these rules are expressed and enforced varies considerably. The differences reflect not only institutional capacity and market maturity but also distinct policy priorities, whether the emphasis lies on promoting innovation, defending monetary sovereignty, or safeguarding financial stability.

This section examines the regulatory frameworks adopted across key jurisdictions, focusing on the European Union, the United Kingdom, the United States of America, Singapore, Hong Kong, the Kingdom of Bahrain, and the UAE, including the CBUAE and ADGM. These jurisdictions have taken leading roles in defining how stablecoins should be treated within their respective financial systems, setting examples that are likely to shape global practice in the years ahead.

Prohibition and Permission: Policy Stances on Stablecoins

National approaches to stablecoins fall along a spectrum that ranges from outright prohibition to carefully calibrated permission. A small number of jurisdictions have chosen to ban stablecoin activity altogether, typically citing the risks of illicit finance, capital flight, or inadequate supervisory capacity. Others have opted for selective restrictions that target specific risks while allowing limited experimentation under supervision. This more nuanced approach enables regulators to mitigate immediate dangers without foreclosing future innovation.

Kuwait represents one of the most conservative examples. In July 2023, its Capital Markets Authority issued a circular imposing a complete ban on the use of cryptocurrencies and stablecoins as either payment tools or investment assets (Al-Melhem, 2023). The prohibition reflects a cautious stance aimed at insulating the domestic financial system from risks associated with unregulated digital assets.

Argentina has taken a markedly different path. Through *Resolution 1058/2025,* its Securities and Exchange Commission established a regulatory framework for VASPs, requiring mandatory registration and compliance with its existing AML / CFT laws (National Securities Commission, 2025). This approach signals a willingness to bring the sector into the formal regulatory fold rather than exclude it entirely.

In contrast, most advanced economies have adopted comprehensive regulation in lieu of prohibition. Their objective is to bring stablecoins within the legal perimeter, mitigating risks through oversight rather than suppression. Within this regulatory approach, two main strategies can be observed. Some jurisdictions extend existing financial regulations (such as those governing electronic money, payments, or banking) to encompass stablecoins. Others enact bespoke frameworks tailored specifically to digital assets. Often, the result is a hybrid system in which new laws set out stablecoin-specific requirements while existing rules continue to apply to cross-cutting issues such as anti-money-laundering, data protection, or consumer rights.

Regulatory Scope

The definitional foundations of stablecoins have been established earlier through the lens of statutory language and regulatory taxonomy. Building on that groundwork, the discussion now turns to how these definitions are applied in practice—how jurisdictions determine which stablecoin activities fall within the regulatory perimeter, how far that perimeter extends across borders, and how oversight is exercised once a token is captured by domestic rules. Scope is therefore not merely a question of terminology but one of jurisdictional reach, enforcement capability, and policy design.

Across major frameworks, a clear pattern has emerged. Most regulators concentrate on fiat-referenced or payment-oriented stablecoins, bringing them under explicit supervision as instruments of exchange or settlement while leaving other token forms, such as commodity-pegged, algorithmic, or governance tokens, to separate regimes or outside the regulated sphere altogether. The key variations lie in how widely the perimeter is drawn and how far domestic laws extend to foreign-issued stablecoins.

In the United States, the GENIUS Act limits its perimeter to "payment stablecoins," covering fiat-pegged instruments intended for payments and extending accountability to foreign issuers offering access to U.S. users (United States Congress, 2025). In the UAE, the CBUAE regulates the issuance of DPT and the use of FPT within the UAE mainland (CBUAE, 2024). Separately, the FSRA supervises the issuance of FRTs that may reference foreign currencies (ADGM, 2015).

The Monetary Authority of Singapore regulates only Single-Currency Stablecoins pegged to the Singapore Dollar or major G10 currencies (Monetary Authority of Singapore, 2023). The European Union takes a wider approach under the MiCA by creating two categories of regulated stablecoins: ARTs and EMTs (European Union, 2023).

The CBB's SIO Module applies to any stablecoin issued "in or from the Kingdom," allowing pegs to the Bahraini Dinar, the U.S. Dollar, or other approved currencies, thereby ensuring comprehensive oversight while remaining accessible to both local and foreign participants (Central Bank of Bahrain, 2025).

The delineation of regulatory scope is not an abstract exercise; it determines tangible outcomes. Inclusion within the regulatory perimeter triggers obligations relating to licensing, governance, reserves, redemption, and reporting. Exclusion, on the other hand, restricts access to banking services, payment systems, and consumer markets. In practice, the boundary of scope defines the line between legitimacy and limitation. It determines which tokens can integrate into mainstream financial infrastructure and which remain peripheral, confined to speculative or unregulated environments.

Across jurisdictions, the global trajectory is toward expanding inclusion within structured oversight. Stablecoins are increasingly permitted to operate, but only within defined parameters that ensure accountability, transparency, and systemic integrity. Regulatory scope has thus become the principal tool through which authorities manage innovation while preserving confidence in the stability of money itself.

Exclusions and Exemptions

Virtually all stablecoin frameworks include explicit exclusions or exemptions to delineate the regulatory perimeter. These carve-outs prevent duplication, reduce regulatory burden, and focus oversight on activities that pose material risks.

A common exclusion applies to instruments already regulated under other financial regulations. MiCA, for example, does not apply to crypto-assets that qualify as traditional financial instruments (like securities, money market funds, or debentures) or as deposits, structured deposits. This prevents overlapping with existing EU securities laws (i.e., MiFID II) or banking laws. Likewise, if a so-called "stablecoin" were actually a form of bank deposit or stored-value facility, it would be regulated as such rather than under the new crypto regime.

Hong Kong's *Stablecoin Ordinance* (hereinafter referred to as "Ordinance") exempts stablecoins that constitute securities or futures contracts, since such stablecoins are to be overseen by the Hong Kong Securities and Futures. ADGM FSRA's FRT framework does not include under its purview tokens classified as Virtual Assets or Digital Securities or other types of digital assets like utility tokens or governance tokens, which are addressed under their respective applicable provisions under the ADGM's regulatory framework. In other practice, ADGM has parallel regimes for virtual assets (covering cryptocurrencies), for digital securities (security tokens), and for fiat-referenced stablecoins, and each regime is mutually exclusive.

Some frameworks also exempt technical service providers or certain support activities from being considered regulated stablecoin activities. The UAE's CBUAE's PTSR excludes, for instance, pure technology providers: activities like providing IT security, operating blockchain nodes or infrastructure, or privacy protection services are not considered "Payment Token Services" if they do not themselves constitute issuing or transacting in tokens. This ensures that companies that are merely offering software or technology services are not forced to become licensed as financial institutions.

Another typical exemption is for closed-loop or limited-use tokens. The CBUAE allows tokens used in customer loyalty programs (e.g., airline miles or supermarket reward tokens that might technically be tokenised and have some monetary-like function) to be exempt from the PTSR so long as they are not redeemable for cash and only used for limited purposes. Similarly, tokens used as means of payment for strictly the issuer's own non-financial goods or services (for example, a token only accepted within a specific platform or game) can be exempted. These carve-outs acknowledge that not every token that has a stable value or payment-like function needs heavy regulation, if the risk to the wider public or financial system is limited (due to limited scope or very small scale), regulators prefer to leave them unregulated or lightly regulated.

Several jurisdictions may also establish de minimis thresholds. For example, some may not enforce full stablecoin issuer requirements if the total outstanding value is below a certain small amount, or if there are fewer than a certain number of users, etc., on the reasoning that the risk is limited. For instance, if the reserve assets of a stablecoin will not exceed AED 500,000 and the aggregate number of token holders is less than 100, the CBUAE may exempt such a Payment Token issuer.

In sum, exclusions are designed to avoid regulatory duplication and to focus regulatory effort on areas of real risk. By excluding tokens already covered as securities or e-money, regulators ensure the stablecoin rules target novel gaps. By exempting limited-use or small-scale tokens, they avoid overburdening innovation or clogging regulators' resources with cases. These exclusions also clarify the regulatory perimeter, an important point for industry, which needs to know whether a given token or activity falls under the stablecoin regulations or not.

Prohibited Stablecoin Variants

While regulators have generally embraced fully backed, fiat-referenced stablecoins, many have drawn clear boundaries around designs deemed incompatible with financial stability and consumer protection. Two categories stand out as targets of explicit prohibition: algorithmic stablecoins and privacy-enhanced stablecoins.

Algorithmic stablecoins attempt to maintain value parity through automated issuance and redemption mechanisms rather than through full reserve backing. Following a series of high-profile failures, regulators worldwide have come to regard these models as inherently fragile. The UAE's CBUAE explicitly prohibits any person in the UAE from issuing algorithmic Payment Tokens or even providing any services related to algorithmic Payment Tokens. Similarly, the ADGM FSRA bans any regulated activity involving algorithmic stablecoins (as well as privacy tokens) within its jurisdiction. These blanket prohibitions reflect the judgment that algorithmic stablecoins present unacceptable risk and volatility as they purport to be stable without the fundamental underpinning of tangible assets, which can be viewed as an inherent consumer fraud risk in the worst case, or at least a systemic threat if they grow large and then collapse.

By banning them, regulators aim to prevent a repeat of failure events and send a clear signal that only fully asset-backed stablecoins are considered legitimate. Indeed, most regimes now either require the term "stablecoin" to be used only if the coin is fully backed. The rationale often given is investor protection and financial stability, as algorithmic designs can create a false sense of security and then unravel rapidly, undermining trust in the broader crypto market and potentially affecting retail users who treated them like safe assets.

Privacy tokens or privacy-enhanced stablecoins have also been targets of restrictions due to ML / TF risks and law enforcement concerns. These are stablecoins that incorporate features (such as cryptographic mixing or zero-knowledge proofs) to obscure transaction details and user identities. While not many stablecoins are currently privacy-oriented, regulators have concerns with regard to the development of a widely used anonymous stablecoin that could facilitate illicit transactions at scale. As a result, the CBUAE's PTSR bans the issuance or servicing of privacy tokens alongside the ban on algorithmic coins.

The ADGM FSRA similarly disallows activities involving privacy tokens. Other jurisdictions have not needed to separately ban privacy stablecoins, since their broader crypto regulations (and FATF Travel Rule implementation) would not permit licensed entities to deal in fully anonymous tokens. Nonetheless, the effect is the same. A stablecoin that does not allow compliance with AML/CFT requirements is not permitted. This ensures that stablecoins cannot become a loophole to evade financial surveillance that applies to traditional e-money or bank transfers.

In essence, regulators have drawn a red line at stablecoins that do not have adequate asset backing or transparency. Algorithmic stablecoins are seen as inherently misleading (since stability is only maintained by market confidence and arbitrage, not hard assets) and prone to collapse, so they are barred to protect users and markets. Privacy-enhanced stablecoins are blocked to pre-empt an avenue for illicit finance that would be extremely difficult to control. These prohibitions show that while regulators are open to innovation in payments, there are boundaries beyond which they are not willing to compromise core financial integrity or stability principles. This distinction underscores the philosophy guiding most modern regulatory frameworks: innovation is encouraged, but only within the bounds of stability, accountability, and trust.

Reserve Asset Requirements and Custody Safeguards

A defining feature of stablecoin regulation worldwide is the requirement that issuers must maintain reserves of high quality and sufficient liquidity to back the value of stablecoins in circulation. Most frameworks mandate a one-to-one backing at all times, ensuring that for every unit of stablecoin issued, an equivalent amount of underlying assets is held in secure custody. This fundamental rule reflects a shared regulatory objective: to guarantee that redemption is always possible, thereby preserving stability and user confidence.

Across jurisdictions, regulators have converged on the principle that eligible reserve assets must comprise high-quality liquid assets (HQLA), such as cash, cash equivalents, or short-term sovereign securities. These instruments can be quickly liquidated at a predictable value even under stress, supporting immediate redemption obligations and mitigating the risk of runs.

Under CBB's SIO Module, reserve assets must be "high quality and high liquidity with minimal market, credit, and concentration risk.". The SIO Module specifies an allowable list: (a) cash or on-demand deposits at banks with high credit ratings (AA- or above); (b) debt securities issued by the central bank of the reference currency with maturity 90 days or less; (c) very short-term repurchase agreements (≤7 days) collateralized by those central bank securities; and (d) money market funds investing in government debt. This list closely mirrors classic definitions of HQLA, ensuring reserves are insulated from market volatility.

ADGM's FSRA adopts comparable principles for FRTs. It requires reserves to be denominated in the same fiat as the FRT's reference value (eliminating currency mismatch risk) and to be held in certain secure forms like cash equivalents and debt securities with up to three-month residual maturity issued by governments and central banks; money-market funds which invest in government debt; and overnight reverse repurchase agreements overcollateralized by debt securities issued by a government or central bank of pegged currency.

The GENIUS Act similarly requires reserve backing of outstanding payment stablecoins on a 1:1 basis. The GENIUS Act permits reserves to comprise US currency, funds held as demand deposits, treasury notes, money received under repurchase agreements, and reverse repurchase agreements.

In the UAE, the CBUAE requires reserves to be held as cash in a segregated escrow account. Where the issuer is a wholly-owned subsidiary of a UAE bank, it may hold up to 50% of reserves in UAE government bonds or central bank bills (with average duration ≤6 months), provided it holds extra regulatory capital as well. This carve-out presumably acknowledges that bank-affiliated issuers can prudently manage some investment of reserves, and it aligns with the idea that reserves can earn a return to fund operations, as long as safety is maintained.

Custody and segregation of reserves is another critical component of these requirements. Regulators consistently insist that reserve assets be bankruptcy-remote from the issuer, meaning that if the issuer fails, reserve assets are insulated and can be used to repay coin holders. To achieve this, reserves must be held with licensed custodians or trusted third parties, separate from the issuer's own operational funds. For example, the EU MiCA requires issuers to safeguard reserve assets either with credit institutions or qualified custodians and to have them fully segregated from other assets. UAE's CBUAE requires an escrow account setup (likely with a bank) for reserves and prohibits any encumbrance of those reserves, i.e., they cannot be pledged or used as collateral.

The consistency across jurisdictions in requiring fully backed, high-quality, and liquid reserves illustrates a fundamental convergence in regulatory philosophy. Stablecoins are intended to function like stored-value facilities or near-deposit instruments; regulators aim to ensure that their backing is equally sound. Strict reserve and custody requirements not only protect users but also mitigate systemic contagion: if a major stablecoin failed to meet redemption requests, it could undermine confidence across both crypto and traditional financial markets. To prevent such instability, regulators favour conservative investment constraints, short maturities, and top-tier credit standards that prioritise preservation of value over yield.

Complementing these reserve obligations, capital requirements are imposed to ensure that issuers maintain a financial buffer against operational or market risks. For instance, the FSRA mandates a paid-up capital of USD 2 million, CBUAE requires an initial and ongoing capital of AED 15 million and an additional ongoing capital of at least 0.5% of the fiat currency face value of outstanding Payment Tokens, and CBB requires a capital of BHD 250,000.

Redemption Rights and Consumer Protection

Robust redemption rights form the other pillar of stablecoin regulation. A stablecoin can only be considered truly stable if holders can reliably exchange it for its equivalent fiat value at any time. Redemption guarantees protect user confidence, distinguish payment-oriented stablecoins from investment tokens, and prevent systemic contagion in the event of stress.

Regulators have therefore enshrined a clear, enforceable right of redemption at par value. For fiat-pegged stablecoins, the standard is one-to-one convertibility, that is, one token redeemable for one unit of the corresponding currency within a specified timeframe.

Under CBB's SIO Module, stablecoin issuers must ensure holders have a direct legal right to redeem at par (1:1) for the pegged fiat currency, within a maximum of 5 business days of request. This five-day window balances immediacy with practical processing time. It is short enough to prevent confidence erosion, but allows the issuer to manage liquidity (especially if offloading reserve assets is needed). In practice, many issuers might offer much faster redemption (even same day) in normal conditions, but the regulation sets an outer limit.

Some jurisdictions push for even faster redemption. The UAE's CBUAE requires redemption "without delay and in any case by the next business day" after the request, unless the CBUAE allows otherwise. This essentially means a 24-hour turnaround for redemption. The stricter timeline reflects perhaps an alignment with how e-money redemptions work (immediate to next-day) and an emphasis on strong consumer protection in the UAE's new framework. ADGM FSRA's regulatory framework for FRTs requires redemption at par no later than T+2 days after completion of any necessary customer due diligence (CDD) checks. The KYC caveat means that if a holder isn't already identified, the period only starts after they comply with AML / CFT checks. However, once CDD, the ADGM FSRA mandates a two-day limit.

The EU's approach under MiCA has an interesting nuance. For ARTs, redemption can be in fiat or by delivering the underlying reference assets, and it must equal the market value of the reference assets at the time of redemption. This suggests that if, say, an ART references a basket of assets, an issuer could redeem by delivering the actual assets or cash of equivalent current value. For EMTs (which are stablecoins pegged to a single currency), redemption must be at par in cash at any time, similar to e-money directives (and notably, it prohibits any redemption fee for EMTs and ARTs, as discussed below).

To prevent the erosion of redemption rights through excessive charges, most regulators either prohibit or cap fees. MiCA explicitly prohibits charging a fee for redemption of EMTs, and also bans fees for ART redemption. While the CBUAE permits fees if "proportionate and commensurate with the actual costs incurred" by the issuer, it effectively disallows profit-making fees. The FSRA and CBB allow modest redemption charges provided they are reasonable, transparent, and clearly disclosed in advance. ADGM FSRA similarly allows a fee for FRT redemption, provided it reflects actual costs and was clearly stated upfront in the white paper.

CBB requires that any redemption fees not be set so high as to deter customers from redeeming; they must be reasonable and clearly communicated. In the US, the GENIUS Act adopts a disclosure-based approach. It does not cap fees but requires issuers to clearly disclose all fees and give notice of fee changes 7 days in advance, ensuring market discipline and consumer awareness. In practice, many major stablecoins did not charge redemption fees directly (instead, they had high minimum redemption amounts for non-institutional users, etc.), but regulators want to formalize protections so that, especially for retail-facing stablecoins, individuals can redeem without undue cost barriers.

Another core consumer protection measure is the prohibition on paying interest or yield to stablecoin holders. The idea is that stablecoins are meant as a means of payment or value transfer, not an investment product, as offering interest could make them resemble deposit accounts or securities and encourage users to treat them as savings vehicles, which raises different regulatory implications. MiCA states that issuers of asset-referenced tokens "shall not grant interest" to holders of those tokens, and similarly, issuers of e-money tokens are forbidden from paying interest.

Hong Kong's Ordinance also provides that a stablecoin licensee must not pay any interest on the stablecoins it issues (HKSA, 2025). Further, the GENIUS Act explicitly prohibits both payment stablecoin issuers from paying any form of interest or yield "whether in cash, tokens, or other consideration" to a stablecoin holder just for holding the stablecoin. The rationale is to prevent regulatory arbitrage around banking laws. If stablecoin issuers could pay interest, they would be competing with bank deposits but without the same guarantees or potentially the same level of oversight, unless they basically become banks. Also, an interest-bearing stablecoin might be deemed a security (an investment contract), which opens another regulatory can of worms. By prohibiting interest, regulators keep stablecoins purely as payment mechanisms, not investment products, which supports their legal classification as something other than securities.

An exception appears in Bahrain's framework, which permits "yield-bearing" stablecoins under certain conditions. Bahrain's rules say an issuer may offer stablecoins that pay passive returns to holders, but only out of the interest or rewards earned on the reserve assets (and for Sharia-compliant structures, rewards rather than interest). In other words, a Bahraini stablecoin could pass through the interest it earns on, say, its reserve treasury bills to the coin holders. This approach is likely to accommodate Islamic finance considerations and to allow innovation in product design, as long as it is transparent and truly based on actual reserve income.

Even so, Bahrain would treat such a stablecoin as a regulated product and subject it to all the same reserve and disclosure requirements. The yield feature is merely allowed so long as it does not transform the risk profile (the prohibition would probably be on promising any return beyond what the conservative reserves yield). Similarly, the ADGM FSRA does not forbid an issuer from passing on reserve income to FRT holders, but it emphasizes that the FRT must not be promoted as an investment or savings product. Essentially, they allow it technically but discourage any marketing that would make people buy stablecoins for yield.

The proscription on interest ties back to monetary policy concerns as well. Central bankers worry that if private stablecoins could pay interest, they might compete strongly with bank deposits and even with sovereign money (cash does not yield interest). A non-interest-bearing design makes stablecoins useful for payments but less attractive purely as a store of wealth compared to bank accounts when interest rates are high, thereby limiting potential disruption to banking funding and credit creation.

Transparency obligations complement these protections. Issuers are generally required to publish detailed disclosures on the mechanism for maintaining stability, the composition of reserves, the rights of holders, and the associated risks. Many frameworks, including MiCA, mandate a detailed white paper for each token offering, along with periodic reserve attestations and immediate disclosure of material changes. These measures enhance accountability and foster market discipline by allowing users and regulators to verify that reserves remain intact and redemptions are honoured.

Taken together, these requirements establish a common regulatory baseline across jurisdictions. Full reserve backing ensures solvency, redemption rights guarantee convertibility, and interest prohibitions maintain the payment-oriented nature of stablecoins. Differences in redemption timelines or yield allowances reflect local market structures rather than divergence in core principles. The overarching intent is consistent: users should always be able to redeem stablecoins promptly and at face value, without exposure to investment risk or uncertainty. In essence, regulators are constructing a framework in which holding a regulated stablecoin is as secure, transparent, and predictable as holding its equivalent fiat currency in a stored-value facility.

Licensing and Authorisation of Stablecoin Activities

A core feature of emerging stablecoin regulation is the establishment of clear licensing and authorisation requirements. The period in which stablecoin issuers operated without formal financial licences has effectively ended. Across major jurisdictions, authorities now require that any entity issuing or providing key services in relation to stablecoins be regulated under an appropriate framework. The precise model differs, but the policy goal is consistent: to bring stablecoin activities within the perimeter of financial supervision and ensure prudential and consumer protection standards comparable to those applied to traditional payment institutions.

Licensing models generally fall into two categories. Some jurisdictions integrate stablecoin issuers into existing regulatory classes such as banks or electronic money institutions, while others have introduced bespoke licence types for stablecoin or digital-asset service providers. In either case, the issuance of stablecoins is now almost universally treated as a regulated activity.

Within the European Union, MiCA requires any issuer of an ART or EMT to obtain authorization from a competent authority. For EMTs, the issuer must be a credit institution or e-money institution, thus holding a banking or e-money licence. For ARTs, MiCA creates a distinct category of authorisation specifically for such issuers. The framework thus embeds stablecoin issuance within existing prudential regulation while recognising the need for a dedicated supervisory regime for asset-linked structures.

In the US, the GENIUS Act similarly requires authorisation but offers flexibility between bank-linked and independent issuers. Only a permitted payment stablecoin issuer can issue stablecoins, effectively limiting issuance to (A) insured depository institution subsidiaries approved for stablecoin issuance; (B) a federal qualified payment stablecoin issuer; or (C) a state qualified payment stablecoin issuer. This structure integrates stablecoin issuance into the banking and payments ecosystem without mandating that every issuer become a full bank, thereby preserving competition while ensuring robust oversight.

The United Kingdom, through its *Draft Financial Services and Markets Act 2000 (Regulated Activities and Miscellaneous Provision) (Cryptoassets) Order 2025* (Draft Order), has proposed to bring stablecoin issuance into the regulatory net via an amendment to the Financial Services and Markets Act ("FSMA") and new UK FCA authorization regimes (Meakin et al., 2025). The Draft Order will make activities such as issuing a "qualifying" stablecoin, safeguarding or operating a crypto-asset wallet, and running a crypto-asset trading platform regulated activities in the United Kingdom (HM Treasury, 2025). Firms will need to get permission from the FCA to undertake such regulated activities. The HM Treasury's policy notes on the *Future financial services regulatory regime for crypto assets* provide that payments using stablecoins will remain unregulated for the time being. As wider payments reform use-cases and user adoption develop over time, the Government will respond accordingly (HM Treasury, 2025).

Hong Kong's Ordinance creates a new licensing regime under the HKMA for stablecoin issuers. Any person who issues a stablecoin in Hong Kong, or actively markets to the public in Hong Kong an overseas-issued stablecoin that is pegged to HKD, is considered to be conducting a regulated stablecoin activity and must obtain a license. The HKMA will be the regulator, and it has also published draft guidelines for applicants. The Ordinance also allows the HKMA to specify additional regulated activities by notice.

The CBB, through its SIO Module, has introduced a license for stablecoin issuance and offering. As such, the issuance or offering of stablecoins to the public, by way of business, from or in Bahrain, is now a specific licensable activity and accordingly, requires a license from the CBB for being an "approved stablecoin". The SIO Module also covers guidelines for marketing stablecoins to the public. CBB further clarifies that even incidental services like managing the reserve or providing custody of stablecoins are considered part of the licensed activity. Thus, a stablecoin issuer's responsibilities extend to such functions.

In the UAE, the CBUAE regulates stablecoins under the PTSR in the mainland UAE. Specifically, an entity issuing a DPT must be licensed by the CBUAE as a Payment Token Issuer. Issuers of foreign-currency-referenced stablecoins must register with the CBUAE to operate within the UAE, subject to defined criteria and disclosure requirements. Related services such as Payment Token Custody and Transfer, and Payment Conversion are likewise regulated and require specific licences. Notably, the CBUAE requires that issuers located in financial free zones (like ADGM or Dubai International Financial Centre (DIFC) that wish to offer stablecoins in the UAE mainland must also register with the CBUAE, to ensure onshore oversight even if the entity is primarily regulated elsewhere.

Within the ADGM, the FSRA updated its framework to include FRT issuance as a regulated activity. Firms wishing to issue an FRT must obtain a Financial Services Permission (FSP) from the FSRA specifically for this activity. For an ADGM FSRA-authorized firm to deal with or use FRTs in their fund flows, such proposed FRTs must go through an ADGM FSRA-led assessment and meet criteria before being accepted as an Accepted FRT. The ADGM FSRA shall assess the proposed FRT on factors such as traceability/monitoring, security, market profile, exchange connectivity, DLT infrastructure and ecosystem, innovation/efficiency, and practical application/functionality. This effectively is a form of registration/approval for FRTs. It means ADGM-authorised exchanges or firms can only deal in FRT that the FSRA has vetted and accepted, which adds a layer of quality control.

Although the legal structures differ, all regimes share a convergent philosophy: stablecoin issuance and related activities must be subject to prior authorisation. Whether integrated into banking law, payments regulation, or bespoke digital-asset frameworks, the common outcome is the elimination of unlicensed issuance. Exchanges, custodians, and wallet providers handling stablecoins are likewise brought under licensing requirements either as VASPs or as specialised payment institutions.

Across jurisdictions, the regulatory trajectory is clear. Stablecoin activities are no longer peripheral to the financial system, but are a part of it. Consequently, regulators now demand that entities engaging in issuance, custody, or conversion meet the same prudential, governance, and consumer-protection standards as other regulated financial actors. The licensing perimeter has become the foundation for ensuring stability, accountability, and confidence in the use of digital money.

Table 1. Simplified comparison of licensing approaches

Jurisdiction	Who Can Issue Stablecoins / License Type	Other Regulated Activities	Regulatory Authority
EU (MiCA)	EMT issuers must be credit institutions or e-money institutions (thus need a banking or e-money license). ART issuers require authorization as a crypto-asset issuer by a national competent authority.	• Issuance of ART/EMT • Custody and administration • Operation of a trading platform • Exchange of crypto-assets for funds / other crypto-assets • Execution of orders • Placing of crypto-assets • Reception and transmission of orders; • Providing advice; • Portfolio management • Transfer services	National financial regulators (with the European Banking Authority coordinating for significant tokens).
UK (proposed)	Any person issuing a qualifying stablecoin (used for payments) must be authorized.	• Issuing qualifying stablecoins • Safeguarding of qualifying crypto assets • Operating a qualifying crypto asset trading platform • Dealing in qualifying crypto assets as principal • Dealing in qualified crypto assets as an agent • Arranging deals in qualifying Cryptoassets • Qualifying crypto asset staking	FCA (primary supervisor for firms), with the Bank of England overseeing systemic payment systems.
US (GENIUS Act)	Only a "Permitted Payment Stablecoin Issuer" can issue. This includes: (A) insured depository bank subsidiaries (with approval); (B) Federal qualified payment stablecoin issuers; or (C) State-qualified stablecoin issuers (licensed under state law equivalent to federal). All issuers are subject to prudential regulation.	Banks and money service businesses engaging in stablecoin-related services might need appropriate charters. The Act focuses on the issuance and governance of stablecoin arrangements; exchanges dealing in stablecoins remain regulated by existing securities/ commodities laws as applicable.	Treasury Department, Office of the Comptroller of the Currency

continued on following page

Table 1. Continued

Jurisdiction	Who Can Issue Stablecoins / License Type	Other Regulated Activities	Regulatory Authority
Hong Kong	Stablecoin issuers must obtain a license from HKMA under the new regime. Only approved licensees can issue or operate stablecoins in HK or market HKD-linked stablecoins.	HKMA can designate other activities as regulated (e.g., operating a reserve management service, wallet provider). Likely, wallet providers and exchanges handling stablecoins will either need this license or an existing Money Service Operator license, depending on function.	Hong Kong Monetary Authority – will supervise stablecoin issuers (and potentially coordinate with Securities and Futures Commission if any stablecoin resembles securities, though such would be handled as securities).
Bahrain	Must have a license from CBB for regulated stablecoin offering service. Both domestic and foreign entities can apply, but need a local presence. Only licensees can issue/offer stablecoins to the public in or from Bahrain.	Incidental services (reserve management, custody of the stablecoin or its reserve) are covered under the same license.	The Central Bank of Bahrain regulates and supervises licensees under its SIO Module.
UAE – CBUAE	Licensed Payment Token Issuer – required for issuing any stablecoin (Payment Token) in the mainland UAE. Dirham-backed token issuers need a full license; foreign stablecoin issuers need to register with CBUAE to operate (lighter touch than a full license, but still a form of authorization). Banks can issue tokens, subject to certain conditions must get approval.	Separate licenses for Payment Token Custody & Transfer and Payment Token Conversion services (for wallet providers, exchanges dealing in tokens). Any entity doing those in the UAE must be licensed. Issuers from ADGM/DIFC or abroad must register to offer tokens onshore.	Central Bank of the UAE – oversees payment token regulatory framework, licensing, and supervision. Coordinates with Securities and Commodities Authority (hereinafter referred to as SCA) and financial free zone regulators for comprehensive coverage.
UAE – ADGM (FSRA)	Issuing an FRT is a regulated activity requiring an FSP from ADG, FSRA. Only firms approved by FSRA can issue FRTs in ADGM. ADGM encompasses a regulator-led assessment model to whitelist FRTs that can be issued/used.	ADGM regulates financial services activities under its existing framework. Those can involve stablecoins that are on the FSRA's Accepted list. Such other activities include: • Operating a Multi-lateral Trading Facility • Arranging in Deals • Dealing in Investments as Agent • Dealing in Investments as Principal • Providing Custody	ADGM FSRA licenses firms for FRT issuance and related financial services. Coordinates with CBUAE regarding AED-pegged tokens.

Note: Licensing approaches to stablecoin issuance and related activities. Jurisdictions either integrate stablecoin issuers into existing licensing categories (e.g. banks/e-money in EU) or create new categories (US stablecoin charter, Bahrain stablecoin licence, ADGM FRT issuer). All require regulatory approval before issuance, and most regulate key intermediaries (exchanges, brokers, and custodians) under either general crypto law or stablecoin-specific provisions.

As Table 1 suggests, the regulatory trend is to ensure no significant stablecoin activity is unlicensed. Now, whether through banking law, payments law, or bespoke crypto-asset law, regulators assert authority over issuance and usually also over the wallets, exchanges, and custody providers that handle stablecoins.

Innovation and Sandboxing: Regulatory Sandboxes for Stablecoins

Regulators have tightened standards around stablecoin issuance and use, yet most are equally intent on cultivating responsible innovation. To strike that balance, jurisdictions have built regulatory sandboxes and innovation hubs, which are essentially mechanisms that allow fintech developers to trial new financial products in a controlled and supervised environment. A sandbox is, in essence, a live testing framework: limited scope, explicit safeguards, and close engagement with the supervisor. The aim is to enable experimentation without compromising consumer protection or financial stability. This approach has proved especially useful for blockchain and stablecoin models that do not map neatly onto traditional regulatory categories.

In stablecoin contexts, sandboxes let issuers and technology developers run limited-scale pilots while deferring some obligations until a design has been validated. A cross-border payments prototype, for example, might operate with a few hundred users under modified requirements, giving regulators direct visibility into reserve management, on-chain mechanics, operational resilience, and user behaviour. This shared learning shortens feedback loops: supervisors see risks and mitigants in practice; innovators refine architecture and controls before seeking full authorization.

Admission to a sandbox typically requires an application that explains the innovation, the test plan, the consumer benefit, and the risk controls. Entry criteria emphasise genuine novelty, potential public value, and credible safeguards. During the trial, the regulator maintains active supervision, collecting performance data and verifying consumer protection measures such as informed consent and compensation limits. Following completion, the trial is evaluated with successful applicants transitioning to full authorization, while those that reveal operational flaws can either modify their models or terminate projects without systemic repercussions.

For regulators and governments, sandboxes deliver four strategic benefits. First, they provide empirical evidence about how new technologies behave, which is vital for instruments whose risk profile depends on code, reserves, and network dynamics. Second, they enable contained experimentation, with caps and contingency plans that limit spillovers. Third, they function as regulatory laboratories: outcomes inform calibration of future rules, revealing where obligations are too heavy, too light, or misaligned. Fourth, they signal openness to innovation, which attracts talent and investment and fosters a collaborative supervisory posture.

For market participants, the advantages are equally compelling. Sandboxes reduce time-to-market and early compliance cost for pilots, particularly for startups. Direct, iterative feedback from supervisors operates as regulatory mentorship, aligning design choices with eventual rulebooks. Participation can also de-risk credibility with customers and investors, since testing occurs under visible oversight. And because trials are bounded, firms can validate demand and resilience before scaling, limiting reputational and financial downside.

Several jurisdictions now run operational sandbox frameworks. The FCA, MAS, have long-standing sandboxes that have hosted digital-asset pilots. In the UAE, both financial free zones operate programs such as the ADGM RegLab and the DIFC Innovation Testing Licence have admitted to running crypto pilots.

Hong Kong offers a focused example with the HKMA Stablecoin Sandbox Initiative (2023–2024) (HKMA, 2024). Launched alongside policy formation, it invited prospective issuers to conduct supervised pilots while the stablecoin regime was being finalized. The initiative had three objectives: (i) to enable constructive dialogue between industry and the HKMA on draft requirements; (ii) to permit genuine stablecoin projects to operate within a restricted, risk-contained environment; and (iii) to use the empirical feedback from these trials to ensure that the eventual rulebook would be proportionate, risk-sensitive, and technologically informed.

Applicants needed to demonstrate both innovation and operational readiness, specifically, the ability to manage reserves, implement sound governance, and ensure compliance with AML / CFT and consumer protection standards. Admission did not constitute licensing or endorsement; rather, it created a pathway to inform the HKMA's policy work and to prepare participants for subsequent authorization. Assessment criteria included consumer benefit and innovation, technical robustness, and readiness to comply with the final framework. In practice, the sandbox allowed the HKMA to stress-test policy assumptions, for instance, how reserve segregation or wallet protection requirements might work in operational reality, before enacting binding regulations. This participatory approach exemplified how supervised experimentation can align industry development with regulatory objectives.

The outcomes of sandbox participation generally benefit both regulators and innovators. Regulators can craft more targeted, effective regulations grounded in empirical evidence rather than abstract risk scenarios. Firms, in turn, gain insight into compliance expectations and reduce the likelihood of costly post-launch regulatory conflicts. However, sandboxes are not without limitations: small-scale trials may fail to reveal issues that emerge under mass adoption, and regulators must vigilantly maintain consumer protection, often restricting participation size or mandating disclosure that the test is experimental.

Applied to stablecoins, sandbox pilots can be particularly useful where innovation touches core prudential questions. Authorities can evaluate stabilisation mechanisms under stress, test reserve compositions and custody models against liquidity needs, pilot automated Travel Rule compliance on-chain, and validate operational resilience under node or oracle failure. The result is a clearer distinction between architectures that enhance transparency and robustness and those that amplify systemic risk.

In summary, regulatory sandboxes act as bridges between innovation and oversight. They empower regulators to keep pace with fast-evolving technologies through empirical learning while giving firms a responsible route to market entry. For the stablecoin ecosystem, where technological change often outpaces legal adaptation, this iterative approach is essential. Ultimately, consumers also benefit: the products reaching them are those tested under regulatory supervision rather than unregulated experimentation, while innovation itself is not stifled by premature rigidity. Consequently, many jurisdictions now regard sandboxes as indispensable tools for adaptive, evidence-based regulation, ensuring that financial governance evolves in tandem with technological progress.

CONCLUSION

The global regulatory architecture for stablecoins is entering a period of consolidation. A clear convergence has emerged around fundamental safeguards such as full reserve backing, transparent custody, redemption at par, strong governance, and the principle of "same risk, same regulation". These features, now embedded in the frameworks of major jurisdictions, signal the formal integration of stablecoins into the broader regulated financial system. What began as an experimental innovation on the margins of crypto markets is being transformed into a supervised financial instrument grounded in prudential oversight and consumer protection.

Despite this alignment in core objectives, national regimes continue to diverge on points of implementation. Some, like the European Union, restrict issuance to banks and e-money institutions, embedding stablecoins within existing financial law. Others, such as the United States, Bahrain, and the UAE, permit non-bank issuers under bespoke authorisation regimes that expand market participation while retaining supervisory control. Approaches to foreign stablecoins also differ. Larger economies increasingly insist on domestic registration to ensure enforceability, while smaller jurisdictions remain open to cross-border issuers so long as they meet equivalent standards.

Differences in scope persist as well. Singapore and the UAE confine regulation to tokens pegged to major currencies to preserve monetary sovereignty. However, the European Union's inclusion of multi-asset and commodity-referenced tokens reflects a broader tolerance for structural innovation. Algorithmic designs remain prohibited across nearly all frameworks, though limited accommodation for yield-sharing models, such as those in the ADGM or Bahrain, demonstrates that regulators can permit incremental innovation where prudential safeguards are intact.

The trend, however, points unmistakably toward greater alignment over time. Once-contested questions such as whether issuers require a licence and whether reserves must be held in cash or cash equivalents are now largely settled. International standard setters such as the FSB and IOSCO are already steering jurisdictions toward consistency, particularly for cross-border stablecoins with systemic potential. Within a few years, a globally recognized baseline of prudential and conduct requirements may well emerge, implemented through nationally tailored but interoperable regimes.

For financial policymakers, the regulation of stablecoins has become a test case for integrating crypto-native innovation into public law frameworks. The evolving regimes exhibit a measured approach, neither prohibitionist nor permissive, aimed at capturing the benefits of programmable, low-cost digital money while constraining risks of runs, misuse, or consumer loss. Innovation tools such as sandboxes and regulatory pilots have accelerated this adaptation, creating a dynamic feedback loop between supervision and experimentation. The experience of Hong Kong and the UAE illustrates how such iterative mechanisms can translate policy learning into proportionate, evidence-based rulemaking.

Ultimately, the stablecoin's legitimacy will depend on the confidence that regulation instils. By aligning reserve, redemption, and governance requirements with established prudential norms, regulators are turning stablecoins into a safe component of financial infrastructure that can be used by consumers, payment institutions, and capital markets participants alike. The effect will likely be a concentration of activity among well-capitalized, compliant issuers and a gradual exit of weaker, unregulated actors.

Unresolved policy questions remain, including how to manage systemic stablecoins at scale, what backstops exist if they fail, and how their role will evolve alongside central bank digital currencies. Yet the direction of travel is clear. Stablecoins are moving from the periphery of financial innovation to the centre of financial regulation, subject to the same accountability, transparency, and prudential discipline that underpin the stability of modern monetary systems.

REFERENCES

Abu Dhabi Global Market. (2015). *Financial Services and Markets Regulations 2015 | Rulebook*. Thomsonreuters.com. https://en.adgm.thomsonreuters.com/rulebook/financial-services-and-markets-regulations-2015-0

Al-Melhem, A. (2023). *Capital Markets Authority-Resolutions and Circulars - CMA*. Cma.gov.kw. https://www.cma.gov.kw/en/web/cma/cma-board-releases/resolutions-and-regulations/-/cmaboardreleases/detail/1384960

Bank for International Settlement. (2022). *Application of the Principles for Financial Market Infrastructures to stablecoin arrangements*. Bis.org. https://www.bis.org/cpmi/publ/d206.htm

Central Bank of Bahrain. (2025). *SIO Stablecoin Issuance & Offering | Rulebook Volume 6: Capital Markets*. Thomsonreuters.com. https://cbben.thomsonreuters.com/rulebook/sio-stablecoin-issuance-offering

Central Bank of the United Arab Emirates. (2024). *Payment Token Services Regulation | CBUAE Rulebook*. Centralbank.ae. https://rulebook.centralbank.ae/en/rulebook/payment-token-services-regulation

European Union. (2023). *Regulation - 2023/1114 - EN - EUR-Lex*. Europa.eu. https://doi.org/DOI: 10/1093/2024-12-30

Financial Action Task Force. (2020). *FATF Report to G20 on So-called Stablecoins*. Fatf-Gafi.org. https://www.fatf-gafi.org/publications/virtualassets/documents/report-g20-so-called-stablecoins-june-2020.html

Financial Stability Board. (2020, October 13). *Regulation, Supervision, and Oversight of "Global Stablecoin" Arrangements*. Www.fsb.org. https://www.fsb.org/2020/10/regulation-supervision-and-oversight-of-global-stablecoin-arrangements/

Hong Kong Money Authority. (2024). *HKMA launches the stablecoin issuer sandbox arrangement*. Hong Kong Monetary Authority. https://www.hkma.gov.hk/eng/news-and-media/press-releases/2024/03/20240312-4/

Hong Kong Special Administrative. (2025). *Hong Kong e-Legislation| Stablecoins Ordinance (Cap. 656)*. Elegislation.gov.hk. https://www.elegislation.gov.hk/hk/cap656?p0=1&p1=1

Meakin, H., Edwards, A., & Lovegrove, S. (2025). *HMT publishes draft legislation for regulating cryptoassets*. Global Regulation Tomorrow. https://www.regulationtomorrow.com/eu/hmt-publishes-draft-legislation-for-regulating-cryptoassets/

Money Authority of Singapore. (2023). *MAS Finalizes Stablecoin Regulatory Framework*. https://www.sgpc.gov.sg/api/file/getfile/Media%20Release_MAS%20Finalises%20Stablecoin%20Regulatory%20Framework.pdf?path=/sgpcmedia/media_releases/mas/press_release/P-20230815-2/attachment/Media+Release_MAS+Finalises+Stablecoin+Regulatory+Framework.pdf

National Securities Commission. (2025). *Regulations (NT 2013 and amendments). Amendment*. Argentina.gob.ar. https://www.argentina.gob.ar/normativa/nacional/resoluci%C3%B3n-1058-2025-410635/texto

Treasury, H. M. (2025a). *Future financial services regulatory regime for cryptoassets (regulated activities) Policy Note*. https://assets.publishing.service.gov.uk/media/680f6397b0d43971b07f5bfd/20250428_RAO_SI_draft_policy_note.pdf

Treasury, H. M. (2025b). *The Financial Services and Markets Act 2000 (Regulated Activities etc.) (Amendment) Order 2025*. Legislation.gov.uk. https://www.legislation.gov.uk/ukdsi/2025/9780348272055

United States Congress. (2025). *S.1582 - 119th Congress (2025-2026): GENIUS Act*. Congress.gov. https://www.congress.gov/bill/119th-congress/senate-bill/1582/text

Chapter 4
A Stablecoin Framework for the Future

Maxine L. Binns
Commonwealth Secretariat, UK

ABSTRACT

Stablecoins are rapidly transforming the global financial landscape, offering programmable, low-cost, and borderless transactions. Yet their proliferation has outpaced regulatory responses, exposing jurisdictions to systemic risks and legal ambiguity. This chapter presents a modular legislative framework designed to accommodate diverse capacities while promoting legal interoperability and cross-border enforceability. It also examines the consequences of regulatory inertia—including financial instability, loss of sovereignty, and exclusion from innovation ecosystems. Drawing on comparative case studies and international standards, the chapter provides actionable recommendations for policymakers, emphasizing the strategic imperative of proactive reform in the digital asset space.

EXECUTIVE OVERVIEW

This chapter presents a forward-looking, modular framework for the regulation and deployment of stablecoins, designed to equip jurisdictions, particularly those navigating legal pluralism and capacity constraints, with practical tools for responsible innovation. Grounded in principles of operational clarity, stakeholder empowerment, and legal resilience, this framework offers a phased approach to implementation that respects local traditions while enabling global interoperability.

At its core, the framework is guided by a philosophy of stewardship and service for the common good. It seeks to ensure that digital financial systems are not only technically sound and legally robust, but also inclusive, transparent, and anchored in

DOI: 10.4018/979-8-3373-6655-5.ch004

the public interest. By translating complex legal and regulatory concepts into actionable overlays, the chapter empowers policymakers, regulators, and legal drafters to build systems that foster trust, protect communities, and promote equitable access to opportunity.

This framework employs a comparative analysis and real-world consultation with jurisdictions implementing both the Commonwealth Model Law on Virtual Assets, the principle Act, and the Commonwealth Model Law on Stablecoins, together the Model Laws (Commonwealth Secretariat, 2024). This was done while reflecting global coordination efforts led by the Financial Stability Board (FSB, 2020) and the International Monetary Fund (IMF, 2021). These references inform the chapter's approach to definitional precision, risk segmentation, and institutional accountability, while embedding safeguards for financial integrity, consumer protection, and systemic stability.

Ultimately, this chapter advocates for a stewardship-based approach to digital financial law as a blueprint for building resilient, future-ready monetary systems that serve not just markets, but people. Furthermore, it is described as a framework that balances innovation with inclusion, modularity with meaning, and ambition with accountability.

INTRODUCTION

The rapid expansion and innovation within the realm of Web3, encompassing blockchain technology, distributed ledgers, VAs require legal and regulatory frameworks that can keep pace with evolving risks and market structures. This challenge is crucial for the diverse Commonwealth member countries, comprising fifty-six countries with varying economic profiles, legal systems, and market maturities, which face the task of responding to disruptive innovation while safeguarding their financial sectors, protecting consumers, and ensuring market integrity (The Commonwealth, 2024a).

As digital assets become increasingly woven into global finance, piecemeal or overly rigid regulations fail to adequately address both the opportunities and the risks of financial digitalisation. Stablecoins emerged as a cornerstone of digital finance, and their appeal lies in the ability to facilitate real-time, low-cost transactions across borders, support programmable financial instruments, and offer alternatives to volatile cryptocurrencies. Yet their rapid adoption has exposed significant gaps in legal and regulatory oversight. Without clear rules, stablecoins risk undermining monetary sovereignty, enabling illicit finance, and destabilising payment systems (IMF, 2021).

The Commonwealth Secretariat Modular Approach

For Commonwealth member countries, the challenge is particularly acute. Many operate within diverse legal traditions, varying levels of institutional capacity, and distinct financial infrastructures. A rigid, one-size-fits-all regulatory model is neither feasible nor equitable. Instead, what is needed is a framework that is legally sound, operationally flexible, and scalable across jurisdictions.

Since VAs are borderless, regulatory efforts needed a coordinated approach to avoid gaps and loopholes in Anti-money Laundering/Countering the Financing of Terrorism (AML/CFT) regulation and supervision of virtual asset service providers (VASPs) and financial institutions (FIs). In Commonwealth member countries, there was also a need to maintain the jurisprudential consistency that has been a hallmark of common law legal systems.

To accommodate jurisdictional diversity while preserving regulatory coherence, the framework incorporates the principle of *functional equivalency*. This concept allows jurisdictions to adopt different legal instruments or supervisory mechanisms that nonetheless achieve comparable outcomes in terms of consumer protection, financial stability, and market integrity. Equivalency enables mutual recognition and interoperability without imposing uniformity, reinforcing the framework's commitment to legal pluralism and operational flexibility (EY, 2025).

While aware of the need to regulate emerging landscape changes, the Commonwealth Secretariat developed an umbrella modular framework implementing international standards for the regulation of VASPs and FIs. The Model Laws are landmark initiatives and the Commonwealth Model Law on Stablecoins (the Model Laws) are landmark initiatives designed to provide templates and articulate a cohesive legal philosophy (Commonwealth Secretariat, 2024). By adopting an "umbrella modular" framework, the Model Laws address regulatory challenges through a flexible system of interconnected modules. Unlike monolithic statutes, a modular approach allows policymakers to tailor laws according to the stage of market development, the nature of local risks, and evolving international standards, while remaining anchored to core legal principles.

The Commonwealth Model Law on Virtual Assets serves as the principal legislation (the principal Act) governing the regulation of VASPs, offering member countries a harmonised approach to licensing, supervision, AML/CFT compliance and operation conduct. This foundational law establishes the baseline legal and regulatory framework for AML/CFT compliance, licensing, supervision, and operational conduct of VASPs. Building upon the principal Act, the proposed new Commonwealth Model Law on Stablecoins (the Stablecoin Model Law) acts as an extension specifically tailored to address the unique characteristics and systemic implications of stablecoins. It defines, among other things, the scope of application of the law and sets out who may lawfully issue stablecoins within relevant Commonwealth member countries. This applies to centralised and decentralised actors, including DAOs (e.g. MakerDAO) and AI-driven protocols developing algorithmic or autonomous Stablecoin models. It reflects the growing adoption of VAs across Commonwealth nations, from remittance use in lower-income economies to institutional investment in advanced markets, and aligns with international standards set by bodies such as the FATF, FSB, IOSCO, and BIS.

While anchored in the principles and obligations set out under the principal Act, the Stablecoin Model Law introduces its own comprehensive legal and regulatory framework. It encompasses distinct provisions for, among others, reserve management, disclosure, algorithmic mechanisms, and cross-border interoperability and corroboration between different networks. Furthermore, it defines the scope of application of the principal Act and prescribes which entities are lawfully authorised stablecoin issuers within the relevant Commonwealth member country. This applies to centralised and decentralised actors, including DAOs (e.g. MakerDAO) and AI-driven protocols developing algorithmic or autonomous stablecoin models.

A layered approach ensures coherence with the overarching VA regime while providing the specialised legal architecture necessary to effectively regulate stablecoins. In this regard, the FATF has clarified that most stablecoins generally fall within the definition of VAs, particularly where they do not represent legal tender fiat currency and are used for payments or trading. If a stablecoin does not qualify as a "financial asset" under another FATF definition (e.g., e-money, securities), it generally falls under the VA category. Accordingly, the activities surrounding stablecoins (issuance, transfer, exchange, custody, etc.) are subject to FATF Recommendations 15 and 16 and VASP obligations.

Aligned closely with the best practices set forth by the international standard-setting bodies, including the FSB, BIS, Basel II framework, IOSCO, and FATF, the Model Law highlights the importance of transparent reserve asset management, rigorous governance standards, and stringent transparency requirements to prevent systemic financial risks. It mandates that stablecoin issuers maintain reserves consisting of short-term High-Quality Liquid Assets to ensure stability and redemption certainty.

While both stablecoins and central bank digital currencies (CBDCs) seek to deliver price-stable digital representations of value, they diverge fundamentally in their issuance, governance, and legal status. Stablecoins are typically issued by private entities and backed by fiat reserves, commodities, or algorithmic mechanisms, whereas CBDCs are sovereign instruments issued directly by central banks and constitute legal tender. Accordingly, where CBDCs are referenced within this framework, they are treated as a distinct category requiring separate regulatory and institutional pathways.

Decentralised Autonomous Organisations (DAOs), though structurally different from CBDCs, may also benefit from modular legal architecture, particularly in areas of governance, accountability, and operational clarity. Their decentralised nature demands tailored modules that reflect dynamic stakeholder participation and evolving consensus mechanisms. Hence, jurisdictions considering the deployment of stablecoins, CBDCs, or DAO-like structures may find value in modular frameworks that support parallel development tracks while maintaining definitional integrity and legal coherence.

BACKGROUND

Guiding Principles Underpinning the Commonwealth Modular Framework

A core innovation of the Commonwealth Model Laws is its explicit commitment to principle-based regulation. This chapter articulates the legal rationale for choosing such a modular, umbrella framework and examines how the guiding principles set by the Commonwealth Secretariat (2023) are embodied within this approach, especially when integrating virtual assets into a unified legal environment:

(a) **Principle-Based**: The regulatory framework is results-driven and offers sufficient flexibility to minimise its intrusiveness on innovation. It adopts a light-touch approach to support the development of new technologies rather than hinder them.

(b) **Protection-Focused**: The framework protects market participants from counterparty risks and covers market integrity, surveillance, fair pricing, custody, clearing, disclosure of conflicts of interest, and systems and business continuity planning.

(c) **Balanced and Proportionate**: This framework balances the need for regulation with the need for protection. It should be proportionate to allow innovative entities in the development stages to succeed while ensuring financial stability and integrity.

(d) **Comprehensive**: The framework incorporates the entire ecosystem of Web3 technologies and avoids an exclusive focus on virtual assets. Even if the Model Law is limited in scope, Commonwealth countries can align on regulatory next steps.

(e) **Flexible and Adaptable**: It maintains technology neutrality and respects varying levels of regulatory readiness and resources across member countries. It avoids prescribing administrative requirements and allows customisation through delegated legislation by implementing regulations, guidance, circulars, rules, codes, and FAQs. This preserves sovereignty and upholds the authority of member countries to legislate independently.

Advantages of Principle-Based Regulation

The advantages of a core principle-based regulatory approach include:

- **Flexibility**: Responds to innovation without requiring constant legislative amendment.
- **Outcome-Oriented**: Focuses regulatory attention on behavioural and substantive outcomes, not mere compliance with form.
- **Enables Proportionality**: Allows supervisors to scale interventions according to evolving risks and market context.
- **Supports Modular Drafting**: Principles can be restated in each module (e.g., consumer protection, AML/CFT, operational resilience), providing thematic unity without overburdening any individual segment of the law.

Examples in Practice

The Model Laws outline foundational principles in their preliminary sections, which are cross-referenced in modules for enforcement, licensing, and market conduct. This approach aligns with modern legal drafting practices that emphasise clarity, accessibility, and plain language, bridging diverse audiences, from technical regulators to business operators and the judiciary.

Where traditional financial regulation relies on detailed prescriptive rules, a principle-based approach articulates high-level regulatory aims, such as ensuring fair markets or preventing illicit finance practices. This design seeks harmonisation and modernisation of laws in tandem with international standards, thereby providing a regulatory compass for countries balancing opportunity and risk in the digital asset sector. The framework proposed is modular in design, grounded in legal rationale, and aligned with international standards. It exposes the risks of regulatory lag, arguing that delay is not a neutral stance but a strategic vulnerability.

The Model Laws allow jurisdictions to adopt core regulatory components while tailoring specific provisions to local contexts. This flexibility supports legal harmonisation without imposing uniformity. By integrating legal interoperability mechanisms and fostering institutional collaboration, these frameworks aim to support financial resilience, consumer protection, and inclusive innovation. Legal interoperability requires mutual recognition clauses, standardised definitions, and dispute resolution protocols that function across borders.

Advancements in blockchain and distributed ledger technology have ushered in a transformative era for global finance, redefining how currency, transactions, and economic interactions are conceived and executed. These innovations have introduced unprecedented efficiency, transparency, and security across financial systems, while also raising complex challenges around financial integrity, market stability, and illicit finance. In response, jurisdictions worldwide, particularly within the Commonwealth, are accelerating efforts to establish robust regulatory frameworks across financial, prudential, and AML/CFT domains.

To support policymakers, legal professionals, and regulators across Commonwealth countries, this chapter draws together insights from the Model Laws and comparative international regulatory analysis. The analysis follows best practices in legal drafting for clarity, accessibility, and practical implementation. Furthermore, the Commonwealth Secretariat recognises the urgency and opportunity presented by these developments and introduced the Commonwealth Model Law on Virtual Assets in 2024 as a foundational legal framework (Commonwealth Secretariat, 2024).

Building upon the principal Act, the Commonwealth Secretariat now presents a specialised extension, particularly part two of the VASP framework, with a focus on the unique characteristics and systemic implications of stablecoins. The advent of stablecoins represents a pivotal evolution in digital finance, offering the potential to overcome volatility barriers that have historically limited the use of VAs as a medium of exchange. By maintaining a stable value relative to a referenced asset, stablecoins are increasingly positioned to support global payment arrangements, especially when sponsored by major technology or financial firms.

The Stablecoin Model Law introduces a comprehensive legal and regulatory framework tailored to stablecoins, including provisions for reserve management, algorithmic mechanisms, disclosure obligations, and cross-border interoperability. It adopts a technology-neutral stance to ensure adaptability and relevance amid rapid innovation, while reinforcing the coexistence of public and private money, acknowledging the complementary role stablecoins can play alongside sovereign digital currencies.

Stablecoin Regulation and Modular Architecture

In line with FATF guidance, most stablecoins are treated as VAs unless classified otherwise under financial asset definitions such as e-money or securities. The Stablecoin Model Law mandates that issuers, VASPs and FIs, maintain reserves in short-term High-Quality Liquid Assets to ensure redemption certainty and systemic stability (Zavalko, 2025). It also introduces clear regulatory classifications for different stablecoin types, mandatory independent audits, and transparency requirements to verify reserve adequacy.

Recognising the heightened ML/TF/PF risks posed by stablecoins, especially due to their potential for mass adoption, cross-border functionality, and anonymity, the Model Laws reinforce the need for pre-launch risk assessments and ongoing mitigation strategies. In arrangements with higher decentralisation, governance bodies must still meet FATF standards, either as VASPs or FIs, and ensure compliance with international regulatory obligations (FATF, 2021).

Importantly, the Model Laws position stablecoins as tools for financial inclusion, especially in regions lacking robust traditional infrastructure. By enabling cost-efficient, accessible financial services, stablecoins can expand economic participation and reduce dependency on volatile fiat systems or external aid. Through proportionate oversight, cross-border coordination, and rigorous governance standards, the Model Laws set a global benchmark for stablecoin regulation, advancing the Commonwealth's commitment to a secure, innovative, and inclusive digital financial future (The Commonwealth, 2024b).

Legal Rationale for a Modular, Umbrella Approach to Web3 Regulation

Lessons from the Commonwealth Model Laws

The Model Laws emerge as landmark initiatives to provide a template and articulate a cohesive legal philosophy. By adopting an "umbrella modular" architecture, the Model Laws address regulatory challenges through a flexible system of interconnected modules. Unlike statutes, a modular approach enables policymakers to tailor laws according to the stage of market development, the nature of local risks, and evolving international standards, while remaining anchored to core legal principles.

This chapter articulates the legal rationale for choosing such a modular, umbrella framework and examines how the guiding principles set by the Commonwealth Secretariat are embodied within this approach, especially when integrating virtual assets into a unified legal environment (The Commonwealth, 2024b).

Responding to a Transforming Financial Ecosystem

The transformation driven by blockchain and related technologies is unlike prior episodes of financial innovation. Unlike centralised institutions or traditional market structures, the Web3 paradigm involves inherently decentralised, global, and often pseudonymous systems, such as cryptocurrencies, decentralised finance (DeFi), stablecoins, and non-fungible tokens (NFTs). These innovations present both profound benefits, such as efficiency, transparency, and expanded financial inclusion, and new types of risks, including market integrity threats, illicit finance, and heightened consumer vulnerability.

Legal and regulatory frameworks grounded in pre-digital models struggle to keep up. Static, entity-based or activity-based rules that once sufficed are outmoded by the borderless and programmable speed of digital assets. Moreover, innovation in Web3 does not fit neatly into traditional financial categories, demanding new forms of functional and technology-neutral regulation.

A modular approach is the logical response to this environment. In a modular framework, the law is structured into discrete sections or modules, each addressing a core regulatory element, such as licensing, AML/CFT, consumer protection, enforcement, or, critically, the separate treatment of different asset classes —most notably Vas. Modules can be implemented incrementally or in a bespoke manner, allowing for easier adaptation across jurisdictions and over time, as risks and technologies change (IOSCO, 2020).

Benefits of Umbrella, Modular Legal Architecture

The benefits of umbrella, modular legal architecture are:

(a) **Legal Clarity and Consistency**: Modular laws facilitate clarity of purpose by separating distinct regulatory concerns. This allows for precise drafting, greater transparency, and easier subsequent amendment. Consistency is enhanced because each module can clearly define key terms, responsibilities, and the scope of obligations.

(b) **Adaptability**: Modular systems allow rapid adaptation to market changes or emergent risks, without requiring wholesale legislative reform each time a structural adjustment is needed. For example, if DeFi presents a novel risk, a new module can be crafted and inserted into the umbrella structure.

(c) **Jurisdictional Customisation**: Commonwealth countries represent a spectrum of regulatory readiness and market sophistication. The umbrella modular format enables each country to customise its implementation, selecting or modifying modules according to local context, while benefiting from a harmonised base structure.

(d) **Facilitation of International Alignment**: By organising laws into functionally separated modules, the umbrella framework allows for alignment with standards from global standard-setters (e.g., FATF, FSB, BIS), regional frameworks (e.g., MiCA in the EU), and interoperability with other jurisdictions (Boar et al., 2021).

(e) **Efficient Supervision and Enforcement**: Supervisory authorities can act within well-defined modules, such as enforcement, licensing, or market surveillance, enabling targeted and proportionate intervention. This enhances both regulatory efficiency and legal certainty for market participants (Financial Stability Board, 2020).

Structure and Scope of the Commonwealth Model Laws

The Commonwealth Secretariat's modular approach is one of the most advanced efforts to provide a comprehensive, principle-aligned, and modular regulatory framework for VASPs and FIs. The Model Laws were drafted in close alignment with the recommendations of international standard-setting bodies, most notably FATF, FSB, and IOSCO.

Core modules of the Model Laws include:

- **Preliminary Provisions** – Definitions, scope, and purpose.
- **Regulatory Authority** – Functions, powers, and objectives.
- **Licensing/Registration** – Procedures for VASP authorisation, criteria, public registers.
- **AML/CFT** – Obligations aligned to FATF, travel rule, due diligence.
- **Initial Virtual Asset Offerings** – Disclosure and conduct of issuers.
- **Supervision and Enforcement** – Investigative, remedial, and sanctioning powers.
- **Financial System Integration and cross-border compatibility** – recognition of the regulatory and supervisory framework of a foreign country for stablecoins as equivalent, and information sharing.
- **Information and Communication Technology** – establish and maintain secure, resilient, recoverable and scalable ICT systems within the stablecoin ecosystem that conform to international ICT standards.
- **Miscellaneous and Delegated Legislation** – Provisions for further regulation and adaptation.

Understanding the rationale for implementing such modular legal architecture is set out in more detail in Chapter 10 (The Commonwealth, 2024b).

Exclusions and Special Cases

Certain asset classes — such as stablecoins fully backed by fiat, CBDCs, closed-loop tokens (e.g., loyalty points), and tokens regulated as securities — are expressly excluded or referred for separate treatment. This modular delineation provides clarity and allows for stablecoin-specific modules to be incorporated within the umbrella structure, rather than conflating stablecoins with more volatile or less transparent VAs.

Integrating the Stablecoin Module

The Stablecoin Model Law builds upon the principal Act's foundation to propose a specific legal module for stablecoins. It highlights the increasing strategic and systemic importance of stablecoins, their distinct risk profile, and taxonomy (fiat-collateralised, crypto-collateralised, algorithmic, commodity-backed, and hybrid).

Key features include:

- **Legal Classification and Taxonomy**: Clear definitions, segregated from other VAs.
- **Reserve Requirements**: High-quality, liquid assets (e.g., cash, short-term government bonds) with restrictions on other forms of collateral.
- **Redemption and Consumer Protections**: Binding frameworks for redemption rights, disclosure, complaint handling, and insolvency protocols.
- **Operational Resilience and Cybersecurity**: Standards for network, data, and business continuity.
- **Enforcement, Supervision, and Governance**: Rulemaking and remedial modules, combined with strong oversight.
- **International Coordination**: Reference to the FATF travel rule for cross-border transactions and interoperable regulatory standards.

This modular overlay for stablecoins permits seamless integration into the broader VA umbrella law, providing both regulatory clarity and adaptability. The architecture encourages tailored risk mitigation commensurate with the stablecoin's size, complexity, and economic significance.

Protection-Focused Regulation

Consumer and investor protection is foregrounded as a central legal rationale, given the complex and sometimes opaque risks of the VA sectors. The Commonwealth framework mandates:

- **Counterparty and Custodial Risk Protections**: Ensuring clear obligations for VASPs regarding safekeeping, disclosure, and business continuity.
- **Market Integrity and Surveillance**: Standardised requirements for transaction monitoring, fair pricing, and anti-fraud protocols.

- **Complaint Handling and Redress**: Mechanisms for dispute resolution, complaint escalation, and restitution (EU, 2023).

Stablecoin modules, in particular, embed protections around redemption rights and reserve transparency, modelled on the best practices outlined by international standards and leading jurisdictions (e.g., Singapore, UK, Japan, EU's MiCA).

Balanced, Comprehensive, and Adaptable Regulation

A central challenge in digital asset regulation is achieving a balance between excessive regulation risks driving innovation offshore or underground and insufficient oversight, because it invites systemic vulnerabilities and reputational harm. The Commonwealth Secretariat's modular umbrella architecture offers a solution by enabling tailored legal responses that scale with market maturity and risk exposure. Modules can be selectively implemented or adapted based on a jurisdiction's development stage, allowing for proportionality in oversight. Regulatory sandboxes embedded within delegated legislative modules provide safe environments for experimentation, enabling innovation without compromising financial integrity.

Supervisory authorities are empowered to apply differentiated standards based on risk scoring, market impact, and institutional capacity, ensuring that small-scale innovators and systemic actors are regulated appropriately. Unlike minimalist or monolithic approaches, the Model Laws pursue comprehensive coverage through a constellation of specialised modules. These address the full spectrum of digital asset activity from exchangers and custodians to stablecoin providers, NFTs, and DeFi operators. Each module is aligned with global standards (FATF, FSB, and IOSCO) and includes provisions for financial, prudential, and AML/CFT risks. Ancillary areas such as API governance, data management, and AI oversight are also incorporated, ensuring future-proofing as the ecosystem evolves.

Flexibility is another cornerstone of this architecture. Technology neutrality, statutory placeholders, and mechanisms for modular insertion allow member countries to issue implementing regulations, FAQs, and subordinate guidance tailored to local needs, while maintaining fidelity to the umbrella's core legal principles. This ensures that emerging risks or novel business models can be addressed promptly without destabilizing the broader framework.

The Model Laws are structured into discrete modules, each with a clear legal rationale and implementation pathway:

Table 1. Modular architecture in practice

Module	Main Contents	Legal Rationale	Implementation Features
Preliminary	Objectives, definitions, exclusions	Establishes clarity and tailored scope	Harmonised definitions across modules for interoperability
Regulatory Authority	Powers, duties, objectives	Enables accountable supervision and rulemaking	Supports sandboxes and international cooperation
Licensing/ Registration	Procedures, fit-and-proper, public registers	Ensures qualified market entry and risk-based gatekeeping	Jurisdiction-specific licenses with common minimum criteria
AML/CFT	Due diligence, travel rule, internal controls	Aligns with FATF standards and cross-border crime prevention	Risk-based KYC tailored to local contexts
Stablecoin Module	Collateralization, redemption rights, and consumer disclosures	Addresses systemic risk and ensures user trust	Legal classification, reserve management, stress testing
Initial Offerings	White paper requirements, risk disclosure	Promotes transparency and investor protection	Consistent with global best practices for token launches
Enforcement/ Supervision	Investigation, sanctions, revocation	Enables proportionate remedial action	Clear administrative and judicial processes
Miscellaneous/ Delegation	Adapting, amending, and regulatory sandboxes	Supports continuous modernisation	Mechanism for inserting new modules as technology evolves

Commonwealth Model Laws Table *"Author's own synthesis based on Commonwealth Secretariat Model Laws framework.*

This structure allows member countries to customise the selection and sequencing of modules based on their legal, economic, and technological circumstances, ensuring agility without sacrificing coherence.

Comparative Analysis: Commonwealth vs. International Frameworks

The EU's Markets in Crypto-Assets Regulation (MiCA) offers a comprehensive, rules-based framework with cross-border passporting and unified supervision (EU, 2023). However, its monolithic design limits jurisdictional flexibility and may struggle to accommodate rapid innovation. In contrast, the Commonwealth's modular approach:

- Allows incremental integration based on local readiness.
- Emphasises principle-based drafting for broader applicability.
- Preserves jurisdictional sovereignty while promoting harmonisation.

Both frameworks align with FATF's AML/CFT recommendations, the FSB's financial stability guidance, and BIS principles on settlement and monetary policy. Yet the Commonwealth Secretariat's modular approach offers unique advantages:

- Integration with broader Commonwealth anti-corruption and asset recovery frameworks.
- Customizable compliance thresholds for smaller economies.
- Explicit interoperability for emerging technologies like AI, DeFi, and NFTs.

The GENIUS Act represents a distinctly American approach to stablecoin regulation, emphasising dual federal-state oversight, flexible licensing pathways, and integration with existing financial laws like the Bank Secrecy Act (USC, 2025). In contrast, the Model Laws patterned on jurisdictions such as Bermuda, Singapore, and the Eastern Caribbean tend to favour modular, principle-based frameworks that prioritise clarity, interoperability, and cross-border harmonisation.

While both aim to ensure reserve integrity and consumer protection, the GENIUS Act leans toward prescriptive compliance and national competitiveness. On the other hand, the Model Laws emphasise adaptability, legal clarity, and alignment with international standards. This divergence reflects differing regulatory philosophies: one rooted in systemic risk containment, the other in enabling innovation within a globally coherent legal architecture.

Table 2. Global stablecoin regulatory comparison (2025)

Dimension	GENIUS Act (U.S.)	EU MiCA	UK FCA Proposals	Singapore PSA	Japan FSA Framework	Commonwealth Model Laws	UAE VARA + CBUAE
Regulatory Philosophy	Prescriptive, risk-containment focused	Harmonised, rules-based across 27 states	Outcome-focused, balancing innovation and stability	Risk-based, tiered licensing with strong AML/CFT controls	Prudential and systemic risk-focused; cautious but open to innovation	Principle-based, modular, enabling innovation and legal clarity	Dual-track: activity-based innovation (VARA) + prudential payment oversight (CBUAE)
Oversight Structure	Dual federal-state licensing and supervision	Centralised EU authority with national implementation	FCA-led with systemic oversight for large issuers	MAS-led with phased licensing and sandbox options	FSA-led with coordination across banking and securities regulators	Centralised or delegated authority with sandbox flexibility	VARA for Dubai VASPs; CBUAE for mainland payment tokens
Legal Architecture	Integrates with existing financial laws (e.g., BSA, FDIC, SEC)	Standalone crypto-assets regulation with stablecoin provisions	Embedded in financial services and payments regulation	Integrated into the Payment Services Act with digital token provisions	Integrated into the Payment Services Act and Financial Instruments Act	Modular overlays tailored to virtual assets and stablecoins	Separate rulebooks: VARA's activity-based modules + CBUAE's PTSR

continued on following page

Table 2. Continued

Dimension	GENIUS Act (U.S.)	EU MiCA	UK FCA Proposals	Singapore PSA	Japan FSA Framework	Commonwealth Model Laws	UAE VARA + CBUAE
Reserve Requirements	Full fiat backing; high-quality liquid assets; strict collateral rules	Reserve transparency; limits on algorithmic coins	Emphasis on prudential backing and redemption assurance	Mandates safeguarding and segregation of customer assets	Requires full backing; prohibits algorithmic models; reserves must be held in Japan	Proportional reserve models based on scale and risk	1:1 backing; highly liquid, low-risk assets; strict segregation and audit
Consumer Protection	Redemption rights, disclosures, complaint protocols, and insolvency safeguards	Strong consumer rights, disclosures, and redemption guarantee	Focus on transparency, redemptions, and systemic risk mitigation	Disclosure, dispute resolution, and safeguarding mechanisms	Disclosure mandates, redemption guarantees, and insolvency protocols	Embedded in financial conduct codes and insolvency protocols	T+1 redemption, no interest, clear disclosures, and retail safeguards
Cross-Border Coordination	FATF travel rule reference; limited foreign issuer access	Harmonised across the EU; FATF-aligned	Open to equivalence and interoperability with foreign regimes	Regional coordination with FATF and APAC standards	FATF-aligned; cautious on foreign stablecoin issuers	Strong FATF alignment and regional harmonisation (e.g., CARICOM, OECS)	FATF-aligned; foreign stablecoins restricted unless approved; local-first issuance preference
Governance and Enforcement	Federal rulemaking authority; remedial powers; competitive positioning	EU-wide enforcement with national regulators	FCA enforcement with systemic oversight for large issuers	MAS supervision with AML/CFT and operational resilience mandates	FSA enforcement with emphasis on financial stability and investor protection	Collaborative governance; emphasis on legal clarity and stakeholder trust	VARA-led licensing and supervision; CBUAE-led enforcement for payment tokens
Adaptability to Innovation	Slower due to layered compliance pathways	Moderate agility via delegated rulemaking	High agility through consultation and sandboxing	Agile via sandbox and phased licensing	Moderate agility; innovation allowed within prudential guardrails	High agility; modular updates and principle-based evolution	High agility; VARA's modular rulebooks + CBUAE's phased compliance windows

Global Stablecoin Regulatory Comparison (2025) *"Author's own comparative table synthesizing global stablecoin regulatory frameworks (2025), based on public regulatory texts and proposals.*

Strategic Takeaways from Select Jurisdictions:

- Singapore offers one of the most innovation-friendly yet risk-aware environments, with MAS balancing agility and consumer protection.
- Japan takes a conservative but clear stance: algorithmic stablecoins are banned, and reserve assets must be held domestically, reflecting a strong emphasis on financial stability.
- Commonwealth jurisdictions like Bermuda and the Eastern Caribbean continue to lead in modular legal design, offering clarity and interoperability for cross-border use.

- The GENIUS Act remains the most prescriptive, while MiCA sets the global benchmark for harmonised regulation.

Implementation and Case Studies

In emerging markets such as Nigeria, India, Bangladesh, and Pakistan, VA adoption is driven by remittances, inflation hedging, and digital entrepreneurship. The modular approach enables these jurisdictions to implement foundational modules such as licensing, AML/CFT, and consumer protection, while deferring more complex components until market conditions mature.

Regulatory sandboxes play a pivotal role here, as they allow new business models to be tested under supervision before full legal authorisation. These sandboxes foster harmonisation, facilitate knowledge exchange, and create a pathway from pilot to scale (Jenik & Duff, 2020).

Globally, frameworks like Singapore's Payment Services Act, Japan's Payment Services Act, and the UK's layered amendments to the Financial Services and Markets Act reflect similar modular principles. Commonwealth member countries participating in international standard-setting bodies are well-positioned to achieve mutual recognition and cross-border interoperability by adhering to the umbrella structure.

Alignment to Global and Regional Regulatory Trends

Beyond the EU's MiCA, several leading frameworks are shaping Commonwealth uptake and reinforcing the modular design of the Model Law, such as:

- **Singapore's Payment Services Act (PSA):** Stablecoin issuers must be licensed, maintain 100% reserve backing in highly liquid assets, undergo regular audits, and comply with stringent AML/CFT obligations. Redemption must occur within five business days, and interest-bearing activities are prohibited.
- **Japan's Payment Services Act:** Stablecoins are classified as Electronic Payment Instruments (EPIs), requiring mandatory redemption rights, full reserve backing, and legal segregation of assets. Issuers must be licensed banks, trust companies, or fund transfer providers.
- **UK Policy Evolution:** Amendments to the Financial Services and Markets Act (FSMA) are progressively incorporating stablecoins and VAs through layered statutory instruments and consultation papers. The UK's two-tiered approach, FCA for non-systemic and BoE for systemic stablecoins, mirrors the modular adaptation strategy of the Commonwealth framework.

- **UAE's Dual Framework (VARA + CBUAE):** The UAE combines Dubai's activity-based licensing under VARA with the Central Bank's Payment Token Services Regulation (PTSR) for mainland oversight. Issuers must be locally licensed, maintain a 1:1 reserve backing in segregated, low-risk assets, and process redemptions within one business day. Interest payments are prohibited, and a local-first issuance preference (e.g., Dirham-backed stablecoins) is embedded.

Commonwealth member states participating in global standard-setting bodies are thus better positioned to attain mutual recognition and cross-jurisdictional interoperability by adhering to the core, modular design of the Model Laws (Jenik & Duff, 2020). These frameworks demonstrate that legal pluralism and regulatory maturity can coexist provided that outcome-based equivalency and shared safeguards are embedded from the outset.

Challenges and Opportunities in Modular Web3 Regulation

Jurisdictional Challenges in Implementing Modular Web3 Regulation

One of the biggest challenges in implementing modular Web3 regulation is the fragmented nature of global legal frameworks. While the Commonwealth umbrella approach offers a harmonised foundation, many jurisdictions operate outside its scope, resulting in inconsistent regulatory expectations for cross-border firms. This fragmentation complicates compliance, increases legal risk, and can deter innovation due to uncertainty around jurisdictional overlap and enforcement. Enforcing decentralised systems presents another layer of complexity.

Modules designed to govern DAOs, smart contracts, and permissionless protocols often lack traditional enforcement mechanisms. Regulators must explore novel strategies, such as integrating trusted oracles, establishing voluntary codes of conduct, and negotiating international memoranda of understanding, to ensure accountability without undermining decentralisation's core principles (BIS, 2007).

Resource constraints further hinder the rollout of comprehensive regulatory modules, especially in emerging markets. These jurisdictions may lack the institutional capacity, technical infrastructure, or financial resources to implement full-spectrum frameworks. As a result, modular regulation must be adaptable, allowing for phased deployment, localised customisation, and prioritisation of high-impact modules that align with national readiness (Erik et al., 2025).

Finally, stakeholder education remains a persistent challenge. Effective regulation depends not only on legal clarity but also on widespread understanding among industry participants, public sector actors, and the judiciary. Continuous engagement, training programs, and collaborative forums are essential to build regulatory literacy and foster a culture of compliance that supports innovation rather than stifling it (OECD, 2019).

Recognising the importance of financial inclusion, especially within regions lacking robust traditional financial infrastructures, stablecoins offer substantial opportunities to enhance economic participation through accessible, cost-efficient financial services. Hence, the regulatory approach is designed to nurture innovation responsibly without compromising financial stability or industry, customer and investor protection.

Additional key points incorporated into the Stablecoin Model Law include:

- Clear regulatory classifications distinguishing between different classes of stablecoins, allowing for proportionate regulatory oversight.
- mandatory independent audits and transparency requirements to verify that stablecoin reserves adequately back the circulating supply.
- promotion of cross-border regulatory coordination to prevent regulatory arbitrage and maintain international market integrity.

This Model Laws represent the Commonwealth Secretariat's proactive commitment to establishing a secure, innovative, and inclusive digital financial future, setting a global benchmark for stablecoin governance and regulatory standards.

Opportunities in Modular Web3 Regulation

Despite these challenges, the modular approach to Web3 regulation unlocks significant opportunities for innovation, agility, and future-readiness. One of the most promising avenues is the integration of regulatory technology (RegTech). By leveraging APIs, risk engines, and real-time reporting tools, regulators can automate supervision, streamline compliance checks, and enhance transparency across modules. This technological backbone not only reduces administrative burden but also enables dynamic oversight in fast-evolving digital ecosystems (PwC, 2023).

Collaboration is another key opportunity. Modular frameworks naturally lend themselves to cooperative development through regulatory sandboxes, legal drafting clinics, and knowledge-sharing platforms. These forums allow stakeholders to test new ideas, refine legal language, and build consensus across jurisdictions. Such collaboration fosters interoperability and accelerates the adoption of best practices, especially in areas like digital identity, token classification, and cross-border data governance (OECD, 2019).

Perhaps most compelling is the potential for future-proofing. Modular regulation equips Commonwealth countries with the flexibility to respond proactively to emerging technologies. Whether it's programmable CBDCs, quantum-resilient cryptography, or AI-governed financial instruments, the modular structure allows for targeted updates without overhauling entire legal systems. This agility ensures that regulatory frameworks remain relevant, resilient, and responsive to technological change (Auer et al., 2025).

Stakeholder Communication and the Importance of Plain Language Drafting

In a domain as complex and fast-moving as Web3, effective stakeholder communication is considered a luxury and a necessity. Legal texts must be intelligible to lawyers, regulators, technologists, entrepreneurs, and civil servants. The Commonwealth Secretariat's emphasis on plain language drafting reflects a commitment to accessibility, usability, and democratic transparency.

Plain English ensures that laws are understood by their intended users, reducing reliance on intermediaries and minimising misinterpretation. This clarity supports broader compliance, enabling stakeholders to act confidently within the bounds of regulation. It also enhances judicial interpretation, lowering the risk of litigation and promoting consistent enforcement across jurisdictions.

To achieve this, several drafting practices are essential. Modules should employ short, direct sentences and clear headings that guide readers through complex provisions. Purpose clauses at the beginning of each module help contextualise the legal intent, anchoring technical rules in real-world objectives. Jargon should be avoided unless necessary for international alignment, such as when referencing FATF definitions or standardised risk classifications.

Finally, the language must be flexible enough to accommodate technological evolution. Emerging concepts such as zero-knowledge proofs, decentralised insurance, or AI-mediated dispute resolution require regulators to adapt modules without sacrificing coherence or legal integrity. This balance between precision and adaptability is the hallmark of resilient, stakeholder-friendly regulation (IOSCO, 2023).

Integrating Stablecoin-Specific Modules into the Umbrella Framework

The rationale for handling stablecoins with dedicated legal modules within the umbrella framework is two-fold:

- Stablecoins pose unique risks regarding reserves (potential runs, redemption assurance, T-bill dependence), cross-border transmission, and monetary policy interaction.
- The technology and business models underlying stablecoins rapidly evolve (e.g., algorithmic designs, hybrid collateralization).

By integrating dedicated stablecoin modules, member countries can:

- Specify reserve, redemption, disclosure, and consumer protection obligations.
- Adjust prudential, operational, and governance requirements as new risks or use-cases (e.g., DeFi lending, payment integration) emerge.
- Align modules with international developments, such as the FSB's recommendations for "same risk, same rules," or emergent BIS standards (FSB, 2023).
- Support legal clarity by avoiding confusion over whether a digital asset is governed under VA, stablecoin, or payment law, and allowing separate, specialised enforcement tracks.

KEY ISSUES, CONTROVERSIES AND PROBLEMS

Financial Instability and Consumer Harm

Unregulated stablecoins pose significant risks to financial stability. For example, the collapse of TerraUSD in 2022, which relied on an algorithmic peg without sufficient reserves, triggered a market-wide downturn and eroded public trust (Laverdure, 2023). Jurisdictions without reserve requirements or redemption guarantees are particularly vulnerable to similar shocks. Retail users in low-capacity jurisdictions may treat stablecoins as savings instruments, unaware of the risks. Without clear disclosure standards or consumer protection laws, they face potential losses with limited recourse. The absence of prudential oversight also increases systemic risk, especially where stablecoins are used for payroll, remittances, or government transfers.

Regulatory Arbitrage and Loss of Sovereignty

Issuers often exploit gaps in global regulation by domiciling in jurisdictions with weak oversight, passing local laws, and undermining domestic policy. This erodes regulatory sovereignty and creates enforcement blind spots. Jurisdictions without robust frameworks risk becoming passive recipients of foreign digital assets, unable to shape their own financial ecosystem. This dynamic is particularly acute in small island states and developing economies, where enforcement capacity is limited and cross-border coordination is weak (The Commonwealth, 2024a). For example, global stablecoin issuers have historically registered in lightly regulated jurisdictions, issuing tokens that circulate globally but remain outside local control.

Illicit Finance and Cyber Threats

Stablecoins are attractive vectors for illicit finance due to their pseudonymity and global reach. Jurisdictions lacking cybercrime legislation or digital forensics capacity struggle to investigate and prosecute such offences. FATF has warned that jurisdictions without VA regulation risk being "grey-listed," which can deter investment and raise transaction costs (FATF, 2023). For instance, the UN report of 2023 on North Korean cybercrime estimated over $1 billion stolen from crypto platforms, with the majority laundered through stablecoins (UN Security Council, 2024). Without mandatory security standards or incident reporting protocols, users and platforms remain exposed, with cybersecurity breaches posing operational risks.

Missed Opportunities for Innovation and Inclusion

Stablecoins can support financial inclusion, reduce remittance costs, and enable programmable finance. The Philippines' regulatory sandbox has enabled rural banks to pilot stablecoin-based lending, while Kenya's mobile money ecosystem is exploring stablecoin integration for cross-border payments. Without enabling frameworks for growth, various jurisdictions miss out on intended benefits, further widening the digital divide. Innovation clusters tend to gravitate toward regulatory certainty. Without it, local fintechs may relocate or stagnate, and foreign investment may bypass the jurisdiction entirely.

Legal Uncertainty and Judicial Overload

Ambiguous laws lead to inconsistent enforcement and litigation. Courts may struggle to interpret digital asset disputes without clear statutory guidance. India's lack of a comprehensive crypto law has led to conflicting decisions, regulatory confusion, and investor hesitation (Mukherjee & Mukherjee, 2025). Judicial overload is a growing concern. Without specialised training or digital asset jurisprudence, judges may rely on analogies to outdated financial instruments, resulting in unpredictable outcomes. This undermines legal certainty and deters innovation.

Strategic Vulnerability in Global Finance

Jurisdictions without modern frameworks risk marginalisation in global finance. They may be excluded from international networks, lose influence in standard-setting bodies, and face barriers to cross-border trade. Strategic autonomy requires proactive legal and regulatory engagement. The EU's MiCA regulation and the U.S. Treasury's stablecoin proposals are shaping global norms (FATF, 2023). Jurisdictions that fail to engage run the risk of having their interests overlooked. Participation in forums like IOSCO, FATF, and the Commonwealth Fintech Toolkit initiative is essential for shaping inclusive standards.

SOLUTIONS AND RECOMMENDATIONS

Modular Legislative Design

A modular framework offers a scalable solution. Tiered legislative modules enable jurisdictions to adopt core provisions initially, such as definitions, licensing, and reserve requirements, and subsequently expand over time. This approach mirrors successful models in Bermuda, Mauritius, and the EU's MiCA regulation. It enables scalability, legal clarity, and policy flexibility. Model laws and template clauses can support harmonisation. The Commonwealth Secretariat and UNIDROIT have developed tools for legal convergence that can be adapted to VAs (UNIDROIT, 2023).

Legal Interoperability Mechanisms

Cross-border functionality requires standardised definitions, mutual recognition clauses, and dispute resolution protocols. Embedding international standards, such as ISO 20022 for messaging, NIST SP 800-53 for cybersecurity, and FATF's Travel Rule for AML, ensures consistency and trust (FATF, 2021).

Institutional Collaboration

Effective regulation requires coordination among ministries, regulators, central banks, and academic institutions. Joint drafting committees, inter-agency task forces, and regional working groups can support coherence and capacity building. Academic engagement is critical. Universities can support legal research, curriculum development, and judicial training. The University of the West Indies and the University of Nairobi have pioneered digital finance programs that support regulatory literacy. *(University of the West Indies, 2021; University of Nairobi, 2020).*

Public Consultation and Digital Literacy

Inclusive engagement builds legitimacy. Public consultations, town hall meetings, and multilingual outreach ensure that frameworks reflect user needs. The Bank of Ghana's eCedi pilot included extensive stakeholder engagement, including rural communities and informal sector workers (Bank of Ghana 2019) (Design Paper 2022 and Pilot Report 2024).

Public consultation and digital literacy are not peripheral concerns in stablecoin and CBDC design because they are foundational to legal legitimacy, operational success, and public trust. The Bank of Ghana's 2022 eCedi pilot offers a cautionary example; despite its ambition to foster financial inclusion, the initiative fell short by not embedding deep public engagement or digital education into its rollout. This created a disconnect between the currency's intended benefits and the public's readiness to adopt it, raising legal concerns around procedural fairness, consumer protection, and equitable access.

In contrast, Hungary's Digital Student Safe pilot (MNB, 2025) and Uganda's nationwide CBDC consultations demonstrate the strategic value of early engagement. Hungary prioritised digital literacy as a core design element, while Uganda's structured outreach surfaced critical usability and privacy concerns that shaped its legal roadmap (Bank of Uganda, 2025).

Digital Literacy as a Pillar of Legal Legitimacy and Financial Inclusion

Digital literacy campaigns should accompany regulatory rollouts. Users must understand the risks, rights, and responsibilities associated with stablecoins. Civil society organisations and fintech associations can support outreach and education. Digital literacy is more than technical competence. It is the gateway to equitable participation in digital finance and a foundational element of legal legitimacy. In the context of stablecoins and central bank digital currencies (CBDCs), digital literacy determines whether individuals can understand, access, and safely use these new monetary tools. Without it, even the most well-designed systems risk excluding the very populations they aim to serve (OECD, 2019).

This challenge is especially acute in regions with low smartphone penetration, limited internet access, or generational gaps in digital fluency. If users cannot grasp how to store, transfer, or redeem digital currency or how to protect themselves from fraud, they are effectively locked out of the financial system. This raises legal concerns around consumer protection, financial inclusion mandates, and the right to access public infrastructure. Moreover, digital literacy ought to evolve alongside technology. As stablecoins introduce features such as smart contracts, programmable wallets, and cross-chain interoperability, literacy programs must expand to address usage and comprehension of risks, rights, and responsibilities.

Public consultation and education are therefore not peripheral, but they are essential to the legal durability and operational success of digital currencies. The Bank of Ghana's 2022 eCedi pilot offers a cautionary example: despite its ambition to foster financial inclusion, the initiative fell short by not embedding deep public engagement or digital education into its rollout. In contrast, Hungary's Digital Student Safe pilot and Uganda's nationwide CBDC consultations demonstrate the strategic value of early engagement (Beecher et al., 2018; Julius & Peter, 2024). These examples show that embedding digital literacy and inclusive consultation from the outset is not optional; instead, it is necessary to ensure that innovation is inclusive.

FUTURE RESEARCH DIRECTIONS

Jurisdictions should begin with legal scoping and gap analysis, followed by stakeholder mapping and pilot programs. Legislative drafting should incorporate enabling clauses and model laws. Capacity building must include training for regulators, law enforcement, and judiciary officials.

Monitoring and evaluation mechanisms should support iterative refinement. Regulatory sandboxes and pilot programs can test provisions before full implementation. Regional harmonisation through peer learning and technical assistance can accelerate adoption.

Strategic engagement with international standard-setting bodies ensures that local priorities are reflected in global norms. Jurisdictions should participate in FATF mutual evaluations, IOSCO consultations, and Commonwealth fintech initiatives (FATF 2024; IOSCO 2024; Commonwealth Secretariat 2024).

Legal Issues Facing Stablecoins Without a Proper Framework

Stablecoins sit at a legal crossroads. Designed to emulate the stability of fiat currencies, they nonetheless operate on decentralised blockchain infrastructure that often circumvents traditional financial systems. This dual nature, part currency, part code, creates a complex regulatory vacuum. Without a clear legal framework, stablecoins risk undermining both market integrity and consumer protection, as their growing systemic relevance collides with unresolved legal ambiguities.

Key legal gaps include:

- **Legal Identity and Accountability**: Stablecoin ecosystems involve issuers, custodians, developers, governance bodies, and sometimes DAOs. Without a coherent framework, regulators may struggle to identify a legally accountable party when things go wrong (IOSCO, 2023).

- **Contractual Enforceability**: Many stablecoins rely on smart contracts to automate issuance, redemption, and collateral management. However, smart contracts are not universally recognised as legally binding. Jurisdictional inconsistencies impair enforcement and erode trust (UNIDROIT, 2023).
- **Custody and Property Rights**: The legal ownership of underlying assets is often unclear. If a custodian fails or assets are misappropriated, users may lack enforceable claims. This undermines the promise of stability (IMF, 2025).
- **Cross-Border Enforcement**: Stablecoins are global, but legal systems are jurisdiction-bound. Without international coordination, enforcement gaps persist. Issuers domiciled abroad may evade local oversight (IMF, 2021).
- **Classification Ambiguity**: Is a stablecoin a currency, commodity, security, or novel instrument? Without clarity, issuers and users face uncertainty around licensing, taxation, and disclosure. This stifles innovation and complicates compliance (IOSCO, 2023; USC, 2023).
- **Insolvency and Resolution Protocols**: If an issuer becomes insolvent, token holders may lack legal recourse. Without codified resolution protocols, users risk holding worthless tokens with no claim to reserves.
- **Consumer Protection Deficits**: Promises of "1:1 backing" or "instant liquidity" may be marketing claims, not enforceable guarantees. Without legal safeguards, users are exposed to misrepresentation, loss, and systemic contagion (CS, 2024).

Taken together, these gaps underscore the urgent need for a comprehensive legal framework for stablecoins that clarifies roles, enforces accountability, and harmonises cross-border rules. Such a framework is not merely a compliance tool; it is foundational to building trust, resilience, and long-term viability in the digital asset ecosystem.

Reclaiming Economic Sovereignty: Barter Logic Meets Stablecoin Infrastructure

For slower-developing economies, the path to financial resilience must move beyond dependency on foreign aid, volatile fiat currencies, or the goodwill of stronger nations. One compelling strategy is to build a self-sustaining financial system rooted in the logic of barter, where value is exchanged based on available resources, and enhanced by stablecoin technology. This hybrid model allows communities to trade goods and services directly, while using stablecoins as a digital ledger, store of value, and medium of exchange. This preserves the dignity and autonomy of local economies, enabling them to function even when disconnected from global financial networks

To educate and empower nations toward this vision, the focus must shift from abstract monetary theory to practical, community-based literacy. This means teaching local leaders, cooperatives, and youth how to identify and map their resource base. This includes agriculture, labour, crafts, energy, and land, while assigning digital value to these assets using stablecoins (though IMF 2025 cautions that risks such as currency substitution and capital flow volatility must be managed). Platforms like Celo, Stellar, and mobile-based wallets offer low-cost, accessible infrastructure for issuing community-backed stablecoins pegged to baskets of local goods or services.

Education must also emphasise economic storytelling, showing how barter-based systems sustained civilisations for centuries and how digital tools now allow these models to scale, track, and evolve. Workshops, radio programs, and mobile learning hubs can demystify stablecoins, teach wallet usage, and build trust in decentralised finance (The Commonwealth, 2018). Ultimately, this approach reframes stablecoins as speculative instruments and digital barter tokens anchored in real value, circulating within resilient networks, and governed by the communities they serve. It is a future path that honours tradition, embraces innovation, and restores economic agency to those who have long been positioned as recipients rather than architects of their own prosperity.

Strategic Benefits for Developed Nations

The implementation of stablecoin legislative frameworks in slower-developing nations carries profound strategic implications for those jurisdictions and developed nations seeking to foster resilient global partnerships. Stablecoins offer a predictable, transparent medium of exchange that can be pegged to real assets, reducing reliance on volatile local currencies or cumbersome barter arrangements. This digital infrastructure lowers friction in cross-border transactions and opens new markets for goods, services, and technology exports from developed economies (Rey, 2025).

Beyond commerce, stablecoin adoption reduces aid dependency and fiscal pressure on donor nations. As developing countries become less reliant on foreign aid and emergency funding, wealthier nations can redirect resources toward strategic investments, innovation, or domestic priorities (OECD, 2024). Global financial stability is also enhanced when nations become digitally literate and economically autonomous. In a world where local economies can function independently during global downturns, supply chain disruptions, or currency crises, the ripple effects on developed markets are significantly reduced (BIS, 2007).

Moreover, the adoption of stablecoin systems generates demand for infrastructure, consulting, and technical expertise sectors, where developed nations often lead. This creates new export channels for fintech solutions, cybersecurity services, and digital education platforms. From a diplomatic perspective, supporting self-sustaining models based on digital barter and stablecoins allows developed nations to reframe their global role. Rather than acting as benefactors, they become enablers of sovereignty. This repositioning enhances diplomatic relationships, builds trust, and strengthens soft power by aligning with principles of dignity, autonomy, and mutual respect (Smith, 2024).

Finally, stablecoin ecosystems often come with real-time data visibility, offering developed nations improved tools for assessing creditworthiness, investment potential, and geopolitical risk. Transparent digital ledgers enhance the quality of foreign direct investment decisions and reduce exposure to opaque financial systems (Elliptic, 2025).

In sum, when slower-developing nations rise through resource-based stablecoin systems, developed nations gain more than moral satisfaction. They gain stronger partnerships, reduced liabilities, and a more resilient global economy. The legislative scaffolding that enables these systems is both a technical necessity and a strategic imperative.

Pathway to Legal and Institutional Readiness for Stablecoins

Establishing a legally sound and institutionally resilient foundation for stablecoins and CBDC requires regulatory ambition and a deliberate, multi-phase legal architecture. This pathway begins with legal scoping and gap analysis, where jurisdictions assess the compatibility of existing laws with digital asset ecosystems. Currency issuance statutes, payment system regulations, securities laws, consumer protection codes, and anti-money laundering frameworks must be reviewed to identify where digital assets fit and where they fall through the cracks.

For example, the BIS Innovation Hub has conducted gap analyses across multiple digital asset pilots, revealing missing definitions and enforcement mechanisms for digital cash equivalents (Hogan, 2025). These insights have helped central banks pinpoint areas requiring legislative reform before pilot deployment.

Once legal gaps are mapped, stakeholder engagement becomes essential. Governments must identify and consult a wide spectrum of actors (financial institutions, technology providers, civil society groups, and end-users) to ensure inclusive design and legitimacy. Uganda's consultation process exemplifies this approach, involving regional outreach and sectoral surveys to understand the needs of rural populations, fintech startups, and regulators (BoU, 2021). This inclusive mapping informed both the technical design and legal framing of their pilot, ensuring that the digital currency reflected local realities and institutional capacity.

Pilot programs serve as the next critical phase, enabling jurisdictions to stress-test legal assumptions in controlled environments. These pilots reveal how laws interact with technology, user behaviour, and institutional workflows. Hungary's Digital Student Safe pilot, for instance, embedded legal safeguards into a sandboxed environment, testing wallet functionality, redemption rights, and dispute resolution protocols before scaling. Such pilots transform abstract legal principles into operational realities, surfacing friction points and informing legislative refinement.

Legislative drafting must follow with precision and foresight. Laws should include enabling clauses that allow regulators to adapt rules as technology evolves, avoiding rigidity and obsolescence. Model laws can offer templates for interoperability and cross-border alignment, especially in regions pursuing monetary integration. The Eastern Caribbean Central Bank's DCash initiative illustrates this approach: enabling legislation permitted digital currency issuance under existing monetary authority laws while preserving flexibility for future amendments (ECCB, 2024). This balance between legal continuity and technological adaptability is essential for long-term viability.

Finally, capacity building ensures that legal frameworks are not only written but also enforceable. Training programs must equip regulators, law enforcement, and judiciary officials with the tools to interpret, supervise, and adjudicate digital asset laws. The BIS Innovation Hub has partnered with central banks to deliver workshops on digital asset supervision, forensic tracing, and smart contract interpretation. These programs build institutional muscle, ensuring that legal readiness translates into operational effectiveness. Taken together, this pathway moves jurisdictions from conceptual ambition to legal and institutional execution. It anchors digital currency initiatives in clarity, inclusion, and enforceability, laying the groundwork for sovereign, resilient, and interoperable financial ecosystems.

To move from conceptual ambition to operational execution, jurisdictions must follow a structured pathway that ensures legal clarity, stakeholder inclusion, and enforceability. This pathway reflects the Commonwealth Secretariat's modular philosophy and supports digital asset readiness.

To illustrate the varying degrees of regulatory maturity across jurisdictions, the following chart categorises selected countries by their current stage of stablecoin and CBDC implementation. This comparative snapshot supports modular adaptation and highlights opportunities for phased engagement.

Table 3. Current stablecoin implementation status

Status	Jurisdictions
Regulations in Force	U.S., Canada, Chile, Japan, Hong Kong, Philippines, Thailand, Singapore, EU, UAE, Bermuda
Regulations Proposed	China, South Korea, Australia, UK, Brazil, Türkiye, Malaysia, Israel, Kenya
No Specific Regulation	India, Pakistan, Mexico, Argentina, Colombia, Venezuela, Bangladesh, Indonesia

Current Stablecoin Implementation Status *"Author's own table, categorizing jurisdictions by current stablecoin regulatory status (2025), based on public regulatory announcements.*

While legal and institutional readiness provides the scaffolding for stablecoin integration, jurisdictions require a structured yet adaptable pathway to operationalise reform. The following five-step roadmap distils complex regulatory transitions into actionable phases, enabling policymakers, regulators, and stakeholders to navigate adoption with clarity, confidence, and contextual sensitivity. Each step is designed to accommodate pluralist legal environments, support iterative refinement, and reinforce resilience across financial and institutional systems. By aligning modular design with phased execution, this roadmap empowers jurisdictions to move from conceptual preparedness to sustained, inclusive implementation.

Table 4. Five-step roadmap to readiness

	Focus Area	Key Actions	Real-World Example
1	Legal Scoping & Gap Analysis	Identify gaps in currency issuance, payments, AML, and consumer protection.	BIS Innovation Hub identified missing legal definitions in CBDC pilots.
2	Stakeholder Mapping & Engagement	Map agencies, fintechs, civil society, and end-users.	Uganda's CBDC outreach shaped pilot design via regional surveys
3	Pilot Programs for Legal Stress Testing	Test wallet functionality, redemption rights, and dispute protocols.	Hungary's Digital Student Safe embedded legal safeguards pre-launch.
4	Legislative Drafting with Enabling Clauses	Use model laws, allow adaptive rulemaking.	Eastern Caribbean's DCash used enabling legislation for digital issuance.
5	Capacity Building for Enforcement & Oversight	Train regulators, law enforcement, judiciary.	BIS workshops on smart contract interpretation and forensic tracing.

Five-Step Roadmap to Readiness *"Author's own five-step roadmap synthesizing global CBDC and stablecoin readiness initiatives, drawing on public pilot reports and case studies*

This roadmap ensures that legal frameworks are conceptually sound and practically enforceable, anchored in clarity, inclusion, and institutional capacity. By embedding this pathway into national strategies, Commonwealth jurisdictions can accelerate their readiness for digital currencies while maintaining legal integrity and public trust. The modular architecture supports phased implementation, allowing jurisdictions to tailor their approach based on market maturity, technological infrastructure, and institutional capacity.

This section reinforces the chapter's central thesis: that modular, principle-based legal frameworks combined with inclusive engagement and strategic capacity-building offer the most resilient path forward for regulating stablecoins, CBDCs, and the broader Web3 ecosystem.

Closing Reflection: Stewardship, Sovereignty, and the Modular Mandate

The journey toward digital asset regulation is a technical exercise and a test of legal stewardship, institutional imagination, and strategic resolve. Jurisdictions must navigate a rapidly evolving landscape where innovation outpaces legislation, and where the stakes include not only financial stability but economic sovereignty, public trust, and global relevance.

Modular legal architecture offers more than flexibility because it contributes to a philosophy of governance rooted in clarity, adaptability, and inclusion. It empowers jurisdictions to regulate at their own pace, build capacity incrementally, and respond to emerging risks without sacrificing coherence or credibility (UNIDROIT, 2023). It also enables legal pluralism, allowing diverse systems to converge around shared principles while respecting local traditions and institutional realities (The Commonwealth, 2018).

The Commonwealth Secretariat's modular framework exemplifies this approach. It offers a scaffold for sovereign decision-making, a toolkit for operational readiness, and a blueprint for global interoperability. Its emphasis on stakeholder engagement, plain-language drafting, and phased implementation reflects a deep understanding of what it takes to move from ambition to execution.

As digital currencies become embedded in the fabric of everyday life, from remittances and payroll to savings and trade, the legal frameworks that govern them must be equally embedded in the lived realities of those they serve. This requires not only legal clarity but institutional empathy, not only technical precision but democratic legitimacy.

The modular mandate is clear: regulate with purpose, adapt with agility, and legislate with foresight. In doing so, jurisdictions can reclaim control over their financial futures, foster innovation on their own terms, and contribute meaningfully to a more resilient, inclusive, and harmonised global financial ecosystem.

CONCLUSION

Toward a Harmonised, Scalable, and Flexible Regulatory Future

As Web3 technologies continue to redefine the architecture of finance, value exchange, and governance, the need for effective, future-ready regulatory frameworks has never been more urgent. The Model Laws, anchored in principle-based, protection-focused, balanced, comprehensive, and adaptable standards, offer a pragmatic and visionary roadmap for jurisdictions seeking to harness innovation while safeguarding systemic integrity.

The adoption of modular, tiered legislative frameworks for stablecoin regulation represents a synthesis of market realities, technological evolution, and policy imperatives.

At its foundation, the core module is the indispensable anchor of any stablecoin regime, with its focus on legal taxonomies, prudential reserves, and issuer eligibility (Commonwealth Secretariat, 2024). Surrounding modules on governance, transparency, interoperability, and innovation are critical for maintaining public trust, financial stability, and dynamic resilience, but must be built upon sound foundational requirements.

Tiered modularity ensures scalability and operational flexibility. Jurisdictions can "activate" advanced modules as their markets mature, risks evolve, or innovations emerge, allowing frameworks to remain fit-for-purpose without stifling competition or disproportionately burdening emerging participants. Real-world success stories from the Bahamas Sand Dollar and MiCA's pilot-to-license pathway, to Singapore's and Switzerland's tiered licensure models, demonstrate that modular legislative architecture is not only feasible but increasingly necessary.

Global standard-setters such as the BIS and FSB now recommend modularity not as an academic ideal, but as a practical strategy for harmonising cross-border expectations while accommodating local contexts and innovation cycles (FSB, 2023).

Regulatory sandboxes and pilot programs further enable rapid, evidence-based calibration, allowing authorities to gather feedback, detect emergent risks, and refine provisions before full-scale implementation. Looking ahead, legislative and supervisory developments will certainly expand the use and sophistication of modular approaches as stablecoins and digital currencies become a universal feature of the financial landscape. The trend is toward global harmonisation with common core minimums and interoperable modules balanced by local adaptation and support for experimentation.

The cost of inaction is steep. Jurisdictions that fail to modernise their VA frameworks risk financial instability, loss of sovereignty, exposure to illicit finance, and missed opportunities for innovation. Legal uncertainty and strategic vulnerability compound these risks. Inaction is not neutrality; it is a choice with profound consequences.

By adopting modular, interoperable, and inclusive frameworks, Commonwealth member states and jurisdictions beyond can shape a digital financial future that serves the public interest. The Commonwealth Model Laws' dynamic architecture position its adopters at the forefront of responsible digital transformation, offering a model with growing global appeal. Proactive reform is feasible and imperative for the common good.

REFERENCES

Auer, R., Dodson, D., Dupont, A., Haghighi, M., Margaine, N., Marsden, D., Mccarthy, S., & Valko, A. (2025). *BIS Papers No 158 Quantum-readiness for the financial system: a roadmap* (p. 17). https://www.bis.org/publ/bppdf/bispap158.pdf

Bank for International Settlement. (2007). *Basel Committee on Banking Supervision Principles for home-host supervisory cooperation and allocation mechanisms in the context of Advanced Measurement Approaches (AMA).* https://www.bis.org/publ/bcbs135.pdf

Bank of Uganda. (2025). *Final Report of the Consultation on Central Bank Digital Currency for Uganda* (pp. 1–49). https://www.bou.or.ug/export/sites/default/.gallery/CBDC-Consultations/CBDC-Consultation-Final-Report-June-30-2025-Submitted.pdf

Beecher, W., Bissessar, S., & Julien, M. (2018). *Business Environment Reform Facility.* https://assets.publishing.service.gov.uk/media/5c76731f40f0b603d45dd9c7/BERF-Caribbean-Fintech-Companies-Regulation-Review-Jan-2019.pdf

Boar, C., Claessens, S., Kosse, A., Leckow, R., & Rice, T. (2021). *BIS Bulletin No 49: Interoperability between payment systems across borders.* https://www.bis.org/publ/bisbull49.pdf

Commonwealth Secretariat. (2024). *The Commonwealth Model Law on Virtual Assets.* Commonwealth. https://thecommonwealth.org/publications/model-law-virtual-assets

Eastern Caribbean Central Bank. (2024). *D-Cash - Eastern Caribbean Central Bank.* Www.eccb-Centralbank.org. https://www.eccb-centralbank.org/d-cash

Elliptic. (2025). *Stablecoin Security Risks in 2025: Full Risk Assessment Guide | Elliptic.* Elliptic.co; Elliptic. https://www.elliptic.co/blockchain-basics/stablecoin-2025-risk-assessment-guide

Erik, F., Natarajan, H., & Saal, M. (2025). *Fintech and the Future of Finance: Market and Policy Implications.* World Bank. https://documents.worldbank.org/curated/en/099450005162250110

European Union. (2023). *Markets in Crypto Assets Regulation.* Europa.eu. https://eur-lex.europa.eu/legal-content/EN/TXT/?uri=CELEX%3A32023R1114

EY. (2025). *Global approaches to stablecoin regulation* (p. 24). https://www.ey.com/content/dam/ey-unified-site/ey-com/en-gl/industries/banking-capital-markets/documents/ey-gl-global-stablecoin-regulation-comparison-09-2025.pdf

FATF. (2021). *Updated Guidance for a Risk-Based Approach to Virtual Assets and Virtual Asset Service Providers*. Www.fatf-Gafi.org. https://www.fatf-gafi.org/en/publications/Fatfrecommendations/Guidance-rba-virtual-assets-2021.html

FATF. (2023). *Virtual Assets: Targeted Update on Implementation of the FATF Standards on VAs and VASPs*. Www.fatf-Gafi.org. https://www.fatf-gafi.org/en/publications/Fatfrecommendations/targeted-update-virtual-assets-vasps-2023.html

Financial Stability Board. (2020). *Regulation, Supervision and Oversight of "Global Stablecoin" Arrangements*. Www.fsb.org. https://www.fsb.org/2020/10/regulation-supervision-and-oversight-of-global-stablecoin-arrangements/

Financial Stability Board. (2023). *High-level Recommendations for the Regulation, Supervision and Oversight of Global Stablecoin Arrangements: Final report*. Www.fsb.org. https://www.fsb.org/2023/07/high-level-recommendations-for-the-regulation-supervision-and-oversight-of-global-stablecoin-arrangements-final-report/

Hogan Lovells. (2025). *Hogan Lovells | How can we help you?* Hoganlovells.com. https://digital-client-solutions.hoganlovells.com/resources/blockchain/insight/key-takeaways-from-the-bis-innovation-summit-2024

International Monetary Fund. (2021). The Rise of Digital Money. *Policy Papers, 2021*(054), 27. DOI: 10.5089/9781513589558.007

International Organisation of Securities Commission. (2020). *Global Stablecoin Initiatives Public Report*. https://www.iosco.org/library/pubdocs/pdf/IOSCOPD650.pdf

IOSCO. (2023). *Policy Recommendations for Crypto and Digital Asset Markets Final Report*. https://www.iosco.org/library/pubdocs/pdf/IOSCOPD747.pdf

Jeník, I., & Duff, S. (2020). *How to build a regulatory sandbox a practical guide for policy makers*. https://digitalfinance.worldbank.org/sites/default/files/2022-11/How-to-Build-a-Regulatory-Sandbox-A-Practical-Guide-for-Policy-Makers.pdf

. Julius, M., & Peter, N. (2024). Effect Of Financial Literacy On Investment Decisions Among Digital Customers Of Microfinance Banks In Nairobi Kenya. *IOSR Journal of Economics and Finance, 15*(6), 01-11. DOI: 10.9790/5933-1506040111

Laverdure, B. (2023). *How the TerraUSD Collapse Affects Stablecoin Regulation and Community Banks*. ICBA.org. https://www.icba.org/w/how-the-terrausd-collapse-affects-stablecoin-regulation-and-community-banks

Mukherjee, P., & Mukherjee, P. (2025). *Supreme Court of India declines appeal on "crypto" regulation*. CoinGeek. https://coingeek.com/supreme-court-of-india-declines-appeal-on-crypto-regulation/

OECD. (2019). *Digital Disruption in Financial Markets*. Oecd.org. https://www.oecd.org/en/events/2019/06/digital-disruption-in-financial-markets.html

OECD. (2024). *Development Co-operation Report 2024 Tackling Poverty and Inequalities Through the Green Transition*. https://www.oecd.org/content/dam/oecd/en/publications/reports/2024/07/development-co-operation-report-2024_b9cb300f/357b63f7-en.pdf

PricewaterhouseCoopers. (2023). *Digital assets regulatory and compliance: PwC*. PwC. https://www.pwc.com/us/en/services/digital-assets/digital-assets-regulations.html

Rey, H. (2025, September 3). *Stablecoins, Tokens, and Global Dominance*. IMF. https://www.imf.org/en/Publications/fandd/issues/2025/09/stablecoins-tokens-global-dominance-helene-rey

Seunghwan, K., Miksjuk, A., Suryakumar, N., Tuladhar, A., Velculescu, D., Wu, Y., Zuniga, J., & Hallmark, N. (2024). *IMF Digital Money*. Cross-Border Payments, International Reserves, and the Global Financial Safety Net Preliminary Considerations., https://www.imf.org/-/media/Files/Publications/IMF-Notes/2024/English/INSEA2024001.ashx

Smith, S. (2024). *Here's Why Stablecoin Policy Is Essential For US Dollar Leadership*. Crypto Council for Innovation. https://cryptoforinnovation.org/heres-why-stablecoin-policy-is-essential-for-us-dollar-leadership/

The Commonwealth. (2018). *Multi-sector support and related toolkits*. Commonwealth. https://thecommonwealth.org/multi-sector-support-and-related-toolkits

The Commonwealth. (2024a). *Commonwealth Ministerial Meeting on Small States: Paving the Way for Resilient Futures*. Commonwealth. https://thecommonwealth.org/news/chogm2024/commonwealth-ministerial-meeting-small-states-paving-way-resilient-futures

The Commonwealth. (2024b). *Model Law on Virtual Assets Office of Civil and Criminal Justice Reform 2*. https://production-new-commonwealth-files.s3.eu-west-2.amazonaws.com/s3fs-public/2024-04/commonwealth-model-law-on-virtual-assets.pdf?VersionId=Mpvonk_fe1DW64Bo1.LqpmSvvxSe430o

The Commonwealth. (2024c). *New Commonwealth model law to help countries regulate virtual assets*. Commonwealth. https://thecommonwealth.org/news/new-commonwealth-model-law-help-countries-regulate-virtual-assets

UN Security Council. (2024). *UN Documents for DPRK (North Korea): Sanctions Committee Documents*. Securitycouncilreport.org. https://www.securitycouncilreport.org/un_documents_type/sanctions-committee-documents/?ctype=DPRK%20%28North%20Korea%29&cbtype=dprk-north-korea

UNIDROIT. (2023). *UNIDROIT PRINCIPLES ON DIGITAL ASSETS AND PRIVATE LAW*. https://www.unidroit.org/wp-content/uploads/2024/01/Principles-on-Digital-Assets-and-Private-Law-linked-1.pdf

United States Congress. (2025). *GENIUS Act*. Congress.gov. https://www.congress.gov/bill/119th-congress/senate-bill/1582/text

Zavalko, M. (2025). *Blockchain Security & Stablecoins: Emerging Standards in the Commonwealth - Commonwealth Chamber of Commerce*. Commonwealth Chamber of Commerce. https://commonwealthchamber.com/blockchain-security-stablecoins-emerging-standards-in-the-commonwealth/

APPENDIX

Illustrative Modular Legal Structure

Table 5. (Commonwealth Model Laws for Web3 Regulation)

Section/Module	Key Focus Areas	Notable International Benchmarks
Preliminary	Definitions, Scope, Exclusions, Purpose	FATF, MiCA, Model Law on Int. Commercial Arbitration
Regulatory Authority	Powers, Functions, Objectives, Delegations	IOSCO, FSB, Singapore MAS
Licensing/ Registration	Application, Fit-and-Proper, Public Registers	AMLD5, FCA Guidance UK
AML/CFT	Risk-based KYC, Travel Rule, Counterparty Diligence	FATF, US FinCEN, MAS, EU TFR
Stablecoins Module	Legal Classification, Reserve Rules, Redemption, Consumer Protection	FSB, BIS, MiCA, JP FSA, US SEC/ CFTC
Initial Offerings	Disclosure, White Paper, Transparency	MiCA, SEC, FCA
Enforcement/ Supervision	Investigation, Sanctions, License Suspension/ Revoke	FSB, NAIC, IOSCO
Miscellaneous/ Delegation	Implementing Regulations, Sandboxes, and Amendments	Global good practices—RegTech, sandboxes

Chapter 5

Technology, Security, and Cyber Risks: Implementing the Commonwealth Model Law on Stablecoins

Marc Gunar Krisjanous
https://orcid.org/0009-0006-0447-1231
SixBlocks Audit, New Zealand

ABSTRACT

This chapter translates the Commonwealth Model Law on Stablecoins into an actionable, technically focused supervisory playbook by linking its legal mandates to the technical realities that drive financial stability outcomes. It deconstructs the stablecoin technology stack—blockchain infrastructure, smart contracts, oracle dependencies, and custody/wallet controls—to identify discrete risk surfaces and the cross-layer failure paths that can trigger rapid, system-wide losses. Anchored in recent case studies of algorithmic collapse and governance-enabled exploits, the chapter advances the principle that technological risk is financial risk and shows how vulnerabilities in bridges, oracle design, key management, and protocol governance can undermine reserves, redemption, and peg maintenance.

INTRODUCTION: FROM LEGAL PRINCIPLES TO TECHNICAL REALITIES

The advent of stablecoins represents a significant innovation in the virtual asset landscape, promising to merge the technological efficiencies of virtual assets with the price stability traditional fiat currencies. Recognising both the transformative potential and inherent risks, the Commonwealth has developed a Model Law on

DOI: 10.4018/979-8-3373-6655-5.ch005

Stablecoins, providing a robust, principles-based framework to guide member nations in crafting effective regulation (The Commonwealth, 2025). This model law focuses on critical areas, including reserve management, governance, consumer protection, and financial stability.

However, the ultimate efficacy of this or any legal framework for stablecoins is inextricably linked to a deep and nuanced understanding of the technology upon which these systems are built. Financial stability in the digital age is as much a function of Information and Communications Technology (ICT) and, most importantly, cybersecurity as it is of prudential oversight.

The history of virtual assets is replete with catastrophic losses stemming not from poor financial management in the traditional sense, but from subtle flaws in software code, the exploitation of economic logic within protocols, and failures in critical third-party services.

The dramatic collapse of TerraUSD (UST) and LUNA in May 2022, erasing tens of billions of dollars in value, was driven by an undercollateralised algorithmic design and a reflexive mint-burn death spiral, triggered by liquidity shocks and a run on the Anchor Protocol (Briola et al., 2023). Similarly, the $182 million exploit of Beanstalk Farms was not a simple theft but a sophisticated attack that leveraged a flash loan to manipulate the protocol's own governance system, effectively making the theft "legal" within the rules of the code (CertiK, 2022). These events serve as stark reminders that for stablecoins, technological risk is financial risk (Austin & Bank Policy Institute, 2025.).

This chapter aims to bridge the critical gap between the high-level principles articulated in the Commonwealth Model Law and the granular, technical realities of the stablecoin technical architecture it seeks to govern. While the Model Law correctly mandates crucial controls such as "ICT Operational Resilience" (Section 39), "Smart Contract Security" (Section 44), and "Oracle Security" (Section 46), these principles require a corresponding framework for assessment and enforcement (The Commonwealth, 2025). Mandating "adequate security" is insufficient without a clear understanding of what constitutes adequacy in the complex, interconnected, and often adversarial environment of Web3 technologies.

This chapter will deconstruct the stablecoin technology stack, examine the unique cybersecurity risks at each layer, and provide a practical guide for policymakers and regulators on how to translate the Model Law's legal principles into concrete supervisory actions. The central argument is that regulatory competence in technology is no longer an optional specialisation but a fundamental prerequisite for effective market supervision. The failure of a systemically important stablecoin has the potential to trigger contagion, not only within the virtual asset ecosystem but, as linkages grow, into the traditional financial system, elevating this from a consumer protection issue to a matter of national and global financial stability (International Monetary Fund, 2023).

THE STABLECOIN TECHNOLOGY STACK: A REGULATORY PRIMER

To effectively regulate stablecoin arrangements, supervisors must first understand the foundational architecture of a stablecoin. A stablecoin is not a monolithic entity but a complex system of interconnected technological layers, each presenting a distinct risk-surface. A vulnerability in one layer can be exploited to create a cascading failure across the entire system. In this section, we break down the foundational technical layers of the stablecoin architecture to provide a map for regulators to identify and assess these risks in a structured manner.

The Blockchain Layer: The Foundation of Trust and Risk

The blockchain, or distributed ledger technology (DLT), is the foundational layer upon which most stablecoins are currently built and transacted. It serves as the immutable and transparent record of ownership and transfers. The choice of blockchain architecture, for instance, a public and permissionless network like Ethereum versus a private and permissioned one, fundamentally defines the stablecoin's security model and risk profile (Basel Committee on Banking Supervision, 2024).

Public, permissionless blockchains offer unparalleled transparency and censorship resistance, as anyone can participate in validating transactions. However, they are also subject to network-wide risks such as congestion, which can lead to prohibitively high transaction fees during periods of peak demand, potentially impeding critical functions like redemption or collateral management. While consensus-level attacks (e.g., a 51% attack) are theoretically possible, they are exceedingly rare and costly on major, established networks.

A more pressing and contemporary risk at this layer arises from the growing need for stablecoins to exist on multiple different chains, to facilitate interoperability with the wider digital economy, which is made up of countless public permissionless blockchains. To expand their reach and utility, issuers often deploy their stablecoin across multiple, distinct blockchains. While this strategy broadens the user base, it introduces significant technical complexity and new vectors for attack. A primary concern is the fragmentation of liquidity; reserves and trading pools are spread thin across different stablecoin ecosystems, which can negatively impact price stability and the ability to settle large transactions efficiently on any single blockchain.

The most critical vulnerability introduced by a multi-blockchain architecture is the reliance on cross-blockchain bridges. These are protocols designed to transfer assets between otherwise incompatible blockchains. Historically, bridges have been a primary target for hackers (Behnkw, 2025) and the source of some of the largest exploits in the history of decentralised finance (DeFi). A vulnerability in a bridge's smart contract or validation mechanism can allow an attacker to mint unbacked "wrapped" versions of the stablecoin on a destination blockchain or drain the assets locked on the source blockchain. Such an exploit would instantly undermine the stablecoin's core promise of full backing, potentially triggering a system-wide loss of confidence and a run on the stablecoin. This risk directly implicates an issuer's ability to fulfil its obligations under Part IV Reserve Management and Transparency of the Model Law, which mandates the maintenance of sufficient reserve assets (The Commonwealth, 2025).

The Smart Contract Layer: The Automated Law

The smart contract layer contains the self-executing software code that governs the stablecoin's functions. Smart contracts, in effect, are the automated law of the protocol, managing critical functions such as issuance (minting), redemption (burning), the mechanics of the stability mechanism, and governance procedures. For a stablecoin backed by a basket of virtual assets, for example, a smart contract could automate the process of locking collateral and minting a corresponding amount of stablecoins, and vice versa for redemption. This layer is the primary source of bespoke software vulnerabilities. Due to the generally immutable nature of most blockchains, a bug deployed in a smart contract is exceptionally difficult to patch or remediate (Akartuna, 2025). A flaw in the code can be permanent, creating a persistent vulnerability that can be exploited at any time. Common coding errors that have led to catastrophic losses include re-entrancy attacks, integer overflows and underflows, and vulnerabilities related to unchecked external calls (Open Web Application Security Project, n.d.d). The security of this layer is so fundamental that the Model Law dedicates Section 44 specifically to "Smart Contract Security" (The Commonwealth, 2025). A failure in this layer does not just cause a system outage; it can lead to the instantaneous and irreversible loss or theft of assets controlled by the affected contracts, potentially at a system-wide scale, depending on the safeguards in place.

The Oracle Layer: The Link to the Real World

Blockchains are closed-loop systems; they cannot natively access external, real-world information such as the price of the US dollar or the market value of reserve assets (Duley et al., 2023). Oracles are essential third-party services that act as a bridge, fetching external data and feeding it into the blockchain for smart contracts to use. A stablecoin pegged to an off-chain asset is therefore only as secure and reliable as the oracle data feed that informs its stability mechanism. This creates a critical dependency and a potential single point of failure.

The "Oracle Problem" refers to the fundamental challenge of ensuring that the data provided by an oracle is accurate, timely, and resistant to manipulation. If an oracle is compromised, is fed malicious data, or simply fails to update during periods of extreme market volatility, it can have catastrophic consequences for the stablecoin arrangement. A smart contract executing its flawless software-based logic based on flawed data will produce a flawed outcome (garbage-in, garbage-out). For example, an incorrect price feed could cause the protocol to issue stablecoins against undervalued collateral, allow for the liquidation of solvent positions, or completely break the arbitrage mechanism designed to maintain the peg (Akartuna, 2025). The Model Law acknowledges this critical dependency in Section 46, "Oracle Security" (The Commonwealth, 2025).

The Custody and Wallet Layer: Securing the Assets

This layer addresses the safeguarding of the key material that controls both the stablecoin's reserve assets and the tokens held by stablecoin users. In the virtual asset world, control of the private key is synonymous with ownership of the asset (Bitcoin.org, n.d.). There is no central intermediary to reverse a fraudulent transaction; a compromised private key almost invariably leads to an irreversible loss of funds.

The risks at this layer are twofold. First, there are custodial risks associated with managing reserve assets. If an issuer uses a third-party custodian to manage the stablecoin's reserves, the security of those reserves depends entirely on that custodian's operational security, key management practices, and internal controls. Second, the issuer itself must secure its own operational wallets, which are used for managing liquidity, processing redemptions, and administering the stablecoin arrangements. A breach of these wallets due to poor key management could allow an attacker to drain operational funds or, in some cases, execute unauthorised administrative functions. The Model Law addresses these fundamental risks through specific provisions on "Key Management" (Section 42) and "Wallet Security" (Section 43) (The Commonwealth, 2025).

It is crucial to recognise that these layers are not independent silos. Sophisticated attacks often exploit vulnerabilities across multiple layers in a causal chain of cause and effect. For instance, consider a collateralised stablecoin. An attacker utilises a flash loan (on the smart-contract layer) to inflate the decentralised exchange (DEX) price of Token A, the collateral asset. A single-source oracle (oracle layer), reading only that exchange, ingests the manipulated price and feeds it to the stablecoin's smart contracts. The protocol then overvalues the attacker's collateral, allowing them to mint stablecoins without adequate backing or to borrow against effectively worthless collateral. A risk assessment that treats each layer in isolation would miss this cross-component failure path. Regulators should therefore adopt a holistic approach, analysing not only the security of each component but also the systemic risks that emerge from their interactions.

Smart Contract and Protocol-Level Risks: Enforcing the Model Law's Mandates

The smart contract layer serves as the essential foundation of a stablecoin's functions; however, it also encompasses the most direct and significant technical risks associated with its implementation. The Commonwealth Model Law's provisions for "Smart Contract Security" (Section 44) and "Secure Coding Practices" (Section 45) provide the legal mandate for robust protection (The Commonwealth, 2025). However, translating these mandates into effective supervision requires a granular understanding of the specific vulnerabilities that plague these systems and the economic exploits that target their logic.

SOFTWARE VULNERABILITIES: THE ANATOMY OF A CODE FLAW

Even with the best intentions, software can contain bugs. In the immutable world of smart contracts, these bugs can become permanent, billion-dollar vulnerabilities (Nethermind, 2024). Two of the most notorious and historically significant types of vulnerabilities are re-entrancy attacks and integer overflows.

Re-entrancy Attacks

A re-entrancy attack is a classic smart contract exploit that occurs when a contract's function makes an external call to another, potentially malicious, contract *before* it updates its own internal state variables (such as a user's balance) (Open Web Application Security Project, n.d.b; Kaia Docs, n.d.). The malicious smart contract, upon receiving the call, can immediately call back into the original function. Because the original function has not yet updated its state, the attacker's balance appears unchanged, allowing them to withdraw funds repeatedly until the contract is drained. The canonical example of this vulnerability was the 2016 hack of "The DAO", an early decentralised investment fund, which led to the theft of approximately $60 million worth of Ether and resulted in a contentious hard fork of the Ethereum blockchain (Pratap, 2022).

Integer Overflow and Underflow

This class of vulnerability arises from the way computers handle numbers with fixed-size data types. For example, an 8-bit unsigned integer (uint8) can only represent numbers from 0 to 255. If an arithmetic operation attempts to store a value of 256 in a uint8, the value will "wrap around" and become 0 (an overflow). Conversely, subtracting 1 from 0 will cause it to wrap around to 255 (an underflow) (Howell, 2024). Attackers can exploit this behaviour to manipulate token balances, bypass security checks, or trigger unintended state changes. The Proof of Weak Hands Coin (PoWH) and BeautyChain exploits are prominent examples where these arithmetic errors led to significant financial losses.

Fortunately, this is a largely solved problem in modern smart contract development. Since version 0.8.0, the Solidity programming language compiler automatically includes checks that cause a transaction to revert if an overflow or underflow occurs (Open Web Application Security Project, n.d.a). For contracts written in older versions of Solidity, the standard practice is to use a "SafeMath" library, which provides arithmetic functions with built-in overflow and underflow checks. From a regulatory perspective, enforcing compliance with Section 45 ("Secure Coding Practices") can be as straightforward as mandating the use of up-to-date compilers or verifying the consistent use of safe math libraries in the codebase.

ECONOMIC AND GOVERNANCE EXPLOITS: ATTACKING THE LOGIC

As the developer community has become more adept at preventing simple code bugs, attackers have shifted their focus to more sophisticated exploits that target a stablecoin's underlying economic or governance logic. These attacks often use the stablecoin's own features against it, making them particularly insidious.

Flash Loan Attacks

Flash loans are a unique innovation of DeFi that allow a user to borrow a vast amount of cryptocurrency with zero collateral, under the single condition that the loan is repaid within the same blockchain transaction (Open Web Application Security Project, n.d.c; Fraud.net, n.d.; Akartuna, 2022). If the loan is not repaid by the end of the transaction, the entire transaction fails, as if it never happened. While this has legitimate uses in arbitrage and collateral swapping, it has also become the weapon of choice for attackers, providing them with the massive, temporary capital required to manipulate markets or governance systems.

The April 2022 exploit of Beanstalk Farms provides a stark case study. In April 2022, Beanstalk Farms was exploited when an attacker, having seeded a malicious governance proposal ~24 hours earlier, flash-borrowed nearly $1 billion in stablecoins via Aave, used them to buy enough governance tokens to control roughly 67% of votes, then used the emergencyCommit mechanism to vote through and execute the proposal in the same transaction, transferring about $182 million of protocol funds to their own address before repaying the loan and walking away with an estimated $76–80 million profit.

The critical point for regulators is that the smart contracts functioned exactly as they were written. The vulnerability was not a bug in the code, but a fatal flaw in the design of the governance mechanism, which did not account for the possibility of a flash loan-funded hostile takeover. This demonstrates that a narrow focus on code security is insufficient. The Model Law's broader provisions on "Governance" (Section 50) and "Risk Management" (Section 21) must be interpreted to include a thorough assessment of a stablecoin's resilience to economic manipulation and governance attacks (The Commonwealth, 2025).

BEYOND AUDITS: THE CASE FOR FORMAL VERIFICATION

An external third-party security audit is an essential part of the software development lifecycle, involving expert review and testing to identify known vulnerabilities. However, for critical financial infrastructure like a systemically important stablecoin, a higher standard of assurance may be necessary. Formal verification is a rigorous technique borrowed from mission-critical fields like aerospace and hardware design. It uses mathematical methods to create a formal model of a program and *prove* that its behaviour conforms to a precise set of specifications under all possible conditions (CertiK, 2023). Unlike auditing, which seeks to find flaws, formal verification seeks to prove their absence. It can uncover subtle logic errors, race conditions, and edge-case vulnerabilities that even skilled human auditors might miss (Behnkw, 2023). While it is a more complex and resource-intensive process, its ability to provide mathematical certainty about a contract's correctness makes it an invaluable tool for securing high-value systems.

For stablecoin issuers classified as Tier 1 (systemically important) under the Model Law's framework, regulators should consider elevating the expectation from a standard audit to the formal verification of the core smart contracts governing issuance, redemption, and reserve management. This would represent the highest possible standard of care and would be the most robust way to enforce the mandate for "Smart Contract Security" under Section 44 (The Commonwealth, 2025).

The progression of attacks from simple coding errors to complex economic and governance exploits reveals a dynamic and escalating threat landscape. This creates an "arms race" where static, checklist-based regulation is destined to fail. Early exploits targeted well-defined bugs that are now largely preventable with standard tools. Attackers then evolved to use novel financial primitives like flash loans to attack a stablecoin's economic assumptions, for instance, by manipulating price oracles. The Beanstalk attack represents a third generation of exploit, where economic tools were used to subvert the governance layer itself. This trend implies that a regulator's duty extends beyond asking, "Is the code secure?" to the more complex questions of "Is the economic model resilient?" and "Is the governance structure defensible against manipulation?". Consequently, the risk management frameworks required by the Model Law must be dynamic, incorporating ongoing modelling of these novel threats, not just a one-time, static analysis of the code.

THE ORACLE PROBLEM: MANAGING CRITICAL THIRD-PARTY DEPENDENCIES

The integrity of a stablecoin pegged to an external asset is fundamentally dependent on its ability to access accurate, real-time data about that asset's value. This dependency creates one of the most significant and challenging risks in the DeFi ecosystem, known as the Oracle Problem. The Commonwealth Model Law identifies this risk in Section 46 ("Oracle Security") and Section 50(5) (covering third-party service providers), but effective supervision requires framing this technical challenge as a core issue of third-party risk management, a concept familiar to financial regulators (The Commonwealth, 2025).

Defining the Oracle Problem

Blockchains, by design, are deterministic and isolated environments. They cannot independently access external data from the internet, such as financial market price feeds (Duley et al., 2023). Oracles are the necessary middleware that serve as a bridge, fetching data from off-chain sources and delivering it to on-chain smart contracts and vice versa. This function is essential, but it introduces a critical vulnerability: the trustless, decentralised security of a smart contract becomes reliant on the trustworthiness of a potentially centralised or manipulatable data source.

Oracle manipulation can occur through several vectors (Gate.com, 2025). An attacker could directly compromise a centralised oracle provider. They could interfere with the data transmission process. Or, in a more common DeFi attack pattern, they can manipulate the underlying data source itself. For example, an attacker could use a flash loan to execute a massive trade on a single, low-liquidity decentralised exchange, momentarily distorting the price of an asset. If a stablecoin's oracle is naively configured to pull its price data from that one exchange, it will feed the manipulated price to the smart contract, triggering flawed liquidations or enabling the minting of unbacked tokens.

Case Study in Oracle Failure: DAI (MakerDAO) on "Black Thursday"

As ETH crashed ~43% in a single day (Friday, March 13, 2020), MakerDAO's liquidation machinery was pushed to the limit. Keepers struggled to participate in auctions amid extreme network congestion, and DAI briefly became partially unbacked (≈$4.5M) while also trading above $1 as demand for safety spiked. The episode shows how oracle behaviour under stress can amplify instability in otherwise well-designed systems (Glassnode, 2020).

MakerDAO's design intentionally inserts a one-hour delay between the oracle price and the "system price" used for liquidations via the Oracle Security Module (OSM). Under normal conditions, this buffers the protocol against short-lived price wicks; under extreme, fast moves, it creates oracle latency risk, as positions can be economically underwater at market prices while still appearing solvent to the protocol until the delayed price rolls forward. That timing gap shaped liquidation dynamics on Black Thursday. With gas prices spiking and MEV competition intensifying, many keepers couldn't submit timely bids. Thousands of auctions cleared at zero DAI because no valid bid landed before the timers expired. Blocknative's forensics counted 3,994 auctions, 1,462 of which (≈36.6%) were won at zero, translating to about $8.32M in collateral value lost. The oracle delay didn't "break," but in combination with network congestion, it magnified liquidation slippage and losses. The peg wobbled upward as users scrambled for DAI, highlighting how collateral shocks plus delayed oracle updates can propagate into the stablecoin's market price. Governance responded within days by admitting USDC as emergency collateral to restore market liquidity, and later formalised tooling like the Peg Stability Module (MIP-29) to tighten the peg during stress.

Why this matters: The case is a concrete example that the oracle problem is real, not just about wrong prices, but about *when* prices arrive and how the rest of the system behaves during that window. Risk controls should assume stressed latency: e.g., buffered liquidation parameters, circuit breakers, robust keeper diversity, and contingency collateral/PSM levers. Black Thursday didn't stem from an oracle "failure," yet oracle latency under duress was a key accelerant of losses and peg deviation.

Mitigation: Decentralised Oracle Networks (DONs)

The primary solution to the Oracle Problem is decentralisation. Rather than relying on a single source of data or a single entity to report it, Decentralised Oracle Networks (DONs), such as Chainlink, provide a more resilient model. DONs achieve this resilience through two layers of decentralisation:

- **Source-Level Decentralisation:** Data is aggregated from a multitude of high-quality, independent data providers and exchanges, rather than a single source. This makes it prohibitively expensive to manipulate the aggregate price.
- **Node-Level Decentralisation:** A network of independent, geographically distributed, and reputation-staked node operators fetches the data from these sources. These nodes use a consensus mechanism to agree on a single, validated data point before it is delivered to the smart contract (Gorawska & Swierzy, 2024).

Under Section 50(5) of the Model Law, which requires due diligence and ongoing monitoring of third-party service providers, the choice of an oracle should be a primary focus of supervisory review. Regulators should require stablecoin issuers to provide a robust justification for their oracle architecture. For any stablecoin of moderate to systemic importance, reliance on a single, centralised oracle should be considered an unacceptable risk. The due diligence documentation should demonstrate that the chosen oracle solution is decentralised, resistant to the types of manipulation seen in flash loan attacks and has proven mechanisms for maintaining data quality and timeliness, especially during periods of extreme network congestion and market volatility.

The Oracle Problem highlights a fundamental tension in the stablecoin arrangement. It is the precise point where the chaotic, unpredictable dynamics of off-chain markets collide with the rigid, automated logic of on-chain smart contracts. The oracle is the translator between these two worlds. This means that the technical design and resilience of the oracle are just as critical to financial stability as the economic design of the stabilisation algorithm itself. An issuer cannot simply outsource this risk to a third party; under the Model Law, they retain full accountability for the integrity of their data dependencies, making the regulator's scrutiny of this relationship a core prudential concern.

KEY MANAGEMENT AND CUSTODY: SECURING THE CORE ASSETS

While smart-contract and oracle risks are systemic threats, operational control of on-chain stablecoin funds depends on who can satisfy the wallet's authorisation policy, whether with a single private signing key, a threshold/distributed signing scheme, a multi-signature quorum, or any other cryptographic mechanism that yields a valid authorisation. Those parties have effective spending authority, subject to contract-level controls (e.g., issuer freeze/clawback) and the blockchain's finality rules. Securing the generation, storage, and use of key material is therefore a critical objective of operational security, alongside issuer governance/solvency and protocol correctness. For brevity, this chapter uses "private key" to refer to any signing authority mechanism capable of authorising a transaction (including threshold/ distributed shares, co-signature schemes, and future authorisation mechanisms). The Commonwealth Model Law places significant emphasis on this foundation through its detailed requirements for "Multi-Party Authorisation Controls" (Section 41), "Key Management" (Section 42), and "Wallet Security" (Section 43) (The Commonwealth, 2025).

The Primacy of the Private Key

Every transaction on a blockchain must be digitally signed using a private key. This signature serves as mathematical proof that the owner of the assets has authorised the transaction (Bitcoin.org, n.d.). Consequently, anyone who gains access to a private key can steal the associated assets with impunity. This makes the private key the single most valuable target for malicious actors. For a stablecoin issuer, this risk exists at multiple levels: keys controlling vast reserve assets, keys for operational wallets managing daily liquidity, and keys that hold administrative privileges to upgrade smart contracts or alter protocol parameters. A single point of failure, where one private key is all that is required to sign a transaction, poses an unacceptable risk for any entity managing significant value.

Institutional Custody Technologies: Multi-Sig vs. MPC

To eliminate single points of failure, institutional-grade custody solutions employ multi-party approval schemes. The two dominant technologies currently for achieving this are Multi-Signature (Multi-Sig) wallets and Multi-Party Computation (MPC).

Multi-Signature (Multi-Sig) Wallets

Multi-signature (multisig) requires approvals from multiple independent keys for a single transaction. On account-based chains like Ethereum, this is enforced by smart-contract wallets; on UTXO chains like Bitcoin, it's enforced by spending scripts. Multisig is transparent and verifiable on-chain, and common setups include 2-of-3. Drawbacks include higher fees versus single-sig and (on some chains, notably Bitcoin) operational inflexibility; changing signers often requires a new address and fund migration (CoinGecko, 2024.). By contrast, modern smart-contract multisigs (e.g., Safe) let you change owners/thresholds without redeploying.

Multi-Party Computation (MPC)

MPC (threshold signatures) achieves the same "no single point of private-key compromise" goal by distributing both key generation and signing across multiple parties. A full private key is never constructed on any one device. Instead, a distributed key-generation protocol creates secret shares held by different parties. To authorise a transaction, any t-of-n parties run an interactive signing protocol that outputs a standard ECDSA/EdDSA signature; the shares are never combined to reconstruct the key.

The primary advantages of MPC are its superior security and flexibility compared to multi-signature mechanisms. Since the full key never exists, there is no single point of compromise for an attacker to target. It is also blockchain-agnostic, as the final signature produced is a standard, single signature that is compatible with any blockchain. This makes it operationally efficient, allowing for signing quorums and policies to be changed off-chain without moving funds. The main trade-off is its complexity; its security relies on the soundness of the underlying cryptography and the secure implementation by the MPC provider.

From a regulatory standpoint, both multi-signature and MPC are valid technologies for fulfilling the Model Law's mandate for multi-party authorisation in Section 41 (The Commonwealth, 2025). A regulator's assessment should focus not on prescribing one over the other, but on evaluating whether the issuer's chosen solution is appropriate for their scale of operations and whether it is implemented with robust procedural controls.

Hardware Security Modules (HSMs): The Physical Root of Trust

To provide an additional layer of defence, particularly against software-based attacks, the cryptographic key material itself should be protected within specialised hardware. Hardware Security Modules (HSMs) are dedicated, tamper-resistant devices designed for the sole purpose of securely generating, storing, and using cryptographic keys (Thales, n.d.). The critical security feature of an HSM is that the private keys never leave the secure, certified hardware environment. All cryptographic operations, such as signing a transaction, are performed inside the HSM. This isolates the keys from vulnerabilities that might exist on the host operating system of a general-purpose server. For any Tier 1 or Tier 2 stablecoin issuer, the use of HSMs to protect the private keys (in a multisig setup) or the key shards (in an MPC setup) should be considered a baseline requirement for institutional-grade security.

Trusted Execution Environments (TEEs) / Secure Enclaves

TEEs (often called secure enclaves) provide hardware-enforced isolation within a general-purpose processor or cloud instance. Code and data inside the enclave are protected from the host OS/hypervisor, and remote attestation allows systems to verify the exact code and configuration before releasing secrets. TEEs can generate, hold, and use keys or MPC shares in an isolated context and are well-suited to scalable, low-latency signing or MPC computation. However, unlike HSMs, TEEs typically lack dedicated physical tamper-resistance and the same level of formal certification; they are best used alongside HSMs, for example, storing keys/shares non-exportably in an HSM and permitting use only by an attested enclave, or running MPC parties in TEEs while the HSM enforces policy (rate limits, approvals).

PROCEDURAL SECURITY AND INSIDER THREATS

Technology alone cannot solve the security challenge. Rigorous and auditable human procedures must complement it. The Model Law's Section 47 on "Human Resource Security" is critical in this regard (The Commonwealth, 2025). Insider threats, whether malicious or negligent, are a significant risk. Strong controls must be in place, including:

- **Key Generation Ceremonies:** The initial creation of key material must be conducted in a formal, multi-person ceremony, with auditable records to ensure no single individual ever has access to the complete key material.
- **Background Checks:** As mandated by the Model Law, thorough pre-employment and periodic background checks must be conducted for all personnel with access to sensitive systems or key material (The Commonwealth, 2025).

- **Segregation of Duties:** No single person should have the ability to both initiate and approve a high-value transaction. This principle should be enforced both technologically (via multi-signature/MPC) and procedurally.

The choice between multi-signature and MPC presents an interesting trade-off for regulators. For EVM chains, the choice between contract multi-signature and MPC creates a clear trade-off for regulators. Contract multi-signature provides on-chain transparency: the owner sets a signature threshold that is stored on-chain, and executed transactions include the owners' signatures so observers can see who approved. MPC/TSS, by contrast, controls a single EOA (Externally Owned Account) key: the resulting blockchain transaction is a standard single-signature, with all multi-party coordination off-chain, keeping approval policies private. This prevents malicious actors from mapping out an organisation's governance structure. A sophisticated regulatory approach, in the spirit of the Model Law, would not mandate a specific technology but would instead assess whether the issuer's choice and its inherent trade-offs between transparency and privacy are appropriate and well-justified for its specific risk profile and use case.

OPERATIONAL RESILIENCE AND CONTAGION RISK IN AN INTERCONNECTED ECOSYSTEM

The risks facing a stablecoin issuer do not exist in a vacuum. They operate within the broader DeFi ecosystem, a highly interconnected and "composable" environment where protocols are built on top of one another like "money legos". This interconnectedness is a source of innovation, but it is also a powerful amplifier of risk. A failure in one protocol can trigger a domino effect, causing cascading failures across the ecosystem. This phenomenon, known as contagion risk, requires regulators to look beyond the security of a single issuer and consider its resilience to systemic shocks, a core tenet of the Model Law's provisions on operational resilience.

The "Daisy-Chain" Effect: Understanding Contagion Risk

The concept of composability means that a stablecoin issuer can integrate with numerous other DeFi protocols to perform various functions. For example, the issuer might deposit some of the reserve assets into a lending protocol to generate yield, or the issuer might accept another protocol's liquid staking token as a form of collateral. This creates a "daisy-chain" of dependencies (The Commonwealth, 2025). If the lending protocol is hacked, the stablecoin's reserves are at risk. If the liquid staking token de-pegs from its underlying asset, the stablecoin's collateral becomes worthless. This deep-seated interconnectedness is a primary vector for systemic risk in DeFi, and a stablecoin, by virtue of its role as a core liquidity and settlement asset, is often at the centre of these chains (International Monetary Fund, 2023).

Case Study in Systemic Collapse: The Terra/Luna De-Peg

The collapse of Terra/Luna was the catalyst for one of the most significant contagion events in the history of crypto-assets. Its failure was not contained within its own stablecoin ecosystem. It triggered a broad wave of distress and insolvencies across the industry, most notably affecting the hedge fund Three Arrows Capital and centralised crypto lenders such as Celsius and Voyager. While Three Arrows Capital had concentrated exposure to UST and LUNA, the lenders were hit through interconnected counterparty exposures and severe liquidity mismatches (including Three Arrows Capital's default), leading to suspended withdrawals, bankruptcies, and the freezing of funds for millions of retail customers.

The technical roots of this contagion lie in the fundamental design flaws of the Terra protocol:

- **Flawed Algorithmic Design:** The reflexive relationship between UST and LUNA created a "death spiral". As market stress reduced demand for UST, the protocol minted and sold massive amounts of LUNA to defend the peg. This hyperinflation of LUNA's supply crashed its price, further eroding confidence in UST and reinforcing the feedback loop.
- **Peg-Defence and Redemption Breakdown Under Stress:** Under extreme volatility, limits and spreads in Terra's market module made redemptions uneconomic; as LUNA collapsed via hyperinflation, validator halts and other emergency measures effectively disabled on-chain redemptions, sealing the collapse (Kurovskiy, G. & Rostova, N.,2023)

The lesson for regulators is that the failure of a single, large stablecoin arrangement can have far-reaching consequences, impacting entities that seem only tangentially related. Assessing an issuer's operational resilience, therefore, requires understanding its dependencies and exposures to the wider ecosystem. A saying attributed to Warren Buffett is "Only when the tide goes out do you discover who's been swimming naked," which appears to be applicable in this case study.

Implementing Resilience: Business Continuity and Incident Response

The Model Law's requirements for "Business Continuity and Disaster Recovery" (BC/DR) in Section 50(4) and "Monitoring and Incident Response" in Section 49 must be interpreted and applied within the unique context of Web3 (The Commonwealth, 2025). Traditional BC/DR planning often focuses on recovering from data centre outages or hardware failures. For a stablecoin issuer, the more relevant disaster scenarios involve market crises, exploits, and contagion events.

A resilient operational framework for a stablecoin issuer should include:

- **Continuous On-Chain Monitoring:** Blockchain markets operate 24/7/365. Issuers must have systems for real-time, continuous monitoring of on-chain activity, the health of their own protocol, and the status of critical dependencies (The Commonwealth, 2025). This includes tracking transaction volumes, redemption flows, collateral health, and oracle price feeds.
- **Pre-defined "Circuit Breakers":** In the event of a sudden, severe de-pegging event or a suspected security breach, issuers should have well-defined and tested procedures to pause certain critical functions. This might involve temporarily halting minting or borrowing functions to contain the damage and give the team time to respond. While this seems to run counter to the ethos of decentralisation, it is a crucial risk management tool.
- **Comprehensive Stress Testing:** As required by the Model Law, stress tests are vital. However, these tests must go beyond simple market volatility scenarios. They must model the failure of critical third-party dependencies, such as the de-pegging of a major stablecoin used as collateral, the failure of a key oracle provider, or an exploit in a protocol where reserves are deposited.

A challenge for regulators in this space is the "decentralisation illusion" (Aramonte et al., 2021). Many protocols are promoted as being fully decentralised and governed by unstoppable code. However, in practice, this is rarely the case. There are almost always centralised points of control: a core development team, a foundation that funds development, or a small group of holders of a multi-signature key with administrative privileges. The Beanstalk Farms attack was a prime example of how a governance process, a key point of control, could be exploited. This centralisation is a significant vulnerability. However, it is also the essential leverage point for effective regulation. The Model Law anticipates this by requiring that even Decentralised Autonomous Organisations (DAOs) must appoint an identifiable legal person or representative to interface with regulators (The Commonwealth, 2025). Regulators should not be deterred by superficial claims of decentralisation. Instead, their task is to identify the true loci of power and control within any stablecoin ecosystem and apply the Model Law's fit and proper requirements, governance standards, and accountability measures directly to those individuals and entities.

A SUPERVISORY FRAMEWORK FOR ASSESSING TECHNICAL AND CYBER RISK

The Commonwealth Model Law provides a comprehensive and forward-looking legal foundation for stablecoin regulation. To translate its principles into effective and consistent supervision, regulators require a practical framework for assessing the technical and cyber risks of licensed issuers. A one-size-fits-all, checklist-based approach is ill-suited to the diverse and dynamic nature of the stablecoin market. Instead, a sophisticated, risk-based approach is necessary, where the intensity of supervision and the stringency of technical requirements scale in proportion to the systemic importance and risk profile of the stablecoin issuer. This aligns directly with the tiered licensing framework established in Sections 13 and 14 of the Model Law, which classifies issuers from Tier 3 (limited or niche use cases) to Tier 1 (systemically important) (The Commonwealth, 2025). The following framework is a basic example that operationalises this tiered approach for the specific domain of technology and cybersecurity, providing clear, actionable, and proportionate expectations for each tier. It aligns the mandates outlined in Part IX of the Model Law and its accompanying exhibits with the technical realities and best practices discussed throughout this chapter.

Table 1. Tiered cybersecurity and governance requirements under the commonwealth model law

Control Area (Relevant Model Law Section)	Tier 3 (Limited/Niche)	Tier 2 (Moderate Scale)	Tier 1 (Systemically Important)
ICT Operational Resilience (Sec. 39, 50(4))	Documented ICT strategy, Business Continuity, and Disaster Recovery plans. Annual testing of recovery procedures.	All Tier 3 requirements, PLUS: Use of redundant systems for critical components. Documented stress tests modelling severe market volatility and de-pegging scenarios.	All Tier 2 requirements, PLUS: A comprehensive, independently audited operational resilience framework. Stress tests must explicitly model contagion risk, including the failure of critical third-party protocols. Predefined and regularly tested "circuit breaker" mechanisms.
Access Control (Sec. 40)	Documented access control policy based on the principle of least privilege, separation of duties, and need-to-know principles. Use of multi-factor authentication (MFA) for all administrative access.	All Tier 3 requirements, PLUS: Automated logging and monitoring of privileged access with alerts for suspicious activity. Formal, documented processes for granting and revoking access, subject to periodic review.	All Tier 2 requirements, PLUS: Implementation of a full Privileged Access Management (PAM) solution. Regular, independent audits of access controls and privileged activity.
Key Management & Custody (Sec. 41-43)	Use of institutional-grade Multi-Signature (Multi-Sig) or Multi-Party Computation (MPC) for all operational and reserve wallets. Documented key management policies and procedures.	All Tier 3 requirements, PLUS: Use of Hardware Security Modules (HSMs) or Trusted Execution Environments (TEEs) for the storage of cryptographic key material for critical operational and reserve management wallets.	All Tier 2 requirements, PLUS: Use of HSMs is mandatory for all key material. Geographically distributed storage of keys or key shards to mitigate physical risks. Formally documented and independently audited key generation and recovery ceremonies.
Smart Contract Security (Sec. 44)	Independent third-party audit of all smart contracts before deployment. Publicly available audit reports.	All Tier 3 requirements, PLUS: Mandatory bug bounty program to incentivise continuous security research. Regular re-audits for any material upgrades to the smart contracts.	All Tier 2 requirements, PLUS: Formal verification of core smart contract logic for issuance, redemption, and reserve management to provide mathematical proof of correctness.

continued on following page

Table 1. Continued

Control Area (Relevant Model Law Section)	Tier 3 (Limited/Niche)	Tier 2 (Moderate Scale)	Tier 1 (Systemically Important)
Secure Coding Practices (Sec. 45)	Adherence to a documented secure software development lifecycle (SDLC). Use of well-audited, standard libraries where possible.	All Tier 3 requirements, PLUS: Mandatory peer code reviews for all changes to production code. Use of static and dynamic application security testing tools within the development pipeline.	All Tier 2 requirements, PLUS: A dedicated application security team responsible for overseeing secure coding practices. Regular, in-depth manual code reviews of critical components by independent security experts.
Oracle Security (Sec. 46, 50(5))	Use of a reputable, established oracle provider. Clear public disclosure of all oracle dependencies.	All Tier 3 requirements, PLUS: Mandatory use of a Decentralized Oracle Network (DON) with multiple independent data sources and nodes to prevent single points of failure. Documented due diligence on the oracle provider's security, reliability, and resilience.	All Tier 2 requirements, PLUS: Real-time, automated monitoring of oracle price feeds for significant deviations from a market-wide consensus price. A documented and tested contingency plan to be executed in the event of an oracle failure or manipulation.
Human Resource Security (Sec. 47)	Documented HR security policy, including role-specific responsibilities. Mandatory security awareness training for all staff upon hiring.	All Tier 3 requirements, PLUS: Pre-employment background checks for all personnel with access to sensitive systems or funds, conducted by an approved third party. Annual security awareness refresher training.	All Tier 2 requirements, PLUS: Periodic background checks for personnel in critical roles. A formal insider threat management program, including monitoring and response procedures.

continued on following page

Table 1. Continued

Control Area (Relevant Model Law Section)	Tier 3 (Limited/Niche)	Tier 2 (Moderate Scale)	Tier 1 (Systemically Important)
Technology and Cybersecurity Framework (Sec. 48, 50)	Annual cybersecurity self-assessment against a regulator-approved framework. Documented due diligence process for all critical third-party service providers.	All Tier 3 requirements, PLUS: An independent, annual cybersecurity audit against a recognized international standard (e.g., ISO/IEC 27001:2022, CryptoCurrency Security Standard (CCSS)). Ongoing monitoring of the security posture of critical third parties.	All Tier 2 requirements, PLUS: A board-level risk committee with formally documented cybersecurity expertise. Proactive integration of threat intelligence feeds into the risk management framework. Periodic, independent red-teaming exercises to test defences against sophisticated, simulated attacks.
Monitoring and Incident Response (Sec. 49)	Documented Incident Response Plan.	All Tier 3 requirements, PLUS: 24/7 on-chain monitoring systems with automated alerting for anomalous activity (e.g., large, rapid outflows).	All Tier 2 requirements, PLUS: A dedicated Security Operations Centre (SOC), either in-house or outsourced, for continuous threat monitoring and response.

This tiered framework provides regulators with a defensible and consistent methodology for supervision. It clarifies and predicts regulatory expectations for issuers, allowing them to scale their stablecoin systems in line with their growth and systemic footprint. For example, it justifies why a Tier 1 issuer, whose failure could have broad financial repercussions, should be held to the highest standards of assurance, such as formal verification and dedicated SOCs, while a smaller Tier 3 issuer can meet its obligations with robust but less intensive controls like third-party audits and documented procedures. This approach fosters a healthier and more resilient stablecoin ecosystem by applying regulatory pressure where it is most needed, thereby promoting responsible innovation while diligently safeguarding market integrity and financial stability.

CONCLUSION: FROM PRINCIPLES TO PRACTICE

The Commonwealth Model Law on Stablecoins represents a landmark achievement in the global effort to create a coherent and future-proof regulatory framework for stablecoins. Its principle-based, technology-neutral approach provides the essential legal scaffolding to balance innovation with financial stability, consumer protection, and market integrity. The law correctly identifies the critical pillars of a safe and sound stablecoin arrangement: robust reserve management, transparent governance, clear redemption rights, and strong technological and cybersecurity foundations.

However, as this chapter has argued, the success of this framework will not be determined by the detailed coverage of the stablecoin arrangement, but by the rigour and technical sophistication of its implementation. The history of stablecoin failures, from the algorithmic collapse of Terra/Luna to the governance exploit of Beanstalk Farms, demonstrates unequivocally that in this domain, technological risk is closely tied to financial risk. A regulator who verifies an issuer's reserve asset attestations but lacks the capacity to assess the security of its smart contracts or the resilience of its oracle dependencies is only seeing half of the picture. They risk missing the very vulnerabilities that could lead to a catastrophic and instantaneous failure.

The analysis of the stablecoin technology layers, from the underlying blockchain to the smart contracts, oracles, and custody solutions, reveals a complex, deeply interconnected system where risks can cascade in unpredictable ways. The evolution of exploits from simple code bugs to sophisticated, multi-stage economic attacks underscores the dynamic nature of the threat landscape. This reality demands a shift in the practice of financial supervision. Regulators must move beyond traditional, paper-based compliance and cultivate in-depth technical and cybersecurity expertise within their organisations. This involves not only hiring staff with expertise in blockchain technology, smart contract auditing, and cryptography but also fostering a culture of continuous learning to keep pace with rapid innovation. Where in-house expertise is not feasible, regulators must establish robust frameworks for relying on and critically evaluating the work of trusted, expert third-party auditors and security firms.

The supervisory framework proposed in this chapter provides a practical pathway for implementing the Model Law's principles in practice. By adopting a tiered, risk-based approach, regulators can apply a rigorous audit methodology and require controls that are proportionate to the systemic importance of each stablecoin issuer. This ensures that systemically critical financial infrastructure is held to the highest standards of cybersecurity, including advanced techniques such as formal verification and comprehensive contagion risk modelling without stifling innovation from smaller, emerging projects.

Ultimately, the challenge and opportunity presented by stablecoins lie in bridging the gap between law and code. A proactive, technically informed, and adaptive supervisory approach is the essential ingredient for navigating this new frontier. By embracing this challenge, Commonwealth nations can leverage the Model Law to foster an environment of responsible innovation, building a digital financial future that is not only more efficient and inclusive but also fundamentally secure and resilient.

REFERENCES

Akartuna, A. (2022, April 19). $76 million stolen from Beanstalk Farms DeFi stablecoin protocol. *Elliptic*. https://www.elliptic.co/blog/76-million-stolen-from-beanstalk-farms-defi-stablecoin-protocol

Aramonte, S., Wenqiuan, H., & Schrimpf, A. (2021, December). DeFi risks and the decentralisation illusion. *Bank for International Settlements. Quarterly Review*. https://www.bis.org/publ/qtrpdf/r_qt2112b.pdf

Austin, A. Bank Policy Institute. (2025, September 19). *Banks urge SEC to apply proven safeguards to crypto custody rules*. Retrieved September 24, 2025, from https://bpi.com/banks-urge-sec-to-apply-proven-safeguards-to-crypto-custody-rules/

Basel Committee on Banking Supervision. (2024). *Novel risks, mitigants and uncertainties with permissionless distributed ledger technologies (Working Paper No. 44)*. Bank for International Settlements. https://www.bis.org/bcbs/publ/wp44.pdf

Behnkw, R. (2023, June 15). *A guide to formal verification of smart contracts*. Halborn. Retrieved September 26, 2025, from https://www.halborn.com/blog/post/a-guide-to-formal-verification-of-smart-contracts

Behnkw, R. (2025, September 8). *Multi-chain stablecoins: Security, risks and best practices*. Halborn. Retrieved September 10, 2025, from https://www.halborn.com/blog/post/multi-chain-stablecoins-security-risks-and-best-practices

Bitcoin.org. (n.d.). *Transactions*. Bitcoin Developer Guide. Retrieved September 25, 2025, from https://developer.bitcoin.org/devguide/transactions.html

Certi, K. (2022, July 28). *Revisiting Beanstalk Farms exploit*. Retrieved September 18, 2025, from https://www.certik.com/resources/blog/revisiting-beanstalk-farms-exploit

Certi, K. (2023, February 2). *What is formal verification in smart contract auditing?* Retrieved October 1, 2025, from https://www.certik.com/resources/blog/what-is-formal-verification

CoinGecko. (2024, April 15). *MPC wallets vs. multi-sig wallets: A deep dive*. Retrieved

Duley, C., Gambacorta, L., Garratt, R., & Wilkens, P. K. (2023, September 7). The oracle problem and the future of DeFi. *Bank for International Settlements Bulletin, No 76*. https://www.bis.org/publ/bisbull76.pdf

Eichholz, L. (2020, March 17. *What really happened to MakerDAO?* Glassnode Insights. https://insights.glassnode.com/what-really-happened-to-makerdao/

Elliptic. (2025, September 11). Stablecoin security risks in 2025: Full risk assessment guide. Retrieved September 23, 2025, from https://www.elliptic.co/blockchain-basics/stablecoin-2025-risk-assessment-guide

Evans, D. Fireblocks. (2024,). *MPC vs. multi-sig*. Retrieved September 19, 2025, from https://www.fireblocks.com/blog/mpc-vs-multi-sig/

Fraud.net. (n.d.). *Flash loan attacks definition*. Retrieved September 3, 2025, from https://www.fraud.net/glossary/flash-loan-attacks

Gate.com. (2024, July 10). *What is formal verification of smart contracts?* Retrieved September 30, 2025, from https://www.gate.com/learn/articles/what-is-formal-verification-of-smart-contracts/4291

Gate.com. (2025, October 1). *Types of blockchain oracle attacks, cases, and multi-layer defense strategies*. Retrieved September 5, 2025, from https://www.gate.com/learn/articles/types-of-blockchain-oracle-attacks-cases-and-multi-layer-defense-strategies/5498

Gorawska, A., & Swierzy, P. (2024). Decentralized oracle network for enhanced user authentication security. *Proceedings of the 57th Hawaii International Conference on System Sciences*. https://aisel.aisnet.org/cgi/viewcontent.cgi?article=1558&context=hicss-57

Howell, J. (2024, January 19). An overview of integer overflow attacks. *101 Blockchains*. Retrieved September 8, 2025, from https://101blockchains.com/integer-overflow-attacks/

Kaia Docs. (n.d.). *Best practices for smart contract security*. Retrieved September 10, 2025, from https://docs.kaia.io/build/smart-contracts/fundamentals/best-practices-for-smart-contract-security/

Kurovskiy, G., & Rostova, N. (2023, April 23). *How algorithmic stablecoins fail* [Conference presentation]. Swiss National Bank, Zurich, Switzerland. https://www.snb.ch/dam/jcr:5140cb30-3c8c-433d-8619-0354b8f1036e/sem_2023_05_26_rostova.n.pdf

Li, B., & Sugimoto, N. (2023, January 19). *Crypto contagion underscores why global regulators must act fast to stem risk*. International Monetary Fund Blog. https://www.imf.org/en/Blogs/Articles/2023/01/18/crypto-contagion-underscores-why-global-regulators-must-act-fast-to-stem-risk

Nethermind. (2024, November 18). Smart contract vulnerabilities and mitigation strategies. https://www.nethermind.io/blog/smart-contract-vulnerabilities-and-mitigation-strategies

Open Web Application Security Project. (n.d.-a). *Integer overflow and underflow*. OWASP Smart Contract Top 10. Retrieved September 10, 2025, from https://owasp.org/www-project-smart-contract-top-10/2023/en/src/SC02-integer-overflow-underflow.html

Open Web Application Security Project. (n.d.-b). *Reentrancy attacks*. OWASP Smart Contract Top 10. Retrieved September 16, 2025, from https://owasp.org/www-project-smart-contract-top-10/2025/en/src/SC05-reentrancy-attacks.html

Open Web Application Security Project. (n.d.-c). *Flash loan attacks*. OWASP Smart Contract Top 10. Retrieved September 10, 2025, from https://owasp.org/www-project-smart-contract-top-10/2025/en/src/SC07-flash-loan-attacks.html

Open Web Application Security Project. (n.d.-d). *OWASP Smart Contract Top 10*. Retrieved September 23, 2025, from https://owasp.org/www-project-smart-contract-top-10/

Pratap, Z. (2022, August 31). Reentrancy attacks and The DAO hack. *Chainlink*. Retrieved September 4, 2025, from https://blog.chain.link/reentrancy-attacks-and-the-dao-hack

September 8, 2025, from https://www.coingecko.com/learn/mpc-wallet-vs-multi-sig-wallets

Thales. (n.d.). *Hardware security modules (HSMs)*. Retrieved August 29, 2025, from https://cpl.thalesgroup.com/encryption/hardware-security-modules

The Commonwealth. (2025). *Model Law on Stablecoins*. Briola, A., Vidal-Tomás, D., Wang, Y., & Aste, T. (2023). Anatomy of a Stablecoin's failure: The Terra-Luna case. *Finance Research Letters, 51*, 103358.

Chapter 6
Financial Stability and Systemic Risks of Stablecoins

Harvesh Kumar Seegolam
Bank of Mauritius, Mauritius

Loretta Joseph
Mcdonell-Nadeau Consultants, Australia

ABSTRACT

Stablecoins represent a defining innovation in twenty-first-century finance. Their market capitalisation, which peaked above USD 180 billion in 2022, continues to hover around USD 150–160 billion. These instruments now sit at the intersection of technology, money, and systemic risk. While their adoption accelerates financial innovation and cross-border efficiency, their rapid growth introduces challenges analogous to those historically associated with unregulated money-market instruments and private banknotes. This chapter provides a comprehensive examination of the financial-stability implications of stablecoins, integrating the policy and legal logic embedded within the Commonwealth Model Law on Stablecoins (July 2025). It expands prior analyses by introducing explicit macroprudential stress-testing regimes, systemic-risk surveillance, and potential central-bank liquidity arrangements to ensure complete conceptual convergence between economic assessment and legislative design (Financial Stability Board, 2023).

DOI: 10.4018/979-8-3373-6655-5.ch006

INTRODUCTION

Stablecoins—digital tokens designed to maintain stable value, often pegged to sovereign currencies—have rapidly grown from niche instruments into a significant segment of the financial system. Global stablecoin market capitalization, once negligible, surged past $180 billion in early 2022 before retrenching to roughly $130–160 billion in 2024. This expansion has elevated stablecoins from peripheral curiosities to potentially systemically important elements of the crypto-financial ecosystem. Their appeal lies in combining the speed and programmability of crypto-assets with the assured value of fiat money. Stablecoins promise more efficient payments (especially cross-border transfers) and greater financial inclusion. Yet, as this chapter details, they also pose significant financial stability risks and policy challenges. These risks crystallized dramatically in recent years—notably in the Terra/Luna collapse of 2022, which erased tens of billions of dollars in value virtually overnight and sent shockwaves through crypto markets. Policymakers worldwide have responded with heightened scrutiny, regulatory proposals, and calls for comprehensive oversight of stablecoin arrangements.

This chapter provides an in-depth analysis of the financial stability implications of stablecoins, written from the perspective of a seasoned central banker. It begins by surveying the evolving stablecoin landscape—tracing their growth, changing composition, and increasing integration with traditional finance. It then examines the myriad risks to financial stability, including run and liquidity risks, reserve asset contagion, operational vulnerabilities, and the potential for risk transmission between the crypto sector and traditional financial markets. Detailed case studies—including Terra/Luna's failure and other episodes—illustrate how stablecoin failures can propagate distress. A comparative analysis contrasts the systemic risk profiles of private stablecoins with those of Central Bank Digital Currencies (CBDCs) (both retail and wholesale), highlighting the different risk dynamics of public versus private digital money.

The chapter also addresses regulatory responses and challenges. Thus far, regulatory approaches have been fragmented across jurisdictions, raising concerns about arbitrage, monetary sovereignty, and gaps in oversight. International bodies such as the Financial Stability Board (FSB), Bank for International Settlements (BIS), and International Monetary Fund (IMF) have underscored the need for globally coordinated frameworks. Emerging standards—from the FSB's high-level recommendations on "global stablecoins" to new laws like the EU's MiCA—seek to mitigate risks while allowing innovation. However, achieving consistency across borders remains difficult, especially amid divergent views (for example, the United States' market-driven stance favoring regulated dollar stablecoins versus Europe's emphasis on a public CBDC solution).

In conclusion, the chapter offers forward-looking policy recommendations. These include ensuring robust reserve management and transparency, instituting bank-like or money-market-like safeguards for major stablecoin issuers, and exploring mechanisms (such as access to central bank balance sheets or deposit insurance structures) to backstop stablecoin stability. The recommendations stress balancing innovation with stability—recognizing stablecoins' potential benefits in payments and inclusion but insisting that appropriate guardrails and oversight are non-negotiable to prevent destabilizing runs or loss of monetary control. Continued research, international dialogue, and adaptive regulation will be crucial as technology and markets evolve. Ultimately, the goal is a coherent approach that harnesses useful financial innovations while preserving trust in money and stability in the global financial system.

BACKGROUND

The rise of stablecoins represents a new frontier in the age-old interplay between public money and private innovation. Stablecoins are typically defined as crypto-assets designed to maintain a stable value relative to a reference asset (most commonly a fiat currency such as the U.S. dollar) (Financial Stability Board, 2020). By marrying the digital, borderless nature of cryptocurrencies with the stability of trusted fiat units, stablecoins have quickly become pivotal bridging instruments between the traditional financial world and the nascent digital asset economy. As of 2024, the stablecoin universe encompasses a variety of designs—from fiat-collateralized tokens like Tether (USDT) and USD Coin (USDC) that hold reserves in bank deposits and high-quality securities to crypto-collateralized and algorithmic stablecoins that attempt to maintain pegs through other mechanisms (Kosse et al., 2023). Market adoption has been striking: after a meteoric 30-fold increase during 2020–2021, stablecoin issuance peaked around $180+ billion in early 2022 (CoinGecko, 2024) before stabilizing in the $120–160 billion range by mid-2024 (CoinGecko, 2024) Today stablecoins form the lubricant of the crypto markets – used as a unit of account and store of value in decentralized finance, as a vehicle for crypto trading, and as a payment medium in some remittance and e-commerce networks.

This rapid growth, however, comes with significant concerns. Stablecoins have effectively introduced a parallel form of *private money* that, at scale, could replicate functions traditionally served by commercial bank deposits or even cash. Historically, private monies (from wildcat banknotes to money market fund shares) have been prone to crises of confidence and runs, absent robust safeguards. Policymakers see echoes of these historical risks in today's stablecoins. A widely adopted stablecoin (especially one not subject to prudential regulation) could become systemically important, meaning a sudden loss of confidence or failure of the coin's stabilizing mechanism might destabilize markets or institutions. The implosion of TerraUSD in May 2022 underscored these dangers: what was touted as a "stable" algorithmic currency collapsed to near-zero, inflicting heavy losses on investors and triggering broader contagion in crypto markets. While the fallout was largely contained to the crypto sector, it served as a cautionary tale—had such an event occurred with a larger, more entwined stablecoin, the shock could have transmitted to the real economy (CoinGecko, 2024).

Central bankers and regulators are therefore examining stablecoins through the lens of financial stability and systemic risk. Key questions have arisen: Could stablecoin runs force fire sales of reserve assets, disrupting bond or funding markets? Might stablecoins facilitate "digital dollarization" in emerging economies, undermining local monetary control? Are banks or payment systems becoming indirectly exposed to stablecoin-related volatility? And how do stablecoins compare to potential CBDCs, which are public sector alternatives to digital currency provision? The answers are being actively researched, even as regulatory bodies begin to craft rules. The Financial Stability Board warned in early 2022 that fast-evolving crypto-asset markets—including stablecoins – *"could reach a point where they represent a threat to global financial stability"* if their scale and links to the core financial system continue to grow (Financial Stability Board, 2020). In 2023, after extensive consultation, the FSB issued updated high-level recommendations to guide jurisdictions in regulating and supervising stablecoins, particularly those with potential global reach (Financial Stability Board, 2020). Likewise, the BIS has critically evaluated stablecoins against fundamental principles of sound money and found them wanting in several respects.

This chapter proceeds to explore these issues systematically. We first map out the current stablecoin landscape – its size, composition, and integration with traditional finance – setting the stage with data on how 2024–2025 has continued to evolve from the tumultuous events of 2022. We then delve into the core financial stability risks, breaking down the mechanisms by which stablecoin distress could transmit to the broader system. Real-world episodes are analyzed to ground the discussion: the Terra/Luna collapse and its cascading effects in crypto markets; the near-miss of USDC's temporary de-peg during the 2023 U.S. banking scare; and the saga of Facebook's Libra (Diem), which prompted a global regulatory backlash even before launch. The comparative section on stablecoins versus CBDCs evaluates how the risk profile of a well-designed central bank digital currency might differ from (or mitigate) the risks of stablecoins, including issues of bank disintermediation and credit risk. We then assess the regulatory landscape – highlighting the current patchwork of national approaches, concerns about regulatory fragmentation and sovereignty, and efforts to build a coherent international framework for stablecoins. Finally, we offer policy recommendations aimed at safeguarding stability while allowing beneficial innovation. In doing so, we emphasize the need for ongoing vigilance: stablecoins sit at the intersection of technology and finance, a space that is rapidly evolving. A proactive yet flexible regulatory posture will be essential to navigate the promise and peril of this new form of digital private money.

KEY ISSUES AND QUESTIONS

Growth, Market Size, and Composition

From humble beginnings less than a decade ago, stablecoins have become a cornerstone of the crypto economy and an increasingly discussed element of global finance. In the mid-2010s, only a handful of stablecoins existed (Tether's USDT being the pioneer, launched in 2014). They remained relatively obscure until the late 2017–2018 crypto boom, when demand for a digital dollar substitute spiked. Since then, the growth has been exponential. As noted, the total market capitalization of stablecoins ballooned from roughly $5 billion at the start of 2020 to a peak of about $182 billion in March 2022 (CoinGecko, 2024). This coincided with a broad crypto-market bull run and the rise of decentralized finance (DeFi), which heavily relies on stable-valued tokens for trading, lending, and yield farming. The TerraUSD (UST) algorithmic stablecoin contributed significantly to that growth in late 2021 – early 2022, temporarily becoming the third-largest stablecoin and driving stablecoins' share of total crypto market value up to 15% by April 2022 (CoinGecko, 2024).

However, 2022 proved to be a volatile year. In May, TerraUSD's collapse erased roughly $45 billion in combined market value of UST and its sister token LUNA within a week. This event punctured the narrative that all stablecoins can maintain stability, and precipitated a contraction in the overall stablecoin market. By mid-2022, stablecoin capitalization had fallen by over 20% from its peak (Kosse *et al.*, 2023, p.5), as investors retreated to the most established fiat-backed stablecoins or cashed out to fiat. The bankruptcy of crypto exchange FTX in November 2022 further dented confidence, though its direct impact on stablecoins was less severe than Terra's failure (Kosse et al., 2023). By the end of 2022, the market stabilized with fiat-collateralized stalwarts – Tether (USDT) and USD Coin (USDC) – commanding the lion's share. Indeed, the top three dollar-pegged coins (USDT, USDC, and Binance USD) came to account for over 90% of the stablecoin market by late 2022 (Kosse et al., 2023), a concentration that increased after weaker players and algorithmic designs fell by the wayside.

In 2023 and 2024, the trajectory turned modestly positive again. As crypto markets partially recovered and new entrants emerged, stablecoin usage grew, albeit at a slower, more mature pace. By August 2024, fiat-backed stablecoins' market cap had rebounded to about $161 billion, regaining some ground from a trough of roughly $119 billion after the Terra crash (CoinGecko, 2024). This remained below the 2022 peak, indicating a more cautious environment. Tether (USDT) strengthened its dominance – rising to about 70% of total stablecoin value by 2024, with a circulation exceeding $110 billion (CoinGecko, 2024). USDT's resiliency (despite past controversies about its reserves) and perhaps its offshore, less-regulated status allowed it to absorb demand as others retrenched. USD Coin (USDC), issued by Circle and known for its transparency and U.S. regulatory compliance, peaked around $50+ billion in early 2022 but then saw a decline to roughly $25–30 billion by late 2023. USDC's market share fell partly due to a March 2023 loss of confidence (addressed later) and also a general shrinking of crypto trading activity (CoinGecko, 2024). DAI, the largest crypto-collateralized stablecoin (from MakerDAO), oscillated in supply and stood near $5 billion in 2024 (CoinGecko, 2024) – notable as a decentralized alternative, though in practice DAI became heavily backed by USDC itself, blurring the lines between fiat-backed and crypto-backed. Other players include Binance USD (BUSD), which was significant (~$20B at its height) but entered a forced wind-down in 2023 after regulatory action against its issuer; algorithmic stablecoins beyond Terra, such as Tron's USDD or various smaller experiments, which have struggled to gain trust post-Terra; and a growing array of asset-backed stablecoins for other currencies or commodities (e.g., euro-backed stablecoins like EURt or precious-metal tokens). These non-USD stablecoins remain a tiny fraction (under 1%) of the market (CoinGecko, 2024), underscoring that the stablecoin phenomenon is primarily a dollar-based one.

Importantly, stablecoins are now an integral part of the crypto-market infrastructure. They consistently represent a significant portion of crypto trading volume, often *the* highest volume assets on exchanges, as traders treat them as on-chain cash. In early 2023, for example, it was common for USDT or USDC trading pairs to dominate volumes, effectively serving as the quote currency for crypto asset prices. Moreover, stablecoins have become the backbone of DeFi protocols – used for borrowing, lending, and as collateral. The adoption is not limited to crypto-native circles: 8.7 million blockchain addresses held stablecoins as of 2024, a figure which, while not directly equal to users, indicates a broad base of holders; of these, the vast majority hold one of the top three USD stablecoins (USDT, USDC, or DAI) (CoinGecko, 2024). This reach, combined with stablecoins' role as a bridge between fiat and crypto, means their stability and integrity are of paramount importance. A breakdown of a major stablecoin could not only wipe out holders' wealth but also freeze large swathes of crypto-market liquidity and disrupt businesses that rely on stablecoins for payments.

Use Cases and Integration With Traditional Finance

Initially conceived to facilitate trading on crypto exchanges, stablecoins have steadily expanded into broader use cases. These include:

- **Crypto Trading and Investment:** This remains the primary use of stablecoins. By providing a stable "parking place" between volatile crypto trades, stablecoins enable investors to stay in the crypto ecosystem without converting back to fiat. They also serve as collateral for derivative products and margin lending, meaning any instability in a major stablecoin can quickly reverberate through leveraged positions.
- **Decentralized Finance (DeFi):** Many DeFi lending platforms (e.g., Aave, Compound) and decentralized exchanges use stablecoins as core liquidity. Users lend stablecoins to earn yield or borrow them against crypto collateral. The promised stability of value is crucial for these financial contracts to function as intended. When Terra's UST was flying high, it was deeply embedded in a DeFi lending protocol (Anchor), which offered extremely high yields on UST deposits – a fact that turbocharged Terra's growth but also its collapse (Azar et al., 2022).
- **Payments and Remittances:** An increasing number of payment arrangements use stablecoins to transfer value, especially across borders. For instance, USD stablecoins are used by individuals in emerging markets to send money internationally at a lower cost than traditional remittance channels. Some merchants and payroll providers in the digital economy have begun accepting payment in USDC or USDT, settling invoices or salaries in stablecoins. The appeal is 24/7, near-instant settlement, and bypassing of costly correspondent banking rails. There is evidence of stablecoin use in corridors where local currency is unstable – effectively a form of dollarization via technology. In countries with high inflation or strict capital controls, residents have turned to dollar-linked stablecoins as a store of value or to move funds, which raises policy concerns (discussed later).
- **Integration with Banks and Payment Networks:** A notable trend in 2022–2025 is the closer integration of stablecoins with traditional financial institutions. Several developments exemplify this convergence:
    - o Major payment networks have started to experiment with stablecoin settlements. For example, Visa and Mastercard announced pilot programs to settle transactions in USD Coin on blockchain networks, signaling a bridge between card networks and stablecoin infrastructure.
    - o Some FinTech and Big Tech firms have launched or explored their own stablecoins. A prominent case is PayPal's USD stablecoin (PYUSD),

launched in 2023, which is fully backed by dollar deposits and equivalents and intended for use within PayPal's ecosystem and beyond. This move by a global payments company underscores the perceived demand for stable digital cash and has the potential to significantly increase stablecoin usage among mainstream users if it gains traction.

- Traditional financial institutions have also shown interest in issuing or using stablecoins. Several U.S. banks (earlier Silvergate and Signature, and now others on a limited basis) provided settlement networks for stablecoin issuers, holding their reserves and processing large redemption flows. In 2021, a consortium of U.S. banks even announced plans for a jointly issued stablecoin (USDF) under a regulatory umbrella, though progress has been slow. Meanwhile, JPMorgan's JPM Coin, though not public, is an example of a bank-issued digital token for internal wholesale settlement, akin to a stablecoin for institutional clients.
- Money market funds have indirect connections to stablecoins: for instance, Circle's USDC reserves are partly managed in a dedicated short-term government bond fund. Thus, shifts in USDC supply led to flows into or out of traditional money markets. This raises the question of whether a run on a stablecoin could cause a run on the money market fund that holds its assets, or vice versa. So far, these funds are extremely liquid and conservative, but the link is being watched by regulators.
- Bank deposits vs. Stablecoins: Some users and businesses now face a choice between holding funds in a bank account (earning interest, protected by insurance up to a limit, but with regulated access) versus holding in stablecoins (earning yield in DeFi or at crypto platforms, usable globally 24/7, but without formal insurance or lender-of-last-resort support). The allure of stablecoins for higher yield and flexibility has to be weighed against their higher risk. Nonetheless, this competition has not gone unnoticed by bankers, who worry about disintermediation – a scenario where substantial deposits shift into stablecoins, depriving banks of funding.

The integration is a two-way street: crypto-native firms have one foot in traditional finance (holding reserves in bank accounts, treasury bills, etc.), and traditional firms are dipping their toes into blockchain-based money. This creates interlinkages that form potential channels for contagion. A disruption in stablecoins could affect the balance sheets of the banks holding their reserves; conversely, distress in a bank can affect a stablecoin, as vividly demonstrated in March 2023 when the failure of Silicon Valley Bank (SVB) temporarily broke USD Coin's 1:1 peg.

Case in point: Circle, issuer of USDC, held a portion of its cash reserves (about $3.3 billion) at SVB. When SVB suddenly collapsed, that cash was temporarily inaccessible, raising doubts about USDC's redeemability. Over a panicked weekend, USDC holders rushed to sell, driving USDC's market price down to ~$0.87 at the low (Helmore, 2023). This "depeg" was reversed only after U.S. authorities intervened to guarantee SVB's deposits, reassuring USDC holders that reserves were safe. The episode highlighted how a traditional banking shock transmitted instantaneously into the stablecoin realm, causing crypto-market turmoil, though fortunately, *"concerns about contagion to other areas of the financial system appeared limited"* once the intervention calmed markets (Helmore, 2023). In essence, a stablecoin, which was considered one of the safest (fully reserved in cash and treasuries), was knocked off course by a banking event – underscoring that stablecoins are *only as stable as their backing and the institutions holding that backing*. It also underscored why regulators worry about stablecoin issuers' reliance on a small set of banks and the need for robust liquidity management.

In summary, the stablecoin landscape as of 2025 is one of growing prominence and entanglement with mainstream finance. Stablecoins have proven their product-market fit in crypto trading and are expanding into payment use cases, with support or interest from major players in the financial industry. This diffusion into everyday financial plumbing means that the risks stablecoins carry can no longer be viewed as contained to a fringe community. The subsequent sections explore those risks in detail – how they might materialize and transmit, and why they matter for financial stability at large.

Risks to Financial Stability and Risk Transmission Mechanisms

While stablecoins aim to import stability into the volatile crypto world, they also import well-known financial risks into the digital realm. In many respects, the risks of stablecoins resemble those of traditional financial intermediaries (banks, money market funds, and payment systems), but they are potentially amplified by technology, opacity, and the global, instantaneous reach of crypto networks. A crucial difference is that most stablecoins operate outside the full scope of bank-like regulation and safety nets, making them more fragile when confidence erodes. Here we break down the key risk categories and how distress in stablecoins could transmit to the wider financial system.

Run Risk and Liquidity Crises

The foremost risk of stablecoins is the classic risk of a "run"—a sudden loss of confidence leading holders to redeem en masse, analogous to a bank run. If users doubt that a stablecoin can hold its peg (e.g., due to questions about the issuer's reserves or solvency), each has an incentive to be among the first to exit, redeeming their tokens for the underlying assets or swapping into other stablecoins or fiat. This dynamic can turn a small disturbance into a self-fulfilling crisis of redemption.

- For fully reserve-backed stablecoins (fiat-collateralized): A run would force the issuer to liquidate reserve assets rapidly to honor redemptions. If reserves are held in highly liquid forms (cash, overnight reverse repos, short-term Treasuries), an orderly wind-down is possible in theory. However, under stress, even high-quality assets might need to be sold at a discount (especially if redemptions occur faster than the assets mature). In extreme cases, if the reserve assets include anything less liquid or risk-free—e.g., longer-term bonds, corporate debt, or loans—a fire sale could ensue, potentially transmitting stress to those asset markets. The BIS and central banks have cautioned that large-scale redemptions of stablecoins could entail *"the tail risk of fire sales of safe assets,"* such as government bonds, if reserve holdings are liquidated abruptly. This is a direct channel to traditional markets: a forced sale of, say, tens of billions in U.S. Treasury bills by a stablecoin issuer under duress could spike yields and reduce market liquidity, analogous to runs on money market funds in 2008 or March 2020.
- For partially or opaquely backed stablecoins, if there is uncertainty about the quality or quantity of reserves, runs are even more likely. Tether (USDT), for instance, in the past faced periods of doubt regarding its holdings of commercial paper and other assets. Though it has not broken the peg significantly in recent years, the risk remains that if a major holder or the market loses trust, USDT could see rapid outflows, and its ability to maintain parity would hinge on its reserve liquidity. The less transparent the issuer, the more quickly trust can evaporate.
- For algorithmic or crypto-collateralized stablecoins: These are even more vulnerable. As the IMF observed, *"algorithmic stablecoins...are extremely risky. They are susceptible to de-pegging in the event of a large shock that becomes self-perpetuating once it starts, as the TerraUSD experience shows."* Without a concrete reserve pool, these designs rely on market arbitrage and/or faith in a supporting asset. TerraUSD maintained its peg through arbitrage with LUNA; once confidence in that mechanism broke, there was nothing to stop a run, and indeed bank-like runs by users caused its collapse. Terra's case illustrates how an algorithmic stablecoin can go into a death spiral: falling price leads to users rushing to redeem (minting huge amounts of the volatile reserve token), which further crashes the reserve token's price, making redemptions worth less and prompting even more redemption attempts.

Within days, TerraUSD went from $1 to a few cents. Contagion within crypto was severe – other algorithmic coins lost value, and even the prices of major crypto assets fell amid forced selling and loss of confidence (Kosse et al., 2023).

It is worth noting that even ostensibly fully backed stablecoins may impose gates, fees, or limits on redemption in stress scenarios (similar to how money market funds can impose liquidity fees or redemption gates). Contracts often allow issuers to pause redemptions or only process a certain amount per period. Such measures can slow a run but can also panic investors further. So far, major stablecoins have generally honored redemptions promptly (Circle, during the SVB incident, for example, processed large outflows once banking resumed). But the potential for illiquidity or suspension is a risk factor.

Credit and Counterparty Risk

Stablecoin holders effectively take on the credit risk of the issuer and its reserve custodians. If a stablecoin's reserves are insufficient due to losses or mismanagement, holders may not be made whole. This risk can arise from several sources:

- **Reserve Asset Risk**: A stablecoin's assets could lose value. For fiat-backed coins, this could happen if they hold interest-bearing instruments that default or drop in market value. For example, an issuer holding corporate paper or extending loans to generate yield could face defaults. Even government securities have interest rate risk—if forced to sell before maturity during a rate spike, the issuer might incur losses. Traditionally, banks and money funds manage such risks with capital buffers or regulations (e.g., restricting investments to very safe assets), but stablecoin issuers until recently had few such constraints beyond their own policies.
- **Issuer Default or Fraud**: Users rely on the issuer's promise that 1 stablecoin = $1 in reserve. If an issuer were to misappropriate reserves, suffer an operational hack, or become insolvent (e.g., due to unrelated activities on its balance sheet), stablecoin holders would be unsecured creditors in bankruptcy. This is a legal and operational risk—for instance, if reserves are commingled or pledged elsewhere. The regulatory void in some jurisdictions means there is no deposit insurance or guaranteed protection for stablecoin holders. Some proposed laws aim to treat stablecoins similarly to bank deposits or e-money, which would impose fiduciary duties and ring-fencing of reserves.
- **Custodial and Banking Risk**: Stablecoin issuers typically rely on banks and other institutions to hold reserve assets. This introduces a counterparty risk –

if the bank fails or assets are seized/frozen, the stablecoin may be impaired. The USDC-SVB incident demonstrated this tangibly (Helmore, 2023). Another example: if a significant portion of Tether's reserves were held in a particular institution or sovereign instruments that default, USDT could be under-collateralized. Additionally, regulatory actions can freeze reserves: in 2021, reserve accounts of certain stablecoins were reportedly closed by banks under regulatory pressure, although issuers managed to move funds elsewhere. Such disruptions could affect redemption capacity in the short term.

- **Interconnectedness with Traditional Finance**: As stablecoin issuers invest in traditional instruments (like money market funds and treasury bills), they become part of the broader credit network. A large stablecoin issuer could be a significant participant in short-term funding markets. If it suddenly withdraws funds (during a contraction in stablecoin supply), it could tighten conditions in those markets. Conversely, if it suddenly has to raise liquidity, it might borrow or sell assets, affecting interest rates. These linkages mean stablecoin issuers could themselves become systemically important financial institutions (SIFIs) if their scale grows, warranting the kind of oversight applied to large banks or clearinghouses.

Market and Concentration Risks

The stablecoin ecosystem also presents certain structural market risks:

- **Concentration of Players**: The dominance of a few issuers (with Tether and Circle together representing a majority of value) means the failure of any single large stablecoin could have systemic repercussions. If, for example, Tether—the largest stablecoin – were to fail to maintain its peg, the trust in all stablecoins could be shaken, leading to sector-wide runs. Moreover, many crypto trading and lending arrangements might unravel (since USDT is widely used as collateral and quote currency). The knock-on effect could be comparable to the failure of a major bank in a traditional system. Currently, no stablecoin issuer is officially designated as a SIFI globally, but their scale in the crypto market suggests they are *crypto*-systemically important and potentially important to real markets via reserve linkages.
- **Fire-sale of Reserve Assets**: As mentioned, concentrated selling of reserve holdings is a key transmission mechanism. Notably, a recent BIS study found that flows in and out of dollar-backed stablecoins had measurable effects on short-term U.S. Treasury yields, indicating that arbitrage and reserve adjustments by issuers were moving markets (BIS Annual Economic Report,

2025). In times of stress, this could be magnified. For instance, if multiple stablecoins faced redemptions concurrently (say, due to a regulatory shock affecting trust in all stablecoins), they might collectively dump assets, which could disrupt short-term funding markets or bond markets. This is analogous to what happens when money market funds face redemptions (as in 2008), necessitating central bank interventions to stabilize the commercial paper and T-bill markets. Stablecoins are, in effect, becoming a new class of shadow bank or money fund, but one that operates largely outside the regulated perimeter so far.

- **Volatility and Wealth Effects**: Although stablecoins themselves are meant not to fluctuate, if one breaks its peg or collapses, holders incur losses. Given that a large portion of stablecoins is held by crypto investors, the immediate wealth effect of a stablecoin collapse may mostly concern that domain. However, as crypto becomes more intertwined with portfolios (retail and institutional), sharp losses can dampen investor confidence broadly. The FSB has noted that wealth effects and confidence channels are one-way; crypto market turmoil could spill over (Financial Stability Board, 2020). A stablecoin collapse could, for example, hurt the balance sheets of crypto companies (exchanges, funds) that hold it, potentially pushing some into insolvency and causing losses for their creditors or clients in traditional finance.
- **Operational and Technological Risk**: Stablecoins rely on underlying blockchain infrastructure (typically public blockchains like Ethereum, Tron, etc., or in some cases proprietary ledgers). Outages, hacks, or forks on these networks could freeze or misdirect stablecoin transactions. We have seen instances where certain blockchain bridges or smart contracts related to stablecoins were exploited, though major stablecoins have so far avoided any fundamental tech failure. A significant risk is cybersecurity – an attacker who gains the keys or control to a stablecoin issuer's treasury wallet could theoretically mint or steal large amounts of coins, destabilizing the system. Similarly, if the blockchain that a stablecoin primarily uses were to suffer a prolonged outage or attack, the stablecoin's usability could be impaired, causing panic. While these are more technical risks, they contribute to systemic risk if they trigger loss of confidence or inability to use the stablecoin when needed (especially in a crisis scenario when liquidity is paramount).

Confidence and Monetary System Concerns

Beyond immediate financial market risks, stablecoins pose more diffuse but profound risks to monetary stability and integrity:

- **Undermining Monetary Sovereignty**: In countries with unstable currencies or weak banking sectors, citizens might gravitate towards stablecoins denominated in a major foreign currency (typically USD). The IMF has warned of the risk of "cryptoization" – effectively, digital dollarization via stablecoins that bypass the official financial system. Unlike traditional dollarization, which might be constrained by access to physical cash or foreign bank accounts, stablecoins offer a borderless, electronic avenue to hold dollars. If a large share of deposits or transactions in an economy migrated to dollar stablecoins, the central bank could lose control over money supply and credit conditions, hampering monetary policy transmission. Moreover, such usage often evades capital flow management rules, potentially increasing volatility of capital in/outflows. From a sovereignty perspective, widespread adoption of a foreign-currency stablecoin (especially one issued by an entity outside the jurisdiction) raises difficult questions: the country in effect imports another's monetary policy and depends on the stability of a privately managed coin. Emerging markets and developing economies (EMDEs) are particularly concerned; some have already seen uptake of USDT/USDC for saving and commerce under high inflation. The FSB in 2023 examined stablecoin use in EMDEs and noted the need to address these cross-border stability risks (Financial Stability Board, 2020).
- **Fragmentation of the Monetary System and "Singleness of Money"**: Central bankers stress the importance of the singleness of money – the idea that money in an economy is uniform and interchangeable (bank deposits, cash, central bank reserves all convert 1:1 at par) (Kosse et al., 2023). Stablecoins potentially fragment this if different coins trade at different values or carry different credit risks. Indeed, at times, stablecoins have traded away from par with each other (e.g., USDT vs USDC at slight deviations). The BIS argues stablecoins "lack the settlement finality and guarantee of par exchange provided by central bank money", resulting in an inferior form of money that could circulate but not command universal trust (Kosse et al., 2023). In extreme cases, a stablecoin could introduce a "two-tier" monetary system where some transactions occur in this private token at perhaps a discount to official money. That undermines the unity of the currency and could create confusion or loss of confidence in the monetary unit if not managed.
- **Illicit Finance and Operational Integrity**: Without proper oversight, stablecoins can be used for illicit activities (money laundering, sanctions evasion, fraud) given their pseudonymous, cross-border nature. This is a concern for financial integrity, and large-scale illicit use could have knock-on stability implications (e.g., if sanctions lead to freezes of stablecoin assets or networks). Additionally, stablecoin arrangements often concentrate opera-

tional control in an issuer or governance body, which might have the power to freeze addresses or alter rules. This centralization, paradoxically, introduces points of operational failure or misuse. For example, an issuer might face legal orders to blacklist certain addresses (which has happened for USDT and USDC in certain cases involving hacks or criminal investigations). Such actions, while often justified, break the fungibility of the coin to some extent and could cause user panic if done unpredictably.

Risk Transmission to Traditional Finance

Bringing these threads together, how could a stablecoin problem become a broader financial stability problem? We outline a plausible transmission sequence:

1. **Shock to Stablecoin Confidence**: This could be triggered by news of reserve inadequacy, a large hack, a ban by regulators, or an external shock (like a related bank failure). Suppose a top stablecoin loses trust.
2. Runs and Redemption Pressure: Holders rush to redeem or sell the stablecoin. Its market price falls below par on exchanges. Arbitrageurs might attempt redemptions if possible, draining reserves.
3. **Asset Liquidation and Market Impact**: The issuer liquidates reserve assets to meet redemptions. If the amounts are large, this puts pressure on those asset markets (e.g., selling Treasury bills en masse drives prices down/yields up). Fire-sale dynamics may emerge (Azar et al., 2022). Other investors in those markets react to the volatility, possibly pulling back, which could reduce market liquidity further. If multiple stablecoins or funds hold similar assets, there could be a broader sell-off (analogous to how troubles at one money market fund in 2008 led investors to withdraw from others, forcing them to sell assets).
4. **Contagion to Crypto Markets and Investors**: Within the crypto ecosystem, the stablecoin's collapse causes major losses. Crypto asset prices may fall as confidence drops and as automated liquidations occur (many loans in DeFi use stablecoins; if their value swings, loans can default or be liquidated, causing further asset sales). Crypto firms holding the stablecoin (exchanges, hedge funds) may suffer hits to their balance sheet. Some may become insolvent, which is what happened after Terra–hedge fund Three Arrows Capital failed and took several brokers/lenders down with it (Azar *et al.,* 2022). While such crypto-sector failures might be insulated from traditional finance in 2022, by 2025, more traditional players (venture funds, even banks or payment companies) will have some exposure to crypto ventures. Losses could propagate to them – e.g., a venture fund might face losses that affect its investors, some of whom could be pension funds or banks.

5. **Banking System Linkages**: If the stablecoin issuer's reserve accounts are large relative to a bank's size, rapid outflows could stress that bank's liquidity. For example, when investors redeem a stablecoin, money might be pulled out from the issuer's account at a commercial bank to send to the redeemer. If that bank is mid-sized and stablecoin reserves form a big chunk of its deposits, this could create strain. This scenario is not far-fetched – Circle kept significant deposits at a few U.S. banks; Signature Bank and Silvergate Bank were heavily involved in crypto, and in fact, collapsed in 2023, partly due to crypto deposit flight and concentration risk (Azar *et al.,* 2022). Even larger banks could feel a pinch if redemptions are huge (tens of billions in a day) – they may need to scramble for cash or rely on central bank facilities if available. In the extreme, if stablecoins became widespread as a store of value, a run on stablecoins is akin to a shadow banking run that could have macroeconomic effects, prompting central banks to consider interventions.
6. **Payment System Disruption**: If businesses and individuals have started using a particular stablecoin for transactions and suddenly it fails, there could be short-term payment disruptions. Imagine remittances or e-commerce transactions that get stuck or lose value. Confidence in digital payment solutions could be dented, potentially pushing users back to less efficient channels in panic, causing operational bottlenecks.
7. **Monetary Policy and Interest Rates**: If stablecoin usage is large, shifts between stablecoins and bank deposits could affect bank funding. For instance, a movement out of deposits into stablecoins (during times of crypto optimism) could force banks to raise deposit rates or other funding costs, marginally influencing credit conditions. Conversely, a panic out of stablecoins back into bank deposits or cash (during a stablecoin scare) could briefly flood banks with liquidity. While these effects are secondary, they could complicate monetary policy implementation at the margin. Central banks may need to monitor such flows if they grow in scale.

It's important to note that as of late 2024, most authorities (IMF, FSB) assess that crypto-asset markets' direct risks to global financial stability have been limited, mainly because traditional financial institutions' exposure to crypto is relatively small and contained. However, they consistently caution that this could change if crypto (and stablecoins in particular) continue to grow and intertwine with core markets (Financial Stability Board, 2020). The tail risk – however seemingly low-probability – of an unregulated stablecoin of massive scale failing is something regulators aim to head off before it materializes.

In sum, stablecoins compress a combination of liquidity risk, credit risk, and operational risk into new digital wrappers. They illustrate how old vulnerabilities morph into new forms: a run is a run, whether on a 19th-century bank or a 21st-century stablecoin – the difference is that a stablecoin run can happen at internet speed and globally. The next sections explore how these risks have played out in real cases, and how the advent of CBDCs could offer a different risk paradigm.

Case Studies: Lessons From Recent Stablecoin Episodes

To ground the analysis of risks, we turn to several key episodes and scenarios involving stablecoins. These case studies shed light on failure modes, market responses, and regulatory reactions in practice.

Terra/Luna Collapse (2022): The Demise of an Algorithmic Stablecoin

One of the most dramatic events in crypto history was the collapse of the TerraUSD (UST) stablecoin and its sister token LUNA in May 2022. TerraUSD was an *algorithmic stablecoin* that relied on a mint-and-burn arbitrage mechanism with LUNA (a float-valued asset) to maintain its $1 peg, rather than holding fiat reserves. At its peak, TerraUSD had a market capitalization of around $18 billion, making it the third-largest stablecoin at the time (Azar *et al.*, 2022). It grew rapidly by attracting users with the Anchor protocol, a DeFi lending platform on the Terra blockchain that offered near-20% yields on UST deposits – an unsustainably high rate that nonetheless drew in huge sums (Azar et al., 2022).

The collapse unfolded within days. In early May 2022, large UST withdrawals and selling pressure led the stablecoin to break its peg, dropping below $0.99 and then precipitously to 70 cents by May 9 (Azar et al., 2022). This sparked a classic run dynamic: UST holders rushed for the exits, each trying to redeem UST for $1 worth of new LUNA tokens (as per the protocol design). The sudden redemption wave caused an enormous increase in LUNA supply, crashing LUNA's price (it plunged from $80+ to nearly zero in a week). As LUNA's value evaporated, the theoretical backing for UST vanished – a death spiral. Within roughly one week, UST was virtually worthless (trading at a few cents) and LUNA's market cap had fallen by over $40 billion. The Terra blockchain was halted twice amid the chaos, and confidence in algorithmic stablecoins was shattered.

Financial stability and contagion effects: Terra's failure, though confined to the crypto sector, had far-reaching consequences there. Over $60 billion in combined market value of UST and LUNA was obliterated (Azar et al., 2022), inflicting heavy losses on investors ranging from retail users to crypto funds. It triggered a cascade of liquidations in other crypto assets: as Terra's reserve backers (the Luna Foundation Guard) sold off billions in Bitcoin in a futile attempt to defend the peg, they contributed to a sharp crypto market downturn (Azar et al., 2022). Major cryptocurrencies like Bitcoin and Ether saw steep declines (Bitcoin dropped by over 50% in the following weeks, Azar *et al.*, 2022), partly due to these forced sales and partly due to a crisis of confidence. Several crypto lending platforms and hedge funds that had invested in or lent against UST/LUNA were swept into bankruptcy in the aftermath. Notably, Three Arrows Capital (3AC), a prominent crypto hedge fund with reportedly over $18 billion AUM at its peak, was heavily exposed to Terra and could not recover from the losses (Azar et al., 2022). Its collapse in June 2022, in turn, caused a chain reaction: crypto brokers and lenders (Voyager Digital, Celsius Network, etc.) that had lent to 3AC suffered huge losses and also entered insolvency. In essence, Terra's collapse was the first domino in a broader crypto credit crisis of 2022.

From a traditional finance perspective, Terra's collapse fortunately did not have direct systemic impacts – it was a contained implosion in an emerging sector. However, it served as a stark warning of how fast and far contagion can spread in an unregulated financial network. The New York Federal Reserve's analysis noted that Terra's case illustrated the fragility and interconnectedness of the crypto ecosystem, and that if stablecoins hold traditional assets, a run could also force fire sales in those assets with potential effects beyond crypto (Azar et al., 2022). In Terra's case, its primary backing was crypto-based (LUNA and some Bitcoin reserves), so the impact stayed within crypto markets (aside from the general hit to investor wealth). But the episode prompted urgent reassessments by regulators globally about the need to rein in stablecoin risks.

Regulatory and market response: The Terra debacle was a catalyst for action:

- **International bodies**: The FSB fast-tracked its review of stablecoin oversight recommendations. By October 2022, it had issued updated proposals, and in July 2023, it finalized 10 high-level recommendations for regulating "global stablecoin" arrangements, explicitly informed by Terra's failure and others (Financial Stability Board, 2020). These recommendations call for end-to-end governance, risk management, redemption rights, and interoperability with national regimes, ensuring stablecoins are subject to supervision commensurate with the risks they pose. The FSB Chairman at the time emphasized that Terra's collapse showed stablecoins' potential *"to make threats to financial stability more acute"* without proper regulation (Financial Stability Board, 2020).
- **National regulators**: Several jurisdictions that had been taking a wait-and-see approach moved to propose stricter rules. In the United States, lawmakers cited Terra's crash in renewed efforts to draft a Stablecoin Act. By 2023, draft bills emerged in Congress aiming to regulate stablecoin issuers like banks or

special purpose institutions, require 100% reserves, and ban algorithms that mimic deposits without backing. While legislation has not yet been passed (as of 2025), there is bipartisan acknowledgement post-Terra that something must be done to prevent a similar incident from hitting U.S. consumers and markets. U.S. regulatory agencies (the Fed, OCC, and FDIC) also warned banks under their purview to exercise caution with crypto deposits and stablecoin reserves, partly in response to volatility events like Terra.

- South Korea, where Terraform Labs (the creator of Terra/LUNA) was based, launched investigations and eventually issued arrest warrants for Terra's founder Do Kwon (who was later detained abroad). The episode became a high-profile enforcement case, highlighting potential fraud and regulatory arbitrage. Korean regulators also accelerated crypto regulatory frameworks to provide better investor protection.
- Europe's regulators (and lawmakers finalizing the MiCA regulation) used Terra as an example of the dangers of unbacked crypto tokens. MiCA, passed in 2023, includes strict provisions for stablecoins (termed "asset-referenced tokens" and "e-money tokens" in the regulation). It effectively outlaws algorithmic stablecoins marketed as stable by requiring that any stable-value token must have redeemability and be backed by a reserve of assets. Under MiCA, something like TerraUSD would simply not be permitted to operate as a stablecoin without reserve backing. Additionally, MiCA places caps on issuance and volume for stablecoins not denominated in EU currencies, reflecting concern about euro area reliance on foreign (especially USD) tokens – a nod to sovereignty issues.
- **Market discipline**: In the aftermath, the crypto market itself became wary of algorithmic designs. Several planned algorithmic stablecoins shelved their launches. Investors gravitated even more to fiat-backed stablecoins, and issuers of those rushed to bolster transparency. For instance, Circle (USDC) began providing daily disclosure of reserve composition and moved more cash into insured banks and overnight repo to reassure holders. Tether reduced its riskier reserve assets (commercial paper), replacing them with treasury bills by late 2022, aiming to restore confidence in its 1:1 backing (likely under regulatory and market pressure). In short, Terra's flameout reinforced the market axiom that "stablecoin is only as good as its reserves and governance" – and that trust, once lost, is hard to regain.

Terra's story is a cautionary tale of innovation running ahead of prudence. It vividly illustrated how a stablecoin can go from "stable" to zero in days, and why regulators insist that anything carrying the stablecoin label must meet high standards of stability. As we move on to other cases, Terra forms a backdrop that has influenced virtually all subsequent policy thinking on stablecoins.

Libra/Diem (2019-2020): A Global Stablecoin Thwarted by Regulators

Around 2019, a very different stablecoin saga unfolded – not one of collapse, but one of regulatory preemption. Libra, later rebranded Diem, was a stablecoin proposed by Facebook (via the Libra Association consortium) that aimed to be a global digital currency. Announced in mid-2019, Libra was envisioned as a "global stablecoin" (GSC): a token backed by a basket of bank deposits and government bonds in various currencies, intended to serve Facebook's billions of users for payments and remittances. Unlike the decentralized ethos of Terra, Libra was a corporate-backed initiative with potentially immediate scale given Facebook's reach.

Regulators worldwide reacted with swift and near-universal alarm. The prospect of a tech giant issuing a borderless currency raised multifaceted concerns:

- **Monetary sovereignty**: Countries feared Libra could quickly achieve wide adoption, effectively outsourcing monetary control to a private network dominated by a U.S. tech firm and its partners. Particularly, emerging economies worried about currency substitution, as people might prefer Libra over volatile local currencies.
- **Financial stability**: A global stablecoin used broadly for payments and savings could become systemically important overnight. If Libra were insufficiently backed or if there were a run on it, the ramifications would be global. Moreover, the basket design meant Libra's value was tied to multiple currencies, potentially introducing exchange rate volatility for users in any single country and complicating central banks' tasks.
- **AML/CFT and data privacy**: Officials raised issues about how Libra would adhere to anti-money laundering rules, and how Facebook's involvement might leverage user data.
- **Fair competition:** There were also worries that Libra could reinforce Facebook's market power and undermine the banking system by drawing deposits away.

As a result, central banks and governments, from the U.S. Treasury to the European Central Bank and many others, essentially issued a collective "not on our watch". The Financial Stability Board in 2020 specifically highlighted "global stablecoins" and developed regulatory principles largely with Libra in mind (Financial Stability Board, 2020). The FSB noted that a widely adopted stablecoin with a potential global reach could become systemically important across multiple jurisdictions and *"challenge the comprehensiveness and effectiveness of existing oversight"* Financial Stability Board, 2020). In response, they crafted international recommendations to ensure any GSC is subject to rigorous regulation and "responsible innovation" (FSB, 2020)

Under intense regulatory scrutiny and lacking support, the Libra project radically altered course: it first shifted from a basket to proposing single-currency stablecoins (like a USD Diem) to appease concerns, and promised strong compliance measures. Yet skepticism remained high. Key partners pulled out. By late 2020 and into 2021, the project stalled, and eventually, in early 2022, Diem's assets were sold off without launching. Libra/Diem is thus a case where regulatory action effectively preempted a potential stablecoin risk before it materialized. It underscores the principle that size and reach are crucial factors in stablecoin risk – regulators drew a line when a stablecoin threatened to scale into the mainstream financial and monetary system immediately.

The Libra episode also had positive impacts: it arguably spurred central banks to accelerate CBDC research and development, seeing a private competitor looming. It also catalyzed international cooperation – the formation of standards and the aforementioned FSB recommendations – to ensure any future Libra-like proposal would have to meet high standards or be stopped. The term "global stablecoin" remains in policy vocabularies as essentially *"what if a Big Tech issues a stablecoin that catches on?"* Regulators learned not to be complacent about such prospects. In a way, the stern response to Libra laid the groundwork that made later regulatory reactions (e.g., to Terra, or to smaller stablecoin issues) more decisive. It demonstrated the resolve to protect monetary sovereignty and stability from incipient threats. As one Atlantic Council analysis noted, US and EU perspectives diverged on whether to encourage private stablecoins or a public CBDC, but both agreed that a widely adopted private coin like Libra posed serious concerns to the global financial order (Matthews & Tran, 2025).

USD Coin's De-Peg during the U.S. Banking Turmoil (2023): Stablecoin Meets Bank Run

In March 2023, the normally steady USD Coin (USDC) experienced a temporary loss of its dollar peg, triggered not by crypto issues, but by the collapse of a traditional bank – Silicon Valley Bank (SVB). This incident is instructive as a case of stablecoin vulnerability to TradFi shocks and the importance of transparency and trust.

What happened: On March 10, 2023, SVB failed and was taken over by regulators, sparking wider fears about mid-sized U.S. banks. Circle, the issuer of USDC, promptly revealed that about $3.3 billion of USDC's reserves (approximately 8% of its total ~$40 billion reserves at that time) were held as deposits at SVB (Helmore,

2023). With SVB's status in limbo that weekend, those funds were at risk (the FDIC only insures up to $250k per depositor; Circle's $3.3B far exceeded that, and immediate access was frozen). This disclosure shook confidence in USDC's full backing. Within hours, USDC – normally tightly $1.00 – began trading down on exchanges. It fell to roughly $0.87 at its nadir on March 11, 2023 (Helmore, 2023) as panicked sellers exchanged USDC for other stablecoins or cash. In essence, this was a stablecoin run precipitated by a bank run – an unprecedented crossover event.

On crypto trading platforms globally, arbitrageurs and speculators drove wild swings among stablecoin prices: USDC down, Tether (which claimed no direct SVB exposure) traded slightly above $1 as demand for it spiked. Many decentralized protocols saw turbulence; for instance, automated market maker pools that assumed 1 USDC ≈ $1 suffered imbalances. Circle publicly assured that it would cover any shortfall and was looking for ways to access its funds. Importantly, this drama happened over a weekend when banks were closed, so direct redemptions of USDC for dollars were largely paused until markets opened.

Resolution: On Sunday, March 12, U.S. authorities (the Fed, Treasury, and FDIC) jointly announced that all SVB depositors would be made whole as part of a systemic risk exception, effectively backstopping the bank's deposits. This decision meant Circle's $3.3B would be fully recoverable. Confidence rapidly returned. By Monday, March 13, USDC's price climbed back toward $1.00. Circle processed large redemption requests once normal banking resumed, and within days, USDC's supply shrank by about 10% as some investors chose to exit to be safe. The peg had been restored, and no losses were incurred by USDC holders – but the scare was a vivid demonstration of stablecoin fragility.

Implications and lessons:

- **Interconnectedness**: USDC's depeg highlighted how even a conservative, fully-collateralized stablecoin can be only as stable as the traditional banking underpinnings it relies on. A failure of a single mid-sized bank nearly unraveled a major stablecoin. The incident echoed the warnings of the BIS and others that stablecoins' "bearer" nature allows them to circulate outside the banking system, but their stability ultimately ties back to that very system (through reserves) (Kosse et al., 2023). It underscored that stablecoin issuers are effectively large financial intermediaries whose choices of banking partners and investment of reserves create potential concentrations of risk.
- **Market functioning under stress**: During the depeg, the stablecoin market structure itself came under strain. Liquidity became thin in trading pairs. Some protocols had to be paused or adjusted (e.g., MakerDAO's DAI, partly backed by USDC, saw its own stability mechanism kick in to avoid DAI dropping in tandem). Yet, broader contagion was contained. The Guardian noted

that beyond the crypto sphere, fears of contagion from SVB's failure to other areas of finance "appeared limited" that weekend (Helmore, 2023) – a statement that became true largely due to the swift government intervention. Had authorities not guaranteed the deposits, Circle would have faced a significant loss, potentially impairing USDC's redemption 1-for-1. In that counterfactual, one can imagine a deeper run and more severe impact on crypto markets, possibly even lawsuits or broader loss of trust in stablecoins.

- **Regulatory response**: The event added fuel to regulators' arguments that stablecoin reserves should be held in safe, central bank-backed places. Some have suggested that stablecoin issuers be given access to central bank accounts (as issuers of a form of public interest money), so that reserves are risk-free and runs become less likely. Short of that, more stringent rules on asset custody and liquidity for stablecoins were called for. In the U.S., the incident was cited in Congressional hearings as evidence that stablecoins, even when well-intentioned, carry systemic considerations and thus need federal oversight.
- **Transparency and trust**: Circle's relatively transparent approach (promptly disclosing its exposure) may have actually contributed to the initial shock (had they kept silent, markets might not have known of the SVB link immediately). However, transparency is crucial for long-term trust. Circle's actions and the recovery likely preserved USDC's reputation more than if information had been hidden. This highlights an important principle: stablecoin issuers must manage not just assets but information and expectations to prevent panic.

Overall, the USDC-SVB episode served as a real world test of a stablecoin under duress from a traditional financial event. It validated concerns that stablecoins can act as a transmission channel between the crypto and banking worlds. Conversely, it also showed that the implicit or explicit support of public authorities can stop a stablecoin run – in this case, by securing the reserves via bank deposit guarantees, essentially a central-bank-like action. This raises interesting questions: to what extent should stablecoins be integrated into the official safety net (as banks are) versus being required to structure themselves to never need it? We revisit this in policy recommendations.

Other Notable Incidents and Near-Misses

Beyond the big three cases above, a few other incidents shed light on stablecoin risks and market dynamics:

- Tether's Peg Wobbles and Scrutiny: Tether (USDT), the largest stablecoin, has historically had moments where its $1 peg was doubted. In April 2019, for example, news of legal action against Tether's parent (accusing it of misusing reserves to cover losses at an affiliated exchange) caused USDT to trade at ~$0.97 briefly. In more recent times, USDT dipped to $0.99 during the worst of the COVID-19 market crunch in March 2020 and again amid the Terra panic in May 2022, but these were slight and quickly corrected. What's notable is that Tether has faced persistent questions about its reserves' quality and transparency – culminating in a 2021 settlement with the New York Attorney General, where Tether admitted no wrongdoing but agreed to provide reports and not do business in NY, and revelations that at times Tether held riskier assets. Tether's ability to maintain stability despite skeptics suggests a somewhat paradoxical market confidence that, even if not fully transparent, it will honor redemptions. However, regulators are not sanguine – the risk remains that if a shock undermines user confidence (perhaps a sudden reveal of losses or a large investor pulling out), USDT's sheer size ($80+ billion) could make a loss of peg very destabilizing. Tether's example demonstrates the market's adaptive expectations – many users treat it as stable because it has been so, but that stability is ultimately underpinned by belief and an expectation of liquidity that could be tested.
- **Binance USD (BUSD) Wind-Down:** BUSD was a dollar stablecoin issued by Paxos in partnership with the Binance exchange. In early 2023, New York regulators ordered Paxos to stop issuing BUSD, citing unregistered security concerns. Paxos complied, and BUSD's supply, about $16 billion at its height, began shrinking as redemptions and conversions took place. This episode was not a run or peg failure – BUSD held its value during the phase-out – but it showed regulatory power in effect: a stablecoin can be killed off through enforcement if not compliant. It also concentrated the stablecoin market further (funds flowed primarily into USDT and USDC). For financial stability, an orderly wind-down like BUSD is not problematic; indeed, it could be seen as a template for how to remove a stablecoin without panic. However, it also underscores how regulatory fragmentation (U.S. SEC vs. others) can create sudden changes in stablecoin availability.
- **DAI and Decentralized Stablecoins**: DAI, unlike others, is over-collateralized by crypto (mainly Ethereum and USDC). It weathered several crises, including the 2020 crypto crash ("Black Thursday" in March 2020), which caused some instability in its mechanism, but ultimately DAI held close to $1. One risk with DAI and similar is that they often rely heavily on centralized stablecoins as collateral (DAI became ~50% backed by USDC at one point). This creates a circular dependency – if USDC had failed, DAI would

likely lose its peg too. Recognizing this, MakerDAO has tried to diversify collateral and even invest part of its reserves in real-world assets (even government bonds). DAI illustrates both the promise and complexity of decentralized approaches to stablecoins: they avoid a single issuer and can be more transparent, but they inherit volatility from their collateral and often indirectly depend on the centralized coins they intended to sidestep.

Each of these cases adds a piece to the puzzle of stablecoin risks. They reinforce that stablecoins, despite the name, are not inherently stable – stability must be designed, managed, regulated, and sometimes enforced through external intervention. The experiences have informed regulators' comparative thinking about CBDCs versus stablecoins, which we discuss next, as well as the push for cohesive global regulatory frameworks.

ISSUES, CONTROVERSIES, PROBLEMS

Stablecoins Versus Central Bank Digital Currencies: Comparative Systemic Risk Analysis

As private stablecoins have proliferated, central banks worldwide have been researching and experimenting with Central Bank Digital Currencies (CBDCs) – digital forms of central bank money – to potentially offer a safer alternative or complement to stablecoins. Both stablecoins and CBDCs represent digital currency innovations, but their risk profiles differ fundamentally due to who issues them and how they are designed. This section compares the two through a financial stability lens, including both retail CBDCs (for general public use) and wholesale CBDCs (for interbank use).

Issuer and Credit Risk: Public Liability vs Private Liability

The most significant difference is that a CBDC is a direct liability of the central bank, whereas a stablecoin is a liability of a private issuer (or governed network) (Chavanette, 2024). This has profound implications:

- **Credit Risk**: A retail CBDC, like physical cash or central bank reserves, carries (virtually) no credit risk – it is backed by the full faith and credit of the sovereign issuer. Holders of CBDC would not have to worry about the central bank defaulting in their domestic currency. In contrast, stablecoin holders are exposed to issuer credit risk. Even fully backed stablecoins depend on the issuer's ability to manage and safeguard assets and fulfill redemption obligations. If the issuer fails (financially or operationally), stablecoin holders could suffer losses. Thus, from a pure creditworthiness standpoint, CBDCs are safer. They provide the ultimate risk-free asset in digital form, which could enhance stability by eliminating the risk of runs that stem from doubts about backing. As Fed Governor Christopher Waller (a skeptic of CBDC) has noted, stablecoins by private issuers inherently involve credit and liquidity risks, whereas a well-designed CBDC does not, because it's essentially digital cash (Matthews & Tran, 2025).

- **Stability of Value**: By definition, a domestic CBDC would be in the national unit and always worth its face value in that unit. Stablecoins aim for the same, but history (as we've seen) shows they can deviate or collapse in value due to issuer problems or market dynamics. So, in terms of maintaining par value, CBDC has an intrinsic advantage – there is no need for collateral or redemption because it *is* the money. Stablecoins need mechanisms (reserves or algorithms) to maintain value, and those mechanisms can fail, meaning stablecoins can lose parity (as UST and even USDC did briefly). The BIS succinctly points out that stablecoins "perform badly against the integrity and singleness of money" tests, failing the no-questions-asked trust that sovereign money enjoys (Kosse et al., 2023).

Liquidity and "Run" Dynamics

Another divergence is how each would behave under stress:

- **Runs on CBDC**: In the traditional sense, a run on a CBDC doesn't quite apply, since one cannot "run" away from the safest asset. However, there is a different systemic risk concern: *runs to CBDC*. If a frictionless retail CBDC exists, in a crisis, people might rapidly convert bank deposits into CBDC (seen as safer). This could disintermediate banks, depriving them of funding when they need it. Thus, while a CBDC itself is stable, its introduction could create new dynamics. Central banks are acutely aware of this, and many design proposals include limits or discouragements on large-scale conversions to CBDC (tiered remuneration, holding caps, etc.) specifically to mitigate bank run risks in stress scenarios. In a steady state, a modest level of CBDC might not threaten banks, but in a panic, the existence of a risk-free digital option could accelerate a digital bank run. This is a systemic risk of CBDC often debated – albeit a very different one from stablecoin runs (the latter are about a run out of the asset; the former is about a run into the asset, causing problems elsewhere).

- **Runs on Stablecoins**: As extensively described, stablecoins are prone to classic runs out of them if confidence falters. In this sense, stablecoins are more analogous to bank deposits or money fund shares – their stability relies on redemption assurances and backing. If credible, fine; if not, runs occur. And unlike banks (which have lenders of last resort and deposit insurance) or regulated money funds (which have liquidity requirements and sometimes sponsor support), stablecoins currently lack formal backstops. Thus, stablecoins pose a more direct run risk *within their own ecosystem*, which could then spill over. A CBDC doesn't suffer from internal run risk (no one questions central bank money in normal conditions), but as noted, it can be a "run destination". From a systemic perspective, a run on stablecoins could be chaotic and hard to stem unless authorities stepped in – whereas a run to CBDC might be more manageable by policy (though still highly disruptive to banks).

Role in Payments and Settlement

CBDCs and stablecoins both aspire to improve payments, but their integration into the financial system would differ:

- **Retail payments:** A retail CBDC (say a digital dollar or digital euro) would be legal tender, universally accepted for payments by law, and likely integrated into the banking/payment system (possibly via wallets provided by banks or the central bank). This means high confidence in acceptance and usability, but also likely a more conservative innovation pace. Stablecoins, being private, have in some cases moved faster technologically, offering features like programmability (smart contracts) on day one. However, stablecoins struggle with universal acceptance – merchants must choose to accept them, and they may prefer ones that are regulated or guaranteed. In terms of systemic risk, if a retail CBDC is widely used, the central bank must ensure resilience (cybersecurity, capacity) as any outage or breach could disrupt the economy. For stablecoins, such outages or failures are a real risk too (think of a top stablecoin's blockchain network freezing – payments could halt for those relying on it). But if stablecoins are not universally adopted, the impact is more limited. The central bank's involvement in CBDC likely ensures robust contingency planning and oversight, whereas stablecoin operators might not reach the same level of reliability without strong regulation.
- **Wholesale settlement**: Many stablecoin advocates propose using stablecoins for settling trades or moving funds between financial institutions, effectively replacing or complementing existing interbank payment systems. For in-

stance, some investment firms use stablecoins to move dollars quickly between exchanges. However, central banks are developing wholesale CBDCs or similar innovations (like tokenized central bank deposits) to serve the same purpose with ultimate safety. A wholesale CBDC, used only by banks and perhaps large institutions, could improve settlement speed without introducing credit risk (since it's central bank money). In contrast, a wholesale stablecoin (like JPM Coin or consortium coins) still carries some credit risk of the issuer bank(s), albeit small if fully collateralized. The systemic risk question here is: do we trust the private sector to run critical wholesale plumbing, or central banks? Historically, central bank RTGS systems are the backbone for final settlement because they eliminate counterparty risk. A proliferation of different wholesale stablecoins might fragment liquidity and complicate interoperability – whereas a central bank digital settlement asset could unify it (assuming international coordination for cross-border use). Integration with DeFi: Notably, some experiments (like Project Mariana by BIS Innovation Hub) have looked at using wholesale CBDCs in DeFi protocols for FX trading, merging the benefits of stablecoins (automated on-chain execution) with the safety of CBDC. This suggests a possible future where CBDCs and private innovation intersect, rather than compete.

Financial Inclusion and Innovation vs Stability Trade-offs

Some proponents argue stablecoins have demonstrated real-world utility (e.g., in emerging markets, as mentioned earlier, providing access to dollars digitally) and technology features (smart contracts, interoperability across platforms) that a central-bank-issued currency might be slower to adopt. Indeed, stablecoins have been at the forefront of exploring programmable money, allowing complex conditional payments in DeFi. They also operate globally by default, whereas CBDCs will be jurisdiction-bound (though potentially interoperable).

However, with that innovation came significant risks, as we have seen – both for users (who can lose money in a collapse) and for the system (runs, etc.). Central banks, by design, prioritize stability and trust over speed of innovation. A central banker might argue that the public sector innovation (CBDC) may be slower but ultimately safer and more aligned with public interest, while private stablecoins innovate faster but can undermine stability if not properly regulated. As one BIS report put it, stablecoins have *"inherited limitations from crypto more broadly"* and cannot guarantee the same level of safety as central bank money (Kosse et al., 2023). For example, stablecoins can circulate pseudonymously, which raises financial integrity issues, whereas a CBDC would likely have an identity/account-based model that complies with AML laws, albeit raising privacy debates.

One view is that CBDCs and stablecoins could coexist, each serving different niches – stablecoins perhaps for certain platform ecosystems or as synthetic forms of foreign currency in some regions, and CBDC as the sovereign bedrock of digital payments. In fact, some countries contemplate a model of "synthetic CBDC" or public-private partnership, where private institutions issue stablecoins, but those coins are fully backed by central bank balances. This would combine innovation with the safety of central bank money, effectively making stablecoins mere wrappers for CBDC. That model addresses many stability risks (no credit risk, no liquidity risk, as backing is in central bank money) but requires legal and operational frameworks to implement. It's analogous to a system where banks issue e-money fully backed by central bank reserves – an idea gaining attention.

From a systemic risk perspective, if a retail CBDC is widely adopted, central banks will have to manage the transitional risk to banks (ensuring it doesn't cause unhealthy disintermediation). But once established, a CBDC-based system could be very robust – no risk of stablecoin-type runs, clear unit of account, etc. It might, however, concentrate more power and responsibility in the central bank, which is a different kind of systemic consideration (operational risk at the central bank and potential political risk if misuse of transaction data, etc.). Stablecoins, if left purely to market forces, could drive innovation but at the cost of recurrent crises that could, in the worst case, erode trust in digital money overall.

Political economy also plays a role: as of 2025, we see divergent approaches – the U.S. has influential voices suggesting that a well-regulated stablecoin ecosystem (with many USD stablecoins) could bolster the dollar's international role and that a U.S. CBDC is unnecessary or even risky (Matthews & Tran, 2025). In contrast, the Eurozone and others see a CBDC as essential to provide a safe anchor and to avoid reliance on foreign or private digital monies (Matthews & Tran, 2025). These choices will shape how systemic risks evolve: heavy reliance on private stablecoins puts the onus on strong regulation to prevent crises, whereas going the CBDC route puts the onus on careful design to avoid unintended disruption to banks and privacy.

In summary, stablecoins carry more intrinsic financial stability risks than CBDCs because of their private, credit-risk-bearing nature and tendency toward fragmentation. CBDCs, being sovereign and uniform, avoid many of those issues but introduce other concerns, primarily around the structure of the banking system and the central bank's role. Many central bankers see CBDCs as a potential solution to stablecoin risks – a way to provide the benefits of digital currency without the instability. Others believe a regulated stablecoin can achieve similar safety with less direct central bank involvement. The policy direction likely will include elements of both: encourage or require stablecoins to operate in a way more akin to risk-free money (or back them with it), and possibly issue CBDCs to provide a public option that raises the bar for what private issuers must offer to remain competitive.

REGULATORY FRAGMENTATION, SOVEREIGNTY CONCERNS, AND CROSS-BORDER IMPLICATIONS

The regulatory response to stablecoins is complicated by the very characteristics that make them attractive: their borderless circulation and diverse designs. This has led to a fragmented regulatory landscape internationally, raising sovereignty issues and cross-border challenges.

Fragmented Regulatory Approaches

Different jurisdictions have taken different stances on stablecoins, reflecting varying priorities and risk perceptions:

- **United States**: As of 2025, the U.S. has not yet enacted federal legislation specific to stablecoins, despite several proposals. Regulatory oversight has been patchwork. Some stablecoin issuers (like Paxos for BUSD, or Gemini for GUSD) obtained Trust charters or licenses under state law, meaning they must hold reserves 100% and undergo audits (similar to e-money rules). Others, like Tether, operate offshore outside direct U.S. oversight, though U.S. users still utilize them. U.S. regulators have mostly used existing laws (securities law, banking law, etc.) to nudge or take action case-by-case basis. For example, the SEC and NY regulators are stepping in on Facebook's Libra or Binance's stablecoin. The President's Working Group on Financial Markets (2021) recommended that Congress legislate so that stablecoins are issued only by insured depository institutions or similar entities to ensure prudence. But absent a new law, agencies have tried to restrict banks from taking on too much stablecoin-related risk (e.g., the OCC under one administration allowed banks to use stablecoins for settlement, only for that to be quietly walked back under the next). This regulatory uncertainty has arguably hampered some development (no U.S. bank has yet launched a major stablecoin product for retail), but conversely, U.S.-regulated Circle has thrived with its transparent approach, even as it awaits clearer rules. The U.S. thus showcases a regulatory gap: stablecoins aren't neatly within the mandate of any one agency (they straddle banking, securities, and payments), leading to a slow response, even as stablecoins grew big. This gap is widely acknowledged – both Congress and the Financial Stability Oversight Council (FSOC) have stated stablecoins need a regulatory framework to avoid risks.
- **European Union**: The EU moved more decisively via the Markets in Crypto-Assets (MiCA) regulation (approved in 2023, with effect in 2024/25). MiCA will impose a comprehensive regime for "asset-referenced tokens" (stable-

coins tied to multiple assets or currencies) and "e-money tokens" (stablecoins tied to a single fiat currency). Issuers will require authorization, must have governance and capital standards, must maintain reserves, and, in the case of e-money tokens, offer redemption rights similar to e-money institutions. There are also provisions to limit the scale of stablecoins: any stablecoin not denominated in euros that becomes widely used in payments can face transaction volume caps (an element clearly targeted at protecting monetary sovereignty in the Eurozone). Algorithmic stablecoins are essentially disallowed from marketing themselves as stable. With MiCA, the EU aims to eliminate regulatory ambiguity – stablecoin issuers will know exactly what is required (e.g., publication of a white paper, reserve custody with little risk, etc.) to operate across the single market. However, MiCA is region-specific; non-EU stablecoins can still be offered from abroad to EU users in theory (though if they get large, they'd violate volume rules without authorization).

- **United Kingdom**: The UK similarly signaled a pro-innovation but cautious approach. It has stated intentions to bring systemic stablecoins into the Bank of England's supervision, and passed laws in 2023 that will recognize stablecoins as a form of payment once certain conditions are met. The BoE and FCA will have authority to oversee major stablecoin firms, ensuring they meet standards akin to payment systems or banks. The UK has been keen to make London a hub for fintech and digital currency; thus, balancing that with stability (especially after seeing Terra and others) is a priority. They have also mused about requiring stablecoin issuers to hold reserves at the central bank, which would dramatically reduce risk (effectively making them narrow intermediaries of central bank money).
- **Asia**: Approaches vary. Japan legislated that stablecoins must be linked to yen and be issued only by licensed banks, trust companies, or licensed money transfer agents, thereby effectively banning offshore dollar stablecoins from being freely marketed. Japan's law (passed in 2022) was one of the first clear, stablecoin-focused acts, motivated by consumer protection and anti-money laundering. Singapore and Hong Kong – major financial centers – have been developing bespoke regimes as well. The Monetary Authority of Singapore (MAS) proposed guidelines for stablecoins, aiming for high-quality reserves and redemption at par. Hong Kong, in its 2023 consultations, indicated it would initially allow only fully backed stablecoins (no algorithmic) and might restrict denominations (e.g., primarily HKD or major currencies) while placing them under a licensing regime. These jurisdictions emphasize proper governance and reserve audits, due to their role as international financial hubs.

- **Developing economies**: Some have moved to outright prohibitions on crypto and stablecoins (China notably banned cryptocurrency trading and stablecoins by extension, while pushing forward its own CBDC). Others have few or no specific rules, and stablecoin use operates in a gray area, which can pose a risk of regulatory arbitrage where issuers choose the lightest-touch jurisdiction.

This patchwork leads to regulatory arbitrage: for instance, if one country enforces stringent rules that an issuer finds onerous, the issuer might domicile in a more permissive jurisdiction and still access the global market via the internet. This was the case with Tether (nominally based in the Caribbean) and several others. It undermines the effectiveness of any single country's rules when a stablecoin can be issued from essentially anywhere and still be used domestically. The FSB explicitly warned that inconsistent national approaches could be exploited, and that only a coordinated global framework can adequately address stablecoin risks (Financial Stability Board, 2020). As a result, the FSB's 2023 final recommendations call on jurisdictions to implement regulations by a set timeline and to cooperate on oversight, especially for any stablecoin that operates in multiple countries.

Sovereignty and Geopolitical Implications

Monetary sovereignty concerns arise chiefly when stablecoins pegged to a foreign currency gain traction in a local economy. If, say, a USD stablecoin becomes a common medium of exchange in a country with a weak currency, that country effectively cedes a part of its monetary sovereignty: transactions and savings shift into a currency the central bank doesn't control, and a form (token) the central bank doesn't issue or supervise. This not only affects macroeconomic control (dollarization has long limited some countries' policy freedom) but also can be seen as a challenge to national currency identity and the seigniorage the state normally enjoys from issuing money.

Libra's specter particularly raised this issue: had a global stablecoin tied to a basket (dominated by USD, EUR, etc.) been launched, smaller nations feared their currencies could be displaced or their people's savings siphoned into this new global currency. Even now, widely used USD stablecoins essentially extend U.S. dollar influence. IMF officials pointed out that unchecked stablecoin adoption could threaten monetary policy effectiveness in some markets (Financial Stability Board, 2020). There is also a geopolitical dimension: if Western-issued stablecoins (or a Chinese CBDC, for another example) become prevalent in third countries, it may alter economic alliances or dependencies. This has led to calls that any global stablecoin arrangement needs to consult and involve all jurisdictions affected (one of the FSB's principles is cooperation in supervision across home/host of the stablecoin's activities).

Another sovereignty aspect is who controls the platform. A stablecoin from a Big Tech might leverage the network effects of tech platforms to dominate payments (as Alipay/WeChat did with mobile payments in China, albeit using RMB). Governments are wary of ceding such control to private companies – it could make enforcement of laws (like anti-money laundering, counter-terror finance) harder if the stablecoin network isn't fully compliant. It also intersects with data sovereignty – the issuer or operator of a stablecoin might glean vast data on transactions that governments typically only see through banking reports. These concerns, in part, drive interest in CBDCs: they keep the sovereign at the helm of digital money innovation.

Cross-Border Regulatory Challenges

Stablecoins are by nature cross-border: even if issued in one jurisdiction, they can be held and transferred globally by anyone with an internet connection. This creates several challenges:

- **Regulatory Perimeter and Enforcement**: If a stablecoin issuer is in country A but has users in country B, whose rules apply? Country B can ban or restrict its citizens from using it (via exchanges or banking channels), but enforcement is tricky if peer-to-peer use is possible. If something goes wrong (fraud, collapse), users in country B might have little recourse if country A's laws were lax. International law around such digital instruments is still developing. One suggestion has been to treat major stablecoins almost like international payment systems, with cooperative oversight of regulators from multiple jurisdictions (similar to how the CLS system for FX settlement is overseen by central banks jointly). But that level of coordination doesn't exist yet for stablecoins.
- **Differences in Definitions and Standards**: Some countries might classify stablecoins as securities, others as deposit equivalents, others as commodities. These differences affect how they are regulated and under what agency. It can also lead to conflicting requirements for a global stablecoin. A concrete example: one jurisdiction might require a stablecoin to hold 100% reserves in local currency assets; another might restrict it to only domestic currency issuance to locals. A stablecoin trying to operate in both must navigate these or potentially fragment into different versions per region.
- **AML/CFT and Illicit Flows**: Cross-border stablecoin flows raise concerns about evading capital controls or sanctions. For instance, stablecoins have reportedly been used in jurisdictions like Russia or Iran to circumvent certain

restrictions. Regulators stress that stablecoin arrangements must adhere to the FATF Travel Rule (collecting/transmitting sender and receiver info for transactions) just as banks do. But implementing this on decentralized networks is hard. Without global alignment, bad actors may exploit the weakest link jurisdiction to launder money through stablecoins that then circulate globally. This is a stability concern insofar as large-scale illicit use could provoke draconian measures (like shutting down access to entire networks) that in turn shock markets.

- **Emerging Markets and Capital Flight**: For countries with capital controls, stablecoins offer a new avenue to move capital. Authorities in such countries (e.g., China, India, to an extent) are extremely cautious about stablecoins for this reason. We may see more countries limiting access to open stablecoins, especially foreign ones, to protect their financial stability. This could bifurcate the world: jurisdictions where stablecoin usage is open vs those where only tightly controlled or domestic stablecoins are allowed. Such fragmentation might reduce some global systemic risk by containing usage, but if a major stablecoin breaks, even users in banned jurisdictions could be indirectly affected (through trade or offshore markets).
- **Global Regulatory Framework Efforts**: The FSB and international standard setters (IOSCO, CPMI, etc.) have been working on global principles. The FSB's 2020 and 2023 recommendations for global stablecoins essentially serve as a template that can be adopted into national law. Similarly, IOSCO (which sets securities market standards) has looked at whether stablecoins that function like payment systems or collective investment schemes should follow analogous rules. The IMF has also engaged, especially focusing on macroeconomic impacts for emerging markets and how to handle digital dollarization. In Sept 2023, the IMF and FSB jointly published a synthesis paper aligning their stance, clearly opposing any accommodation of unchecked cryptoization and urging comprehensive regulation rather than any outright ban (except perhaps for the most dangerous forms) (Financial Stability Board, 2020). One challenge is that these recommendations are not legally binding – it's up to each jurisdiction to implement them. So far, some (EU, UK, etc.) have moved in alignment with them, while others lag behind.

EMERGING GLOBAL REGULATORY FRAMEWORKS

Building on the above, it's worth summarizing the main elements that a global framework for stablecoins is converging towards, as seen in various documents by BIS, FSB, and others:

- **Prudential Requirements**: Stablecoin issuers, especially those deemed significant, should be subject to capital and liquidity requirements akin to banks or payment institutions. This could include holding a capital buffer against operational risks or unexpected losses in reserves.
- **Reserve Composition and Safekeeping**: Reserves must be conservative, liquid, and segregated. Many proposals call for 100% high-quality liquid assets (short-term government debt, central bank reserves, or cash). Reserves should be custodied in regulated entities, ideally with some protection from insolvency of the issuer (trust accounts, for instance). Some jurisdictions might mandate holding reserves at the central bank (effectively converting stablecoin float into central bank money deposits).
- **Redemption Rights**: Stablecoins that function like money should give holders a clear legal claim to redeem at par in fiat, within a reasonable timeframe (say T+1 or T+5 days). This is to assure users and reduce run incentives. If redemption can be legally suspended or denied, the stablecoin is more like an investment product than cash.
- **Transparency and Disclosures**: Regular reporting of reserves (composition, amounts, any lending or reuse of collateral) is essential. Some regulators want daily or real-time public disclosures; at a minimum, monthly audited statements are becoming standard. Transparency builds trust and allows markets to discipline issuers.
- **Governance and Operational Resilience**: Issuers need strong governance (fit and proper management, board oversight, risk management frameworks). They should have plans for operational continuity, cybersecurity, handling hacks or incidents, etc. Also, there should be clarity on how a stablecoin could be wound down in a crisis (who oversees the return of funds, etc.), akin to resolution planning in banking.
- **Conduct and Consumer Protection**: Rules against misleading marketing (e.g., an algorithmic coin calling itself "stable" with no explanation of risks), safeguards for user assets (if held in custody), and complaint redress mechanisms.
- **Domestic Coordination**: Within countries, agencies (central bank, securities regulator, etc.) must coordinate on who oversees what part of a stablecoin arrangement (the issuer, the wallet providers, exchanges). Some countries might designate stablecoins as systematically important payment systems if they reach a threshold, which brings central bank oversight directly.
- **Cross-Border Cooperation**: For stablecoins operating across borders, regulators should share information and possibly coordinate actions (for example, if an issuer in one country is failing, authorities in other countries where it's used should be informed or involved). Also, recognizing each other's regula-

tions to avoid double compliance burdens would help create a global framework. The goal is an environment where a stablecoin can't escape scrutiny by moving to a less regulated jurisdiction.

- **No Fragmentation of the Unit of Account**: BIS, in particular, emphasizes that stablecoins should not undermine the unity of the currency. One way to enforce this is to ensure conversion at par to the fiat currency is always honored for domestic use, and perhaps to discourage multiple competing private monies that aren't interoperable. If stablecoins are too fragmented (say, every big tech has its own coin that isn't 1:1 interchangeable), that's a problem. Standards for interoperability or a requirement to clear through a common platform could be considered.

One novel idea to manage sovereignty concerns is to restrict or oversee foreign currency stablecoins. For instance, some emerging markets might say: only stablecoins pegged to our currency are allowed (to promote our currency's digital use), and foreign ones (like USD stablecoins) are banned or limited. However, enforcement is tricky. Alternatively, they could allow foreign stablecoins but require licenses and maybe even some reserves to be held locally as collateral against macro risks.

Finally, a note on taxonomy: Not all stablecoins are equal, and regulation might differentiate:

- **Global Stablecoin (GSC)**: one with multinational reach (Libra-like). FSB wants the highest standards here.
- **Systemic stablecoin (domestic SIFI)**: one that is critical in a single country's financial system (e.g., a stablecoin that a lot of payments rely on). This might be regulated akin to a systemically important payment system or bank.
- **Smaller stablecoins**: These might be allowed under lighter regimes (like sandbox environments) if their scale is limited, to foster innovation. But triggers would exist that, if they grow, they must beef up compliance.

As of 2025, we see alignment in principle globally (the risk awareness is high everywhere), but uneven implementation. The risk is that if some major economies don't put in place adequate rules quickly, a stablecoin incident there could still have global repercussions. Conversely, if one region's rules are too onerous relative to others, it might push activity to less regulated shores (for example, if the EU limits non-EU stablecoin volumes, will usage shift to ones outside EU jurisdiction?).

In conclusion, addressing regulatory fragmentation is a work in progress. There is momentum toward a more harmonized approach, but bridging differences in legal systems and policy preferences takes time. Meanwhile, the stablecoin market continues to innovate (e.g., introducing things like real-world asset backing, variable interest stablecoins), which poses a moving target for regulators.

SOLUTIONS AND RECOMMENDATIONS

Having examined the landscape, risks, case studies, and regulatory responses, this final section outlines policy recommendations to harness the benefits of stablecoins while mitigating their systemic risks. The overarching aim is to balance innovation with financial stability – ensuring that the financial system can safely accommodate useful innovations like stablecoins without undermining trust, consumer protection, or monetary and financial stability. Additionally, given the rapidly evolving nature of digital finance, a stance of ongoing research and adaptive regulation is vital.

1. Strengthen Regulatory Oversight and Standards for Stablecoin Issuers

Bring stablecoin issuers into the regulatory perimeter with clear and robust requirements. At a minimum:

- **Prudential regulation**: Require significant issuers to be licensed and subject to prudential oversight (potentially as a new category of payment institution or bank-like entity). They should hold capital against operational and credit risks and maintain transparent, high-quality reserves. For large stablecoins, consider regulation akin to narrow banking or money market funds, meaning strictly limit what assets reserves can be invested in (e.g., only cash, central bank reserves, and short-term sovereign debt of the highest quality). This eliminates riskier investments and aligns stablecoins with a low-risk profile.
- **Redemption and liquidity**: Mandate clear redemption rights at par, and impose liquidity requirements so that a high percentage of reserves are immediately accessible (cash or overnight instruments) to meet surges in redemption demand. Basically, stablecoins must be "as good as cash" for redemption purposes to avoid panic; that might involve central bank support indirectly (for instance, allowing issuers access to central bank deposit facilities or emergency liquidity lines in return for compliance with strict rules – a controversial but potentially stabilizing measure).
- **Supervision and enforcement**: Designate a lead supervisory agency (or a college if cross-border) to conduct regular audits, oversee risk management, and enforce compliance. Examiners should verify reserve holdings and look at operational resiliency. Violations (like misrepresenting reserves) should

carry strict penalties to deter negligence or fraud. In essence, the stablecoin sector must not remain a regulatory "wild west" – it should be held to standards comparable to similarly risky activities in traditional finance.

By formalizing oversight, authorities can preempt problems – for example, detecting if an issuer is straying from 100% backing or if its governance is weak – rather than waiting for a crisis. As the BIS notes, regulators *"need to adapt quickly, both to monitor and assess risks from stablecoins"* and to enforce standards (Kosse et al., 2023). An important benefit of strong regulation is market discipline via transparency: if issuers must publish audited reserve breakdowns and are known to be supervised, users can make informed choices, and the ecosystem will gravitate to the most sound and compliant coins, squeezing out fringe operators.

2. Enhance Cross-Border Regulatory Coordination

Because stablecoins easily cross borders, international coordination is essential. Building on the FSB's work, policymakers should:

- **Adopt global standards**: Jurisdictions should implement the FSB's high-level recommendations for stablecoins in a consistent manner (Financial Stability Board, 2020). This includes exchange of information among regulators about stablecoin activities, cooperative oversight arrangements for any global stablecoin, and agreement on key principles (like 1:1 backing, redemption rights, and so forth).
- **Close regulatory gaps**: Identify any countries that might become havens for unregulated stablecoin issuance and engage them through the G20 or IMF to encourage adoption of the standards. If a jurisdiction refuses and a stablecoin poses risk elsewhere, consider defensive measures (like not allowing that coin to interface with regulated institutions).
- **Bilateral and multilateral supervision**: For stablecoins operating in multiple markets, set up supervisory colleges (similar to those for multinational banks) where relevant regulators share findings and coordinate actions. If an issuer in Country A has a failure that affects citizens in Country B, there should be a framework for resolution that protects those users, too. This could mean legal arrangements for ring-fencing reserves per jurisdiction or priority of claims for foreign users – areas requiring international legal cooperation.
- **Harmonize definitions**: Strive for alignment in how stablecoins are classified (as e-money, as securities, etc.) to avoid arbitrage. International standard setters like IOSCO and the Basel Committee can clarify how existing frame-

works (like securities laws for tokenized funds, or bank exposure rules for stablecoins) should be applied uniformly.

The IMF-FSB synthesis paper (2023) emphasized a comprehensive policy approach and included a roadmap for implementation, urging authorities not to delay since crypto markets evolve fast (Financial Stability Board, 2020). The global community should heed this and act in concert – a fragmented regulatory regime is an open invitation for instability.

3. Address Sovereignty and Macro-Financial Risks

Policymakers in each jurisdiction should consider measures to mitigate monetary sovereignty risks:

- **Encourage local-currency stablecoins and/or CBDCs**: If there is genuine demand for digital currency, providing a domestic CBDC or well-regulated domestic stablecoins could offer citizens a safe digital alternative, reducing reliance on foreign stablecoins. For instance, a retail CBDC in an emerging economy could be an official answer to the populace's desire for digital dollars, thus keeping them in the local currency ecosystem (assuming the local currency is reasonably stable).
- **Capital flow management**: Treat large stablecoin flows as part of capital flow monitoring. If evidence of "cryptoization" (flight to foreign stablecoins) emerges, central banks might use macroprudential tools or even targeted restrictions. For example, some countries might limit banks from integrating with certain foreign stablecoins or require any fiat on/off ramps to report and perhaps impose limits on conversions to stablecoins. These are sensitive measures (too heavy-handed can stifle innovation or push activity underground) – so they must be calibrated. But a country facing rapid dollarization via stablecoins might need such tools to manage the transition gradually.
- **Diplomacy and agreements**: Just as currency substitution has been discussed in forums like the IMF, digital dollarization should be too. Perhaps agreements can be made, say between the U.S. and some emerging markets, on standards for USD stablecoin usage abroad or sharing information on flows to help those countries manage the impact. The providers of major global stablecoins (often based in the U.S. or EU) should be mindful of international implications; regulators there could factor global spillovers into their oversight.

4. Foster Coexistence and Integration of CBDCs and Stablecoins

Rather than viewing CBDCs and stablecoins purely as competitors, policy can shape an environment where they coexist with appropriate roles:

1. **Leverage private sector innovation**: If a central bank develops a CBDC, allow it to be used in the same programmable environments that stablecoins operate in (APIs, smart contract platforms). Encourage private intermediaries (banks, fintechs) to build services on top of CBDC (like wallets, payment apps) so that they can match stablecoins in convenience and features. Interoperability is key – e.g., if CBDC can be easily exchanged for stablecoins and vice versa, then market forces can decide the mix, and risk can be balanced (with CBDC as ultimate safe asset).
2. **Regulated liability networks**: Explore frameworks where tokenized bank deposits, CBDCs, and stablecoins operate on common platforms with shared standards, as some consortia have proposed. In such a model, stablecoins issued by banks or licensed entities could be one form of digital money, but every transaction ultimately settles via central bank oversight (either directly or through synchronized ledgers). This ensures stability (every token is a claim on a supervised entity or the central bank) while preserving competition and innovation in front-end services.
3. **Gradual introduction of CBDC to manage transition**: If rolling out a retail CBDC, central banks might do so gradually or in pilot phases, closely watching for impacts on bank disintermediation. They can adjust features (like holding limits) as needed. The presence of CBDC also forces stablecoins to up their game or find new niches – which is healthy. For example, maybe stablecoins focus on cross-border or multi-currency scenarios, whereas CBDC handles domestic retail. Each can play to its strengths if guided well.

The Atlantic Council report suggests that at least in some jurisdictions (e.g., the US), policy is leaning toward stablecoins over CBDC for extending dollar reach (Matthews & Tran, 2025), whereas in others, the opposite. Ultimately, the best outcome might be a synergy: a CBDC provides the safe foundation, and stablecoins innovate on top in a regulated way. Policies should remain flexible to adjust this balance as technology and usage patterns evolve.

5. Improve Infrastructure for Stablecoin Transparency and Resilience

Even with regulation, certain industry-led or public sector-supported improvements could reduce risks:

- **Real-time audits and monitoring**: Encourage or require stablecoin issuers to use technology for real-time attestations of reserves (for instance, some have proposed blockchain-based proofs of reserve). Regulators might even integrate reporting systems that continuously monitor large stablecoin flows or reserve account balances. If an issuer deviates from required backing or a sudden drop in reserves occurs, supervisors can intervene early.
- **Enhanced clearing mechanisms**: If multiple stablecoins exist, fragmentation can be reduced by establishing interoperable clearing or conversion channels. Perhaps a central bank or trusted third party could host a platform where stablecoins can be redeemed or swapped efficiently for each other or for central bank money. This could act like a clearinghouse that dampens swings – e.g., if one stablecoin falls in price, arbitrage can quickly trade it for another via the clearing platform, keeping prices aligned. Essentially a stability backstop facility: not to bail out issuers, but to ensure holders can always migrate to safer money easily (reducing panic).
- **Emergency planning:** Regulators should plan for worst-case scenarios: what if the largest stablecoin fails? Similar to bank resolution plans, authorities could have a strategy – whether to orchestrate an orderly wind-down, facilitate an acquisition by a more stable entity, or, in extreme cases, provide temporary liquidity to avert fire-sales of assets (Azar *et al.*, 2022). Having such plans ready would mean faster action and clearer communication in a crisis, which can itself prevent system-wide loss of confidence.

6. Public Education and Market Discipline

Users of stablecoins span from sophisticated crypto traders to ordinary citizens seeking dollar stability in weak-currency countries. Education about the risks is crucial:

- Regulators and central banks should clearly communicate that stablecoins are not risk-free money (unless and until a particular one is officially backed). Just as governments often run campaigns about deposit insurance limits or scam awareness, they might issue guidance on what protections do or don't exist for stablecoins. For example, clarifying that stablecoins are not legal tender and are not protected by deposit insurance.

- This transparency can foster market discipline: if users are aware of differences between, say, a regulated fully-reserved stablecoin and an unregulated one, they may favor the former, pressuring the latter either to improve or lose market share. Already, we see some market discipline: post-Terra, purely algorithmic coins have found little trust; users flocked to stablecoins with clearer backing. Regulators can reinforce that dynamic by promoting information availability.
- On the industry side, best practice standards can be developed (perhaps via an industry association or with official backing) for disclosures, risk management, and consumer protection features (like complaint handling, or maybe even voluntary insurance pools).

7. Continuous Research and Dialogue

Finally, given how novel this area is, authorities must remain in a learning and adaptive posture:

- **Monitor trends**: Keep abreast of technology developments (e.g., emerging algorithmic ideas, integration of stablecoins with social media or new payment apps, etc.), as well as usage patterns (like which countries see rising stablecoin use and why).
- **Data gathering**: Improve data on stablecoin holdings and flows. The global official community might need new reporting frameworks – for example, encouraging banks and funds to report any significant exposures to stablecoins, or tracking on-chain data with advanced analytics (the way some firms do, but for policy use).
- **Scenario analysis and stress tests**: Conduct exercises simulating stablecoin run scenarios and their impact on financial markets. Central banks and the IMF could incorporate these into their stability assessments (indeed, some have started doing so in reports). This will help quantify potential spillovers and convince any doubters in the regulatory community to take preemptive action. The New York Fed's paper (2024), adapting a systemic risk framework to digital assets, is a good example of the analytical approaches needed (Azar *et al.*, 2022).
- **Stakeholder dialogue**: Engage not just domestically (with industry, consumer groups, etc.) but internationally. Use forums like the BIS committees, G20, and others to regularly discuss progress and adjust the global roadmap. Private sector input is valuable too – stablecoin issuers and blockchain devel-

opers can highlight practical challenges or innovations that regulators should consider (for instance, technical ways to implement regulatory requirements on-chain).

- **Adaptive regulation**: Be prepared that initial regulations might need updates. The crypto field evolves quickly; regulatory sandboxes can be used to allow experimentation under watch. If, say, someone develops a stablecoin truly immune to runs through novel design, regulators should study it and possibly refine rules to accommodate beneficial innovation (while keeping guardrails). Conversely, if new risks emerge (like stablecoins linked to novel underlying assets that could be systemic), rules should expand to cover them.

The principle is that policymaking should not be one-and-done; it's an iterative process to keep the regulatory framework in line with market reality and risks. A good comparison is the evolution of banking regulation over decades – stablecoin and crypto regulation will similarly need constant refinement.

FUTURE RESEARCH DIRECTIONS

In implementing all the above, the challenge is to avoid stifling useful innovation while preventing instability. There is a middle path:

- Encourage competition and diversity of solutions (multiple regulated issuers, different technology approaches) so that no single failure is catastrophic. At the same time, enforce baseline safety standards for all.
- Promote beneficial uses (like cheaper remittances, inclusion) by perhaps supporting pilot projects or public-private partnerships, even while clamping down on reckless speculative projects (like unbacked algorithmic coins promising unrealistic yields).
- Global public good considerations: Stablecoins addressing payment frictions are solving a real problem. If regulation or CBDCs can solve that problem in a safer way, that's ideal. But if it will take time, perhaps allow interim solutions with oversight. For example, where cross-border payments are costly, allowing a regulated stablecoin to operate can be positive as long as the risks are managed.

In the end, achieving the right balance will likely be an ongoing negotiation. Policymakers must weigh the public interest in financial stability, which is paramount, as a crisis in money can undermine economies, against the potential benefits of technological innovation that could make financial services more efficient and accessible. As one IMF commentary framed it, stablecoins are a "double-edged sword" (instagram.com): they point to inefficiencies in current systems and offer new solutions, but also carry familiar dangers in new forms. The goal of policy should be to sharpen the useful edge and blunt the harmful one.

CONCLUSION

Stablecoins have emerged from the fringes of cryptocurrency to become a focal point of discussions on the future of money and finance. Their rapid ascent – fueled by demand for digital, dollar-denominated value in a fast-paced online economy – demonstrates the innovative potential of private-sector-led monetary evolution. By providing liquidity and stability within the crypto ecosystem, stablecoins have enabled new markets and financial products to flourish. They hint at how payments and settlements could be more efficient and borderless, addressing pain points in traditional finance such as costly remittances or slow cross-border transfers.

Yet, as this chapter has detailed, stablecoins also epitomize the age-old risks of banking and finance, transplanted into a new setting. They raise the specter of runs, of credit failures, of fragmentation of the monetary unit – the very problems that 20th-century financial regulation and central banking strove to solve in traditional contexts. The events of 2022–2024, from Terra's collapse to the USDC depeg, served as clarion calls that unchecked stablecoin growth can indeed threaten financial stability. What was initially a hypothetical concern has become tangible: billions can be lost, markets can be roiled, and confidence can be shaken if stablecoins falter. Moreover, as stablecoins increasingly interface with the traditional financial system (through reserve assets and institutional adoption), the distinction between "crypto risks" and "traditional risks" is blurring. A shock in one realm can quickly transmit to the other.

For central bankers and regulators, the mandate is clear. Financial stability must be preserved. This does not mean stifling innovation – rather, it means channeling it responsibly. The chapter's recommendations underscore a philosophy of same risk, same regulation: if stablecoins function like money or like bank deposits, they should be safeguarded and supervised similarly to those instruments. The frameworks being developed aim to erect guardrails so that, for instance, a stablecoin widely used for payments cannot suddenly implode due to poor backing or mismanagement. In parallel, the exploration of CBDCs offers a public sector path to modernize money without the credit risk that plagues private stablecoins. Many central banks view CBDCs not as anathema to stablecoins, but as part of a broader strategy to ensure the "singleness of money" and trust in the currency in a digital age (Kosse et al., 2023).

The coexistence model – where CBDCs provide a stable core and private players innovate around it – appears both viable and attractive from a stability standpoint.

Looking forward into 2025 and beyond, we can anticipate a few key developments:

- Regulatory clarity and enforcement will increase. By end-2025, major jurisdictions will likely have enforceable stablecoin regulations in place. Some existing large stablecoins might need to adjust (e.g., more disclosure, changes in reserve structure) to comply or risk being restricted.
- Market adjustments will occur. We may see consolidation (perhaps weaker stablecoins exit, stronger ones grow). New entrants from the traditional finance world could emerge (for example, consortia of banks issuing tokenized deposit coins, or fintech firms launching fully regulated stablecoins, perhaps in multiple currencies). Competition from CBDCs may also shape the market – for instance, if a digital euro launches, euro-backed private stablecoins might diminish in relevance.
- Innovation in risk mitigation. The industry, in dialogue with authorities, might devise novel ways to make stablecoins safer – for instance, technologies for instant redemption through smart contracts tied to central bank money, or hybrid models where stablecoins automatically convert into CBDC under stress. Such ideas, once mere theory, could be piloted in the coming years.
- Cross-border cooperation will be tested and hopefully strengthened. If a stablecoin aspires to be global, it will face a gauntlet of regulatory expectations globally. Conversely, if global coordination is insufficient and a systemic stablecoin incident occurs, it will serve as a painful lesson, reinforcing the necessity for joint action (much as 2008 did for banking). The G20 and institutions like the IMF will remain critical venues for forging consensus on these issues.

Throughout all these changes, the priority must remain to safeguard the stability and integrity of the financial system. Stablecoins, like any financial innovation, must ultimately serve the public interest – which includes not just efficiency and inclusion, but also safety and reliability. The chapter's perspective – that of a central bank governor – inherently puts weight on caution and systemic risk awareness. This is appropriate: central bankers are the custodians of monetary stability and lenders of last resort; they know that trust, once lost, is hard to regain. As one IMF article noted, *"if this common knowledge fails, so does coordination, and the monetary system becomes unmoored, with large societal costs"* (Kosse et al., 2023). Stablecoins, if they are to be part of the future monetary system, must not be allowed to undermine that common knowledge of value.

In conclusion, stablecoins sit at a crossroads of promise and peril. With prudent governance, international cooperation, and adaptive policy, we can envisage a future where stablecoins (or their evolutions) contribute to a more efficient and inclusive financial system – one that embraces the benefits of technology while upholding the bedrock of stability that underpins global economic prosperity. The journey requires vigilance, dialogue, and an unwavering commitment to sound principles of money and finance. The coming years will be critical in determining whether stablecoins fulfill their transformative potential as a trusted bridge between old and new finance, or whether they remain a source of systemic anxieties. The work of balancing innovation with stability will persist, but armed with the lessons so far and guided by a clear vision of the public good, policymakers and industry together can steer this innovation toward a sustainable and secure path.

REFERENCES

Annual Economic Report, B. I. S. (2025). The next-generation monetary and financial system. In *Bis.org* (pp. 1–38). BIS., https://www.bis.org/publ/arpdf/ar2025e3.htm

Azar, P. D., Baughman, G., Carapella, F., Gerszten, J., Lubis, A., Perez-Sangimino, J. P., & Werman, A. (2022). *The financial stability implications of digital assets (No. 1034)*. Staff Reports.

Chavanette. (2024). *CBDC and Regulated Stablecoins: Friend or Foe? Pt2 - Ep. 9 - Chavanette Advisors*. Chavanette Advisors. https://chavanette.com/blog/cbdc-and-regulated-stablecoins-friend-or-foe-part-2/

CoinGecko. (2024). *State of Stablecoins: 2024*. CoinGecko. https://www.coingecko.com/research/publications/state-of-stablecoins-2024 – Report.

Financial Stability Board. (2020). *Crypto-assets and Global "Stablecoins."* www.fsb.org. https://www.fsb.org/work-of-the-fsb/financial-innovation-and-structural-change/crypto-assets-and-global-stablecoins/

Financial Stability Board. (2022). "Assessment of Risks to Financial Stability from Crypto-assets" – Report.

Financial Stability Board. (2023). *High-level recommendations for the regulation, supervision and oversight of global stablecoin arrangements*. Financial Stability Board.

Financial Stability Board. (2024). "Cross-border issues of Global Stablecoins in Emerging Markets" – Report.

Helmore, E. (2023). USD Coin value falls after revealing $3.3bn held at Silicon Valley Bank. *The Guardian*. https://www.theguardian.com/technology/2023/mar/11/usd-coin-depeg-silicon-valley-bank-collapse

Kosse, A., Glowka, M., Mattei, I., & Rice, T. (2023). *Will the real stablecoin please stand up?* BIS Papers.

Matthews, B., & Tran, H. (2025). Central bank digital currencies versus stablecoins: Divergent EU and US perspectives. Atlantic Council. https://www.atlanticcouncil.org/blogs/econographics/central-bank-digital-currencies-versus-stablecoins-divergent-eu-and-us-perspectives/

President's Working Group on Financial Markets. (2021). "Report on Stablecoins." (Recommended that Congress enact legislation to limit stablecoin issuance to insured depository institutions or similar, to ensure prudential oversight and protection, citing potential runs and payments systemic risk in absence of such regulation).

Chapter 7
Cross Border Coordination

Kokila Alagh
KARM Legal Consultants, UAE

ABSTRACT

This chapter analyses cross-border coordination in the regulation and supervision of stablecoins. Stablecoins challenge jurisdiction-based regulatory frameworks by operating across multiple legal and monetary regimes. Drawing upon the perspectives of the FSB, FATF, and the CPMI, the chapter explores how these international standard-setting bodies converge on the need for globally consistent oversight to mitigate systemic, prudential, and financial integrity risks. It examines the macroeconomic and microeconomic vulnerabilities associated with fragmented regulation, including risks to monetary sovereignty, financial stability, and consumer protection. The chapter further identifies implementation challenges in supervision and enforcement, proposes key policy principles for achieving coordinated oversight, and highlights emerging models of international cooperation such as supervisory colleges, memoranda of understanding, and mutual-recognition frameworks. Ultimately, it argues that structured, institutionalised cooperation is the cornerstone of credible global stablecoin governance.

INTRODUCTION

Following the global convergence on prudential safeguards for stablecoins, a further challenge arises in ensuring that regulation is effective across borders. Stablecoins, by design, are digital and borderless instruments that transcend jurisdictional boundaries. They may be issued in one jurisdiction, traded on a platform authorised by a regulator in another, and used by individuals and corporations across several

DOI: 10.4018/979-8-3373-6655-5.ch007

others. This combination of technological reach and jurisdictional fluidity challenges traditional regulatory paradigms built on territoriality. As stablecoin arrangements increasingly operate across legal, regulatory, and monetary frontiers, they blur established lines of oversight. Consequently, the application of a purely domestic regulatory framework may prove inadequate to address the systemic, prudential, and conduct-related risks arising from stablecoin arrangements whose reach extends beyond the jurisdiction of issuance or primary regulation.

The absence of robust cross-border coordination introduces vulnerabilities to financial stability and market integrity. These include the risk of regulatory arbitrage, where entities exploit inconsistencies between national frameworks and fragmented supervision, undermining enforcement and enabling systemic risk. Recognising these challenges, the SSBs, including the FSB, the FATF, and the Bank for International Settlements' Committee on Payments and Market Infrastructures (CPMI), have underscored that stablecoins, particularly those used for cross-border payments, require coordinated global oversight. Their concerns encompass AML/CFT, consumer protection, data privacy, and cybersecurity. Addressing these challenges requires not only sound domestic frameworks but also mechanisms for consistent international cooperation, information sharing, and coordinated supervision (Financial Stability Board, 2023; Financial Stability Board, 2025).

Stablecoins move instantly across borders through decentralised networks that often bypass correspondent banking systems. While this may enhance efficiency and inclusion, it also increases the risk of illicit activity and regulatory evasion. The effectiveness of any domestic regime therefore depends not only on its internal controls but also on its interoperability with other jurisdictions' frameworks. Without cross-border alignment, inconsistent oversight enables undesirable actors to migrate to weaker jurisdictions, fragmenting global supervision.

The FATF, FSB, and CPMI each approach the question of cross-border coordination from distinct but complementary perspectives. FATF focuses on financial integrity and AML/CFT supervision; the FSB examines systemic stability and global policy coherence; and the CPMI evaluates implications for cross-border payments and financial infrastructure.

The FATF's Updated Guidance for a Risk-Based Approach to Virtual Assets and Virtual Asset Service Providers (FATF Guidance) serves as the foundation for contemporary global AML/CFT oversight of virtual assets and VASP(s) (The Financial Action Task Force, 2021). FATF recognises that such activities are inherently transnational, enabling frictionless movement of value across jurisdictions. This very quality, while promoting innovation and inclusion, heightens the risk of money laundering, terrorist financing, and proliferation financing. FATF therefore stresses that no jurisdiction, regardless of its sophistication, can mitigate these risks in isolation. A coordinated approach is essential.

FATF calls upon countries to establish formal and informal supervisory cooperation mechanisms to facilitate timely exchange of information and mutual assistance. These should extend beyond financial intelligence units to include securities regulators, central banks, and law enforcement authorities. FATF's risk-based philosophy encourages regulators to calibrate oversight to risk while ensuring international consistency. Without proactive cooperation, virtual assets, including stablecoins, could become channels for illicit finance and systemic opacity.

Complementing FATF's focus on financial integrity, the FSB adopts a systemic and prudential lens. In its Thematic Review on the FSB Global Regulatory Framework for Crypto-Asset Activities (FSB Review), the FSB evaluates global progress in implementing international policy measures, particularly those concerning stablecoin arrangements (Financial Stability Board, 2025). This review builds upon earlier frameworks such as the FSB's High-Level Recommendations for the Regulation, Supervision and Oversight of Global Stablecoin Arrangements, offering a comprehensive assessment of how jurisdictions have operationalised these principles (Financial Stability Board, 2023). It observes that stablecoin arrangements are structurally cross-border, with issuers, custodians, and users distributed across multiple legal regimes. This fragmentation generates oversight gaps and inconsistent supervision. To address these risks, the FSB underscores the need for supervisory and regulatory responses that extend beyond national borders and rely on structured international coordination (Financial Stability Board, 2025). Achieving this parity requires information exchange, aligned supervisory standards, and coordinated interpretation of equivalent risks.

The FSB notes that few jurisdictions have adopted specific cooperation tools such as memoranda of understanding (MoUs) for crypto-asset supervision. It recommends that members establish bilateral and multilateral arrangements covering prudential, conduct, operational resilience, and AML/CFT oversight. Effective supervision, the FSB argues, must integrate prudential and consumer-protection concerns and avoid both duplication and regulatory gaps. Strengthened cooperation enhances both national frameworks and the collective resilience of the global financial system.

The CPMI, by contrast, frames cross-border coordination through the lens of payment efficiency and financial infrastructure. Its 2023 Report on Considerations for the Use of Stablecoin Arrangements in Cross-Border Payments (CPMI Report) forms a crucial part of the G20 cross-border payments programme and situates stablecoins at the intersection of innovation and systemic risk (The Committee on Payments and Market Infrastructures, 2023). Properly designed and regulated stablecoins could improve cross-border payments by reducing costs and increasing speed and transparency. However, in the absence of consistent international regulation, these same characteristics could amplify systemic vulnerabilities, fragment payment systems, and undermine monetary sovereignty.

The CPMI's analysis reinforces the principle that cross-border coordination is not merely supportive but essential to ensuring payment system safety and integrity.

Together, the FATF, FSB, and CPMI perspectives converge on a shared conclusion: fragmented or inconsistent regulation cannot effectively manage cross-border stablecoin risks. FATF provides the baseline for financial integrity, the FSB extends it into systemic stability, and the CPMI anchors it in payment infrastructure. Their institutional priorities differ, but their mandates are complementary. When harmonised, they form a coherent framework for global stablecoin governance that integrates AML/CFT, financial stability, and operational interoperability.

Against this background, the chapter proceeds to explore the multifaceted dimensions of cross-border regulatory cooperation in the context of stablecoins. It will: examine why cross-border regulatory coordination and cooperation are particularly important for stablecoin activities; analyse the macro- and microeconomic risks associated with cross-border stablecoin activities; identify the core challenges of implementation, supervision, and enforcement across jurisdictions; outline key policy considerations and principles that may assist in mitigating such challenges; assess how regulators in leading jurisdictions are operationalising cross-border coordination; and set out the future outlook for cross-border coordination and international cooperation in this industry.

WHY CROSS-BORDER COORDINATION IS IMPORTANT?

The need for cross-border coordination arises directly from the decentralised and distributed structure of stablecoins. A single transaction may involve an issuer incorporated in one jurisdiction, a reserve custodian in another, and users across several others. This dispersion of functions creates layers of legal and compliance complexity. Measures relating to AML/CFT, data protection, cybersecurity, and consumer protection become difficult to enforce consistently when entities are subject to distinct national standards.

No single regulator can supervise the entire operational chain of a stablecoin arrangement without cooperation with foreign counterparts. The absence of structured coordination creates blind spots that enable regulatory arbitrage and obscure accountability when breaches occur. At a macro level, the extensive use of foreign-currency-pegged stablecoins in domestic economies could weaken monetary sovereignty, hinder liquidity management, and undermine transmission of monetary policy. At the micro level, fragmented enforcement leaves consumers vulnerable to products outside their jurisdiction's perimeter, limiting redress in cases of fraud or insolvency. For these reasons, regulators such as the CBUAE have introduced registration requirements for FPT issuers under the PTSR, ensuring that such issuers remain subject to domestic supervision even when operating across borders.

At a macroeconomic level, the widespread use of foreign-currency-pegged stablecoins in domestic payment systems may have far-reaching implications for monetary sovereignty and financial stability. If households and businesses increasingly transact or store value in a stablecoin pegged to an external currency, central banks could face difficulties in managing liquidity, transmitting monetary policy, and maintaining confidence in the national currency. At the micro level, the absence of consistent cross border enforcement could expose consumers and investors to products that fall outside their jurisdiction's regulatory perimeter, diminishing recourse in the event of fraud or insolvency. Thus, effective cross-border coordination is not merely an issue of regulatory efficiency; it is a precondition for maintaining both financial stability and the credibility of domestic monetary frameworks in a globalised financial environment (Financial Stability Board, 2023).

The FATF warns that some stablecoins could achieve global scale before adequate safeguards are in place. It therefore underscores the necessity of cooperation across the entire value chain, including issuers, reserve custodians, wallet providers, exchanges, and other intermediaries. Coordination should extend beyond financial intelligence units to securities and payments supervisors, central banks, and law enforcement.

The FATF also acknowledges the enforcement complexities created by the cross border distribution of stablecoin functions and encourages the formation of dedicated supervisory groups, akin to cooperation frameworks used for systemically important institutions, to facilitate information exchange, joint risk assessments, and mutual assistance. It calls for closer collaboration among international organisations, including the FSB, BIS, World Bank, and IMF, to harmonise approaches and close jurisdictional gaps that enable misconduct to migrate. Without such coordination, the risks of arbitrage, illicit finance, and market distortion could undermine both domestic and global financial stability (The Financial Action Task Force, 2021).

The FSB approaches the issue from a systemic perspective. In its thematic review of the global regulatory framework for crypto-asset activities, the FSB observes that stablecoin markets are inherently transnational, with functions distributed across multiple legal regimes and often lacking a clear geographic locus of control. This fragmentation produces oversight gaps and divergent approaches that create financial stability risks. To counter these risks, the FSB reiterates the principle of same activity, same risk, same regulation (Financial Stability Board, 2025). Achieving parity requires efficient exchange of supervisory information and coordinated interpretations of equivalent risk. The FSB notes that only a limited number of jurisdictions currently rely on tools such as memoranda of understanding tailored to crypto-asset supervision and recommends the use of bilateral and multilateral arrangements that encompass prudential, conduct, operational resilience, and AML and CFT oversight (Financial Stability Board, 2025).

The FSB further emphasises that supervisory coordination must be holistic, integrating prudential concerns with consumer protection, competition policies, and cybersecurity. Fragmented oversight leads to gaps where agencies assume another is responsible, as well as overlaps where conflicting mandates cause friction. These inefficiencies magnify vulnerabilities and reduce the capacity for collective response during market stress. The FSB's recommendations therefore articulate a cooperative architecture based on continuous dialogue, reciprocal data access, and clearly delineated responsibilities. The aim is not uniform law but equivalent outcomes under harmonised principles so that domestic discretion aligns with global standards and reduces contagion risk.

The CPMI provides a payments-infrastructure vantage point. Its report on stablecoin arrangements in cross-border payments examines how stablecoins might be integrated into the global payments ecosystem without compromising stability or sovereignty. Properly designed and regulated arrangements could reduce costs and settlement times and expand access to digital payments, while on-chain transparency could, in principle, enhance traceability across borders. These benefits materialise only where international regulations are consistent and coordinated. In its absence, the very features that make stablecoins efficient can amplify systemic vulnerabilities, fragment payment systems, and erode monetary sovereignty. The CPMI therefore views cross-border coordination as a precondition for safe interoperability, settlement finality, and the orderly interaction between public and private payment systems (The Committee on Payments and Market Infrastructures, 2023).

Taken together, the perspectives of FATF, the FSB, and the CPMI converge on a single, unambiguous conclusion: stablecoin regulation cannot succeed without structured international coordination. While each institution views the issue through its own mandate - FATF from the standpoint of financial integrity, FSB from systemic stability, and CPMI from payment efficiency - all recognise that the borderless architecture of stablecoins collapses the distinction between domestic and international financial activity. The effectiveness of national regulation is therefore contingent on the collective willingness of jurisdictions to cooperate, share information, and enforce consistent standards.

Taken together, the perspectives of the FATF, FSB, and CPMI converge on a clear conclusion. Stablecoin regulation cannot succeed without structured international coordination. Each institution's mandate is distinct, with the FATF focused on financial integrity, the FSB on systemic stability, and the CPMI on payment system safety and efficiency, yet their approaches are complementary. The FATF provides the baseline for AML and CFT compliance and risk mitigation. The FSB extends its reach into financial stability and market integrity. The CPMI situates both within the operational realities of cross-border payments. Combined, they form a multi-layered framework for addressing the risks and opportunities associated with stablecoins. The absence of coordination would not merely hinder supervisory efficiency. It would undermine the core objectives of financial stability, consumer protection, and monetary sovereignty that these institutions collectively seek to preserve.

MACRO AND MICRO ECONOMIC RISKS ASSOCIATED WITH STABLECOINS

Stablecoins introduce interconnected macroeconomic and microeconomic risks that demand coordinated global oversight. At the macro level, they influence monetary policy transmission, currency substitution, and systemic stability. At the micro level, they expose users to governance, operational, and redemption risks. Because stablecoins circulate globally, no single authority can effectively monitor their full lifecycle across issuance, trading, and redemption.

From a macroeconomic perspective, widespread use of foreign-denominated stablecoins within domestic economies can erode monetary sovereignty and reduce the effectiveness of national monetary policy. In jurisdictions with weaker financial systems, households and businesses may increasingly rely on stablecoins pegged to global reserve currencies such as the US dollar or the euro for savings and transactions. This dynamic can lead to "digital dollarisation," where private, foreign-backed tokens compete directly with sovereign currencies. As a result, central banks may find it difficult to manage liquidity, influence interest rates, and respond to macroeconomic shocks.

The failure or loss of confidence in a widely used stablecoin could have systemic implications far beyond the crypto market. Disruptions in redemption mechanisms or reserve management could trigger investor panic and spill over into payment systems, DeFi protocols, and other market infrastructures that depend on the stablecoin as a settlement asset. This interconnection between private and public payment networks transforms stablecoin stability into a macro-financial concern. For this reason, SSBs have consistently emphasised that cross-border regulatory coordination is not an adjunct to monetary policy, it is a precondition for safeguarding global financial stability. For this reason, the Financial Stability Board (FSB) and other international bodies view cross-border regulatory coordination as a precondition for safeguarding global financial stability (Financial Stability Board, 2023).

The FSB explicitly links microeconomic vulnerabilities to macroeconomic outcomes. Global stablecoins can affect capital flows, exchange rates, and liquidity distribution across jurisdictions. Divergent national approaches to supervision or prudential standards may encourage regulatory arbitrage, distort competition, and fragment liquidity. To mitigate these risks, the FSB recommends joint monitoring by central banks and regulators, supported by comprehensive data-sharing arrangements capturing reserve distributions, user activity, and cross-border flows (Financial Stability Board, 2025).

At the micro level, vulnerabilities arise from inadequate redemption mechanisms, poor governance, and opaque reserve management. When reserve holdings are insufficiently liquid or concentrated in volatile assets, or when redemption rights are unclear, user confidence can deteriorate rapidly, prompting run-like behaviour. Where issuers, custodians, and service providers are distributed across multiple jurisdictions, regulators may face barriers to accessing key financial data, especially under restrictive data-localisation laws. The FSB emphasises that strong transparency and governance standards—together with cooperative supervision—are essential to address these risks.

The CPMI approaches these issues from a central banking and payment-systems perspective. Its analysis highlights three domains affected by cross-border stablecoin use (The Committee on Payments and Market Infrastructures, 2023).

First, with respect to payment system integrity, central banks bear the mandate of ensuring that payment infrastructures remain reliable and resilient. Cross-border stablecoins, depending on their design and governance, could either complement or destabilise these systems. If oversight is fragmented, a failure in the settlement process or operational malfunction in one jurisdiction could rapidly spill over across markets,

undermining trust and causing systemic disruption. The CPMI thus views regulatory coordination as a prerequisite for integrating stablecoins into the payment ecosystem safely.

Second, in terms of monetary stability, the CPMI highlights the danger of currency substitution in jurisdictions where stablecoins pegged to major international currencies become widely used in domestic payments. Such substitution weakens the transmission of monetary policy and erodes central banks' control over the money supply. The CPMI Report calls for enhanced policy coordination among central banks to monitor the extent of stablecoin adoption and to design complementary macroprudential measures, such as limits on foreign-currency exposure in domestic markets. The CPMI's recommendation reflects an underlying concern that while stablecoins can promote efficiency and inclusion, their uncontrolled proliferation could compromise the sovereignty and effectiveness of national monetary systems.

Third, in the realm of financial stability, the CPMI draws attention to the potential for runs on reserve-backed stablecoins. Because stablecoin issuers often hold reserve assets in traditional financial institutions, a sudden surge in redemption requests could strain liquidity and transmit stress to the broader banking system. Given that these reserves are frequently distributed across multiple jurisdictions, a liquidity shortfall in one market could cascade into others, creating a cross-border contagion effect. The CPMI therefore advocates for coordinated supervisory responses among central banks and financial regulators. This includes establishing mechanisms to share data on reserve composition, redemption volumes, and liquidity positions, as well as aligning crisis management procedures across jurisdictions. Coordination, in this sense, extends beyond supervision to encompass joint policymaking and contingency planning.

The CPMI further stresses that effective oversight requires not only prudential and technical regulation but also macroeconomic policy coordination among central banks. Stablecoins operate at the intersection of monetary, technological, and regulatory domains, making isolated supervision ineffective.

Collectively, the analyses of the FATF, FSB, and CPMI reveal that macroeconomic and microeconomic risks are deeply interlinked. Failures in reserve management can trigger liquidity shortages that propagate internationally, while macroeconomic instability can accelerate user withdrawals and governance breakdowns. Stablecoins thus test the limits of existing regulatory architectures, compelling central banks and supervisors to move beyond jurisdictional silos toward a genuinely global system of oversight.

The overarching lesson from international standard setters is clear: effective management of stablecoin risks cannot occur in isolation. It requires continuous, structured, and cooperative engagement among authorities, founded on mutual trust and a shared commitment to financial stability. Without such collaboration, the promise of innovation risks being eclipsed by the dangers of fragmentation and systemic contagion.

CHALLENGES IN CROSS-BORDER IMPLEMENTATION, SUPERVISION AND ENFORCEMENT

Although the need for cross-border coordination in regulating stablecoins is widely recognised, its practical implementation remains complex. National authorities face multiple challenges ranging from information and data asymmetries to divergent legal definitions, institutional capacity constraints, and limited enforcement powers beyond national borders. These difficulties delay supervision, weaken enforcement, and undermine confidence in the effectiveness of global oversight mechanisms. The decentralised, borderless design of stablecoin arrangements exposes the structural limitations of the traditional jurisdiction-based financial regulatory model.

One of the foremost challenges is the persistent asymmetry of information and data. Key operational components of a stablecoin arrangement—transaction flows, reserve holdings, and governance structures—often lie outside the jurisdiction of domestic authorities. In traditional financial systems, licensing and prudential reporting enable comprehensive oversight. In contrast, stablecoin ecosystems disperse critical functions across jurisdictions: an issuer may be incorporated in one country, intermediaries may be in another, and validators may operate globally through decentralised networks. This dispersion prevents any single regulator from maintaining a consolidated view of operations, complicating both real-time supervision and ex post enforcement.

A related obstacle stems from divergent regulatory definitions and the inconsistent scope of application across jurisdictions. Some countries treat stablecoins as payment instruments or e-money, others classify them as securities, and many still operate without any clear legal framework. The absence of definitional harmony obstructs cooperation between authorities by preventing mutual recognition of licensing, supervisory findings, or enforcement measures. Differences in institutional mandates further complicate engagement: in some jurisdictions, oversight rests with central banks; in others, with securities regulators or financial intelligence units. This fragmentation creates uncertainty over which authority should lead cross-border engagement, delays cooperation, and opens opportunities for regulatory arbitrage.

Institutional and resource limitations compound these challenges. Supervisory authorities, particularly in smaller or developing economies, often lack the technical capacity to monitor blockchain-based activities or to analyse smart contracts in real time. Stablecoins pegged to foreign currencies and issued through decentralised or offshore structures make it even harder to identify a legally accountable entity. This accountability gap undermines supervision and enforcement and weakens the ability of regulators to act when systemic risks or consumer harm arise.

Enforcement mechanisms for cross-border stablecoin activities also remain underdeveloped. Even where domestic laws exist, regulators frequently lack jurisdiction to compel offshore entities to comply with information requests or enforcement orders. The absence of clear authority over cross-border entities creates uncertainty, particularly in crisis situations that demand rapid, coordinated action. This fragmentation leaves users exposed and undermines regulatory credibility.

The FATF's Guidance, acknowledges progress since its 2019 standards but emphasises that cross-border implementation remains inconsistent. Many jurisdictions have not yet transposed FATF's recommendations fully into domestic law or they lack the institutional infrastructure for effective enforcement. FATF identifies several impediments that continue to obstruct coordinated supervision (The Financial Action Task Force, 2021). Chief among them is the divergence in definitions of "virtual assets" and "virtual asset service providers". In some countries, the term encompasses a broad range of entities from exchanges to custodians, while in others it is limited to intermediaries. Such inconsistencies hinder mutual recognition of licensing regimes and equivalent regulatory treatment across borders.

FATF also observes that many jurisdictions lack clarity on which domestic authority leads cross-border supervision, especially where multiple agencies share responsibility for crypto oversight. This institutional overlap weakens coordination both nationally and internationally. Another constraint lies in cross-border enforcement: regulators often cannot compel offshore entities to respond to enquiries or orders if those entities have no legal presence in the jurisdiction. Consequently, compliance gaps persist, and authorities remain reliant on voluntary cooperation.

Limited technical capacity further constrains regulatory effectiveness. Monitoring blockchain transactions requires advanced analytical tools and expertise that many regulators have yet to acquire. Without the means to trace transactions or interpret complex smart contracts, supervisors face blind spots in detecting illicit finance or systemic vulnerabilities. FATF's "Travel Rule", which mandates that virtual asset service providers collect and transmit originator and beneficiary information for all transfers, exemplifies these challenges. Implementation remains uneven due to varying technological readiness, privacy laws, and interpretations of compliance requirements. FATF stresses that achieving interoperability among national implementations of the Travel Rule is critical to preventing fragmentation and regulatory loopholes that could facilitate illicit activity.

The FSB adopts a systemic and institutional perspective. Its review identifies persistent barriers to establishing coherent global supervision (Financial Stability Board, 2025). Foremost among these is regulatory fragmentation: jurisdictions classify stablecoins and crypto assets differently—under securities laws, payment system frameworks, or e-money regulations—and many still lack dedicated oversight regimes. This heterogeneity impedes consistent supervision, complicates enforcement, and undermines confidence in the predictability of regulation.

Legal barriers to information sharing remain another key obstacle. Confidentiality, data protection, and bank secrecy laws in several jurisdictions limit regulators' ability to exchange information on entities or transactions, especially when stablecoin issuers or custodians are located offshore. Without harmonised data-sharing protocols or legal gateways, cooperation remains slow and reactive. The FSB also highlights resource constraints: many supervisory agencies lack the personnel and technical tools to engage in international coordination, participate in supervisory colleges, or conduct joint inspections. This imbalance creates a two-tier system where advanced economies can sustain robust oversight, while smaller jurisdictions become weak links in the global supervisory network.

To address these gaps, the FSB recommends that jurisdictions establish national coordination mechanisms, such as inter-agency task forces or joint supervisory units, to streamline communication and clarify roles. Each jurisdiction should designate a lead authority for crypto-asset supervision to serve as the main point of contact for cross-border cooperation. By strengthening domestic coherence, regulators can enhance their ability to participate effectively in global coordination and ensure information flows both vertically and horizontally across networks. The FSB's approach reflects a core principle: meaningful international coordination begins with clear and well-resourced domestic governance.

The CPMI categorises the challenges of cross-border supervision into organisational, market, and regulatory domains (The Committee on Payments and Market Infrastructures, 2023). At the organisational level, stablecoin arrangements often comprise multiple entities—issuers, custodians, technology operators, and governance bodies—each located in different jurisdictions. This fragmentation leads to gaps where certain functions fall outside supervision and overlaps where several authorities claim jurisdiction. The CPMI urges regulators to conduct coordinated mapping exercises to delineate which components of a stablecoin arrangement fall under their remit and to establish structured cooperation channels with foreign counterparts.

From a market perspective, the CPMI warns of rapid scaling and concentration risks. A stablecoin denominated in a major reserve currency could quickly achieve global reach, creating systemic dependencies that transcend national boundaries. Disruptions in one jurisdiction could therefore propagate across the global financial system.

At the regulatory level, the CPMI concludes that the lack of consistent oversight remains the greatest obstacle to the safe and efficient cross-border use of stablecoins. Differing classifications and supervisory approaches fragment markets and hinder cooperation. The CPMI thus calls for "strongly coordinated efforts at the international level" to promote convergence while allowing flexibility to address jurisdiction-specific risks (The Committee on Payments and Market Infrastructures, 2023). Balancing harmonisation with national discretion remains one of the central tensions in stablecoin regulation.

Taken together, the analyses of the FATF, FSB, and CPMI reveal that challenges in implementing, supervising, and enforcing cross-border stablecoin regulation are not merely administrative but structural. They expose the limits of applying territorially bound regulation to globally distributed financial networks. The challenge is not only that of coordination but of governance itself. Stablecoins have demonstrated that risk, information, and accountability no longer align neatly with jurisdictional borders. Addressing this reality requires a paradigm shift toward collective responsibility, shared supervision, and mutual trust among regulators. Only through such a cooperative framework can the international community ensure that innovation in the stablecoin ecosystem develops within an environment of stability, integrity, and global coherence.

KEY POLICY CONSIDERATIONS AND REGULATORY PRINCIPLES FOR EFFECTIVE CROSS-BORDER COORDINATION

Building an effective cross-border regime for stablecoins requires more than broad commitments to cooperation; it demands a practical framework through which supervisors can identify risks simultaneously and act in concert. This section sets out a coherent suite of considerations and regulatory principles that, together, can narrow information asymmetries, strengthen supervisory access to data, and enable timely, proportionate interventions across jurisdictions.

At the centre of an effective model lies structured cooperation among national authorities. Stablecoin activity spans multiple domains (payments, prudential supervision, securities regulation, and AML and CFT oversight) and cannot be monitored effectively by siloed agencies acting independently. Supervisors therefore require durable information

sharing arrangements that go beyond case-specific requests, as well as coordinated supervisory mechanisms and joint enforcement protocols. Such mechanisms are particularly critical where risks are inherently cross-jurisdictional, including AML and CFT compliance, sanctions screening, data privacy, cyber incident response, and operational resilience across globally distributed technology infrastructures. Without intentional governance structures linking these areas, blind spots persist and accountability becomes diluted (The Committee on Payments and Market Infrastructures, 2023; The Financial Action Task Force, 2021; Financial Stability Board, 2023).

A second organising principle is the establishment of minimum international standards to anchor consistent supervisory outcomes. While the form of implementation will differ across jurisdictions, convergence on core prudential and conduct parameters can materially reduce fragmentation and the incentive for regulatory arbitrage. Key minimum standards include requirements on reserve composition and disclosure (quality, liquidity, segregation, and custody location), enforceable redemption mechanisms and timeframes, and baseline governance measures such as board accountability, conflicts management, audit, and fit-and-proper standards for management. Agreement on these fundamentals provides a common floor from which regulators can adapt additional safeguards to local contexts (The Committee on Payments and Market Infrastructures, 2023; Financial Stability Board, 2023).

A third pillar is capacity building. Jurisdictions most exposed to foreign-issued stablecoins (often those dependent on remittance corridors) are also those least equipped to oversee complex cross-border arrangements. A credible framework therefore combines standards with technical assistance, including training on blockchain analytics, supervisory technology for real-time monitoring, and guidance for cross-border investigations and crisis management. Parallel investment in digital payment infrastructure, interoperability standards, and settlement finality frameworks further embeds compliance at the system level, making risks more visible and regulatory expectations more consistent across markets (The Committee on Payments and Market Infrastructures, 2023; Financial Stability Board, 2025).

The FATF Recommendations provide detailed guidance on what meaningful supervisory coordination should entail, particularly for AML and CFT purposes. It underscores that supervisors should not operate in isolation, as virtual-asset activities involve globally distributed entities and shared technology infrastructures. Information exchanged across borders must go beyond public enforcement notices to include licensing status, beneficial ownership data, risk assessments, inspection outcomes, and transactional intelligence on cross-border flows. FATF encourages authorities to leverage existing platforms such as the Egmont Group and regional FATF bodies while also establishing bilateral and multilateral channels among prudential, conduct, and payments supervisors to ensure both strategic and operational intelligence can circulate promptly (The Financial Action Task Force, 2021).

FATF identifies several categories of barriers that impede this exchange: legal (privacy and confidentiality restrictions), technical (non-standard data formats), institutional (resource and expertise gaps), and relational (deficits of trust). Remedies begin with common information-sharing protocols, use of mutual legal assistance mechanisms where appropriate, and the appointment of liaison points within agencies to ensure requests are processed quickly and predictably. FATF stresses timeliness as a supervisory virtue: in markets where value moves within seconds, delayed responses amount to non-responses.

Anchoring cooperation within a risk-based framework, FATF expects supervisors to identify foreign VASPs with material cross-border exposure to local residents, require registration or authorisation where appropriate, and coordinate with home supervisors on risk assessments and compliance outcomes. This approach closes regulatory blind spots and ensures that all significant actors fall under effective supervision. FATF's Travel Rule exemplifies this model: by mandating transmission of originator and beneficiary information for virtual-asset transfers, it enables traceability of cross-border flows— provided that national implementations are interoperable. To this end, FATF advocates supervisory colleges and joint inspections for major cross-border VASPs and stablecoin operators, applying the principle of "same activity, same risk, same regulation" across technologies and jurisdictions (The Financial Action Task Force, 2021).

The FSB Review situates these supervisory mechanics within a broader governance framework. Recognising that stablecoin activities intersect payments, securities, and banking mandates, the FSB warns against domestic overlaps and underlaps that impede coherent engagement with foreign regulators. Its principal remedy is institutional clarity: for each global stablecoin arrangement, a designated lead supervisor should coordinate relevant domestic agencies and serve as the principal point of contact for host authorities. This structure integrates oversight throughout the lifecycle of authorisation, supervision, and resolution, without displacing other mandates (Financial Stability Board, 2025).

The FSB Review also calls for cross-border crisis-management frameworks tailored to stablecoins. Given the global distribution of users and reserves, authorities require pre agreed communication channels, escalation protocols, and playbooks for orderly wind down or resolution, including recognition of foreign enforcement measures. To operationalise these expectations, the FSB recommends annual reporting on national implementation, participation in cross-jurisdictional assessments of cooperation effectiveness, and maintenance of an implementation repository tracking use of memoranda of understanding, supervisory colleges, and data-sharing mechanisms (Financial Stability Board, 2025). Central to these efforts is data: the FSB highlights that stablecoin oversight depends on granular, harmonised reporting of reserve composition and location, redemption flows, cross-border transactions, and the network of intermediaries facilitating issuance and custody. Without such inputs, supervisors cannot construct a consolidated risk view.

The FSB's Recommendation 3 explicitly centres cross-border cooperation as a cornerstone of regulation. It directs authorities to coordinate domestically and internationally to achieve consistent oversight across borders and sectors. Several operational principles follow: cooperation must be systematic and cross-sectoral, institutionalised through memoranda of understanding, supervisory colleges, and crisis management groups; outcome consistency must be the goal, ensuring comparable protections for equivalent activities; information exchange must be timely and comprehensive, covering reserves, governance, and operational incidents; and crisis coordination must be pre-defined through clear escalation paths and communication protocols. Recommendation 3 is designed to interlock with sectoral standards such as the IOSCO' principles for cross-border cooperation and the Principles for Financial Market Infrastructures.

Other FSB recommendations reinforce this cooperative posture. Recommendation 1 links coordination to mandate clarity and resources; Recommendation 2 calls for comprehensive oversight of all functions across jurisdictions; Recommendation 6 addresses cross-border access to operational data; and Recommendation 7 requires prearranged coordination on recovery and resolution strategies. The FSB sets a structured implementation cycle, including a review of national compliance by the end of 2025 and annual progress reporting thereafter, supported by a shared repository of best practices to accelerate convergence (Financial Stability Board, 2023).

From the payments-system vantage point, the CPMI emphasises that stablecoin interoperability among stablecoin arrangements and between those arrangements and existing payment rails depends on harmonised legal, technical, and regulatory frameworks. Without convergence on messaging standards, settlement finality, and compliance expectations, cross-border fragmentation intensifies, and operational risk migrates across systems. The CPMI's coordination blueprint operates across several layers: global coordination between the FSB and CPMI on standard-setting and implementation monitoring, regional adaptation of global principles to local market structures, and bilateral cooperation through home-host memoranda of understanding and joint supervisory arrangements (The Committee on Payments and Market Infrastructures, 2023).

These considerations amount to a governance design rather than a checklist. Cooperation, through formalised information-sharing, supervisory colleges, lead supervisor models, and crisis-management groups, supplies the institutional muscle that makes coordination routine rather than ad hoc. The standards layer, such as minimum expectations for reserves, redemption, governance, and disclosure, anchors consistent outcomes even as domestic law varies. The capability layer, such as common data taxonomies, interoperable Travel Rule implementations, and capacity building, turns visibility from aspiration into practice (The Committee on Payments and Market Infrastructures, 2023; The Financial Action Task Force, 2021; Financial Stability Board, 2023; Financial Stability Board, 2025).

Most importantly, this architecture must be inclusive. If only advanced economies can implement it, vulnerabilities will re-emerge through weaker links. Technical assistance and shared tooling are therefore not ancillary but essential, ensuring cooperation is truly global. In a stablecoin ecosystem where issuance, custody, validation, and user activity are rarely co-located, inclusivity determines whether supervisors can view the entire system or continue to chase its fragments.

In summary, effective cross-border coordination in the stablecoin ecosystem rests on institutionalised cooperation, outcome-orientated minimum standards, sustained investment in supervisory capacity, and interoperable compliance infrastructure. These principles do not seek to erase domestic legal diversity but to secure equivalence of outcomes—financial integrity, consumer protection, and systemic stability—across jurisdictions that remain legally distinct yet operationally interconnected. This is the foundation of a credible international regime for stablecoins and the necessary precondition for realising their benefits without compromising the resilience of the global financial system.

FORMS OF INTERNATIONAL COOPERATION AND FUTURE OUTLOOK

The path toward credible cross-border oversight of stablecoin arrangements rests on cooperation that is formalised, well-resourced, and capable of producing consistent supervisory outcomes across jurisdictions. A practical toolkit is emerging from the institutional frameworks and experiences already surveyed: passporting and mutual recognition models that reduce duplicative licensing; joint supervision for globally active arrangements; and a dense fabric of MoUs, supervisory colleges, and secure data-sharing systems that make cooperation routine rather than reactive. These mechanisms align with the operational realities of leading financial centres and form the foundation for a sustainable international supervisory architecture.

A first pillar is outcome-based recognition. Mutual recognition, equivalence, or passporting mechanisms can allow authorised stablecoin service providers to operate across multiple jurisdictions subject to common safeguards, provided that host authorities are confident that home-state oversight delivers comparable protections. Recognition does not require identity of rules; it requires confidence in outcomes. Where a jurisdiction's framework demonstrably satisfies core expectations, such as high-quality and liquid reserves, enforceable and timely redemption, transparent governance, robust AML/CFT controls, and operational resilience, host supervisors can streamline access while retaining the right to impose targeted, risk-based add-ons to address local conditions. This approach simultaneously reduces regulatory friction for responsible actors and deprives bad actors of arbitrage opportunities that arise from patchwork transposition of international standards (The Committee on Payments and Market Infrastructures, 2023; The Financial Action Task Force, 2021; Financial Stability Board, 2023; Financial Stability Board, 2025).

A second pillar is institutionalised joint supervision for arrangements with a truly global footprint. In practice, a global stablecoin's core functions – issuance, reserve management, transfer, custody, governance, and redemption – will often be split across several legal entities and multiple countries. No single authority will ever have a complete line of sight without cooperation. Formal colleges and crisis-management groups, convened under a clear lead-supervisor model, can align supervisory expectations during licensing and material change approvals, perform coordinated examinations in steady state, and coordinate escalation and resolution ex post during stress (The Committee on Payments and Market Infrastructures, 2023; The Financial Action Task Force, 2021; Financial Stability Board, 2025).

A third pillar comprises the legal plumbing of cooperation: MoUs, bilateral/multilateral treaties, and protected data channels that move beyond public pronouncements. Without this, cooperation remains dependent on emails and goodwill; with it, supervisors can build a shared risk picture and coordinate interventions on the same facts at the same time.

These institutional building blocks become most powerful when coupled with greater alignment in domestic classification and strengthened operational and technical capabilities. Harmonising key definitional touchpoints, such as what constitutes a "stablecoin", a "reserve asset", "redemption", a "custodian", or "significant user base", reduces friction at the border and allows supervisors to compare like-for-like. Equally, capacity matters: host and home authorities alike need appropriate tools capable of parsing blockchain data at scale, linking addresses to real-world entities, and surfacing cross-border interconnections that would otherwise remain opaque. Improvements in digital payments infrastructure and interoperability further shrink the room for arbitrage, embed compliance into the rails, and make high-standard cross-border operation commercially viable (The Committee on Payments and Market Infrastructures, 2023; The Financial Action Task Force, 2021; Financial Stability Board, 2025).

The FATF provides the foundation for AML and CFT cooperation in the virtual asset and VASP sector. The FATF Guidance reiterates that countries should offer the broadest possible range of international cooperation to counter illicit finance in virtual assets and translates that principle into operational expectations for regulators (The Financial Action Task Force, 2021). Supervisors should be able to exchange licensing and registration data, ownership and beneficial-ownership information, compliance examination results, and sanctions notices, as well as transactional intelligence where lawfully permitted. FATF encourages reliance on established platforms such as the Egmont Group for FIU-to-FIU communication, while urging prudential, conduct, and payment-system regulators to form bilateral and multilateral channels of their own. Effective AML and CFT coordination now depend on full ecosystem participation rather than isolated agency action.

The FSB Review broadens the discussion of international cooperation beyond AML/CFT considerations to encompass the full spectrum of prudential, conduct, operational, and market integrity risks associated with stablecoins and other crypto assets. The FSB underscores that close coordination among international SSBs is essential to ensuring a coherent and comprehensive global framework. In this respect, the FSB identifies IOSCO, the Basel Committee on Banking Supervision ("BCBS"), and the FATF as relevant actors whose mandates cover distinct, yet interrelated, areas of crypto-asset oversight.

According to the FSB Review, cooperation among regulators in the crypto-asset sector remains limited and largely ad hoc. Existing MoUs and information-sharing agreements primarily support traditional functions—such as authorisation, licensing, and registration—and are seldom extended to financial-stability monitoring or enforcement. A few jurisdictions have begun to expand these mechanisms: for instance, Bermuda plans to include enforcement within its cooperation frameworks, while Chile has introduced bilateral arrangements enabling cross-border on-site inspections.

Regional initiatives are also gaining traction. In Latin America, countries such as Chile participate in the Pacific Alliance MoUs and the Ibero-American Securities Markets Institute's FinTech MoU. Across the Asia-Pacific region, several IOSCO members have adopted a regional supervisory MoU to facilitate cross-border authorisation, information sharing, and the identification of emerging risks. Within the European Union, the European Securities and Markets Authority (ESMA) coordinates cooperation among national competent authorities under its own MoU, providing a framework for exchanging confidential information on authorisation, supervision, and enforcement (Financial Stability Board, 2025).

Jurisdictions where crypto-assets fall within the remit of securities regulators are most likely to rely on IOSCO's multilateral MoUs for cross-border information exchange. In contrast, countries with less regulatory clarity or without a designated market supervisor tend to make limited use of these mechanisms, even when they are signatories. In some instances, central banks have taken the lead in coordinating with foreign counterparts; for instance, the Saudi Central Bank has used bilateral communication to address challenges related to offshore service providers (Financial Stability Board, 2025).

The FSB observes that, despite positive momentum, existing cooperative efforts remain insufficient to safeguard global financial stability. The interconnectedness between crypto-asset markets, non-bank financial intermediaries, and the traditional banking sector increases the risk of systemic spillovers, while persistent data gaps hinder timely risk assessments. As regulatory frameworks mature, jurisdictions are encouraged to expand the scope and depth of cooperation tools beyond their traditional confines, building toward comprehensive oversight aligned with the FSB's broader objectives of financial stability and market integrity.

Table 1. Key forms of cross-border coordination, with case studies

Type of Cooperation	Jurisdiction/Institution & Explanation
Investigative Frameworks	**United States.** U.S. law enforcement agencies and federal departments collaborate extensively with foreign partners on investigations, arrests, and asset seizures involving digital-asset crimes. These partnerships support multi-jurisdictional cases that often include foreign-based actors, VASPs, and transnational criminal networks. Mutual Legal Assistance Requests remain the principal channel for cross-border evidence exchange and enforcement cooperation. Recognising that digital assets and transactional data can be quickly transferred or obscured across borders, U.S. authorities have implemented policies to expedite evidence gathering and asset restraint abroad, addressing the jurisdictional and procedural gaps that traditional legal tools do not cover (The Financial Action Task Force, 2021).
Mutual Recognition	**Dubai International Financial Centre (DIFC).** When assessing whether to recognise a foreign-issued fiat-referenced crypto token, the Dubai Financial Services Authority (hereinafter referred to as DFSA) considers whether the token's reserves are maintained in segregated accounts with regulated banks or custodians in jurisdictions whose prudential and AML/CFT frameworks meet standards equivalent to those of the DFSA and the FATF. It also examines the token's regulatory standing in other recognised jurisdictions, including whether it has received approval or authorisation from a competent regulator. This mutual-recognition process ensures that only tokens operating under comparable safeguards are admitted into the DIFC market (Dubai Financial Services Authority, 2025).
Memoranda of Understanding (MoUs)	While many jurisdictions maintain bilateral or regional MoUs, the IOSCO Multilateral MoU (hereinafter referred to as MMoU) and its Enhanced MMoU (hereinafter referred to as EMMoU) remain the most widely adopted global cooperation frameworks. Signed by over 130 member authorities, they enable the exchange of supervisory and enforcement information in securities-related investigations and proceedings. These MoUs constitute the backbone of international regulatory collaboration, fostering trust, consistency, and coordinated oversight among securities regulators (Financial Stability Board, 2025).

Viewed in this light, "international cooperation" is not a single instrument; it is a layered architecture. The recognition layer reduces friction for compliant firms while preserving host safeguards. The college layer aligns expectations and actions across home and host authorities. The legal layer (MoUs and bilateral/multilateral agreements) and the data layer (secure, standardised feeds) make cooperation operational.

The future outlook therefore turns on execution. International bodies have articulated the principles; supervisors now need to institutionalise them—domestically, by clarifying mandates and resourcing lead authorities, and internationally, by making colleges, MoUs, and data rails part of business-as-usual supervision. These actions will allow stablecoins to contribute to cheaper, faster, and more transparent cross-border payments while protecting monetary sovereignty, market integrity, and consumer welfare. Done piecemeal, it will invite the very fragmentation that these frameworks were designed to prevent.

CONCLUSION

Across the international reports reviewed, a single theme resounds with clarity: the effective oversight of stablecoins depends on structured, predictable, and institutionalised cross-border cooperation. This is not an ancillary consideration but the central organising principle of any credible regulatory framework for assets that are, by their very design, borderless. Each of the principal standard-setting bodies approaches this imperative from within its own institutional mandate—whether grounded in financial stability, payment system safety, or the prevention of illicit finance—yet their conclusions converge on the same fundamental point: stablecoins operate across jurisdictions, and therefore, their regulation must do the same.

The FSB provides perhaps the most direct articulation of this necessity. It observes that despite notable progress in domestic regulation, national frameworks for stablecoins remain fragmented, creating both gaps and overlaps in supervision that undermine collective oversight. In the FSB's analysis, such fragmentation allows risks to migrate across borders faster than regulators can respond, while duplicative requirements stifle innovation without necessarily enhancing stability. The FSB therefore calls for the transformation of cooperation tools—from informal, reactive exchanges into formal, standing mechanisms embedded in supervisory practice. These mechanisms include supervisory colleges that bring together home and host authorities overseeing global stablecoin issuers; memoranda of understanding that provide structured channels for information exchange and joint enforcement; coordinated on-site inspections to align supervisory findings; and information-sharing networks capable of supporting continuous, rather than episodic, dialogue among regulators.

Through its reports and recommendations, the FSB advances a consistent message: that regulatory consistency across jurisdictions is essential not merely to sustain market confidence but to preserve the stability of the international financial system. The oversight of cross-border stablecoin arrangements, in its view, cannot be accomplished in isolation. Because these instruments integrate issuance, redemption, custody, and transfer functions that are frequently distributed across several legal regimes, effective supervision depends on regulators being able to access the same information, reach consistent assessments, and act in coordination. Global cooperation, in this sense, is not an abstract ideal but a functional necessity. No jurisdiction, acting alone, can credibly regulate a cross-border stablecoin that operates beyond its territorial reach.

The CPMI situates this requirement within a broader architecture of payment system integrity and safety. It views stablecoins not merely as financial products but as emergent components of the global payment ecosystem whose design, if uncoordinated, could affect the resilience of established financial infrastructures. The CPMI argues that interoperability between stablecoin arrangements and traditional payment systems must rest on coordinated legal, technical, and regulatory foundations. Where reserve composition, redemption rights, or disclosure standards diverge between jurisdictions, payment systems risk fragmentation, and the potential for contagion increases. A stablecoin operating under inconsistent standards can generate uncertainty over settlement finality, liquidity coverage, and reserve adequacy, thereby weakening the trust that underpins cross border transfers. The CPMI thus positions harmonisation not as an aspirational goal but as a precondition for operational safety: a coherent legal and regulatory foundation is essential to ensuring that stablecoins reinforce, rather than destabilise, global payment networks.

The FATF, meanwhile, approaches the issue through the prism of financial integrity and AML/CFT supervision. The FATF says that effective oversight in this area depends fundamentally on international cooperation and timely information exchange. It identifies the establishment of both formal and informal channels among financial intelligence units, prudential supervisors, securities regulators, and payment-system authorities as indispensable to ensuring that illicit finance does not exploit regulatory gaps between jurisdictions. The FATF's perspective extends beyond policy design to the operational mechanics of cooperation, particularly through its emphasis on interoperability in the implementation of the so-called Travel Rule. This rule requires the transmission of originator and beneficiary information for virtual asset transfers, and its efficacy depends on jurisdictions adopting compatible data standards and secure communication protocols. In the FATF's analysis, therefore, regulatory coordination is not only a matter of aligning laws but of ensuring that compliance infrastructures themselves are interoperable across borders.

Viewed together, the analyses of the FSB, CPMI, and FATF delineate a coordinated model of global governance in which cross-border supervision, data exchange, and mutual recognition are not exceptional exercises but routine features of regulatory life. The envisioned framework is one where domestic laws are reinforced by international coordination and where regulators, through supervisory colleges, memoranda of understanding, and shared data infrastructures, can act upon a unified understanding of risk. It is a model that transforms international cooperation from a principle into a practice, embedding it in the day-to-day functioning of oversight institutions.

The future of stablecoin regulation will therefore depend not only on the content of national legislation but also on the capacity of authorities to cooperate through shared standards, interoperable data systems, and joint risk assessments. The evolution of this cooperative infrastructure will determine whether stablecoins can mature into trusted instruments that enhance the efficiency, inclusivity, and transparency of cross-border payments or whether they will remain a fragmented experiment prone to regulatory arbitrage and instability. In this respect, international coordination ceases to be an aspirational goal and becomes the foundation upon which stability, integrity, and confidence in the global digital-asset ecosystem must rest.

REFERENCES

Dubai Financial Services Authority. (2025). *The DFSA Rulebook* (Rulebook No. GEN/VER67/03-25; p. 212). https://dfsaen.thomsonreuters.com/rulebook/general -module -gen-ver6703-25

Financial Stability Board. (2023). *High-level Recommendations for the Regulation, Supervision and Oversight of Global Stablecoin Arrangements* (Reports to the G20, p. 24). https://www.fsb.org/uploads/P170723-3.pdf

Financial Stability Board. (2025). *Thematic Review on FSB Global Regulatory Framework for Crypto-asset Activities* (p. 111) [Peer Review Report]. https://www .fsb.org/2025/10/thematic-review-on-fsb-global-regulatory-framework-for-crypto-asset-activiactivities/

The Committee on Payments and Market Infrastructures. (2023). *Considerations for the Use of Stablecoin Arrangements in Cross-Border Payments* (CPMI Report No. 220; CPMI Papers, p. 37). Bank for International Settlements. https://www.bis .org/cpmi/publ/d220.pdf

The Financial Action Task Force. (2021). *Updated Guidance for a Risk-Based Approach to Virtual Assets and Virtual Asset Service Providers* (p. 111). https:// www.fatf gafi.org/content/dam/fatf-gafi/guidance/Updated-Guidance-VA-VASP.pdf .coredownload. inline.pdf

Chapter 8
Strengthening AML/CFT and Proliferation Financing Frameworks for Stablecoins:
Global Policy Recommendations Anchored in the Commonwealth Model Law

Loretta Joseph
Mcdonell-Nadeau Consultants, Australia

Rick McDonell
Mcdonell-Nadeau Consultants, Canada

Paul Derham
Holley Nethercote Lawyers, Australia

Stuart Davis
Scotiabank, Canada

ABSTRACT

Stablecoins are rapidly transforming digital finance by enabling fast, low-cost transactions, cross-border payments, and greater financial inclusion in remittance-dependent Commonwealth economies. However, their pseudonymous nature, integration with decentralised finance, and global accessibility introduce significant vulnerabilities to money laundering, terrorist financing, and proliferation financing. Illicit actors

DOI: 10.4018/979-8-3373-6655-5.ch008

increasingly exploit stablecoins to bypass traditional financial controls, sanctions, and oversight. This chapter evaluates these emerging risks and advances a coherent regulatory response anchored in the Commonwealth Model Law. It recommends risk-based supervision, stronger licensing and enforcement for issuers and intermediaries, Travel Rule compliance, enhanced due diligence, and mandatory transparency in reserves and governance. It also calls for improved data sharing, cyber-resilience standards, and capacity building for smaller jurisdictions. Case studies from across the Commonwealth illustrate both challenges and successful approaches.

OVERVIEW

Stablecoins, digital assets designed to maintain a stable value relative to fiat currencies or other reference assets, have moved from the periphery of crypto markets into the centre of global finance. Their combined market capitalisation has grown from niche levels a decade ago to hundreds of billions of US dollars, with daily volumes rivaling those of major payment networks. They are now used for cross-border remittances, trade settlement, decentralised finance (DeFi), and, increasingly, as cash-like instruments within digital ecosystems.

This evolution offers clear benefits for the Commonwealth. Properly regulated stablecoins can reduce the cost and friction of remittances, support regional trade, improve financial inclusion in small states, and reduce dependence on correspondent banking relationships that have been eroded by global de-risking. However, the same features that make stablecoins attractive for legitimate users—speed, global reach, programmability, and 24/7 availability—also make them highly attractive for money laundering (ML), terrorist financing (TF), and proliferation financing (PF).

Chain analytics and law enforcement cases already show stablecoins frequently used in ransomware, darknet markets, sanctions evasion and high-risk offshore structures. The growing integration of stablecoins into DeFi, tokenised real-world asset (RWA) markets, and cross-chain bridges further complicates supervision. In particular, multi-chain stablecoins—those issued or represented on several blockchains, often connected by complex bridging infrastructure—create new attack surfaces and supervisory blind spots. These are no longer hypothetical scenarios: regulators have confronted real investigations in which stablecoins have been rapidly moved across chains and wrapped into new forms to frustrate tracing and asset recovery.

The Commonwealth has a unique opportunity to respond in a coordinated, principled way. The Commonwealth Model Law on Virtual Assets (CMLVA) (Commonwealth Secretariat (2024) provides a robust foundation for licensing, supervision, and cross-border cooperation regarding virtual asset service providers (VASPs). Building on that, the emerging Commonwealth Model Law on Stablecoins

(CMLS) (Commonwealth Secretariat, 2025) will offer a dedicated framework for fiat-referenced and other systemically important stablecoin arrangements, aligning with standards from the Basel Committee on Payments and Market Infrastructures, (Bank for International Settlement. (2007).

This chapter translates those model laws into concrete global policy recommendations for strengthening AML/CFT and PF frameworks around stablecoins, with a special focus on the needs of small and vulnerable Commonwealth states. It:

- maps the global and Commonwealth regulatory landscape, highlighting alignment and gaps relative to international standards;
- analyses key ML, TF, PF and cyber-enabled risks posed by stablecoins, including DeFi, RWAs and multi-chain designs;
- proposes a toolkit of regulatory and supervisory measures, including licensing criteria, reserve and redemption requirements, governance and risk-management standards, transaction-monitoring expectations, and PF-specific metrics;
- offers practical case studies from Mauritius, Singapore, the Eastern Caribbean and The Bahamas; and
- sets out an Implementation Roadmap to help member states sequence reforms, build capacity, and cooperate through a proposed Commonwealth Stablecoin Observatory and PF Dashboard.

The central message is that stablecoins are not inherently incompatible with robust AML/CFT and PF objectives. On the contrary, if appropriately regulated, they can be brought into the rule-of-law architecture, with stronger transparency than many legacy payment channels. But this is not automatic. It requires clear legislation, risk-based supervision, cross-border information sharing, and sustained technical assistance for those Commonwealth members that face the greatest capacity constraints while also being disproportionately exposed to global ML and PF pressures.

Grounded in the Commonwealth's tradition of collaborative law reform, the chapter calls for a coordinated, standards-based approach that treats stablecoins (including multi-chain and DeFi-linked variants) as part of the formal financial system, subject to proportionate but firm controls. In doing so, it aims to ensure that stablecoins become tools for inclusive growth, not channels for illicit finance or financial instability.

INTRODUCTION

The Imperative for Robust AML/CFT and PF Frameworks

Stablecoins are no longer experimental instruments used only by sophisticated traders. They now support a growing share of global crypto activity, cross-border payments, and on-chain markets. For many Commonwealth citizens, particularly in small island developing states and lower-income countries, dollar-referenced stablecoins are becoming a de facto savings and transaction instrument, used to hedge local currency volatility, receive remittances, and access global platforms.

Yet most existing regulatory frameworks were designed for traditional banking and securities markets, not for programmable money that moves borderlessly through public and permissioned chains. Conventional AML/CFT controls—such as bank-centric customer due diligence, manual transaction monitoring, and static sanctions lists—are stretched by pseudonymous wallets, complex transaction chains, wrapping and re-issuance of stablecoins across chains, and the use of mixers, privacy tools and nested services.

Proliferation financing (PF) risks require particular attention. Proliferation networks have historically exploited gaps in export controls, trade finance and shell entities. Stablecoins add a new dimension: they allow rapid, cross-border payments with limited friction, which can be layered through DeFi, NFTs, gaming platforms or other digital interfaces. If not addressed, these channels could undermine the effectiveness of sanctions and export-control regimes.

For Commonwealth states reliant on correspondent banking, tourism, trade and offshore financial services, reputational risk is acute. Grey-listing or black-listing by FATF, or negative assessments in mutual evaluations, can trigger capital flight, reduced investment, and higher costs of international finance. It is therefore essential that Commonwealth jurisdictions demonstrate credible, risk-based approaches to stablecoins and other virtual assets.

Within this context, this chapter has four main objectives:

1. Clarify how global standards apply to stablecoins.
2. Anchor stablecoin reforms in Commonwealth model laws.
3. Provide a risk-based analysis of ML, TF and PF threats.
4. Offer a practical roadmap for implementation.

GLOBAL AND COMMONWEALTH REGULATORY LANDSCAPE

Evolution of International Standards

International standard-setters have progressively clarified expectations for virtual assets and stablecoins. FATF's revisions to Recommendation 15 and its Interpretive Note introduced the concepts of virtual assets and VASPs, requiring licensing or registration and risk-based supervision (FATF (2021). Subsequent FATF guidance emphasised the Travel Rule, sanctions screening, and heightened due diligence for higher-risk products, including privacy-enhancing coins and certain DeFi arrangements.

The BIS CPMI-IOSCO guidance on stablecoin arrangements applies the Principles for Financial Market Infrastructures (PFMI) to those stablecoins that reach systemic scale or play critical roles in payments and settlement (International Organization of Securities Commissions (CPMI–IOSCO) 2021). The FSB and IOSCO have issued complementary guidance on global stablecoins and crypto-asset markets more broadly (Financial Stability Board. (2020); Financial Stability Board. (2023); International Organisation of Securities Commission. (2020). International Organisation of Securities Commission (2023)).

Regionally, the EU's Markets in Crypto-Assets Regulation (MiCA) sets a detailed regime for asset-referenced tokens and e-money tokens, providing for licensing, capital requirements, reserve composition and custody, governance rules, redemption rights, and public disclosure (European Union, 2023).

The Commonwealth's Pioneering Role

The CMLVA was developed to help member states transpose FATF standards into their domestic legal systems in a coherent and context-appropriate way. It defines virtual assets and VASPs, sets out licensing and supervisory powers, and includes detailed provisions on AML/CFT, consumer protection, and cross-border cooperation.

The forthcoming CMLS builds on this foundation by providing a specialised framework for stablecoin arrangements. It recognises the diversity of models—fiat-backed, crypto-collateralised, algorithmic and hybrid—and classifies them based on risk, introducing requirements for reserve management, governance and risk management, AML/CFT and PF controls, and supervisory and resolution powers.

Gaps and Opportunities

Despite progress, gaps remain. Many Commonwealth countries still lack comprehensive legislation on virtual assets and stablecoins, or have partially implemented regimes that do not clearly cover newer phenomena such as DeFi, RWAs, or multi-chain stablecoins. Key gaps include undefined perimeters, limited PF focus, capacity constraints and inconsistent treatment of cross-border activity.

RISKS POSED BY STABLECOINS TO AML/CFT AND PF FRAMEWORKS

Money Laundering Vulnerabilities

Stablecoins can facilitate money laundering through pseudonymous transfers and rapid layering, nested and unregistered VASPs, DeFi protocols and token swaps, and cash-in/cash-out interfaces. To manage these risks, NRAs and supervision should focus on identifying and licensing all material VASPs, enforcing the Travel Rule, targeting cash-in/cash-out points, and requiring the use of blockchain analytics tools.

Tokenised Assets and DeFi Risks

Tokenised RWAs frequently use stablecoins as the settlement leg, creating concentrated corridors of ML risk. DeFi protocols add further complexity through liquidity pools and automated market makers. Supervisors should assess whether tokenisation platforms and RWA issuers fall within existing regimes, require enhanced analytics for DeFi-exposed VASPs, and consider special reporting thresholds for large, short-duration RWA positions funded via stablecoins.

Terrorist Financing Threats

Terrorist organisations and associated networks experiment with virtual assets, including stablecoins, for donations, micro-payments and procurement. TF risks may be modest in volume but are strategically significant. Authorities should ensure TF risks associated with stablecoins are explicitly considered in national risk assessments, that VASPs are trained to detect TF indicators, and that FIUs and law enforcement have access to blockchain analytics focused on TF typologies.

Proliferation Financing Exposures

Proliferation networks use layered corporate structures, trade-based schemes and complex payment chains. Stablecoins add a further tool: they can be used to circumvent conventional banking channels, settle invoices for controlled goods, and move funds through or around sanctions regimes. PF-relevant patterns can include payments for high-risk goods, use of stablecoins to settle freight and logistics costs, sanctions evasion, and movement of profits back to proliferation-sensitive jurisdictions.

Multi-Chain Stablecoins and Cross-Chain Risks

Multi-chain stablecoins are available on several networks, either through native issuance or through wrapped and bridged representations. For users, this offers advantages; for AML/CFT and PF frameworks, it creates new challenges.

First, cross-chain bridges and interoperability protocols are complex systems and have been the source of major hacks. In the context of stablecoins, such incidents can lead to unauthorised minting or double issuance of wrapped tokens and unlawful release of locked assets, generating substantial illicit proceeds.

Second, multi-chain stablecoins rely on centralised reserves and governance mechanisms that may be vulnerable if key management or custody practices are weak. A single compromise can affect balances across all chains simultaneously.

Third, multi-chain issuance can fragment liquidity and supervisory visibility. Criminals may route funds through chains where supervision is weaker, then bridge back to more liquid networks.

To mitigate these risks, the CMLS and national frameworks should treat multi-chain stablecoin arrangements as single economic systems, subject to integrated oversight, including secure bridge design and auditing, transparent mapping of chains and reserves, cross-chain analytics and monitoring, multi-chain governance and incident response, and, where appropriate, embedded compliance-by-design features.

POLICY AND REGULATORY RECOMMENDATIONS

Establish Clear Legal and Regulatory Perimeters

- Define stablecoin categories in law.
- License or register all material actors.
- Address foreign and offshore arrangements.

Strengthen AML/CFT and PF Controls

- Implement risk-based CDD and Travel-Rule compliance.
- Integrate PF-specific risks into NRAs and supervision.
- Issue guidance on DeFi, RWAs and multi-chain activity.

Prudential, Governance and Consumer-Protection Measures

- Mandate reserve and redemption requirements for fiat-referenced stablecoins.
- Impose governance and operational resilience standards.
- Require transparency and disclosure, including for multi-chain designs.

Technology, Data and Supervisory Co-operation

- Invest in on-chain analytics and RegTech.
- Develop regional and Commonwealth platforms, including a Stablecoin Observatory and PF Dashboard.
- Establish supervisory colleges and information-sharing mechanisms.

Capacity Building and Technical Assistance

Many Commonwealth states require support to design, implement and enforce stablecoin frameworks. Priority areas include legislative drafting, training of supervisors and FIUs, national digital finance strategies, and public-private collaboration.

PF Dashboard and Data Architecture for Stablecoins

A central lesson from recent assessments is that many jurisdictions struggle not because they lack laws, but because they lack timely, structured data on which to base PF risk assessments and supervisory decisions. A dedicated PF Dashboard for stablecoins can help bridge this gap. In its simplest form, a PF Dashboard is a set of data feeds, analytics and visualisations that bring together information from VASPs, banks, customs and FIUs on a single platform.

For stablecoins, such a Dashboard should be able to track:

- aggregate inflows and outflows of major stablecoins through locally supervised VASPs, broken down by jurisdiction, sector and counterparty type;
- exposure to high-risk jurisdictions, trans-shipment hubs and sectors associated with dual-use goods and sensitive technologies;
- use of cross-chain bridges and multi-chain stablecoin arrangements, including sudden spikes in activity or flows to or from higher-risk chains;
- sanctions-relevant indicators, such as repeated small-value transfers linked to designated entities, known typologies for sanctions evasion, or addresses flagged by international partners.

Developing such a Dashboard does not require every Commonwealth state to build its own advanced analytics laboratory. Smaller jurisdictions can participate in shared or regional solutions, including a Commonwealth Stablecoin Observatory hosted by the Secretariat or a regional body. The key is to ensure that national authorities retain the ability to query data relevant to their own risk profile, receive alerts on PF-related events, and feed local intelligence back into the regional system.

From a governance perspective, the PF Dashboard should be supported by:

- clear legal gateways for data sharing between supervisors, FIUs, customs and law enforcement;
- protocols for engaging with private-sector analytics providers and VASPs, including data standards and quality controls;
- documented procedures for responding to alerts, including which agency leads on operational follow-up and how decisions are recorded; and
- regular reviews to ensure that indicators and typologies are updated as stablecoin markets and PF threats evolve.

A well-governed PF Dashboard turns on-chain transparency into actionable insight. It enables supervisors to move from reactive, case-by-case responses to a more strategic, intelligence-led approach to PF risks in stablecoin markets.

Mauritius

Mauritius has positioned itself as a regional fintech hub, using a regulatory sandbox and progressive legislation to attract responsible innovation while strengthening AML/CFT controls.

Singapore

Singapore combines a comprehensive legislative framework with a strong emphasis on technology and public-private collaboration, including specific proposals for fiat-backed stablecoins.

Eastern Caribbean

The Eastern Caribbean Currency Union's experience with digital currency and VASP licensing provides insights into regional approaches, shared infrastructure and common standards.

The Bahamas

The Bahamas' early move into CBDC and digital asset regulation highlights both opportunities and the need for continual refinement of frameworks in light of market developments and enforcement experience.

ILLUSTRATIVE IMPLEMENTATION ROAD MAP

Phase 1 (0–12 Months): Foundations

In the first phase, authorities focus on building a shared understanding of the issues and on identifying gaps in existing frameworks. A structured legal gap analysis should compare current laws and regulations with the CMLVA and CMLS, FATF standards, and relevant regional instruments. This analysis should be practical rather than purely academic: it should identify exactly which types of stablecoin activity are already covered, which fall into grey areas, and which lie entirely outside the current perimeter.

At the same time, an inter-agency working group should be established, ideally under a clear mandate from the Minister of Finance or equivalent authority. The group should bring together the central bank, financial regulators, FIU, customs, law enforcement, and, where appropriate, ministries responsible for technology and national security. Early engagement with industry—banks, VASPs, payments providers, telecoms and consumer groups—helps ensure that policy is grounded in real-world use-cases and that market participants understand the reform trajectory.

Phase 2 (12–24 Months): Legislation and Licensing

The second phase centres on drafting, enacting and beginning to implement legislation. Using the CMLVA and CMLS as templates can significantly accelerate this work, allowing drafters to focus on local adaptations rather than starting from a blank page. Key decisions include whether to integrate stablecoin provisions into existing financial laws or to create a dedicated statute; how to allocate responsibilities between authorities; and how to sequence commencement dates so that industry has time to adapt.

Transitional licensing regimes are critical. They allow existing VASPs and stablecoin projects to continue operating within a clear framework while their full applications are assessed. Conditions can be attached to transitional licences—for example, restrictions on retail activity or on certain high-risk products—until the supervisor is satisfied that all requirements have been met. During this phase, supervisors should also issue initial guidance notes and FAQs to clarify expectations and reduce uncertainty.

Phase 3 (24–36 Months): Supervision, Technology and PF Focus

By the third phase, the focus shifts from legislative design to operational effectiveness. Supervisors and FIUs should move from ad hoc monitoring to structured, risk-based supervision of licensed entities. This includes developing annual and multi-year examination plans; creating standardised templates for off-site reporting; and conducting thematic reviews on topics such as travel-rule implementation, sanctions screening, or the management of multi-chain stablecoin exposures.

Technology becomes a cornerstone of this phase. Authorities should ensure access to reliable on-chain analytics, either through in-house tools or shared regional platforms. Staff must be trained not only to operate these tools, but also to interpret their outputs in the context of broader financial intelligence. PF-specific risks require particular attention: supervisors should work with FIUs, customs and export-control agencies to identify indicators of proliferation-related activity in stablecoin flows and to integrate these into the PF Dashboard described above.

Phase 4 (36+ Months): Consolidation and Continuous Improvement

Once the core framework is in place, the challenge becomes one of consolidation and continuous improvement. Jurisdictions should periodically evaluate the effectiveness of their stablecoin regime, including feedback from mutual evaluations, peer reviews and industry consultations. Questions to consider include: Are licensing criteria appropriately calibrated? Are enforcement tools being used in a timely and proportionate way? Are PF and other high-risk typologies being detected and disrupted?

Regional and Commonwealth integration deepens in this phase. Participation in a Commonwealth Stablecoin Observatory, regional supervisory colleges and information-sharing networks can significantly enhance the impact of national efforts. Finally, authorities should not neglect the importance of clear communication with the public. Explaining the benefits and risks of stablecoins, the protections that regulation provides, and the responsibilities of users helps to build trust and supports the long-term legitimacy of the framework.

ROLES AND RESPONSIBILITIES OF KEY STAKEHOLDERS

Legislature and Executive

Parliament or the national legislature plays the foundational role of creating the legal framework for stablecoins and virtual assets. It enacts or amends primary laws that define how stablecoins are classified, which authorities have supervisory powers, and what remedies and sanctions are available when things go wrong. In many Commonwealth jurisdictions this includes amending the core AML/CFT Act, the Proceeds of Crime legislation, securities laws, banking laws and, in some cases, foreign-exchange or payments statutes. Without clear, modern primary legislation, supervisors and courts are forced to stretch old concepts to new technologies, creating legal uncertainty that criminals and bad actors can exploit.

The executive – Cabinet, the Minister of Finance, the Attorney-General and other relevant ministers – provides high-level policy direction. The executive decides, for example, whether the national strategy is to become a regional hub for well-regulated digital finance, or whether the immediate priority is defensive: protecting the jurisdiction from being used as a conduit for ML, TF and PF while domestic capacity is still being built. The executive also authorises inter-agency working groups, endorses national AML/CFT and PF strategies that explicitly address stablecoins, and represents the jurisdiction in Commonwealth and FATF-style regional fora.

Central Bank and Financial Regulators

The central bank and financial regulators are at the front line of day-to-day implementation. Where a stablecoin functions as a payment instrument or e-money, the central bank will usually have a leading role in licensing the issuer, approving reserve structures and supervising operational resilience. Where a stablecoin is integrated with trading platforms, derivatives or tokenised securities, securities or investment regulators will be more prominent. Insurance and pensions regulators may also have a role where stablecoins are used as collateral or investment assets within regulated funds or insurance products.

Together, these authorities must translate broad legislative objectives into concrete, enforceable rules: licence conditions, prudential requirements, governance standards and detailed reporting templates. They must decide whether particular stablecoin arrangements are systemically important; how to calibrate reserve requirements and redemption rights; and how to treat multi-chain and DeFi-linked products that blur boundaries between payment, investment and speculation. Importantly, they are responsible for building the supervisory teams and techniques – including on-chain analytics – that make the rules meaningful in practice.

Financial Intelligence Unit (FIU)

The FIU occupies a unique position in the ecosystem. It receives suspicious transaction reports (STRs) and other information from banks, VASPs, payment institutions and gatekeepers, and turns these into financial intelligence products that can be used by law enforcement, supervisors and policymakers. In the stablecoin context the FIU has to adapt its analytical toolkit: traditional bank-statement analysis is no longer sufficient when funds move through multiple exchanges, wallets and chains in minutes.

A modern FIU therefore needs at least a basic capability in blockchain analytics, or access to a regional or Commonwealth platform that can provide this on demand. It must be able to map how stablecoins feature in domestic predicate crimes, TF networks and potential PF schemes. It should also work with supervisors and the private sector to develop red-flag indicators and typologies – for example, repeated use of high-risk mixers, rapid bridging of funds between chains, or stablecoin flows linked to suspicious trade routes for dual-use goods. Finally, the FIU is the main interface with foreign counterparts for tracing cross-border flows and securing intelligence on foreign-domiciled stablecoin issuers or exchanges.

Law Enforcement and Prosecutorial Authorities

Law enforcement agencies and prosecutors turn intelligence into cases. Their role in the stablecoin framework includes investigating underlying crimes that generate illicit funds, tracing those funds through stablecoins and other virtual assets, seizing and freezing digital wallets where permitted by law, and presenting coherent cases in court. They are also critical for building case law on questions such as who owns stablecoin balances held in omnibus accounts, how to prove control of private keys, and how to value seized tokens for confiscation purposes.

Many Commonwealth law enforcement agencies are still building experience in digital-asset investigations. Targeted training, joint task forces with FIUs and regulators, and practical guidance on seizing and storing digital evidence are therefore essential. Without the ability to follow through on the most serious cases, even the best legislative framework risks being perceived as largely symbolic.

VASPs and Stablecoin Issuers

VASPs and stablecoin issuers are the primary gatekeepers within the system. They see customer behaviour first-hand and have the tools to implement robust control frameworks. Their responsibilities include risk-based onboarding and customer due diligence; screening customers and transactions against sanctions lists;

implementing the Travel Rule for transfers; monitoring transactions for ML, TF and PF indicators; and filing timely, high-quality STRs when warranted. For stablecoin issuers there is the additional responsibility of managing reserves prudently, maintaining transparent reporting, and ensuring that redemption commitments can be honoured even under stress.

In practice, the quality of AML/CFT and PF controls in the stablecoin ecosystem will often be determined by the culture and governance of these private actors. Boards and senior management must understand that compliance is not a "tick-box" exercise but a core part of the licence to operate. Regulators should therefore assess not only written policies but also the tone from the top, the independence and resourcing of compliance functions, and the incentives created by remuneration and business strategies.

Banks, Payment Institutions and Other Gatekeepers

Traditional financial institutions remain crucial. Banks provide settlement accounts to exchanges and stablecoin issuers; payment institutions act as on-ramps and off-ramps; lawyers, accountants and company-service providers create and administer structures that may hold or transact in stablecoins. These entities must integrate stablecoin-related risks into their own enterprise-wide risk assessments. For example, a bank that services several exchanges needs to understand not only the direct credit and operational risks but also the reputational and correspondent-banking risks if those exchanges are lax on AML/CFT and PF controls.

Supervisors should encourage banks and other gatekeepers to adopt a "risk-aware engagement" model. Blanket de-risking of all VASPs and stablecoin businesses may push activity into opaque channels, while indiscriminate onboarding can expose the jurisdiction to heightened ML/PF risk. A middle path – where services are offered to well-governed, well-supervised entities subject to stringent risk mitigants – is more consistent with the risk-based approach.

Private-Sector Analytics Providers and Technical Partners

Specialist analytics and RegTech providers now play an indispensable role across the ecosystem. They label addresses and clusters, identify mixers and high-risk services, and build tools for transaction monitoring and Travel Rule compliance. For smaller Commonwealth jurisdictions, partnering with reputable providers can provide capabilities that would be difficult or uneconomic to build domestically. However, authorities should pay close attention to issues such as data protection, confidentiality, the risk of over-reliance on a single vendor, and the need for public-sector staff to understand – and if necessary challenge – the outputs generated by commercial tools.

Civil Society, Academia and International Partners

Civil society organisations and academic institutions contribute independent research, policy critique and public education. They can highlight unintended consequences of regulation, such as exclusion of vulnerable groups or overreach in surveillance. Their engagement helps to ensure that the design of AML/CFT and PF frameworks respects human rights, privacy and due-process principles.

International partners – including the Commonwealth Secretariat, FATF and FSRBs, development banks and bilateral donors – can support member states with technical assistance, training, funding for shared infrastructure such as PF Dashboards, and platforms for peer learning. Over time, these partnerships can help to reduce the capacity gap between larger and smaller jurisdictions, ensuring that all Commonwealth members can participate meaningfully in the governance of stablecoins and other digital assets.

ADDITIONAL TECHNICAL CONSIDERATIONS FOR IMPLEMENTATION

Sequencing Reforms in Resource-Constrained Environments

Many Commonwealth members face acute capacity constraints: limited staff, small budgets, and competing priorities across the entire financial sector. Attempting to implement a fully fledged stablecoin regime overnight is neither realistic nor desirable. Instead, authorities should focus on sequencing reforms so that the most critical building blocks are put in place first. For example, it may be more impactful to start by ensuring that major domestic VASPs and stablecoin issuers are licensed, supervised and capable of filing high-quality STRs, before moving to very sophisticated stress-testing of multi-chain liquidity risks.

Sequencing also has a political dimension. Early quick wins – such as issuing clear guidance on the legal status of stablecoins, or successfully supervising a small number of high-profile entities – can build confidence among foreign partners and correspondent banks that the jurisdiction is taking financial integrity seriously. These visible steps can buy time to implement more complex reforms, such as the establishment of a PF Dashboard or comprehensive cross-border supervisory colleges.

Integrating Human Rights and Inclusion Considerations

Stablecoin regulation should not be designed in a vacuum. Many Commonwealth countries see stablecoins as a potential tool for reducing remittance costs, improving access to digital payments, and giving households a hedge against local currency instability. Overly restrictive rules, or blanket bans on self-hosted wallets, can inadvertently undermine financial inclusion and drive vulnerable users into unregulated channels that are even harder to supervise.

Authorities should therefore integrate human-rights and inclusion perspectives into their policy process. This may involve consulting consumer groups and civil-society organisations; assessing how proposed rules affect women, rural communities and micro-entrepreneurs; and considering safeguards for legitimate privacy and data protection. A well-designed framework can both protect the financial system from abuse and expand safe access to useful innovations.

Coherence With Broader Digital and Data Strategies

Stablecoin policy is only one part of a wider digital transformation agenda. Many Commonwealth members are pursuing parallel initiatives on open banking, digital identity, cybersecurity, data protection, cloud computing and AI. Poorly coordinated reforms can create gaps and overlaps that criminals exploit. For example, if digital-identity systems are weak or fragmented, VASPs may struggle to perform robust remote onboarding; if data-protection rules are unclear, information sharing between authorities and private firms may be hampered.

Policymakers should therefore situate stablecoin reforms within a broader digital and data strategy. This might include aligning customer due diligence with national digital-ID schemes, ensuring that PF Dashboards comply with data-protection standards, and harmonising incident-response protocols for cyber events across banks, VASPs and other critical infrastructure. A coherent approach reduces compliance costs and improves the overall resilience of the digital economy.

Learning From Incidents and Near-Misses

No framework will be perfect from day one. Even in advanced jurisdictions, stablecoin markets have experienced de-peggings, liquidity squeezes, cyber incidents and governance failures. These events are painful but valuable sources of learning. Authorities should put in place mechanisms to capture lessons from incidents and near-misses – domestically and abroad – and feed them into future reforms.

This might involve post-incident reviews of how supervisors, FIUs and law enforcement responded; debriefs with industry participants; and contributions to

Commonwealth or regional case-study repositories. Where appropriate, anonymised summaries can be shared publicly to help other jurisdictions avoid similar pitfalls. A culture of open learning and honest reflection is more effective than one of blame and denial.

Measuring Success

Finally, jurisdictions should think carefully about how they will measure the success of their stablecoin and virtual-asset frameworks. Simple metrics, such as the number of licences issued or the number of inspections conducted, are useful but incomplete. Authorities should also consider indicators such as: reductions in unlicensed activity; improvements in the quality and usefulness of STRs; evidence that PF-relevant typologies are being detected earlier; feedback from correspondent banks and international partners; and, on the positive side, uptake of safe, regulated stablecoin-based services that reduce costs for households and businesses.

These metrics should feed into periodic reviews of the strategy. Where goals are not being met, authorities can adjust course – for example by reallocating resources, simplifying overly complex rules, or investing in additional technology or training. A dynamic, evidence-based approach is essential in a fast-moving area such as stablecoins.

Taken together, the elements described in this chapter – robust laws based on Commonwealth model texts, risk-based supervision, practical tools such as PF Dashboards, and a clear allocation of roles – provide a pathway for Commonwealth members to harness the opportunities of stablecoins while managing their risks. The journey will look different in each jurisdiction, but the destination is shared: a financial system that is more inclusive, more efficient and more resilient to abuse.

STABLECOIN RISK TYPOLOGIES AND RED FLAG INDICATORS

Purpose and Use of Typologies

Typologies and red-flag indicators are practical tools that help supervisors, FIUs, law enforcement and reporting entities recognise how stablecoins are being misused in real life. While every case is different, certain patterns recur across investigations and jurisdictions. Systematically capturing and sharing these patterns allows authorities and industry to move from an abstract understanding of "ML/TF/PF risk" to concrete, operational vigilance.

The aim of this section is not to create an exhaustive or static list. Criminals, terrorists and proliferators adapt quickly and will change techniques once old ones become too visible. Rather, the goal is to illustrate the kinds of behaviour that should prompt questions, additional due diligence or suspicious transaction reports. Commonwealth members are encouraged to adapt these typologies to their own risk profiles and to feed back new patterns into Commonwealth and regional knowledge-sharing platforms.

Money Laundering Typologies Involving Stablecoins

A first set of typologies concerns classic money laundering: placement of illicit funds, layering to disguise origin, and integration into the legitimate economy. Stablecoins can feature in each stage.

Use of Stablecoins as a Cross-Border Layering Tool

In many cases, illicit funds are still generated in fiat – for example through fraud, corruption, tax evasion, environmental crime or drug trafficking. The proceeds may be deposited into bank accounts or held as cash. One common pattern is for criminals to convert these funds into stablecoins through OTC brokers, unlicensed exchanges or complicit staff within regulated institutions. Once in stablecoin form, the funds can be rapidly moved across borders and across chains, taking advantage of 24/7 markets and low fees.

Layering may involve:

- using multiple exchanges and swap services in different jurisdictions;
- routing funds through privacy tools, including mixers and privacy coins, before returning to stablecoins;
- bridging between chains to exploit gaps in supervision and analytics coverage; and
- temporarily placing funds into DeFi protocols to generate yield, obscure the transaction trail, or both.

Red flags for VASPs and banks include:

- rapid conversion of large fiat balances into stablecoins followed by transfers to high-risk exchanges or newly created self-hosted wallets;
- customers with limited economic profile engaging in high-volume cross-border stablecoin activity;
- repeated use of high-risk mixers or services that have been publicly associated with ransomware or darknet markets; and

- complex routing of funds with no clear economic purpose, especially where the ultimate destination is a high-risk jurisdiction.

Trade-Based Money Laundering with Stablecoins

Stablecoins can also be used as the settlement leg for trade-based money laundering schemes. For example, an exporter and importer may collude to over-invoice or under-invoice goods. The "true" value of the transaction may be settled in stablecoins through offshore wallets or VASPs that are not visible to banks handling documentary credits or shipping documents. In other cases, shell companies may appear to pay for legitimate goods in stablecoins while actually moving value connected with criminal activities. Indicative red flags include:

- companies with limited history or real operations engaging in large stablecoin payments for high-value goods;
- mismatches between shipping routes, commodity types and payment patterns – for example, repeated stablecoin payments to hubs unrelated to the underlying trade;
- use of stablecoins to settle invoices for goods that are commonly used as cover in TBML schemes (such as easily over- or under-valued consumer goods); and
- repeated partial payments in stablecoins that do not align with normal commercial practice.

Professional Money Laundering Networks and Stablecoins

Professional money launderers increasingly offer "virtual asset cleaning" services. They may advertise on encrypted forums that they can receive funds in fiat or one crypto-asset and return them "cleaned" in another, often stablecoins. These networks use a combination of OTC brokers, nested VASPs, complex DeFi routes and cross-chain bridges. Red flags include:

- customers that appear to operate as intermediaries for multiple unrelated third parties;
- flows in which stablecoins move rapidly through accounts and are withdrawn without European Union 2023, "Regulation (EU) 2023/1114 of the European Parliament and of the Council of 31 May 2023 on markets in crypto-assets, and amending Regulations (EU) No 1093/2010 and (EU) No 648/2012 (MiCA)", Official Journal of the European Union.any clear business rationale;

- use of repeated "choreographed" patterns of transfers involving the same set of addresses and services; and
- connections to addresses that analytics tools identify as part of known professional laundering networks.

Terrorist Financing Typologies

Stablecoins have begun to feature in terrorist financing in several ways, although volumes remain comparatively small. Because even small amounts can have outsized impact, these typologies warrant careful attention.

Online Donations and Propaganda-Linked Addresses

Terrorist organisations and extremist groups may publish stablecoin addresses on websites, social media, messaging apps or propaganda materials, encouraging supporters to donate. These campaigns sometimes emphasise the perceived anonymity and resilience of stablecoins to censorship. Donations can be collected in one stablecoin and then converted or bridged into others. Red flags include:

- inflows of small stablecoin donations from many different addresses, followed by consolidation and onward transfer;
- customer links to publicly known extremist or terrorist propaganda channels;
- account activity that is dormant for long periods and then exhibits bursts of donation-related inflows; and
- use of stablecoins linked to higher-risk ecosystems or services that have previously been used for extremist financing.

Stablecoins in Cross-Border Movement of TF Funds

Stablecoins can also be used to move funds between cells or associated networks across borders. A facilitator in one country may buy stablecoins from an OTC broker and send them to a wallet controlled by an associate in another jurisdiction. The recipient can then convert the stablecoins back into local currency, or into goods and services, through informal exchangers or local VASPs. Potential indicators include:

- stablecoin flows between locations with known or emerging TF concerns, particularly where senders and recipients lack clear economic ties;
- use of self-hosted wallets with minimal on-chain history for cross-border transfers;

- repeated patterns of transfers just below reporting thresholds in conjunction with other TF indicators; and
- involvement of individuals or entities already flagged for TF-related risk in bank or law-enforcement databases.

Proliferation Financing Typologies

Proliferation networks are often sophisticated users of trade, finance and corporate structures. Their use of stablecoins is still evolving, but plausible and emerging typologies include:

Stablecoins for Procurement of Dual-Use Goods

Front companies or brokers may arrange the purchase of dual-use goods – for example, machine tools, electronic components or laboratory equipment – and settle all or part of the value in stablecoins. This may be done to avoid scrutiny from banks, to route payments through jurisdictions with weaker controls, or to decrease the visibility of the ultimate end-user. Red flags include:

- stablecoin payments to suppliers of high-risk goods that do not align with the stated business profile of the buyer;
- involvement of shipping routes, free zones or trans-shipment hubs associated with past proliferation cases;
- repeated under- or over-invoicing combined with off-ledger stablecoin payments; and
- connections to designated entities, proliferating states or their known networks of front companies.

Sanctions Evasion and Stablecoins

Proliferation-related sanctions evasion may involve the use of stablecoins to pay for shipping, insurance, bunkering or other services related to controlled goods. Actors may use nested relationships with compliant-looking intermediaries, but settle side-payments in stablecoins moved through high-risk VASPs or self-hosted wallets. Indicators can include:

- stablecoin flows to or from entities involved in shipping, logistics or maritime services with ties to sanctioned jurisdictions;
- payments for services linked to vessels that have engaged in ship-to-ship transfers, AIS spoofing or other suspicious maritime behaviour;

- use of multiple high-risk exchanges in quick succession; and
- patterns where funds move from regulated environments into opaque chains and then re-emerge near entities or sectors associated with proliferation concern.

Fraud, Scams and Consumer Harm

Beyond ML, TF and PF, stablecoins are heavily used in fraud and scams, including romance scams, investment fraud, fake "crypto trading platforms" and pyramid schemes. While not always captured as ML/TF/PF risk, these activities can undermine trust in digital finance and damage the reputation of jurisdictions that appear to tolerate them. Common patterns include:

- overseas call centres or online platforms instructing victims to buy stablecoins from reputable exchanges and then transfer them to external addresses supposedly linked to investment accounts;
- fake "stablecoin savings programmes" promising unrealistically high yields, often combined with multi-level marketing tactics;
- fraudulent stablecoin issuers claiming to be fully backed without independent audits or clear legal rights for holders; and
- use of stablecoins in advance-fee frauds, where victims are asked to pay upfront "taxes", "release fees" or "processing charges" in stablecoins to unlock non-existent funds.

Using Typologies and Red Flags in Practice

Typologies and red flags only add value if they are integrated into day-to-day processes. For authorities and reporting entities this means:

- incorporating relevant indicators into internal risk-assessment methodologies and customer-risk scoring models;
- configuring transaction-monitoring systems – including on-chain analytics – to detect patterns described in typologies;
- providing regular training for front-line staff and investigators using real or anonymised case examples; and
- establishing feedback loops so that STRs, supervisory findings and law-enforcement cases continuously refine and update the typologies.

Commonwealth members can amplify the impact of their efforts by contributing anonymised typologies to a shared repository, coordinated through the Secretariat or regional bodies. Over time, a living library of stablecoin-related typologies can significantly improve the ability of all members to detect and disrupt misuse.

COMPARATIVE OVERVIEW OF KEY INTERNATIONAL APPROACHES

Why Comparative Perspective Matters

No jurisdiction designs its stablecoin framework in a vacuum. Policymakers, supervisors and industry actors are aware of developments in major financial centres and increasingly look to those frameworks – positively or negatively – as reference points. A basic comparative understanding helps Commonwealth members to benchmark their own regimes, avoid obvious pitfalls and identify where they may be able to position themselves as credible, well-regulated alternatives.

This section does not attempt a detailed legal commentary on any particular jurisdiction. Instead, it sketches key features of leading approaches in the European Union, the United Kingdom, the United States and selected Asian centres, and then contrasts these with a potential "Commonwealth approach" anchored in the model laws.

European Union – MiCA as a Comprehensive Framework

The European Union's Markets in Crypto-Assets Regulation (MiCA) represents one of the first comprehensive, region-wide regimes for crypto-assets, including stablecoins. MiCA distinguishes between different categories – such as asset-referenced tokens and e-money tokens – and imposes tailored requirements on each.

Key features relevant to AML/CFT and PF objectives include:

- a licensing regime for issuers of certain stablecoins, with conditions on governance, capital, reserves and disclosure;
- rules on redemption rights and the treatment of reserves, including requirements for safekeeping and investment;
- limitations on large-scale stablecoins that could pose risks to monetary policy or financial stability within the euro area; and
- strong links to the EU's broader AML/CFT framework, including the forthcoming EU Anti-Money Laundering Authority.

For Commonwealth members, MiCA offers a useful reference point but is not a blueprint. The scale and institutional complexity of the EU differ from most member states, and some MiCA provisions – such as detailed disclosure templates – may be overly burdensome if transplanted wholesale. However, the overall structure, with clear categories of stablecoins, unified licensing and strong emphasis on reserves and redemption, aligns closely with the principles embedded in the CMLS.

United Kingdom – A Gradual, FSMA-Based Approach

The United Kingdom has taken a more incremental route, building on its existing Financial Services and Markets Act (FSMA) framework. Rather than creating a completely new code for crypto-assets, the UK is progressively bringing certain types of stablecoins and related activities within the perimeter of existing payment and banking regulation, while consulting on future treatment of broader crypto-assets and DeFi.

Key elements include:

- proposals to regulate certain fiat-referenced stablecoins used for payments under the payments and banking regime, with the Bank of England playing a leading role for systemic arrangements;
- plans to extend the regulatory perimeter to encompass broader crypto-asset activities, including exchange, custody and lending, under a modified FSMA framework;
- a strong focus by the Financial Conduct Authority (FCA) on conduct, disclosure and consumer protection, particularly in response to mis-selling and fraud risks; and
- continued emphasis on risk-based AML/CFT supervision, including thematic work on sanctions screening and Travel Rule implementation.

For Commonwealth states with legal systems influenced by UK models, this path – using existing financial-services legislation as the foundation and layering stablecoin-specific provisions on top – may be particularly attractive. The CMLS is designed to be compatible with such an approach, allowing legislators to integrate key concepts into pre-existing Acts rather than starting entirely anew.

United States – Fragmented but Influential

The United States does not yet have a single, unified stablecoin statute. Instead, the regulatory landscape is fragmented across federal and state authorities, with overlapping and sometimes contested mandates for the Securities and Exchange Commission, the Commodity Futures Trading Commission, banking regulators, state money-transmitter supervisors and others. Several draft bills on stablecoins have been introduced in Congress but not yet enacted.

From an AML/CFT and PF perspective, however, the United States remains highly influential. Major global stablecoin issuers often have significant US connections, and US sanctions and law-enforcement tools have a strong extraterritorial impact. Key features include:

- Bank Secrecy Act and related obligations for exchanges, custodians and payment institutions;
- aggressive use of sanctions, forfeiture and enforcement powers in relation to stablecoin issuers, mixers and high-risk exchanges;
- emphasis on due diligence for cross-border correspondent relationships, including where counterparties have significant exposure to stablecoin markets; and
- public guidance and enforcement actions that signal expectations for governance, reserves and disclosures even in the absence of a dedicated stablecoin statute.

For Commonwealth members, the main lesson from the US experience is the importance of clarity. Fragmentation can create opportunities for regulatory arbitrage and uncertainty, while clear allocation of responsibilities and a coherent legislative framework – such as that offered by the CMLVA and CMLS – can provide more predictable outcomes for both industry and international partners.

Selected Asian Approaches – Japan, Singapore and Hong Kong

Several Asian jurisdictions have moved quickly to address stablecoins within broader digital-asset reforms.

Japan has amended its payments legislation to clarify that certain categories of stablecoins are treated as electronic money, subject to issuance and redemption requirements, while still allowing for innovation in other types of crypto-assets. This approach emphasises consumer protection and the stability of payment instruments, reflecting Japan's experience with past exchange failures and its desire to maintain confidence in the financial system.

Singapore, as discussed in the case studies, is moving towards a dedicated framework for well-regulated fiat-backed stablecoins while maintaining a broader licensing regime for digital-payment-token services under its Payment Services Act. Its focus on technology-risk management, operational resilience and public–private cooperation offers valuable lessons for smaller states seeking to do "more with less" in supervision.

Hong Kong has likewise developed proposals for regulating stablecoin issuers and intermediaries, aiming to balance its ambitions as a digital-asset hub with lessons learned from past volatility and platform failures. Its approach underlines the importance of linking stablecoin regulation to prudential oversight, market-conduct rules and broader financial stability mandates.

Towards a Distinctive Commonwealth Approach

Against this backdrop, what might a distinctively "Commonwealth approach" look like? The model laws and the discussions reflected in this chapter suggest several guiding principles:

- Alignment with global standards: Commonwealth frameworks should be clearly compatible with FATF, FSB, BIS and IOSCO principles, reducing the risk of negative assessments or perceptions of regulatory arbitrage.
- Proportionality and flexibility: Rules must be robust but also tailored to local capacity and market size. Smaller states may focus first on core AML/CFT and PF safeguards, leaving more complex prudential features for later phases.
- Emphasis on financial inclusion and development: Many Commonwealth members are emerging or developing economies that see stablecoins as tools for remittances, trade and savings. Regulatory design should protect consumers without unnecessarily stifling legitimate use-cases that advance development goals.
- Regional cooperation and shared infrastructure: Rather than each jurisdiction attempting to build everything alone, the Commonwealth can facilitate shared PF Dashboards, training programmes, supervisory colleges and typology repositories.
- Legal clarity and rule of law: A key comparative advantage of the Commonwealth is its strong tradition of legal certainty and judicial independence. By grounding stablecoin frameworks in clear legislation, supported by explanatory materials and model texts, members can provide a predictable environment for responsible innovators and international partners alike.

In practice, a Commonwealth approach anchored in the CMLVA and CMLS could sit comfortably alongside EU, UK, US and Asian regimes while retaining its own character. It would speak the same "language" of international standards but would do so in a way that recognises the realities of small and vulnerable states, prioritises financial integrity and inclusion, and leverages the unique convening power of the Commonwealth family.

Using Comparative Insights in Domestic Reform

Comparative analysis should not lead to uncritical copying. Instead, authorities should ask:

- Which elements of foreign regimes are genuinely applicable to our context?
- Where would transplantation create complexity or burdens without commensurate benefit?
- How can we use international examples to explain and justify our choices to domestic stakeholders and external partners?

A well-informed domestic debate, drawing on comparative insights but rooted in local realities and the Commonwealth model laws, is more likely to produce stablecoin frameworks that are both effective and sustainable.

CONCLUSION AND CALL TO ACTION

Stablecoins sit at the intersection of innovation and risk. For the Commonwealth, they offer the prospect of cheaper remittances, more efficient trade, improved financial inclusion and new digital-economy opportunities. But without coherent regulation and supervision—especially for multi-chain designs, DeFi interfaces, and cross-border flows—they risk becoming channels for ML, TF, PF and broader financial instability.

The call to action is threefold:

1. Legislate: Enact or update national laws to incorporate the CMLVA and CMLS.
2. Supervise: Invest in supervisory capacity, technology and regional cooperation.
3. Collaborate: Work through the Commonwealth and regional bodies to share data, tools, training and best practices.

REFERENCES

Bank for International Settlement. (2007). *Basel Committee on Banking Supervision Principles for home-host supervisory cooperation and allocation mechanisms in the context of Advanced Measurement Approaches (AMA).* https://www.bis.org/publ/bcbs135.pdf

European Union (2023). "Regulation (EU) 2023/1114 of the European Parliament and of the Council of 31 May 2023 on markets in crypto-assets, and amending Regulations (EU) No 1093/2010 and (EU) No 648/2012 (MiCA)", Official Journal of the European Union.

FATF. (2021). *Updated Guidance for a Risk-Based Approach to Virtual Assets and Virtual Asset Service Providers.* Www.fatf-Gafi.org. https://www.fatf-gafi.org/en/publications/Fatfrecommendations/Guidance-rba-virtual-assets-2021.html

Financial Stability Board. (2020). *Regulation, Supervision and Oversight of "Global Stablecoin" Arrangements.* Www.fsb.org. https://www.fsb.org/2020/10/regulation-supervision-and-oversight-of-global-stablecoin-arrangements/

Financial Stability Board. (2023). *High-level Recommendations for the Regulation, Supervision and Oversight of Global Stablecoin Arrangements: Final report.* Www.fsb.org. https://www.fsb.org/2023/07/high-level-recommendations-for-the-regulation-supervision-and-oversight-of-global-stablecoin-arrangements-final-report/

International Organisation of Securities Commission. (2020). *Global Stablecoin Initiatives Public Report.* https://www.iosco.org/library/pubdocs/pdf/IOSCOPD650.pdf

International Organization of Securities Commissions (CPMI–IOSCO). (2021). *Application of the Principles for Financial Market Infrastructures to stablecoin arrangements.* Bank for International Settlements.

IOSCO. (2023). *Policy Recommendations for Crypto and Digital Asset Markets Final Report.* https://www.iosco.org/library/pubdocs/pdf/IOSCOPD747.pdf

Secretariat, C. (2024). *The Commonwealth Model Law on Virtual Assets.* Commonwealth. https://thecommonwealth.org/publications/model-law-virtual-assets

Secretariat, C. (2025 forthcoming). *Commonwealth Model Law on Stablecoins (draft).* Commonwealth Secretariat.

Chapter 9
Licensing and Supervision Made Simple:
The Why and How We Need Licensing

Jonathan Hatch
https://orcid.org/0009-0002-7142-2852
Independent Researcher, Australia

ABSTRACT

This chapter provides a comprehensive roadmap for designing robust licensing and supervisory frameworks for stablecoins. The authors examine at a high level who should be licensed, licensing requirements, proportionate supervision, exemptions, innovation support, enforcement, cross-border cooperation, and future directions. Drawing on international principles from the Financial Stability Board, International Organization of Securities Commissions, Financial Action Task Force, and comparative experiences from the EU's Markets in Crypto-Assets Regulation, Singapore's Payment Services Act, and Commonwealth jurisdictions, this chapter argues for functional, risk-based, and technologically neutral frameworks. The authors emphasize that licensing establishes accountability rather than control, enabling innovation within appropriate guardrails. Key themes include proportionality through tiered requirements, technology-enabled supervision via RegTech and SupTech tools, graduated enforcement, and essential cross-border coordination for inherently global instruments

DOI: 10.4018/979-8-3373-6655-5.ch009

INTRODUCTION

Stablecoins have emerged as one of the most significant—and contentious—innovations in contemporary digital finance. Designed to bridge the volatility of cryptocurrencies with the stability of traditional fiat currencies, they promise low-cost, near-instant, and programmable settlement capabilities that could fundamentally reshape payment systems, cross-border remittances, and even monetary policy transmission (Financial Stability Board, 2020; International Monetary Fund, 2021). Yet this promise comes with considerable regulatory uncertainty. Are stablecoins simply digital versions of existing payment instruments, or do they represent something fundamentally new that challenges the boundaries of traditional financial regulation?

Financial regulators worldwide find themselves navigating uncharted territory. The challenge is not merely technical—it is conceptual. How should authorities classify instruments that function like money but are issued by private entities outside the banking system? What licensing thresholds make sense for arrangements that may involve distributed ledgers, algorithmic stabilisation mechanisms, or cross-border issuance without a clear jurisdictional anchor? And perhaps most fundamentally: should regulators seek to fit stablecoins into existing frameworks designed decades ago for banks and payment institutions, or do these instruments demand entirely new regulatory architectures (Financial Action Task Force, 2021; IOSCO, 2020)?

These questions are not merely academic. The answers will determine whether stablecoins evolve into integral components of the global financial system or remain relegated to niche markets due to regulatory fragmentation and compliance uncertainty. They will shape the competitive dynamics between traditional financial institutions and technology-driven newcomers. And they will influence whether innovation occurs within well-supervised frameworks or migrates to less regulated jurisdictions—a pattern that has characterised financial innovation for centuries.

This chapter adopts a deliberately practical approach to these complex questions. Rather than proposing a single "correct" regulatory model, it examines the core functions that licensing and supervision must fulfil, regardless of the specific legal form a jurisdiction chooses. The focus throughout is on simplicity—not in the sense of oversimplification, but in the pursuit of regulatory clarity that enables both compliance and innovation. Drawing on emerging international principles from the Bank for International Settlements (Basel Committee on Banking Supervision, 2021), the Monetary Authority of Singapore (Monetary Authority of Singapore, 2021), and comparative experiences from the European Union, Japan, and Commonwealth jurisdictions, this chapter provides a roadmap for designing proportionate, risk-sensitive, and technologically neutral regulatory frameworks.

The chapter's central argument is straightforward yet frequently overlooked: licensing is not primarily about control—it is about responsibility. When designed well, licensing frameworks create clear lines of accountability, establish minimum standards for operational competence, and provide regulators with the supervisory tools necessary to respond when things go wrong. The challenge lies in calibrating these requirements so they are neither so onerous that they stifle innovation nor so permissive that they fail to protect consumers and financial stability.

BACKGROUND

The regulatory treatment of stablecoins has been characterised by confusion, experimentation, and occasional crisis. When early stablecoins like Tether first appeared in 2014, regulators were largely unprepared. The instruments did not fit neatly into existing categories. Were they securities, requiring registration under securities laws? Were they a form of electronic money, subject to e-money regulations? Or were they something else entirely—perhaps closer to bank deposits, given their promise of stable value and redemption on demand?

This taxonomic uncertainty led to predictable regulatory fragmentation. Jurisdictions responded differently based on their existing legal frameworks, institutional structures, and tolerance for regulatory innovation. In the United States, stablecoins faced a patchwork of federal and state requirements, with different agencies claiming jurisdiction depending on the instrument's specific features (U.S. Securities and Exchange Commission, 2023). The European Union initially addressed stablecoins indirectly through its e-money directive, though many arrangements fell outside its scope (ECB, 2020). Singapore took a more integrated approach, incorporating stablecoins into its Payment Services Act framework alongside other digital payment tokens (Monetary Authority of Singapore, 2019; Monetary Authority of Singapore, 2021). Japan distinguished between stablecoins backed by bank deposits—which it treated as a form of electronic prepaid payment instrument—and other arrangements that might fall under its cryptocurrency exchange licensing regime (Financial Services Agency of Japan, 2020; Financial Services Agency of Japan, 2022).

This fragmentation was not merely an academic problem. It created real market distortions. Issuers engaged in regulatory arbitrage, structuring their arrangements to fall into the most favourable regulatory category or jurisdiction. Some moved operations offshore to avoid licensing requirements entirely. Consumers struggled to understand what protections, if any, applied to their holdings. And regulators found themselves playing catch-up as the market evolved faster than their frameworks could adapt.

The inadequacy of this piecemeal approach became starkly apparent in 2022 with the collapse of TerraUSD, an algorithmic stablecoin that lost its peg spectacularly, wiping out approximately $60 billion in value within days (Zadeh, 2022). While

TerraUSD was not representative of all stablecoins—its algorithmic design differed fundamentally from asset-backed models—its failure catalysed regulatory urgency. Policymakers recognised that the "wait and see" approach had run its course. The question was no longer whether stablecoins should be regulated, but how.

International standard-setting bodies responded with unusual speed and coordination. The Financial Stability Board (FSB) issued recommendations for the regulation, supervision, and oversight of "global stablecoin" arrangements, emphasising the need for comprehensive regulatory frameworks that address both prudential and financial integrity risks (Financial Stability Board, 2020, 2023). The International Organization of Securities Commissions (IOSCO) provided guidance on the application of its principles to stablecoin arrangements, particularly those with securities-like features (IOSCO, 2020). The Financial Action Task Force (FATF) clarified how its anti-money laundering and counter-terrorism financing standards apply to stablecoin service providers, introducing the concept of "virtual asset service providers" to capture entities that might otherwise fall outside traditional financial institution definitions (Financial Action Task Force, 2021; Financial Action Task Force, 2023).

Perhaps most significantly, major jurisdictions began developing comprehensive, bespoke frameworks specifically for stablecoins and related crypto-assets. The European Union's Markets in Crypto-Assets Regulation (MiCA), which entered into force in 2023 with phased implementation through 2024-2025, established a dedicated regulatory regime covering authorisation requirements, reserve asset rules, governance standards, and conduct obligations for both issuers and service providers (European Parliament & Council, 2023). Singapore continued refining its Payment Services Act framework, introducing specific provisions for digital payment token services and stablecoin arrangements (Monetary Authority of Singapore, 2021; Monetary Authority of Singapore, 2023). Japan amended its Payment Services Act to create a distinct category for "electronic payment instruments" backed by deposits or assets, with clear licensing and custody requirements (Financial Services Agency of Japan, 2022).

Despite their different approaches, these frameworks share important commonalities. Most fundamentally, they reject the notion that stablecoins should be treated as entirely unregulated instruments simply because they use novel technology. Instead, they embrace what has become known as the principle of "same activity, same risk, same regulation"—though this principle, while rhetorically appealing, proves more complex in application than in theory (Financial Action Task Force, 2021; Basel Committee on Banking Supervision, 2021).

The principle assumes we can identify when stablecoin arrangements engage in the "same activity" as traditional financial services. But what constitutes equivalence? A stablecoin that promises redemption at par resembles a bank deposit in function, yet it may lack deposit insurance, operate across borders seamlessly, and be issued by an entity with no banking licence. Is this the "same" as deposit-taking? Similarly, a stablecoin arrangement might involve multiple parties—an issuer, a reserve manager, a technology provider, a wallet operator—each performing functions that partially overlap with traditional financial intermediation but without clear analogues in legacy regulatory frameworks.

These complexities reveal a deeper tension in stablecoin regulation: the tension between functional equivalence and institutional form. Traditional financial regulation has long been organised around institutional types—banks, securities firms, payment institutions—each with distinct licensing requirements and supervisory regimes. Stablecoins, however, often unbundle and recombine functions performed by different types of institutions. This poses a fundamental question: should regulation follow function (regulating the economic activity regardless of who performs it) or institution (regulating based on the legal form of the entity)?

The answer, increasingly, is "both." Modern stablecoin frameworks adopt a hybrid approach, identifying key functions that require licensing—such as issuance, custody of reserve assets, and redemption services—while also imposing institutional requirements on entities performing those functions. This functional-institutional synthesis represents an evolution in regulatory thinking, one that may have implications well beyond stablecoins for the broader regulation of decentralised finance and digital assets.

Understanding this evolution requires appreciating that licensing is not a novel regulatory tool invented for stablecoins. Rather, it is one of the oldest mechanisms by which societies have sought to manage risk in activities involving public trust. The next section examines this deeper history and explains why licensing remains relevant—indeed, essential—in the context of digital financial innovation.

STRUCTURE OF THE CHAPTER

This chapter provides a comprehensive, academically grounded, and practical roadmap for designing robust licensing and supervisory frameworks for stablecoins. It integrates historical insights, regulatory theory, and comparative international practice to assist policymakers, regulators, and legal scholars in crafting proportionate, risk-sensitive approaches that promote innovation while safeguarding market integrity and consumer trust.

1. Who Should Be Licensed – Rationale, Scope, and Thresholds

This section examines why licensing is essential for stablecoin-related activities, tracing its conceptual and historical foundations in financial regulation. It explains how licensing functions as a societal tool to manage risk, allocate responsibility, and ensure accountability in systems involving public trust, such as payment and deposit services. It outlines a function-based framework for identifying entities that require licensing—issuers, custodians, smart contract controllers, wallet providers, and liquidity agents—based on their operational roles and systemic risk implications. White-label and Banking-as-a-Service models are addressed, with emphasis on preventing regulatory arbitrage and ensuring consumer-facing entities remain within the regulatory perimeter.

2. What Licensing Should Require – Principles and Pillars

Building on the "who," this section sets out eight foundational pillars of what licensing frameworks for stablecoins should require: legal status and governance, risk management, reserve asset safeguards, prudential requirements, redemption rights, transparency and disclosure, interoperability, and consumer/data protection. The section balances regulatory effectiveness and innovation by highlighting proportionality, tiering, and alignment with evolving international standards (e.g. FATF, IOSCO, EU MiCA). Particular attention is given to reserve audits, capital buffers, redemption enforceability, and the secure custody of private keys.

3. How Supervision Should Work – Proportionality, RegTech, and Dynamic Oversight

This section explores the architecture of supervision, differentiating between ex-ante licensing and ex-post monitoring. It addresses tiered supervisory models based on systemic footprint, average transaction volumes, or user base. It considers the use of RegTech and SupTech tools for real-time monitoring, risk flagging, and dynamic disclosures. Lessons are drawn from Singapore's Payment Services Act, the EU's MiCA supervisory tiering, and emerging Commonwealth guidance. It also considers cross-functional supervisory teams involving prudential, conduct, AML/CFT, and cyber specialists.

4. Who Should Be Exempt – Narrow Carveouts and Residual Responsibility

This section discusses when and how certain actors may be exempt from direct licensing, such as back-end technical service providers, infrastructure nodes, or software developers. Drawing on proportionality principles and FATF's functional guidance, it sets out criteria for exemptions based on risk, remoteness from control, and functional equivalence. It clarifies the residual responsibility of licensed entities for their agents, delegates, and technology partners, with analogies to outsourcing rules in banking and payments.

5. Guidance, Sandboxes, and Pathways to Compliance – Supporting Innovation Without Compromising Standards

This section provides a deep dive into non-enforcement-based tools for regulatory support and innovation enablement, including:

- **Regulatory guidance documents** and FAQs to support early compliance.
- **Innovation support functions** (ISFs) such as ASIC's Innovation Hub or the MAS FinTech Office, which facilitate **early contact and problem-solving**, often with better results than limited sandboxes (see Buckley, Arner & Zetzsche, 2020).
- **Regulatory sandboxes**, differentiated into:
    - o *Testing environments* for limited-market pilots;
    - o *Guidance-based sandboxes* focused on interpretive clarity;
    - o *Exemption-based sandboxes* granting time-bound relief;
    - o *Coordination platforms* (e.g., FCA sandbox cohort model) facilitating multi-party engagement.

The section also discusses pathways to compliance, including transitional licensing, "if not, why not" self-assessment models, and alignment with international standards such as ISO/IEC 42001 and MiCA Titles III–IV as alternative compliance pathways.

Key academic sources include Gromilova (2021), Buckley et al. (2020), Arner & Zetzsche (2021), and comparative sandbox evaluations by the World Bank and OECD.

6. Supervisory Tools, Remedies, and Offences – Enforcement Without Overreach

This section outlines the regulatory toolkit available post-licensing, including:

- On-site and off-site inspections;
- Mandated audits or third-party reviews;
- Freezing of redemptions or trading;
- Penalties, licence suspensions, and criminal offences for fraud or misrepresentation.

It proposes a graduated enforcement approach aligned with supervisory objectives and operational proportionality.

7. Cross-Border Cooperation and Enforcement – A Coordinated Global Response

Given the **borderless nature of stablecoin ecosystems**, this section explores international cooperation mechanisms for information sharing, mutual recognition, and coordinated enforcement. It discusses:

- Common reporting templates and data interoperability;
- Crisis coordination via IOSCO or FSB platforms;
- Legal assistance in AML/CFT and fraud cases;
- Issues around forum shopping and enforcement jurisdiction for DAOs and stateless issuers.

Examples from the EU's passporting regime, ASEAN cross-border cooperation, and the Commonwealth Virtual Assets Model Law are analysed.

8. Conclusion and Future Directions – Building a Resilient, Innovation-Ready Framework

The final section synthesises the chapter's core arguments, affirming that licensing and supervision are **not designed to mimic bank regulation**, but to ensure stablecoin ecosystems meet equivalent standards where similar risks arise. It emphasises the need for **principled regulatory pluralism**—offering different pathways to compliance while converging on core outcomes like redemption certainty, reserve integrity, and user protection. The section also sketches future directions, including alignment with emerging global stablecoin standards, integration with central bank digital currency (CBDC) frameworks, and the role of AI in managing dynamic risk surfaces.

1. WHO SHOULD BE LICENSED – RATIONALE, SCOPE, AND THRESHOLDS

Why Societies License Financial Conduct

Licensing is not merely a bureaucratic gatekeeping function—it represents something far more fundamental: a mechanism for enforcing the social contract between private actors and public trust. When the state grants a financial licence, it makes an implicit bargain: it allows an entity access to public capital, payment systems, and consumer trust in exchange for adherence to conduct standards, regulatory oversight, and legal accountability.

This bargain exists because certain financial activities, if conducted without regulatory guardrails, create negative externalities that markets alone cannot efficiently manage. A failed bank does not merely harm its shareholders—it can trigger contagion, destroy depositor savings, and threaten macroeconomic stability. An unscrupulous payment provider does not simply damage its own reputation—it can facilitate money laundering, fraud, and erosion of confidence in payment systems more broadly. These are classic examples of market failures where private incentives diverge from social welfare, justifying regulatory intervention (Stiglitz, 1993).

The core public interest objectives that financial licensing serves include:

- **Reducing information asymmetry** between providers and consumers, particularly where technical complexity makes informed decision-making difficult;
- **Protecting consumers** from fraud, loss, and exploitation, especially where fiduciary relationships or custody of funds creates vulnerability;
- **Ensuring financial stability** by supervising institutions whose failure could trigger systemic contagion or disrupt critical payment infrastructure;
- **Enforcing prudential norms** where public funds, household savings, or retirement assets are at risk; and
- **Maintaining integrity** of payment systems, preventing illicit financial flows, and preserving monetary sovereignty.

Yet licensing also carries symbolic weight that extends beyond its technical functions. It signals to the public that a provider has met minimum standards of competence, integrity, and financial soundness. This symbolic legitimacy is particularly critical in trust-sensitive environments like money issuance, asset custody, and payment services, where confidence itself becomes the currency that enables the system to function.

As Coffee (2006) observed, "licensing transforms private actors into semi-public fiduciaries," imposing obligations that transcend ordinary commercial relationships. A licensed bank cannot simply walk away from depositors when business conditions deteriorate—it operates under a regulatory framework that mandates capital buffers, liquidity reserves, and resolution procedures designed to protect depositors even in failure. This transformation from purely private actor to quasi-public trustee is the essence of what licensing accomplishes.

However, this transformation comes at a cost. Licensing requirements impose compliance burdens, create barriers to entry, and can protect incumbents from competition. The challenge for regulators is ensuring that licensing serves genuine public interest objectives rather than merely entrenching existing market structures or imposing costs that exceed benefits.

Historical Evolution of Financial Licensing

Understanding why stablecoins require licensing requires appreciating the historical arc of financial regulation more broadly. Financial licensing did not emerge from abstract regulatory theory—it evolved as a pragmatic response to repeated crises where unregulated financial activity caused widespread social harm.

The origins of modern financial licensing can be traced to the era of "wildcat banking" in 19th century United States. During this period, state-chartered banks issued their own banknotes as currency, often with minimal capital backing and inadequate reserves. When banks failed—which they did with alarming frequency—their notes became worthless, wiping out the savings of ordinary citizens who had accepted them as payment. The result was a cycle of bank runs, financial panics, and economic instability that plagued the American economy for decades (Calomiris & Gorton, 1991).

This experience catalyzed fundamental reforms. States began imposing charter requirements, minimum capital standards, and reserve obligations on banks. The National Banking Acts of 1863 and 1864 created federal banking licenses, establishing uniform currency and stricter prudential standards. Later, the creation of the Federal Reserve System in 1913 and deposit insurance in 1933 further strengthened the regulatory architecture, but licensing remained its foundation—the mechanism for determining who could accept deposits and issue payment instruments.

The 20th century saw financial licensing expand beyond traditional banks to encompass new types of financial intermediaries as they emerged and reached systemic significance. Insurance companies came under state regulation following widespread failures in the late 1800s. Securities dealers and broker-dealers became subject to federal licensing after the 1929 stock market crash revealed how unregulated securities markets could destabilize the broader economy. Money transmitters faced licensing requirements as they grew to handle significant payment flows, particularly for immigrant remittances.

The 2008 Global Financial Crisis marked another watershed. It revealed how non-bank financial institutions—mortgage originators, structured investment vehicles, credit default swap dealers—could create systemic risks comparable to traditional banks while operating outside the banking regulatory perimeter. The regulatory response included expanding oversight to these "shadow banking" entities, though implementation has varied across jurisdictions and remains incomplete (International Monetary Fund, 2010; Financial Stability Board, 2020).

More recently, technological intermediation of financial services has triggered the latest expansion of licensing frameworks. Electronic money issuers like PayPal came under regulation through the EU's E-Money Directive. Digital wallet providers operating at scale—WeChat Pay in China, GCash in the Philippines—became subject to licensing requirements as regulators recognized their systemic importance. Cryptocurrency exchanges and custodians increasingly face licensing obligations under anti-money laundering frameworks and investor protection regimes.

A pattern emerges across these historical waves: each significant financial innovation that touches public trust, payment finality, or savings custodianship eventually triggers a licensing response, usually following a crisis that demonstrates the inadequacy of existing frameworks (Zetzsche et al., 2020a). Stablecoins represent the latest iteration of this pattern.

Why Stablecoins Require Licensing

Stablecoins are not merely technical innovations—they are functional substitutes for traditional forms of money and payment instruments, carrying similar risks that have justified licensing requirements throughout financial innovation (Potts, 2017) history. When stablecoins are issued to the public with promises of stable value and redemption for fiat currency, they replicate core functions of deposit-taking, money issuance, and payment settlement infrastructure—often without the transparency, capital buffers, or compliance systems required of traditional financial institutions performing these same functions.

The case for licensing becomes especially compelling when stablecoin issuers:

- **Accept and custody customer funds**, acting as de facto deposit-takers without the prudential safeguards that apply to banks;
- **Offer redemption guarantees**, creating liquidity and maturity mismatch risks similar to those that trigger bank runs;
- **Operate infrastructure for peer-to-peer settlement**, functioning as unregulated payment systems that could fail or be exploited for illicit purposes;

- **Rely on fractional reserves or risky asset portfolios** to generate returns, exposing users to credit and market risks they may not understand or consent to.

The systemic risks posed by stablecoins arise not primarily from their use of blockchain technology or cryptographic security—these are implementation details that may actually enhance resilience in some respects. Rather, the risks stem from their fundamental economic promise: to be as safe, liquid, and stable as sovereign money, while operating outside the regulatory constraints that make sovereign money credible (Gorton & Zhang, 2023).

Without licensing and the supervisory framework it enables, stablecoin arrangements can undermine multiple regulatory objectives:

Consumer protection suffers when users lack clarity about redemption rights, reserve backing, or who bears losses when things go wrong. The sudden freeze of redemptions or collapse of an issuer can wipe out household savings with no recourse.

Financial stability is threatened when large-scale stablecoins create the potential for mass redemptions that trigger fire sales of reserve assets, transmit stress across markets, or disrupt critical payment functions.

Market integrity erodes when stablecoins enable regulatory arbitrage—allowing functionally equivalent services to operate under different standards depending on their legal structure or jurisdictional location.

Monetary sovereignty faces challenges when private stablecoins facilitate large-scale substitution away from national currencies, potentially undermining monetary policy transmission and central bank control over the money supply.

Case in Point: TerraUSD

The collapse of TerraUSD in May 2022 serves as a stark illustration of why licensing matters. TerraUSD was an algorithmic stablecoin that relied on arbitrage mechanisms and a complementary volatile token (LUNA) to maintain its dollar peg, rather than holding conventional reserves. Operating without a license or regulatory oversight in most jurisdictions, TerraUSD grew to a market capitalization exceeding $18 billion before losing its peg catastrophically in a matter of days.

The unwinding destroyed approximately $60 billion in value across TerraUSD and LUNA, triggered severe volatility in cryptocurrency markets more broadly, and contributed to the failures of several crypto-focused financial firms. Individual investors—many attracted by promises of 20% yields on TerraUSD deposits—lost life savings. The contagion rippled through to other stablecoins, causing temporary de-pegging and widespread loss of confidence.

As the IMF observed in the aftermath, "Terra's collapse demonstrated the need for regulatory frameworks that are proportionate to the risks and functions of crypto-assets" (International Monetary Fund, 2023). Had TerraUSD been subject to licensing requirements—mandating reserve backing, capital buffers, redemption rights, and ongoing supervision—the scale of the collapse might have been contained or prevented entirely.

Risks of Overreach and Misaligned Licensing

Yet licensing is not without risks of its own, and policymakers must approach stablecoin licensing with clear-eyed recognition of potential downsides. Critics of heavy-handed licensing regimes raise several legitimate concerns that deserve serious consideration.

Innovation stifling: Licensing requirements that are overly prescriptive or impose disproportionate compliance costs can stifle beneficial innovation, particularly where startups or community-based financial models lack the resources to navigate complex regulatory processes. If licensing effectively requires hiring teams of compliance officers and lawyers before launching, only well-capitalized incumbents will enter the market.

Incumbent entrenchment: Licensing can create a moat around established players by raising barriers to entry that protect existing market participants from competition rather than genuinely improving standards. Incumbent institutions may even lobby for stricter licensing requirements as a competitive strategy, knowing smaller competitors cannot bear the costs.

Regulatory capture: Where licensing processes become complex and opaque, opportunities for regulatory capture increase. Licensed entities may exert undue influence over regulators, shaping rules to favor their business models and exclude alternative approaches that might better serve consumers.

Misaligned requirements: Perhaps most fundamentally, applying bank-like licensing regimes wholesale to all stablecoins risks mischaracterizing risks and creating poorly calibrated regulation. Not all stablecoins pose equivalent risks—a small-scale, fully reserved stablecoin used for niche cross-border payments differs fundamentally from a large-scale, fractionally-reserved stablecoin integrated into multiple payment systems. Treating them identically makes little sense (Arner et al., 2017).

These concerns point toward an essential principle: licensing must be risk-based, proportionate, and technologically neutral. Regulators should focus not on the label "stablecoin" or the specific technology employed, but on the functions performed and risks created. As Zetzsche et al. (2020b) argue, "Regulators must avoid applying old labels to new products and instead ask: What risks are being created? What regulatory objectives are implicated?"

This functional, risk-based approach requires careful analysis of who within stablecoin ecosystems controls critical risks and should therefore be subject to licensing requirements.

Who Should Be Licensed: A Functional Approach

A functional approach to stablecoin licensing begins with a simple but powerful question: who in the stablecoin ecosystem exercises control over critical risks to users or the financial system? Licensing should attach to entities whose actions—or failures to act—can cause material harm that regulatory intervention aims to prevent.

The following table provides a framework for identifying licensing triggers based on functions performed and risks controlled:

Table 1. Functional licensing framework for stablecoin participants

Function	Risk	Licensing Trigger
Issuer	Redemption obligation, reserve adequacy, governance of issuance/ destruction	Primary licensure required (e.g., MiCA Title III/IV, Singapore PSA)
Reserve Custodian	Loss, theft, or misappropriation of reserve assets	Subject to separate custody licence or equivalent prudential requirements
Wallet Provider (Custodial)	Control of user private keys, access to funds, execution of transactions	Licensing required where provider holds customer assets or facilitates redemption
Liquidity Provider / Market Maker	Peg maintenance, market manipulation, sudden liquidity withdrawal	Licensing required where proprietary trading creates conflicts or systemic dependencies
Smart Contract Controller	System operation, ability to modify code, pause/resume functions, redirect funds	Licensing required where control implies fiduciary responsibility or material operational risk
Governance Token Holder (DAO)	Protocol upgrades, changes to risk parameters, treasury management	Legal wrapper or licensing may be required to ensure accountability

Let us examine each category in greater depth.

Issuers

Issuers are the most straightforward candidates for licensing. An issuer creates stablecoins and assumes—whether through explicit legal obligation, contractual commitment, or merely implied representation—the responsibility to maintain their value and facilitate redemption. This is functionally indistinguishable from deposit-taking or e-money issuance, both of which are universally subject to licensing requirements across developed financial systems (European Parliament & Council, 2023; Monetary Authority of Singapore, 2021).

The issuer sits at the center of the stablecoin arrangement and controls fundamental risks: whether reserves are adequate, how redemption requests are processed, what happens during stress events, and ultimately whether users can convert their stablecoins back into fiat currency. Without robust licensing of issuers that establishes minimum standards for capital, reserves, governance, and operational resilience, consumer protection and financial stability objectives cannot be achieved.

Reserve Asset Custodians

The entities that custody reserve assets backing stablecoins perform a critical function that may be separate from issuance itself. If reserve assets are stolen, mismanaged, or simply prove inadequate, the stablecoin loses its backing and users face losses—regardless of how responsibly the issuer otherwise operates (Financial Stability Board, 2020).

Some stablecoin arrangements use third-party custodians—often regulated banks or trust companies—who already hold appropriate licenses and are subject to prudential supervision. In these cases, existing regulatory frameworks may provide adequate oversight of the custody function. However, where issuers custody reserves internally or through unregulated affiliates, the custody function itself may require specific licensing, or at minimum the custodian must be subject to prudential standards equivalent to those applying to regulated depositary institutions.

Wallet Providers

Wallet providers facilitate user access to stablecoins and fall into two distinct categories with very different regulatory implications.

Custodial wallet providers hold private keys on behalf of users and execute transactions at their direction. This is functionally analogous to payment institutions or broker-dealers who hold client assets in custody. The risk is clear: a custodial wallet provider that suffers a hack, becomes insolvent, or acts dishonestly can cause users to lose access to their stablecoins entirely (Organisation for Economic Co-operation and Development, 2012).

Most jurisdictions already license custodial wallet services under payment services frameworks or virtual asset service provider regimes.

Non-custodial wallet providers, by contrast, offer software tools that enable users to maintain direct control over their own private keys. Since these providers never take custody of user assets and cannot unilaterally access or transfer funds, the case for licensing them as financial service providers is much weaker. However, they may face different regulatory obligations around software liability, disclosure of risks, or prevention of use for illicit purposes.

Liquidity Providers and Market Makers

Large-scale liquidity providers and market makers play an important role in maintaining stablecoin price stability through continuous trading operations. While not typically part of the core issuance mechanism, major market makers can significantly influence stablecoin stability. If dominant liquidity providers suddenly withdraw from markets during stress periods, the resulting illiquidity can cause stablecoins to lose their peg and trigger broader instability (Financial Stability Board, 2023).

Whether such entities require stablecoin-specific licensing or can operate under existing securities dealer, trading platform, or market maker licenses depends on jurisdictional frameworks. The key principle is that entities providing material liquidity to systemically important stablecoins should operate within some regulatory perimeter that enables supervisory oversight of their risk management, capital adequacy, and conduct.

Smart Contract Controllers

Smart contract controllers present one of the most conceptually challenging licensing questions. In many stablecoin arrangements, critical functions—issuance, redemption, reserve management—are executed through smart contracts deployed on distributed ledgers. The question becomes: who, if anyone, controls these contracts?

If a single entity or small group can modify contract parameters, pause operations, upgrade code, or redirect funds, that entity exercises control functionally equivalent to a traditional financial intermediary (Financial Action Task Force, 2021). Such control warrants licensing, even if the entity characterizes itself as merely providing "technology services" or "protocol governance."

Conversely, if smart contracts are genuinely immutable and their governance is sufficiently decentralized that no single party exercises effective control, the case for licensing becomes more complex. Regulators cannot license no one. However, they might focus on licensing the initial deployers of contracts, requiring ongoing governance mechanisms that ensure accountability, or mandating that critical functions involve licensed intermediaries even if smart contracts automate execution.

Governance Token Holders and DAOs

Some stablecoin protocols are governed by decentralized autonomous organizations (DAOs) where decisions about protocol upgrades, risk parameters, and treasury management are made through token-holder voting. These governance structures challenge traditional notions of licensing, which presume identifiable legal entities that can be held accountable.

One approach involves requiring DAOs to establish legal wrappers—such as foundations, associations, or specialized DAO legal entities—that can hold licenses and be subject to regulatory obligations. Another approach focuses on licensing key service providers to the DAO, such as the entities operating critical infrastructure, managing treasury assets, or implementing governance decisions. The goal is ensuring that meaningful accountability exists somewhere in the structure, even if governance is distributed.

Licensing and White-Label Models

The functional approach becomes particularly important when examining white-label and Banking-as-a-Service (BaaS) models, which have proliferated in both traditional fintech and emerging stablecoin contexts. In these arrangements, a licensed entity—typically a bank or regulated payment institution—provides the regulatory infrastructure and license, while a technology company or other non-regulated entity handles customer-facing operations, product design, user experience, and sometimes key business decisions.

Such arrangements create obvious opportunities for regulatory arbitrage if not carefully supervised. Consider a technology company that partners with a small, lightly supervised bank to issue stablecoins nominally under the bank's license. The technology company designs the product, controls the user interface, makes decisions about reserve management and redemption policies, and builds the business—yet claims it need not be licensed because it operates "through" a licensed bank. Meanwhile, the bank may exercise minimal actual oversight, viewing its role as merely providing regulatory compliance as a service.

If something goes wrong—reserves prove insufficient, redemptions are delayed, or users suffer losses—who bears responsibility? The licensed bank may claim it merely provided infrastructure and relied on the technology partner for operational management. The technology company insists it was not the regulated entity and therefore not responsible for regulatory compliance failures. Users are left in a accountability vacuum.

Regulatory frameworks must close this gap through several mechanisms:

First, licensing requirements should include explicit provisions that licensed entities remain fully responsible for all functions performed by technology partners, white-label operators, or outsourced service providers (European Parliament & Council, 2023). Accountability cannot be outsourced even if operations can be. The licensed entity must maintain effective oversight, establish clear service level agreements, ensure business continuity provisions exist, and remain liable for failures anywhere in the service chain.

Second, regulators can require that consumer-facing entities—those whose brand appears on the stablecoin and with whom users reasonably believe they are transacting—be licensed directly, even if they partner with other licensed entities for specific functions. If a technology company markets a stablecoin under its own brand, solicits users, and controls the user experience, it should not be able to avoid licensing merely by routing transactions through a licensed partner.

Third, supervisory practice should emphasize substance over form, looking through corporate structures and partnership arrangements to identify who truly controls key decisions and holds material risks. Supervisors should have authority to require licensing of any entity that exercises effective control over stablecoin functions, regardless of formal licensing arrangements or contractual labels.

The EU's MiCA Regulation incorporates these principles, requiring clear allocation of responsibilities in outsourcing arrangements and empowering supervisors to assess whether entities are evading licensing obligations through complex structures (European Parliament & Council, 2023). Singapore's framework similarly emphasizes substance over form, with the Monetary Authority of Singapore maintaining authority to require licensing of any entity performing regulated payment functions regardless of how it characterizes its activities (Monetary Authority of Singapore, 2021).

A useful analogy exists in traditional Banking-as-a-Service models. When a technology company offers banking services through partnership with a licensed bank:

- The **backend provider** (holding deposits, managing settlement systems, maintaining capital) must be a fully licensed and supervised financial institution;
- The **front-end provider** (interfacing with customers, offering branded services, making product decisions) must either hold its own license or operate under clearly governed agency or outsourcing arrangements where the licensed bank maintains effective control and accountability.

The same principles should apply to stablecoin arrangements: no regulatory vacuum should exist between backend and frontend, and the entity exercising material control over user outcomes must be subject to regulatory oversight.

Avoiding Arbitrage and Ensuring Minimum Standards

Even with clear functional licensing requirements, risks of regulatory arbitrage remain. Sophisticated actors can structure arrangements to appear to fall outside licensing thresholds or to benefit from exemptions intended for genuinely low-risk activities. Several design principles help minimize these arbitrage opportunities.

Consumer-facing functions should not operate unlicensed: Regardless of backend arrangements, entities that directly interact with users, solicit funds, or make representations about stablecoin features should generally be within the regulatory perimeter. This prevents the "licensed partner" arbitrage where consumer-facing companies avoid regulation by claiming to operate through licensed intermediaries who exercise minimal actual control.

Critical infrastructure must meet operational standards: Even where infrastructure providers—node operators, oracle providers, smart contract developers—are not directly licensed, licensed entities that depend on them should be required to ensure these providers meet appropriate operational, cybersecurity, and business continuity standards. This creates incentive structures where licensed issuers must vet and supervise their technology stack, even if individual infrastructure providers are not themselves regulated.

Minimum controls apply to all: Even exempt or sandbox participants should be subject to baseline requirements around customer identification, anti-money laundering controls, and basic operational resilience. These minimum standards prevent "race to the bottom" dynamics where regulatory arbitrage creates systemic weaknesses exploitable by illicit actors or vulnerable to operational failures.

Substance-over-form supervision: Supervisory authorities should have clear legal authority to look through corporate structures, partnership arrangements, and technical architectures to identify where risks truly lie and who exercises effective control. Bright-line rules alone cannot capture all regulatory arbitrage strategies—supervisory judgment informed by functional analysis remains essential.

The Commonwealth Model Law on Virtual Assets reflects these principles, requiring licensing for any provider of "virtual asset services" including issuance, transfer, safekeeping, or exchange of virtual assets, while allowing only narrow, risk-based exemptions (Commonwealth Secretariat, 2024). Importantly, the Model Law grants supervisors discretion to require licensing even where activities might technically fall within exemptions if the scale, business model, or risk profile warrants regulatory oversight.

Summary

Licensing is not simply about categorizing stablecoin entities into regulatory boxes—it is about managing risks, establishing accountability, and maintaining societal trust in money-like instruments that operate outside traditional banking systems. This section has traced the historical evolution of financial licensing, from wildcat banking through successive waves of financial innovation, demonstrating that licensing consistently emerges when activities touching public trust and payment systems reach systemic significance.

The case for stablecoin licensing rests on functional equivalence: when stablecoins replicate the economic functions of deposits, payment instruments, or money issuance, they create similar risks that justify similar regulatory treatment. The TerraUSD collapse starkly illustrated the consequences of allowing large-scale stablecoin arrangements to operate without licensing or prudential oversight.

Yet licensing carries risks of its own—stifling innovation, entrenching incumbents, enabling regulatory capture—that demand careful calibration. The solution lies in functionally aligned, proportionate, and technologically neutral licensing frameworks that target entities controlling material risks without sweeping in low-risk activities or imposing unduly burdensome requirements on genuinely innovative approaches.

A functional licensing framework focuses on key roles within stablecoin ecosystems: issuers who create obligations and control reserves; custodians who safeguard backing assets; wallet providers who control user access; liquidity providers whose sudden withdrawal could destabilize markets; smart contract controllers who can modify critical functions; and governance structures that make material decisions about protocol operation.

Special attention must be paid to white-label and Banking-as-a-Service models, where risks of regulatory arbitrage are particularly acute. Clear allocation of responsibility, substance-over-form supervision, and requirements that consumer-facing entities remain within the regulatory perimeter help close accountability gaps.

Ultimately, effective licensing frameworks establish clear perimeters around activities that warrant oversight while providing regulatory certainty for compliant actors and maintaining flexibility to address evolving business models. This foundation enables the supervisory architecture explored in subsequent sections.

2. WHAT LICENSING SHOULD REQUIRE – PRINCIPLES AND PILLARS

Once a jurisdiction determines which entities should be licensed, the next critical question emerges: what should licensing actually require? This is where regulatory design becomes particularly challenging. Requirements must be stringent enough to address genuine risks and protect public interests, yet not so burdensome that they stifle beneficial innovation or create barriers that only well-capitalized incumbents can overcome.

This section examines eight foundational pillars that licensing frameworks for stablecoins should incorporate, drawing on emerging international standards and comparative regulatory practice. Throughout, it highlights the inherent tensions in regulatory design—the trade-offs between safety and innovation, between prescriptive rules and principles-based flexibility, between comprehensive requirements and proportionate application.

The goal is not to obstruct innovation, but to impose baseline standards of trust and accountability in markets characterized by significant information asymmetries, potential failure modes, and systemic externalities (Financial Action Task Force, 2021; Organisation for Economic Co-operation and Development, 2012). Getting this balance right determines whether stablecoin regulation enables responsible innovation or inadvertently pushes activity into less supervised channels.

Legal Status, Governance, and Accountability

Theoretical Rationale and Core Tensions

At the most fundamental level, licensing requires that stablecoin issuers exist as legally accountable entities. This may seem obvious, but it represents a significant departure from the ethos of decentralization that animates much cryptocurrency innovation. The regulatory imperative is clear: enforcement mechanisms, consumer redress procedures, and systemic oversight all require identifiable legal persons or organizations to which obligations can attach and against which remedies can be pursued.

Licensing should not be available to pseudonymous developers, anonymous decentralized autonomous organizations (DAOs), or purely code-based protocols without an identifiable legal wrapper (Financial Stability Board, 2022). This principle links to foundational concepts in regulatory theory: rules must attach to identifiable agents to enable both deterrence of misconduct and remedies when harm occurs (Black, 2008). A regulatory framework cannot function if the entities it seeks to regulate can simply operate pseudonymously or structure themselves to avoid legal personality.

Yet this requirement immediately creates tension with decentralized and open-source development models. If regulation requires legal wrapping too strictly, it may exclude important classes of innovation or drive them to jurisdictions with less robust oversight. Some protocols genuinely lack centralized control—no single entity can modify code, freeze operations, or redirect funds. Requiring such protocols to create artificial legal entities merely to satisfy licensing requirements may be both impractical and potentially counterproductive.

Some scholars therefore propose **functional attribution rules**, under which control over certain key functions—such as upgrade authority, reserve management, or ability to pause operations—triggers legal liability and licensing requirements, regardless of how decentralized the protocol claims to be (Arner et al., 2022). If identifiable parties control material aspects of the stablecoin arrangement, those parties should be subject to licensing even if they characterize themselves as merely providing technical services or governance frameworks.

This functional approach aligns with the "substance over form" principle discussed in Section 1: regulatory requirements should attach based on what entities actually do and what risks they control, not merely how they describe themselves or structure their legal arrangements.

Governance Criteria

Beyond mere legal existence, licensing should require robust governance structures that ensure competent, ethical management and appropriate checks and balances. Key governance requirements should include:

Fit-and-proper standards for directors, beneficial owners, and controllers. These standards, common in financial services licensing across jurisdictions, assess whether key individuals possess the integrity, competence, and independence necessary to manage a stablecoin arrangement responsibly. Criminal backgrounds, previous regulatory violations, conflicts of interest, or demonstrated incompetence in prior roles should disqualify individuals from controlling licensed entities.

Organizational separation of critical functions. Risk management, compliance, technology operations, reserve management, and custody should be organizationally separated to prevent conflicts of interest and ensure appropriate checks and balances. The individuals responsible for generating profits should not be the same individuals responsible for ensuring adequate reserves or managing compliance risks.

Board oversight of technological risks. Given that stablecoins are fundamentally technology-dependent, boards of directors must possess sufficient technical expertise—either directly or through qualified advisors—to provide meaningful oversight of technology decisions. Licensing requirements might mandate that boards explicitly approve significant protocol upgrades, review incident response procedures, and regularly assess cybersecurity posture.

Conflict-of-interest disclosure and transparency. The full ownership structure, including beneficial owners, should be transparent to regulators and, to an appropriate degree, to the public. Sources of funding, related-party transactions, and potential conflicts must be disclosed. This prevents situations where stablecoin issuers are controlled by entities with incentives that diverge from user protection or systemic stability.

These governance requirements appear in banking regulation—the Basel Core Principles specifically address governance and risk management—and have been adapted for payment institutions and e-money issuers (Basel Committee on Banking Supervision, 2012). However, they must be calibrated appropriately for stablecoin contexts. Requiring the same governance structures for a startup issuing a limited-scope stablecoin as for a systemically important global payment institution would be disproportionate and likely counterproductive.

The challenge lies in establishing minimum governance standards applicable to all licensed entities while allowing for tiered requirements that scale with the size, complexity, and systemic importance of the stablecoin arrangement.

Risk Management Frameworks

Purpose and Dimensions

A comprehensive, dynamic risk management framework represents a core licensing requirement, one that reflects the multidimensional risks inherent in stablecoin arrangements. Unlike traditional financial instruments where risks are relatively well understood and standardized, stablecoins present novel risk combinations that require careful analysis and ongoing adaptation.

Key risk categories that licensing frameworks must address include:

Operational risk, particularly cybersecurity threats, smart contract vulnerabilities, oracle failures, and protocol exploits. Stablecoin arrangements are fundamentally dependent on software systems operating continuously and correctly. A successful cyberattack, coding error, or manipulation of price oracles can cause catastrophic failures. Licensed entities must demonstrate robust operational risk management, including secure software development practices, regular security audits, incident response procedures, and business continuity planning.

Liquidity risk, especially during redemption stress events. When large numbers of users simultaneously seek to redeem stablecoins for fiat currency, issuers must have sufficient liquid reserves to meet demand without triggering fire sales or breaking the peg. This risk is analogous to bank run dynamics, where confidence effects can become self-fulfilling. Risk management frameworks must include liquidity stress testing under various scenarios, clear escalation procedures, and predetermined responses to redemption surges.

Credit and market risk, when reserves include securities, derivatives, or other assets beyond cash. To generate returns, some stablecoin issuers invest reserves in short-term securities, repurchase agreements, or other instruments. While this can make business models more sustainable, it introduces credit risk (the possibility that reserve asset issuers default) and market risk (the possibility that reserve asset values decline). Risk management frameworks must assess, monitor, and limit these exposures appropriately.

Legal risk, including enforceability of redemption obligations, cross-border legal uncertainty, and regulatory change risk. Stablecoins often operate across multiple jurisdictions, creating complex legal questions about which laws apply, whether contracts are enforceable, and how regulatory changes in one jurisdiction might affect global operations. Licensed entities must have legal risk management processes that identify potential legal exposures and establish appropriate mitigants.

Technology and protocol risk, including consensus failures, network partitions, software bugs, and failed upgrades. Stablecoins built on blockchain infrastructure inherit the reliability characteristics of that infrastructure. Protocol upgrades can introduce vulnerabilities if not properly tested. Network splits can create confusion about which version of transaction history is authoritative. Risk management must encompass not just the stablecoin itself but the entire technology stack on which it depends.

A substantial body of regulatory literature supports the necessity of comprehensive risk management frameworks in financial services (Llewellyn, 2006; Masciandaro & Quintyn, 2013). The key principle is dynamic adaptation: risk management frameworks cannot be static documents that satisfy licensing requirements and then sit on shelves. They must evolve continuously as stablecoin arrangements add new features—such as cross-chain bridging, wrapped token mechanisms, or integration with decentralized finance protocols—and as risk landscapes change.

Critical Considerations and Challenges

Several challenges complicate the design and implementation of risk management requirements for stablecoins:

Model risk poses particular challenges for algorithmic stablecoins or those using complex stabilization mechanisms. These arrangements depend on models—mathematical relationships, assumed behavioral responses, arbitrage dynamics—that may break down under stress or when underlying assumptions prove incorrect. The Terra/Luna collapse illustrated how algorithmic models relying on arbitrage and reflexive token dynamics can fail catastrophically when faced with coordinated selling pressure and loss of confidence (Briola et al., 2023). Supervisors must scrutinize model assumptions, require sensitivity analysis, and demand robust stress testing that includes scenarios where key assumptions break down.

Data quality and oracle dependence create vulnerabilities that risk management must address. Many stablecoins depend on price oracles—external data feeds that inform smart contracts about real-world prices or conditions. If oracles provide inaccurate data, whether due to manipulation, technical failure, or time lags, smart contracts may execute incorrectly with serious consequences. Risk management frameworks must assess oracle reliability, implement multiple data source strategies, and establish procedures for detecting and responding to oracle failures.

Backward compatibility and upgrade governance require careful management as protocols evolve. When stablecoin systems undergo upgrades—whether to add features, fix bugs, or improve security—there is risk that legacy code interactions create vulnerabilities or that upgrade processes themselves introduce errors. Risk management must include rigorous testing procedures, staged rollouts, and ability to roll back failed upgrades.

Counterparty and supply chain dependencies extend risk beyond the immediate issuer. Reserve managers, custodians, payment processors, liquidity providers, and technology infrastructure providers all represent potential points of failure. If a third-party custodian is hacked or becomes insolvent, reserve assets may be lost regardless of how well the issuer manages its own operations. Risk management must include thorough due diligence on all critical service providers, ongoing monitoring of counterparty health, and contingency plans for replacing failed service providers.

The empirical evidence from stablecoin failures underscores the importance of sophisticated risk management. The Terra/Luna collapse destroyed approximately $60 billion in value largely due to inadequate risk modeling and overconfidence in stabilization mechanisms. The temporary de-pegging of USDC in March 2023 following Silicon Valley Bank's failure illustrated how reserve asset risks can materialize even for reputable, well-managed stablecoins. These episodes demonstrate that risk management frameworks must be comprehensive, stress-tested, and regularly updated based on emerging threats and near-miss events.

Reserve Asset Safeguards

Core Design Principles

For asset-backed stablecoins—those promising redemption at par value based on holdings of fiat currency or other assets—reserve safeguards represent perhaps the single most critical licensing requirement. Without adequate, properly managed reserves, redemption promises become empty, and the stablecoin ceases to function as intended. History provides ample evidence of how inadequate reserve practices can cause catastrophic failures, from 19th century wildcat banking through modern e-money failures.

Licensing frameworks should anchor reserve requirements to clear, verifiable standards rather than allowing vague marketing claims or unaudited self-reporting. Key elements include:

Full or near-full backing with liquid, low-risk assets. The most robust approach requires that every stablecoin in circulation be backed by highly liquid reserves—cash, central bank deposits, or short-term government securities—held in amounts sufficient to meet all redemptions on demand (Gorton & Zhang, 2023). This approach mirrors requirements for e-money under EU regulations and provides maximum confidence in redemption capability. However, as discussed below, full backing creates trade-offs that must be carefully considered.

Legal segregation and independent custody. Reserve assets must be legally separated from the issuer's operating capital and other business assets. This ensures that if the issuer becomes insolvent, reserve assets remain available to satisfy redemption obligations rather than being seized by general creditors. Segregation typically requires holding reserves in bankruptcy-remote structures—special purpose vehicles, trusts, or similar arrangements—that legally ring-fence these assets. Additionally, reserves should be held by independent custodians rather than the issuer itself, providing both operational separation and additional oversight.

Independent audits and attestation. Periodic audits by qualified, independent third-party auditors should verify reserve holdings, confirm legal segregation, and assess compliance with reserve requirements. These audits must go beyond simple balance confirmations to examine the quality, liquidity, and valuation of reserve assets. Furthermore, audit results should be made available to regulators and, in appropriately summarized form, to the public to enable market discipline. The frequency of audits should scale with risk—monthly or even more frequent attestations for larger or more complex stablecoins.

Conservative valuation disciplines. Reserve assets should be valued using conservative methodologies that reflect their true liquidation value under stress conditions rather than optimistic mark-to-model approaches. This may require haircuts—reducing the stated value of assets to account for potential losses upon forced sale—and stress buffers that provide cushions against adverse market movements. Mark-to-market valuation using observable market prices provides more reliable information than mark-to-model approaches, particularly for less liquid securities.

Liquidity management and stress buffers. Beyond full backing in the aggregate, reserves must include sufficient highly liquid components to meet anticipated redemptions without forced asset sales. Licensing requirements might specify minimum percentages of reserves that must be held in overnight or near-overnight liquidity, with the remainder allowed in slightly longer-dated but still high-quality instruments. Stress testing should inform these buffer requirements, examining redemption patterns under various adverse scenarios.

Some jurisdictions, particularly those applying e-money frameworks, require 100% redemption on demand with no exceptions. While this provides maximum user protection, it may prove challenging for certain business models or during extreme stress events. Licensing frameworks might allow for limited grace periods or temporary suspension of redemptions under extraordinary circumstances, but only with immediate regulatory notification, strict time limits, and mandatory compensatory measures.

Trade-offs and Tensions

Reserve requirements involve difficult trade-offs between safety and other objectives:

Returns versus risk: Requiring issuers to hold only cash or overnight government securities maximizes safety but generates minimal or even negative returns (when interest rates are low or negative). This makes stablecoin business models economically challenging, particularly when issuers face significant operational costs. Allowing some investment of reserves in higher-yielding but still high-quality securities—such as short-term corporate paper or longer-dated government bonds—can improve business viability but introduces credit risk and market risk. The regulatory challenge is calibrating what asset mix appropriately balances these considerations.

Audit frequency versus cost: More frequent audits provide more current assurance about reserve adequacy but impose substantial costs that may be prohibitive for smaller issuers. Quarterly audits represent common practice in financial services, but monthly or even continuous real-time verification through technological means may be appropriate for systemically important stablecoins. Licensing frameworks might tier audit requirements based on size and systemic importance.

Transparency versus competitive sensitivity: Full public disclosure of reserve composition provides maximum transparency and enables market discipline, but issuers sometimes argue that detailed disclosure of investment strategies or specific securities holdings reveals proprietary information that competitors could exploit. Licensing frameworks must balance these concerns, perhaps requiring full disclosure to regulators with more aggregated public disclosure, while maintaining that the public has sufficient information to assess reserve quality.

Rigid rules versus adaptive management: Highly prescriptive reserve requirements—such as specifying exact percentages that must be held in each asset category—provide clarity but may not adapt well to changing market conditions or financial innovation. Principles-based approaches allow more flexibility but create uncertainty and potential for regulatory arbitrage. Hybrid approaches that establish clear floors and ceilings while allowing discretion within bounds may offer the best balance.

A well-designed approach likely combines minimum liquid backing requirements (perhaps 80-90% in cash and overnight instruments) with dynamic buffer reserves determined by stress testing, regular attestations supplemented by real-time monitoring where feasible, and detailed regulatory reporting with appropriately aggregated public disclosure.

Prudential and Capital Requirements

Justification and Application

Although stablecoin issuers are not banks and should not be regulated identically to banks, they face liquidity, redemption, and operational risks functionally similar to those that justify prudential regulation of banking. Capital buffers—funds that can absorb losses or support orderly wind-down—provide a critical shock absorber when things go wrong.

The Basel principles for banking supervision indicate that entities exposed to credit, liquidity, and operational risks must hold capital proportionate to those exposures (Basel Committee on Banking Supervision, 2019). While stablecoins need not meet bank capital standards, licensing regimes should adapt these principles appropriately. The fundamental logic is straightforward: entities that can fail in ways that harm consumers or threaten financial stability should maintain buffers that reduce the probability and severity of such failures.

Capital serves several purposes in a stablecoin context:

Operational loss absorption: When operational failures occur—cyberattacks, fraud, system outages—capital provides funds to make users whole rather than requiring users to bear losses. This is particularly important for stablecoins, where technology failures can occur suddenly and affect large numbers of users simultaneously.

Orderly wind-down funding: If a stablecoin arrangement becomes unviable and must shut down, capital provides resources to complete final redemptions, pay wind-down costs, and ensure orderly exit rather than chaotic collapse. Without such funding, users may face "last-mover" problems where late redeemers cannot be satisfied after reserves are exhausted.

Confidence effects: The very existence of capital requirements signals regulatory seriousness and issuer commitment to user protection, potentially reducing the likelihood of confidence-driven runs. Users may be more willing to hold and use stablecoins from well-capitalized issuers than from thinly capitalized entities operating at the edge of viability.

However, capital requirements must be calibrated carefully. Excessive capital requirements would make stablecoin issuance economically unviable, particularly for smaller players, potentially concentrating the market among a few large, well-capitalized entities. Insufficient capital requirements fail to provide meaningful protection.

Tiered Application Based on Risk and Scale

Proportionality demands tiered capital requirements that scale with the risks and systemic importance of different stablecoin arrangements:

Tier 1 or small issuers (perhaps those with outstanding issuance below $10-50 million or operating within limited geographic or use case scope) might face minimal capital requirements initially—perhaps sufficient to cover six months of operating expenses or a small percentage of outstanding issuance. The logic is that these arrangements pose limited systemic risk, and heavy capital requirements would prevent entry entirely.

Tier 2-3 issuers (medium-scale operations with broader reach but not yet systemically important) might face escalating capital requirements as they grow, perhaps 2-5% of outstanding stablecoin liabilities or amounts determined by stress testing and operational risk assessments. These issuers should also face increasing expectations around resolution planning—documented procedures for orderly wind-down should business become unviable.

Tier 4 or systemic stablecoins (those with very large scale, significant integration into payment systems, or cross-border reach that creates systemic dependencies) might face capital requirements approaching those for banks, potentially 8-10% of risk-weighted exposures, along with additional requirements for loss-absorbing liabilities and detailed resolution planning. The Financial Stability Board's recommendations for global stablecoins contemplate such heightened requirements for arrangements that pose systemic risks (Financial Stability Board, 2020; Financial Stability Board, 2023).

One important caveat: imposing overly aggressive capital requirements too early may preclude new entrants entirely, especially in jurisdictions with limited capital markets or where investors are unfamiliar with stablecoin business models. Regulatory frameworks should allow for transitional periods during which smaller issuers can build capital gradually as they grow, while ensuring that systemic risks are addressed promptly as they emerge.

Redemption Rights and Terms

Foundations and Critical Importance

The ability to redeem stablecoins for fiat currency at par value represents the anchor of user confidence and market stability. If users cannot reliably redeem, the "stable" aspect of stablecoins evaporates, potentially triggering cascading failures as users rush to exit before redemptions become impossible. Licensing must therefore codify clear, enforceable redemption rights and terms.

Key elements should include:

Unambiguous right to redemption: Users must have a clear legal right to redeem stablecoins for fiat currency at par (perhaps minus reasonable fees to cover actual costs). This right should be contractually binding and enforceable through legal action if necessary, not merely a discretionary service that issuers can suspend at will.

Clear disclosure of redemption mechanics: Users must understand how to initiate redemptions, what processing times to expect, what fees apply, and under what circumstances (if any) redemptions might be delayed or denied. Ambiguity around redemption processes creates vulnerability to issuer opportunism and user confusion during stress periods.

Reasonable processing times: While instant redemption may not be feasible for all arrangements, processing times should be clearly specified and limited—perhaps one to three business days for standard redemptions, with expedited options available at higher cost. Extended or indefinite processing times should require specific regulatory approval based on operational necessity.

Limited exceptions with regulatory oversight: If circumstances exist where redemptions might legitimately be delayed or temporarily suspended—such as extreme market dislocations or technical failures—these should be narrowly defined, require immediate regulatory notification, and be subject to strict time limits. Issuers should not be able to unilaterally freeze redemptions indefinitely without consequences.

Dispute resolution and consumer redress: Clear procedures must exist for resolving disputes about denied or delayed redemptions, including access to independent dispute resolution mechanisms and, ultimately, judicial remedies.

Failures to honor redemption promises—whether through outright freezes, inability to deliver fiat currency, or de facto denials through excessive delays or fees—risk triggering precisely the loss of confidence and bank run dynamics that licensing seeks to prevent. The TerraUSD collapse and subsequent contagion to other stablecoins illustrate how redemption failures can cascade across markets.

Complexity and Boundary Cases

Several challenging design questions arise around redemption rights:

Stressed conditions and temporary suspensions: Should regulation permit temporary suspension of redemptions during extreme stress—for example, when market dislocations make liquidating reserve assets impossible without catastrophic losses? Banking regulation typically allows for such suspensions under extraordinary circumstances, but they must be tightly controlled. Stablecoin licensing might similarly allow time-limited suspensions (perhaps 24-72 hours) when clearly defined conditions are met, but only with immediate regulatory notification and required compensatory measures such as enhanced transparency or priority redemption for smaller holders when resumed.

Tiered redemption priorities: Some have proposed that during stress events, smaller individual holders should have priority redemption rights over large institutional holders or speculators who might be triggering runs. While this could protect retail users, it creates complexity and might itself trigger strategic behavior—large holders might split holdings across many small accounts to evade restrictions. Whether such tiering is desirable depends on regulatory objectives and enforcement capabilities.

Fees and economic redemption denials: Issuers should not be able to effectively deny redemptions by imposing economically prohibitive fees. Licensing requirements might cap redemption fees at actual processing costs or establish that fees above certain thresholds require justification and regulatory approval.

Algorithmic redemption mechanisms: For algorithmic stablecoins that maintain pegs through arbitrage rather than direct redemption for fiat, licensing must carefully assess whether these mechanisms are sufficiently robust. The Terra/Luna experience suggests that purely algorithmic redemption without asset backing creates fundamental vulnerabilities that licensing should address through requirements for hybrid models or additional safeguards.

The core principle remains that redemption at par should be the default expectation, with deviations permitted only under narrow, well-defined circumstances subject to regulatory oversight.

Transparency, Disclosure, and Auditability

The Backbone of Accountability

Transparency serves as the backbone of regulatory accountability and market discipline in stablecoin markets. Without meaningful disclosure, users cannot assess risks, regulators cannot supervise effectively, and market discipline cannot function.

Licensing should therefore impose comprehensive transparency requirements across multiple dimensions:

Reserve composition and valuation: Detailed, regular disclosure of what assets back stablecoins, how they are valued, where they are held, and how valuations have changed over time. This should include not just aggregate totals but breakdowns by asset type, maturity, credit quality, and custodian. Users need to understand whether they hold claims on cash, government securities, corporate bonds, or riskier assets.

Governance structures and conflicts: Clear disclosure of ownership structures, beneficial owners, related-party relationships, and potential conflicts of interest. Users should know who controls the stablecoin arrangement and whether those parties have incentives that might diverge from user protection.

Technology architecture and smart contract logic: While complete disclosure of proprietary code may not be feasible, licensing should require sufficient technical disclosure that qualified parties can assess security and operational risks. This might include disclosure of smart contract addresses, audit reports from security firms, and explanations of key protocol mechanisms.

Historical performance data: Regular reporting of redemption volumes, processing times, any instances of delayed or denied redemptions, operational incidents, and how they were resolved. This performance data enables users and regulators to identify deteriorating conditions before they become crises.

Stress testing and risk metrics: Results from stress tests, liquidity coverage ratios, and other risk metrics that indicate financial health and resilience. While detailed stress testing methodologies might remain confidential to prevent gaming, high-level results should be disclosed.

These disclosure requirements align with IOSCO's principles for stablecoin transparency (Organisation for Economic Co-operation and Development, 2012) and help mitigate the information asymmetries that otherwise leave users unable to distinguish between sound and risky stablecoin arrangements.

Balancing Transparency Against Competitive Concerns

However, over-disclosure can create legitimate competitive concerns. Requiring real-time disclosure of detailed reserve investment strategies might enable competitors or speculators to front-run issuer transactions or exploit proprietary trading approaches. Requiring complete disclosure of all technical architecture might expose security vulnerabilities before they can be patched.

Licensing frameworks can balance these tensions through tiered disclosure:

Full disclosure to regulators: Supervisors should have access to complete, real-time information about all material aspects of stablecoin operations, without commercial confidentiality restrictions. Effective supervision requires this comprehensive information flow.

Detailed but somewhat aggregated public disclosure: Public disclosure might provide detailed information about reserve composition and governance while allowing some aggregation of specific securities holdings or technical implementation details. For example, disclosing that 80% of reserves are in overnight government repurchase agreements and 20% in Treasury bills maturing within 30 days provides meaningful information without revealing specific counterparties or transaction timing.

Confidential competitive information: Truly proprietary information that provides competitive advantage might be shared only with regulators under confidentiality protections, but the scope of such exceptions should be narrow and carefully scrutinized. The presumption should favor transparency unless specific, justified competitive harms can be demonstrated.

The fundamental principle is that users deserve sufficient information to make informed decisions about whether to hold and use stablecoins, while regulators require comprehensive information to supervise effectively.

Interoperability and Technical Standards

Promoting Open Systems

Interoperability—the ability of different stablecoin arrangements to work together seamlessly and integrate with broader payment systems—provides significant benefits for users and financial efficiency. Stablecoins that operate as closed, proprietary systems create fragmentation, increase costs, and reduce network effects that make payment systems valuable.

Licensing can promote interoperability through several mechanisms:

Technical standards adoption: Requiring or incentivizing adoption of open technical standards for messaging, identity, and transaction processing. For example, alignment with ISO 20022 messaging standards could facilitate integration between stablecoins and traditional payment systems. Shared standards for wallet connectivity and blockchain interoperability can enable users to move value across different stablecoin arrangements without friction.

API requirements: Mandating that licensed issuers provide documented, non-discriminatory application programming interfaces (APIs) that allow wallets, payment processors, and other service providers to interact with stablecoins programmatically. This prevents issuers from maintaining closed systems that lock users into proprietary ecosystems.

Identity and compliance data portability: Establishing standards for how customer identification and compliance information can be securely shared across licensed entities, reducing redundant compliance processes when users move between different service providers while maintaining appropriate privacy protections.

Cross-chain bridging standards: As multiple blockchain networks host stablecoins, standards for securely bridging value across chains become important. Licensing could require that bridge mechanisms meet minimum security standards and undergo independent audits.

However, imposing overly rigid or premature technical standards creates risks:

Innovation stifling: If licensing mandates specific technical architectures or protocols before they mature, it may lock in suboptimal approaches and prevent beneficial innovation. Technology evolves rapidly, and regulatory standards often lag behind best practices.

One-size-fits-all problems: Different use cases may benefit from different technical approaches. Requirements appropriate for retail payment stablecoins may not make sense for wholesale settlement tokens or specialized applications.

Implementation challenges: Smaller issuers may lack resources to implement complex technical standards, potentially creating barriers to entry that benefit large, established players.

A balanced approach might establish minimum interoperability principles—such as requirements that systems be capable of integrating with open standards—while avoiding overly prescriptive technical mandates. Regulators could facilitate industry working groups that develop technical standards voluntarily, later codifying successful standards into licensing requirements once they mature and gain broad adoption.

Consumer and Data Protection

Beyond Technical Compliance

Even when stablecoin issuers are technically compliant with financial soundness requirements, consumer outcomes depend on additional protections that address information asymmetries, power imbalances, and behavioral realities. Licensing should therefore incorporate consumer protection requirements comparable to those in other financial services contexts:

Data privacy obligations: Stablecoin issuers collect significant personal and financial information about users. Data privacy obligations comparable to GDPR in the EU or similar frameworks in other jurisdictions should apply, including requirements for user consent, limitations on data use and sharing, security safeguards against breaches, and rights for users to access and correct their data.

Error correction and fraud protection: Clear procedures must exist for users to report errors, unauthorized transactions, or fraud, with time-bound requirements for issuers to investigate and resolve complaints. While blockchain transactions are generally irreversible, licensed issuers should maintain reserves or insurance to compensate users for losses due to system errors or security breaches within the issuer's control.

Restrictions on misleading marketing: Licensing should prohibit marketing that makes misleading claims about safety, guarantees, or regulatory status. Terms like "stable" or "backed" must be accurate and substantiated. Claims about being "as safe as bank deposits" should be prohibited unless the arrangement actually carries deposit insurance or equivalent protections.

Simplified disclosure for retail users: While comprehensive disclosure serves important purposes, retail users may not understand technical financial disclosures. Licensing could require simplified disclosure documents—comparable to Key Information Documents in EU financial services regulation—that summarize key risks, costs, and features in plain language accessible to non-experts.

Vulnerable consumer safeguards: Special protections might apply for particularly vulnerable populations—such as cooling-off periods allowing cancellation of large transactions, warnings about risks before significant purchases, or enhanced disclosure requirements when marketing to less sophisticated users.

Dispute resolution mechanisms: Access to independent dispute resolution—such as financial ombudsman services—provides important recourse when users believe they have been treated unfairly. Licensing could require participation in dispute resolution schemes and compliance with their decisions.

Without these consumer protections, stablecoin markets risk reputational damage and regulatory backlash that could undermine even well-designed prudential frameworks. Retail users who suffer losses due to misleading marketing, inadequate security, or poor service may generate political pressure for harsh regulatory responses that could stifle beneficial innovation along with problematic practices.

Summary and Critical Observations

Licensing requirements for stablecoins should be comprehensive, proportionate, and enforceable. They must address the full range of risks—financial, operational, technological, legal—that stablecoin arrangements create while remaining sufficiently flexible to accommodate different business models and scales of operation. The eight pillars examined in this section—legal status and governance, risk management, reserve safeguards, prudential requirements, redemption rights, transparency, interoperability, and consumer protection—provide a framework for designing robust licensing regimes.

However, several critical observations should inform regulatory design:

One-size-fits-all approaches are perilous: Stablecoins vary enormously in their scale, technology, business models, and risk profiles. Licensing requirements appropriate for a global stablecoin with billions in outstanding issuance would be absurdly burdensome for a small, specialized stablecoin serving a niche cross-border payment corridor. Tiered, proportionate requirements that scale with risk remain essential, even as they create complexity and potential for regulatory arbitrage.

Cross-border complications are inevitable: Stablecoins often operate seamlessly across borders, creating challenges when different jurisdictions impose inconsistent requirements. Passporting arrangements or mutual recognition frameworks can help, but they require substantial regulatory coordination and may impose the strictest requirements across entire regions. International standard-setting through bodies like FSB, IOSCO, and FATF helps but cannot eliminate jurisdictional differences entirely.

Regulatory capacity constraints matter: Sophisticated licensing frameworks mean little if supervisory authorities lack capacity to enforce them. Smaller jurisdictions or those new to digital asset regulation may need to adopt narrower licensing permission sets initially, gradually expanding obligations as regulatory capacity builds. Technical assistance and regulatory cooperation can help address capacity gaps.

Threshold gaming requires vigilance: Sophisticated actors will optimize their arrangements to fall just below licensing thresholds or exploit exemptions intended for genuinely low-risk activities. This creates a "regulatory cliff" where dramatically different requirements apply to similar arrangements based on technical distinctions. Regulators must monitor these dynamics and adjust thresholds and exemptions based on experience.

Licensing is necessary but insufficient: Even the best-designed licensing requirements cannot ensure safety and soundness without effective ongoing supervision, enforcement capabilities, and coordination with other regulatory authorities. The next sections examine how supervision should work in practice and what tools regulators need to enforce licensing requirements effectively.

The ultimate test of licensing requirements is not their technical sophistication but whether they achieve regulatory objectives—protecting consumers, maintaining financial stability, preventing illicit activity—while enabling beneficial innovation to flourish within appropriate guardrails. Getting this balance right remains the central challenge of stablecoin regulation.

3. HOW SUPERVISION SHOULD WORK – PROPORTIONALITY, REGTECH, AND DYNAMIC OVERSIGHT

Licensing establishes who can operate and what minimum standards they must meet. But licensing alone cannot ensure ongoing compliance, identify emerging risks, or respond when problems arise. This is where supervision enters—the continuous oversight function that monitors licensed entities, detects deteriorating conditions, and intervenes when necessary to protect regulatory objectives.

The challenge in designing supervisory frameworks for stablecoins lies in achieving multiple, sometimes competing goals simultaneously: ensuring robust oversight of systemically important arrangements while not crushing innovation with disproportionate burdens; maintaining sufficient regulatory intensity to catch problems early while working within realistic resource constraints; and creating frameworks flexible enough to adapt as technology and business models evolve.

This section explores how supervision should work in practice, emphasizing three core principles: proportionality (matching supervisory intensity to risk), technological enablement (using RegTech and SupTech tools to enhance efficiency), and dynamic adaptation (evolving supervisory approaches as the ecosystem matures).

Proportional and Risk-Based Supervision: Core Principles

The global regulatory community has increasingly coalesced around risk-based, proportionate supervision as a fundamental regulatory principle. The Financial Stability Board, Basel Committee, and IOSCO all emphasize that supervisory intensity and focus should be tailored to the potential impact that regulated entities could have on consumer outcomes, financial stability, market integrity, and systemic risk (Financial Stability Board, 2022; Basel Committee on Banking Supervision, 2023; Organisation for Economic Co-operation and Development, 2012).

This approach builds on foundational concepts in regulatory theory. Proportionality requires that regulatory burdens be justified by regulatory benefits, aligning with principles of regulatory justice and economic efficiency—we arguable should not impose $1 million in compliance costs to prevent $10,000 in potential harm (Black, 2008; Organisation for Economic Co-operation and Development, 2012). Risk-based supervision directs limited regulatory resources toward higher-risk entities and activities, allowing regulators to manage complexity and uncertainty despite having finite supervisory capacity (Masciandaro & Quintyn, 2013).

In practical terms, this means that a small stablecoin used for remittances in a single corridor, with perhaps $5 million in outstanding issuance and a few thousand users, should face periodic reporting requirements and basic disclosure obligations—but not the intensive, real-time oversight appropriate for a globally systemically important stablecoin with billions in circulation integrated into major payment systems worldwide. Note consideration should be given to who wears the cost and how often however.

The logic is straightforward but sometimes politically difficult to defend: different risks warrant different responses. A collapse of the small remittance stablecoin would harm its users, certainly, but would not threaten financial stability or create contagion effects. Devoting scarce supervisory resources to intensive oversight of such arrangements makes little sense when those same resources could be monitoring genuinely systemic risks. Conversely, treating a globally important stablecoin with light-touch oversight because "we want to encourage innovation" would be regulatory malpractice.

This proportionate approach serves several important objectives:

Preserves space for responsible innovation: Startups and new entrants can test business models and demonstrate viability without immediately facing the full compliance burden of systemically important institutions. This matters because some of the most beneficial financial innovations historically came from new entrants rather than established players.

Avoids regulatory overreach on low-risk activities: Not everything that looks like a stablecoin poses significant risk. Community currencies, gaming tokens, or specialized corporate payment instruments may have "stablecoin-like" features but limited potential for systemic harm. Proportionate supervision allows these to operate with appropriate but not excessive oversight.

Enables dynamic escalation: As businesses grow and their risk profiles change, supervisory intensity can increase correspondingly. A stablecoin that starts small but achieves rapid adoption can transition smoothly to more intensive supervision rather than facing a sudden "regulatory cliff" where dramatically different requirements suddenly apply.

Makes efficient use of limited resources: No regulator has unlimited capacity. Risk-based approaches ensure that supervisory attention concentrates where it matters most—on entities whose failure or misconduct would cause the greatest harm.

However, proportionate supervision is not a license for regulatory laxity. Even small, low-risk arrangements must meet minimum standards around consumer protection, anti-money laundering controls, and basic operational resilience. The question is not whether to supervise, but how intensively to supervise.

Tiered Regulatory Obligations: Operationalizing Proportionality

A tiered regulatory framework provides the practical architecture for implementing proportionate supervision. Rather than having a single licensing category with uniform requirements, tiering creates graduated categories—each with progressively more stringent obligations calibrated to the risks that entities in each tier pose.

Consider the following illustrative framework, which draws on elements from the EU's MiCA Regulation, Singapore's Payment Services Act, and emerging Commonwealth guidance:

Table 2. Illustrative tiered supervisory framework for stablecoins

Tier	Entity Type	Key Thresholds	Supervisory Focus	Core Obligations
Tier 1	Prototype / Limited Use	≤\$1M outstanding, ≤1,000 users, single jurisdiction	Innovation support and basic consumer protection	Registration, consumer risk warnings, basic AML/KYC, quarterly reporting
Tier 2	Retail-Scale	\$1M–\$100M outstanding, retail users, limited geographic scope	Consumer protection and operational soundness	Full licensing, reserve attestations, complaint handling, monthly reporting, conduct supervision
Tier 3	General Purpose	≥\$100M outstanding, cross-border operation, wholesale and retail use	Financial stability and prudential soundness	Capital buffers, stress testing, redemption SLAs, real-time reserve monitoring, recovery planning
Tier 4	Systemically Important	Determined by systemicity assessment (size, interconnectedness, substitutability)	Macroprudential risk and systemic resilience	Central bank supervision, resolution planning, systemic stress testing, enhanced capital, supervisory college

This tiered structure offers several advantages:

Scalability for growing businesses: Startups can enter at Tier 1 with manageable compliance requirements, then graduate through tiers as they grow. This avoids forcing new entrants to immediately meet requirements designed for systemic players, while ensuring that regulatory intensity increases as risks materialize.

Risk containment matched to impact: Higher tiers face more demanding standards precisely because they pose greater potential harm. A Tier 4 systemically important stablecoin might be required to hold capital equivalent to 10% of outstanding liabilities, maintain resolution plans, and participate in international supervisory colleges—requirements that would be absurd for a Tier 1 prototype but entirely appropriate given systemic risks.

Market clarity and signaling: Tiering provides useful information to users, investors, and business partners. A Tier 4 designation signals both that an arrangement is systemically important and that it faces correspondingly intensive supervision. This can actually enhance market confidence rather than stigmatize the entity.

Regulatory flexibility: As experience with stablecoin supervision accumulates, regulators can adjust tier definitions and requirements more easily than if all entities faced identical obligations. Different experiments can be tried in different tiers, with successful approaches scaled up.

This tiered approach mirrors structures already adopted in other contexts. The EU's MiCA Regulation distinguishes between ordinary asset-referenced tokens and "significant" e-money tokens that face enhanced requirements (European Parliament & Council, 2023, Article 43). Singapore's Payment Services Act links obligations to transaction volumes and nature of services (Monetary Authority of Singapore, 2019). The UK's proposed regime for systemic payment systems similarly contemplates graduated requirements (HM Treasury, 2023).

However, tiering creates its own challenges. Determining appropriate thresholds requires balancing multiple considerations—set them too low and too many entities face burdensome requirements; too high and significant risks accumulate below the threshold. Entities will inevitably optimize their operations to remain just below tier thresholds, requiring regulators to monitor for such gaming and adjust thresholds accordingly. And transitions between tiers must be managed carefully to avoid creating sudden, disruptive changes in requirements.

RegTech and SupTech: Technological Enablers of Efficient Oversight

Regulatory technology (RegTech) and supervisory technology (SupTech) are not merely nice-to-have innovations—they are essential enablers of proportionate, tiered supervision in stablecoin contexts. Without technological tools to reduce compliance costs and enhance supervisory efficiency, tiered frameworks risk becoming administratively unworkable.

RegTech for Regulated Entities

For stablecoin issuers and service providers, RegTech tools can dramatically reduce the marginal cost of compliance, making it feasible for smaller entities to meet regulatory requirements that might otherwise be prohibitively expensive:

Automated reporting systems allow entities to submit required data to regulators through standardized APIs rather than manually preparing reports. If regulatory reporting requirements are designed with machine-readable formats from the outset, compliance becomes a matter of configuring systems rather than employing teams of compliance staff to compile quarterly reports.

Compliance-by-design architectures embed regulatory requirements directly into operational systems. For example, smart contracts can be designed to automatically segregate reserve assets, enforce redemption priorities, or flag suspicious transaction patterns. When compliance is built into core systems rather than layered on top as an afterthought, costs decrease and effectiveness increases.

Identity and AML tools leverage existing KYC utilities, shared databases, and advanced analytics to streamline customer identification and transaction monitoring. Rather than each stablecoin provider building its own AML infrastructure from scratch, shared utilities and specialized service providers offer economies of scale.

Regulatory intelligence platforms help smaller providers track changing requirements across multiple jurisdictions, reducing the risk of inadvertent non-compliance in rapidly evolving regulatory landscapes.

These tools particularly benefit Tier 1 and Tier 2 entities, for whom compliance costs represent a larger percentage of operating budgets. If RegTech can reduce compliance costs from prohibitive to manageable levels, more innovation can occur within regulated frameworks rather than migrating to unregulated offshore jurisdictions.

SupTech for Regulatory Authorities

For supervisors, technology enables differentiated, risk-based oversight that would be impossible with traditional manual approaches:

Real-time data ingestion and monitoring allows regulators to track reserve adequacy, redemption patterns, and concentration risks continuously rather than reviewing periodic reports that may be weeks or months old. Automated systems can flag concerning trends—such as declining reserve quality or increasing redemption requests—before they become crises.

Risk dashboards and analytics provide supervisors with comprehensive views of individual entities and systemic risks. Rather than reviewing hundreds of pages of text reports, supervisors can use visualization tools that highlight key metrics, compare entities against benchmarks, and identify outliers warranting attention.

Scenario simulation and stress testing capabilities allow supervisors to model how stablecoin arrangements might respond to various shock scenarios—rapid redemptions, reserve asset price declines, counterparty failures—using actual operational data. This supports forward-looking supervision rather than merely backward-looking compliance checking.

Pattern recognition and anomaly detection using machine learning can identify suspicious activities, emerging risks, or potential misconduct that might not be apparent through manual review. These tools support both prudential supervision (detecting financial stress) and conduct supervision (identifying potential fraud or market manipulation).

Regulatory sandboxes and innovation functions can be enhanced with digital tools that facilitate communication, data sharing, and monitoring of entities operating under temporary licensing relief or experimental frameworks.

The Bank for International Settlements has been particularly active in exploring SupTech applications for crypto-asset and stablecoin supervision, including proof-of-concept projects demonstrating real-time reserve monitoring and cross-border supervisory data sharing (Basel Committee on Banking Supervision, 2023).

Important Caveats and Limitations

However, enthusiasm for RegTech and SupTech must be tempered by several important considerations:

Technology is not a substitute for judgment: Automated systems can flag risks and highlight patterns, but human supervisors must still exercise judgment about what actions to take. Over-reliance on algorithmic decision-making without appropriate governance and oversight risks missing context-specific factors that algorithms cannot capture.

Interoperability challenges: For RegTech and SupTech to work across jurisdictions—which is essential given stablecoins' cross-border nature—data standards and technical protocols must be harmonized. This requires international coordination that has proven difficult historically.

Regulatory resilience requirements: Supervisors cannot become entirely dependent on complex technological systems that might fail during exactly the stress events when supervision matters most. Dual systems—maintaining capability to supervise manually even while using advanced tools—provide important resilience.

Explainability and accountability: When regulatory decisions are informed by AI systems or complex analytics, it must remain possible to explain the basis for those decisions and identify who is accountable. "Black box" decision-making is incompatible with principles of regulatory accountability and due process.

Resource requirements: While technology can increase supervisory efficiency, implementing SupTech systems requires upfront investment in infrastructure, skills, and ongoing maintenance. Resource-constrained regulators may struggle with these investments even as they promise long-term benefits.

The role of RegTech and SupTech, then, is to enhance and enable proportionate supervision—not to replace human judgment or allow supervisors to avoid difficult resource allocation decisions.

Avoiding Innovation Stifling and Market Entrenchment

Tiered supervision, while necessary for proportionality, creates risks of its own that regulators must consciously address. Poorly designed tiering can inadvertently stifle innovation or entrench incumbents, defeating the very objectives that proportionate regulation seeks to achieve.

Several dynamics warrant attention:

Compliance costs as barriers to entry: Even with RegTech tools reducing costs, the absolute burden of meeting Tier 2 or Tier 3 requirements may deter new entrants, particularly in smaller markets or for specialized use cases. If only large, well-capitalized entities can afford compliance, the market concentrates around a few dominant players who face limited competitive pressure to innovate or serve users well.

Regulatory incumbency bias: Systemically important institutions often have greater resources to invest in regulatory relationships, can afford more sophisticated lobbying, and may even influence regulatory design in ways that make entry harder for competitors. Supervisors must remain alert to these dynamics and resist pressure to design requirements that disproportionately favor incumbents (Zetzsche et al., 2020b).

Threshold gaming and cliff effects: When tier thresholds create significant differences in requirements, entities will optimize to remain just below thresholds—perhaps by structuring operations across multiple legal entities, limiting growth, or moving certain activities offshore. These behaviors can create inefficiencies and undermine regulatory objectives.

Delayed innovation in specialized niches: A tiered system optimized for large, general-purpose stablecoins may inadvertently impose inappropriate requirements on specialized applications—remittance corridors, supply chain finance, gaming economies, or community currencies. These niches may generate important social benefits even if they never achieve massive scale.

To mitigate these risks, several design features can help:

Phase-in and transitional arrangements: Rather than requiring immediate compliance with all Tier 2 or Tier 3 requirements the moment a threshold is crossed, regulators can allow reasonable transition periods—perhaps 6-12 months—during which entities can build the necessary infrastructure and processes. This smooths the transition and reduces cliff effects.

Supervisory coaching over punishment: Especially for Tier 1 and Tier 2 entities, supervisory approach should emphasize helping entities understand and meet requirements rather than immediately moving to enforcement when deficiencies are identified. This "supervisory support" model has proven effective in other contexts, particularly for new entrants unfamiliar with regulatory requirements.

Multiple pathways to compliance: Rather than prescribing exactly how requirements must be met, regulators can establish outcomes that must be achieved while allowing flexibility in how entities get there. This "principles-based" approach, combined with clear guidance and examples, can accommodate diverse business models while ensuring core objectives are met.

Functional equivalence recognition: Where entities use genuinely different approaches to achieve similar risk mitigation—for example, different technical architectures for reserve management or redemption processing—supervisors should be willing to recognize these as equivalent rather than insisting on uniform methods.

Attention to special categories: Regulators might create specific exemptions or modified requirements for clearly defined specialized uses—such as closed-loop corporate payment systems or community currencies with natural circulation constraints—that pose limited systemic risks even if they technically meet size thresholds.

The academic literature has highlighted how regulatory structures can inadvertently protect systemically important providers from competition, a phenomenon sometimes called "too big to fail" subsidy or regulatory capture (Gorton & Zhang, 2023). Effective supervisory design must actively resist these dynamics, ensuring that tiered systems serve public policy objectives rather than private interests.

Supervisory Capacity and Sustainable Funding

Even the most elegantly designed supervisory framework means little if regulatory authorities lack the capacity—human resources, technical capabilities, funding—to implement it effectively. This challenge is particularly acute for stablecoin supervision, which requires expertise spanning financial regulation, technology, cryptography, and international coordination.

Many jurisdictions, particularly in developing economies and smaller states, face significant capacity constraints:

Skills shortages in digital asset expertise, protocol auditing, reserve assurance, and cybersecurity assessment. Financial regulators historically recruited economists, accountants, and lawyers—not the computer scientists and cryptographers now needed to assess stablecoin arrangements effectively.

Budget limitations, especially where regulators operate on fixed government appropriations rather than industry-funded models. Building SupTech infrastructure, hiring specialized staff, and participating in international supervisory coordination all require resources many regulators lack.

Coordination challenges across multiple regulatory authorities—prudential supervisors, conduct regulators, competition authorities, AML/CFT agencies, data protection authorities—each of whom may have legitimate interests in stablecoin oversight. Without effective coordination mechanisms, regulatory gaps or duplicative requirements emerge.

Several approaches can help address these capacity constraints:

Capacity-Building Models

Regional supervisory cooperation through pooled resources or shared supervisory centers. For example, smaller jurisdictions within regional blocs (ASEAN, CARICOM, East African Community) might establish joint supervisory units with specialized stablecoin expertise available to member states. The Commonwealth Secretariat has explored similar models for virtual asset supervision (Commonwealth Secretariat, 2024).

Technical assistance programs from international organizations like the IMF, World Bank, and BIS Innovation Hub can provide training, analytical tools, and policy guidance tailored to jurisdictions' specific circumstances. The Asian Development Bank has been particularly active in supporting digital finance supervisory capacity building in Asia-Pacific (Arner et al., 2017).

Supervisory sandboxes for regulators (not just firms) where regulatory authorities can experiment with new supervisory approaches, share lessons learned, and build expertise in lower-stakes environments before applying techniques to systemically important entities.

Public-private partnerships where industry associations or technology providers assist in developing supervisory tools, standards, and training—though with appropriate governance to prevent regulatory capture.

Sustainable Funding Mechanisms

Supervisory capacity requires sustainable funding. Several models warrant consideration:

Tiered fee structures where licensed entities pay annual fees proportionate to their scale and systemic importance. Tier 4 systemically important stablecoins might pay substantially higher fees than Tier 1 entities, both because they require more intensive supervision and because they can better afford to contribute to regulatory infrastructure. This approach creates a direct link between supervisory costs and the entities being supervised.

Transaction-based fees or levies collected on stablecoin transactions, similar to how some payment system operators fund their supervisory oversight. Even very small per-transaction fees—fractions of a penny—can generate significant revenue at scale while remaining imperceptible to users.

Innovation levies where a small percentage of revenues from digital asset activities fund regulatory innovation and capacity building. The UK has explored similar models in its approach to cryptoasset financial promotions (Financial Conduct Authority, 2023c).

International assistance and cost-sharing for smaller jurisdictions that cannot realistically self-fund sophisticated supervision. Larger economies with systemically important stablecoin issuers might partially fund supervisory capacity in smaller jurisdictions where those stablecoins also operate, recognizing the global public good of effective supervision.

The fundamental principle is that supervision should be adequately funded to match the scale and complexity of the activities being supervised. Expecting regulators to supervise multi-billion-dollar global stablecoin arrangements with shoestring budgets and generalist staff is a recipe for regulatory failure.

Summary: Execution Layer of Stablecoin Regulation

Supervision represents the execution layer of stablecoin regulation—where principles become practice, where requirements are enforced, and where problems are detected and addressed. The design of supervisory frameworks determines whether licensing requirements remain paper commitments or become operational reality.

This section has argued for graduated, risk-based, innovation-compatible supervision resourced adequately to fulfill its functions. Key principles include:

Proportionality matching oversight intensity to risk, ensuring that systemically important arrangements receive intensive supervision while low-risk innovations are not crushed by disproportionate burdens.

Tiering that operationalizes proportionality through clear categories, graduated requirements, and paths for entities to scale up through tiers as they grow.

Technological enablement through RegTech and SupTech that reduces compliance costs, enhances supervisory efficiency, and enables risk-based oversight that would be impossible manually.

Active resistance to dynamics that would stifle innovation or entrench incumbents, through transitional arrangements, supervisory coaching, and recognition of functional equivalence.

Realistic attention to capacity constraints and sustainable funding mechanisms that ensure regulators have the resources necessary to supervise effectively.

The goal is not to regulate every stablecoin identically—that would be neither proportionate nor effective. Rather, the goal is ensuring that every stablecoin is supervised according to its actual risk profile and potential impact. Getting this balance right remains central to effective stablecoin regulation that protects public interests while enabling beneficial innovation.

4. WHO SHOULD BE EXEMPT – NARROW CARVEOUTS AND RESIDUAL RESPONSIBILITY

In any licensing regime, defining who must be licensed is only half the equation. Equally important—and often more politically contentious—is determining who should be exempt. Exemptions serve legitimate regulatory purposes: they prevent disproportionate burdens on genuinely low-risk activities, enable experimentation and innovation, and allow regulators to focus limited resources on entities that pose material threats to regulatory objectives.

Yet exemptions also create risks. They can become loopholes that sophisticated actors exploit to evade oversight. They can create uneven competitive conditions where exempt entities undercut licensed competitors by avoiding compliance costs. And they can generate confusion among users who may not understand that exempt providers lack the protections associated with licensed entities.

This section examines how exemptions should be designed in stablecoin contexts—narrowly framed, carefully monitored, and paired with baseline safeguards that apply even to exempt entities. The goal is creating space for beneficial innovation while preventing exemptions from becoming escape hatches that undermine regulatory effectiveness.

Reframing the Purpose and Limits of Exemptions

Exemptions from licensing requirements are typically justified on several grounds:

Proportionality: Imposing full licensing requirements on very small-scale or clearly low-risk providers would be disproportionate—the compliance costs would exceed any plausible regulatory benefit. A stablecoin used by 50 people for local community exchange does not warrant the same regulatory intensity as a global payment instrument with millions of users.

Innovation enablement: Allowing new entrants to test business models and demonstrate viability before facing full compliance burdens can facilitate beneficial innovation that might not occur if licensing requirements apply from day one. This is particularly important in rapidly evolving sectors where business models are still being discovered.

Regulatory efficiency: Finite regulatory resources should concentrate on entities whose failure or misconduct would cause significant harm. Exempting demonstrably low-risk activities allows supervisors to focus attention where it matters most.

These are legitimate rationales, but experience from early fintech and decentralized finance eras demonstrates how exemptions can backfire. Actors initially operating below regulatory thresholds can scale rapidly, becoming functionally systemic before regulators notice or respond. Services marketed as "not financial products" accumulate millions of users and billions in value before regulatory frameworks catch up. What begins as a reasonable exemption for small-scale experimentation becomes an avenue for regulatory arbitrage.

As Buckley et al. (2020) observe, exemptions too often "become escape hatches" in fast-moving digital ecosystems, where actors deliberately structure operations to exploit gaps between laws, between regulatory agencies, or between jurisdictional thresholds. The result is that significant risks accumulate outside regulatory perimeters until a crisis forces reactive intervention.

This history suggests that exemptions must be carefully designed with several features:

Narrow framing and clear boundaries: Exemptions should be defined precisely, with clear criteria determining when they apply and when they do not. Vague or open-ended exemptions invite interpretive disputes and strategic structuring to qualify for exempt status.

Dynamic monitoring and escalation triggers: Exempt entities that grow beyond initial assumptions or whose risk profiles change should automatically trigger licensing requirements. Exemptions should not be permanent safe harbors but rather transitional categories subject to ongoing assessment.

Baseline safeguards for all participants: Even exempt entities should meet minimum standards around consumer disclosure, anti-money laundering controls, and basic operational resilience. Complete exemption from all requirements creates ecosystem-wide vulnerabilities that threaten even well-regulated participants.

The challenge lies in implementing these principles without creating such complex exemption frameworks that the administrative burden defeats the purpose of exemptions in the first place.

Threshold-Based Exemptions: Necessary but Requiring Vigilance

Many regulatory regimes use threshold-based exemptions—objective criteria like total issuance volume, transaction amounts, or number of users that determine when licensing requirements apply. These thresholds provide clarity and enable proportionate treatment, but they also create opportunities for gaming and require careful calibration.

Singapore's Payment Services Act, for instance, allows certain limited-purpose providers to operate with lighter obligations below specified transaction volumes, though they remain subject to basic anti-money laundering requirements (Monetary Authority of Singapore, 2019). The EU's MiCA Regulation exempts small-scale issuers of asset-referenced tokens and e-money tokens under Article 15, though with restrictions on cross-border activities and requirements to notify authorities if growth approaches thresholds (European Parliament & Council, 2023).

Common threshold approaches include:

Total circulation caps (e.g., less than $5-10 million in outstanding stablecoins) that exempt genuinely small-scale operations while capturing larger arrangements that pose greater consumer protection or stability risks.

Transaction volume limits (e.g., less than $1 million monthly transaction volume) that identify entities operating at commercially insignificant scales unlikely to create systemic concerns.

User base restrictions (e.g., fewer than 1,000 active users) that exempt truly niche or experimental services while ensuring that mass-market offerings face appropriate oversight.

Geographic limitations that exempt arrangements operating only within single jurisdictions or limited regions, reducing cross-border complexity and contagion risks.

These thresholds serve useful purposes but create several challenges:

Rapid growth dynamics: Digital services can scale exponentially, crossing exemption thresholds in weeks or months. Without mechanisms to detect such growth promptly and trigger licensing requirements, significant risks can materialize faster than regulatory responses.

Strategic structuring: Sophisticated actors can structure operations to remain just below thresholds—perhaps by fragmenting services across multiple legal entities, imposing artificial limits on growth, or routing activities through different jurisdictions. This gaming undermines the integrity of threshold-based systems.

Differential treatment of similar risks: Arbitrary thresholds inevitably create situations where very similar activities face dramatically different requirements based on small differences in scale. This can feel unfair to entities just above thresholds who face full compliance costs while competitors just below thresholds operate with minimal burdens.

To address these challenges, threshold-based exemptions should incorporate several features:

Graduated requirements rather than binary exemption: Instead of complete exemption below thresholds and full licensing above them, intermediate categories with modest requirements can smooth the transition and reduce cliff effects. This approach appears in tiered licensing frameworks discussed in Section 3.

Universal baseline standards: Certain requirements—particularly anti-money laundering controls, consumer disclosures about regulatory status, and basic operational security—should apply universally regardless of exemption status. This prevents exempt entities from becoming weak links that threaten the entire ecosystem.

Mandatory notification and transition periods: Entities approaching exemption thresholds should be required to notify regulators and begin transition toward full licensing, with reasonable time periods (perhaps 6-12 months) to come into compliance. This prevents sudden disruptions while ensuring regulatory coverage expands as risks materialize.

Regular threshold review and adjustment: Thresholds appropriate when initially established may become too permissive or too restrictive as markets evolve. Regulators should systematically review and adjust thresholds based on experience, ensuring they continue serving their intended purposes.

Notably, exemptions from prudential requirements (capital, reserves, stress testing) may be more tolerable for genuinely small-scale entities than exemptions from conduct requirements (disclosure, redress, AML controls). A small stablecoin serving 500 users may not need bank-like capital buffers, but it should still identify its customers, disclose its limitations, and maintain basic security. This suggests that different types of requirements warrant different exemption thresholds.

White-Label Arrangements and the Question of Accountability

White-label models—where technology providers or infrastructure operators enable third parties to offer branded stablecoin services—present particularly difficult exemption questions. These arrangements blur traditional lines between service providers and infrastructure, creating ambiguity about who should be licensed and who might qualify for exemptions.

Consider a typical white-label structure: a technology company operates a stablecoin platform, managing reserves, maintaining blockchain infrastructure, and handling redemptions. Multiple retail-facing companies partner with this provider, each offering stablecoins under their own brands to their own customer bases. The retail brands market the stablecoins, onboard customers, and handle customer service. Who should be licensed? Can any party claim exemption?

Several regulatory questions arise:

Who controls the customer relationship? The retail-facing entity interacts directly with users, makes representations about the product, and handles complaints. Yet it may have limited actual control over reserves, redemptions, or protocol operations.

Who controls critical functions? The backend provider manages reserves, determines redemption mechanics, and can modify smart contracts. Yet it may claim to merely provide technology services without being in the "stablecoin business."

Who bears responsibility when things go wrong? If reserves are mismanaged, redemptions are delayed, or users suffer losses, both parties may point to the other, leaving users without clear recourse.

To prevent white-label arrangements from enabling regulatory evasion, licensing frameworks should adopt a **dual accountability model** where responsibilities are clearly allocated based on actual functions performed:

The customer-facing entity (the retail brand) should be licensed or at minimum registered for conduct-related obligations including:

- Marketing and disclosure requirements ensuring users understand what they're buying and from whom
- Customer identification and anti-money laundering controls
- Complaint handling and dispute resolution procedures
- Ensuring redemption requests are processed appropriately

The infrastructure provider (the backend platform) should be licensed for technical and prudential obligations including:

- Reserve safeguarding and segregation
- System resilience, security, and business continuity
- Redemption mechanics and liquidity management
- Smart contract security and upgrade governance

This dual licensing approach aligns with precedents from e-money regulation and Banking-as-a-Service frameworks, where agent-principal relationships are regulated distinctly with each party's obligations mapped to their actual roles (World Bank, 2021). The key principle, as Zetzsche et al. (2020a) emphasize, is that function—not form—should drive regulatory obligations. All entities performing core financial functions must be held accountable regardless of how they label themselves.

Importantly, neither party should be able to claim exemption merely because the other is licensed. The retail brand cannot avoid licensing by pointing to its licensed infrastructure partner, and the infrastructure provider cannot avoid oversight by claiming it merely provides technology to licensed distributors. Both perform critical functions; both should be regulated appropriately for those functions.

Infrastructure Providers and the Question of Systemic Importance

Some entities in stablecoin ecosystems never issue tokens or interact with end users, yet they perform functions critical to system operation. These infrastructure providers present difficult questions about whether they should be licensed, exempt, or subject to indirect oversight through the licensed entities that depend on them.

Infrastructure providers include:

Reserve custodians holding fiat currency or securities backing stablecoins. If custody fails—through theft, insolvency, or misappropriation—stablecoins lose backing regardless of how well issuers manage other aspects of operations.

Smart contract developers or protocol controllers who can modify code, upgrade systems, or pause operations. Effective control over these technical functions creates power over user outcomes comparable to traditional financial intermediation.

Oracles providing external data—such as asset prices or redemption rates—that smart contracts depend on to function correctly. Oracle manipulation or failures can cause widespread system malfunctions.

Cloud service providers or blockchain infrastructure operators hosting critical components. If Amazon Web Services suffers an outage, stablecoins dependent on AWS-hosted systems may become temporarily unavailable.

The traditional approach would exempt these infrastructure providers as mere technology or custody service providers not themselves in the stablecoin business. However, this approach breaks down when infrastructure providers become systemically important—where their failure would disrupt multiple stablecoin arrangements simultaneously or where they exercise effective control over critical functions.

The EU's Digital Operational Resilience Act (DORA) offers a useful model, placing third-party ICT (information and communication technology) providers under direct regulatory oversight when they are deemed critical to financial system functioning (European Commission, 2022). Similarly, IOSCO's principles on operational risk and outsourcing emphasize that licensed entities cannot outsource accountability, and regulators may need direct oversight of critical service providers (Organisation for Economic Co-operation and Development, 2012).

Applying this logic to stablecoins suggests several principles:

Concentration creates supervisory interest: When a single infrastructure provider supports multiple stablecoin issuers, its failure creates systemic risk warranting direct regulatory attention. A custodian holding reserves for dozens of stablecoins represents a single point of failure demanding supervisory oversight.

Effective control trumps formal labels: Entities that can modify smart contracts, pause redemptions, or redirect funds exercise control that should trigger licensing requirements regardless of whether they call themselves "infrastructure providers" or "technology companies."

Indirect oversight through licensed entities: Where direct licensing of infrastructure providers is impractical, regulators can require that licensed issuers conduct thorough due diligence on critical service providers, maintain oversight of their operations, include strong contractual protections, and report material incidents. This creates incentive structures where licensed entities themselves monitor and manage infrastructure risks.

Residual regulatory authority: Supervisors should retain authority to examine critical infrastructure providers, require remediation of deficiencies, or even prohibit use of providers that pose unacceptable risks—even if those providers are not themselves licensed. This residual authority provides backstop protection when indirect oversight proves insufficient.

The goal is ensuring no critical function operates entirely outside regulatory visibility. Whether through direct licensing, indirect oversight, or contractual requirements flowing through licensed entities, regulators need mechanisms to address infrastructure risks that threaten the stability and integrity of stablecoin arrangements.

Managing Arbitrage Between Exempt and Licensed Entities

A subtle but important risk in exemption design involves competitive dynamics between exempt and licensed entities. If exemptions are too generous or poorly monitored, they can distort markets in ways that undermine regulatory effectiveness:

Cost-based undercutting: Exempt entities that avoid compliance costs can offer services more cheaply than licensed competitors, potentially attracting users away from better-regulated, safer providers. This dynamic punishes compliance and rewards regulatory avoidance.

Misleading marketing: Exempt entities may market themselves in ways that suggest regulatory protections they don't actually possess, leaving users confused about what safeguards apply. Terms like "regulated" or "licensed" should be reserved for entities actually subject to oversight.

Regulatory reputation spillover: If exempt entities fail or engage in misconduct, public perception may not distinguish between properly licensed entities and exempt ones, potentially damaging trust in the entire stablecoin ecosystem including well-regulated participants.

Strategic threshold management: Sophisticated actors may deliberately structure operations to remain just below exemption thresholds indefinitely, creating permanent competitive advantages while avoiding regulatory obligations that apply to slightly larger competitors.

Several regulatory tools can mitigate these arbitrage risks:

Mandatory disclosure of regulatory status: Exempt entities should be required to clearly disclose that they are not licensed and do not possess protections associated with licensed providers. This disclosure should appear prominently in marketing materials, user agreements, and interfaces where users make decisions about whether to use the service.

Restrictions on misleading marketing: Exempt entities should be prohibited from using terminology that suggests regulatory oversight they don't have—words like "regulated," "licensed," "safe," or "guaranteed" should be restricted or heavily qualified. Enforcement against misleading marketing protects both users and compliant competitors.

Automatic escalation mechanisms: When exempt entities approach threshold limits, automatic licensing reviews should trigger, with burden placed on the entity to either demonstrate continued exemption eligibility or begin transition to licensed status. This prevents prolonged operation just below thresholds.

Periodic review of exemption criteria: Regulators should systematically review exemption frameworks to assess whether they're being used as intended or have become avenues for large-scale arbitrage. If significant value or activity accumulates among exempt entities, thresholds or criteria may need adjustment.

Cross-entity monitoring for related-party structures: Where multiple nominally separate exempt entities share common ownership, management, or operational infrastructure, regulators should have authority to aggregate their activities when assessing whether licensing thresholds are met. This prevents simple fragmentation strategies from evading oversight.

These measures support what might be called a **graduated, adaptive regulatory perimeter**—one that expands naturally as activities grow or risks materialize, while maintaining clear distinctions between exempt and licensed status that users can understand and rely upon.

Summary: Surgical Exemptions Within Comprehensive Frameworks

Exemptions remain vital regulatory tools when designed and implemented carefully. They enable proportionate regulation that doesn't crush small-scale or genuinely low-risk activities under disproportionate compliance burdens. They create space for experimentation and innovation that can ultimately benefit users and financial systems. And they allow regulators to focus limited resources on entities posing the greatest threats to regulatory objectives.

However, exemptions are not regulatory free passes. Several principles should guide their design:

Universal baseline standards: Certain minimum requirements—particularly around customer identification, disclosure of regulatory status, and basic operational security—should apply to all participants regardless of exemption status. Complete exemption creates ecosystem-wide vulnerabilities.

Dual accountability in white-label models: Both customer-facing entities and infrastructure providers should face appropriate oversight for their respective functions, with neither able to claim exemption merely because the other is licensed.

Direct or indirect oversight of critical infrastructure: When infrastructure providers become systemically important or exercise effective control over critical functions, they should be subject to regulatory oversight—either through direct licensing or through robust indirect supervision via the licensed entities that depend on them.

Dynamic monitoring and escalation: Exemptions should not be permanent safe harbors but rather transitional categories subject to ongoing monitoring and automatic escalation when thresholds are approached or risk profiles change.

Clear communication preventing confusion: Users should understand which entities are licensed and which are exempt, with mandatory disclosures and restrictions on misleading marketing protecting against arbitrage and reputation spillovers.

By embedding these features, regulatory frameworks can allow beneficial innovation to flourish within appropriate guardrails while preventing exemptions from becoming escape hatches that undermine market fairness, consumer protection, or financial stability. The next section examines how regulators can further support innovation through guidance, sandboxes, and pathways to compliance that help entities navigate requirements effectively.

5. GUIDANCE, SANDBOXES, AND PATHWAYS TO COMPLIANCE – SUPPORTING INNOVATION WITHOUT COMPROMISING STANDARDS

Licensing establishes the regulatory perimeter and supervision ensures ongoing compliance, but between these formal mechanisms and the realities of innovation lies a critical gap. New entrants often face genuine uncertainty about how regulatory requirements apply to novel business models. Regulators themselves may need to observe new technologies in practice before determining appropriate oversight approaches. And the transition from experimentation to full-scale operation requires pathways that neither expose users to undue risk nor impose such sudden compliance burdens that viable innovations cannot scale.

This section examines the tools regulators can deploy to bridge this gap: guidance that clarifies regulatory expectations, innovation support functions that facilitate dialogue between regulators and innovators, regulatory sandboxes that enable controlled experimentation, and graduated pathways to full compliance that smooth transitions as entities mature. These are not alternatives to robust licensing and supervision—they are complementary mechanisms that make regulatory frameworks more effective and innovation-friendly.

Beyond Sandboxes: The Critical Role of Innovation Support Functions

Much regulatory discussion of fintech innovation focuses on sandboxes—controlled environments where firms can test new products under regulatory oversight with temporary relief from certain requirements. Sandboxes have become fashionable, with jurisdictions worldwide establishing programs they characterize as innovation-friendly. However, recent research suggests that much of what makes jurisdictions genuinely supportive of innovation comes not from sandboxes themselves but from broader **innovation support functions** that facilitate ongoing regulatory engagement.

Buckley et al. (2019) make a compelling empirical case that innovation hubs—dedicated regulatory functions providing advice, feedback, and ecosystem coordination—often deliver greater benefits than sandboxes alone, particularly in resource-constrained jurisdictions. Their research on fintech ecosystems across Asia, Europe, and Africa found that the jurisdictions most successful at fostering innovation maintained continuous regulatory contact and advisory relationships with innovators, not merely time-limited sandbox experiments.

Innovation support functions can include:

Pre-application advisory services where potential applicants can discuss business models with regulators informally before committing resources to formal applications. This dialogue helps clarify whether licensing is required, what category might apply, and what concerns regulators might have—allowing firms to adjust approaches before investing heavily in compliance infrastructure.

Technical consultation and feedback loops where regulators with specialized expertise (or access to expert advisors) can assess novel technical approaches—algorithmic stabilization mechanisms, smart contract architectures, oracle designs—and identify potential regulatory concerns or opportunities for regulatory recognition.

Facilitation and matchmaking where regulatory authorities help connect innovators with potential partners—licensed banks willing to provide custody services, compliance technology vendors, legal advisors familiar with regulatory requirements, or other firms facing similar challenges who might collaborate.

Educational programs and capacity building where regulators organize workshops, publish guidance materials, and create forums for dialogue between industry participants and regulatory staff. These activities build shared understanding and reduce information asymmetries that impede innovation.

Pilot programs and proof-of-concept trials that may or may not constitute formal sandboxes but allow regulators and firms to jointly test whether novel approaches can meet regulatory objectives through different means.

The key insight from Buckley et al.'s research is that these ongoing support functions—what they term "innovation hubs" or "innovation support functions"—

often matter more than the existence of formal sandboxes. Many benefits attributed to sandboxes actually derive from the continuous regulatory engagement that surrounds them, not from the temporary relief from requirements that sandboxes formally provide.

For stablecoin regulation, this suggests that jurisdictions should invest at least as much in building robust innovation support capabilities—dedicated staff, clear contact points, advisory processes—as in designing elaborate sandbox programs. A small regulatory team providing consistent, accessible guidance may foster more innovation than a complex sandbox program that few firms can navigate successfully.

Types of Regulatory Sandboxes and Their Functions

That said, sandboxes remain valuable tools when designed appropriately. However, not all sandboxes serve the same purposes or operate through the same mechanisms. Understanding different sandbox models helps regulators select approaches appropriate to their objectives and constraints.

Table 3. Typology of regulatory sandboxes for stablecoin innovation

Sandbox Type	Primary Purpose	Key Features	Relevance to Stablecoins
Testing Environment Sandbox	Validate technical approaches and business models with limited real-world exposure	Time-limited, volume-capped, intensive monitoring, selected users only	Useful for novel stabilization mechanisms, hybrid governance models, or cross-chain architectures requiring empirical validation
Guidance-Based Sandbox	Provide structured regulatory feedback and interpretive clarity without formal exemptions	Advisory relationship, iterative design feedback, no formal waivers from requirements	Helps early-stage issuers refine designs and understand requirements before committing to full licensing process
Exemption-Based Sandbox	Grant temporary forbearance from specific compliance requirements subject to safeguards	Limited exemptions (e.g., reduced audit frequency, lower capital requirements), strict volume and time limits	Enables startups to demonstrate viability while building compliance infrastructure gradually
Coordination Sandbox	Facilitate multi-party experimentation and interoperability testing	Multiple participants, infrastructure providers, potential real-money transactions, complex governance	Particularly valuable for stablecoin networks requiring coordination among issuers, banks, payment systems, or CBDC pilots

Testing Environment Sandboxes

These sandboxes create controlled spaces where firms can operate with real users and real transactions, but under strict constraints that limit potential harm. Participation typically requires detailed proposals, supervisory approval, and ongoing monitoring. Volume caps, user limits, and time restrictions ensure that if experiments fail, damage remains contained.

The value lies in generating empirical evidence about how products work in practice. A stablecoin issuer might test whether an algorithmic stabilization mechanism maintains pegs during simulated stress conditions, whether redemption processes function smoothly, or whether users understand the product as intended. Regulators gain direct observation of operations, allowing them to assess risks that theoretical analysis cannot fully capture.

However, testing sandboxes are resource-intensive for both regulators and participants. Supervisory oversight of live experimentation requires specialized expertise and attention. And results from small-scale tests may not translate reliably to full-scale operations—behaviors that work with 1,000 users may break down with 1 million users.

Guidance-Based Sandboxes

These involve structured advisory relationships where regulators provide feedback on proposed designs, clarify how existing rules apply, and identify potential regulatory concerns—without granting formal exemptions or approving live operations. The "sandbox" is conceptual rather than operational.

Guidance-based approaches have lower regulatory risk exposure than testing sandboxes since firms operate either in simulation or do not operate at all until they achieve full compliance. They enable broader participation since regulatory capacity constraints around monitoring live operations do not limit how many firms can receive guidance. And they create continuous dialogue that builds regulatory understanding of innovation while helping firms design compliant products from the outset.

The limitation is that guidance alone cannot validate operational assumptions. A stablecoin design that looks sound in concept may encounter unanticipated problems in practice. Firms may delay full compliance indefinitely while seeking additional guidance, and without clear boundaries, the "guidance phase" can become prolonged limbo.

Exemption-Based Sandboxes

These grant temporary relief from specific regulatory requirements—perhaps reduced audit frequency, lower capital buffers, or delayed implementation of certain technical standards—while firms operate in real markets subject to volume or user limits. The goal is bridging the gap between zero compliance burden and full requirements that may be prohibitive for startups.

Exemption sandboxes enable real-world market exposure and revenue generation while compliance capabilities mature. They help address "first-mover" problems where being the first to seek licensing means bearing costs that fast-follower competitors might avoid if regulation changes.

However, exemption sandboxes create moral hazard risks. Firms may become dependent on exemptions, delaying investment in full compliance. Some may exploit "sandbox cover" to operate with inadequate safeguards. And determining which requirements can be safely waived versus which are essential even for small-scale operations proves difficult.

Empirical evidence on exemption sandboxes remains mixed. Studies of digital banking sandboxes in the UK found that while sandbox participation initially reduced regulatory burden, complexity and costs often increased later as firms transitioned to full licensing (Bromberg et al., 2022). This suggests that exemption sandboxes work best when paired with clear transition pathways and sunset provisions that prevent indefinite temporary status.

Coordination Sandboxes

These facilitate multi-party experimentation where multiple entities—issuers, infrastructure providers, financial institutions, sometimes even competing firms—test interoperability, information sharing, or joint operations. The UK's Financial Conduct Authority sandbox has evolved substantially in this direction, creating cohort-based programs where participants collaborate and regulators facilitate coordination rather than merely monitor individual firms (Financial Conduct Authority, 2023b).

For stablecoins, coordination sandboxes hold particular promise. Many regulatory challenges involve coordination problems—establishing common technical standards, ensuring interoperability across different stablecoin arrangements, integrating with traditional payment systems, or collaborating with central bank digital currency initiatives. These challenges cannot be resolved by individual firms working in isolation.

Coordination sandboxes require more complex governance structures and often involve multiple regulatory authorities with different mandates. They are harder to contain since network effects and interconnections create channels through which problems could spread. But they enable learning and standard-setting that benefits entire ecosystems, not just individual participants.

Pathways to Compliance: Graduating From Innovation to Full Regulation

However well-designed sandboxes and innovation support functions are, they must ultimately connect to mainstream regulatory frameworks. Firms cannot operate indefinitely in experimental status—at some point, successful innovations must transition to full compliance with licensing and supervisory requirements, while failed experiments must exit gracefully without harming users.

The challenge lies in designing transition pathways that are clear, predictable, and calibrated to enable smooth graduation without creating permanent regulatory limbo. Several models warrant consideration:

Provisional or Conditional Licensing

Rather than treating licensing as binary—either fully licensed or not licensed at all—regulators can grant provisional licenses with explicit conditions attached. These might include volume caps, requirements for third-party oversight, restrictions on user types (e.g., only sophisticated investors initially), or mandatory review periods after which full licensing or exit is required.

Provisional licensing reduces the "cliff effect" where startups face sudden, overwhelming compliance burdens the moment they seek regulatory approval. It provides oversight and consumer protection during growth phases while allowing requirements to scale gradually. And it gives regulators visibility into operations during periods when risks are emerging but not yet fully mature.

The EU's MiCA Regulation incorporates elements of this approach, allowing issuers of asset-referenced tokens to begin under less stringent oversight with automatic escalation to enhanced requirements when they cross significance thresholds based on size, interconnectedness, or cross-border reach (European Parliament & Council, 2023). Singapore's tiered licensing under the Payment Services Act similarly enables graduated entry with increasing requirements as operations scale (Monetary Authority of Singapore, 2019).

Potential downsides include uncertainty about renewal conditions—firms may be reluctant to invest in scaling if provisional status might not be extended—and risks of regulatory arbitrage if conditions are loosely enforced. Clear, objective criteria for transitioning from provisional to full licensing help address these concerns.

Staged Escalation of Requirements

A complementary approach involves automatic intensification of regulatory obligations as objectively measured characteristics change—outstanding issuance volume, transaction counts, number of jurisdictions served, integration into critical payment infrastructure. Firms understand from the outset that crossing these thresholds triggers enhanced requirements, allowing them to prepare rather than facing surprises.

This approach aligns well with tiered licensing frameworks discussed in Section 3. As a stablecoin grows from Tier 1 to Tier 2 to Tier 3, specific additional requirements activate—perhaps moving from quarterly to monthly reporting, from self-attestation to independent audits, from principles-based capital guidance to quantitative capital ratios.

The advantage is transparency and predictability—both regulators and firms know what triggers enhanced oversight. The risk is that firms might deliberately structure operations to remain just below escalation thresholds indefinitely, or that ambiguous threshold definitions create disputes about when escalation is required. Regular review and adjustment of thresholds based on experience helps address these concerns.

"If Not, Why Not" Compliance Models

Another approach allows firms to either comply with specified standards—perhaps international norms like ISO/IEC standards for information security or operational resilience—or publicly disclose their deviations and explain compensating controls they have implemented. This model borrows from corporate governance frameworks in securities regulation where "comply or explain" approaches provide flexibility while maintaining accountability.

For stablecoins, this might mean requiring issuers to either meet comprehensive reserve attestation standards or explain why their alternative approach provides equivalent assurance. Either adopt recognized smart contract security auditing practices or document why their internal processes achieve similar objectives. Either implement standard KYC procedures or justify alternative identity verification methods.

The strength of this approach lies in enabling innovation and recognizing functional equivalence—there may be multiple valid ways to achieve regulatory objectives. It maintains transparency and market discipline since disclosures allow users, investors, and competitors to assess whether "why not" justifications are credible.

Weaknesses include potential for firms to overclaim equivalence of non-compliant approaches and the risk that disclosure becomes formulaic box-checking rather than meaningful accountability. Supervisory review of "why not" justifications and willingness to challenge inadequate explanations remains essential.

Sunset Provisions and Mandatory Review Points

Perhaps most important for preventing permanent experimental status, every provisional license, sandbox participation, or exemption should incorporate mandatory review points—dates by which firms must either demonstrate progress toward full compliance or exit. These sunset provisions ensure that temporary arrangements remain temporary and that firms cannot indefinitely avoid full regulatory obligations.

Well-designed sunset provisions include:

Clear deadlines established at the outset, not open-ended "when the regulator is satisfied" criteria that create uncertainty.

Defined demonstration requirements specifying what evidence of compliance readiness firms must present—not vague "good faith effort" standards.

Explicit consequences for non-compliance at review points, whether that means transition to full licensing, wind-down requirements, or license revocation.

Reasonable timelines that recognize compliance infrastructure takes time to build but prevent indefinite delay—perhaps 12-24 months for provisional status with one potential extension rather than rolling indefinite provisional arrangements.

The risk is that firms may underinvest in compliance if they believe they can repeatedly extend temporary status, or that regulatory review capacity becomes bottlenecked when many firms reach transition points simultaneously. Staggering review timelines and maintaining adequate supervisory capacity for transition assessments helps manage these dynamics.

Critical Observations on Sandbox Effectiveness

While sandboxes and innovation support functions offer genuine value, it is important to maintain realistic expectations based on emerging evidence. Several observations warrant attention:

Selection bias in outcomes: Firms accepted into sandboxes typically already possess stronger resources, better regulatory sophistication, and more viable business models than rejected applicants. Positive outcomes among sandbox participants may reflect this selection rather than sandbox benefits per se. Studies comparing sandbox participants to similar firms operating outside sandboxes show smaller outcome differences than proponents often claim (Bromberg et al., 2022).

Resource intensity for regulators: Meaningful sandbox oversight requires significant regulatory capacity—specialized staff, technological capabilities, monitoring systems. Jurisdictions with limited supervisory resources may find that operating sandboxes effectively requires diverting capacity from supervision of licensed entities, potentially creating net risks rather than benefits.

Limited scalability of results: What works in a sandbox with 1,000 users and $5 million in issuance may break down entirely at scale. Behavioral dynamics change, technical systems face different stresses, and risk management approaches that seem adequate at small scale prove insufficient when volume increases orders of magnitude.

Time-limited learning windows: Sandbox participation typically lasts 6-24 months—not long enough to observe how stablecoin arrangements perform through full economic cycles, stress events, or long-term operational challenges. Successful sandbox graduation does not guarantee sustained viability.

These observations suggest that sandboxes work best when:

- Embedded within broader innovation support ecosystems rather than operating in isolation
- Focused on specific, well-defined learning objectives rather than serving as general innovation promotion tools
- Paired with robust transition pathways and willingness to require exit when experiments fail
- Complemented by strong ongoing supervision after sandbox graduation rather than treating successful sandbox participation as evidence that lighter oversight suffices

Summary: Complementary Tools in a Comprehensive Framework

Guidance, innovation support functions, sandboxes, and compliance pathways serve vital purposes in stablecoin regulatory frameworks, but they are not substitutes for robust licensing and supervision. Rather, they are complementary mechanisms that make regulatory frameworks more effective by:

Reducing information asymmetries between regulators and innovators, enabling both parties to understand novel approaches and their regulatory implications before committing to formal processes.

Providing space for experimentation within appropriate safeguards, allowing empirical validation of innovative approaches that purely theoretical analysis cannot adequately assess.

Smoothing transitions from experimentation to full-scale operation through graduated pathways rather than sudden compliance cliffs that make scaling prohibitively difficult.

Building regulatory capacity and expertise through ongoing engagement with innovation, ensuring regulatory frameworks evolve based on practical experience rather than becoming ossified.

Several principles should guide design of these mechanisms:

Innovation support functions deserve equal investment with formal sandboxes—continuous advisory relationships and ecosystem facilitation often deliver greater benefits than time-limited sandbox experiments.

Clear objectives and evaluation criteria should define what each sandbox or pathway is meant to achieve, with honest assessment of whether objectives are being met.

Sunset provisions and mandatory transitions prevent regulatory limbo where firms operate indefinitely in experimental status without graduating to full compliance or exiting.

Proportionate design matching jurisdictional capacity—sophisticated multi-tier sandbox programs make little sense in jurisdictions lacking supervisory resources to operate them effectively, while simple innovation contact points may deliver substantial benefits at much lower cost.

The goal is not maximizing the number of sandbox participants or creating the appearance of innovation-friendliness. Rather, it is facilitating genuine innovation that benefits users and financial systems while maintaining appropriate safeguards against risks. Getting this balance right requires recognizing that supporting innovation and protecting users are complementary objectives, not competing ones—robust regulatory frameworks enable sustainable innovation by creating confidence and clarity that purely unregulated environments cannot provide.

6. SUPERVISORY TOOLS, REMEDIES, AND OFFENCES – ENFORCEMENT WITHOUT OVERREACH

Licensing establishes who can operate, supervision monitors ongoing compliance, and guidance supports innovation—but without credible enforcement mechanisms, regulatory frameworks become merely aspirational. Rules that cannot be enforced are suggestions, not requirements. Yet enforcement design itself poses difficult challenges: sanctions must be severe enough to deter misconduct without being so harsh that they stifle beneficial innovation or drive activity into unregulated channels.

This section examines the toolkit regulators require to enforce stablecoin frameworks effectively: information-gathering powers that provide visibility into operations, corrective mechanisms that address deficiencies before they become crises, and sanctions that punish serious misconduct appropriately. Throughout, it emphasizes graduated approaches that match enforcement intensity to violation severity, procedural safeguards that protect against arbitrary action, and practical realities that constrain what enforcement can achieve in decentralized, cross-border contexts.

Types of Supervisory Tools

Effective supervision depends on access to timely, accurate information about licensed entities' operations, financial conditions, and risk exposures. Without this visibility, supervisors cannot detect emerging problems, assess compliance, or intervene appropriately. Stablecoin supervision requires tools adapted to digital operations while building on established supervisory practices from traditional financial regulation.

Reporting, Disclosure, and Audit Powers

Regular reporting requirements form the foundation of supervisory visibility. Licensed stablecoin issuers should submit periodic reports—monthly for larger or higher-risk entities, quarterly for smaller ones—covering critical operational and financial metrics:

- Reserve compositions broken down by asset type, maturity, credit quality, and custodian, enabling supervisors to assess whether backing meets requirements and identify concentration risks
- Liquidity buffer levels and stress testing results showing capacity to meet redemption demands under adverse scenarios
- Redemption and issuance activity including volumes, processing times, any delayed or denied redemptions, and geographic patterns
- Operational incidents such as system outages, security breaches, smart contract bugs, or oracle failures—even if resolved without user harm, these incidents provide early warning of vulnerabilities
- Governance changes including key personnel appointments, ownership transfers, or modifications to decision-making processes

Material change notifications should be required before significant operational changes occur—not merely after the fact. Upgrading smart contract logic, changing reserve custodians, restructuring governance mechanisms, or adding new features create risks that supervisors should assess proactively. Requiring advance notice enables supervisory dialogue about potential concerns before changes become irreversible.

Audit rights and independent attestation empower supervisors to verify self-reported information through third parties. Supervisors should have authority to require independent audits of reserves, review audit reports and working papers, and commission specialized audits when concerns arise. For stablecoins operating on distributed ledgers, this may include verification of on-chain data through blockchain analytics and examination of oracle reliability.

These reporting and audit powers provide the visibility supervisors need to detect anomalies, identify emerging stress, or discover divergence from regulatory commitments before problems escalate (Financial Stability Board, 2023). However, reporting requirements must be designed carefully—overly burdensome reporting that generates more data than supervisors can meaningfully analyze serves no useful purpose while imposing costs on regulated entities.

On-Site and Off-Site Inspections

Traditional financial supervision distinguishes between off-site monitoring (analysis of submitted reports and data) and on-site inspections (direct examination of entity premises, systems, and personnel). Both remain relevant for stablecoins, though adapted to digital contexts.

Off-site monitoring can be substantially enhanced through technology. Real-time dashboards fed by APIs from licensed entities enable continuous monitoring of key indicators—reserve levels, redemption patterns, transaction volumes, concentration metrics. Blockchain analytics tools allow supervisors to independently verify on-chain activities without relying solely on entity self-reporting. Automated anomaly detection systems can flag concerning patterns—sudden reserve drops, unusual redemption surges, divergence between reported and observable on-chain data—triggering supervisory attention.

On-site inspections provide deeper assessment through direct examination. Supervisory teams visit operations to review internal systems, interview key personnel, examine custody arrangements and business continuity plans, inspect smart contract version control and upgrade procedures, assess oracle reliability mechanisms, and verify that reported practices match actual operations. For stablecoins, "on-site" may involve remote technical audits of systems and code rather than purely physical presence, but the principle of direct supervisory examination remains important.

The integration of RegTech and SupTech tools enhances both off-site and on-site supervision. Machine learning algorithms can identify patterns human reviewers might miss. Automated data collection reduces reporting burdens while increasing timeliness. Real-time monitoring enables faster supervisory responses than periodic reporting alone would allow. However, technology supplements rather than replaces human supervisory judgment—automated systems flag potential issues, but humans must assess context and determine appropriate responses.

Variation, Conditions, and License Amendments

Supervisory frameworks should provide flexibility to adjust requirements as circumstances change, without requiring complete license revocation and reapplication processes. Powers to vary license conditions allow supervisors to impose additional requirements when risks increase—perhaps requiring enhanced reserve buffers during stress periods, more frequent audits when concerns emerge, or restrictions on new activities while deficiencies are addressed.

This flexibility enables calibrated responses to evolving risks (International Monetary Fund, 2021). A stablecoin that initially operated domestically but begins expanding internationally might face additional requirements around cross-border reporting or foreign exchange risk management. One that experiences rapid growth might transition from quarterly to monthly reporting and become subject to stress testing requirements. Variation powers enable these adjustments without the disruption of complete license revocation and reapplication.

However, variation powers must be exercised transparently with clear justification. Arbitrary or unexplained condition changes undermine regulatory certainty and may be challenged through administrative review processes. The balance lies in maintaining flexibility while ensuring predictability.

Warnings, Directives, and Corrective Orders

Before imposing formal sanctions, supervisors should typically issue warnings and corrective directives that provide opportunities for remediation. Formal warnings put licensed entities on notice that practices are concerning or approaching non-compliance, documenting supervisory concerns without yet imposing penalties. Directives require specific corrective actions within defined timeframes—perhaps strengthening governance processes, addressing audit findings, or enhancing reserve management practices.

Cease-and-desist orders provide stronger intervention for more serious deficiencies, requiring entities to stop specific activities until problems are resolved:

- Directives to cease issuance until reserve coverage is restored to required levels
- Orders suspending algorithmic stabilization features that have proven unreliable until they can be strengthened
- Mandates for enhanced disclosure or engagement of third-party experts to address governance weaknesses

These intermediate tools enable graduated responses. Not every deficiency warrants immediate license revocation—many can be corrected through supervisory dialogue and directed remediation. Providing opportunities for correction before imposing severe sanctions aligns with principles of proportionality and reduces unnecessary disruption.

License Suspension and Revocation

When entities fail to remediate serious deficiencies, engage in misconduct, or pose unacceptable risks, supervisors require ultimate authority to suspend or revoke licenses. License suspension temporarily prohibits operations, perhaps allowing only redemptions but no new issuance, while issues are addressed. License revocation permanently terminates authorization to operate in the jurisdiction.

These are serious interventions with significant consequences—for the entity, for its users, potentially for financial stability if the entity is large or interconnected. They should be used judiciously, after other corrective measures have failed or proven inadequate, and with procedures ensuring fair treatment. However, the credible threat of suspension or revocation is essential for enforcement effectiveness. Without it, less severe sanctions may be ignored by entities that calculate compliance costs exceed sanction risks.

Revocation procedures should address orderly wind-down, ensuring users can redeem holdings and that reserve assets are protected during resolution. This may involve appointing administrators, transferring operations to solvent entities, or requiring detailed wind-down plans as part of initial licensing.

Public Disclosure and Reputational Mechanisms

Public censure—formally naming non-compliant entities through regulatory announcements, website postings, or consumer alerts—imposes reputational costs that can exceed monetary penalties, particularly for technology-forward businesses where reputation matters intensely. Users may move to competitors, investors may withdraw support, and business partners may terminate relationships when regulatory concerns become public.

Public disclosure serves multiple purposes: it protects users by informing them of risks, creates market discipline by enabling informed choices, and deters misconduct through reputational consequences. However, it must be used carefully—premature or inaccurate public accusations can cause severe harm, and procedural fairness requires opportunities for entities to respond before reputational damage occurs.

Some regulatory regimes publish all enforcement actions as a matter of course, while others disclose only the most serious cases or maintain confidentiality to encourage cooperation and remediation. The balance depends on regulatory culture and legal frameworks, but transparency generally enhances accountability and public confidence in supervision.

Referral to Enforcement and Prosecution Authorities

When misconduct crosses into criminal territory—fraud, embezzlement, money laundering, market manipulation—supervisors must coordinate with criminal prosecutors and specialized enforcement agencies. Supervisors typically focus on prudential and conduct regulation rather than criminal prosecution, but they often discover criminal activity through supervisory examinations and must have clear referral mechanisms.

Effective coordination requires established protocols for information sharing, joint investigations when appropriate, and clarity about which authorities lead in which circumstances. Some jurisdictions embed shared enforcement powers or create integrated agencies combining supervisory and prosecutorial functions, while others maintain separate institutions requiring formal referral procedures.

Remedial and Corrective Powers: Graduated Enforcement

Effective enforcement does not rely solely on severe sanctions. **Graduated approaches** that match intervention intensity to violation severity prove more effective at achieving compliance while minimizing unnecessary disruption. A spectrum of remedial powers enables supervisors to calibrate responses appropriately:

Enforceable undertakings or supervisory agreements allow entities to commit to remediation plans under regulatory oversight—improving governance structures, strengthening reserve management, enhancing audit processes—with supervisory monitoring of implementation. These voluntary but legally binding commitments can resolve deficiencies cooperatively without formal sanctions.

Compensation and restitution orders require entities to make users whole when regulatory violations cause harm—refunding losses from failed redemptions, compensating for unauthorized transactions, or providing remedies for misleading disclosures. Restitution directly benefits harmed parties while sanctioning violators, serving both corrective and punitive purposes.

Restriction orders temporarily limit specific high-risk activities without suspending entire operations—perhaps disabling algorithmic rebalancing features that have proven unreliable, capping redemption processing times to ensure timely service, or restricting cross-border expansion until compliance capabilities mature. Restrictions enable continued operation in lower-risk areas while addressing specific concerns.

Structural remedies or divestiture requirements may be appropriate when business structures create unmanageable conflicts or risks—perhaps requiring separation of reserve custody from operations, divestiture of unrelated high-risk activities, or changes to governance structures that concentrate excessive control.

Financial penalties impose monetary sanctions proportionate to violation severity and entity revenue, serving as deterrents without necessarily destroying viable businesses. Penalty frameworks should specify how amounts are calculated—perhaps based on revenue derived from violations, harm caused to users, or prescribed ranges for different violation types—providing predictability while enabling supervisory discretion.

The aim throughout is to correct problematic practices and deter violations without imposing disproportionate consequences for minor technical lapses. A reporting deadline missed by a day warrants different response than deliberate misrepresentation of reserve backing. Graduated approaches enable nuanced responses reflecting these differences.

Civil, Administrative, and Criminal Offences

Well-designed enforcement frameworks distinguish between civil/administrative violations and criminal offences, reserving criminal prosecution for the most serious misconduct while handling less severe violations through administrative processes.

Civil and Administrative Offences

These address violations that may involve negligence, technical non-compliance, or operational failures without necessarily involving criminal intent. Administrative processes can resolve these matters more quickly and efficiently than criminal prosecutions:

- **False or misleading disclosures** about reserve backing, redemption capabilities, or operational safeguards that may reflect negligence or recklessness rather than intentional fraud
- **Operating without required licenses** through misunderstanding of requirements or regulatory changes rather than deliberate evasion
- **Failures to notify material changes** due to inadequate compliance processes rather than intentional concealment
- **Minor deviations from reserve, redemption, or reporting requirements** that don't cause user harm or threaten stability

Administrative sanctions—fines, license restrictions, required remediation—can be imposed through streamlined processes without meeting criminal burden of proof standards. This enables timely responses to deficiencies while reserving resource-intensive criminal processes for conduct warranting them.

Criminal Offences

Criminal prosecution should be reserved for intentional wrongdoing, large-scale consumer harm, or conduct threatening systemic stability:

- **Fraudulent issuance or misappropriation of reserve assets**—stealing user funds, using reserves for unauthorized purposes, or operating Ponzi-like schemes under guise of legitimate stablecoins
- **Knowing misrepresentation of redemption guarantees or reserve backing** with intent to deceive users and regulators about fundamental product characteristics
- **Deliberate circumvention of AML/CFT controls** to facilitate money laundering or terrorist financing
- **Tampering with audit records, forensic data, or transaction logs** to conceal misconduct or obstruct regulatory oversight
- **Operating unlicensed at significant scale** after clear notice that licensing is required, demonstrating willful disregard for regulatory requirements

Criminal prosecution carries severe consequences—imprisonment, criminal records, entity dissolution—justifying the high procedural protections and proof standards criminal processes require. The threat of criminal liability provides important deterrence for egregious misconduct that administrative sanctions alone cannot adequately address, but it should not be the primary enforcement mechanism for routine compliance matters.

Challenges, Safeguards, and Best Practices

Implementing supervisory tools and enforcement mechanisms in stablecoin contexts presents several distinctive challenges requiring thoughtful responses.

Attribution in Decentralized and Automated Systems

When stablecoins operate through smart contracts with governance distributed across multiple parties, determining accountability becomes complex. Who bears responsibility when automated code executes incorrectly—the original developers, current protocol controllers, governance token holders who approved parameters, oracles providing faulty data, or users who deployed the contracts?

Legal frameworks must provide clarity about liability attribution in code-driven systems. Some approaches include:

- **Primary responsibility on licensed issuers** regardless of technological implementation, creating incentives for issuers to ensure all technology components function appropriately
- **Joint and several liability** for entities sharing control over critical functions, preventing accountability gaps where multiple parties each claim others are responsible
- **Contractual allocation** of responsibilities among participants with regulatory approval, provided allocations ensure someone is clearly accountable for each critical function

Some regulatory proposals include requirements for "circuit breakers" or emergency override mechanisms enabling human intervention when automated systems malfunction. While this potentially compromises decentralization benefits, it ensures that regulators and courts have identifiable parties to hold accountable.

Consistency, Predictability, and Proportionality

Enforcement credibility depends on consistency—similar violations receiving similar treatment regardless of violator identity. Inconsistent enforcement where some entities face harsh sanctions while others receive lenient treatment for comparable conduct breeds cynicism and undermines compliance incentives.

Enforcement guidelines that specify how sanctions will be calculated based on objective factors—violation severity, harm caused, entity cooperation, remediation efforts, prior compliance history—enhance predictability while allowing appropriate discretion. **Published enforcement decisions** (with appropriate confidentiality protections) provide precedent helping entities understand expectations.

Proportionality requires that sanctions match violation severity. Technical violations causing no user harm should not trigger the same responses as deliberate fraud causing substantial losses. Graduated sanction frameworks with clear escalation principles help ensure proportionate responses.

Due Process and Appeal Rights

Enforcement actions that lack procedural fairness risk being overturned on administrative or judicial review, wasting resources and undermining regulatory authority. Due process safeguards should include:

- **Notice of alleged violations** with sufficient detail enabling entities to understand charges and prepare responses
- **Opportunities to present evidence and arguments** before sanctions are imposed, either through hearings or written submissions
- **Reasoned decisions** explaining factual findings and legal conclusions supporting sanctions
- **Appeal mechanisms** enabling independent review of enforcement determinations, whether through specialized tribunals or courts

These protections serve both fairness and accuracy—they reduce erroneous enforcement while enhancing legitimacy and acceptance of properly justified actions. However, procedural requirements must be balanced against enforcement timeliness—emergency situations threatening users or stability may warrant expedited processes with post-action review rather than extensive pre-action proceedings.

Avoiding Overreach and Market Chilling Effects

Overly aggressive enforcement can produce unintended consequences—driving innovation to less regulated jurisdictions, encouraging firms to avoid regulatory engagement entirely, or creating such risk aversion that beneficial experimentation ceases. Several practices help avoid these chilling effects:

Proportionate sanctions that correct problems without destroying viable businesses encourage compliance over evasion. A correctable deficiency should not trigger license revocation if less severe interventions would achieve regulatory objectives.

Enforcement discretion allowing prosecutors to decline cases or supervisors to accept remediation for minor violations without formal sanctions reduces over-criminalization of technical non-compliance.

Safe harbors and guidance clarifying what conduct is permissible provide confidence that compliant firms won't face unexpected enforcement, reducing incentives to avoid regulation entirely.

Graduated approaches that escalate from warnings through corrective orders before imposing severe sanctions give entities opportunities to remediate before suffering irreparable harm.

The goal is maintaining credible deterrence against serious misconduct while avoiding such extreme risk aversion that innovation becomes impossible within regulated frameworks.

Cross-Border Enforcement Coordination

Stablecoins' cross-border nature creates enforcement challenges when entities operate from multiple jurisdictions or lack clear territorial connection to any specific regulator. Effective enforcement increasingly requires international cooperation:

Memoranda of understanding between regulatory authorities facilitate information sharing about entities operating across borders, enabling coordinated surveillance and investigation.

Mutual recognition and enforcement agreements allow one jurisdiction's enforcement actions to be given effect in others, preventing entities from evading sanctions by moving operations or assets across borders.

Joint investigations and coordinated actions enable multiple regulators to act simultaneously against entities operating internationally, preventing firms from playing regulators against each other.

Common enforcement standards and frameworks developed through international bodies like FSB, IOSCO, and FATF provide foundation for cooperation by creating shared understanding of regulatory objectives and appropriate enforcement responses (Financial Stability Board, 2023).

However, cross-border enforcement faces limitations—jurisdictional boundaries constrain regulatory authority, and cooperation depends on willing partners with compatible legal frameworks. Entities that structure themselves to avoid clear jurisdictional connections can prove difficult to regulate effectively even with international cooperation.

Supervisory Capacity and Technical Expertise

The most sophisticated enforcement toolkit proves ineffective if supervisors lack capacity to use it. Effective stablecoin supervision requires specialized expertise:

- **Blockchain analytics capabilities** enabling independent verification of on-chain activities
- **Smart contract auditing expertise** to assess whether code functions as claimed and identify vulnerabilities
- **Cryptographic knowledge** sufficient to evaluate security architectures
- **Financial analysis skills** appropriate for novel business models and reserve structures

- **Cross-border coordination experience** managing investigations spanning multiple jurisdictions

Building this capacity requires investment in training, recruitment of specialized personnel, adoption of SupTech tools, and potentially engagement of external experts. Resource-constrained regulators may struggle to develop comprehensive capabilities, potentially limiting enforcement effectiveness despite having appropriate legal authorities.

International technical assistance programs, regulatory cooperation enabling smaller jurisdictions to leverage larger partners' expertise, and industry-funded supervisory levies can help address capacity constraints, but they remain significant practical limitations on enforcement in many jurisdictions.

Summary: Layered and Proportionate Enforcement

Supervisory tools, corrective mechanisms, and sanctions form an indispensable component of stablecoin regulatory frameworks. Without credible enforcement, licensing requirements and supervisory standards become aspirational rather than binding. However, enforcement design itself requires careful calibration—sanctions must be severe enough to deter misconduct without being so draconian that they stifle innovation or drive activity into unregulated channels.

Several principles should guide enforcement framework design:

Graduated approaches that escalate from monitoring through warnings and corrective orders before imposing severe sanctions enable proportionate responses matched to violation severity.

Clear distinction between administrative violations handled through streamlined processes and criminal offences requiring full procedural protections ensures efficient enforcement while reserving criminal prosecution for serious misconduct.

Procedural safeguards including notice, opportunities to respond, reasoned decisions, and appeal rights protect against arbitrary action while enhancing enforcement legitimacy.

Technological capabilities enabling effective supervision of blockchain-based operations ensure enforcement keeps pace with technological evolution.

International cooperation addressing cross-border enforcement challenges through information sharing, mutual recognition, and coordinated action.

The strongest enforcement frameworks recognize that the goal is not maximizing penalties but achieving compliance. Most entities prefer to comply with clear requirements rather than face sanctions. Effective enforcement provides that clarity, demonstrates serious consequences for willful non-compliance, but calibrates responses to encourage correction rather than merely punish failures. Getting this balance right remains central to regulatory effectiveness in stablecoin markets as in financial regulation more broadly.

7. CROSS-BORDER COOPERATION AND ENFORCEMENT – A COORDINATED GLOBAL RESPONSE

Stablecoins present a fundamental challenge to traditional regulatory approaches: they operate globally while regulation remains largely national. A stablecoin issued by an entity in one jurisdiction, using reserve custodians in several others, operating on blockchain infrastructure distributed across dozens of countries, and accessible to users worldwide defies neat categorization into any single regulatory territory. This creates a coordination problem that no individual regulator can solve alone.

The stakes are significant. Without effective cross-border cooperation, stablecoin regulation risks becoming a race to the bottom where operators migrate to the least regulated jurisdictions while serving users globally. Alternatively, inconsistent requirements across jurisdictions could fragment markets, increase costs, and limit the cross-border benefits that make stablecoins attractive. This section examines why cross-border cooperation matters, what mechanisms can enable it, and what practical challenges constrain its effectiveness.

The Risks of Regulatory Fragmentation

When stablecoin operators face dramatically different requirements across jurisdictions—some demanding comprehensive licensing, others imposing minimal oversight—several predictable problems emerge:

Regulatory arbitrage becomes attractive and feasible. Sophisticated operators can establish legal presence in jurisdictions with light regulation while serving users in jurisdictions with stricter requirements, claiming they fall under the permissive regime. This pattern appeared repeatedly in early cryptocurrency exchange regulation, where entities incorporated in offshore jurisdictions provided services to users in major economies while avoiding those economies' regulatory requirements. Stablecoins face similar dynamics—issuers can structure operations to benefit from the most favorable regulatory treatment while maintaining global reach through internet access.

Inconsistent consumer protection creates confusion and unfairness. Users in some countries may benefit from redemption guarantees, reserve requirements, and complaint mechanisms while users elsewhere accessing the same stablecoin lack these protections. This inconsistency is particularly problematic given that stablecoins market themselves as borderless—users may reasonably expect similar protections regardless of their location, yet fragmented regulation cannot deliver this.

Market instability can result from divergent reserve rules and redemption expectations. If one jurisdiction requires full backing with liquid assets while another permits fractional reserves or risky collateral, the same stablecoin may have different risk profiles depending on where scrutiny occurs. During stress events, these inconsistencies could trigger contagion as users in well-regulated jurisdictions lose confidence due to problems originating in poorly regulated ones.

Enforcement gaps emerge when no regulator has clear authority or practical ability to oversee critical functions. A stablecoin issuer might be incorporated in one jurisdiction, custody reserves in several others, operate technology infrastructure from yet another, and be controlled by individuals or entities in additional locations. If each regulator assumes others are handling oversight, the result may be that no effective supervision occurs anywhere.

These risks have been highlighted repeatedly by international standard-setting bodies. The Financial Stability Board's recommendations for global stablecoin arrangements emphasize the need for comprehensive regulation that does not leave gaps (Financial Stability Board, 2023). The International Monetary Fund has warned that regulatory fragmentation could undermine financial stability as stablecoins scale (International Monetary Fund, 2021). And scholars like Zetzsche et al. (2020a) caution that uneven global standards create parallel systems of trust and value that can undermine market confidence and generate systemic vulnerabilities.

The question, then, is not whether cross-border cooperation is necessary—it clearly is—but rather how to achieve it given the political, legal, and practical obstacles to regulatory coordination.

Mutual Recognition and Equivalence Frameworks

One approach to reducing regulatory fragmentation involves mutual recognition—allowing stablecoin services licensed in one jurisdiction to operate in another without duplicating the entire licensing process. This approach offers administrative efficiency and reduces barriers to legitimate cross-border service provision while maintaining regulatory oversight.

Several models exist with different levels of integration:

Passporting within regional frameworks provides the most comprehensive mutual recognition. The European Union's Markets in Crypto-Assets Regulation (MiCA) establishes passporting rights allowing issuers licensed in any EU member state to operate throughout the EU without separate licensing in each country (European Parliament & Council, 2023). This approach creates a single market for stablecoins within the EU while maintaining common standards all participants must meet. Similar regional integration appears in other contexts—the ASEAN Economic Community has explored mutual recognition arrangements for digital financial services, and Gulf Cooperation Council states have discussed coordinated crypto-asset frameworks.

Regional passporting works best where jurisdictions share legal traditions, enforcement capabilities, and regulatory philosophies, and where political integration provides mechanisms to resolve disputes and harmonize standards. These conditions exist more readily within regional blocs than globally.

Recognition of comparable regimes offers a less integrated alternative where individual jurisdictions assess whether foreign regulatory frameworks achieve equivalent outcomes even if requirements differ in detail. A jurisdiction might recognize that another country's stablecoin licensing regime, while structured differently, imposes substantially similar capital requirements, reserve standards, and supervisory oversight. Recognition agreements would allow issuers licensed under the recognized regime to operate with streamlined approval processes rather than complete re-licensing.

This approach preserves regulatory sovereignty—each jurisdiction decides whose frameworks it recognizes as equivalent—while reducing duplication. However, it requires detailed assessment of foreign regimes and ongoing monitoring to ensure equivalence is maintained as frameworks evolve. Regulatory drift over time can undermine initial equivalence findings.

Bilateral memoranda of understanding between regulatory authorities create frameworks for cooperation on specific matters—information sharing, coordinated inspections, mutual assistance in enforcement—without necessarily creating formal recognition of licensing regimes. MoUs facilitate case-by-case cooperation while preserving each regulator's independent authority. They work particularly well for investigatory cooperation and information exchange but provide less predictability for regulated entities than formal recognition frameworks.

The Commonwealth Model Law on Virtual Assets proposes equivalence-based recognition frameworks particularly suited to smaller jurisdictions seeking to avoid duplicating sophisticated regulatory infrastructure while maintaining standards (Commonwealth Secretariat, 2024). For small island or developing states, mutual recognition enables access to international markets without requiring each jurisdiction to build comprehensive supervisory capacity from scratch.

However, all mutual recognition approaches face an inherent tension: they rely on trust that foreign regulators are competent, independent, and adequately resourced. When this trust proves misplaced—when a jurisdiction's supervision is less robust than advertised, or when regulatory capture compromises oversight—problems in one jurisdiction can spread to others through recognition relationships. The global financial crisis illustrated how recognition of credit rating agencies and regulatory frameworks in some jurisdictions proved unjustified, with consequences spreading internationally.

International Standards as Foundation for Cooperation

Cross-border cooperation becomes more feasible when jurisdictions align around shared standards that provide common frameworks for assessing risks and coordinating oversight. Several international standard-setting initiatives provide this foundation for stablecoins:

FATF guidance on virtual assets establishes anti-money laundering and counter-terrorism financing requirements for virtual asset service providers, including stablecoin issuers and intermediaries (Financial Action Task Force, 2023). FATF Recommendation 15 requires that jurisdictions license or register VASPs, implement preventive measures comparable to those for traditional financial institutions, and enable cross-border supervisory cooperation. While not all jurisdictions have fully implemented FATF standards, the guidance provides a common baseline that facilitates international cooperation on financial integrity matters.

IOSCO principles and recommendations address securities aspects of crypto-assets and stablecoins, particularly those with investment features (Organisation for Economic Co-operation and Development, 2012). IOSCO's framework emphasizes disclosure, conflicts management, operational resilience, and consumer protection obligations that apply across borders. When jurisdictions implement IOSCO-consistent frameworks, they create common ground enabling regulatory cooperation.

Basel Committee guidance establishes prudential expectations for banks' exposures to crypto-assets, including holdings of stablecoins as reserves or investments (Basel Committee on Banking Supervision, 2022). While not directly regulating stablecoins themselves, Basel standards influence how banks interact with stablecoin arrangements, creating indirect pressure for stablecoins to meet standards banks require for counterparty relationships.

Technical standards from bodies like the International Organization for Standardization provide common frameworks for security, risk management, and technical architecture. ISO/TC 307 develops blockchain and distributed ledger technology standards. ISO/IEC 27001 addresses information security management. ISO/IEC 42001 covers AI management systems increasingly relevant to algorithmic stablecoin mechanisms. When stablecoin arrangements implement recognized technical standards, supervisors across jurisdictions can more easily assess whether appropriate controls exist.

These international standards serve multiple functions. They create common vocabulary enabling regulators to communicate effectively about risks and requirements. They provide benchmarks against which different national frameworks can be compared to assess equivalence. And they offer neutral, technically grounded criteria for supervision that can transcend differences in legal systems or regulatory traditions.

However, international standards also have limitations. They represent consensus positions that may not address cutting-edge risks quickly. Implementation varies across jurisdictions, sometimes undermining their utility as common frameworks. And standards developed in international forums may not adequately reflect perspectives from smaller or less influential jurisdictions, potentially embedding developed-country assumptions that prove ill-suited elsewhere.

Mechanisms for Information Sharing and Coordinated Action

Beyond common standards, effective cross-border supervision requires practical mechanisms enabling regulators to share information, coordinate oversight, and support each other's enforcement actions. Several institutional and technical tools facilitate this cooperation:

Supervisory colleges bring together regulators from jurisdictions where systemically important financial institutions operate to coordinate oversight. Originally developed for global banks and insurance groups, the Financial Stability Board now recommends supervisory colleges for global stablecoin arrangements (Financial Stability Board, 2023). These colleges would include prudential supervisors, conduct regulators, AML/CFT authorities, and potentially central banks from all major jurisdictions where a stablecoin operates.

Colleges facilitate information sharing about supervisory findings, coordinate examination activities to avoid duplication or gaps, discuss emerging risks and appropriate responses, and develop coordinated crisis management approaches. For truly global stablecoins integrated into multiple payment systems, supervisory colleges could prove essential for maintaining comprehensive oversight no single regulator can provide alone.

Cross-border regulatory sandboxes enable coordination on innovation support, not just enforcement. The Global Financial Innovation Network facilitates cross-border testing where firms can pilot products in multiple jurisdictions simultaneously under coordinated supervisory oversight (Financial Conduct Authority, 2023a). While still developing, these cross-border sandboxes could help regulators jointly assess novel stablecoin arrangements and coordinate regulatory responses rather than each jurisdiction making independent determinations that might conflict.

Intelligence sharing platforms and joint investigations address financial crime dimensions of stablecoin regulation. Bodies like the Egmont Group (a network of financial intelligence units) and Interpol facilitate information sharing about suspicious transactions, money laundering typologies, and enforcement actions. For stablecoins potentially used in illicit finance, these networks enable coordinated responses that purely national efforts cannot achieve. Recent examples include coordinated actions by European and Asian authorities against crypto exchanges facilitating money laundering, demonstrating how intelligence sharing can enable effective enforcement across borders.

Technical cooperation mechanisms leverage technology itself to facilitate oversight. Regulators can deploy blockchain analytics tools providing visibility into on-chain activities across jurisdictions. "Regulator nodes" could provide authorities with real-time read access to transaction data and reserve holdings without depending on issuer reporting. Shared audit standards and recognition of qualified auditors enable reliance on attestations across borders. Common technical approaches to reserve verification, smart contract auditing, and cyber security assessment help regulators coordinate oversight of distributed systems.

Access to several types of information proves particularly critical for cross-border supervision:

- Corporate control structures including beneficial ownership, board composition, and key personnel
- Reserve custody arrangements specifying where assets are held and under what legal protections
- Audit trails for reserve management, redemption processing, and governance decisions
- Smart contract code, upgrade mechanisms, and administrative key controls
- Operational incident reports including security breaches, system failures, or oracle manipulations

When this information is accessible to all relevant supervisors through cooperative frameworks, comprehensive oversight becomes feasible even for globally distributed operations.

Challenges in Establishing Enforcement Jurisdiction

Despite growing international cooperation, fundamental challenges remain in establishing clear enforcement jurisdiction over stablecoins. Many arrangements are structured specifically to obscure accountability or fragment control across multiple jurisdictions:

Decentralized autonomous organizations claim no single entity controls operations, making traditional regulatory concepts of licensable entities difficult to apply. A DAO might describe itself as a community-governed protocol with no legal person to hold accountable. Yet someone typically controls smart contract upgrade keys, manages reserve assets, or operates infrastructure—the challenge lies in identifying these control points and establishing which jurisdiction has authority over them.

Complex corporate structures involving foundations in one jurisdiction, operating companies in another, technology providers in a third, and users globally create ambiguity about where enforcement should occur. Each entity in the structure may claim it performs only limited functions not warranting licensing, while collectively the structure provides complete stablecoin services. Determining which jurisdiction should take primary enforcement responsibility becomes difficult.

Pseudonymous or anonymous operations where developers, operators, or controllers use pseudonyms rather than revealing identities make enforcement actions challenging even when jurisdiction is clear. How does a regulator sanction an entity it cannot identify or serve with legal process? While blockchain analytics and investigatory techniques can sometimes identify individuals behind pseudonyms, truly anonymous operations pose enforcement difficulties.

These challenges led Gorton and Zhang (2023) to warn that without enforceable accountability, stablecoins risk becoming modern versions of 19th century "wildcat banks"—private issuers whose collapse caused widespread harm precisely because enforcement jurisdiction remained unclear and mechanisms for holding issuers accountable proved inadequate.

Several approaches can help address these jurisdiction challenges:

Functional regulation focuses on requiring that a legally accountable entity be designated in every jurisdiction where material services are offered, regardless of decentralization claims or complex structures (Arner et al., 2022). If a stablecoin is marketed to users in a jurisdiction, someone must accept responsibility for compliance with that jurisdiction's requirements. This approach treats regulatory obligations as attaching to functions performed rather than legal forms adopted.

Control-based attribution assigns regulatory responsibility based on who actually controls critical functions—upgrade keys, reserve management, redemption mechanisms—rather than formal corporate structure. If an identifiable entity can pause operations, modify code, or redirect funds, that entity should be subject to licensing regardless of whether it characterizes itself as merely providing technical services.

Mandatory legal representation requires that stablecoin arrangements designate legal representatives in each major jurisdiction who can be served with legal process, face enforcement actions, and ensure compliance with local requirements. This ensures regulators have identifiable parties to engage with even if ultimate control lies elsewhere.

Forum-shopping limitations through agreements among regulators about which jurisdiction should take primary responsibility for oversight based on factors like where issuers are incorporated, where significant operations occur, or where the largest user base exists. Clear allocation of primary jurisdiction prevents regulatory arbitrage while enabling coordinated secondary oversight from other affected jurisdictions.

None of these approaches perfectly resolves jurisdictional challenges, but they help ensure that truly global operations face coordinated international oversight rather than evading accountability by claiming no single jurisdiction can effectively regulate them.

Summary: Building Effective Cross-Border Architecture

Cross-border cooperation represents not a luxury but a necessity for effective stablecoin regulation. The borderless nature of these instruments means that purely national approaches will inevitably prove inadequate, leaving gaps that enable regulatory arbitrage and allowing risks to accumulate outside supervisory visibility.

Several elements are essential for effective cross-border regulatory cooperation:

Common standards through international bodies like FSB, IOSCO, FATF, and Basel Committee that provide shared frameworks for assessing risks and designing requirements.

Mutual recognition frameworks that reduce duplication while maintaining oversight, whether through regional passporting arrangements or bilateral equivalence agreements.

Supervisory colleges and coordination mechanisms enabling regulators to share information, coordinate examinations, and develop joint responses to systemically important stablecoin arrangements.

Clear jurisdiction allocation ensuring that globally distributed operations face comprehensive oversight without leaving gaps where no regulator accepts responsibility.

Technical cooperation tools leveraging blockchain analytics, shared audit standards, and potentially direct regulatory access to transaction data and reserves.

Capacity building support ensuring that smaller or less-resourced jurisdictions can participate effectively in international cooperation rather than becoming weak links exploited for regulatory arbitrage.

The challenge ahead involves building these cooperative frameworks while respecting regulatory sovereignty and accommodating legitimate differences in national priorities and approaches. Perfect global harmonization remains neither achievable nor necessarily desirable—different jurisdictions may reasonably make different trade-offs between innovation and protection, or face different risk profiles requiring adapted approaches.

The goal should be preventing coordination failures that allow significant risks to fall outside regulatory oversight, while enabling innovation that benefits from stablecoins' global reach. Getting this balance right requires sustained commitment to international cooperation from both regulators and the stablecoin industry itself. The next section concludes by synthesizing these themes and examining future directions for stablecoin regulatory frameworks.

8. CONCLUSION AND FUTURE DIRECTIONS – BUILDING A RESILIENT, INNOVATION-READY FRAMEWORK

Stablecoins occupy a unique position in financial history—instruments that promise the stability of traditional money while leveraging the technological possibilities of decentralized systems. This duality creates both their appeal and their regulatory challenge. They are not simply a new payment technology requiring modest adaptations to existing frameworks, nor are they so fundamentally novel that entirely new regulatory paradigms must be invented. Rather, they demand thoughtful application of established regulatory principles—licensing, supervision, consumer protection, prudential safeguards—adapted to digital, often decentralized, frequently cross-border contexts.

This chapter has examined the core components of effective licensing and supervisory frameworks for stablecoins, arguing throughout for approaches that balance protection of legitimate regulatory interests with recognition that innovation can serve public welfare. From initial questions about who should be licensed through detailed requirements for what licensing should entail, from supervisory architecture enabling proportionate oversight to pathways supporting compliance and innovation, the framework outlined here rests on several foundational principles:

Function over form: Regulatory requirements should attach based on activities performed and risks created, not labels adopted or corporate structures chosen. An entity that accepts funds, promises redemption at par, and operates payment infrastructure performs functionally equivalent activities to traditional money issuers regardless of whether it calls itself a technology company rather than a financial institution.

Proportionality and tiering: Not all stablecoin arrangements pose equivalent risks. Regulatory intensity should scale with actual risk profiles—small-scale, limited-purpose arrangements warrant lighter oversight than systemically important global payment instruments, with graduated tiers enabling smooth transitions as operations grow.

Technology-enabled supervision: Traditional supervisory approaches must be enhanced with RegTech and SupTech capabilities that enable real-time monitoring, reduce compliance costs, and provide visibility into blockchain-based operations. Technology should facilitate rather than impede effective oversight.

International cooperation: The borderless nature of stablecoins means national regulatory approaches alone cannot suffice. Cross-border coordination through common standards, mutual recognition, supervisory colleges, and information sharing becomes essential rather than optional.

Dynamic adaptation: Both regulatory frameworks and individual licensing decisions must evolve as technologies, business models, and risk profiles change. Static approaches that assume stability in rapidly evolving markets will inevitably prove inadequate.

As stablecoin markets continue maturing and regulatory frameworks solidify, several trends and directions warrant attention.

Emerging Trends Shaping Stablecoin Regulation

Convergence Around International Standards

The fragmented early regulatory responses to stablecoins are giving way to increasing convergence around international standards and principles. The Financial Stability Board's recommendations for global stablecoin arrangements, IOSCO's principles for crypto-asset markets, FATF's guidance on virtual asset service providers, and the Basel Committee's treatment of cryptoasset exposures provide common frameworks that national regulators increasingly reference when designing domestic requirements (Financial Stability Board, 2023; Organisation for Economic Co-operation and Development, 2012; Financial Action Task Force, 2023; Basel Committee on Banking Supervision, 2022).

This convergence serves multiple purposes. It reduces regulatory arbitrage opportunities by creating more consistent baseline standards across jurisdictions. It facilitates mutual recognition and cross-border cooperation by providing common reference points for assessing equivalence. And it creates clearer expectations for international stablecoin operations about what requirements they must meet regardless of where they operate.

Technical standards from bodies like ISO are likely to form baseline layers for operational requirements around security, auditability, and interoperability (ISO, 2023). When jurisdictions require compliance with recognized international technical standards, they create objective criteria that transcend differences in legal systems while enabling assessment of whether appropriate controls exist. This proves particularly valuable for mutual recognition frameworks where authorities must assess foreign regulatory regimes without deep familiarity with their details.

However, convergence should not mean complete uniformity. Different jurisdictions face different risk profiles, possess different institutional capacities, and may make legitimate different choices about trade-offs between various regulatory objectives. The goal should be sufficient coordination to prevent major gaps and enable cooperation, not elimination of all regulatory diversity.

Rise of Embedded Supervision and Real-Time Monitoring

Traditional financial supervision operates largely through periodic reporting—licensed entities submit quarterly or annual reports that supervisors review retrospectively. By the time problems appear in reports, they may have existed for months. For stablecoins operating on distributed ledgers with continuous transaction flows and potentially rapid changes in reserve composition or redemption demands, periodic retrospective reporting proves inadequate.

Supervisory technology (SupTech) increasingly enables real-time or near-real-time monitoring that fundamentally changes supervisory capabilities. Reserve verification can occur continuously through direct observation of custody accounts rather than relying on quarterly audits. Smart contract auditing tools can automatically flag concerning code changes or parameter modifications. Redemption flow monitoring can detect surges that might indicate emerging stress before they become crises. Blockchain analytics provide independent verification of on-chain activities without depending on entity self-reporting (Zetzsche et al., 2020; Arner et al., 2017).

This shift toward embedded, continuous supervision requires investment in technological capabilities, access to relevant data sources (potentially including "regulator nodes" providing direct read access to blockchain data), and analytical capacity to process large volumes of real-time information. Not all jurisdictions can make these investments immediately, but the direction is clear—supervision will increasingly leverage technology to move from periodic retrospective review toward continuous forward-looking monitoring.

This evolution also changes the nature of supervisory relationships. Rather than adversarial interactions where supervisors discover problems through examinations that entities tried to hide, continuous monitoring enables more collaborative relationships where supervisors and regulated entities jointly identify emerging issues and address them before they cause harm. This shift from episodic enforcement toward ongoing cooperation could prove as significant as the technological capabilities enabling it.

Shift Toward Functional Regulation

The collapse of algorithmic stablecoins like TerraUSD, the failure of several centralized exchanges claiming to operate outside regulatory perimeters, and the opacity of many decentralized finance protocols have all reinforced regulatory interest in functional approaches that focus on economic substance rather than legal form.

Functional regulation asks what activities an entity actually performs and what risks it creates, then applies appropriate requirements regardless of how the entity structures itself legally or what label it adopts. A DAO that controls protocol upgrades, manages reserve assets, and determines redemption policies performs functionally equivalent activities to a corporate stablecoin issuer—it should face equivalent regulatory requirements regardless of its decentralized structure or claim to be merely a "technology protocol" (International Monetary Fund, 2021; Commonwealth Secretariat, 2024).

This approach proves particularly relevant for white-label platforms where multiple entities share functions but each claims limited responsibility, for embedded financial services where technology companies provide financial functionality without being financial institutions, and for decentralized protocols that fragment control across multiple parties hoping to avoid clear regulatory accountability.

Implementing functional regulation requires moving beyond bright-line rules based on entity types toward principles-based assessment of actual activities and risks. It demands supervisory capacity to analyze complex structures and trace control through technical and corporate arrangements. And it requires legal frameworks providing clear authority to regulate based on functional analysis rather than merely formal categorization.

From Static Licensing to Dynamic Oversight

A critical theme throughout this chapter has been the need to view licensing not as a one-time gate that entities pass through and then operate indefinitely under unchanged conditions, but rather as the entry point into ongoing regulatory relationships that evolve as circumstances change.

This reflects both the rapid pace of technological evolution and the changing business models in digital finance. A stablecoin arrangement that begins as a small-scale remittance tool may expand into general-purpose payments, add programmable features enabling complex financial applications, or integrate into critical payment infrastructure. Its risk profile changes fundamentally through this evolution—static licensing requirements established at inception cannot remain appropriate indefinitely.

Several mechanisms enable more dynamic oversight:

Tiered frameworks with automatic escalation: As discussed in Section 3, tiering based on objective metrics like outstanding issuance volume, transaction counts, or cross-border reach enables automatic intensification of requirements as risks materialize. Entities understand from the outset that growth triggers enhanced obligations, allowing planning while ensuring oversight scales with risk.

Machine-readable regulatory reporting: When supervisory reporting uses standardized, machine-readable formats rather than narrative text, automated analysis becomes feasible. This enables real-time assessment of compliance and rapid detection of concerning trends, supporting dynamic supervisory responses.

Conditional or provisional licensing: Rather than permanent licenses granted after initial assessment, conditional licenses subject to periodic review or specific performance requirements create ongoing incentives for compliance and provide natural points for reassessing whether requirements remain appropriate.

Regulatory feedback loops: Regular structured dialogue between supervisors and licensed entities about emerging risks, technological changes, or operational challenges enables proactive adaptation rather than reactive crisis responses.

These mechanisms point toward what might be called "regulation-as-a-platform"—integrated, interactive frameworks where the boundary between private innovation and public oversight becomes more fluid and collaborative rather than adversarial. Success depends on both regulators and regulated entities embracing this more dynamic model rather than treating licensing as a fixed state to be achieved and maintained indefinitely.

Toward Coordinated Global Architecture

Throughout this chapter, the challenge of regulating inherently global instruments through nationally bounded regulatory authorities has been a recurring theme. Section 7 examined cross-border cooperation mechanisms in detail, but the fundamental tension warrants emphasis in conclusion: stablecoins will not wait for perfect global regulatory harmonization before scaling internationally, yet purely national approaches cannot provide adequate oversight.

Several elements appear essential for effective global coordination:

Mutual recognition frameworks that allow services licensed in one jurisdiction to operate in others without complete re-licensing, whether through regional passporting arrangements like MiCA or bilateral equivalence agreements between major financial centers. These frameworks must balance reducing duplication against ensuring all jurisdictions maintain adequate standards.

International standard-setting through bodies like FSB, IOSCO, FATF, and the Basel Committee provides common frameworks enabling coordination even absent formal recognition agreements. When jurisdictions implement substantially similar requirements based on shared international standards, coordination becomes feasible even without explicit treaties.

Supervisory colleges and coordination mechanisms for systemically important stablecoin arrangements enable regulators from multiple jurisdictions to share information, coordinate examinations, and develop joint crisis responses. These proved effective for global banks and should be adapted for globally significant stablecoins.

Technical cooperation including shared analytical tools, common data standards, and potentially direct regulatory access to blockchain data creates practical infrastructure for coordination. When regulators can independently verify on-chain activities using common tools, coordination becomes more feasible than when each depends on entity reporting in different formats.

Capacity building for smaller jurisdictions ensures that regulatory cooperation does not require all participants to maintain equivalent sophisticated infrastructure. Shared supervisory platforms, templated licensing frameworks, and technical assistance from international institutions like the IMF, World Bank, and Commonwealth Secretariat can enable effective participation in global coordination despite limited domestic resources.

Small and developing jurisdictions face particular challenges—they often lack resources for sophisticated regulation yet may be attractive locations for entities seeking light-touch oversight. International cooperation that provides capacity-building support while establishing minimum baseline standards helps prevent races to the bottom while enabling these jurisdictions to participate meaningfully in global markets.

The Essential Role of Innovation Support Functions

Finally, Section 5's examination of regulatory sandboxes and innovation support functions deserves emphasis in conclusion. As Buckley et al. (2020) demonstrated empirically, much of what enables successful innovation in regulated contexts comes not from formal sandbox programs but from ongoing regulatory engagement through innovation hubs and support functions.

These functions—providing pre-application guidance, facilitating connections between innovators and licensed entities, offering technical consultations on novel approaches, organizing forums for dialogue—create the knowledge flows essential for effective regulation of rapidly evolving technologies. They enable regulators to understand innovations before they scale to systemic importance, while helping innovators understand regulatory expectations before committing resources to approaches that may prove non-compliant.

Future regulatory frameworks should therefore not merely permit but actively encourage establishment of well-resourced innovation support functions. These should be recognized as core supervisory capabilities, not peripheral activities that supervisors undertake when resources allow. For jurisdictions with limited capacity, regional or international cooperation on innovation support—perhaps through shared facilities or technical assistance programs—can provide benefits that individual jurisdictions could not achieve alone.

The distinction between sandboxes (time-limited experiments with specific entities) and innovation support functions (ongoing engagement with broader ecosystems) proves important. While sandboxes serve useful purposes for testing specific approaches, innovation support functions provide the continuous dialogue, knowledge building, and relationship development that enable regulatory frameworks to evolve appropriately. Both have value, but support functions may deliver greater benefit per unit of regulatory resource invested.

Final Reflection: Licensing as Enabler of Trust and Innovation

Licensing and supervision are often portrayed as bureaucratic obstacles that innovation must overcome. This framing fundamentally misunderstands their purpose and potential. Well-designed licensing frameworks are not barriers to innovation—they are enablers of trust that allows innovation to scale responsibly.

Users adopt new financial services when they trust they will work as promised and that recourse exists if problems arise. Investors fund innovations they believe can operate sustainably under legal frameworks rather than in regulatory gray areas. Traditional financial institutions partner with new entrants they know meet baseline standards and face appropriate oversight. None of this occurs without credible regulatory frameworks that establish clear rules, ensure baseline competence and integrity, and provide mechanisms for addressing problems.

The goal is not suppressing innovation but ensuring it can scale inclusively and responsibly, underpinned by transparent governance and credible oversight. As stablecoins become more integrated into global financial systems—supporting remittances, enabling payments, facilitating commerce, potentially serving as components of monetary systems—the frameworks discussed in this chapter will serve as foundations of their long-term viability.

The choice is not between innovation and regulation. It is between chaotic, crisis-prone innovation that ultimately loses public trust and collapses under its own contradictions, versus innovation that occurs within frameworks enabling it to serve genuine public purposes while managing attendant risks. Stablecoins have potential to provide real benefits—reducing payment costs, improving financial inclusion, enabling new business models. Realizing this potential requires regulatory frameworks that protect against risks without stifling beneficial development.

The licensing and supervisory approaches outlined in this chapter—proportionate, risk-based, technologically enabled, internationally coordinated, dynamically adaptive—provide a roadmap for achieving this balance. Whether they succeed depends on continued commitment from both regulators and the stablecoin industry

REFERENCES

Arner, D. W., Barberis, J., & Buckley, R. P. (2017). FinTech, RegTech and the Reconceptualization of Financial Regulation. *Northwestern Journal of International Law & Business, 37*(3), 371–413.

Arner, D. W., Buckley, R. P., Zetzsche, D. A., & Didenko, A. (2022). *Artificial Intelligence, RegTech and Financial Inclusion.* Asian Development Bank Working Paper Series.

Basel Committee on Banking Supervision. (2012). *Core principles for effective banking supervision.* Bank for International Settlements. https://www.bis.org/publ/bcbs230.htm

Basel Committee on Banking Supervision. (2019). *Basel III: Finalising post-crisis reforms.* Bank for International Settlements. https://www.bis.org/bcbs/publ/d424.htm

Basel Committee on Banking Supervision. (2021). *Prudential treatment of cryptoasset exposures.* Bank for International Settlements. https://www.bis.org/bcbs/publ/d531.pdf

Basel Committee on Banking Supervision. (2022). *Prudential treatment of cryptoasset exposures.* Bank for International Settlements. https://www.bis.org/bcbs/publ/d545.htm

Basel Committee on Banking Supervision. (2023). *SupTech applications for crypto-asset supervision.* Bank for International Settlements.

Black, J. (2008a). Constructing and contesting legitimacy and accountability in polycentric regulatory regimes. *Regulation & Governance, 2*(2), 137–164. DOI: 10.1111/j.1748-5991.2008.00034.x

Black, J. (2008b). Forms and paradoxes of principles based regulation. *Capital Markets Law Journal, 3*(4), 425–457. DOI: 10.1093/cmlj/kmn026

Briola, A., Vidal-Tomás, D., Wang, Y., & Aste, T. (2023). Anatomy of a Stablecoin's failure: The Terra-Luna case. *Finance Research Letters, 51*, 103358. DOI: 10.1016/j.frl.2022.103358

Bromberg, L., Godwin, A., & Ramsay, I. (2022). Fintech sandboxes: Achieving a balance between regulation and innovation. *Journal of Banking Regulation, 23*(1), 71–92.

Buckley, R. P., Arner, D. W., Veidt, R., & Zetzsche, D. A. (2019). Building fintech ecosystems: Regulatory sandboxes, innovation hubs and beyond. *SSRN*, *61*, 55–98. DOI: 10.2139/ssrn.3455872

Buckley, R. P., Arner, D. W., Zetzsche, D. A., & Selga, E. (2020). The dark side of digital financial transformation: The new risks of FinTech and the rise of TechRisk. *Singapore Journal of Legal Studies*, *2020*, 423–445.

Calomiris, C. W., & Gorton, G. (1991). The Origins of Banking Panics: Models, Facts, and Bank Regulation. In Hubbard, G. (Ed.), *Financial Markets and Financial Crises* (pp. 109–173). University of Chicago Press.

Coffee, J. C. (2006). *Gatekeepers: The Professions and Corporate Governance*. Oxford University Press. DOI: 10.1093/oso/9780199288090.001.0001

Commonwealth Secretariat. (2024). *Commonwealth Model Law on Virtual Assets* (Draft). https://production-new-commonwealth-files.s3.eu-west-2.amazonaws.com/s3fs-public/2024-07/commonwealth-model-law-on-virtual-assets_d19821.pdf

European Commission. (2022). *Digital Operational Resilience Act (DORA)*. Regulation (EU) 2022/2554.

European Parliament & Council. (2023). Regulation (EU) 2023/1114 of the European Parliament and of the Council of 31 May 2023 on markets in crypto-assets, and amending Regulations (EU) No 1093/2010 and (EU) No 1095/2010 and Directives 2013/36/EU and (EU) 2019/1937 (Text with EEA relevance). *Official Journal of the European Union, L 150*, 9.6.2023, pp. 40–205. https://eur-lex.europa.eu/legal-content/EN/TXT/?uri=CELEX%3A32023R1114

Financial Action Task Force. (2021). *Updated Guidance for a Risk-Based Approach to Virtual Assets and Virtual Asset Service Providers*. FATF, Paris. https://www.fatf-gafi.org/en/publications/Fatfrecommendations/Guidance-rba-virtual-assets-2021.html

Financial Action Task Force. (2023). *Targeted Update on Implementation of the FATF Standards on Virtual Assets and Virtual Asset Service Providers*. FATF, Paris. https://www.fatf-gafi.org/en/publications/Fatfrecommendations/targeted-update-virtual-assets-vasps-2023.html

Financial Conduct Authority. (2023a). *Regulatory sandbox*. FCA.

Financial Conduct Authority. (2023b). *Financial promotions for cryptoassets*. FCA.

Financial Conduct Authority. (2023c). *Global Financial Innovation Network (GFIN).* FCA, London. https://www.fca.org.uk/firms/innovation/global-financial-innovation-network

Financial Services Agency of Japan. (2020). *Payment Services Act: Treatment of cryptoassets.* FSA Japan.

Financial Services Agency of Japan. (2022). *Payment Services Act amendments.* FSA Japan.

Financial Stability Board. (2020). *Regulation, Supervision and Oversight of "Global Stablecoin" Arrangements.* FSB, Basel. https://www.fsb.org/2020/10/regulation-supervision-and-oversight-of-global-stablecoin-arrangements/

Financial Stability Board. (2022). *Assessment of Risks to Financial Stability from Crypto-assets.* FSB.

Financial Stability Board. (2023). *High-Level Recommendations for the Regulation, Supervision and Oversight of Global Stablecoin Arrangements: Final Report.* FSB, Basel. https://www.fsb.org/2023/07/high-level-recommendations-for-the-regulation-supervision-and-oversight-of-global-stablecoin-arrangements-final-report/

Gorton, G. B., & Zhang, J. Y. (2023). Taming Wildcat Stablecoins. *The University of Chicago Law Review. University of Chicago. Law School, 90*(3), 909–974. https://chicagounbound.uchicago.edu/uclrev/vol90/iss3/3

International Monetary Fund. (2010). *Global Financial Stability Report: Meeting New Challenges to Stability and Building a Safer System.* IMF, Washington, DC. https://www.imf.org/en/Publications/GFSR/Issues/2016/12/31/Global-Financial-Stability-Report-April-2010-Meeting-New-Challenges-to-Stability-and-23794

International Monetary Fund. (2021). *The Rise of Digital Money: A Strategic Plan to Continue Delivering On The IMF's Mandate.* IMF Policy Paper 2021/054, IMF, Washington, DC. DOI: 10.5089/9781513589558.007

International Monetary Fund. (2023). *Global Financial Stability Report – Crypto: Risk, Regulation, and the Road Ahead.* IMF, Washington, DC. https://www.imf.org/en/Publications/GFSR/Issues/2023/04/11/global-financial-stability-report-april-2023

International Organization for Standardization. (2023). *ISO/TC 307 Blockchain and distributed ledger technologies.* ISO.

International Organization of Securities Commissions. (2020). *Global Stablecoin Initiatives: Consultation Report.* IOSCO, Madrid. https://www.iosco.org/library/pubdocs/pdf/IOSCOPD645.pdf

International Organization of Securities Commissions. (2021). *Principles on Outsourcing*. IOSCO.

International Organization of Securities Commissions. (2023). *Policy Recommendations for Crypto and Digital Asset Markets: Final Report.* FR03/2023, IOSCO, Madrid. https://www.iosco.org/library/pubdocs/pdf/IOSCOPD747.pdf

Llewellyn, D. (2006). Institutional structure of financial regulation and supervision: The basic issues. *World Bank seminar Aligning Supervisory Structures with Country Needs*, 6-7.

Masciandaro, D., & Quintyn, M. (2013). The governance of financial supervision: Recent developments. *Journal of Economic Surveys*, *27*(4), 734–769.

Monetary Authority of Singapore. (2019). *Payment Services Act 2019.* MAS, Singapore. https://www.mas.gov.sg/regulation/acts/payment-services-act

Monetary Authority of Singapore. (2021). *Payment Services Act 2019.* MAS, Singapore. https://www.mas.gov.sg/regulation/explainers/payment-services-act-explained

Monetary Authority of Singapore. (2023). *Regulatory framework for digital payment token services*. MAS.

Organisation for Economic Co-operation and Development. (2012). *Recommendation of the Council on Regulatory Policy and Governance*. OECD.

Potts, J. (2017). Governing the innovation commons. *Journal of Institutional Economics*, *13*(2), 249–269. DOI: 10.1017/S1744137416000448

U.S. Securities and Exchange Commission. (2023). *Framework for "Investment Contract" Analysis of Digital Assets.* SEC, Washington, DC.

Stiglitz, J. E. (1993). The Role of the State in Financial Markets. *Proceedings of the World Bank Annual Conference on Development Economics* (pp. 19–52). World Bank. DOI: 10.1093/wber/7.suppl_1.19

Treasury, H. M. (2023). *Future financial services regulatory regime for cryptoassets*. UK Government.

Zadeh, A. H. (2022). An analysis of the Terra-Luna crash and its contagion effects. SSRN *Electronic Journal.* DOI: 10.2139/ssrn.4145551

Zetzsche, D. A., Arner, D. W., & Buckley, R. P. (2020a). Decentralized Finance. *Journal of Financial Regulation*, *6*(2), 172–203. DOI: 10.1093/jfr/fjaa010

Zetzsche, D. A., Buckley, R. P., & Arner, D. W. (2020b). Regulating Libra: The Transformative Potential of Facebook's Cryptocurrency and Possible Regulatory Responses. *European Banking Institute Working Paper Series* 2020/45. https://ssrn.com/abstract=3414401

Zetzsche, D. A., Buckley, R. P., Arner, D. W., & Barberis, J. N. (2017). Regulating a revolution: From regulatory sandboxes to smart regulation. *SSRN*, *23*(1), 31–103. DOI: 10.2139/ssrn.3018534

Chapter 10
How to Implement a Stablecoin Framework

Maxine L. Binns
Commonwealth Secretariat, UK

ABSTRACT

This chapter outlines the legal and institutional process required to implement virtual asset legislation—including stablecoins—with a focus on jurisdictions adopting the Commonwealth Secretariat's Model Laws. It presents a modular, principle-based approach to legislative design, emphasising legal clarity, proportionality, and adaptability. Drawing on comparative practices and implementation case studies, the chapter explores how governments can translate conceptual ambition into enforceable law—through legal scoping, stakeholder engagement, modular drafting, and capacity-building. The goal is to equip policymakers, legal drafters, and institutional leaders with a roadmap for embedding digital asset frameworks into domestic law while preserving sovereignty, enabling innovation, and ensuring cross-border coherence.

EXECUTIVE OVERVIEW

This chapter presents a practical roadmap for Commonwealth member countries seeking to implement a virtual asset (VA) legal and regulatory regime using the Model Laws, as guidance. Anchored in legal pluralism (Harper, 2011) and modular design, the framework enables governments to legislate with precision, flexibility, and strategic foresight—without compromising local legal traditions or institutional realities.

The chapter begins by outlining six key phases of legislative implementation: legal scoping, stakeholder consultation, modular drafting, institutional capacity-

DOI: 10.4018/979-8-3373-6655-5.ch010

building, pilot deployment, and iterative reform. Each phase offers jurisdictions a step-by-step guide to translating the Model Laws into enforceable, usable, and context-sensitive legislation. From mapping existing statutes to stress-testing legal provisions for enforceability, the implementation process is framed as a dynamic act of legal stewardship.

To support operational clarity, the chapter then examines five core provisions of the Model Laws—licensing, redemption, consumer protection, enforcement, and cross-border recognition. These provisions are unpacked in detail, with guidance on how to adapt them to domestic systems, anticipate institutional dependencies, and navigate common challenges. The emphasis throughout is on usability: making the law not only technically sound, but accessible to regulators, practitioners, and users alike.

Recognising that implementation is rarely linear, the chapter concludes by addressing legal challenges and controversies that may arise. These include definitional ambiguity, institutional overlap, political resistance, and cross-border friction. Rather than treating these as obstacles, the chapter frames them as opportunities for refinement, dialogue, and adaptive reform.

Taken together, this chapter equips the Commonwealth jurisdictions with the tools, insights, and strategic framing needed to implement stablecoin legislation responsibly and effectively. It reinforces the principle that legal modernisation is not a one-time event but also an ongoing process—one that demands clarity, collaboration, and a commitment to resilience.

INTRODUCTION

This chapter is written for those tasked with the real work of implementation—legislators, legal drafters, and institutional actors charged with translating the Model Laws into enforceable, context-sensitive legislation. At the same time, it remains intelligible to a broader audience: scholars, civil society advocates, and policy observers seeking to understand the rationale behind the Commonwealth model law frameworks and the strategic choices that shaped their architecture.

Stablecoin legislation is not merely a regulatory exercise; it is a foundational act of legal stewardship in the digital age. The rise of virtual assets, including stablecoins, has prompted a global wave of legislative activity. Yet for many jurisdictions—particularly those navigating developmental constraints or institutional fragmentation—the challenge is not simply to regulate but to legislate with precision, flexibility, and foresight. The Model Laws offer a blueprint for doing so: a modular legal framework that enables jurisdictions to adopt tailored provisions while aligning with international standards (Financial Action Task Force, 2012; Financial Stability

Board, 2023; The International Organization of Securities Commissions, 2023). Implementation requires a coordinated process spanning legal diagnostics, stakeholder mapping, statutory drafting, institutional readiness, and iterative refinement.

Each phase must be grounded in the realities of the member country—its legal traditions, technological infrastructure, regulatory capacity, and economic priorities. The modular structure of the Model Law allow for phased adoption, enabling governments to legislate at their pace while maintaining interoperability with global norms.

This chapter explores that process in detail. It begins by examining the legal rationale behind modular legislation, then walks through the steps required to translate model provisions into enforceable domestic law. Along the way, it highlights key challenges—such as definitional ambiguity, institutional gaps, and cross-border enforcement—and offers strategies for overcoming them. The aim is to provide a practical, legally grounded roadmap for jurisdictions seeking to embed virtual asset and stablecoin frameworks into their national legal systems.

Why a Non-Prescriptive, Modular Approach Was Essential

The Model Laws were deliberately designed to avoid prescriptive legal transplants from any single jurisdiction—including the United Kingdom. This intention reflects both principled and practical considerations. The Commonwealth comprises fifty-six member countries or member countries with diverse legal traditions, spanning common law, civil law, mixed systems, and customary frameworks. Imposing a framework rooted in one country's legal architecture would risk incompatibility with domestic laws, institutional mandates, and constitutional norms across the membership.

For instance, transplanting UK-style enforcement mechanisms into a civil law jurisdiction such as Rwanda or Cameroon could conflict with procedural safeguards or judicial structures built on entirely different premises. Likewise, the UK's Financial Conduct Authority operates within a mature regulatory ecosystem with substantial resources and technical capacity (the Financial Services Act 2021). Replicating its supervisory model in smaller or emerging Commonwealth economies could overwhelm local institutions or misalign with existing mandates.

Instead, the Model Laws adopt a principle-based, modular design that enables jurisdictions to tailor implementation to their contexts. Member states can adjust licensing thresholds, integrate the framework with existing financial and consumer protection laws, scale obligations according to institutional capacity and, at the same time, adhere to international standards (Commonwealth Secretariat, 2024).

Prescriptive laws frequently fail when imported frameworks lack legitimacy among local stakeholders, when enforcement mechanisms are impractical due to resource limitations, or when terminology and concepts are foreign to domestic legal traditions. . A UK-style sandbox regime, for example, may be effective in London, but in a jurisdiction without a robust fintech ecosystem, it could be premature or poorly utilised.

By avoiding prescriptiveness, the Commonwealth Secretariat has empowered member states to co-create their own digital asset regimes. This fosters innovation, encourages legal stewardship, and promotes resilience by allowing experimentation within a safe legal perimeter. It is especially vital for small island states and emerging markets, where stablecoins may serve critical roles in remittances, savings preservation, or financial inclusion—functions that differ markedly from their use in advanced economies. In these contexts, legal stewardship is not just technical—it is a form of economic sovereignty (United Nations Conference on Trade and Development, 2023).

Examples of Successful Adaptable Legal Frameworks

The Model Laws draw inspiration from a lineage of adaptable legal frameworks that have proven effective across jurisdictions. These frameworks succeed not by prescribing uniform rules, but by offering principle-based guidance that can be tailored to local legal traditions, institutional capacities, and policy priorities (Commonwealth Secretariat, 2024).

One prominent example is the suite of model laws developed by the United Nations Commission on International Trade Law (UNCITRAL). The Model Law on International Commercial Arbitration, for instance, has been adopted in over eighty jurisdictions—both common law and civil law—with each country customising its provisions to fit domestic procedural norms. Similarly, UNCITRAL's Model Law on Electronic Commerce has guided digital transaction legislation globally, enabling countries to modernise their laws without abandoning foundational legal principles.

The Basel Core Principles for Effective Banking Supervision, issued by the Basel Committee on Banking Supervision, offer another adaptable framework (Basel Committee on Banking Supervision, 2012; Melo et al., 2024). These principles are scalable, allowing countries with varying levels of financial sector development to strengthen oversight without replicating the full Basel III architecture. Kenya and Bangladesh, for example, have tailored these principles to suit their regulatory environments while maintaining alignment with international standards (K.B.M & Zayed, 2018; Upadhyaya, 2017).

The Financial Action Task Force (FATF) Recommendations on anti-money laundering and counter-terrorist financing provide further precedent. FATF emphasises a risk-based approach, allowing countries to calibrate their controls based on exposure and capacity. Jurisdictions such as Vanuatu and Mauritius have implemented FATF principles in ways that reflect their unique financial ecosystems and vulnerabilities, demonstrating the value of flexible, context-sensitive regulation (Asia/Pacific Group on Money Laundering, 2018; Eastern and Southern Africa Anti-Money Laundering Group, 2022; Financial Action Task Force, 2012).

In the realm of disaster law, the International Federation of Red Cross and Red Crescent Societies (IFRC) has developed adaptable legal frameworks that support national preparedness and response (International Federation of Red Cross and Red Crescent Societies, 2021a). Countries like the Philippines and Fiji have successfully integrated these frameworks into domestic law, enhancing coordination and legal mandates during emergencies (International Federation of Red Cross and Red Crescent Societies, 2021b; International Federation of Red Cross and Red Crescent Societies & University College Cork, 2021).

Finally, the Commonwealth Cybercrime Model Law, adopted in 2002, provides a direct precedent for the stablecoin initiative. Like the Stablecoin Model Law, it avoids prescriptiveness and supports modular adoption. Trinidad and Tobago, for example, adapted the cybercrime model to fit its existing criminal code while aligning with international norms—demonstrating how principle-based frameworks can facilitate legal modernisation without imposing rigid templates (Central Bank of Trinidad and Tobago, 2019; Commonwealth Secretariat, 2002; United Nations Conference on Trade and Development, 2025).

These examples underscore the value of adaptable legal frameworks for promoting harmonisation, resilience, and local ownership. They offer a compelling rationale for the Commonwealth Secretariat's decision to pursue a modular, principle-based approach to stablecoin legislation—one that respects legal pluralism while enabling innovation and stewardship across its diverse membership.

Table 1. Comparative dashboard: Adaptable legal frameworks

Framework	Issuing Body	Legal Modality	Adaptability Features	Jurisdictional Reach	Use Case Examples
UNCITRAL Model Law on Arbitration	UN Commission on International Trade Law	Model Law (non-binding)	Principle-based; modular adoption; compatible with civil and common law systems	80+ jurisdictions	India, Singapore, and Nigeria each adapted procedural rules to fit domestic legal culture.
FATF Recommendations (AML/CFT)	Financial Action Task Force	Soft Law / Global Standard	Risk-based implementation; flexible thresholds; tailored to national risk profiles	200+ jurisdictions via FATF & FSRBs	Mauritius and Vanuatu contextualised controls for offshore finance and remittance flows
Basel Core Principles	Basel Committee on Banking Supervision	Global Principles	Scalable supervision standards; tiered application based on financial sector maturity	Global (esp. IMF/WB member states)	Kenya and Bangladesh adopted proportional oversight for banking sector resilience.

continued on following page

Table 1. Continued

Framework	Issuing Body	Legal Modality	Adaptability Features	Jurisdictional Reach	Use Case Examples
IFRC Disaster Law Frameworks	International Federation of Red Cross	Model Guidelines / Templates	Modular legal preparedness; adaptable to emergency governance structures	30+ jurisdictions	Fiji and the Philippines integrated disaster protocols into national emergency laws.
Commonwealth Cybercrime Model Law	Commonwealth Secretariat	Model Law (non-binding)	Modular provisions; interoperable with existing criminal codes; supports regional harmonisation	Multiple Commonwealth states	Trinidad & Tobago customised provisions to fit domestic criminal procedure.

Strategic Framing for Seamless Transition

This principle-based, non-prescriptive architecture is not merely a theoretical preference—it is a strategic enabler of implementation. By allowing jurisdictions to tailor modules to their legal traditions, institutional capacities, and policy priorities, the Model Laws creates space for phased, context-sensitive adoption (Commonwealth Secretariat, 2024). The following section outlines the key phases through which member states can operationalise the framework, ensuring both legal coherence and practical feasibility.

KEY PHASES OF LEGISLATIVE IMPLEMENTATION

Implementing stablecoin legislation is a layered process requiring legal precision, institutional coordination, and strategic sequencing. For jurisdictions adopting the Model Laws, this process is modular by design—enabling governments to tailor adoption to their legal traditions, economic priorities, and technological capacity. The following phases outline a practical roadmap for translating model provisions into enforceable domestic law.

Phase 1: Legal Scoping and Framework Alignment

Implementation begins with a deliberate, context-sensitive legal scoping exercise. This foundational phase determines whether, how, and where the Model Laws can be integrated into a jurisdiction's existing legal architecture. Legal scoping is not merely a technical audit—it is a strategic inquiry into constitutional frameworks, statutory landscapes, institutional mandates, and regulatory culture.

Jurisdictions should start by mapping current laws and regulations that intersect with digital assets, payments, financial services, and consumer protection (Commonwealth Secretariat, 2024). This includes identifying existing definitions of virtual assets, electronic money, or digital tokens, and reviewing licensing regimes, reserve requirements, and enforcement protocols. The goal is to surface overlaps, contradictions, or gaps that may affect adoption of the Model Law modules.

Constitutional compatibility must also be assessed. In some jurisdictions, introducing a new licensing category or delegating regulatory powers may require parliamentary approval, constitutional amendment, or judicial review (Commonwealth Secretariat, 2024). Legal scoping should therefore include analysis of enabling clauses, legislative authority, and the division of powers across governmental and non-governmental actors. In federal systems, coordination with state or provincial legislatures may be required to ensure harmonious implementation.

Institutional mandates must be clarified. Implementing legislation often engages multiple agencies—central banks, financial regulators, consumer protection bodies, and cybersecurity authorities (Gail, 2007). Legal scoping should identify which institutions are best positioned to lead implementation, which require capacity-building, and where inter-agency coordination mechanisms must be established. This includes reviewing statutory mandates, rulemaking authority, and enforcement jurisdiction.

Member countries may benefit from conducting a legal readiness assessment—a structured tool that evaluates the maturity of legal infrastructure, institutional capacity, and stakeholder alignment (Commonwealth Secretariat, 2024). These assessments can be developed internally or with support from regional bodies or the Commonwealth Secretariat. They help determine whether to adopt the Model Laws in full, in part, or through phased integration.

Legal scoping also provides an opportunity for early stakeholder engagement. By consulting legal practitioners, industry actors, civil society, and academic experts at this stage, governments can identify practical concerns, anticipate resistance, and build legitimacy (Harper, 2011). This engagement lays the groundwork for the consultation phase and signals a commitment to inclusive legal design.

Ultimately, legal scoping is not a box-ticking exercise—it is a strategic act of legal stewardship. It ensures that the Model Laws are not merely transplanted but thoughtfully adapted, aligned with domestic realities, and positioned for sustainable implementation.

Phase 2: Stakeholder Consultation

Building on the legal and institutional mapping conducted in Phase 1, this phase turns outward to engage stakeholders who will shape, interpret, and operationalise the framework. Stakeholder consultation is not a procedural formality—it is a substantive exercise in pluralist governance. It ensures that the stablecoin framework is not only technically sound but socially legitimate, politically feasible, and institutionally grounded (Commonwealth Secretariat, 2024).

Consultation must reflect the jurisdiction's legal culture and governance model. In some contexts, this may involve formal public hearings or parliamentary committee sessions; in others, sectoral roundtables, town halls, or targeted interviews with key actors (Organisation for Economic Co-operation and Development, 2020). Regardless of format, the goal is to surface diverse perspectives, identify operational concerns, and build consensus around the framework's core provisions.

A pluralist approach requires engaging a wide spectrum of stakeholders—financial institutions, fintech startups, consumer advocacy groups, legal practitioners, academic experts, civil society organisations, and, where relevant, traditional authorities or customary legal actors. Each group brings distinct insights into how stablecoins function in practice, how risks are perceived, and how legal protections are understood. Their input helps ensure the framework is not only enforceable but also usable.

Jurisdictions should also engage cross-sectoral regulators—such as central banks, securities commissions, data protection authorities, and competition regulators—to ensure coherence across institutional mandates (The International Organization of Securities Commissions, 2023). This is especially important in environments where digital assets intersect with multiple regulatory domains. Early coordination can prevent fragmentation and reduce the risk of conflicting interpretations.

Consultation should be iterative, not episodic. Initial feedback may inform the drafting of preliminary modules, which can then be circulated for further review. Sandbox regimes and pilot programmes can serve as live consultation platforms, allowing regulators to observe market behaviour and gather real-time feedback (Financial Conduct Authority, 2024). These mechanisms help refine technical standards, clarify definitions, and test enforcement protocols before full-scale implementation.

Transparency is essential. Governments should publish consultation summaries, explain how feedback was incorporated, and clarify why certain recommendations were not adopted (Gail, 2007). This builds trust and reinforces the legitimacy of the process. It also creates a public record that can inform future reforms and comparative analysis.

In Commonwealth jurisdictions, stakeholder consultation is particularly vital given the diversity of legal traditions, economic structures, and institutional capacities. A well-designed consultation process respects this diversity while fostering shared ownership of the legal framework. It transforms implementation from a top-down exercise into a collaborative act of legal modernisation.

Ultimately, stakeholder consultation is where legal pluralism becomes operational. It ensures that the stablecoin framework is not imposed but co-created—reflecting the lived realities of those who will regulate, use, and be protected by it.

Phase 3: Modular Drafting and Legal Integration

With legal scoping completed and stakeholder perspectives gathered, jurisdictions enter the core technical phase of implementation: modular drafting. This phase involves selecting, adapting, and sequencing components of the Model Laws to fit the jurisdiction's legal architecture, policy priorities, and institutional capacity. It is here that the principle of modularity becomes operational—enabling legislation that is precise, flexible, and strategically grounded.

It is essential to stress that modular drafting is not a simple "cut and paste" exercise. While the Model Laws provide ready-to-use modules—covering licensing, redemption, consumer protection, enforcement, and cross-border recognition—each must be carefully adapted to the jurisdiction's legal architecture (Commonwealth Secretariat, 2024). This process often requires multiple redrafts over extended periods, as governments work through constitutional constraints, institutional mandates, and stakeholder concerns. Coordination between legal drafters, regulators, and parliamentary counsel is essential to avoid duplication, contradiction, or gaps.

Modular drafting begins with a decision on scope. Jurisdictions must determine which modules are immediately relevant, which require adaptation, and which may be deferred for future integration. For example, a jurisdiction with an existing licensing regime for payment service providers may adopt only reserve management and redemption modules, while another may prioritise consumer protection and cross-border provisions. Selective adoption ensures the framework complements—rather than disrupts—existing legal structures.

Adaptation is equally critical. Each module must be reviewed for compatibility with domestic terminology, institutional mandates, and enforcement mechanisms. Definitions may need to be aligned with local statutes while remaining interoperable with international standards, licensing thresholds adjusted to reflect market size, and supervisory powers tailored to the jurisdiction's legal culture (The International Organization of Securities Commissions, 2023). In some cases, modules may be merged with existing legislation or enacted as standalone instruments. The goal is not uniformity, but coherence.

Legal structuring must be deliberate and internally consistent. Each module should be drafted with clear definitions, enforceable provisions, and logical sequencing that supports both interpretation and application. For example, stablecoins must be clearly distinguished from other digital assets, such as cryptocurrencies or central bank digital currencies (CBDCs) (Financial Stability Board, 2023b). Definitions should reflect domestic terminology while remaining interoperable with international standards. Jurisdictions should also consider how the stablecoin framework interacts with broader legislative instruments, ensuring seamless integration without ambiguity or duplication.

Drafting should also anticipate legal layering. Stablecoin legislation often intersects with securities law, banking law, data protection, and consumer rights. Modular drafting allows jurisdictions to embed cross-references, enabling clauses, and transitional provisions that facilitate integration across these domains. Such structural tools help ensure the law is not only technically sound but operationally usable. For example, a provision on reserve disclosure may reference existing financial reporting standards, while a clause on smart contract enforceability may draw on electronic transactions legislation.

Jurisdictions may choose to embed modules within existing legislation (e.g., financial services acts or payment systems laws) or enact standalone statutes. Each approach has advantages. Integration may streamline enforcement and reduce legislative burden, while standalone laws can offer greater visibility and thematic coherence. The choice depends on institutional capacity, legal tradition, and political feasibility.

To support usability and transparency, jurisdictions may benefit from developing annotated drafts—versions of the legislation that include commentary, rationale, and implementation notes. These annotations clarify legislative intent, guide judicial interpretation, and support training for regulators and legal practitioners. They also serve as a bridge between technical drafters and policy stakeholders, reinforcing shared understanding (Commonwealth Secretariat, 2024).

Importantly, modular drafting should be iterative. Preliminary drafts should be circulated for review, tested through sandbox environments, and revised based on feedback. This process allows jurisdictions to refine language, resolve ambiguities, and ensure operational usability. It also builds institutional confidence and stakeholder buy-in—essential ingredients for successful implementation.

In Commonwealth contexts, modular drafting offers a pathway to legal modernisation without disrupting the law. It respects pluralism, enables phased reform, and empowers jurisdictions to legislate at their own pace. By treating each module as a building block rather than a mandate, governments can construct stablecoin frameworks that are both principled and practical.

As emphasised in the Commonwealth Legislative Drafting Manual, effective legislation must be "clear, coherent, and contextually appropriate"—qualities that emerge not from replication, but from deliberate design, redrafting, and legal stewardship (Rose, 2017).

Ultimately, modular drafting is a process of legal craftsmanship. It requires time, iteration, and strategic coordination—not just technical skill, but institutional patience and political will. By combining modular design with plain-language drafting and stakeholder-informed integration, jurisdictions can create stablecoin legislation that is enforceable, inclusive, and future-ready.

Phase 4: Institutional Capacity-Building

Even the most carefully drafted legislation will falter without the institutional capacity to implement, supervise, and enforce it. Phase 4 focuses on equipping relevant authorities—regulators, supervisors, adjudicators, and support agencies with the tools, knowledge, and coordination mechanisms required to operationalise the stablecoin framework effectively.

Capacity-building begins with a clear delineation of institutional roles. As stated previously, stablecoin legislation often spans multiple agencies, including central banks, financial services commissions, consumer protection bodies, cybersecurity authorities, and data regulators. Jurisdictions must clarify which entity leads implementation, which ones support it, and how inter-agency coordination will be structured. This may involve formal memoranda of understanding, joint supervisory protocols, or shared data platform.

Training is essential. Regulators and supervisors must understand not only the legal provisions but also the technological underpinnings of stablecoins—such as reserve mechanisms, smart contracts, and distributed ledger systems. Judicial actors, including magistrates and appellate judges, may be sensitised to new legal concepts and dispute resolution pathways. Training programmes should be tailored to each institution's mandate and delivered through workshops, online modules, or peer exchanges (Commonwealth Secretariat, 2024).

Technical assistance can play a catalytic role. Commonwealth member states may benefit from support provided by the Secretariat, regional bodies, or international organisations. This assistance may include model regulations, supervisory toolkits, legal commentary, and implementation dashboards. It can also facilitate access to global best practices and comparative insights from other jurisdictions (Commonwealth Secretariat, 2024).

Institutional readiness must also be assessed. Some agencies may require upgrades to IT systems, staffing models, or legal databases to accommodate the new framework. Others may need to establish new units or task forces dedicated to digital asset oversight. These structural adjustments should be planned in parallel with legislative drafting to avoid implementation delays caused by institutional bottlenecks.

Capacity-building is not limited to government. Industry actors—such as stablecoin issuers, custodians, and payment platforms—must be educated on their obligations, licensing pathways, and compliance expectations. Civil society organisations and consumer advocates should be empowered to monitor implementation, raise concerns, and contribute to public awareness. A well-informed ecosystem strengthens accountability and reinforces the legitimacy of the legal framework (Harper, 2011; Organisation for Economic Co-operation and Development, 2020).

In pluralist jurisdictions, capacity-building must be inclusive. Where customary laws or decentralised governance structures exist, training and sensitisation should extend to traditional authorities and community leaders. This ensures the framework is understood and respected across all layers of society—not just within formal institutions (The International Organization of Securities Commissions, 2023).

Ultimately, institutional capacity-building is the bridge between law and practice. It transforms legislative intent into operational reality—enabling jurisdictions to supervise stablecoin activity with confidence, competence, and credibility.

Phase 5: Pilot Deployment and Legal Stress Testing

Before full-scale implementation, jurisdictions should consider pilot deployment as a strategic bridge between legislative design and operational reality. This phase enables governments to test the framework's functionality, observe market behaviour, and refine enforcement protocols in a controlled environment. Pilot deployment is not a trial run—it is a deliberate exercise in legal calibration, institutional learning, and stakeholder engagement.

Sandbox regimes are a common vehicle for pilot deployment. These regulatory test environments allow selected entities—such as stablecoin issuers, custodians, or payment platforms—to operate under modified compliance conditions while regulators monitor performance (Financial Conduct Authority, 2024). Jurisdictions such as Hong Kong and Bermuda have implemented sandbox regimes specifically tailored to stablecoin innovation. Bermuda's framework, administered under the Digital Asset Business Act (DABA), includes structured consultation phases, embedded supervision pilots, and guidance for fiat-pegged stablecoins. These regimes offer valuable insights into how the law interacts with technology, business models, and user behaviour. Sandboxes may be structured as time-bound programmes, thematic cohorts, or rolling admissions, depending on the jurisdiction's capacity and policy objectives. They provide invaluable understanding of how the law interacts with technology, business models, and user behaviour.

Jurisdictions may also conduct phased rollouts, enacting specific modules of the law in stages. For example, reserve management and redemption provisions may be implemented first, followed by licensing and consumer protection rules. This sequencing enables institutions to build capacity incrementally and reduces the risk of systemic disruption. It also allows regulators to adjust supervisory protocols based on early feedback.

Pilot deployment also functions as a form of legal stress testing. By observing how the framework responds to edge cases—such as redemption delays, reserve volatility, or jurisdictional disputes—regulators can identify structural vulnerabilities and refine provisions before full-scale implementation (The European Parliament and the Council of the European Union, 2023). These stress points may expose gaps in enforcement protocols, inconsistencies in statutory language, or coordination challenges between agencies. Addressing these issues early strengthens the framework's resilience and enhances institutional readiness (Gail, 2007).

Pilot deployment should be accompanied by clear eligibility criteria, performance benchmarks, and exit strategies. Participants must understand the scope of the pilot, the conditions under which it operates, and the expectations for compliance. Regulators, in turn, must establish mechanisms for data collection, risk assessment, and feedback integration. These mechanisms help identify legal ambiguities, operational bottlenecks, and unintended consequences before the framework is scaled.

Feedback loops are essential. Regulators should convene post-pilot reviews with participants, observers, and independent experts to evaluate outcomes and recommend adjustments (Financial Stability Board, 2022; The International Organization of Securities Commissions, 2023). These reviews may lead to revisions in statutory language, updates to technical standards, or the issuance of interpretive guidance. In some cases, pilot findings may inform the development of supplementary regulations or supervisory handbooks.

Pilot deployment also serves a political function. It demonstrates the government's commitment to innovation, responsiveness, and evidence-based policymaking. It builds public confidence in the framework and signals to international partners that the jurisdiction is taking a measured, strategic approach to digital asset legislation.

In the Commonwealth context, pilot deployment offers a pathway for member states with limited resources to engage with stablecoin regulation without overcommitting institutional capacity. It enables experimentation, learning, and adaptation—hallmarks of resilient legal systems. By treating pilot deployment as a core phase of implementation rather than a peripheral exercise, jurisdictions can ensure that their stablecoin frameworks are not only legislated but lived.

Phase 6: Monitoring, Evaluation, and Iterative Reform

The final phase of implementation is not a conclusion—it marks the beginning of continuous legal stewardship. Stablecoin legislation must be treated as a living framework, capable of evolving in response to technological innovation, market behaviour, and societal needs. This requires jurisdictions to embed robust mechanisms for monitoring, evaluation, and reform within the legal architecture itself.

Monitoring begins with the identification of key performance indicators that reflect the law's intended outcomes, such as issuer classification, reserve integrity, and enforcement metrics. These indicators should be tailored to the jurisdiction's economic context and institutional capacity, but certain metrics are broadly applicable. For example, the percentage of stablecoin issuers correctly classified under statutory definitions reflects the clarity and usability of the legal taxonomy. Enforcement metrics—such as the ratio of regulatory actions to licenced entities—can signal whether oversight is proportionate and effective. Reserve integrity may be tracked through the frequency and transparency of audits, while redemption efficiency can be measured by average processing times for fiat conversion.

Consumer protection outcomes may be assessed through the number of complaints resolved via statutory mechanisms, offering insight into the accessibility and legitimacy of legal recourse. Innovation uptake can be gauged by the number of sandbox participants or pilot projects launched under enabling clauses (Commonwealth Secretariat, 2024; Jean-Noel II, 2025).

Cross-border activity, such as transaction volumes involving foreign jurisdictions, reveals the framework's interoperability. Stakeholder engagement should also be monitored—both in terms of frequency and diversity of consultation events—to ensure pluralism is not merely aspirational but operational. Finally, the number of judicial decisions citing the stablecoin law provides a proxy for legal integration and jurisprudential clarity.

Evaluation must go beyond metrics. Jurisdictions should solicit feedback from issuers, users, regulators, civil society, and technical experts. This can be achieved through periodic consultations, public hearings, and targeted surveys. Commonwealth member states may also benefit from peer learning platforms, where jurisdictions share implementation experiences, challenges, and innovations. These exchanges help surface blind spots and foster regional coherence (The Committee on Payments and Market Infrastructures, 2023).

Reform should be triggered not only by performance shortfalls but also by structural shifts in the ecosystem. Technological developments—such as the emergence of synthetic or multi-asset stablecoins—may require updates to definitions and licensing modules (Financial Action Task Force, 2021). Market disruptions, including issuer insolvency or mass redemption events, should prompt a review of reserve requirements and insolvency protocols. Regulatory conflicts—where stablecoin provisions overlap or contradict securities or banking laws—necessitate harmonisation and interpretive guidance.

Cross-border friction, such as disputes over jurisdiction or enforcement, may trigger the negotiation of mutual recognition agreements or legal assistance protocols. Judicial ambiguity—where courts expose gaps or contradictions—should lead to statutory amendments or clarifying regulations. Stakeholder feedback, especially when recurring concerns emerge from users or civil society, must be taken seriously and addressed through consultative reform. Updates to global standards—such as new guidance from FATF, IOSCO, or BIS—should be mirrored in domestic law to maintain alignment (The Committee on Payments and Market Infrastructures, 2023;

Financial Action Task Force, 2023; The International Organization of Securities Commissions, 2023).

To support this process, jurisdictions should embed enabling clauses that authorise regulators to revise technical standards, adjust licensing thresholds, and adapt governance requirements as the ecosystem evolves. Sunset provisions may be used to phase out temporary rules, while review clauses can mandate formal reassessment at regular intervals. In some cases, jurisdictions may establish standing committees or digital asset commissions tasked with overseeing reform and advising Parliament or Cabinet.

The Commonwealth Secretariat can play a catalytic role in supporting reform. Through technical assistance, model amendments, and regional coordination, it can help member states align domestic updates with global developments. This ensures that reform is not only reactive but anticipatory—enabling jurisdictions to stay ahead of emerging risks and opportunities.

Ultimately, monitoring and reform are not peripheral tasks—they are central to the legitimacy and resilience of stablecoin legislation. By embedding feedback loops, stress testing protocols, and adaptive legal mechanisms, jurisdictions can ensure that their frameworks remain fit for purpose in a rapidly changing digital landscape.

OPERATIONALISING KEY PROVISIONS OF THE MODEL LAWS

Licensing and Registration: Legal Foundations and Enforcement Architecture

Licensing and registration provisions form the legal gateway to stablecoin regulation. They establish the perimeter of lawful activity, define the entities subject to oversight, and anchor the framework in enforceable statutory authority. In the Model Laws, these provisions are not merely procedural—they are foundational instruments of legal identity, accountability, and public protection.

From a legislative perspective, licensing must be treated as a statutory obligation, not a discretionary privilege. The law should clearly define the scope of regulated activities—such as issuance, custody, redemption, and platform operation—and specify which entities are required to obtain a licence. This includes natural persons, legal entities, and, where applicable, decentralised arrangements that meet defined thresholds for control or risk.

Eligibility criteria must be codified in statute, including requirements related to legal form, governance structure, reserve backing, and fit-and-proper assessments. The licensing authority—typically a financial regulator or central bank—should be granted explicit powers to grant, suspend, revoke, or condition licences, subject to procedural safeguards and judicial review. These powers must be exercised transparently and proportionately, with clear timelines, appeal mechanisms, and public disclosure obligations.

Registration complements licensing by creating a public record of authorised entities. Jurisdictions may establish digital registries, searchable databases, or licensing dashboards that enable users, counterparties, and regulators to verify compliance. These tools support market integrity and reduce the risk of fraud or misrepresentation.

Legal consequences for operating without a licence must be embedded directly in the legislation. These may include civil penalties, administrative sanctions, and, in serious cases, criminal liability. Unlicenced entities may be subject to cease-and-desist orders, asset freezes, and injunctions. They may also lose legal standing in contractual disputes, rendering their agreements unenforceable in court. These consequences must be proportionate to the risk posed and consistent with constitutional protections.

International standards reinforce the importance of licensing as a legal safeguard. The FSB, IOSCO, and FATF all recommend that stablecoin issuers be subject to "comprehensive regulatory oversight", including licensing and supervision as a prerequisite for AML compliance, consumer protection, and systemic risk mitigation (The Committee on Payments and Market Infrastructures 2023; Financial Action Task Force, 2021; The International Organization of Securities Commissions, 2023). Jurisdictions that fail to implement robust licensing regimes may face reputational harm, reduced interoperability, and diminished access to cross-border recognition frameworks.

To support implementation, jurisdictions may develop annotated application forms, licensing guidance notes, and transitional provisions for legacy entities. These tools help clarify legislative intent, reduce administrative burden, and ensure that licensing is not only enforceable but also accessible.

Ultimately, licensing and registration provisions are the legal scaffolding of the stablecoin framework. They define who may operate, under what conditions, and with what consequences. By embedding these provisions in statute and aligning them with global standards, jurisdictions can build a regulatory perimeter that is clear, credible, and resilient.

Redemption Rights and Reserve Management

Redemption rights and reserve management are the legal pillars that uphold the promise of stablecoin value. Together, they ensure that users can convert digital tokens into fiat currency reliably and that those tokens are backed by verifiable, high-quality assets. In the Commonwealth Model Laws, these provisions are not technical appendices—they are central statutory guarantees that must be drafted with clarity, enforceability, and resilience in mind.

Redemption Rights

Redemption rights must be codified as enforceable entitlements. Users should have a clear statutory right to redeem stablecoins for fiat currency under defined conditions. The legislation should specify:

- The timeframe within which redemption must occur (e.g., on demand, within 24 or 48 hours)
- The entities responsible for fulfilling redemption obligations (e.g., issuers, custodians, authorised agents)
- The channels through which redemption may be executed (e.g., bank transfer, mobile money, in-person cash-out)
- The procedural safeguards available to users in cases of delay, denial, or dispute

These rights must be framed as statutory obligations, not discretionary promises. Failure to honour redemption may constitute breach of fiduciary duty, misrepresentation, or unjust enrichment—triggering civil liability, regulatory enforcement, and reputational harm. In cases of issuer insolvency, jurisdictions should ensure that redemption claims are prioritised in asset recovery proceedings, supported by clear insolvency protocols and reserve segregation rules.

International standards reinforce this approach. The FSB calls for redemption mechanisms that are "timely, transparent, and enforceable", while BIS emphasises the need for legal certainty in redemption pathways, especially in cross-border contexts (Crisanto et al., 2024). MiCA regulation similarly mandates that users be able to redeem stablecoins at par value, with clear disclosures and complaint-handling procedures.

Reserve Management

Reserve management provisions ensure that stablecoins are backed by assets of sufficient quality, liquidity, and transparency. These provisions must be embedded in statute and subject to independent verification. Key legislative elements include:

- Minimum reserve ratios and asset composition requirements (e.g., cash, government securities, short-term deposits)
- Segregation of reserve assets from operating funds and proprietary investments

- Frequency and scope of independent audits, conducted by licenced professionals
- Disclosure obligations to regulators and the public, including real-time reserve snapshots and audit summaries

The law should also specify enforcement mechanisms for reserve breaches. These may include administrative penalties, licence suspension, mandatory remediation plans, and—in cases of fraud or concealment—criminal liability. Reserve mismanagement undermines financial stability and consumer trust and may expose issuers to claims of negligent misstatement, breach of statutory duty, or systemic risk creation.

Global frameworks support robust reserve oversight. The FSB's high-level recommendations call for "comprehensive supervision of reserve assets, including valuation, custody, and liquidity risk" (Financial Stability Board, 2023). The SEC's proposed stablecoin framework in the United States mandates full reserve backing and periodic disclosures (Jean-Noel II, 2025), while MiCA requires issuers to maintain reserves in segregated accounts and submit to regular audits (Katz, 2023).

Legal Integration and Enforcement

To ensure enforceability, redemption and reserve provisions should be embedded in primary legislation, supported by enabling clauses that authorise regulators to issue technical standards, conduct inspections, and initiate enforcement proceedings. Judicial remedies—such as injunctions, damages, and declaratory relief—should be available to users and regulators alike.

Jurisdictions may also consider developing annotated drafts, visual overlays, and supervisory dashboards to track reserve adequacy and redemption performance. These tools support transparency, institutional readiness, and public confidence.

Ultimately, redemption rights and reserve management are not just regulatory mechanisms—they are legal guarantees of value, trust, and accountability. By embedding these provisions in enforceable law and aligning them with international standards, jurisdictions can build stablecoin frameworks that are resilient, transparent, and fit for purpose.

Consumer Protection and Disclosure Obligations

Consumer protection and disclosure obligations are essential to the legitimacy, usability, and resilience of stablecoin legislation. These provisions ensure that users are informed, empowered, and protected from exploitation, misrepresentation, and systemic failure. In the Commonwealth Model Law, they are not peripheral—they are embedded as enforceable statutory safeguards that reflect both domestic legal traditions and global best practices.

Consumer protection provisions must be drafted to guarantee access to redress, transparency in operations, and protection against unfair or deceptive conduct. The legislation should establish clear obligations for stablecoin issuers and service providers, including:

- Transparent disclosure of fees, risks, redemption conditions, and reserve composition
- Statutory complaint-handling procedures with defined timelines and escalation pathways
- Prohibitions on misleading advertising, concealment of material facts, and exploitative contract terms
- Access to remedies such as refunds, compensation, and injunctive relief

These protections must be enforceable through both administrative and judicial channels. Regulators should be empowered to investigate complaints, impose penalties, and compel corrective action. Courts must be able to interpret and enforce consumer rights, award damages, and issue declaratory relief where necessary.

Non-compliance with consumer protection obligations carries significant legal consequences. Entities that violate these provisions may face civil penalties, licence suspension, reputational damage, and—in cases involving fraud or systemic abuse—criminal liability. They may also lose legal standing in contractual disputes, particularly where terms are found to be unconscionable or misleading.

International frameworks reinforce these protections. MiCA regulation requires that stablecoin issuers provide "fair, clear, and not misleading" information and maintain accessible complaint-handling procedures. The GENIUS Act in the United States prioritises consumer claims in insolvency proceedings and prohibits interest-bearing stablecoins without explicit disclosures, These standards reflect a growing consensus that consumer protection must be embedded in law—not relegated to platform policies or discretionary enforcement.

Disclosure Obligations

Disclosure obligations ensure that regulators, users, and counterparties have access to accurate, timely, and relevant information. These obligations must be codified in statute and linked to enforcement mechanisms. Key legislative elements include:

- Periodic reporting on reserve holdings, redemption activity, and operational risks

- Real-time disclosures of material changes, such as governance shifts or reserve rebalancing
- Public transparency tools, such as licensing registries, audit summaries, and supervisory dashboards
- Mandatory filings with regulators, including compliance attestations and incident reports

Failure to meet disclosure obligations may result in administrative penalties, licence revocation, and—in cases of wilful nondisclosure—criminal liability. Disclosure breaches may also expose entities to civil claims for negligent misstatement or breach of statutory duty. In cross-border contexts, nondisclosure may violate mutual recognition agreements or trigger enforcement actions under foreign law.

Global standards support robust disclosure regimes. The FSB calls for "comprehensive and consistent public disclosures" to support market discipline and regulatory oversight (The Committee on Payments and Market Infrastructures, 2023). The SEC's proposed stablecoin framework mandates disclosures covering cybersecurity resilience, business continuity, and dispute resolution mechanisms (U.S. Securities and Exchange Commission, 2025). These elements are essential for legal clarity, systemic stability, and user trust.

Legal Integration and Oversight

To ensure enforceability, consumer protection and disclosure obligations should be embedded in primary legislation, supported by enabling clauses that authorise regulators to issue technical standards, interpretative guidance, and supervisory protocols. Jurisdictions may also establish ombudsman offices, consumer tribunals, or digital asset commissions to oversee compliance and adjudicate disputes.

Annotated drafts may also include commentary on enforcement thresholds, evidentiary standards, and cross-border coordination. Visual overlays can help track complaint volumes, disclosure compliance, and enforcement actions in real time.

Ultimately, consumer protection and disclosure obligations are not regulatory niceties—they are legal guarantees of fairness, transparency, and accountability. By embedding these provisions in enforceable law and aligning them with global standards, jurisdictions can build stablecoin frameworks that are trusted, resilient, and fit for purpose.

Automated Execution and Legal Interfaces: Smart Contracts in Practice

Smart contracts—self-executing code that automates legal obligations—pose both opportunities and challenges for jurisdictions implementing the Model Laws. While they promise efficiency, transparency, and reduced transaction costs, their rigid logic often clashes with the interpretive nuance of legal systems.

To operationalise smart contracts within a model law framework, jurisdictions must address three key dimensions:

1. **Legal Translation and Enforceability**—Smart contracts must be drafted with legal clarity, ensuring that automated execution aligns with enforceable obligations. This requires a dual-layer approach: code that performs and legal text that governs. Jurisdictions like Australia have begun to treat smart contracts as binding where traditional elements of contract law are satisfied (Bacina, 2017), while Mauritius explores hybrid interpretations that accommodate both codified and equitable principles (Fulena, 2025).
2. **Fallback Mechanisms and Dispute Resolution**— Automated execution can fail or produce unintended outcomes. Model Law overlays should include fallback clauses, human override protocols, and embedded dispute resolution pathways. These mechanisms preserve legal integrity while allowing for innovation.
3. **Pluralist Adaptation and Customary Interfaces**— In pluralist environments, smart contracts must interface with non-codified norms. This may involve layered design, where automated functions are supplemented by interpretive guidance or community-based adjudication. Mauritius's pluralist legal culture offers a precedent for such integration.

By embedding smart contract considerations into operational overlays, jurisdictions can future-proof their legal systems while maintaining fairness, transparency, and adaptability. The Model Law's modular architecture is ideally suited to this task, enabling jurisdictions to tailor their approach based on legal tradition, technical capacity, and stakeholder needs.

CROSS-BORDER RECOGNITION AND ENFORCEMENT POWERS

Legal Interoperability and Jurisdictional Authority

Stablecoin ecosystems are inherently transnational. Transactions often span multiple jurisdictions, involve foreign counterparties, and rely on digital infrastructure hosted across borders. Because of this, any stablecoin framework needs cross-border recognition and enforcement powers to be legally valid and trustworthy. In the Model Laws, these provisions are designed to ensure that domestic legislation does not operate in isolation but as part of a globally coherent legal architecture.

Cross-border recognition provisions enable jurisdictions to acknowledge and enforce foreign regulatory actions, licensing decisions, and judicial outcomes—subject to safeguards and reciprocity. These provisions must be carefully drafted to balance legal sovereignty with interoperability. Key legislative elements include:

- Enabling clauses that permit recognition of foreign licences, supervisory actions, or compliance attestations
- Conditions for recognition, such as equivalence of standards, mutual assistance agreements, or treaty obligations
- Procedures for challenging or refusing recognition, including public interest exceptions and due process guarantees

Recognition provisions should be embedded in statute, not left to discretionary memoranda. They must be legally binding, transparent, and subject to judicial oversight. Failure to recognise legitimate foreign actions may result in regulatory fragmentation, enforcement gaps, and reputational risks—particularly in cross-border insolvency, fraud, or consumer protection cases.

International instruments provide guidance. The UNCITRAL Model Law on Recognition and Enforcement of Insolvency-Related Judgements offers a framework for cross-border cooperation while the Hague Convention on the Recognition and Enforcement of Foreign Judgements establishes principles of reciprocity and procedural fairness. Commonwealth jurisdictions may also rely on regional protocols or bilateral agreements to facilitate recognition (Hague Conference on Private International Law, 2019).

Enforcement Powers

Enforcement powers must be clearly defined in legislation, granting regulators the authority to investigate, sanction, and compel compliance. These powers should include:

- Authority to issue administrative penalties, cease-and-desist orders, and asset freezes
- Power to initiate civil proceedings, refer cases for criminal prosecution, and enforce judgements
- Mechanisms for cross-border enforcement, including mutual legal assistance, information sharing, and coordinated supervision

Enforcement provisions must be drafted with attention to constitutional limits, procedural safeguards, and judicial review. Regulators must act within the bounds of statutory authority, and affected parties must have access to appeal or redress. Enforcement should be proportionate, transparent, and consistent with international norms.

Non-compliance with enforcement provisions—whether by regulated entities or regulators themselves—can undermine the entire framework. It may result in legal uncertainty, loss of public trust, and exposure to international dispute resolution. Jurisdictions must ensure that enforcement powers are not only available but also operationally usable and legally defensible.

Global standards reinforce this imperative. FATF calls for "effective, proportionate, and dissuasive sanctions" for non-compliance with AML/CFT obligations (Financial Action Task Force, 2012). The IOSCO Principles on Enforcement emphasise transparency, consistency, and cross-border cooperation (The International Organization of Securities Commissions, 2023). The FSB recommends that enforcement powers be embedded in law and supported by institutional capacity (Financial Stability Board, 2023).

Legal Integration and Oversight

To ensure coherence, cross-border recognition and enforcement powers should be integrated with other modules—such as licensing, consumer protection, and reserve management. Jurisdictions may establish inter-agency coordination protocols, designate lead authorities for cross-border matters, and develop supervisory dashboards to track enforcement actions.

Annotated drafts may include commentary on jurisdictional triggers, recognition thresholds, and procedural safeguards. Visual overlays can help map enforcement pathways across borders, identify gaps, and support training for regulators and judicial actors.

Ultimately, cross-border recognition and enforcement powers are not technical add-ons—they are legal instruments of interoperability, accountability, and resilience. By embedding these provisions in statute and aligning them with international standards, jurisdictions can ensure that their stablecoin frameworks are not only domestically enforceable but also globally credible.

While the Commonwealth Model Laws offer a modular and context-sensitive pathway for regulating virtual assets and stablecoins, their implementation is not without legal complexity. Jurisdictions must navigate a landscape marked by conceptual ambiguity, institutional fragmentation, and evolving global norms. These challenges are not merely technical—they reflect deeper tensions about sovereignty, risk, and the role of law in shaping digital finance.

LEGAL CHALLENGES AND CONTROVERSIES IN IMPLEMENTATION

While the Commonwealth Model Laws offer a modular and context-sensitive pathway for regulating virtual assets, their implementation is not without legal complexity. Jurisdictions must navigate a landscape marked by conceptual ambiguity, institutional fragmentation, and evolving global norms. These challenges are not merely technical—they reflect deeper tensions about sovereignty, risk, and the role of law in shaping digital finance.

One of the most persistent challenges is definitional clarity. Terms such as "stablecoin", "virtual asset", and "decentralised governance" often lack consistent legal meaning across jurisdictions. This creates uncertainty for lawmakers and regulators, particularly when existing statutes—such as those governing securities, banking, or consumer protection—use overlapping or conflicting terminology. Without careful legal scoping, jurisdictions risk creating duplicative or contradictory provisions that undermine enforcement, investor confidence, and cross-border interoperability.

Definitional Ambiguity

A particularly acute source of friction arises from the inconsistent use of terms like *virtual assets*, *digital assets*, and *cryptoassets*. These terms are often used interchangeably in public discourse, yet they carry distinct meanings across regulatory frameworks. The Model Laws adopt the term *virtual asset* in alignment with FATF standards, referring to digital representations of value that can be digitally transferred or used for payment (Financial Action Task Force, 2021). In contrast, jurisdictions focused on securities regulation or broader digital finance often prefer *digital asset* as an umbrella term encompassing tokenised securities, NFTs, and other blockchain-based instruments. The FSB, SEC, and MiCA frameworks each apply different definitions, further complicating legal harmonisation (Financial Stability Board, 2023a; Financial Stability Board, 2023b; Hansen, 2024; U.S. Securities and Exchange Commission (SEC), 2025).

This divergence has practical consequences. Licensing triggers, supervisory scope, and enforcement powers often hinge on asset classification. A stablecoin treated as a payment instrument in one jurisdiction may be classified as a security in another, leading to regulatory mismatches and enforcement gaps. Jurisdictions implementing the Model Laws must therefore clarify their preferred terminology in enabling legislation and ensure consistency across statutes, regulatory guidance, and public disclosures.

Stablecoin classification presents another layer of controversy. Depending on their design, stablecoins may resemble e-money, securities, collective investment schemes, or bank deposits. This ambiguity complicates licensing regimes and supervisory mandates. For example, a fiat-backed stablecoin used for cross-border remittances may fall under payment system regulation in one jurisdiction but be treated as a security in another. The Model Laws' modularity helps mitigate the issue by allowing jurisdictions to define and categorise stablecoins based on function and risk profile—but the underlying tension remains.

Institutional coordination poses a further challenge. In many jurisdictions, regulatory authority over digital assets is fragmented across multiple agencies—central banks, securities commissions, financial intelligence units, and consumer protection bodies. Implementing a coherent framework requires not only legal harmonisation but also inter-agency collaboration, which may be hindered by turf battles, resource constraints, or divergent policy priorities. The establishment of dedicated digital asset units or cross-sectoral task forces can help address this, but such reforms require political will and sustained investment.

Global regulatory uncertainty also shapes domestic implementation. International bodies such as the FSB, FATF, and BIS continue to refine their positions on stablecoins, often in response to market developments and geopolitical shifts. Jurisdictions must balance alignment with global standards against the need to preserve legal autonomy and economic relevance. This is particularly acute for small states and emerging markets, where stablecoins may offer critical financial infrastructure but also pose systemic risks. As noted by BIS, widespread use of foreign-denominated stablecoins may erode monetary sovereignty and disrupt foreign exchange regimes (Aldasoro et al., 2025).

Finally, public trust and political legitimacy are essential but often overlooked. Virtual asset legislation touches on sensitive issues—privacy, monetary sovereignty, financial inclusion—and may provoke public scepticism or resistance. Transparent consultation, inclusive design, and clear communication are vital to building support and ensuring that the law reflects societal values. In some cases, controversies may arise not from the content of the law but from its perceived beneficiaries, especially if legislation is seen to favour large platforms or foreign interests.

These challenges demonstrate the need for a flexible, principle-based approach. The Model Laws do not offer a one-size-fits-all solution—they provide a scaffold for legal stewardship, enabling jurisdictions to navigate complexity with clarity, coherence, and confidence. By anticipating legal tensions and embedding mechanisms for iterative reform, the Model Laws help ensure that virtual asset legislation remains both resilient and responsive.

SOLUTIONS AND RECOMMENDATIONS

To address the legal challenges and implementation barriers outlined above, jurisdictions adopting the Model Laws must pursue a series of strategic legislative and institutional reforms. These recommendations are designed to reinforce legal clarity, preserve sovereignty, and enable inclusive innovation across diverse legal environments:

1. **Codify Stablecoin Classifications**—Legislators should define stablecoin types: fiat-backed, commodity-backed, algorithmic, and hybrid—directly in statute. Modular definitions ensure legal certainty across licensing, taxation, and enforcement. Leaving classification to regulatory interpretation risks inconsistency and undermines predictability.
2. **Embed Enabling Clauses in Each Module**—Modules should authorise regulators to issue secondary rules, conduct pilots, and adapt provisions to evolving technologies. This ensures responsiveness without constant legislative overhaul.
3. **Recognise Smart Contracts as Legally Enforceable**—Legal recognition should be accompanied by safeguards—auditability, dispute resolution protocols, and consumer protection overlays. Bridging code and law enables automated compliance and unlocks efficiencies.
4. **Mandate Tiered Licensing and Oversight Regimes**—Small issuers should operate under simplified requirements, systemically significant actors under enhanced scrutiny. This proportional approach fosters inclusion and enables resource-efficient oversight.
5. **Codify Reserve Management and Redemption Safeguards**—Issuers must maintain transparent, auditable reserves and statutory redemption rights. Insolvency protocols should ensure enforceable user claims.

6. **Enable Hybrid Governance Models**— DAOs and similar entities must be subject to clear rules on liability, decision-making, and dispute resolution. Innovation in governance must not compromise legal clarity or user protection (Charbit, 2011).
7. **Build Cross-Border Legal Coordination Mechanisms**—Mutual recognition agreements, supervisory memoranda, and legal assistance protocols are essential to address enforcement gaps. Commonwealth frameworks can support regional harmonisation and interoperability (Ernst & Young Global Limited, 2025).

Together, these recommendations offer a strategic framework for resilient, inclusive, and future-proof implementation. They reflect the spirit of the Commonwealth Model Laws—not as rigid templates, but as living frameworks for legal stewardship in the digital age.

Legal Pluralism in Stakeholder Engagement

In jurisdictions with plural legal systems, stakeholder engagement must extend beyond formal state institutions. Customary courts, religious councils, and community governance bodies often exercise de facto legal authority over property rights, dispute resolution, and financial conduct. A modular legislative framework enables these actors to be meaningfully included in the design and implementation of stablecoin systems. For example, modules governing custodial arrangements or dispute resolution can be configured to recognise non-state norms—provided they meet the minimum standards of transparency, accountability, and user protection. This approach enhances legitimacy and ensures that digital financial infrastructure reflects the layered realities of law on the ground.

JURISDICTIONAL SNAPSHOTS

Across different jurisdictions, digital finance must be adapted to pluralistic and community-based governance settings. Research on financial innovation shows that token systems and blockchain applications gain legitimacy only when they respect traditional property rights and collective authority structures.

Solomon Islands

Customary land tenure governs over 80% of land holdings, and village courts handle a significant portion of civil disputes. While exploring digital asset legislation, policymakers recognised that any framework for stablecoin custody or asset-backed issuance would need to account for customary ownership structures. By engaging tribal leaders and integrating local dispute resolution protocols into the governance module, the legislative process respected plural legal authority while maintaining statutory coherence. This pluralist accommodation strengthened community trust and ensured smoother implementation (Customs Recognition Act 2000, 2000).

Kenya

Kenya's legal landscape is shaped by a dynamic interplay between statutory law and customary norms, particularly in areas such as land tenure, inheritance, and informal finance. Policymakers recognised that mobile money systems like M-Pesa had already embedded informal trust networks in the financial ecosystem. To ensure legitimacy and adoption, stablecoin frameworks were designed to accommodate community-based savings groups (*chamas*) and local dispute resolution mechanisms. By allowing modules on custody and governance to reflect these pluralistic norms, Kenya's approach reinforced legal inclusion while maintaining regulatory coherence (Virtual Asset Service Providers Bill, 2025).

Trinidad and Tobago

Legal pluralism in Trinidad and Tobago manifests through the coexistence of common law, statutory law, and religious legal traditions—particularly in matters of family law and community finance. During consultations on digital asset legislation, policymakers engaged religious councils and cooperative credit unions to understand how stablecoin systems might interact with existing financial practices. The resulting framework included provisions for faith-based financial institutions to issue or custody stablecoins under tailored licensing regimes. This pluralist accommodation ensured that the law respected diverse normative orders while enabling secure, interoperable digital finance (International Monetary Fund. Monetary and Capital Markets Department, 2023).

Papua New Guinea

Papua New Guinea (PNG) exemplifies legal pluralism, where customary law operates alongside formal statutory law in nearly every domain—from land tenure and dispute resolution to financial obligations and community governance. In implementing digital asset legislation, PNG's policymakers recognised that any framework for stablecoin issuance or custody would need to accommodate customary ownership structures and local dispute resolution norms. For example, land-backed stablecoins or community-based token systems must be legally designed to respect clan-based property rights and traditional compensation mechanisms. By configuring modules on asset custody and governance to reflect these pluralistic norms, PNG's approach reinforces legitimacy and ensures that digital finance is not imposed from above but co-developed with local authority structures (Nao et al., 2023), (NAFSA, 2023; Beyond the Hype, 2023).

Bermuda

Bermuda's legal system blends common law traditions with a sophisticated offshore regulatory regime, making it a global leader in digital asset legislation. While not pluralist in the customary sense, Bermuda's legal pluralism manifests through its layered regulatory architecture—where corporate, trust, and insurance law intersect with digital asset governance. The Bermuda Monetary Authority has pioneered modular licensing structures under the DABA, allowing stablecoin issuers to operate within segregated account frameworks that ensure bankruptcy remoteness and legal clarity. These structures reflect a form of institutional pluralism, where different legal domains are harmonised to support innovation while preserving investor protection. Bermuda's model demonstrates how modular legislation can integrate complex legal instruments—such as incorporated segregated accounts—into a coherent framework for stablecoin issuance and custody (Bermuda Monetary Authority, 2024).

United Kingdom

The United Kingdom's Office of Communications (Ofcom) has long championed pluralism in media and digital regulation, emphasising the need for diverse stakeholder voices in shaping policy. Ofcom's consultation protocols routinely engage civil society, industry actors, and academic experts, reflecting a commitment to deliberative governance (KPMG & Innovate Finance, 2024). This pluralistic ethos is also evident in the UK's approach to digital finance, where sandbox regimes and open calls for evidence have enabled broad-based participation in regulatory innovation (FCA 2024; HM Treasury, 2023).

United States

The United States, through agencies such as the Federal Communications Commission (FCC) and the Securities and Exchange Commission (SEC), demonstrates a pluralistic model grounded in adversarial engagement and public comment. While stakeholder engagement often reflects power asymmetries, mechanisms such as notice-and-comment rulemaking and congressional hearings provide formal avenues for diverse input. Recent debates around stablecoin regulation have seen active participation from consumer advocates, fintech startups, legacy financial institutions, and state regulators—each bringing distinct perspectives to the table.

Canada

Canada's regulatory approach to stablecoins is shaped by federal-provincial jurisdictional dynamics and a securities-focused lens. The Canadian Securities Administrators (CSA) treat fiat-backed stablecoins—referred to as *Value-Referenced Crypto Assets (VRCAs)*—as potential securities or derivatives, subject to registration and disclosure requirements. This classification creates friction for payment use cases, as businesses and consumers face uncertainty over whether stablecoin transactions trigger securities obligations.

Recent CSA Staff Notices (SN 21-332 and SN 21-333) impose interim conditions on crypto asset trading platforms (CTPs) and stablecoin issuers, requiring undertakings and reserve disclosures to continue offering assets like USDC (Canadian Securities Administrators, 2023; Manzer et al., 2023). While this ensures short-term access, it underscores the absence of a dedicated legal framework for stablecoins and highlights Canada's misalignment with jurisdictions such as the EU (MiCA) and Australia, which are pursuing bespoke legislation.

Canada's snapshot illustrates how definitional ambiguity and institutional overlap can hinder stablecoin adoption, especially when digital payment instruments are regulated as investment products. It also reinforces the need for modular legal frameworks that distinguish between payment functionality and investment risk.

European Union

The European Union offers a structured and consensus-orientated model of pluralism. Institutions such as the European Economic and Social Committee (EESC) and the European Parliamentary Research Service (EPRS) facilitate multi-stakeholder dialogues that integrate foresight, ecosystem mapping, and long-term policy planning (European Securities and Market Authorities, 2023). The EU's Digital Finance Strategy and MiCA (Markets in Crypto-Assets) regulation were shaped through extensive consultation with member states, industry groups, and civil society—underscoring the role of pluralism in achieving regulatory legitimacy and coherence across a multi-jurisdictional bloc.

These jurisdictional snapshots highlight a key point: effective stablecoin legislation must be both modular and pluralist. Whether navigating customary land tenure in Papua New Guinea, layered regulatory regimes in Bermuda, or community-based finance in Kenya, the legal environment is rarely uniform. Modular frameworks—

like those offered by the Commonwealth Model Laws—enable jurisdictions to configure legal provisions that respect local authority structures while maintaining global interoperability. This adaptability is not a compromise; it is a strategic asset. By embedding pluralism into the legislative process, governments can build digital financial systems that are not only technically sound but socially grounded and legally legitimate. Pluralism in stakeholder engagement is not monolithic—it manifests differently depending on legal tradition, institutional design, and political culture.

For Commonwealth jurisdictions implementing the Stablecoin Model Law, these examples provide valuable lessons in designing inclusive, context-sensitive consultation processes that reflect local realities while aligning with global best practices.

Stakeholder engagement in digital asset governance is deeply shaped by the legal pluralism embedded within each jurisdiction's constitutional and institutional architecture. Whether through the formal recognition of customary law, the coexistence of federal and tribal systems, or the supranational layering of legal authority, pluralism influences not only who participates in legal reform but also how legitimacy is constructed.

Australia

Australia presents a compelling case study in the evolution of digital asset regulation within a mature common law system. While the country has yet to enact comprehensive legislation specific to virtual assets or stablecoins, its legal infrastructure is actively adapting through interpretive guidance, sectoral regulation, and judicial engagement. The Australian Law Reform Commission has undertaken a multi-phase review of financial services legislation, with particular attention to the integration of blockchain-based instruments and smart contracts. Courts have begun to grapple with the enforceability of automated agreements, often relying on traditional principles of contract formation, intention, and consideration (Australian Law Reform Commission, 2022).

Australia's regulatory posture is shaped by a strong consumer protection ethos and a pragmatic approach to technological innovation. The Australian Securities and Investments Commission (ASIC) has issued targeted guidance on digital asset offerings and custody arrangements, while the Reserve Bank continues to explore CBDC prototypes. Importantly, Australias legal community is actively engaged in translating complex technical constructs into actionable legal frameworks, making it a valuable comparator for jurisdictions seeking to modernise without abandoning foundational legal principles.

Mauritius

Mauritius has emerged as a regional leader in fintech regulation, leveraging its hybrid legal system and strategic positioning within the African and Indian Ocean regions. The enactment of the Virtual Asset and Initial Token Offering Services Act 2021 marked a significant milestone, establishing a licensing regime for service providers and embedding international standards on anti-money laundering and consumer protection (Hossenkhan et al., 2024; Virtual Asset and Initial Token Offering Services Act 2021, 2022). The legislation reflects a modular approach, enabling phased implementation and adaptation to evolving market dynamics.

Mauritius's legal pluralism, which includes parts of French civil law, English common law, and customary norms—has fostered a more flexible regulatory environment. The courts and regulators have shown a willingness to interpret smart contracts and digital instruments through both codified and equitable lenses, recognising the need for legal certainty while accommodating innovation. The jurisdiction's emphasis on capacity-building, stakeholder consultation, and regional harmonisation aligns closely with the Model Law's implementation ethos. Mauritius offers a reform trajectory for small island states seeking to balance resilience, innovation, and legal integrity. This modularity is further illustrated in Bowmans' practitioner summary, which outlines how the Act enables phased licensing and supervisory adaptation in response to market evolution.

The Mauritius IFC's implementation framework reinforces this approach, highlighting the role of technical assistance and regional coordination in supporting legal pluralism and institutional capacity (Mauritius International Financial Centre, 2022).

United Arab Emirates (UAE)

The UAE exemplifies how legal pluralism and stakeholder engagement can be operationalised through modular architecture. Its dual-framework approach—combining Dubai's Virtual Assets Regulatory Authority (VARA) with the Central Bank's Payment Token Services Regulation (PTSR)—reflects a strategic balance between innovation and prudential oversight. Stakeholder consultation is embedded through sandbox pilots, phased licensing, and local-first issuance preferences (Heaver et al., 2025; Pirbhai, 2024; Ringer & Johal, 2024; Rud, 2025). The UAE's emphasis on regulatory clarity, institutional coordination, and cultural responsiveness aligns with the Model Laws' principle-based design and offers a replicable model for jurisdictions navigating plural legal environments.

India

India's approach to digital asset regulation is shaped by its constitutional pluralism and complex financial ecosystem. The country operates under a layered legal framework that accommodates statutory law, personal law systems, and informal financial networks—including mobile money and cooperative finance. While private stablecoins remain cautiously treated, the Reserve Bank of India (RBI) has led stakeholder engagement through sandbox initiatives, public consultations, and inter-agency coordination (Baghel, 2025; Kulkarni & The Economic Times, 2024).

The rollout of India's central bank digital currency (CBDC), the e-Rupee, reflects a sovereignty-first posture, prioritising monetary control and systemic stability (The Economic Times, 2025). At the same time, India's fintech ecosystem continues to push for regulatory clarity on virtual digital assets (VDAs), prompting phased innovation within tightly managed guardrails. Parliamentary committees, industry associations, and civil society actors have all contributed to shaping the discourse, reinforcing India's pluralist governance model.

India's experience draws attention to the importance of balancing innovation with institutional caution—especially in jurisdictions where legal pluralism intersects with high financial inclusion and rapid technological adoption.

Table 2. Comparative dashboard: Legal pluralism in stakeholder engagement

Jurisdiction	Legal Pluralism Context	Stakeholder Engagement Practices	Notable Features /Examples
Solomon Islands	Customary law formally recognised alongside state law; strong village-level legal traditions	Community consultations integrated into justice reform; emphasis on cultural legitimacy and local ownership	The ASIPJ programme supports pluralist justice delivery; family law reforms reflect mixed legal systems.
Papua New Guinea	The Underlying Law Act 2000 promotes integration of customary law into the formal legal system.	Legal reform includes tribal leaders, customary courts, and local dispute resolution networks.	Customary law used in land disputes and restorative justice; pluralism embedded in constitutional design
Kenya	Dual legal system: formal courts and recognised customary tribunals	Public participation mandated in constitutional reform; civil society and religious leaders actively consulted	Traditional dispute resolution mechanisms are recognised under the Constitution; strong NGO involvement
Trinidad & Tobago	Common law base with pluralist overlays in family and customary law	Sectoral roundtables and public forums used in cybercrime and digital finance consultations	Adapted the Commonwealth Cybercrime Model Law through inclusive stakeholder mapping.
Bermuda	British Overseas Territory with common law and local statutory adaptations	Financial sector consultations include insurers, fintechs, and legal experts with an emphasis on regulatory transparency.	Stakeholder engagement is central to the digital asset licensing regime; pluralism is reflected in policy layering.

continued on following page

Table 2. Continued

Jurisdiction	Legal Pluralism Context	Stakeholder Engagement Practices	Notable Features /Examples
United Kingdom	Common law system with devolved legal powers and multicultural legal influences	Open calls for evidence, sandbox regimes, and public consultations across sectors	Ofcom and FCA exemplify pluralist engagement; legal pluralism is evident in devolved jurisdictions.
United States	Federal system with overlapping state, federal, and tribal legal authorities	Notice-and-comment rulemaking; congressional hearings; tribal consultations in federal lawmaking	The SEC and CFTC engage diverse actors in digital asset regulation; pluralism is shaped by adversarial engagement.
European Union	Supranational legal order is layered over member state systems.	Multi-stakeholder dialogues via EESC, EPRS, and public consultations across member states	The MiCA regulation was shaped through extensive engagement, with pluralism being managed through subsidiarity principle.
Canada	Dual-layered governance: federal prudential oversight and provincial securities regulation	Ongoing federal consultations led by the Department of Finance and the Bank of Canada; active input from Web3 Canada, CIRO, and crypto trading platforms	Federal and provincial regulators engage industry, consumer groups, and financial institutions; pluralism is shaped by fragmented oversight and conditional collaboration.
Australia	Common law with strong judicial precedent and sectoral regulation	The Legal profession, the fintech sector, and regulatory agencies	Multi-tiered engagement across legal, regulatory, and fintech sectors. The Australian Law Reform Commission's consultative review process and ASIC's targeted guidance reflect a commitment to iterative reform. Legal practitioners actively contribute to translating blockchain constructs into enforceable legal language.
Mauritius	The hybrid system blending civil law, common law, and customary norms.	Multi-sector consultations, capacity-building, regional forums	Inclusive stakeholder consultations during the drafting of the Virtual Asset and Initial Token Offering Services Act. Emphasis on capacity-building for regulators and the judiciary, supported by regional forums and technical assistance programmes. Engagement spans government, the private sector, and civil society, reinforcing pluralist adaptation.
United Arab Emirates (UAE)	Dual legal system combining Sharia principles with civil and common law; regulatory authority split between federal and emirate levels.	Stakeholder input embedded through sandbox pilots, phased licensing, and consultations via VARA and CBUAE	Modular rulebooks and phased implementation: Dubai's VARA and federal PTSR reflect layered governance and innovation alignment.
India	Coexistence of statutory law, personal law systems, and informal financial networks; strong constitutional pluralism	Stakeholder engagement through RBI consultations, fintech sandboxes, and parliamentary committee reviews	CBDC rollout reflects a sovereignty-first approach; informal finance and mobile money ecosystems shape regulatory priorities.

WAY FORWARD

The successful implementation of virtual asset legislation requires more than technical drafting—it demands legal imagination, institutional choreography, and cultural sensitivity. The Commonwealth Model Laws provide a modular foundation, but its true strength lies in its adaptability. Jurisdictions must treat the framework not as a rigid template, but as a living architecture—capable of reflecting local priorities, plural legal traditions, and evolving technologies.

Moving forward, governments should prioritise inclusive legislative processes, engage diverse stakeholders, and build capacity across regulatory and judicial institutions. Pilot programmes and feedback loops must be embedded into the legal lifecycle, ensuring that laws remain responsive and grounded in real-world experience. Legal pluralism should be embraced as a strategic asset, allowing frameworks to coexist with customary norms, religious practices, and community governance structures—without sacrificing legal clarity or global interoperability.

Ultimately, modular stablecoin legislation is not just about regulating digital assets—it is about designing legal systems that are resilient, equitable, and future-ready. By combining principled structure with contextual flexibility, jurisdictions can build digital financial ecosystems that serve their people, protect their sovereignty, and connect them to the global economy on their own terms.

Closing Reflection: Legislation as a Legal Memory

Stablecoin legislation is more than a regulatory exercise—it is a form of legal memory. It captures a jurisdiction's values, priorities, and institutional readiness at a particular moment in time, while leaving space for future adaptation. The Model Laws, with its modular architecture and pluralist ethos, enable jurisdictions to legislate not only for the present but also for the evolving contours of digital finance.

Implementation is where legal theory becomes operational reality. It is where abstract provisions are translated into enforceable rights, institutional mandates, and public trust. This process is inherently iterative. Jurisdictions must be prepared to revise, refine, and re-engage as technology evolves, market behaviours shift, and new risks emerge. The Model Laws support this through enabling clauses, phased deployment strategies, and stakeholder engagement protocols that embed responsiveness into the legislative fabric.

For small island states and pluralist legal environments, implementation is also a form of economic and cultural agency. It allows jurisdictions to participate in global financial systems on terms that respect local governance structures, customary norms, and community priorities. By integrating legal pluralism into statutory design, the Model Laws affirms that resilience is not achieved through uniformity but through contextual coherence.

Moreover, modular legislation offers a pathway to intergenerational legal stewardship. It enables today's lawmakers to build frameworks that future drafters can expand, recalibrate, or sunset without dismantling the entire legal edifice. This is particularly vital in digital finance, where innovation cycles are rapid and legislative inertia can be costly.

As jurisdictions move from drafting to deployment, they must treat implementation not as a final step but as a living process. It requires legal clarity, institutional choreography, and cultural sensitivity. It demands that lawmakers, regulators, and communities co-create frameworks that are enforceable, inclusive, and future-ready (Commonwealth Secretariat, 2024).

The Commonwealth Model Laws provides the tools. This chapter has offered the roadmap. What remains is the commitment—to steward digital finance through law that is modular, pluralist, and enduring.

CONCLUSION

Stewardship, Sovereignty, and the Future of Digital Asset Governance

The Model Laws represent more than a legal instrument—it is a blueprint for principled innovation, institutional resilience, and inclusive economic transformation. Throughout this chapter, we have explored the rationale behind its non-prescriptive design, the phased pathways for implementation, the legal tensions it must navigate, and the strategic recommendations that can guide jurisdictions toward effective adoption. What emerges is a framework that is not only technically sound but also philosophically grounded in pluralism, stewardship, and legal empowerment.

By avoiding rigid legal transplants and embracing modular architecture, the Model Laws respects the diversity of Commonwealth legal systems while enabling coherence across borders. It empowers jurisdictions to tailor stablecoin regulation to their own constitutional traditions, economic priorities, and technological capacities—without sacrificing interoperability or global alignment. This balance between sovereignty and harmonisation is especially vital in a domain as fluid and contested as digital finance.

The implementation pathway outlined in this chapter underscores the importance of sequencing, consultation, and capacity-building. It recognises that legislation is not a static endpoint but a dynamic process—one that must evolve through feedback, pilot testing, and iterative reform. The legal challenges explored here—from definitional ambiguity to cross-border enforcement—are not obstacles to be avoided but design constraints to be addressed with clarity and foresight.

Looking ahead, the Commonwealth has an opportunity to lead by example. By fostering regional coordination, supporting technical assistance, and promoting legal pluralism, it can help member states build resilient digital asset ecosystems that serve both local needs and global standards. The Model Laws offer a foundation—but their success will depend on how they are interpreted, operationalised, and sustained over time.

Ultimately, digital asset governance is not merely about regulating technology—it is about shaping the legal infrastructure of trust, inclusion, and continuity in an era of rapid change. The Commonwealth's approach, grounded in principle-based modularity and stakeholder engagement, offers a compelling vision for how law can adapt without fragmenting, innovate without destabilising, and empower without excluding.

In the Commonwealth, law is not merely a tool of regulation—it is a vessel of stewardship. The Model Laws invite jurisdictions to legislate with purpose, govern with integrity, and build digital futures that honour both tradition and transformation (Commonwealth Secretariat, 2024).

REFERENCES

Aldasoro, I., Aquilina, M., Lewrick, U., & Lim, S. H. (2025). *Stablecoin Growth – Policy Challenges and Approaches* (BIS Bulletin No. 108; p. 8). Bank for International Settlements (BIS). https://www.bis.org/publ/bisbull108.htm

Asia/Pacific Group on Money Laundering. (2018). *3rd Follow-Up Report: Mutual Evaluation of Vanuatu* (p. 33). The Financial Action Task Force (FATF). https://www.fatf-gafi.org/content/dam/fatf-gafi/fsrb-fur/APG-3rd-Follow-Up%20Report-Vanuatu-2018.pdf

Australian Law Reform Commission. (2022). *Legislative Framework for Corporations and Financial Services Regulation: New Business Models, Technologies, and Practices* (Background Paper No. FSL7; p. 38). Australian Law Reform Commission (ALRC). https://www.alrc.gov.au/wp-content/uploads/2022/10/FSL7-New-Business-Models-Technologies-and-Practices.pdf

Bacina, M. (2017). *Smart contracts in Australia: Just how clever are they?* [Insight]. Piper Alderman. https://piperalderman.com.au/insight/smart-contracts-in-australia-just-how-clever-are-they/

Baghel, B. (2025). RBI Crypto Stance: Sanjay Malhotra Sounds Cautious on Crypto. *CoinGabbar*.https://www.coingabbar.com/en/crypto-currency-news/rbi-crypto-stance-sanjay-malhotra-crypto-stablecoin-warning

Basel Committee on Banking Supervision. (2012). *Core Principles for Effective Banking Supervision*. Bank for International Settlements (BIS). https://www.bis.org/publ/bcbs230.htm

Bermuda Monetary Authority. (2024). *Single Currency Pegged Stablecoins (SCPS) Guidance* (p. 14). Bermuda Monetary Authority. https://cdn.bma.bm/documents/2024-12-06-16-16-15-DAB-Single-Currency-Pegged-Stablecoins-Consultation-Guidance.pdf

Canadian Securities Administrators. (2023). *CSA Staff Notice 21-333: Crypto Asset Trading Platforms: Terms and Conditions for Trading Value-Referenced Crypto Assets with Clients* (Instruments, Rules and Policies, p. 24) [CSA Notice]. Canadian Securities Administrators (CSA). https://www.osc.ca/en/securities-law/instruments-rules-policies/2/21-333/csa-staff-notice-21-333-crypto-asset-trading-platforms-terms-and-conditions-trading-value

Caribbean Regional Technical Assistance Centre. (2021). *CARTAC FY21 Annual Report* (p. 150) [Annual Report]. Caribbean Regional Technical Assistance Centre. https://www.cartac.org/content/dam/CARTAC/AnnualReports/CARTAC_FY21_Annual-Report_Final(2).pdf

Central Bank of Trinidad and Tobago. (2019). *Financial Stability Report 2019* (p. 83). Central Bank of Trinidad and Tobago. https://www.central-bank.org.tt/core-functions/financial-stability/financial-stability-report

Charbit, C. (2011). *Governance of Public Policies in Decentralised Contexts: The Multi-level Approach* (OECD Regional Development Working Papers No. 2011/04; OECD Regional Development Working Papers, Vol. 2011/04). Organisation for Economic Co-operation and Development (OECD). DOI: 10.1787/20737009

Crisanto, J. C., Ehrentraud, J., & Ocampo, D. G. (2024). *Stablecoins: Regulatory Responses to Their Promise of Stability* (Policy Report No. 57; FSI Insights, p. 26). Bank for International Settlements (BIS), Financial Stability Institute. https://www.bis.org/fsi/publ/insights57.pdf

Customs Recognition Act. 2000, No. No 7 of 2000, National Parliament of the Solomon Islands (2000). https://faolex.fao.org/docs/pdf/sol74602.pdf

Eastern and Southern Africa Anti-Money Laundering Group. (2022). *Anti-Money Laundering and Counter-Terrorist Financing Measures – Mauritius: 5th Enhanced Follow-up Report & Technical Compliance Re-Rating* (p. 7). Eastern and Southern Africa Anti-Money Laundering Group (ESAAMLG).https://www.fatf-gafi.org/content/dam/fatf-gafi/fsrb-fur/ESAAMLG-Mauritius-FUR2022. pdf

Ernst & Young Global Limited. (2025). *Global Approaches to Stablecoin Regulation: A Global Stablecoin Regulation Comparison.* (Industry Report Nos 005677-25Gbl; p. 24). Ernst & Young Global Limited. https://www.ey.com/content/dam/ey-unified-site/ey-com/en-gl/industries/banking-capital-markets/documents/ey-gl-global-stablecoin-regulation-comparison-09-2025.pdf

European Securities and Market Authorities. (2025). *ESMA and the European Commission Publish Guidance on Non-MiCA Compliant ARTs and EMTs (stablecoins)* (Public Statement Nos ESMA75-223375936–6099; p. 3). European Securities and Market Authorities (ESMA). https://www.esma.europa.eu/press-news/esma-news/esma-and-european-commission-publish-guidance-non-mica-compliant-arts-and-emts

European Securities and Markets Authority. (2023). *Consultation Paper on the Technical Standards specifying certain requirements of MiCA (3rd package)* (Consultation Paper Nos ESMA75-453128700–1002; p. 101). European Securities and Markets Authority (ESMA). https://www.esma.europa.eu/document/consultation-paper-technical-standards-specifying-certain-requirements-mica-3rd-package

Financial Action Task Force. (2012). *International Standards on Combating Money Laundering and the Financing of Terrorism & Proliferation* (p. 152). Financial Action Task Force (FATF). https://www.fatf-gafi.org/en/publications/Fatfrecommendations/Fatf-recommendations.html Financial Action Task Force. (2020). *FATF Report to G20 on So-called Stablecoins* (p. 32). Financial Action Task Force (FATF). https://www.fatf-gafi.org/content/dam/fatf-gafi/reports/Virtual-Assets-FATF-Report-G20-So-Called-Stablecoins.pdf

Financial Action Task Force. (2021). *Updated Guidance for a Risk-Based Approach to Virtual Assets and Virtual Asset Service Providers* (p. 111). Financial Action Task Force (FATF). https://www.fatf-gafi.org/content/dam/fatf-gafi/guidance/Updated-Guidance-VA-VASP.pdf

Financial Action Task Force. (2023). *Methodology for Assessing Compliance with the FATF Recommendations and the Effectiveness of AML/CFT Systems* (p. 196) [Official Institutional Report]. Financial Action Task Force (FATF). https://www.fatf-gafi.org/publications/mutualevaluations/documents/fatf-methodology.html

Financial Conduct Authority. (2024). *The Regulatory Sandbox* (p. 13) [Organizational Report]. Financial Conduct Authority (FCA). https://www.fca.org.uk/firms/innovation/regulatory-sandbox

Financial Services Act. 2021, https://www.legislation.gov.uk/ukpga/2021/22/enacted, Parliament of the United Kingdom 2019-21, UK Public General Acts, 2021 CBP 8705 192 (2022). https://www.legislation.gov.uk/ukpga/2021/22/enacted

Financial Stability Board. (2023a). *High-level Recommendations for the Regulation, Supervision and Oversight of Global Stablecoin Arrangements* (Reports to the G20, p. 24). Financial Stability Board (FSB). https://www.fsb.org/uploads/P170723-3.pdf

Financial Stability Board. (2023b). *IMF-FSB Synthesis Paper: Policies for Crypto-Assets* (p. 53). Financial Stability Board (FSB) and International Monetary Fund (IMF). https://www.fsb.org/2023/09/imf-fsb-synthesis-paper-policies-for-crypto-assets/

Fulena, V. (2025). Examining Smart Contracts Within Mauritian Contract Law: Assessing Their Compatibility with Existing Legal Frameworks. In Hinkelmann, K., & Smuts, H. (Eds.), *Society 5.0* (Vol. 2173, pp. 123–135). Springer Nature Switzerland., DOI: 10.1007/978-3-031-71412-2_10

Gail, E. (2007). Legal Transplants and Economics: The World Bank and Third World Economies in the 1980s – A Case Study of Jamaica, the Republic of Kenya and the Philippines. *European Journal of Law Reform, 9(2)*, 243–283. https://sas-space.sas.ac.uk/349/1/Gail_Edwards_MA_Thesis.pdf

Guiding and Establishing National Innovation for U.S. Stablecoins Act. (Senate Bill 1582: GENIUS Act), Pub. L. No. 119–27 (2025). https://www.congress.gov/bill/119th-congress/senate-bill/1582/text

Hague Conference on Private International Law. (2019). *Convention on the Recognition and Enforcement of Foreign Judgments in Civil or Commercial Matters* (International Instrument No. 41; p. 13). Hague Conference on Private International Law (HCCH). https://www.hcch.net/en/instruments/conventions/full-text/?cid=137

Hansen, P. (2024). *Analyzing MiCA's significance regime for stablecoins* [Commentary Report]. Circle Internet Group, Inc. https://www.circle.com/blog/analyzing-micas-significance-regime-for-stablecoins

Harper, E. (2011). *Customary Justice: From Program Design to Impact Evaluation*. International Development Law Organization (IDLO). https://www.idlo.int/publications/customary-justice-program-design-impact-evaluation

Heaver, I., Melnichenko, A., & Kamran, Z. (2025). *UAE Crypto Regulation Q3 2025 Update: VARA, SCA & ADGM* [Legal Insights]. NeosLegal. https://neoslegal.co/uae-crypto-regulation-q3-2025-update-vara-sca-adgm/

Hossenkhan, F., Jeehoo, N., Li, K., & Pang, A. K. (2024). *Mauritius: Law and Practice—Trends and Developments* (p. 20). Bowmans. https://www.bom.mu/sites/default/files/virtual-asset-and-initial-token-offering-services-act-2021.pdf

International Federation of Red Cross and Red Crescent Societies. (2021a). *IFRC Annual Report 2021* (p. 62). International Federation of Red Cross and Red Crescent Societies. https://disasterlaw.ifrc.org/media/3835

International Federation of Red Cross and Red Crescent Societies. (2021b). *Strengthening Climate Resilience Through Law and Policy in the Philippines* (p. 4). https://disasterlaw.ifrc.org/sites/default/files/media/disaster_law/2021-12/IFRC Disaster Law_Case Study_Strengthening climate resilience through law and policy in the Philippines.pdf

International Federation of Red Cross and Red Crescent Societies, & University College Cork. (2021). *Global Synthesis Report on Law and Policies for Climate Resilience: Enhancing Normative Integration Between Climate Change Adaptation and Disaster Risk Reduction* (p. 40). International Federation of Red Cross and Red Crescent Societies. https://disasterlaw.ifrc.org/sites/default/files/media/disaster_law/2021-08/20210803_DRR_CCA_FinalDoc_ONLINE.pdf

International Monetary Fund. Monetary and Capital Markets Department. (2023). Trinidad and Tobago. *IMF Staff Country Reports, 2023*(322), 1. DOI: 10.5089/9798400254437.002

Jean-Noel, I. I. D. (2025). *Securing Digital Dollar Dominance: A Comprehensive Framework for Stablecoin Regulation and Innovation* (p. 106) [Working Paper]. U.S. Securities and Exchange Commission (SEC). https://www.sec.gov/files/stablecoin_regulatory_framework.pdf

Katz, E. (2023). *Custody of stablecoin reserves under MiCA* (Legal Development No. 2023). Ashurst (law firm). https://www.ashurst.com/en/insights/custody-of-stablecoin-reserves-under-mica/

K.B.M. R. H., & Zayed, N. M. (2018). The New Basel-III Capital Accord: Capability of The Banks In Adapting and Adopting the New Regime In Bangladesh. *International Journal of Development Research, 8*(9), 22782–22791. https://www.journalijdr.com/new-basel-iii-capital-accord-capability-banks-adapting-and-adopting-new-regime-bangladesh

KPMG & Innovate Finance. (2024). *The Roadmap to Open Finance in the UK* (p. 18). KPMG International Limited and Innovate Finance. https://assets.kpmg.com/content/dam/kpmgsites/uk/pdf/2024/04/the-roadmap-to-open-finance-in-the-uk.pdf

Kulkarni, S., & the The Economic Times. (2024, April 5). Digital Rupee: RBI widens scope of CBDC; non-banking payment companies to facilitate transactions. *Bennett, Coleman & Co. Ltd.* https://economictimes.indiatimes.com/wealth/save/eps-95-pension-is-government-planning-to-increase-minimum-eps-payout-from-rs-1000-to-rs-7500-heres-what-ministry-says/articleshow/125713018.cms

Manzer, A. R., Solomons, M., & Sharma, T. (2023). *CSA Provides Additional Guidance for Stablecoin Regulation*. Cassels Brock & Blackwell LLP., https://cassels.com/insights/csa-provides-additional-guidance-for-stablecoin-regulation/

Mauritius International Financial Centre. (2022). *Toolkit on Mauritius IFC for Ambassadors & High Commissioners* (p. 41). Economic Development Board Mauritius. https://mauritiusifc.mu/index.php/toolkit-mauritius-ifc-ambassadors-high-commissioners

Melo, F., Seal, K., & Salomao, V. (2024). 2024 Revised Basel Core Principles for Effective Banking Supervision. *Policy Papers, 2024*(037), 13. DOI: 10.5089/9798400286636.007

Nao, L., Kabiu, J., Awayang, S., & Kutan, L. P. (2023). *Bankability of Customary Land in Papua New Guinea: Challenges and Prospects* (Discussion Paper No. 210; p. 31). The National Research Institute,PNG. https://pngnri.org/images/Publications/DPNo.210updated_Bankability_of_customary_land_in_Papua_New_Guinea-_challenges_and_prospects_.pdf

Organisation for Economic Co-operation and Development. (2020). *The OECD Digital Government Policy Framework: Six Dimensions of a Digital Government* (OECD Public Governance Policy Papers No. 02; Series: OECD Public Governance Policy Papers Volume: 02, p. 40). Organisation for Economic Co-operation and Development (OECD). DOI: 10.1787/14e1c5e8-en-fr

Pirbhai, H. (2024). CBUAE Payment Token Services Regulation. *Global Regulation Tomorrow*. https://www.regulationtomorrow.com/dubai-and-saudi/cbuae-payment-token-services-regulation/

Ringer, M., & Johal, Y. (2024). *The New CBUAE Payment Token Services Regulation: 10 Things You Need to Know*. CMS Legal., https://cms-lawnow.com/en/ealerts/2024/08/the-new-cbuae-payment-token-services-regulation-10-things-you-need-to-know

Rose, R. (2017). *Commonwealth Legislative Drafting Manual*. Commonwealth Secretariat. https://www.thecommonwealth-ilibrary.org/index.php/comsec/catalog/download/873/873/7305?inline=1

Rud, M. (2025). *UAE Crypto Regulation 2025: Complete Guide to VARA, ADGM, SCA, CBUAE Stablecoin Rules, Security Tokens, & On-Chain Real Estate* [Legal Guide]. ComplyFactor. https://complyfactor.com/uae-crypto-regulation-2025-complete-guide-to-vara-adgm-sca-cbuae/

Secretariat, C. (2002). *Model Law on Computer and Computer Related Crime.*, https://database.cyberpolicyportal.org/api/files/1663937569955dd9j3bxcigh.pdf

Secretariat, C. (2024). *The Commonwealth Model Law on Virtual Assets*. Commonwealth Secretariat. [Legal guidance], https://thecommonwealth.org/publications/model-law-virtual-assets

The Committee on Payments and Market Infrastructures. (2023). *Considerations for the Use of Stablecoin Arrangements in Cross-Border Payments* (CPMI Report No. 220; CPMI Papers, p. 37). Bank for International Settlements (BIS). https://www.bis.org/cpmi/publ/d220.pdf

The Economic Times. (2025). RBI Cautious in Its Approach to Stablecoins, Cryptos Says Governor Sanjay Malhotra. *Bennett, Coleman & Co. Ltd.* https://economictimes.indiatimes.com/industry/banking/finance/banking/rbi-cautious-in-its-approach-to-stablecoins-cryptos-says-governor-sanjay-malhotra/articleshow/125464379.cms

The European Parliament and the Council of the European Union. (2023, May 31). *Regulation (EU) 2023/1114 Of the European Parliament and of the Council of 31 May 2023 on markets in crypto-assets, and amending Regulations (EU) No 1093/2010 and (EU) No 1095/2010 and Directives 2013/36/EU and (EU) 2019/1937.* Official Journal of the European Union (OJ). https://eur-lex.europa.eu/eli/reg/2023/1114/oj/eng

The International Organization of Securities Commissions. (2023). *Policy Recommendations for Crypto and Digital Asset Markets* (No. 747; p. 77). https://www.iosco.org/library/pubdocs/pdf/IOSCOPD747.pdf

The Virtual Asset and Initial Token Offering Services Act. 2021, Government Gazette of Mauritius No. 183 (2022). https://www.bom.mu/sites/default/files/virtual-asset-and-initial-token-offering-services-act-2021.pdf

Treasury, H. M. (2023). *Consultation on the Digital Securities Sandbox.* HM Treasury. [Consultation Paper], https://www.gov.uk/government/consultations/consultation-on-the-digital-securities-sandbox

United Nations Commission on International Trade Law. (1999). *UNCITRAL Model Law on Electronic Commerce with Guide to Enactment 1996 with Additional Article 5 Bis as Adopted in 1998* (No. E.99.V.4; United Nations Publication, p. 86). United Nations. https://uncitral.un.org/en/texts/ecommerce/modellaw/electronic_commerce

United Nations Commission on International Trade Law. (2008). *UNCITRAL Model Law on International Commercial Arbitration 1985: With Amendments as Adopted in 2006* (No. E.08.V.4; United Nations Publication, p. 56). United Nations. https://uncitral.un.org/en/texts/arbitration/modellaw/commercial_arbitration

United Nations Commission on International Trade Law. (2018). *UNCITRAL Model Law on Recognition and Enforcement of Insolvency-Related Judgments with Guide to Enactment* (No. E.19.V.8; United Nations Publication, p. 84). UNITED NATIONS. https://uncitral.un.org/en/texts/insolvency/modellaw/mlij

United Nations Conference on Trade and Development. (2023). *Global Report on Blockchain and Its Implications on Trade Facilitation Performance* (No. UNCTAD/TCS/DTL/INF/2023/1; p. 71). United Nations Conference on Trade and Development (UNCTAD). https://unctad.org/publication/global-report-blockchain-and-its-implications-trade-facilitation-performance

United Nations Conference on Trade and Development. (2025). *Trinidad and Tobago eTrade Readiness Assessment* (Policy Review No. UNCTAD/DTL/ECDE/2024/5; p. 100). United Nations. https://dig.watch/resource/trinidad-and-tobago-etrade-readiness-assessment

Upadhyaya, R. (2017). *The Political Economy of Basel Adoption in Kenya: A Case of Alignment of Donor, Government and Banking Sector Interests* (GEG Working Paper No. 131; p. 37). University of Oxford, Global Economic Governance Programme (GEG). https://hdl.handle.net/10419/196387

U.S. Securities and Exchange Commission. (2025). *Statement on Stablecoins* [Regulatory Statement]. U.S. Securities and Exchange Commission (SEC). https://www.sec.gov/newsroom/speeches-statements/statement-stablecoins-040425

Virtual Asset and Initial Token Offering Services Act 2021, Pub. L. No. 21 of 2021, 183 Government Gazette of Mauritius (2022). Assented 16 December 2021; Proclaimed by Proclamation No. 12 of 2022, effective 7 February 2022 https://www.bom.mu/sites/default/files/virtual-asset-and-initial-token-offering-services-act-2021_0.pdf

Virtual Asset Service Providers Bill, 15 of 2025, Parliament of Kenya, Kenya Gazette Supplement No. 173 Act No. 20 of 2025 489 (2025). https://new.kenyalaw.org/akn/ke/act/2025/20/eng@2025-11-04

APPENDIX

Modular Integration and Readiness Checklist

To support jurisdictions in translating legislative principles into operational practice, this Implementation Readiness Checklist offers a structured diagnostic tool. It is designed to help legislative drafters, regulators, and inter-agency task forces assess their preparedness to implement the Model Law. By identifying key elements—from legal definitions and licensing infrastructure to stakeholder engagement and judicial integration—the checklist enables tailored, phased deployment aligned with local capacities and governance traditions.

Table 3.

Implementation Element	Readiness Question
Legal Definitions	Have you mapped existing definitions of "virtual asset", "stablecoin", and "issuer" across statutes?
Licensing Infrastructure	Is there a designated authority with statutory powers to licence, supervise, and enforce?
Reserve Oversight	Are there mechanisms for independent audits, reserve disclosures, and enforcement of segregation rules?
Redemption Protocols	Have statutory redemption rights been codified, with clear timelines and dispute resolution pathways?
Stakeholder Engagement	Have customary, religious, and community governance bodies been consulted in module design?
Cross-Border Coordination	Are mutual recognition agreements or legal assistance protocols in place or under negotiation?
Enabling Clauses	Does the legislation authorise regulators to issue technical standards and adapt provisions?
Pilot Deployment	Is there a sandbox or phased rollout mechanism embedded in the implementation plan?
Judicial Integration	Are courts equipped to interpret and enforce stablecoin provisions, including consumer claims?
Feedback Mechanisms	Have post-implementation review processes been established to support iterative reform?

Chapter 11
Global Stablecoin Regulation:
Where to From Here?

Jane Thomason
https://orcid.org/0009-0007-3123-7851
University College London, UK

Mu'azu Umar
https://orcid.org/0009-0003-1578-8531
ECOWAS Commisson, Nigeria

ABSTRACT

Stablecoins have firmly established themselves in the core of global digital finance. They now function as payment infrastructure, liquidity tools, and potential public-purpose digital money. Viewed through regulatory, technical, economic, and humanitarian lenses, the chapters in this volume present a consistent conclusion: stablecoins offer significant opportunities for efficiency, inclusion, and financial innovation, but these benefits can only be realised when supported by strong governance frameworks, transparent and high-quality reserves, enforceable redemption rights, and coherent cross-border oversight. At the same time, substantial differences remain in national implementation, supervisory capability, and the treatment of high-risk models such as algorithmic stablecoins. The Commonwealth Model Law on Stablecoins, outlined in this volume, is a forward-looking regulatory blueprint. Its principles of proportionality, transparency, and interoperability offer jurisdictions a foundation for building safe, inclusive, and resilient systems

DOI: 10.4018/979-8-3373-6655-5.ch011

INTRODUCTION

Digital asset innovation reflects a structural transformation in financial architecture, driven by technological change, regulatory arbitrage, and persistent gaps in efficiency and inclusion, giving rise to new forms of private digital money (Arner, Barberis, & Buckley, 2015). Within this context, stablecoins have emerged as privately issued monetary instruments that promise stability; however, without robust prudential safeguards, they risk mirroring historical episodes of wildcat banking and are therefore vulnerable to runs and confidence shocks (Gorton & Zhang, 2021). More broadly, the digitalisation of money entails a reconfiguration of the monetary system, in which stablecoins, alongside central bank digital currencies (CBDCs) and tokenised deposits, reshape the relationship between public and private money, monetary sovereignty, and financial stability (Brunnermeier, James, & Landau, 2021).

The evolution of stablecoins can be understood in three broad phases. Phase 1: Speculative experimentation (2016–2022) was characterised by rapid innovation, limited oversight, and repeated failures, as stablecoins were tested primarily within crypto markets with weak governance, fragile stabilisation mechanisms, and inadequate reserves. Phase 2: Regulated integration (2023–2027) reflects the entry of stablecoins into mainstream payments, remittances, and financial systems, accompanied by increasing regulatory convergence, licensing regimes, prudential requirements, and supervisory coordination. Phase 3: Systemic digital infrastructure (2027–2035) represents the likely next stage, in which stablecoins operate alongside CBDCs and tokenised deposits as interoperable, public-purpose financial infrastructure, contingent on sustained cross-border cooperation and the practical implementation of modular regulatory frameworks.

As the chapters in this book demonstrate, stablecoins are already reshaping payments, remittances, decentralised finance (DeFi), humanitarian disbursements, and cross-border trade by combining the stability of value of fiat currencies with the speed, programmability, and borderless reach of blockchain-based infrastructure. Their rapid expansion reflects growing global demand for digital money that is efficient, reliable, and interoperable.

At the same time, these very characteristics generate significant vulnerabilities that threat actors can exploit. Persistent gaps in consumer protection, heightened exposure to illicit finance, governance weaknesses, limited transparency of reserves, and the potential for systemic contagion all feature prominently in the case studies discussed in this book. Episodes of collapse involving poorly designed stablecoins underscore the need for robust, preemptive oversight before such instruments achieve widespread adoption. For example, the collapse of the TerraUSD stablecoin in 2022 demonstrated how weak stabilisation mechanisms and opaque governance can trigger rapid de-pegging, liquidity spirals, and systemic contagion across interconnected markets (BIS, 2023). More recently, the temporary de-pegging of a major fiat-backed stablecoin following the failure of a U.S. regional bank in 2023 illustrated how concentration risk in reserve assets can transmit traditional banking stress directly into digital money ecosystems (BIS, 2025). These episodes underscore a central message of this book: without high-quality reserves, enforceable redemption rights, robust governance, and adequate cross-border supervision, stablecoins can amplify financial instability.

Areas of Contestation

Despite growing convergence around baseline regulatory principles, stablecoins remain the subject of substantive scholarly, policy, and institutional disagreement. Some scholars view that privately issued stablecoins, even when fully reserved and subject to regulatory oversight, pose inherent challenges to monetary sovereignty and central bank control. From this perspective, the widespread adoption of foreign-denominated stablecoins, particularly in emerging and developing economies, risks accelerating digital dollarisation, weakening monetary transmission mechanisms, and constraining macroeconomic policy autonomy (Brunnermeier et al., 2019). Proponents of this view often argue that central bank digital currencies (CBDCs), rather than regulated private instruments, should form the primary foundation of future digital monetary systems (Agur et al., 2022).

A second area of contestation concerns the feasibility and desirability of integrating private stablecoins into core financial infrastructure. Critics question whether private issuers can credibly perform functions traditionally associated with public money, such as acting as a stable store of value during periods of systemic stress, without ultimately relying on implicit or explicit public backstops. Drawing on historical analogies to pre-deposit-insurance banking and contemporary shadow-banking systems, this literature warns that stablecoins may recreate familiar forms of liquidity and run risk outside the perimeter of conventional banking regulation (Ricks, 2016; Gorton & Zhang, 2023). From this standpoint, stablecoins risk amplifying financial fragility rather than mitigating it, particularly when governance, reserve management, or redemption mechanisms prove inadequate.

There is also ongoing debate regarding the long-term role of algorithmic and partially collateralised stablecoin models. While recent market failures have exposed their vulnerabilities, some scholars contend that dismissing these designs entirely may prematurely foreclose innovation in decentralised monetary mechanisms. Others counter that repeated instability demonstrates structural weaknesses incompatible with financial stability objectives and public trust. As a result, many regulators have adopted a cautious stance, restricting or prohibiting such models while allowing limited experimentation under controlled conditions (Brunnermeier et al., 2019).

More broadly, an emerging body of institutional research suggests that the future of digital money is likely to be plural rather than singular. In this view, CBDCs, regulated stablecoins, tokenised deposits, and commercial bank money may coexist within interoperable payment ecosystems, provided that robust governance, transparency, and supervisory coordination are in place (BIS Innovation Hub, 2023). This perspective reframes the discussion towards the design of resilient, multi-rail monetary architecture capable of supporting innovation while safeguarding financial stability. A multi-rail digital money ecosystem is a financial environment in which stablecoins, CBDCs, tokenised deposits, and traditional bank money coexist and interact across interoperable technical and legal infrastructures, each serving distinct economic functions.

Several contributors further argue that fragmented regulatory approaches across jurisdictions jeopardise interoperability, financial stability, and overall market integrity. Recent BIS research (Ahmed, R. et.al, 2024; and Aldasoro. I, et al 2024) highlights that as central banks accelerate exploration and design of CBDCs in tandem with the rise of stablecoins, preserving central bank money's role, while fostering interoperability across digital monetary systems is critical to ensuring that CBDCs and privately issued stablecoins can coexist without undermining financial stability or fragmenting payment infrastructure.

This volume does not seek to resolve these debates, it reflects an emerging pragmatic consensus that where stablecoins are permitted to operate, they must do so within robust, proportionate, and interoperable regulatory frameworks that prioritise consumer protection, financial integrity, and systemic resilience. The Model Law is examined in this context as one possible regulatory response to these contested dynamics, offering a structured approach to managing risks while enabling responsible innovation, rather than as a universal solution.

The Commonwealth Model Law on Stablecoins

This book should be seen as a companion to the Model Law. It provides a comprehensive and multidisciplinary examination of stablecoins, offering a globally relevant account of their development, functions, and implications. It brings together legal analysis, technical architecture, economic assessment, consumer protection, humanitarian use cases, and geopolitical perspectives within a single, coherent framework. The book combines regulatory insights, detailed technical analysis, and forward-looking policy guidance in a way few existing works do.

The book begins by identifying the economic, technological, and governance challenges posed by stablecoins; it then develops a coherent solution architecture grounded in risk-based, modular, and technology-neutral regulation; and it concludes by translating these principles into an actionable implementation roadmap through the Model Law. This concluding chapter serves as the bridge between analysis and execution, synthesising the volume's insights into practical guidance for policymakers, regulators, and institutional leaders tasked with governing stablecoins as they transition from experimental instruments to systemically relevant financial infrastructure.

This book complements prior policy reports on crypto-assets and stablecoins, which have typically focused either on high-level risk identification or narrow regulatory recommendations (Financial Stability Board (2020, 2023), Bank for International Settlements (2007), Financial Action Task Force (2021). It goes further by integrating legal design, technical architecture, financial stability analysis, and implementation practice into a single, operational framework. Its distinctive contribution lies in translating international standards into a modular, legislatively actionable model law, grounded in real institutional constraints and cross-border realities, and explicitly framing stablecoins as emerging public-purpose digital infrastructure (digital financial systems that perform essential societal functions such as payments, remittances, and value storage at scale).

The book's contribution is framed in clearly differentiated institutional responsibilities. For central banks, it clarifies how stablecoins interact with monetary sovereignty, payment-system oversight, and CBDC strategies within a multi-rail digital-money ecosystem. For financial regulators and supervisors, it provides a risk-tiered, modular blueprint for licensing, prudential supervision, technology oversight, and cross-border coordination that can be operationalised within existing mandates. For finance ministries and policymakers, it offers a legislative architecture that balances innovation, financial stability, and inclusion while remaining adaptable to national legal systems and development priorities. Finally, for regulated private entities (including stablecoin issuers, custodians, wallet providers, and payment intermediaries) the book articulates clear expectations around governance, reserve management, transparency, compliance, and accountability, reducing regulatory uncertainty and supporting responsible innovation.

OVERVIEW OF THE BOOK

This chapter adopts a structured qualitative synthesis methodology. It draws on comparative analysis, cross-jurisdictional policy review, and thematic integration of the preceding chapters to distill common patterns, points of convergence, and unresolved tensions in stablecoin regulation. Rather than presenting new empirical data, the chapter systematically synthesises legal, economic, technical, and policy analyses contributed throughout the volume, situating them within the broader body of international standards and regulatory scholarship. Such an approach enables the identification of cross-cutting principles, implementation challenges, and forward-looking research and policy priorities relevant to diverse institutional and geopolitical contexts.

The book was written by the expert contributors who developed The Model Law. It establishes the conceptual, legal, and regulatory foundations for understanding stablecoins in contemporary digital finance. It provides precise definitions, comparative analysis across major jurisdictions, and a detailed assessment of systemic risks. It provides an in-depth exposition of The Model Law, a fully developed legislative framework designed for adoption by member states and aligned with international standards set by the FATF (2021), the FSB (2020, 2023), and the BIS (2007).

A summary of the individual chapters follows.

In Chapter 1, **"Why Stablecoins Matter,"** Loretta Joseph, Anson Zeall, and Jane Thomason outline the book's purpose, scope, and central arguments, and introduce stablecoins as a pivotal innovation in digital finance, framing the book's core questions around their systemic significance, risks, and regulatory design.

Building on this foundation, Chapter 2, **What Are Stablecoins?** Kokila Alargh establishes a conceptual and regulatory map of stablecoins, showing how diverse designs, taxonomies, and legal definitions shape their risk profiles and policy treatment globally. The chapter shows that although stablecoins share the common objective of maintaining stable value, they vary significantly in design, risk exposure, and legal character. The chapter identifies areas of emerging convergence and ongoing fragmentation in global terminology by examining definitions issued by international bodies, such as the FSB (2020, 2023), the BIS (2007), and the FATF (2021). The chapter further demonstrates how domestic regulatory frameworks - such as the EU's MiCA (2023), Singapore's MAS (MAS, 2022) rules, and the U.S. GENIUS Act (2025) - shape stablecoin design and governance according to local priorities such as financial stability, consumer protection, and monetary sovereignty. A structured typology of stablecoins highlights how different stabilisation mechanisms, whether fiat reserves, diversified asset portfolios, crypto collateral, or algorithmic controls, generate distinct strengths and vulnerabilities. A detailed outline of the stablecoin lifecycle maps the points at which risks arise and clarifies the allocation of regulatory responsibilities across issuance, reserve management, redemption, and secondary-market activity.

In Chapter 3, **Global Regulatory Approaches**, Kokila Alargh demonstrates that international regulation of stablecoins is gradually converging around a common foundation of transparency, prudential discipline, and accountability, even as national approaches continue to diverge in structure and emphasis. She shows how international standard-setting bodies have articulated guiding principles centred on proportionality, technological neutrality, and the doctrine of "same activity, same risk, same regulation." Building on these shared core principles, jurisdictions have developed regulatory models that reflect their own institutional priorities and market conditions, ranging from the EU's comprehensive MiCA (2023) regime to more flexible frameworks in the United States, Bahrain, Singapore, Hong Kong, and the UAE.

Despite these differences, Alargh identifies clear areas of convergence. Most jurisdictions now require full reserve backing with high-quality liquid assets, enforceable redemption at par, licensing and oversight for issuers and intermediaries, stringent AML/CFT compliance, and defined governance standards. Regulators are also establishing firm boundaries by restricting or prohibiting high-risk models, notably algorithmic designs and privacy-enhanced stablecoins, while allowing controlled experimentation through regulatory sandboxes.

The chapter notes that significant divergences remain, including variation in scope, differing treatment of foreign issuers, and contrasting preferences between banking-integrated and bespoke licensing regimes. These differences raise broader questions about monetary sovereignty, financial stability, and cross-border spillovers. Nevertheless, Alargh concludes that the overall trajectory is clear, stablecoins are transitioning into mainstream, supervised financial infrastructure. The emerging global regulatory architecture points toward an increasingly harmonised baseline, one capable of supporting innovation while safeguarding consumers, preserving market integrity, and protecting national monetary systems.

In Chapter 4, **A Stablecoin Framework for the Future**, Maxine Binns argues that the long-term effectiveness of stablecoin regulation rests on legal frameworks that are flexible, principle-based, and interoperable, capable of adapting to rapid technological and market change. She confirms that stablecoins have moved to the centre of modern digital finance. However, jurisdictions continue to grapple with a wide range of regulatory challenges, including reserve transparency, governance standards, systemic risk, cross-border enforceability, and consumer protection. In this context, a rigid, uniform regulatory model is neither practical nor appropriate, particularly given the diversity of legal systems, market structures, and institutional capacities across the Commonwealth.

Binns proposes a modular regulatory framework as a workable and scalable solution. By organising regulation into discrete modules, covering licensing, AML/CFT requirements, reserve management, governance, interoperability, and market conduct, jurisdictions can introduce essential safeguards immediately while expanding or refining their frameworks over time. Modular regulation is a regulatory approach in which legal and supervisory requirements are structured into discrete, function-specific components that jurisdictions can adopt and scale according to risk, capacity, and context while remaining aligned with common global standards. This approach preserves legal clarity and national sovereignty while remaining aligned with global expectations set by the FSB (2020, 2023), BIS (2007), FATF (2021), IOSCO (2023), and leading domestic regimes.

The chapter emphasises that regulatory inaction entails risks. Without timely reform, countries risk destabilising financial markets, weakening monetary autonomy, and falling behind in the emerging global digital economy. In contrast, modular and technology-neutral frameworks enable jurisdictions to support innovation, enhance resilience, and integrate effectively into a harmonising global regulatory environment. Binns concludes that adaptive, inclusive, and interoperable regulation is fundamental to the development of trustworthy, future-ready monetary systems in the digital era.

In Chapter 5, **Technology, Security, and Cyber Risks Implementing the Commonwealth Model Law on Stablecoins**, Marc Krisjanous contends that the successful implementation of The Model Law hinges on recognising technology and cybersecurity as central pillars of financial supervision. Stablecoins rely on a multilayered technological stack, comprising blockchain infrastructure, smart contracts, oracle systems, custody arrangements, and digital wallets -where weaknesses at any layer can precipitate rapid, system-wide failures. Through case studies such as the Terra/Luna algorithmic collapse, the Beanstalk governance exploit, and various oracle and key-management breaches, Krisjanous illustrates that in the stablecoin ecosystem, technological vulnerabilities translate directly into financial vulnerabilities, with the potential to trigger broader contagion across interconnected markets.

The chapter operationalises The Model Law's high-level expectations for ICT resilience, the security of smart contracts and oracles, governance oversight, and third-party risk management by proposing a tiered supervisory framework. Requirements escalate according to the systemic footprint of an arrangement - from basic standards for smaller Tier 3 issuers to advanced controls for systemically important Tier 1 issuers. These enhanced expectations include formal code verification, the use of decentralised oracle networks, custody solutions, continuous monitoring systems, red-team testing, and dedicated security operations centres.

Krisjanous concludes that regulators must build strong internal technical expertise and adopt adaptive, risk-based supervisory practices, supplemented where necessary by specialised external providers. Bridging the gap between legal prescriptions and technical realities is essential. Only by integrating technology, supervision, and governance can jurisdictions support responsible stablecoin innovation while preserving consumer protection, market integrity, and global financial stability.

In Chapter 6, **Financial Stability and Systemic Risks of Stablecoins**, Harvesh Seegolam and Loretta Joseph explain that the financial stability implications of stablecoins are immediate, structural, and global in scope. As stablecoins evolve from niche digital instruments into systemically relevant components of modern financial ecosystems, they introduce new pathways for contagion, liquidity stress, and cross-border spillovers. The chapter demonstrates that vulnerabilities in governance, reserve asset quality, operational resilience, and redemption processes can trigger rapid and widespread destabilisation - patterns already evident in recent market disruptions. Their growing integration with banks, money market funds, payment systems, and decentralised finance only heightens these systemic exposures.

In Chapter 7, **Cross-Border Coordination**, Kokila Alargh argues that effective and sustainable regulation of stablecoins is unattainable without formal, institutionalised cross-border cooperation. She emphasises that, by design, stablecoins are borderless: they may be issued in one jurisdiction, governed in another, and used globally. This structural feature challenges the territorial assumptions underpinning traditional financial regulation. Fragmented national approaches produce supervisory blind spots, facilitate regulatory arbitrage, weaken consumer protection, and elevate systemic risk. Alargh shows that although international standard-setting bodies such as the FATF (2021) and the FSB (2020, 2023) approach the issue from distinct mandates, they reach the same conclusion: coordinated global oversight is essential to protect financial integrity, preserve monetary sovereignty, and maintain the stability of payment systems.

The chapter explains that stablecoins generate both macro-level and micro-level vulnerabilities. At the macro level, the widespread adoption of foreign-denominated stablecoins can undermine domestic monetary policy and accelerate processes of digital dollarisation. At the micro level, deficiencies in governance, reserve management, or redemption mechanisms can transmit shocks across markets and jurisdictions, triggering rapid contagion. No single national authority can adequately manage these interconnected risks.

Alargh identifies several practical barriers to effective cooperation: data asymmetries between regulators, inconsistent definitional frameworks, legal restrictions on information sharing, and substantial disparities in supervisory capacity. To address these issues, she outlines core policy principles, including establishing minimum international standards, creating supervisory colleges, developing mutual recognition mechanisms, and adopting interoperable compliance infrastructures.

The chapter concludes that cross-border cooperation is the foundation of any credible global regulatory regime for stablecoins. Only through coordinated, outcomes-aligned supervision can stablecoins be integrated safely into the international financial system.

In Chapter 8, **Strengthening AML/CFT and Proliferation Financing Frameworks for Stablecoins: Global Policy Recommendations Anchored in the Commonwealth Model Law,** Rick McDonell and his co-authors argue that although stablecoins present meaningful opportunities for financial inclusion, efficiency gains, and the growth of the digital economy across the Commonwealth and many other jurisdictions, they simultaneously introduce substantial money laundering, terrorist financing, and proliferation financing risks. The authors highlight that the speed, global accessibility, pseudonymous nature of transactions, constant interaction with traditional financial systems and deep integration with decentralised finance create vulnerabilities that traditional oversight frameworks are ill-equipped to manage without significant reform. Stablecoins now feature prominently in illicit financial activity, including ransomware payments, sanctions evasion, and proliferation finance-related transactions, with smaller and mid-sized Commonwealth jurisdictions particularly exposed due to high remittance flows and limited supervisory capacity.

The chapter posits that mitigating these risks requires harmonised, technology-neutral regulatory frameworks grounded in global standards set by the FATF (2021), BIS (2007), FSB (2020,2023), and IOSCO (2023), and implemented through The Model Law. Priority measures include enhanced licensing regimes, real-time blockchain analytics, full implementation of the FATF Travel Rule (FATF, 2021), mandatory sanctions-screening mechanisms, proliferation-financing indicators, and coordinated cross-border supervision.

Case studies from Mauritius, Singapore, the Eastern Caribbean, and The Bahamas illustrate that even smaller jurisdictions can develop adequate AML/CFT controls when supported by RegTech tools, regional collaboration, and targeted capacity-building initiatives.

The authors conclude with a call for urgent, coordinated action anchored in a multi-country roadmap, which is provided. They emphasise that only through collective commitment can stablecoins fulfil their potential to support inclusion and innovation while maintaining the integrity of the global financial system and protecting national and international security.

In Chapter 9, **Licensing and Supervision Made Simple: The Why and How We Need Licensing,** Jonathan Hatch argues that the effectiveness of stablecoin regulation depends fundamentally on clear, risk-sensitive licensing and robust supervisory frameworks that balance innovation with public confidence. He notes that stablecoins now carry out economically significant functions, storing value, facilitating payments, rapid transfer, and enabling redemption, activities that have traditionally required strong regulatory safeguards to prevent consumer harm and systemic instability. Within this context, licensing is not a procedural formality but a core accountability mechanism: it determines who is permitted to operate, under what conditions, and with whom responsibility is borne when failures occur.

Hatch's analysis emphasises the necessity of functional regulation, whereby entities are licensed according to the specific risks they face and manage. This approach helps prevent regulatory arbitrage, governance weaknesses, and fragility, which are problems that have characterised earlier phases of financial innovation. Given that issuers, custodians, wallet providers, liquidity agents, and smart-contract controllers each pose distinct risks, licensing frameworks must account for these differences. Precise requirements related to governance, reserve management, redemption rights, capital adequacy, transparency, and consumer protection form the essential pillars of a resilient system.

The chapter further outlines that supervision must be adaptive, proportionate, and technologically informed. RegTech tools, tiered supervisory structures, and international cooperation are necessary to reflect the borderless nature of stablecoin ecosystems. Hatch concludes that well-designed licensing regimes enable innovation rather than restrict it, allowing stablecoins to integrate safely into the global financial system while preserving financial integrity and maintaining user trust.

In Chapter 10, **How to Implement a Stablecoin Framework**, Maxine Binns asserts that implementing stablecoin legislation is, above all, an exercise in legal stewardship. This requires the convergence of principle-based design, institutional capacity, and contextual awareness to produce laws that are both credible and future-ready. She stresses that effective implementation extends far beyond drafting statutory text. It requires a sequenced, pluralistic, and adaptive process that translates The Model Law and similar frameworks into enforceable, legitimate, and operational regulatory systems. Binns outlines six essential phases in this process: legal scoping, stakeholder consultation, modular drafting, capacity-building, pilot deployment, and iterative reform. Each phase must be executed carefully to preserve legal coherence and sustain public trust.

A central theme of the chapter is the importance of modularity. Given the wide variation in legal traditions, institutional maturity, and economic priorities across jurisdictions, no single regulatory model can serve every context. The Model Laws' modular structure allows governments to adopt components tailored to their needs, whether in licensing, redemption, consumer protection, enforcement, or cross-border coordination, while remaining aligned with global standards.

The chapter also emphasises the need for robust enforcement powers, precise definitions, readiness to integrate smart contracts, and cross-border legal interoperability. Binns presents legal pluralism not as an obstacle but as a strategic asset, enabling the development of frameworks that respect community norms and customary practices, thereby supporting a more efficient and accessible digital economy. Ultimately, Binns argues that implementation is an ongoing process. Stablecoin legislation must evolve through continuous monitoring, piloting, and responsive reform to remain effective in a rapidly advancing digital environment.

Binns offers specific strategic legislative and institutional reforms to reinforce legal clarity, preserve sovereignty, and enable inclusive innovation across diverse legal environments, including:

1. Codify stablecoin classifications
2. Embed enabling clauses in each module
3. Recognise smart contracts as legally enforceable

4. Mandate tiered licensing and oversight regimes
5. Codify reserve management and redemption safeguards
6. Enable hybrid governance models
7. Build cross-border legal coordination mechanisms

Together, these recommendations offer a strategic framework for resilient, inclusive, and future-proof implementation.

This concluding chapter summarises the key themes related to The Model Law. It outlines priorities for policymakers, regulators, international institutions, and researchers as the stablecoin ecosystem moves from framework design to operational reality. The volume should be read in conjunction with *"Global Lessons for Stablecoin Regulation and Governance"* (Thomason, 2026 forthcoming), which provides empirical case studies on stablecoins.

KEY THEMES

Stablecoins are Emerging as a Systemic Financial Infrastructure

Across the chapters, stablecoins are portrayed as having moved far beyond speculative crypto instruments. They increasingly function as core components of modern payment systems, remittance channels, humanitarian transfer mechanisms, and DeFi liquidity rails. Their economic role increasingly mirrors that of short-term money market instruments and cross-border payment networks.

Regulatory Convergence is Emerging, yet Fragmentation Persists

While there is broad alignment on core principles from bodies such as the FSB (2020, 2023), FATF (2021), and BIS (2007), national implementation varies substantially. Differences in licensing structures, treatment of foreign issuers, and reserve requirements create risks of regulatory arbitrage and inconsistency in consumer protection.

Risks Range From Micro-Level Consumer Harm to Macro-Level Systemic Threats

Risks range from algorithmic design failures, liquidity spirals, governance weaknesses, reserve opacity, illicit finance and money laundering, terrorist financing and proliferation financing exposure, digital identity exclusion, and monetary sovereignty concerns in emerging markets. These risks underscore the need for comprehensive safeguards and cross-border cooperation, collaboration and coordination. Together, these themes highlight the convergence of scholarly, policy, and technical perspectives on how stablecoins should evolve within a safe, inclusive, and globally coherent digital financial system.

NEXT STEPS: FROM FRAMEWORK TO GLOBAL IMPLEMENTATION

Despite the areas of convergence identified, several significant tensions remain unresolved and continue to drive global debates on the future of stablecoins. The future of stablecoins will depend on how regulators, policymakers, and international institutions navigate these unresolved tensions surrounding them. The ability to balance innovation with stability, sovereignty, and ethical considerations will shape the next phase of global digital finance. Without coordinated action, stablecoins will continue to develop through regulatory arbitrage and fragmentation, leaving reserve risks opaque, consumer protection uneven, and stress events capable of rapidly propagating across borders and systems, with particular consequences for financial stability and monetary sovereignty in vulnerable economies.

A close alignment emerges across contributors that: (i) Stablecoins have become systemically relevant components of the global financial architecture. (ii) Across the contributions, there is broad agreement that effective regulation is more likely to be sustainable when it is risk-based, proportionate, and technology-neutral, anchored in full-reserve backing, enforceable redemption rights, strong governance, and transparent disclosures. (iii) Cross-border coordination is indispensable to prevent fragmentation, regulatory arbitrage, and systemic blind spots. (iv) When properly governed, stablecoins can act as public-purpose infrastructure that reduces costs, promotes financial inclusion, enhances humanitarian operations, and supports secure digital identity ecosystems.

Stablecoins are now central components of the emerging global financial infrastructure. The next phase is coordinated execution. The following steps propose priorities for policymakers, regulators, international institutions, and researchers as the stablecoin ecosystem develops.

1. National Adoption and Localisation of the Commonwealth Model Law

Many jurisdictions are now considering a transition from high-level policy alignment toward more concrete legislative and supervisory responses by adopting and localising The Model Law. This includes mapping existing financial laws to The Model Law's modular components, identifying gaps in licensing, reserve governance, redemption rights, and enforcement powers, and sequencing reforms according to institutional capacity. Pilot jurisdictions, small states, and emerging markets can serve as early adopters, generating implementation lessons for broader global uptake.

2. Establishment of Supervisory Colleges for Systemic Stablecoins

Given the borderless nature of major stablecoin arrangements, regulators should prioritise establishing cross-border supervisory colleges. These colleges would coordinate oversight of reserve management, governance, technology risk, and redemption processes, and enable timely information sharing during stress events. The Model Law provides a legal foundation for such cooperation; operationalising it is now essential to closing supervisory blind spots.

3. Development of Minimum Global Standards for Reserve Transparency and ICT Resilience

While regulatory convergence is emerging, significant variation remains in reserve disclosures, audit practices, and technology risk management. The next step is to articulate minimum, globally interoperable standards for reserve quality, frequency of attestations, custody segregation, smart-contract assurance, and third-party risk. These standards should be scalable, risk-tiered, and aligned with The Model Law's proportional approach.

4. Integration of Stablecoins into Broader Digital Money Strategies

Stablecoin policy should no longer be developed in isolation. Governments and central banks must integrate stablecoin regulation into broader strategies covering CBDCs, tokenised deposits, instant payment systems, and digital identity. Clarifying the complementary roles of public and private digital money will be critical to avoiding fragmentation, preserving monetary sovereignty, and enabling innovation.

5. Operationalisation of Cross-Border Consumer Protection and Redress

As retail users across borders increasingly use stablecoins, regulators should move beyond domestic consumer protection frameworks. Priority actions include piloting interoperable online dispute-resolution mechanisms, defining portable consumer rights for users of digital money, and establishing cooperative enforcement channels. Without credible redress, trust in stablecoins as public-purpose infrastructure will remain fragile.

6. Targeted Capacity Building for Emerging and Developing Economies

The effectiveness of any global framework ultimately depends on supervisory capability. International organisations, development banks, and regional bodies should support targeted capacity-building initiatives focused on RegTech adoption, blockchain analytics, cyber supervision, and macro-financial monitoring. The Model Law is deliberately accessible; sustained technical assistance will determine its real-world impact.

FUTURE RESEARCH DIRECTIONS

Future research is needed to build on this work by examining empirical outcomes of early adoption, stress-testing stablecoin frameworks under real market conditions, and analysing emerging issues such as AI-driven payments, autonomous financial agents, and the long-term interactions among stablecoins, sovereignty, and the global monetary order. Key research priorities are summarised below:

Quantitative Models of Stablecoin Systemic Risk

More advanced modelling is needed to understand the systemic dynamics of stablecoins across both digital and traditional markets. Priority areas include: stress testing under extreme market conditions; redemption cascades and liquidity spirals; shock transmission between stablecoins, DeFi protocols, and banking systems; and real-time contagion modelling in 24/7 markets; network-centrality analysis to identify "too-interconnected-to-fail" nodes. Developing such models will allow regulators to build early-warning systems and design macroprudential tools tailored to digital money.

Interoperability Standards for Multi-Rail Digital Money Ecosystems

As CBDCs, stablecoins, tokenised deposits, and commercial bank money begin to coexist, the next frontier is interoperability. Research is needed on: technical and legal interoperability between CBDCs and stablecoins; integration of tokenised banking deposits into multi-rail payment systems; and harmonised data formats for cross-border compliance and settlement. Interoperability will determine whether digital money evolves as a fragmented ecosystem or a coherent global network.

Regulatory Impact Evaluations Across Jurisdictions

There is a pressing need for comparative studies that assess how different frameworks perform in practice, including: MiCA (EU) (2023), the GENIUS Act (US) (2025), Singapore's PSA (MAS), and the rollouts of The Model Law. Evaluations should examine market integrity, consumer outcomes, compliance effectiveness, innovation trajectories, and systemic-risk profiles.

Consumer Protection and Redress Mechanisms for Borderless Digital Economies

Effective redress will be central to trust in digital money ecosystems. As financial activity becomes more digital and cross-border, future research should explore consumer protection, end-user experience, and micro-risks. The complexity of self-custody, the potential for irreversible loss and the need for redress mechanisms, especially in low-resource settings, is a vital research area. Mechanisms such as interoperable online dispute resolution networks, AI safety and bias mitigation in redress systems, portable consumer rights across jurisdictions, privacy-preserving complaint data-sharing protocols, and harmonised standards for cross-border requirements need empirical evidence.

Stablecoins, Sovereignty, and Digital Dollarisation

Emerging markets face unique macroeconomic risks. Priority research areas include: the effects of stablecoin adoption on monetary transmission; capital-flow volatility linked to stablecoin demand; risks of accelerated dollarisation and policy leakage; hybrid public–private models for digital national currencies; and mechanisms for preserving monetary autonomy amid competing digital rails. These issues are significant for regions with high inflation, large remittance flows, or fragile banking systems.

Cybersecurity, Operational Resilience, and Third-Party Risk

Given that stablecoins operate on layered technology stacks, future research should assess systemic vulnerabilities in oracle networks, custody providers, and smart-contract ecosystems; cascading failures across interoperable networks; minimum global standards for ICT resilience; and stress scenarios involving simultaneous cyberattacks and liquidity shocks. This work is crucial for strengthening digital monetary infrastructure.

Legal Interoperability and Cross-Border Enforcement

As stablecoins circulate globally, research must examine: mutual recognition of licences and supervisory decisions; conflict-of-laws rules for digital money; the enforceability of redemption rights across borders; and international coordination on sanctions compliance and proliferation financing and terrorist financing controls. Legal interoperability will determine the feasibility of global digital financial markets.

These research directions collectively define the next phase of inquiry needed to support safe, resilient, and inclusive global digital money systems.

CONCLUSION

A set of clear organising principles emerges from the contributors of this book for understanding the future of stablecoins and their place within global digital finance.

Regulation must be modular, proportionate, and technology-neutral. The Model Law embodies this approach, offering a flexible framework that jurisdictions can tailor to their institutional capacity, risk tolerance, and sovereignty concerns without imposing a single regulatory template.

Cross-border coordination is a non-negotiable element of global financial stability. Even the most robust national regime will falter without interoperable data standards, supervisory colleges, and harmonised definitions that prevent regulatory arbitrage and systemic blind spots.

The book also highlights the specific opportunities and vulnerabilities facing emerging markets. Stablecoins can expand inclusion, reduce remittance costs, and support financial modernisation, yet they also heighten concerns about dollarisation, capital-flow volatility, and monetary autonomy. Policy must therefore strike a careful balance between innovation and sovereignty.

Equally important is the recognition that stablecoins increasingly function as public-purpose infrastructure. Their use in humanitarian transfers, remittances, and identity-linked services demonstrates significant social value, but these applications also carry risks of surveillance, exclusion, and dependency if governance frameworks are weak. Ethical, rights-based design is essential.

Stablecoins have the potential to evolve into a foundational layer of global digital finance, contingent on governance quality, institutional oversight, and sustained international coordination, provided their development is guided by thoughtful governance, strong institutions, and sustained international cooperation. The aim must be not only to support innovation but also to protect human dignity, market integrity, and economic sovereignty in a rapidly evolving monetary landscape.

In this context, The Model Law provides a forward-looking regulatory framework that operationalises emerging international principles through a modular and adaptable legislative design. It offers a scalable blueprint for licensing, reserve management, disclosures, supervision, and cross-border coordination. Significantly, it reframes stablecoins as potential public goods capable of advancing financial inclusion, humanitarian efficiency, and secure digital identity, if properly regulated.

The future of stablecoins will ultimately hinge on trust, interoperability, and regulatory coherence. The coming decade will redefine the architecture of global finance as digital money shifts from experimentation to public infrastructure. If designed wisely, digital money can expand inclusion, reduce friction, and enhance resilience; if poorly governed, it risks amplifying inequality, eroding sovereignty, and introducing new forms of systemic fragility. The next decade will therefore be defined not by the technology itself, but by collective choices about trust, governance, and cooperation. This book provides a clear, rigorous, and practical guide. It offers the essential foundation for anyone seeking to understand, design, or regulate the next generation of digital monetary systems.

REFERENCES

Ahmed, R., Aldasoro, I., & Duley, C. (2024). Public information and stablecoin runs (BIS Working Paper No. 1164). Bank for International Settlements. https://www.bis.org/publ/work1164.pdf (Accessed 4 January 2026)

Aldasoro, I., Cornelli, G., Ferrari Minesso, M., Gambacorta, L., & Habib, M. M. (2024). Stablecoins, money market funds, and monetary policy (BIS Working Paper No. 1219). Bank for International Settlements. https://www.bis.org/publ/work1219.pdf (Accessed 4 January 2026)

Arner, D. W., Barberis, J. N., & Buckley, R. P. The Evolution of Fintech: A New Post-Crisis Paradigm? (October 1, 2015). University of Hong Kong Faculty of Law Research Paper No. 2015/047, UNSW Law Research Paper No. 2016-62, Available at SSRN: https://ssrn.com/abstract=2676553 DOI: 10.2139/ssrn.2676553

Bank for International Settlements. (2023). The crypto ecosystem: Key elements and risks, June 2023. https://www.bis.org/publ/othp72.pdf(Accessed 5 January 2026)

Bank for International Settlements. (2025) BIS Working Papers No. 1164: Public information and stablecoin runs. Monetary and Economic Department, January 2024 (revised January 2025) https://www.bis.org/publ/work1164.pdf (Accessed 5 January 2026)

Bank for International Settlements (BIS). (2007). *Basel Committee on Banking Supervision Principles for home-host supervisory cooperation and allocation mechanisms in the context of Advanced Measurement Approaches (AMA).* https://www.bis.org/publ/bcbs135.pdf (Accessed 4 January 2026)

Brunnermeier, James, & Landau, 2021., The Digitalisation of Money. BIS Working Papers, No 941, 19 May 2021.https://www.bis.org/publ/work941.htm (Accessed 4 January 2026)

Commonwealth Secretariat. (2025 forthcoming). *Commonwealth Model Law on Stablecoins (draft).* Commonwealth Secretariat.

European Union. (2023). *Regulation - 2023/1114 - EN - EUR-Lex.* Europa.eu. https://eur-lex.europa.eu/eli/reg/2023/1114/oj/eng (Accessed 4 January 2026)

FATF. (2021). *Updated Guidance for a Risk-Based Approach to Virtual Assets and Virtual Asset Service Providers.* Www.fatf-Gafi.org. https://www.fatf-gafi.org/en/publications/Fatfrecommendations/Guidance-rba-virtual-assets-2021.html (Accessed 4 January 2026)

Financial Stability Board. (2020). *Regulation, Supervision and Oversight of "Global Stablecoin" Arrangements*. Www.fsb.org. https://www.fsb.org/2020/10/regulation-supervision-and-oversight-of-global-stablecoin-arrangements/ (Accessed 4 January 2026)

Financial Stability Board. (2023). *High-level Recommendations for the Regulation, Supervision and Oversight of Global Stablecoin Arrangements: Final report*. Www.fsb.org. https://www.fsb.org/2023/07/high-level-recommendations-for-the-regulation-supervision-and-oversight-of-global-stablecoin-arrangements-final-report/ (Accessed 4 January 2026)

Gorton, G. B., Zhang, J. Y., & Stablecoins, T. W. (September 30, 2021). 90 University of Chicago Law Review 909 (2023), Available at SSRN: https://ssrn.com/abstract=3888752 (Accessed 4 January 2026)

IOSCO. (2023). *Policy Recommendations for Crypto and Digital Asset Markets Final Report*. https://www.iosco.org/library/pubdocs/pdf/IOSCOPD747.pdf (Accessed 4 January 2026)

Money Authority of Singapore (MAS). (2022). *Consultation Paper on Proposed Regulatory Approach for Stablecoin-Related Activities* https://www.mas.gov.sg/publications/consultations/2022/consultation-paper-on-proposed-regulatory-approach-for-stablecoin-related-activities (Accessed 4 January 2026)

Thomason, J. (2026 forthcoming). *Global Lessons for Stablecoin Regulation and Governance*. IGI-Global.

United States Congress. (2025). *S.1582 - 119th Congress (2025-2026): GENIUS Act*. Congress.gov. https://www.congress.gov/bill/119th-congress/senate-bill/1582/text (Accessed 4 January 2026)

Compilation of References

Aave Protocol. (n.d.). *Aave — open-source non-custodial liquidity protocol* [Computer software]. https://aave.com/

Abu Dhabi Global Market. (2015). *Financial Services and Markets Regulations 2015 | Rulebook*. Thomsonreuters.com. https://en.adgm.thomsonreuters.com/rulebook/financial-services-and-markets-regulations-2015-0

Abu Dhabi Global Market. (2015, October 4). *Financial Services and Markets Regulations 2015* (ADGM Law No. 4 of 2013) [Regulations]. https://en.adgm.thomsonreuters.com/rulebook/financial-services-and-markets-regulations-2015-0

Adachi, M., Bento Pereira Da Silva, P., Born, A., Cappuccio, M., Czák-Ludwig, S., Gschossmann, I., Pellicani, A., Philipps, S.-M., Plooij, M., Rossteuscher, I., & Zeoli, P. (2022). *Stablecoins' Role in Crypto and Beyond: Functions, Risks and Policy* (Policy Report No. Vol. 18; Macroprudential Bulletin). European Central Bank. https://www.ecb.europa.eu/press/financial-stability-publications/ macroprudential-bulletin/html/ecb.mpbu202207_2~836f682ed7.en.html

Ahmed, R., Aldasoro, I., & Duley, C. (2024). Public information and stablecoin runs (BIS Working Paper No. 1164). Bank for International Settlements. https://www.bis.org/publ/work1164.pdf (Accessed 4 January 2026)

Akartuna, A. (2022, April 19). $76 million stolen from Beanstalk Farms DeFi stablecoin protocol. *Elliptic*. https://www.elliptic.co/blog/76-million-stolen-from-beanstalk-farms-defi-stablecoin-protocol

Aldasoro, I., Aquilina, M., Lewrick, U., & Lim, S. H. (2025). *Stablecoin Growth – Policy Challenges and Approaches* (BIS Bulletin No. 108; p. 8). Bank for International Settlements (BIS). https://www.bis.org/publ/bisbull108.htm

Aldasoro, I., Cornelli, G., Ferrari Minesso, M., Gambacorta, L., & Habib, M. M. (2024). Stablecoins, money market funds, and monetary policy (BIS Working Paper No. 1219). Bank for International Settlements. https://www.bis.org/publ/work1219.pdf (Accessed 4 January 2026)

Al-Melhem, A. (2023). *Capital Markets Authority-Resolutions and Circulars - CMA*. Cma.gov.kw. https://www.cma.gov.kw/en/web/cma/cma-board-releases/resolutions-and-regulations/-/cmaboardreleases/detail/1384960

Annual Economic Report, B. I. S. (2025). The next-generation monetary and financial system. In *Bis.org* (pp. 1–38). BIS., https://www.bis.org/publ/arpdf/ar2025e3.htm

Aramonte, S., Wenqiuan, H., & Schrimpf, A. (2021, December). DeFi risks and the decentralisation illusion. *Bank for International Settlements. Quarterly Review*. https://www.bis.org/publ/qtrpdf/r_qt2112b.pdf

Arner, D. W., Barberis, J. N., & Buckley, R. P. The Evolution of Fintech: A New Post-Crisis Paradigm? (October 1, 2015). University of Hong Kong Faculty of Law Research Paper No. 2015/047, UNSW Law Research Paper No. 2016-62, Available at SSRN: https://ssrn.com/abstract=2676553 DOI: 10.2139/ssrn.2676553

Arner, D. W., Buckley, R. P., & Zetzsche, D. A. (2020). *Programmable Money, Smart Contracts, and the Future of Financial Regulation. Law Working Paper Series*, University of Hong Kong Faculty of Law. https://doi.org/DOI: 10.2139/ssrn.3539057

Arner, D. W., Buckley, R. P., Zetzsche, D. A., & Didenko, A. (2022). *Artificial Intelligence, RegTech and Financial Inclusion.* Asian Development Bank Working Paper Series.

Arner, D. W., Barberis, J., & Buckley, R. P. (2017). FinTech, RegTech and the Reconceptualization of Financial Regulation. *Northwestern Journal of International Law & Business, 37*(3), 371–413.

Asia/Pacific Group on Money Laundering. (2018). *3rd Follow-Up Report: Mutual Evaluation of Vanuatu* (p. 33). The Financial Action Task Force (FATF). https://www.fatf-gafi.org/content/dam/fatf-gafi/fsrb-fur/APG-3rd-Follow-Up%20Report-Vanuatu-2018.pdf

Auer, R., Dodson, D., Dupont, A., Haghighi, M., Margaine, N., Marsden, D., Mccarthy, S., & Valko, A. (2025). *BIS Papers No 158 Quantum-readiness for the financial system: a roadmap* (p. 17). https://www.bis.org/publ/bppdf/bispap158.pdf

Austin, A. Bank Policy Institute. (2025, September 19). *Banks urge SEC to apply proven safeguards to crypto custody rules*. Retrieved September 24, 2025, from https://bpi.com/banks-urge-sec-to-apply-proven-safeguards-to-crypto-custody-rules/

Australian Law Reform Commission. (2022). *Legislative Framework for Corporations and Financial Services Regulation: New Business Models, Technologies, and Practices* (Background Paper No. FSL7; p. 38). Australian Law Reform Commission (ALRC). https://www.alrc.gov.au/wp-content/uploads/2022/10/FSL7-New-Business-Models-Technologies-and-Practices.pdf

Azar, P. D., Baughman, G., Carapella, F., Gerszten, J., Lubis, A., Perez-Sangimino, J. P., & Werman, A. (2022). *The financial stability implications of digital assets (No. 1034)*. Staff Reports.

Bacina, M. (2017). *Smart contracts in Australia: Just how clever are they?* [Insight]. Piper Alderman. https://piperalderman.com.au/insight/smart-contracts-in-australia-just-how-clever-are-they/

Baghel, B. (2025). RBI Crypto Stance: Sanjay Malhotra Sounds Cautious on Crypto. *CoinGabbar*.https://www.coingabbar.com/en/crypto-currency-news/rbi-crypto-stance-sanjay-malhotra-crypto-stablecoin-warning

Bank for International Settlement. (2007). *Basel Committee on Banking Supervision Principles for home-host supervisory cooperation and allocation mechanisms in the context of Advanced Measurement Approaches (AMA)*. https://www.bis.org/publ/bcbs135.pdf

Bank for International Settlement. (2022). *Application of the Principles for Financial Market Infrastructures to stablecoin arrangements*. Bis.org. https://www.bis.org/cpmi/publ/d206.htm

Bank for International Settlements (BIS). (2007). *Basel Committee on Banking Supervision Principles for home-host supervisory cooperation and allocation mechanisms in the context of Advanced Measurement Approaches (AMA)*. https://www.bis.org/publ/bcbs135.pdf (Accessed 4 January 2026)

Bank for International Settlements. (2023). The crypto ecosystem: Key elements and risks, June 2023. https://www.bis.org/publ/othp72.pdf(Accessed 5 January 2026)

Bank for International Settlements. (2025) BIS Working Papers No. 1164: Public information and stablecoin runs. Monetary and Economic Department, January 2024 (revised January 2025) https://www.bis.org/publ/work1164.pdf (Accessed 5 January 2026)

Bank of Uganda. (2025). *Final Report of the Consultation on Central Bank Digital Currency for Uganda* (pp. 1–49). https://www.bou.or.ug/export/sites/default/.gallery/CBDC-Consultations/CBDC-Consultation-Final-Report-June-30-2025-Submitted.pdf

Basel Committee on Banking Supervision. (2012). *Core Principles for Effective Banking Supervision.* Bank for International Settlements (BIS). https://www.bis.org/publ/bcbs230.htm

Basel Committee on Banking Supervision. (2012). *Core principles for effective banking supervision.* Bank for International Settlements. https://www.bis.org/publ/bcbs230.htm

Basel Committee on Banking Supervision. (2019). *Basel III: Finalising post-crisis reforms.* Bank for International Settlements. https://www.bis.org/bcbs/publ/d424.htm

Basel Committee on Banking Supervision. (2021). *Prudential treatment of cryptoasset exposures.* Bank for International Settlements. https://www.bis.org/bcbs/publ/d531.pdf

Basel Committee on Banking Supervision. (2022). *Prudential treatment of cryptoasset exposures.* Bank for International Settlements. https://www.bis.org/bcbs/publ/d545.htm

Basel Committee on Banking Supervision. (2023). *SupTech applications for crypto-asset supervision.* Bank for International Settlements.

Basel Committee on Banking Supervision. (2024). *Novel risks, mitigants and uncertainties with permissionless distributed ledger technologies (Working Paper No. 44).* Bank for International Settlements. https://www.bis.org/bcbs/publ/wp44.pdf

Baughman, G., Carapella, F., Gerszten, J., & Mills, D. C. (2022). *The stable in stablecoins.* Board of Governors of the Federal Reserve System., DOI: 10.17016/2380-7172.3224

Beecher, W., Bissessar, S., & Julien, M. (2018). *Business Environment Reform Facility.* https://assets.publishing.service.gov.uk/media/5c76731f40f0b603d45dd9c7/BERF-Caribbean-Fintech-Companies-Regulation-Review-Jan-2019.pdf

Behnkw, R. (2023, June 15). *A guide to formal verification of smart contracts.* Halborn. Retrieved September 26, 2025, from https://www.halborn.com/blog/post/a-guide-to-formal-verification-of-smart-contracts

Behnkw, R. (2025, September 8). *Multi-chain stablecoins: Security, risks and best practices.* Halborn. Retrieved September 10, 2025, from https://www.halborn.com/blog/post/multi-chain-stablecoins-security-risks-and-best-practices

Bermuda Monetary Authority. (2024). *Single Currency Pegged Stablecoins (SCPS) Guidance* (p. 14). Bermuda Monetary Authority. https://cdn.bma.bm/documents/2024-12-06-16-16-15-DAB-Single-Currency-Pegged-Stablecoins-Consultation-Guidance.pdf

Bitcoin.org. (n.d.). *Transactions*. Bitcoin Developer Guide. Retrieved September 25, 2025, from https://developer.bitcoin.org/devguide/transactions.html

Black, J. (2008a). Constructing and contesting legitimacy and accountability in polycentric regulatory regimes. *Regulation & Governance*, *2*(2), 137–164. DOI: 10.1111/j.1748-5991.2008.00034.x

Black, J. (2008b). Forms and paradoxes of principles based regulation. *Capital Markets Law Journal*, *3*(4), 425–457. DOI: 10.1093/cmlj/kmn026

Boar, C., Claessens, S., Kosse, A., Leckow, R., & Rice, T. (2021). *BIS Bulletin No 49: Interoperability between payment systems across borders*. https://www.bis.org/publ/bisbull49.pdf

Briola, A., Vidal-Tomás, D., Wang, Y., & Aste, T. (2023). Anatomy of a Stablecoin's failure: The Terra-Luna case. *Finance Research Letters*, *51*, 103358. DOI: 10.1016/j.frl.2022.103358

Bromberg, L., Godwin, A., & Ramsay, I. (2022). Fintech sandboxes: Achieving a balance between regulation and innovation. *Journal of Banking Regulation*, *23*(1), 71–92.

Brunnermeier, James, & Landau, 2021., The Digitalisation of Money. BIS Working Papers, No 941, 19 May 2021.https://www.bis.org/publ/work941.htm (Accessed 4 January 2026)

Buckley, R. P., Arner, D. W., Veidt, R., & Zetzsche, D. A. (2019). Building fintech ecosystems: Regulatory sandboxes, innovation hubs and beyond. *SSRN*, *61*, 55–98. DOI: 10.2139/ssrn.3455872

Buckley, R. P., Arner, D. W., Zetzsche, D. A., & Selga, E. (2020). The dark side of digital financial transformation: The new risks of FinTech and the rise of TechRisk. *Singapore Journal of Legal Studies*, *2020*, 423–445.

Calomiris, C. W., & Gorton, G. (1991). The Origins of Banking Panics: Models, Facts, and Bank Regulation. In Hubbard, G. (Ed.), *Financial Markets and Financial Crises* (pp. 109–173). University of Chicago Press.

Canadian Securities Administrators. (2023). *CSA Staff Notice 21-333: Crypto Asset Trading Platforms: Terms and Conditions for Trading Value-Referenced Crypto Assets with Clients* (Instruments, Rules and Policies, p. 24) [CSA Notice]. Canadian Securities Administrators (CSA). https://www.osc.ca/en/securities-law/instruments-rules-policies/2/21-333/csa-staff-notice-21-333-crypto-asset-trading-platforms-terms-and-conditions-trading-value

Caribbean Regional Technical Assistance Centre. (2021). *CARTAC FY21 Annual Report* (p. 150) [Annual Report]. Caribbean Regional Technical Assistance Centre. https://www.cartac.org/content/dam/CARTAC/AnnualReports/CARTAC_FY21_Annual-Report_Final(2).pdf

Central Bank of Bahrain. (2025). *SIO Stablecoin Issuance & Offering | Rulebook Volume 6: Capital Markets*. Thomsonreuters.com. https://cbben.thomsonreuters.com/rulebook/sio-stablecoin-issuance-offering

Central Bank of the UAE. (2024). *Payment Token Services Regulation* (No. 2/2024; p. 101) [Regulations]. https://rulebook.centralbank.ae/en/rulebook/payment-token-services-regulation

Central Bank of the United Arab Emirates. (2024). *Payment Token Services Regulation | CBUAE Rulebook*. Centralbank.ae. https://rulebook.centralbank.ae/en/rulebook/payment-token-services-regulation

Central Bank of Trinidad and Tobago. (2019). *Financial Stability Report 2019* (p. 83). Central Bank of Trinidad and Tobago. https://www.central-bank.org.tt/core-functions/financial-stability/financial-stability-report

Certi, K. (2022, July 28). *Revisiting Beanstalk Farms exploit*. Retrieved September 18, 2025, from https://www.certik.com/resources/blog/revisiting-beanstalk-farms-exploit

Certi, K. (2023, February 2). *What is formal verification in smart contract auditing?* Retrieved October 1, 2025, from https://www.certik.com/resources/blog/what-is-formal-verification

Charbit, C. (2011). *Governance of Public Policies in Decentralised Contexts: The Multi-level Approach* (OECD Regional Development Working Papers No. 2011/04; OECD Regional Development Working Papers, Vol. 2011/04). Organisation for Economic Co-operation and Development (OECD). DOI: 10.1787/20737009

Chavanette. (2024). *CBDC and Regulated Stablecoins: Friend or Foe? Pt2 - Ep. 9 - Chavanette Advisors*. Chavanette Advisors. https://chavanette.com/blog/cbdc-and-regulated-stablecoins-friend-or-foe-part-2/

Circle Internet Financial. (2022). *Circle Announces $400M Funding Round* [Press Release]. Circle Internet Group, Inc. https://www.circle.com/pressroom/circle-announces-400m-funding-round

Coffee, J. C. (2006). *Gatekeepers: The Professions and Corporate Governance.* Oxford University Press. DOI: 10.1093/oso/9780199288090.001.0001

CoinGecko. (2024). *State of Stablecoins: 2024.* CoinGecko. https://www.coingecko.com/research/publications/state-of-stablecoins-2024 – Report.

CoinGecko. (2024, April 15). *MPC wallets vs. multi-sig wallets: A deep dive.* Retrieved

Commonwealth Secretariat. (2024). *Commonwealth Model Law on Virtual Assets* (Draft). https://production-new-commonwealth-files.s3.eu-west-2.amazonaws.com/s3fs-public/2024-07/commonwealth-model-law-on-virtual-assets_d19821.pdf

Commonwealth Secretariat. (2024). *The Commonwealth Model Law on Virtual Assets.* Commonwealth. https://thecommonwealth.org/publications/model-law-virtual-assets

Crisanto, J. C., Ehrentraud, J., & Ocampo, D. G. (2024). *Stablecoins: Regulatory Responses to Their Promise of Stability* (Policy Report No. 57; FSI Insights, p. 26). Bank for International Settlements (BIS), Financial Stability Institute. https://www.bis.org/fsi/publ/insights57.pdf

Customs Recognition Act. 2000, No. No 7 of 2000, National Parliament of the Solomon Islands (2000). https://faolex.fao.org/docs/pdf/sol74602.pdf

Das, A. (2025, November 12). Social Capital Markets. *Stablecoin Statistics 2025.* https://socialcapitalmarkets.net/crypto-trading/stablecoin-statistics

Dubai Financial Services Authority. (2025). *The DFSA Rulebook* (Rulebook No. GEN/VER67/03-25; p. 212). https://dfsaen.thomsonreuters.com/rulebook/general-module -gen-ver6703-25

Duley, C., Gambacorta, L., Garratt, R., & Wilkens, P. K. (2023, September 7). The oracle problem and the future of DeFi. *Bank for International Settlements Bulletin, No 76.* https://www.bis.org/publ/bisbull76.pdf

Eastern and Southern Africa Anti-Money Laundering Group. (2022). *Anti-Money Laundering and Counter-Terrorist Financing Measures – Mauritius: 5th Enhanced Follow-up Report & Technical Compliance Re-Rating* (p. 7). Eastern and Southern Africa Anti-Money Laundering Group (ESAAMLG).https://www.fatf-gafi.org/content/dam/fatf-gafi/fsrb-fur/ESAAMLG-Mauritius-FUR2022. pdf

Eastern Caribbean Central Bank. (2024). *D-Cash - Eastern Caribbean Central Bank.* Www.eccb-Centralbank.org. https://www.eccb-centralbank.org/d-cash

Eichholz, L. (2020, March 17. *What really happened to MakerDAO?* Glassnode Insights. https://insights.glassnode.com/what-really-happened-to-makerdao/

Elliptic. (2025). *Stablecoin Security Risks in 2025: Full Risk Assessment Guide | Elliptic*. Elliptic.co; Elliptic. https://www.elliptic.co/blockchain-basics/stablecoin-2025-risk-assessment-guide

Elliptic. (2025, September 11). Stablecoin security risks in 2025: Full risk assessment guide. Retrieved September 23, 2025, from https://www.elliptic.co/blockchain-basics/stablecoin-2025-risk-assessment-guide

ERC3643 Association. (2025). *ERC-3643 (T-REX Protocol): The standard for permissioned tokens* (Version 4.1.3) [Computer Software]. https://github.com/ERC-3643/ERC-3643

Erik, F., Natarajan, H., & Saal, M. (2025). *Fintech and the Future of Finance: Market and Policy Implications*. World Bank. https://documents.worldbank.org/curated/en/099450005162250110

Ernst & Young Global Limited. (2025). *Global Approaches to Stablecoin Regulation: A Global Stablecoin Regulation Comparison.* (Industry Report Nos 005677-25Gbl; p. 24). Ernst & Young Global Limited. https://www.ey.com/content/dam/ey-unified-site/ey-com/en-gl/industries/banking-capital-markets/documents/ey-gl-global-stablecoin-regulation-comparison-09-2025.pdf

European Commission. (2022). *Digital Operational Resilience Act (DORA).* Regulation (EU) 2022/2554.

European Parliament & Council. (2023). Regulation (EU) 2023/1114 of the European Parliament and of the Council of 31 May 2023 on markets in crypto-assets, and amending Regulations (EU) No 1093/2010 and (EU) No 1095/2010 and Directives 2013/36/EU and (EU) 2019/1937 (Text with EEA relevance). *Official Journal of the European Union, L 150*, 9.6.2023, pp. 40–205. https://eur-lex.europa.eu/legal-content/EN/TXT/?uri=CELEX%3A32023R1114

European Securities and Market Authorities. (2025). *ESMA and the European Commission Publish Guidance on Non-MiCA Compliant ARTs and EMTs (stablecoins)* (Public Statement Nos ESMA75-223375936–6099; p. 3). European Securities and Market Authorities (ESMA). https://www.esma.europa.eu/press-news/esma-news/esma-and-european-commission-publish-guidance-non-mica-compliant-arts-and-emts

European Securities and Markets Authority. (2023). *Consultation Paper on the Technical Standards specifying certain requirements of MiCA (3rd package)* (Consultation Paper Nos ESMA75-453128700–1002; p. 101). European Securities and Markets Authority (ESMA). https://www.esma.europa.eu/document/consultation-paper-technical-standards-specifying-certain-requirements-mica-3rd-package

European Union (2023). "Regulation (EU) 2023/1114 of the European Parliament and of the Council of 31 May 2023 on markets in crypto-assets, and amending Regulations (EU) No 1093/2010 and (EU) No 648/2012 (MiCA)", Official Journal of the European Union.

European Union. (2023). *Markets in Crypto Assets Regulation*. Europa.eu. https://eur-lex.europa.eu/legal-content/EN/TXT/?uri=CELEX%3A32023R1114

European Union. (2023). *Regulation - 2023/1114 - EN - EUR-Lex*. Europa.eu. https://doi.org/DOI: 10/1093/2024-12-30

European Union. (2023). *Regulation - 2023/1114 - EN - EUR-Lex*. Europa.eu. https://eur-lex.europa.eu/eli/reg/2023/1114/oj/eng (Accessed 4 January 2026)

Evans, D. Fireblocks. (2024,). *MPC vs. multi-sig*. Retrieved September 19, 2025, from https://www.fireblocks.com/blog/mpc-vs-multi-sig/

EY. (2025). *Global approaches to stablecoin regulation* (p. 24). https://www.ey.com/content/dam/ey-unified-site/ey-com/en-gl/industries/banking-capital-markets/documents/ey-gl-global-stablecoin-regulation-comparison-09-2025.pdf

FATF. (2021). *Updated Guidance for a Risk-Based Approach to Virtual Assets and Virtual Asset Service Providers*. Www.fatf-Gafi.org. https://www.fatf-gafi.org/en/publications/Fatfrecommendations/Guidance-rba-virtual-assets-2021.html

FATF. (2021). *Updated Guidance for a Risk-Based Approach to Virtual Assets and Virtual Asset Service Providers*. Www.fatf-Gafi.org. https://www.fatf-gafi.org/en/publications/Fatfrecommendations/Guidance-rba-virtual-assets-2021.html (Accessed 4 January 2026)

FATF. (2023). *Virtual Assets: Targeted Update on Implementation of the FATF Standards on VAs and VASPs*. Www.fatf-Gafi.org. https://www.fatf-gafi.org/en/publications/Fatfrecommendations/targeted-update-virtual-assets-vasps-2023.html

Financial Action Task Force. (2012). *International Standards on Combating Money Laundering and the Financing of Terrorism & Proliferation* (p. 152). Financial Action Task Force (FATF). https://www.fatf-gafi.org/en/publications/Fatfrecommendations/Fatf-recommendations.html Financial Action Task Force. (2020). *FATF Report to G20 on So-called Stablecoins* (p. 32). Financial Action Task Force (FATF). https://www.fatf-gafi.org/content/dam/fatf-gafi/reports/Virtual-Assets-FATF-Report-G20-So-Called-Stablecoins.pdf

Financial Action Task Force. (2020). *FATF Report to G20 on So-called Stablecoins.* Fatf-Gafi.org. https://www.fatf-gafi.org/publications/virtualassets/documents/report-g20-so-called-stablecoins-june-2020.html

Financial Action Task Force. (2021). *Updated Guidance for a Risk-Based Approach to Virtual Assets and Virtual Asset Service Providers* (p. 111). Financial Action Task Force (FATF). https://www.fatf-gafi.org/content/dam/fatf-gafi/guidance/Updated-Guidance-VA-VASP.pdf

Financial Action Task Force. (2021). *Updated Guidance for a Risk-Based Approach to Virtual Assets and Virtual Asset Service Providers.* FATF, Paris. https://www.fatf-gafi.org/en/publications/Fatfrecommendations/Guidance-rba-virtual-assets-2021.html

Financial Action Task Force. (2023). *Methodology for Assessing Compliance with the FATF Recommendations and the Effectiveness of AML/CFT Systems* (p. 196) [Official Institutional Report]. Financial Action Task Force (FATF). https://www.fatf-gafi.org/publications/mutualevaluations/documents/fatf-methodology.html

Financial Action Task Force. (2023). *Targeted Update on Implementation of the FATF Standards on Virtual Assets and Virtual Asset Service Providers.* FATF, Paris. https://www.fatf-gafi.org/en/publications/Fatfrecommendations/targeted-update-virtual-assets-vasps-2023.html

Financial Action Task Force. (2025). *Virtual Assets: Targeted Update on the Implementation of the FATF Standards on VAs and VASPs* [Press release]. FATF. https://www.fatf-gafi.org/en/publications/fatfrecommendations/targeted-update-virtual-assets-vasps-2025.html

Financial Conduct Authority. (2023a). *Regulatory sandbox.* FCA.

Financial Conduct Authority. (2023b). *Financial promotions for cryptoassets.* FCA.

Financial Conduct Authority. (2023c). *Global Financial Innovation Network (GFIN).* FCA, London. https://www.fca.org.uk/firms/innovation/global-financial-innovation-network

Financial Conduct Authority. (2024). *The Regulatory Sandbox* (p. 13) [Organizational Report]. Financial Conduct Authority (FCA). https://www.fca.org.uk/firms/innovation/regulatory-sandbox

Financial Conduct Authority. (2025). *Stablecoin Issuance and Cryptoasset Custody* (Consultation Paper No. CP25/14; p. 239). https://www.fca.org.uk/publications/consultation-papers/cp25-14-stablecoin-issuance-cryptoasset-custody

Financial Services Act. 2021, https://www.legislation.gov.uk/ukpga/2021/22/enacted, Parliament of the United Kingdom 2019-21, UK Public General Acts, 2021 CBP 8705 192 (2022). https://www.legislation.gov.uk/ukpga/2021/22/enacted

Financial Services Agency of Japan. (2020). *Payment Services Act: Treatment of cryptoassets*. FSA Japan.

Financial Services Agency of Japan. (2022). *Payment Services Act amendments.* FSA Japan.

Financial Stability Board. (2020). *Crypto-assets and Global "Stablecoins."* www.fsb.org. https://www.fsb.org/work-of-the-fsb/financial-innovation-and-structural-change/crypto-assets-and-global-stablecoins/

Financial Stability Board. (2020). *Regulation, Supervision and Oversight of "Global Stablecoin" Arrangements.* FSB, Basel. https://www.fsb.org/2020/10/regulation-supervision-and-oversight-of-global-stablecoin-arrangements/

Financial Stability Board. (2020). *Regulation, Supervision and Oversight of "Global Stablecoin" Arrangements.* Www.fsb.org. https://www.fsb.org/2020/10/regulation-supervision-and-oversight-of-global-stablecoin-arrangements/

Financial Stability Board. (2020). *Regulation, Supervision and Oversight of "Global Stablecoin" Arrangements.* Www.fsb.org. https://www.fsb.org/2020/10/regulation-supervision-and-oversight-of-global-stablecoin-arrangements/ (Accessed 4 January 2026)

Financial Stability Board. (2020, October 13). *Regulation, Supervision, and Oversight of "Global Stablecoin" Arrangements.* Www.fsb.org. https://www.fsb.org/2020/10/regulation-supervision-and-oversight-of-global-stablecoin-arrangements/

Financial Stability Board. (2022). "Assessment of Risks to Financial Stability from Crypto-assets" – Report.

Financial Stability Board. (2022). *Assessment of Risks to Financial Stability from Crypto-assets*. FSB.

Financial Stability Board. (2023). *High-level Recommendations for the Regulation, Supervision and Oversight of Global Stablecoin Arrangements* (Reports to the G20, p. 24). https://www.fsb.org/uploads/P170723-3.pdf

Financial Stability Board. (2023). *High-level recommendations for the regulation, supervision and oversight of global stablecoin arrangements*. Financial Stability Board.

Financial Stability Board. (2023). *High-Level Recommendations for the Regulation, Supervision and Oversight of Global Stablecoin Arrangements: Final Report.* FSB, Basel. https://www.fsb.org/2023/07/high-level-recommendations-for-the-regulation-supervision-and-oversight-of-global-stablecoin-arrangements-final-report/

Financial Stability Board. (2023). *High-level Recommendations for the Regulation, Supervision and Oversight of Global Stablecoin Arrangements: Final report.* Www.fsb.org. https://www.fsb.org/2023/07/high-level-recommendations-for-the-regulation-supervision-and-oversight-of-global-stablecoin-arrangements-final-report/

Financial Stability Board. (2023). *High-level Recommendations for the Regulation, Supervision and Oversight of Global Stablecoin Arrangements: Final report.* Www.fsb.org. https://www.fsb.org/2023/07/high-level-recommendations-for-the-regulation-supervision-and-oversight-of-global-stablecoin-arrangements-final-report/ (Accessed 4 January 2026)

Financial Stability Board. (2023a). *High-level Recommendations for the Regulation, Supervision and Oversight of Global Stablecoin Arrangements* (Reports to the G20, p. 24). Financial Stability Board (FSB). https://www.fsb.org/uploads/P170723-3.pdf

Financial Stability Board. (2023b). *IMF-FSB Synthesis Paper: Policies for Crypto-Assets* (p. 53). Financial Stability Board (FSB) and International Monetary Fund (IMF). https://www.fsb.org/2023/09/imf-fsb-synthesis-paper-policies-for-crypto-assets/

Financial Stability Board. (2024). "Cross-border issues of Global Stablecoins in Emerging Markets" – Report.

Financial Stability Board. (2025). *Thematic Review on FSB Global Regulatory Framework for Crypto-asset Activities* (p. 111) [Peer Review Report]. https://www.fsb.org/2025/10 /thematic-review-on-fsb-global-regulatory-framework-for-crypto-asset-activiactivities/

Fraud.net. (n.d.). *Flash loan attacks definition*. Retrieved September 3, 2025, from https://www.fraud.net/glossary/flash-loan-attacks

Fulena, V. (2025). Examining Smart Contracts Within Mauritian Contract Law: Assessing Their Compatibility with Existing Legal Frameworks. In Hinkelmann, K., & Smuts, H. (Eds.), *Society 5.0* (Vol. 2173, pp. 123–135). Springer Nature Switzerland., DOI: 10.1007/978-3-031-71412-2_10

Gail, E. (2007). Legal Transplants and Economics: The World Bank and Third World Economies in the 1980s – A Case Study of Jamaica, the Republic of Kenya and the Philippines. *European Journal of Law Reform, 9(2)*, 243–283. https://sas-space.sas.ac.uk/349/1/Gail_Edwards_MA_Thesis.pdf

Gate.com. (2024, July 10). *What is formal verification of smart contracts?* Retrieved September 30, 2025, from https://www.gate.com/learn/articles/what-is-formal-verification-of-smart-contracts/4291

Gate.com. (2025, October 1). *Types of blockchain oracle attacks, cases, and multi-layer defense strategies*. Retrieved September 5, 2025, from https://www.gate.com/learn/articles/types-of-blockchain-oracle-attacks-cases-and-multi-layer-defense-strategies/5498

Gemini. (2025). *2025 Global State of Crypto Report.* Gemini. https://www.gemini.com/state-of-crypto

Gorawska, A., & Swierzy, P. (2024). Decentralized oracle network for enhanced user authentication security. *Proceedings of the 57th Hawaii International Conference on System Sciences*. https://aisel.aisnet.org/cgi/viewcontent.cgi?article=1558&context=hicss-57

Gorton, G. B., Zhang, J. Y., & Stablecoins, T. W. (September 30, 2021). 90 University of Chicago Law Review 909 (2023), Available at SSRN: https://ssrn.com/abstract=3888752 (Accessed 4 January 2026)

Gorton, G. B., & Zhang, J. Y. (2023). Taming Wildcat Stablecoins. *The University of Chicago Law Review. University of Chicago. Law School, 90*(3), 909–974. https://chicagounbound.uchicago.edu/uclrev/vol90/iss3/3

Guiding and Establishing National Innovation for U.S. Stablecoins Act. (Senate Bill 1582: GENIUS Act), Pub. L. No. 119–27 (2025). https://www.congress.gov/bill/119th-congress/senate-bill/1582/text

Hague Conference on Private International Law. (2019). *Convention on the Recognition and Enforcement of Foreign Judgments in Civil or Commercial Matters* (International Instrument No. 41; p. 13). Hague Conference on Private International Law (HCCH). https://www.hcch.net/en/instruments/conventions/full-text/?cid=137

Hansen, P. (2024). *Analyzing MiCA's significance regime for stablecoins* [Commentary Report]. Circle Internet Group, Inc. https://www.circle.com/blog/analyzing-micas-significance-regime-for-stablecoins

Harper, E. (2011). *Customary Justice: From Program Design to Impact Evaluation*. International Development Law Organization (IDLO). https://www.idlo.int/publications/customary-justice-program-design-impact-evaluation

Heaver, I., Melnichenko, A., & Kamran, Z. (2025). *UAE Crypto Regulation Q3 2025 Update: VARA, SCA & ADGM* [Legal Insights]. NeosLegal. https://neoslegal.co/uae-crypto-regulation-q3-2025-update-vara-sca-adgm/

Helmore, E. (2023). USD Coin value falls after revealing $3.3bn held at Silicon Valley Bank. *The Guardian*. https://www.theguardian.com/technology/2023/mar/11/usd-coin-depeg-silicon-valley-bank-collapse

Hogan Lovells. (2025). *Hogan Lovells | How can we help you?* Hoganlovells.com. https://digital-client-solutions.hoganlovells.com/resources/blockchain/insight/key-takeaways-from-the-bis-innovation-summit-2024

Hong Kong Monetary Authority. (2023). *Legislative proposal to implement regulatory regime for stablecoin issuers and announcement on introduction of sandbox arrangement* [Consultation]. https://www.hkma.gov.hk/eng/news-and-media/press-releases/2023/12/20231227-4/

Hong Kong Money Authority. (2024). *HKMA launches the stablecoin issuer sandbox arrangement*. Hong Kong Monetary Authority. https://www.hkma.gov.hk/eng/news-and-media/press-releases/2024/03/20240312-4/

Hong Kong Special Administrative. (2025). *Hong Kong e-Legislation| Stablecoins Ordinance (Cap. 656)*. Elegislation.gov.hk. https://www.elegislation.gov.hk/hk/cap656?p0=1&p1=1

Hossenkhan, F., Jeehoo, N., Li, K., & Pang, A. K. (2024). *Mauritius: Law and Practice—Trends and Developments* (p. 20). Bowmans. https://www.bom.mu/sites/default/files/virtual-asset-and-initial-token-offering-services-act-2021.pdf

Howell, J. (2024, January 19). An overview of integer overflow attacks. *101 Blockchains*. Retrieved September 8, 2025, from https://101blockchains.com/integer-overflow-attacks/

International Federation of Red Cross and Red Crescent Societies, & University College Cork. (2021). *Global Synthesis Report on Law and Policies for Climate Resilience: Enhancing Normative Integration Between Climate Change Adaptation and Disaster Risk Reduction* (p. 40). International Federation of Red Cross and Red Crescent Societies. https://disasterlaw.ifrc.org/sites/default/files/media/disaster_law/2021-08/20210803_DRR_CCA_FinalDoc_ONLINE.pdf

International Federation of Red Cross and Red Crescent Societies. (2021a). *IFRC Annual Report 2021* (p. 62). International Federation of Red Cross and Red Crescent Societies. https://disasterlaw.ifrc.org/media/3835

International Federation of Red Cross and Red Crescent Societies. (2021b). *Strengthening Climate Resilience Through Law and Policy in the Philippines* (p. 4). https://disasterlaw.ifrc.org/sites/default/files/media/disaster_law/2021-12/IFRC Disaster Law_Case Study_Strengthening climate resilience through law and policy in the Philippines.pdf

International Monetary Fund. (2010). *Global Financial Stability Report: Meeting New Challenges to Stability and Building a Safer System.* IMF, Washington, DC. https://www.imf.org/en/Publications/GFSR/Issues/2016/12/31/Global-Financial-Stability-Report-April-2010-Meeting-New-Challenges-to-Stability-and-23794

International Monetary Fund. (2021). The Rise of Digital Money. *Policy Papers, 2021*(054), 27. DOI: 10.5089/9781513589558.007

International Monetary Fund. (2023). *Global Financial Stability Report – Crypto: Risk, Regulation, and the Road Ahead.* IMF, Washington, DC. https://www.imf.org/en/Publications/GFSR/Issues/2023/04/11/global-financial-stability-report-april-2023

International Monetary Fund. Monetary and Capital Markets Department. (2023). Trinidad and Tobago. *IMF Staff Country Reports, 2023*(322), 1. DOI: 10.5089/9798400254437.002

International Organisation of Securities Commission. (2020). *Global Stablecoin Initiatives Public Report.* https://www.iosco.org/library/pubdocs/pdf/IOSCOPD650.pdf

International Organization for Standardization. (2023). *ISO/TC 307 Blockchain and distributed ledger technologies.* ISO.

International Organization of Securities Commissions (CPMI–IOSCO). (2021). *Application of the Principles for Financial Market Infrastructures to stablecoin arrangements.* Bank for International Settlements.

International Organization of Securities Commissions. (2020). *Global Stablecoin Initiatives: Consultation Report.* IOSCO, Madrid. https://www.iosco.org/library/pubdocs/pdf/IOSCOPD645.pdf

International Organization of Securities Commissions. (2021). *Principles on Outsourcing*. IOSCO.

International Organization of Securities Commissions. (2023). *Policy Recommendations for Crypto and Digital Asset Markets: Final Report.* FR03/2023, IOSCO, Madrid. https://www.iosco.org/library/pubdocs/pdf/IOSCOPD747.pdf

IOSCO. (2023). *Policy Recommendations for Crypto and Digital Asset Markets Final Report*. https://www.iosco.org/library/pubdocs/pdf/IOSCOPD747.pdf

IOSCO. (2023). *Policy Recommendations for Crypto and Digital Asset Markets Final Report*. https://www.iosco.org/library/pubdocs/pdf/IOSCOPD747.pdf (Accessed 4 January 2026)

Jean-Noel, I. I. D. (2025). *Securing Digital Dollar Dominance: A Comprehensive Framework for Stablecoin Regulation and Innovation* (p. 106) [Working Paper]. U.S. Securities and Exchange Commission (SEC). https://www.sec.gov/files/stablecoin_regulatory_framework.pdf

Jeník, I., & Duff, S. (2020). *How to build a regulatory sandbox a practical guide for policy makers*. https://digitalfinance.worldbank.org/sites/default/files/2022-11/How-to-Build-a-Regulatory-Sandbox-A-Practical-Guide-for-Policy-Makers.pdf

K.B.M. R. H., & Zayed, N. M. (2018). The New Basel-III Capital Accord: Capability of The Banks In Adapting and Adopting the New Regime In Bangladesh. *International Journal of Development Research, 8*(9), 22782–22791. https://www.journalijdr.com/new-basel-iii-capital-accord-capability-banks-adapting-and-adopting-new-regime-bangladesh

Kaia Docs. (n.d.). *Best practices for smart contract security*. Retrieved September 10, 2025, from https://docs.kaia.io/build/smart-contracts/fundamentals/best-practices-for-smart-contract-security/

Katz, E. (2023). *Custody of stablecoin reserves under MiCA* (Legal Development No. 2023). Ashurst (law firm). https://www.ashurst.com/en/insights/custody-of-stablecoin-reserves-under-mica/

Kosse, A., Glowka, M., Mattei, I., & Rice, T. (2023). *Will the real stablecoin please stand up?* BIS Papers.

KPMG & Innovate Finance. (2024). *The Roadmap to Open Finance in the UK* (p. 18). KPMG International Limited and Innovate Finance. https://assets.kpmg.com/content/dam/kpmgsites/uk/pdf/2024/04/the-roadmap-to-open-finance-in-the-uk.pdf

Kulkarni, S., & the The Economic Times. (2024, April 5). Digital Rupee: RBI widens scope of CBDC; non-banking payment companies to facilitate transactions. *Bennett, Coleman & Co. Ltd.* https://economictimes.indiatimes.com/wealth/save/eps-95-pension-is-government-planning-to-increase-minimum-eps-payout-from-rs-1000-to-rs-7500-heres-what-ministry-says/articleshow/125713018.cms

Kurovskiy, G., & Rostova, N. (2023, April 23). *How algorithmic stablecoins fail* [Conference presentation]. Swiss National Bank, Zurich, Switzerland. https://www.snb.ch/dam/jcr:5140cb30-3c8c-433d-8619-0354b8f1036e/sem_2023_05_26_rostova.n.pdf

Laverdure, B. (2023). *How the TerraUSD Collapse Affects Stablecoin Regulation and Community Banks*. ICBA.org. https://www.icba.org/w/how-the-terrausd-collapse-affects-stablecoin-regulation-and-community-banks

Li, B., & Sugimoto, N. (2023, January 19). *Crypto contagion underscores why global regulators must act fast to stem risk*. International Monetary Fund Blog. https://www.imf.org/en/Blogs/Articles/2023/01/18/crypto-contagion-underscores-why-global-regulators-must-act-fast-to-stem-risk

Llewellyn, D. (2006). Institutional structure of financial regulation and supervision: The basic issues. *World Bank seminar Aligning Supervisory Structures with Country Needs*, 6-7.

Manzer, A. R., Solomons, M., & Sharma, T. (2023). *CSA Provides Additional Guidance for Stablecoin Regulation*. Cassels Brock & Blackwell LLP., https://cassels.com/insights/csa-provides-additional-guidance-for-stablecoin-regulation/

Masciandaro, D., & Quintyn, M. (2013). The governance of financial supervision: Recent developments. *Journal of Economic Surveys*, *27*(4), 734–769.

Matthews, B., & Tran, H. (2025). Central bank digital currencies versus stablecoins: Divergent EU and US perspectives. Atlantic Council. https://www.atlanticcouncil.org/blogs/econographics/central-bank-digital-currencies-versus-stablecoins-divergent-eu-and-us-perspectives/

Mauritius International Financial Centre. (2022). *Toolkit on Mauritius IFC for Ambassadors & High Commissioners* (p. 41). Economic Development Board Mauritius. https://mauritiusifc.mu/index.php/toolkit-mauritius-ifc-ambassadors-high-commissioners

Meakin, H., Edwards, A., & Lovegrove, S. (2025). *HMT publishes draft legislation for regulating cryptoassets*. Global Regulation Tomorrow. https://www.regulationtomorrow.com/eu/hmt-publishes-draft-legislation-for-regulating-cryptoassets/

Melo, F., Seal, K., & Salomao, V. (2024). 2024 Revised Basel Core Principles for Effective Banking Supervision. *Policy Papers, 2024*(037), 13. DOI: 10.5089/9798400286636.007

Monetary Authority of Singapore. (2019). *Payment Services Act 2019.* MAS, Singapore. https://www.mas.gov.sg/regulation/acts/payment-services-act

Monetary Authority of Singapore. (2021). *Payment Services Act 2019.* MAS, Singapore. https://www.mas.gov.sg/regulation/explainers/payment-services-act-explained

Monetary Authority of Singapore. (2023). *Proposed Regulatory Approach for Stablecoin-Related Activities* (Consultation Nos P009-2022; p. 128). https://www.mas.gov.sg/publications/consultations/ 2022/consultation-paper-on-proposed-regulatory-approach-for-stablecoin-related-activities

Monetary Authority of Singapore. (2023). *Regulatory framework for digital payment token services.* MAS.

Money Authority of Singapore (MAS). (2022). *Consultation Paper on Proposed Regulatory Approach for Stablecoin-Related Activities* https://www.mas.gov.sg/publications/consultations/2022/consultation-paper-on-proposed-regulatory-approach-for-stablecoin-related-activities (Accessed 4 January 2026)

Money Authority of Singapore. (2023). *MAS Finalizes Stablecoin Regulatory Framework.* https://www.sgpc.gov.sg/api/file/getfile/Media%20Release_MAS%20Finalises%20Stablecoin%20Regulatory%20Framework.pdf?path=/sgpcmedia/media_releases/mas/press_release/P-20230815-2/attachment/Media+Release_MAS+Finalises+Stablecoin+Regulatory+Framework.pdf

Mukherjee, P., & Mukherjee, P. (2025). *Supreme Court of India declines appeal on "crypto" regulation.* CoinGeek. https://coingeek.com/supreme-court-of-india-declines-appeal-on-crypto-regulation/

Nao, L., Kabiu, J., Awayang, S., & Kutan, L. P. (2023). *Bankability of Customary Land in Papua New Guinea: Challenges and Prospects* (Discussion Paper No. 210; p. 31). The National Research Institute,PNG. https://pngnri.org/images/Publications/DPNo.210updated_Bankability_of_customary_land_in_Papua_New_Guinea-_challenges_and_prospects_.pdf

National Securities Commission. (2025). *Regulations (NT 2013 and amendments). Amendment.* Argentina.gob.ar. https://www.argentina.gob.ar/normativa/nacional/resoluci%C3%B3n-1058-2025-410635/texto

Nethermind. (2024, November 18). Smart contract vulnerabilities and mitigation strategies. https://www.nethermind.io/blog/smart-contract-vulnerabilities-and-mitigation-strategies

OECD. (2019). *Digital Disruption in Financial Markets.* Oecd.org. https://www.oecd.org/en/events/2019/06/digital-disruption-in-financial-markets.html

OECD. (2024). *Development Co-operation Report 2024 Tackling Poverty and Inequalities Through the Green Transition.* https://www.oecd.org/content/dam/oecd/en/publications/reports/2024/07/development-co-operation-report-2024_b9cb300f/357b63f7-en.pdf

Open Web Application Security Project. (n.d.-a). *Integer overflow and underflow.* OWASP Smart Contract Top 10. Retrieved September 10, 2025, from https://owasp.org/www-project-smart-contract-top-10/2023/en/src/SC02-integer-overflow-underflow.html

Open Web Application Security Project. (n.d.-b). *Reentrancy attacks.* OWASP Smart Contract Top 10. Retrieved September 16, 2025, from https://owasp.org/www-project-smart-contract-top-10/2025/en/src/SC05-reentrancy-attacks.html

Open Web Application Security Project. (n.d.-c). *Flash loan attacks.* OWASP Smart Contract Top 10. Retrieved September 10, 2025, from https://owasp.org/www-project-smart-contract-top-10/2025/en/src/SC07-flash-loan-attacks.html

Open Web Application Security Project. (n.d.-d). *OWASP Smart Contract Top 10.* Retrieved September 23, 2025, from https://owasp.org/www-project-smart-contract-top-10/

Organisation for Economic Co-operation and Development. (2012). *Recommendation of the Council on Regulatory Policy and Governance.* OECD.

Organisation for Economic Co-operation and Development. (2020). *The OECD Digital Government Policy Framework: Six Dimensions of a Digital Government* (OECD Public Governance Policy Papers No. 02; Series: OECD Public Governance Policy Papers Volume: 02, p. 40). Organisation for Economic Co-operation and Development (OECD). DOI: 10.1787/14e1c5e8-en-fr

Organisation for European Economic Co-operation. (2021). *Central Bank Digital Currencies and payments: A review of domestic and international implications* (OECD Economics Department Working Papers, Vol. 1655). DOI: 10.1787/18151973

PayPal Inc. (n.d.). *PayPal USD Stablecoin.* PayPal. https://www.paypal.com/us/digital-wallet/manage-money/crypto/pyusd

Pirbhai, H. (2024). CBUAE Payment Token Services Regulation. *Global Regulation Tomorrow*. https://www.regulationtomorrow.com/dubai-and-saudi/cbuae-payment-token-services-regulation/

Potts, J. (2017). Governing the innovation commons. *Journal of Institutional Economics, 13*(2), 249–269. DOI: 10.1017/S1744137416000448

Pratap, Z. (2022, August 31). Reentrancy attacks and The DAO hack. *Chainlink*. Retrieved September 4, 2025, from https://blog.chain.link/reentrancy-attacks-and-the-dao-hack

President's Working Group on Financial Markets. (2021). "Report on Stablecoins." (Recommended that Congress enact legislation to limit stablecoin issuance to insured depository institutions or similar, to ensure prudential oversight and protection, citing potential runs and payments systemic risk in absence of such regulation).

PricewaterhouseCoopers. (2023). *Digital assets regulatory and compliance: PwC.* PwC. https://www.pwc.com/us/en/services/digital-assets/digital-assets-regulations.html

Rey, H. (2025, September 3). *Stablecoins, Tokens, and Global Dominance.* IMF. https://www.imf.org/en/Publications/fandd/issues/2025/09/stablecoins-tokens-global-dominance-helene-rey

Ringer, M., & Johal, Y. (2024). *The New CBUAE Payment Token Services Regulation: 10 Things You Need to Know*. CMS Legal., https://cms-lawnow.com/en/ealerts/2024/08/the-new-cbuae-payment-token-services-regulation-10-things-you-need-to-know

Rose, R. (2017). *Commonwealth Legislative Drafting Manual.* Commonwealth Secretariat. https://www.thecommonwealth-ilibrary.org/index.php/comsec/catalog/download/873/873/7305?inline=1

Rud, M. (2025). *UAE Crypto Regulation 2025: Complete Guide to VARA, ADGM, SCA, CBUAE Stablecoin Rules, Security Tokens, & On-Chain Real Estate* [Legal Guide]. ComplyFactor. https://complyfactor.com/uae-crypto-regulation-2025-complete-guide-to-vara-adgm-sca-cbuae/

Schaaf, J. (2025, July 28). European Central Bank. *From Hype to Hazard: What Stablecoins Mean for Europe*.https://www.ecb.europa.eu/press/blog/date/2025/html/ecb.blog20250728~e6cb3cf8b5.en.html

Secretariat, C. (2024). *The Commonwealth Model Law on Virtual Assets*. Commonwealth. https://thecommonwealth.org/publications/model-law-virtual-assets

Secretariat, C. (2002). *Model Law on Computer and Computer Related Crime.*, https://database.cyberpolicyportal.org/api/files/1663937569955dd9j3bxcigh.pdf

Secretariat, C. (2024). *The Commonwealth Model Law on Virtual Assets*. Commonwealth Secretariat. [Legal guidance], https://thecommonwealth.org/publications/model-law-virtual-assets

Secretariat, C. (2025 forthcoming). *Commonwealth Model Law on Stablecoins (draft)*. Commonwealth Secretariat.

September 8, 2025, from https://www.coingecko.com/learn/mpc-wallet-vs-multi-sig-wallets

Seunghwan, K., Miksjuk, A., Suryakumar, N., Tuladhar, A., Velculescu, D., Wu, Y., Zuniga, J., & Hallmark, N. (2024). *IMF Digital Money*. Cross-Border Payments, International Reserves, and the Global Financial Safety Net Preliminary Considerations., https://www.imf.org/-/media/Files/Publications/IMF-Notes/2024/English/INSEA2024001.ashx

Singh, R. (2025, April 7). J.P. Morgan Wary of Stablecoins' Trillion-Dollar Growth Bets, Cuts Them by Half. *Reuters*. https://www.reuters.com/business/finance/jpmorgan-wary-stablecoins-trillion-dollar-growth-bets-cuts-them-by-half-2025-07-03/

Smith, S. (2024). *Here's Why Stablecoin Policy Is Essential For US Dollar Leadership*. Crypto Council for Innovation. https://cryptoforinnovation.org/heres-why-stablecoin-policy-is-essential-for-us-dollar-leadership/

Stiglitz, J. E. (1993). The Role of the State in Financial Markets. *Proceedings of the World Bank Annual Conference on Development Economics* (pp. 19–52). World Bank. DOI: 10.1093/wber/7.suppl_1.19

Thales. (n.d.). *Hardware security modules (HSMs)*. Retrieved August 29, 2025, from https://cpl.thalesgroup.com/encryption/hardware-security-modules

The Committee on Payments and Market Infrastructures. (2023). *Considerations for the Use of Stablecoin Arrangements in Cross-Border Payments* (CPMI Report No. 220; CPMI Papers, p. 37). Bank for International Settlements (BIS). https://www.bis.org/cpmi/publ/d220.pdf

The Committee on Payments and Market Infrastructures. (2023). *Considerations for the Use of Stablecoin Arrangements in Cross-Border Payments* (CPMI Report No. 220; CPMI Papers, p. 37). Bank for International Settlements. https://www.bis.org/cpmi/publ/d220.pdf

The Commonwealth. (2018). *Multi-sector support and related toolkits*. Commonwealth. https://thecommonwealth.org/multi-sector-support-and-related-toolkits

The Commonwealth. (2024a). *Commonwealth Ministerial Meeting on Small States: Paving the Way for Resilient Futures*. Commonwealth. https://thecommonwealth.org/news/chogm2024/commonwealth-ministerial-meeting-small-states-paving-way-resilient-futures

The Commonwealth. (2024b). *Model Law on Virtual Assets Office of Civil and Criminal Justice Reform 2*. https://production-new-commonwealth-files.s3.eu-west-2.amazonaws.com/s3fs-public/2024-04/commonwealth-model-law-on-virtual-assets.pdf?VersionId=Mpvonk_fe1DW64Bo1.LqpmSvvxSe430o

The Commonwealth. (2024c). *New Commonwealth model law to help countries regulate virtual assets*. Commonwealth. https://thecommonwealth.org/news/new-commonwealth-model-law-help-countries-regulate-virtual-assets

The Commonwealth. (2025). *Model Law on Stablecoins*. Briola, A., Vidal-Tomás, D., Wang, Y., & Aste, T. (2023). Anatomy of a Stablecoin's failure: The Terra-Luna case. *Finance Research Letters, 51*, 103358.

The Economic Times. (2025). RBI Cautious in Its Approach to Stablecoins, Cryptos Says Governor Sanjay Malhotra. *Bennett, Coleman & Co. Ltd.* https://economictimes.indiatimes.com/industry/banking/finance/banking/rbi-cautious-in-its-approach-to-stablecoins-cryptos-says-governor-sanjay-malhotra/articleshow/125464379.cms

The European Parliament and the Council of the European Union. (2023, May 31). *Regulation (EU) 2023/1114 Of the European Parliament and of the Council of 31 May 2023 on markets in crypto-assets and amending Regulations (EU) No 1093/2010 and (EU) No 1095/2010 and Directives 2013/36/EU and (EU) 2019/1937*. Official Journal of the European Union (OJ). https://eur-lex.europa.eu/eli/reg/2023/1114/oj/eng

The European Parliament and the Council of the European Union. (2023, May 31). *Regulation (EU) 2023/1114 Of the European Parliament and of the Council of 31 May 2023 on markets in crypto-assets, and amending Regulations (EU) No 1093/2010 and (EU) No 1095/2010 and Directives 2013/36/EU and (EU) 2019/1937*. Official Journal of the European Union (OJ). https://eur-lex.europa.eu/eli/reg/2023/1114/oj/eng

The Financial Action Task Force. (2020). *FATF Report to G20 on So-called Stablecoins* (p. 32). https://www.fatf-gafi.org/content/dam/fatf-gafi/reports/Virtual-Assets-FATF-Report-G20-SoCalled-Stablecoins.pdf.coredownload.pdf

The Financial Action Task Force. (2021). *Updated Guidance for a Risk-Based Approach to Virtual Assets and Virtual Asset Service Providers* (p. 111). https://www.fatf gafi.org/content/dam/fatf-gafi/guidance/Updated-Guidance-VA-VASP.pdf.coredownload. inline.pdf

The Financial Action Task Force. (2021). *Updated Guidance for a Risk-Based Approach to Virtual Assets and Virtual Asset Service Providers* (p. 111). https://www.fatf-gafi.org/content/dam/fatf-gafi/guidance/Updated-Guidance-VA-VASP.pdf.coredownload.inline.pdf

The International Organization of Securities Commissions. (2023). *Policy Recommendations for Crypto and Digital Asset Markets* (No. 747; p. 77). https://www.iosco.org/library/pubdocs/pdf /IOSCOPD747.pdf

The International Organization of Securities Commissions. (2023). *Policy Recommendations for Crypto and Digital Asset Markets* (No. 747; p. 77). https://www.iosco.org/library/pubdocs/pdf/IOSCOPD747.pdf

The Virtual Asset and Initial Token Offering Services Act. 2021, Government Gazette of Mauritius No. 183 (2022). https://www.bom.mu/sites/default/files/virtual-asset-and-initial-token-offering-services-act-2021.pdf

Thomason, J. (2026 forthcoming). *Global Lessons for Stablecoin Regulation and Governance*. IGI-Global.

Treasury, H. M. (2025a). *Future financial services regulatory regime for cryptoassets (regulated activities) Policy Note*. https://assets.publishing.service.gov.uk/media/680f6397b0d43971b07f5bfd/20250428_RAO_SI_draft_policy_note.pdf

Treasury, H. M. (2025b). *The Financial Services and Markets Act 2000 (Regulated Activities etc.) (Amendment) Order 2025*. Legislation.gov.uk. https://www.legislation.gov.uk/ukdsi/2025/9780348272055

Treasury, H. M. U. K. (2025a). *Future Financial Services Regulatory Regime for Cryptoassets (Regulated Activities)* (p. 19) [Policy Note]. https://assets.publishing.service.gov.uk/media/680f6397b0d43971b07f5bfd/20250428_RAO_SI_draft_policy_note.pdf

Treasury, H. M. U. K. (2025b). *The Financial Services and Markets Act 2000 (Regulated Activities and Miscellaneous Provisions) (Cryptoassets) Order 2025* (No. 2025 No. 000; p. 27). [Draft Statutory Instrument].https://assets.publishing.service.gov.uk/media/680f6387faff81833fcae94b/0302425_draft_RAO_SI.pdf

Treasury, H. M. (2023). *Consultation on the Digital Securities Sandbox*. HM Treasury. [Consultation Paper], https://www.gov.uk/government/consultations/consultation-on-the-digital-securities-sandbox

Treasury, H. M. (2023). *Future financial services regulatory regime for cryptoassets*. UK Government.

U.S. Securities and Exchange Commission. (2023). *Framework for "Investment Contract" Analysis of Digital Assets*. SEC, Washington, DC.

U.S. Securities and Exchange Commission. (2025). *Statement on Stablecoins* [Regulatory Statement]. U.S. Securities and Exchange Commission (SEC). https://www.sec.gov/newsroom/speeches-statements/statement-stablecoins-040425

UN Security Council. (2024). *UN Documents for DPRK (North Korea): Sanctions Committee Documents*. Securitycouncilreport.org. https://www.securitycouncilreport.org/un_documents_type/sanctions-committee-documents/?ctype=DPRK%20%28North%20Korea%29&cbtype=dprk-north-korea

UNIDROIT. (2023). *UNIDROIT PRINCIPLES ON DIGITAL ASSETS AND PRIVATE LAW*. https://www.unidroit.org/wp-content/uploads/2024/01/Principles-on-Digital-Assets-and-Private-Law-linked-1.pdf

United Nations Commission on International Trade Law. (1999). *UNCITRAL Model Law on Electronic Commerce with Guide to Enactment 1996 with Additional Article 5 Bis as Adopted in 1998* (No. E.99.V.4; United Nations Publication, p. 86). United Nations. https://uncitral.un.org/en/texts/ecommerce/modellaw/electronic_commerce

United Nations Commission on International Trade Law. (2008). *UNCITRAL Model Law on International Commercial Arbitration 1985: With Amendments as Adopted in 2006* (No. E.08.V.4; United Nations Publication, p. 56). United Nations. https://uncitral.un.org/en/texts/arbitration/modellaw/commercial_arbitration

United Nations Commission on International Trade Law. (2018). *UNCITRAL Model Law on Recognition and Enforcement of Insolvency-Related Judgments with Guide to Enactment* (No. E.19.V.8; United Nations Publication, p. 84). UNITED NATIONS. https://uncitral.un.org/en/texts/insolvency/modellaw/mlij

United Nations Conference on Trade and Development. (2023). *Global Report on Blockchain and Its Implications on Trade Facilitation Performance* (No. UNCTAD/TCS/DTL/INF/2023/1; p. 71). United Nations Conference on Trade and Development (UNCTAD). https://unctad.org/publication/global-report-blockchain-and-its-implications-trade-facilitation-performance

United Nations Conference on Trade and Development. (2025). *Trinidad and Tobago eTrade Readiness Assessment* (Policy Review No. UNCTAD/DTL/ECDE/2024/5; p. 100). United Nations. https://dig.watch/resource/trinidad-and-tobago-etrade-readiness-assessment

United States Congress. (2025). *GENIUS Act*. Congress.gov. https://www.congress.gov/bill/119th-congress/senate-bill/1582/text

United States Congress. (2025). *Guiding and Establishing National Innovation for U.S. Stablecoins Act (GENIUS Act)* (Pub. L. No. 119-27, S. 1582). https://www.congress.gov/bill/119th-congress/senate-bill/1582/textVirtual Assets Regulatory Authority. (2025). *Virtual Assets and Related Activities Regulations 2023* (p. 50) [Rulebook]. Government of Dubai. https://rulebooks.vara.ae/rulebook/virtual-assets-and-related-activities-regulations-2023

United States Congress. (2025). *S.1582 - 119th Congress (2025-2026): GENIUS Act*. Congress.gov. https://www.congress.gov/bill/119th-congress/senate-bill/1582/text

United States Congress. (2025). *S.1582 - 119th Congress (2025-2026): GENIUS Act*. Congress.gov. https://www.congress.gov/bill/119th-congress/senate-bill/1582/text (Accessed 4 January 2026)

Upadhyaya, R. (2017). *The Political Economy of Basel Adoption in Kenya: A Case of Alignment of Donor, Government and Banking Sector Interests* (GEG Working Paper No. 131; p. 37). University of Oxford, Global Economic Governance Programme (GEG). https://hdl.handle.net/10419/196387

Virtual Asset and Initial Token Offering Services Act 2021, Pub. L. No. 21 of 2021, 183 Government Gazette of Mauritius (2022). Assented 16 December 2021; Proclaimed by Proclamation No. 12 of 2022, effective 7 February 2022 https://www.bom.mu/sites/default/files/virtual-asset-and-initial-token-offering-services-act-2021_0.pdf

Virtual Asset Service Providers Bill. 15 of 2025, Parliament of Kenya, Kenya Gazette Supplement No. 173 Act No. 20 of 2025 489 (2025). https://new.kenyalaw.org/akn/ke/act/2025/20/eng@2025-11-04

Zadeh, A. H. (2022). An analysis of the Terra-Luna crash and its contagion effects. SSRN *Electronic Journal.* DOI: 10.2139/ssrn.4145551

Zavalko, M. (2025). *Blockchain Security & Stablecoins: Emerging Standards in the Commonwealth - Commonwealth Chamber of Commerce*. Commonwealth Chamber of Commerce. https://commonwealthchamber.com/blockchain-security-stablecoins-emerging-standards-in-the-commonwealth/

Zetzsche, D. A., Arner, D. W., & Buckley, R. P. (2020a). Decentralized Finance. *Journal of Financial Regulation*, *6*(2), 172–203. DOI: 10.1093/jfr/fjaa010

Zetzsche, D. A., Buckley, R. P., & Arner, D. W. (2020b). Regulating Libra: The Transformative Potential of Facebook's Cryptocurrency and Possible Regulatory Responses. *European Banking Institute Working Paper Series* 2020/45. https://ssrn.com/abstract=3414401

Zetzsche, D. A., Buckley, R. P., Arner, D. W., & Barberis, J. N. (2017). Regulating a revolution: From regulatory sandboxes to smart regulation. *SSRN*, *23*(1), 31–103. DOI: 10.2139/ssrn.3018534

About the Contributors

Jane Thomason, is a global thought leader in emerging technologies, including AI, Blockchain, Web3, Metaverse, and MedTech. She holds a PhD from the University of Queensland. She currently holds distinguished roles on the editorial boards of three peer reviewed journals and is an Industry Associate: University College London, Centre for Blockchain. She is author of "Blockchain for Global Social Change," "Applied Ethics in a Digital World" and has "Advancements in the New World of Web 3: A Look Toward the Decentralized Future". She has published widely on MedTech, Web3, Blockchain, AI and Metaverse and is at the forefront of the impact of emerging technologies on industry and society.

***

Kokila Alagh has over 20 years of experience as a corporate, commercial, and technology lawyer in the UAE. She is the founder of KARM Legal Consultants, a boutique law firm specializing in fintech, blockchain, and digital transformation. Widely recognized as an industry thought leader, Kokila is also an award-winning lawyer known for her influential contributions to the legal and regulatory landscape of emerging technologies. She serves on the boards of the Middle East Stablecoin Association, the MENA Fintech Association, and D2A2, among others, where she plays a key role in shaping policy, innovation frameworks, and governance across the region's digital assets and fintech sectors. Kokila holds a Master of Laws from Monash University and has completed fintech and blockchain programs from Harvard Business School and the University of Oxford. She has an extensive track record advising on joint ventures, mergers, acquisitions, and foreign direct investments.

Maxine L Binns is a Barrister and Attorney with over four decades of experience in Bermuda's legal and financial sectors, specializing in corporate, commercial, and estate law. Her distinguished career includes senior roles within leading law firms and banking institutions, where she cultivated a reputation for legal acumen, strategic foresight, and professional integrity. In her more recent public service, Maxine served first as a Legislative Analyst and then subsequently as a Legislative Consultant to the Bermuda Government. In these roles, she played a central role in shaping economic development policies, advancing legislative reforms, and supporting strategic initiatives across both the public and private sectors. Her work involved close collaboration with domestic and international stakeholders to modernize Bermuda's legislative framework and enhance its product and service offerings for local and international businesses seeking to conduct business in or from within Bermuda, as a premier international financial centre. These efforts were instrumental in the successful implementation of Bermuda's economic substance regime and the establishment of a robust legislative foundation for digital asset business. Maxine read Law at the University of Buckingham and BPP Law School in the United Kingdom. She is admitted to the Bar of England and Wales and the Bermuda Bar. Her public appointments include service as a Member of Bermuda's Human Rights Commission Board of Inquiry and the Commission of Inquiry into Historic Land Losses in Bermuda — both of which addressed issues of justice, equity and redress. At the Commonwealth level, Maxine served as a Member of the Committee of Experts supporting the development of the Model Law on Virtual Assets. She continues to contribute to the Committee's ongoing work on model laws for stablecoins, real-world assets and artificial intelligence — advancing legal harmonization and cross-border interoperability.

Stuart Davis is the Global Head, Financial Crimes Risk Management for Scotiabank and is based in Toronto, Canada. He has over 28 years banking and regulatory experience including and 16 years in running AML programs. He served previously as the Enterprise Chief Anti-Money Laundering Officer for the BMO Financial Group and has led the Global AML programs for USAA in Texas, for First Data Corporation, which included Western Union Financial Service and for Capital One. Stuart began his career with the Office of the Comptroller of the Currency. Stuart is the Chair of the Toronto Chapter of ACAMS, Chair of the Canadian Banker's Association sub-committee on AML and is the Co-Chair with Canada's Department of Finance Advisory Committee on AML/TF. Stuart is a frequent speaker on AML, blockchain and virtual currency topics and has spoken at the UN, Canada's Parliamentary hearings, OECD, FATF, and other conferences globally.

Paul Derham is the Managing Partner at Holley Nethercote Lawyers. He helps participants in the Australian financial services industry to meet their legal and compliance obligations. Paul regularly assists businesses acquire their Australian financial services licences (AFSLs), and build robust governance systems to help them stay out of court, and out of the hands of regulators. He works closely with global payments, crypto, derivatives, FX and advisory groups, as well as fintech startups. He's involved in regulatory reform work in Australia and on a global scale, helping develop Model Law on Virtual Assets, and then Stablecoins, for the Commonwealth Secretariat. The law is currently being rolled out in 33+ countries. He also sits on compliance committees for a large number of AFSL holders.

Jonathan Hatch is a financial services and technology lawyer with experience in in-house, compliance and regulatory roles with a focus on technology and academic aspects in this area. Jonathan is a highly ethical solicitor who thrives on learning about the law and applying this knowledge in assisting clients through facilitating their understanding of the law and technology and applying his extensive problem solving skills and experience to find alternative solutions to difficult technical issues. He has a special interest in applying existing or reforming laws to new regimes and has advised on a wide range of in-house areas, mostly in financial services, and also dealt with a range of related areas such as probate, employment law, litigation and dispute handling, IP, IT, basic property transactions, contract and a wide range work related to the application of new technologies.

Loretta Joseph is a global Leader in Digital Finance, Virtual Assets, and Financial Regulation Internationally recognised as an expert in digital finance, virtual assets, and regulatory frameworks. Extensive experience advising governments, regulators, and organisations worldwide,I champion the responsible adoption of financial technology to foster inclusion and economic growth. Instrumental in developing regulatory frameworks for Virtual Assets and Virtual Asset Service Providers (VASPs), including the Commonwealth Model Law on Virtual Assets and draft model law on Stablecoins.

Marc Krisjanous is the Associate Director of Audit at SixBlocks Audit, an audit company that provides assessment and audit services to the Web3 sector worldwide. He is a member of the Executive Council of Blockchain New Zealand, a member of the CryptoCurrency Security Standard (CCSS) Steering Committee, and a New Zealand expert and project co-leader for ISO TC307 Blockchain and DLT standards. He contributes to the creation of several standards and model laws, including ISO TC307 - the ISO standards for blockchain and DLT systems, CCSS - a key management standard for blockchain and DLT systems, Singapore Baseline Security Requirements for Blockchain and DLT Systems and the Commonwealth Working Group developing a model law on stablecoins and a model law for tokenisation. He educates the Web3 community on cybersecurity through speaking engagements, webinars, and published articles. He also authored the CCSS v9 Implementation Guide.

Rick McDonnell is Co-CEO and Co-Founder of McDonell-Nadeau, Executive Director of ACAMS and former Executive Secretary of the FATF. Accomplishments as Executive Secretary of the FATF included the negotiation and approval of the revised FATF Standards, the development of a new, standardized assessment methodology for the global FATF network and the start of a new round of FATF country evaluations. The new focus of evaluation now extends beyond the technical implementation of FATF standards to examine their actual effectiveness - a dramatic change, which has enabled strengths and weaknesses of AML regimes to be clearly determined. Also oversaw the expansion of the FATF Global Network to nine FSRBs comprising over 190 countries. Managed and supervised the FATF's new fourth round mutual evaluation program and led the first evaluation under the revised Standards (Spain).

Harvesh Kumar Seegolam, GCSK, is a globally recognized financial systems architect and crisis leadership expert. He contributed significantly over the last 17 years in transforming Mauritius into a premier international financial center. He has more recently served as Governor of the Bank of Mauritius and Chairperson and Chief Executive of the Financial Services Commission of Mauritius. Appointed Governor of the Bank of Mauritius in February 2020, just before the COVID-19 pandemic, his exceptional stewardship of the financial system during unprecedented global turbulence earned him international acclaims from The Banker and The African Banker, amongst many others. His global recognition also culminated in his election as President of the Association of African Central Banks in 2024. As the visionary architect behind Mauritius' pioneering 2018 Fintech strategic roadmap and the Virtual Assets legislation; the revolutionary new monetary policy framework adopted in 2023; the development of payment corridors connecting the Mauritian and Indian payment systems allowing for trade and settlement in domestic currencies; and the setting up of Mauritius as an RMB clearing centre, he has consistently positioned his country and emerging markets at the forefront of global financial innovation. As the Head of the Mauritius delegation, his systematic approach to regulatory excellence, effectiveness and sustainability led Mauritius out of the FATF ICRG Grey List in record time, while establishing world-class AML/CFT frameworks and systems that became regional benchmarks. Beyond traditional central banking, he pioneered the Bank of Mauritius' Innovation Hub as a regional innovation platform for Central Banks. He equally led climate-conscious financial policy through a number of international initiatives and the establishment of the Bank of Mauritius' Climate Change Centre, demonstrating the integration of sustainability with monetary and financial stability. Currently serving as an independent thought leader, he continues to shape global discourse on innovative finance, cross-border payments, and next-generation regulatory frameworks, bringing a unique combination of crisis-tested leadership, regulatory mastery, and technological vision to complex financial challenges.

Mu'azu Umaru is a Nigerian. He obtained his Bachelor's and Master's degree in Counselling from the University of Nigeria, Nsukka and University of Benin, Nigeria, in 1991 and 1995, respectively.

Anson Zeall is the Co-founder and Chair Emeritus of IDAXA (idaxa.org), the global voice for the world's virtual asset associations and service providers, formed during the 2019 G20 Leader's Summit in Osaka, Japan. Anson is also the Co-founder and Chair Emeritus of ACCESS Singapore, the first and most respected crypto and blockchain association in Singapore. He was also the founding board member of the Singapore Fintech Association. In 2020, Anson was appointed to the OECD's Blockchain Expert Policy Advisory Board (BEPAB).

Index

F

G

I

K

L

M

O

P

R

S

T

www.ingramcontent.com/pod-product-compliance
Lightning Source LLC
LaVergne TN
LVHW080911300926
849162LV00003B/643